THE TIMES
Guide to the House of Commons June 1983

Revised edition, 1984

Times Books

Published by
Times Books Ltd
16 Golden Square
London W1R 4BN

Typesetting by
Input Typesetting Ltd
London SW19 8DR

Printed in the UK by
St Edmundsbury Press
Bury St Edmunds
Suffolk

British Library Cataloguing in Publication Data

The Times guide to the House of Commons,
June 1983.—2nd ed.
1. Great Britain. *Parliament—*
Elections, 1983
324.941′0858 JN956

ISBN 0–7230–0257–6

Contents

Her Majesty's Government

The Cabinet

Prime Minister, First Lord of the Treasury and Minister for the Civil Service
Mrs Margaret Thatcher

Lord President of the Council and Leader of the House of Lords
Viscount Whitelaw

Lord Chancellor
Lord Hailsham of St Marylebone

Secretary of State for Foreign and Commonwealth Affairs
Sir Geoffrey Howe

Home Secretary
Mr Leon Brittan

Chancellor of the Exchequer
Mr Nigel Lawson

Secretary of State for Education and Science
Sir Keith Joseph

Secretary of State for Northern Ireland
Mr James Prior

Secretary of State for Energy
Mr Peter Walker

Secretary of State for Defence
Mr Michael Heseltine

Secretary of State for Scotland
Mr George Younger

Secretary of State for Wales
Mr Nicholas Edwards

Secretary of State for the Environment
Mr Patrick Jenkin

Lord Privy Seal and Leader of the House of Commons
Mr John Biffen

Secretary of State for Social Services
Mr Norman Fowler

Secretary of State for Employment
Mr Tom King

Secretary of State for Trade and Industry
Mr Norman Tebbit

Chancellor of the Duchy of Lancaster
Lord Cockfield

Secretary of State for Transport
Mr Nicholas Ridley

Minister of Agriculture, Fisheries and Food
Mr Michael Jopling

Chief Secretary to the Treasury
Mr Peter Rees

Departments of State and Ministers

AGRICULTURE, FISHERIES AND FOOD

Minister
Mr Michael Jopling

Ministers of State
Lord Belstead
Mr John MacGregor

Parliamentary Secretary
Mrs Peggy Fenner

DUCHY OF LANCASTER

Chancellor
Lord Cockfield

DEFENCE

Secretary of State
Mr Michael Heseltine

Minister of State for the Armed Forces
Mr John Stanley
Minister of State for Defence Procurement
Mr Geoffrey Pattie
Under Secretary of State for the Armed Forces
Lord Trefgarne
Under Secretary of State for Defence Procurement
Mr John Lee

EDUCATION AND SCIENCE

Secretary of State
Sir Keith Joseph

Under Secretaries of State
Mr Peter Brooke
Mr Robert Dunn

EMPLOYMENT

Secretary of State
Mr Norman Tebbit

Ministers of State
Mr Peter Morrison
Mr John Selwyn Gummer

Under Secretary of State
Mr Alan Clark

ENERGY

Secretary of State
Mr Peter Walker

Minister of State
Mr Alick Buchanan-Smith

Under Secretaries of State
Earl of Avon
Mr Giles Shaw

ENVIRONMENT

Secretary of State
Mr Patrick Jenkin

Minister of State for Local Government
Lord Bellwin

Minister of State for Housing and Construction
Mr Ian Gow

Under Secretaries of State
Mr Neil Macfarlane
Sir George Young
Mr William Waldegrave

FOREIGN AND COMMONWEALTH

Secretary of State
Sir Geoffrey Howe

Ministers of State
Lady Young
Mr Malcolm Rifkind
Mr Richard Luce

Minister of State for Overseas Development
Mr Timothy Raison

Under Secretary of State
Mr Raymond Whitney

HEALTH AND SOCIAL SECURITY

Secretary of State for Social Services
Mr Norman Fowler

Minister of State for Health
Mr Kenneth Clarke

Minister of State for Social Security
Dr Rhodes Boyson

Under Secretaries of State
Mr Antony Newton
Mr John Patten
Lord Glenarthur

HOME OFFICE

Secretary of State
Mr Leon Brittan

Ministers of State
Mr Douglas Hurd
Mr David Waddington

Under Secretaries of State
Lord Elton
Mr David Mellor

LAW OFFICERS

Attorney General
Sir Michael Havers

Lord Advocate
Lord Cameron of Lochbroom

Solicitor General
Sir Patrick Mayhew

Solicitor General for Scotland
Mr Peter Fraser

MANAGEMENT AND PERSONNEL OFFICE

Prime Minister and Minister for the Civil Service
Mrs Margaret Thatcher

NORTHERN IRELAND OFFICE

Secretary of State
Mr James Prior

Ministers of State
Mr Adam Butler
Earl of Mansfield

Under Secretaries of State
Mr Nicholas Scott
Mr Christopher Patten

PRIVY COUNCIL OFFICE

Lord President of the Council and Leader of the House of Lords
Viscount Whitelaw

Lord Privy Seal and Leader of the House of Commons
Mr John Biffen

Minister of State (and Minister for the Arts)
Earl of Gowrie

SCOTTISH OFFICE

Secretary of State
Mr George Younger

Minister of State
Lord Gray of Contin

Under Secretaries of State
Mr Allan Stewart
Mr John MacKay
Mr Michael Ancram

TRADE AND INDUSTRY

Secretary of State
Mr Norman Tebbit

Minister of State for Trade
Mr Paul Channon
Minister of State for Information Technology
Mr Kenneth Baker

Minister of State
Mr Norman Lamont

Under Secretaries of State
Mr John Butcher
Mr Alexander Fletcher
Mr David Trippier

TRANSPORT

Secretary of State
Mr Nicholas Ridley

Minister of State
Mrs Lynda Chalker

Under Secretary of State
Mr David Mitchell

TREASURY

Prime Minister, First Lord of the Treasury and Minister for the Civil Service
Mrs Margaret Thatcher

Chancellor of the Exchequer
Mr Nigel Lawson

Chief Secretary
Mr Peter Rees

Financial Secretary
Mr John Moore

Minister of State
Mr Barney Hayhoe

Economic Secretary
Mr Ian Stewart

Parliamentary Secretary and Government chief whip in the House of Commons
Mr John Wakeham

Lord Commissioners (Government whips)
Mr Alastair Goodlad
Mr Donald Thompson
Mr David Hunt
Mr Ian Lang
Mr Tristan Garel-Jones

Assistant Government Whips
Mr Archibald Hamilton
Mr John Major
Mr Douglas Hogg
Mr Michael Neubert
Mr Timothy Sainsbury

WELSH OFFICE

Secretary of State
Mr Nicholas Edwards

Minister of State
Mr John Stradling Thomas

Under Secretary of State
Mr Wyn Roberts

HM HOUSEHOLD

Treasurer
Mr John Cope

Comptroller
Mr Carol Mather

Vice Chamberlain
Mr Robert Boscawen

Captain, Gentlemen-at-arms (Government chief whip in the House of Lords)
Lord Denham
Captain, Yeomen of the Guard
Earl of Swinton

Lords in Waiting
Viscount Long
Lord Lyell
Lord Skelmersdale
Lord Lucas of Chilworth

Baroness in Waiting
Lady Trumpington

Second Church Estates Commissioner
Sir William van Straubenzee

The House of Commons

In this list of members returned to the House of Commons at the General Election on June 9, 1983 a † denotes new members. The abbreviations used to designate political parties are:
C – Conservative; Lab – Labour; L – Liberal; SDP – Social Democratic Party; OUP – Official Unionist Party; SDLP – Social Democratic and Labour Party; UPUP – Ulster Popular Unionist Party; DUP – Democratic Unionist Party; SNP – Scottish National Party; Pl C – Plaid Cymru; PSF – Provisional Sinn Fein.

A

	Abse, Leo: *Torfaen*	Lab
	Adams, Allen: *Paisley North*	Lab
†	Adams, Gerry: *Belfast West*	PSF
	Adley, Robert: *Christchurch*	C
	Aitken, Jonathan: *Thanet South*	C
	Alexander, Richard: *Newark*	C
	Alison, Michael: *Selby*	C
	Alton, David: *Liverpool, Mossley Hill*	L
	Amery, Julian: *Brighton, Pavilion*	C
†	Amess, David: *Basildon*	C
	Ancram, Michael: *Edinburgh South*	C
	Anderson, Donald: *Swansea East*	Lab
	Archer, Peter: *Warley West*	Lab
	Armstrong, Ernest: *Durham North West*	Lab
	Arnold, Tom: *Hazel Grove*	C
†	Ashby, David: *Leicestershire North West*	C
†	Ashdown, Paddy: *Yeovil*	L
	Ashley, Jack: *Stoke-on-Trent South*	Lab
	Ashton, Joe: *Bassetlaw*	Lab
	Aspinwall, Jack: *Wansdyke*	C
	Atkins, Humphrey: *Spelthorne*	C
	Atkins, Robert: *South Ribble*	C
	Atkinson, David: *Bournemouth East*	C
	Atkinson, Norman: *Tottenham*	Lab

B

	Bagier, Gordon: *Sunderland South*	Lab
	Baker, Kenneth: *Mole Valley*	C
	Baker, Nicholas: *Dorset North*	C
†	Baldry, Tony: *Banbury*	C
	Banks, Robert: *Harrogate*	C

† Banks, Tony: *Newham North West*	Lab
Barnett, Guy: *Greenwich*	Lab
† Barron, Kevin: *Rother Valley*	Lab
† Batiste, Spencer: *Elmet*	C
Beaumont-Dark Anthony: *Birmingham, Selly Oak*	C
† Beckett, Mrs Margaret: *Derby South*	Lab
† Beggs, Roy: *Antrim East*	OUP
Beith, Alan: *Berwick-upon-Tweed*	L
† Bell, Stuart: *Middlesbrough*	Lab
† Bellingham, Henry: *Norfolk North West*	C
Bendall, Vivian: *Ilford North*	C
Bennett, Andrew: *Denton and Reddish*	Lab
Bennett, Sir Frederic: *Torbay*	C
Benyon, William: *Milton Keynes*	C
† Bermingham, Gerald: *St Helens South*	Lab
Berry, Sir Anthony: *Enfield, Southgate*	C
Best, Keith: *Ynys Môn*	C
Bevan, David: *Birmingham, Yardley*	C
Bidwell, Sydney: *Ealing, Southall*	Lab
Biffen, John: *Shropshire North*	C
Biggs-Davison, Sir John: *Epping Forest*	C
Blackburn, John: *Dudley West*	C
† Blair, Anthony: *Sedgefield*	Lab
Blaker, Sir Peter: *Blackpool South*	C
Body, Richard: *Holland with Boston*	C
Bonsor, Sir Nicholas: *Upminster*	C
Boothroyd, Miss Betty: *West Bromwich West*	Lab
Boscawen, Robert: *Somerton and Frome*	C
Bottomley, Peter: *Eltham*	C
Bowden, Andrew: *Brighton, Kemptown*	C
† Bowden, Gerald: *Dulwich*	C
† Boyes, Roland: *Houghton and Washington*	Lab
Boyson, Dr Rhodes: *Brent North*	C
Braine, Sir Bernard: *Castle Point*	C
† Brandon-Bravo, Martin: *Nottingham South*	C
Bray, Dr Jeremy: *Motherwell South*	Lab
Bright, Graham: *Luton South*	C
Brinton, Timothy: *Gravesham*	C
Brittan, Leon: *Richmond, Yorks*	C
Brooke, Peter: *City of London and Westminster South*	C
† Brown, Gordon: *Dunfermline East*	Lab
Brown, Hugh: *Glasgow, Provan*	Lab
Brown, Michael: *Brigg and Cleethorpes*	C
† Brown, Nicholas: *Newcastle upon Tyne East*	Lab
Brown, Robert: *Newcastle upon Tyne North*	Lab
Brown, Ronald: *Edinburgh, Leith*	Lab
Browne, John: *Winchester*	C
† Bruce, Malcolm: *Gordon*	L
† Bruinvels, Peter: *Leicester East*	C
Bryan, Sir Paul: *Boothferry*	C
Buchan, Norman: *Paisley South*	Lab

Buchanan-Smith, Alick: *Kincardine and Deeside*	C
Buck, Sir Antony: *Colchester North*	C
Budgen, Nicholas: *Wolverhampton South West*	C
Bulmer, Esmond: *Wyre Forest*	C
† Burt, Alistair: *Bury North*	C
Butcher, John: *Coventry South West*	C
Butler, Adam: *Bosworth*	C
† Butterfill, John: *Bournemouth West*	C

C

† Caborn, Richard: *Sheffield Central*	Lab
Callaghan, James: *Cardiff South and Penarth*	Lab
Callaghan, James: *Heywood and Middleton*	Lab
Campbell, Ian: *Dumbarton*	Lab
Campbell-Savours, Dale: *Workington*	Lab
Canavan, Dennis: *Falkirk West*	Lab
† Carlile, Alexander: *Montgomery*	L
Carlisle, John: *Luton North*	C
Carlisle, Kenneth: *Lincoln*	C
Carlisle, Mark: *Warrington South*	C
Carter-Jones, Lewis: *Eccles*	Lab
† Carttiss, Michael: *Great Yarmouth*	C
Cartwright, John: *Woolwich*	SDP
Chalker, Mrs Lynda: *Wallasey*	C
Channon, Paul: *Southend West*	C
Chapman, Sydney: *Chipping Barnet*	C
† Chope, Christopher: *Southampton, Itchen*	C
Churchill, Winston: *Davyhulme*	C
Clark, Alan: *Plymouth, Sutton*	C
Clark, Dr David: *South Shields*	Lab
† Clark, Dr Michael: *Rochford*	C
Clark, Sir William: *Croydon South*	C
Clarke, Kenneth: *Rushcliffe*	C
Clarke, Thomas: *Monklands West*	Lab
† Clay, Robert: *Sunderland North*	Lab
Clegg, Sir Walter: *Wyre*	C
Cockeram, Eric: *Ludlow*	C
Cocks, Michael: *Bristol South*	Lab
† Cohen, Harry: *Leyton*	Lab
Coleman, Donald: *Neath*	Lab
Colvin, Michael: *Romsey and Waterside*	C
Concannon, Don: *Mansfield*	Lab
Conlan, Bernard: *Gateshead East*	Lab
† Conway, Derek: *Shrewsbury and Atcham*	C
† Cook, Frank: *Stockton North*	Lab
Cook, Robin: *Livingston*	Lab
† Coombs, Simon: *Swindon*	C
Cope, John: *Northavon*	C
† Corbett, Robin: *Birmingham, Erdington*	Lab
† Corbyn, Jeremy: *Islington North*	Lab

	Cormack, Patrick: *Staffordshire South*	C
	Corrie, John: *Cunninghame North*	C
†	Couchman, James: *Gillingham*	C
	Cowans, Harry: *Tynebridge*	Lab
	Cox, Thomas: *Tooting*	Lab
	Craigen, James: *Glasgow, Maryhill*	Lab
	Cranborne, Viscount: *Dorset South*	C
	Critchley, Julian: *Aldershot*	C
	Crouch, David: *Canterbury*	C
	Crowther, Stanley: *Rotherham*	Lab
	Cunliffe, Lawrence: *Leigh*	Lab
	Cunningham, Dr John: *Copeland*	Lab
†	Currie, Mrs Edwina: *Derbyshire South*	C

D

	Dalyell, Tam: *Linlithgow*	Lab
	Davies, Denzil: *Llanelli*	Lab
†	Davies, Ronald: *Caerphilly*	Lab
	Davis, Terence: *Birmingham, Hodge Hill*	Lab
	Deakins, Eric: *Walthamstow*	Lab
	Dean, Paul: *Woodspring*	C
	Dewar, Donald: *Glasgow, Garscadden*	Lab
	Dickens, Geoffrey: *Littleborough and Saddleworth*	C
†	Dicks, Terence: *Hayes and Harlington*	C
	Dixon, Donald: *Jarrow*	Lab
	Dobson, Frank: *Holborn and St Pancras*	Lab
	Dormand, Jack: *Easington*	Lab
	Dorrell, Stephen: *Loughborough*	C
	Douglas, Richard: *Dunfermline West*	Lab
	Douglas-Hamilton, Lord James: *Edinburgh West*	C
	Dover, Den: *Chorley*	C
	Dubs, Alfred: *Battersea*	Lab
	du Cann, Edward: *Taunton*	C
	Duffy, Patrick: *Sheffield, Attercliffe*	Lab
	Dunn, Robert: *Dartford*	C
	Dunwoody, Mrs Gwyneth: *Crewe and Nantwich*	Lab
	Durant, Anthony: *Reading West*	C
	Dykes, Hugh: *Harrow East*	C

E

Eadie, Alexander: *Midlothian*	Lab
Eastham, Kenneth: *Manchester, Blackley*	Lab
Edwards, Nicholas: *Pembroke*	C
Edwards, Robert: *Wolverhampton South East*	Lab
Eggar, Timothy: *Enfield North*	C
Ellis, Raymond: *Derbyshire North East*	Lab

Emery, Sir Peter: *Honiton*	C
Evans, Ioan: *Cynon Valley*	Lab
Evans, John: *St Helens North*	Lab
† Evennett, David: *Erith and Crayford*	C
Ewing, Harry: *Falkirk East*	Lab
Eyre, Reginald: *Birmingham, Hall Green*	C

F

Fairbairn, Nicholas: *Perth and Kinross*	C
† Fallon, Michael: *Darlington*	C
Farr, Sir John: *Harborough*	C
† Fatchett, Derek: *Leeds Central*	Lab
Faulds, Andrew: *Warley East*	Lab
† Favell, Anthony: *Stockport*	C
Fenner, Mrs Peggy: *Medway*	C
Field, Frank: *Birkenhead*	Lab
† Fields, Terry: *Liverpool, Broadgreen*	Lab
Finsberg, Geoffrey: *Hampstead and Highgate*	C
† Fisher, Mark: *Stoke-on-Trent Central*	Lab
Flannery, Martin: *Sheffield, Hillsborough*	Lab
Fletcher, Alex: *Edinburgh Central*	C
Fookes, Miss Janet: *Plymouth, Drake*	C
Foot, Michael: *Blaenau Gwent*	Lab
Forman, Nigel: *Carshalton and Wallington*	C
Forrester, John: *Stoke-on-Trent North*	Lab
† Forsyth, Michael: *Stirling*	C
† Forsythe, Clifford: *Antrim South*	OUP
† Forth, Eric: *Worcestershire Mid*	C
Foster, Derek: *Bishop Auckland*	Lab
Foulkes, George: *Carrick, Cumnock and Doon Valley*	Lab
Fowler, Norman: *Sutton Coldfield*	C
Fox, Marcus: *Shipley*	C
† Franks, Cecil: *Barrow and Furness*	C
Fraser, Sir Hugh: *Stafford*	C
Fraser, John: *Norwood*	Lab
Fraser, Peter: *Angus East*	C
† Freeman, Roger: *Kettering*	C
Freeson, Reginald: *Brent East*	Lab
Freud, Clement: *Cambridgeshire North East*	L
Fry, Peter: *Wellingborough*	C

G

† Gale, Roger: *Thanet North*	C
† Galley, Roy: *Halifax*	C
Gardiner, George: *Reigate*	C
Gardner, Sir Edward: *Fylde*	C
Garel-Jones, Tristan: *Watford*	C
Garrett, Edward: *Wallsend*	Lab

George, Bruce: *Walsall South*	Lab
Gilbert, Dr John: *Dudley East*	Lab
Gilmour, Sir Ian: *Chesham and Amersham*	C
Glyn, Dr Alan: *Windsor and Maidenhead*	C
† Godman, Norman: *Greenock and Port Glasgow*	Lab
Golding, John: *Newcastle-under-Lyme*	Lab
Goodhart, Sir Philip: *Beckenham*	C
Goodlad, Alistair: *Eddisbury*	C
Gorst, John: *Hendon North*	C
† Gould, Bryan: *Dagenham*	Lab
Gourlay, Harry: *Kirkcaldy*	Lab
Gow, Ian: *Eastbourne*	C
Gower, Sir Raymond: *Vale of Glamorgan*	C
Grant, Sir Anthony: *Cambridgeshire South West*	C
Greenway, Harry: *Ealing North*	C
† Gregory, Conal: *York*	C
Griffiths, Eldon: *Bury St Edmunds*	C
Griffiths, Peter: *Portsmouth North*	C
Grist, Ian: *Cardiff Central*	C
† Ground, Patrick: *Feltham and Heston*	C
Grylls, Michael: *Surrey North West*	C
Gummer, Selwyn: *Suffolk Coastal*	C

H

Hamilton, Archibald: *Epsom and Ewell*	C
Hamilton, James: *Motherwell North*	Lab
† Hamilton, Neil: *Tatton*	C
Hamilton, William: *Fife Central*	Lab
Hampson, Dr Keith: *Leeds North West*	C
† Hanley, Jeremy: *Richmond and Barnes*	C
Hannam, John: *Exeter*	C
Hardy, Peter: *Wentworth*	Lab
† Hargreaves, Kenneth: *Hyndburn*	C
Harman, Ms Harriet: *Peckham*	Lab
† Harris, David: *St Ives*	C
Harrison, Walter: *Wakefield*	Lab
Hart, Dame Judith: *Clydesdale*	Lab
† Harvey, Robert: *Clywd South West*	C
Haselhurst, Alan: *Saffron Walden*	C
Hattersley, Roy: *Birmingham, Sparkbrook*	Lab
Havers, Sir Michael: *Wimbledon*	C
† Hawkins, Christopher: *High Peak*	C
Hawkins, Sir Paul: *Norfolk South West*	C
Hawksley, Warren: *The Wrekin*	C
† Hayes, Jeremy: *Harlow*	C
Hayhoe, Barney: *Brentford and Isleworth*	C
Haynes, Frank: *Ashfield*	Lab
† Hayward, Robert: *Kingswood*	C
Healey, Denis: *Leeds East*	Lab
† Heathcoat-Amory, David: *Wells*	C
Heath, Edward: *Old Bexley and Sidcup*	C

Heddle, John: *Staffordshire Mid*	C
Heffer, Eric: *Liverpool, Walton*	Lab
Henderson, Barry: *Fife North East*	C
Heseltine, Michael: *Henley*	C
† Hickmet, Richard: *Glanford and Scunthorpe*	C
Hicks, Robert: *Cornwall South East*	C
Higgins, Terence: *Worthing*	C
Hill, James: *Southampton, Test*	C
† Hind, Kenneth: *Lancashire West*	C
† Hirst, Michael: *Strathkelvin and Bearsden*	C
Hogg, Douglas: *Grantham*	C
Hogg, Norman: *Cumbernauld and Kilsyth*	Lab
Holland, Sir Philip: *Gedling*	C
Holland, Stuart: *Vauxhall*	Lab
† Holt, Richard: *Langbaurgh*	C
Home Robertston, John: *East Lothian*	Lab
Hooson, Tom: *Brecon and Radnor*	C
Hordern, Peter: *Horsham*	C
† Howard, Michael: *Folkestone and Hythe*	C
† Howarth, Alan: *Stratford-on-Avon*	C
† Howarth, Gerald: *Cannock and Burntwood*	C
Howe, Sir Geoffrey: *Surrey East*	C
Howell, David: *Guildford*	C
Howell, Denis: *Birmingham, Small Heath*	Lab
Howell, Ralph: *Norfolk North*	C
Howells, Geraint: *Ceredigion and Pembroke North*	L
Hoyle, Douglas: *Warrington North*	Lab
† Hubbard-Miles, Peter: *Bridgend*	C
Hughes, Dr Mark: *Durham, City of*	Lab
Hughes, Robert: *Aberdeen North*	Lab
Hughes, Roy: *Newport East*	Lab
† Hughes, Sean: *Knowsley South*	Lab
Hughes, Simon: *Southwark and Bermondsey*	L
† Hume, John: *Foyle*	SDLP
Hunt, David: *Wirrall West*	C
Hunt, John: *Ravensbourne*	C
† Hunter, Andrew: *Basingstoke*	C
Hurd, Douglas: *Witney*	C

I

Irving, Charles: *Cheltenham*	C

J

† Jackson, Robert: *Wantage*	C
Janner, Greville: *Leicester West*	Lab
Jenkin, Patrick: *Wanstead and Woodford*	C
Jenkins, Roy: *Glasgow, Hillhead*	SDP
Jessel, Toby: *Twickenham*	C
John, Brynmor: *Pontypridd*	Lab

	Johnson Smith, Sir Geoffrey: *Wealden*	C
	Johnston, Russell: *Inverness, Nairn and Lochaber*	L
	Jones, Barry: *Alyn and Deeside*	Lab
†	Jones, Gwilym: *Cardiff North*	C
†	Jones, Robert: *Hertfordshire West*	C
	Jopling, Michael: *Westmorland and Lonsdale*	C
	Joseph, Sir Keith: *Leeds North East*	C

K

	Kaufman, Gerald: *Manchester, Gorton*	Lab
	Kellett-Bowman, Mrs Elaine: *Lancaster*	C
†	Kennedy, Charles: *Ross, Cromarty and Skye*	SDP
	Kershaw, Sir Anthony: *Stroud*	C
†	Key, Robert: *Salisbury*	C
	Kilfedder, James: *Down North*	UPUP
	Kilroy-Silk, Robert: *Knowsley North*	Lab
†	King, Roger: *Birmingham, Northfield*	C
	King, Tom: *Bridgwater*	C
	Kinnock, Neil: *Islwyn*	Lab
†	Kirkwood, Archy: *Roxburgh and Berwickshire*	L
†	Knight, Gregory: *Derby North*	C
	Knight, Mrs Jill: *Birmingham, Edgbaston*	C
†	Knowles, Michael: *Nottingham East*	C
	Knox, David: *Staffordshire, Moorlands*	C

L

	Lambie, David: *Cunninghame South*	Lab
	Lamond, James: *Oldham Central and Royton*	Lab
	Lamont, Norman: *Kingston upon Thames*	C
	Lang, Ian: *Galloway and Upper Nithsdale*	C
	Latham, Michael: *Rutland and Melton*	C
†	Lawler, Geoffrey: *Bradford North*	C
	Lawrence, Ivan: *Burton*	C
	Lawson, Nigel: *Blaby*	C
	Leadbitter, Edward: *Hartlepool*	Lab
	Lee, John: *Pendle*	C
†	Leigh, Edward: *Gainsborough and Horncastle*	C
	Leighton, Ronald: *Newham North East*	Lab
	Lennox-Boyd, Mark: *Morecambe and Lunesdale*	C
	Lester, James: *Broxtowe*	C
	Lewis, Sir Kenneth: *Stamford and Spalding*	C
	Lewis, Ronald: *Carlisle*	Lab
†	Lewis, Terence: *Worsley*	Lab
†	Lightbown, David: *Staffordshire South East*	C
†	Lilley, Peter: *St Albans*	C
	Litherland, Robert: *Manchester Central*	Lab
†	Lloyd, Anthony: *Stretford*	Lab

	Lloyd, Ian: *Havant*	C
	Lloyd, Peter: *Fareham*	C
	Lofthouse, Geoffrey: *Pontefract and Castleford*	Lab
†	Lord, Michael: *Suffolk Central*	C
†	Loyden, Edward: *Liverpool, Garston*	Lab
	Luce, Richard: *Shoreham*	C
	Lyell, Nicholas: *Bedfordshire Mid*	C

M

	Macfarlane, Neil: *Sutton and Cheam*	C
	MacGregor, John: *Norfolk South*	C
†	MacKay, Andrew: *Berkshire East*	C
	MacKay, John: *Argyll and Bute*	C
	Mackenzie, Gregor: *Glasgow, Rutherglen*	Lab
	Maclennan, Robert: *Caithness and Sutherland*	SDP
	Macmillan, Maurice: *Surrey South West*	C
†	Madden, Max: *Bradford West*	Lab
	Madel, David: *Bedfordshire South West*	C
†	Maginnis, Kenneth: *Fermanagh and South Tyrone*	OUP
	Major, John: *Huntingdon*	C
†	Malins, Humfrey: *Croydon North West*	C
†	Malone, Gerald: *Aberdeen South*	C
†	Maples, John: *Lewisham West*	C
†	Marek, Dr John: *Wrexham*	Lab
	Marland, Paul: *Gloucestershire West*	C
	Marlow, Antony: *Northampton North*	C
	Marshall, David: *Glasgow, Shettleston*	Lab
	Marshall, Michael: *Arundel*	C
	Martin, Michael: *Glasgow, Springburn*	Lab
	Mason, Roy: *Barnsley Central*	Lab
	Mates, Michael: *Hampshire East*	C
	Mather, Carol: *Esher*	C
†	Maude, Francis: *Warwickshire North*	C
	Mawhinney, Dr Brian: *Peterborough*	C
	Maxton, John: *Glasgow, Cathcart*	Lab
	Maxwell-Hyslop, Robin: *Tiverton*	C
	Mayhew, Sir Patrick: *Tunbridge Wells*	C
	Maynard, Miss Joan: *Sheffield, Brightside*	Lab
	McCartney, Hugh: *Clydebank and Milngavie*	Lab
†	McCrea, Rev Robert: *Ulster Mid*	DUP
	McCrindle, Robert: *Brentwood and Ongar*	C
†	McCurley, Mrs Anna: *Renfrew, West and Inverclyde*	C
	McCusker, James: *Upper Bann*	OUP
	McDonald, Dr Oonagh: *Thurrock*	Lab
	McGuire, Michael: *Makerfield*	Lab
	McKay, Allen: *Barnsley, West and Penistone*	Lab
	McKelvey, William: *Kilmarnock and Loudoun*	Lab
	McNair-Wilson, Michael: *Newbury*	C

McNair-Wilson, Patrick: *New Forest*	C
McNamara, Kevin: *Hull North*	Lab
McQuarrie, Albert: *Banff and Buchan*	C
McTaggart, Robert: *Glasgow, Central*	Lab
McWilliam, John: *Blaydon*	Lab
Meacher, Michael: *Oldham West*	Lab
† Meadowcroft, Michael: *Leeds West*	L
Mellor, David: *Putney*	C
† Merchant, Piers: *Newcastle upon Tyne, Central*	C
Meyer, Sir Anthony: *Clwyd North West*	C
† Michie, William: *Sheffield, Heeley*	Lab
Mikardo, Ian: *Bow and Poplar*	Lab
Millan, Bruce: *Glasgow, Govan*	Lab
Miller, Hilary: *Bromsgrove*	C
Miller, Dr Maurice: *East Kilbride*	Lab
Mills, Iain: *Meriden*	C
Mills, Sir Peter: *Devon, West and Torridge*	C
Miscampbell, Norman: *Blackpool North*	C
Mitchell, Austin: *Great Grimsby*	Lab
Mitchell, David: *Hampshire North West*	C
Moate, Roger: *Faversham*	C
Molyneaux, James: *Lagan Valley*	OUP
Monro, Sir Hector: *Dumfries*	C
Montgomery, Fergus: *Altrincham and Sale*	C
Moore, John: *Croydon, Central*	C
Morris, Alfred: *Manchester, Wythenshawe*	Lab
Morris, John: *Aberavon*	Lab
Morris, Michael: *Northampton South*	C
Morrison, Charles: *Devizes*	C
Morrison, Peter: *City of Chester*	C
† Moynihan, Colin: *Lewisham East*	C
Mudd, David: *Falmouth and Camborne*	C
Murphy, Christopher: *Welwyn Hatfield*	C

N

Neale, Gerrard: *Cornwall North*	C
Needham, Richard: *Wiltshire North*	C
† Nellist, David: *Coventry South East*	Lab
Nelson, Anthony: *Chichester*	C
Neubert, Michael: *Romford*	C
Newton, Antony: *Braintree*	C
† Nicholls, Patrick: *Teignbridge*	C
† Nicholson, James: *Newry and Armagh*	OUP
Normanton, Tom: *Cheadle*	C
† Norris, Steven: *Oxford East*	C

O

Oakes, Gordon: *Halton*	Lab
† O'Brien, William: *Normanton*	Lab

O'Neill, Martin: *Clackmannan*	Lab
Onslow, Cranley: *Woking*	C
† Oppenheim, Philip: *Amber Valley*	C
Oppenheim, Mrs Sally: *Gloucester*	C
Orme, Stanley: *Salford East*	Lab
Osborn, Sir John: *Sheffield, Hallam*	C
† Ottaway, Richard: *Nottingham North*	C
Owen, Dr David: *Plymouth, Devonport*	SDP

P

Page, Sir John: *Harrow West*	C
Page, Richard: *Hertfordshire South West*	C
Paisley, Rev Ian: *Antrim North*	DUP
Park, George: *Coventry North East*	Lab
Parkinson, Cecil: *Hertsmere*	C
Parris, Matthew: *Derbyshire West*	C
Parry, Robert: *Liverpool, Riverside*	Lab
† Patchett, Terry: *Barnsley East*	Lab
Patten, Christopher: *Bath*	C
Patten, John: *Oxford, West and Abingdon*	C
Pattie, Geoffrey: *Chertsey and Walton*	C
Pavitt, Laurence: *Brent South*	Lab
Pawsey, James: *Rugby and Kenilworth*	C
† Peacock, Mrs Elizabeth: *Batley and Spen*	C
Pendry, Thomas: *Stalybridge and Hyde*	Lab
Penhaligon, David: *Truro*	L
Percival, Sir Ian: *Southport*	C
† Pike, Peter: *Burnley*	Lab
Pink, Bonner: *Portsmouth South*	C
Pollock, Alexander: *Moray*	C
Porter, Barry: *Wirral South*	C
Powell, Enoch: *Down South*	OUP
Powell, Raymond; *Ogmore*	Lab
† Powell, William: *Corby*	C
† Powley, John: *Norwich South*	C
Prentice, Reginald: *Daventry*	C
Prescott, John: *Hull East*	Lab
Price, Sir David: *Eastleigh*	C
Prior, James: *Waveney*	C
Proctor, Harvey: *Billericay*	C
Pym, Francis: *Cambridgeshire South East*	C

R

Radice, Giles: *Durham North*	Lab
† Raffan, Keith: *Delyn*	C
Raison, Timothy: *Aylesbury*	C
† Randall, Stuart: *Hull West*	Lab
Rathbone, Tim: *Lewes*	C
† Redmond, Martin: *Don Valley*	Lab

Rees, Merlyn: *Leeds, South and Morley*	Lab
Rees, Peter: *Dover*	C
Renton, Timothy: *Sussex Mid*	C
Rhodes James, Robert: *Cambridge*	C
Rhys Williams, Sir Brandon: *Kensington*	C
Richardson, Ms Jo: *Barking*	Lab
Ridley, Nicholas: *Cirencester and Tewkesbury*	C
Ridsdale, Sir Julian: *Harwich*	C
Rifkind, Malcolm: *Edinburgh Pentlands*	C
Rippon, Geoffrey: *Hexham*	C
Roberts, Allan: *Bootle*	Lab
Roberts, Ernest: *Hackney North and Stoke Newington*	Lab
Roberts, Wyn: *Conwy*	C
Robertson, George: *Hamilton*	Lab
Robinson, Geoffrey: *Coventry North West*	Lab
† Robinson, Mark: *Newport West*	C
Robinson, Peter: *Belfast East*	DUP
† Roe, Mrs Marion: *Broxbourne*	C
† Rogers, Allan: *Rhondda*	Lab
Rooker, Jeffrey: *Birmingham, Perry Barr*	Lab
Ross, Ernest: *Dundee West*	Lab
Ross, Stephen: *Isle of Wight*	L
Ross, William: *Londonderry East*	OUP
Rossi, Sir Hugh: *Hornsey and Wood Green*	C
Rost, Peter: *Erewash*	C
† Rowe, Andrew: *Kent Mid*	C
Rowlands, Edward: *Merthyr Tydfil and Rhymney*	Lab
Rumbold, Mrs Angela: *Mitcham and Morden*	C
† Ryder, Richard: *Norfolk Mid*	C
Ryman John: *Blyth Valley*	Lab

S

† Sackville, Thomas: *Bolton West*	C
Sainsbury, Timothy: *Hove*	C
St John-Stevas, Norman: *Chelmsford*	C
† Sayeed, Jonathan: *Bristol East*	C
Scott, Nicholas: *Chelsea*	C
† Sedgemore, Brian: *Hackney South and Shoreditch*	Lab
Shaw, Giles: *Pudsey*	C
Shaw, Sir Michael: *Scarborough*	C
Sheerman, Barry: *Huddersfield*	Lab
Sheldon, Robert: *Ashton-under-Lyne*	Lab
Shelton, William: *Streatham*	C
Shepherd, Colin: *Hereford*	C
Shepherd, Richard: *Aldridge-Brownhills*	C
Shersby, Michael: *Uxbridge*	C
Shore, Peter: *Bethnal Green and Stepney*	Lab
† Short, Ms Clare: *Birmingham, Ladywood*	Lab

	Short, Mrs Renée: *Wolverhampton North East*	Lab
	Silkin, John: *Lewisham, Deptford*	Lab
	Silvester, Frederick: *Manchester, Withington*	C
	Sims, Roger: *Chistlehurst*	C
	Skeet, Trevor: *Bedfordshire North*	C
	Skinner, Dennis: *Bolsover*	Lab
†	Smith, Christopher: *Islington South and Finsbury*	Lab
	Smith, Cyril: *Rochdale*	L
	Smith, Sir Dudley: *Warwick and Leamington*	C
	Smith, John: *Monklands East*	Lab
	Smith, Timothy: *Beaconsfield*	C
	Smyth, Rev Martin: *Belfast South*	OUP
	Snape, Peter: *West Bromwich East*	Lab
†	Soames, Nicholas: *Crawley*	C
	Soley, Clive: *Hammersmith*	Lab
	Spearing, Nigel: *Newham South*	Lab
	Speed, Keith: *Ashford*	C
	Speller, Tony: *Devon North*	C
	Spence, John: *Rydale*	C
†	Spencer, Derek: *Leicester South*	C
	Spicer, James: *Dorset West*	C
	Spicer, Michael: *Worcestershire South*	C
	Squire, Robin: *Hornchurch*	C
	Stanbrook, Ivor: *Orpington*	C
	Stanley, John: *Tonbridge and Malling*	C
	Steel, David: *Tweeddale, Ettrick and Lauderdale*	L
	Steen, Anthony: *South Hams*	C
†	Stern, Michael: *Bristol North West*	C
†	Stevens, Lewis: *Nuneaton*	C
	Stevens, Martin: *Fulham*	C
	Stewart, Allan: *Eastwood*	C
†	Stewart, Andrew: *Sherwood*	C
	Stewart, Ian: *Hertfordshire North*	C
	Stewart, Donald: *Western Isles*	SNP
	Stokes, John: *Halesowen and Stourbridge*	C
	Stott, Roger: *Wigan*	Lab
	Stradling Thomas, John: *Monmouth*	C
	Strang, Gavin; *Edinburgh East*	Lab
	Straw, Jack: *Blackburn*	Lab
†	Sumberg, David: *Bury South*	C

T

	Tapsell, Peter: *Lindsey East*	C
	Taylor, Edward: *Southend East*	C
†	Taylor, John D.: *Strangford*	OUP
†	Taylor, John M.: *Solihull*	C
	Tebbit, Norman: *Chingford*	C
	Temple-Morris, Peter: *Leominster*	C
†	Terlezki, Stefan: *Cardiff West*	C
	Thatcher, Mrs Margaret: *Finchley*	C

	Thomas, Dafydd: *Meirionnydd Nant Conwy*	Pl C
	Thomas, Peter: *Hendon South*	C
	Thomas, Dr Roger: *Carmarthen*	Lab
	Thompson, Donald: *Calder Valley*	C
†	Thompson, Patrick: *Norwich North*	C
†	Thompson, John: *Wansbeck*	Lab
	Thorne, Neil: *Ilford South*	C
	Thorne, Stanley: *Preston*	Lab
	Thornton, Malcolm: *Crosby*	C
†	Thurnham, Peter: *Bolton North East*	C
	Tinn, James: *Redcar*	Lab
	Torney, Thomas: *Bradford South*	Lab
	Townend, John: *Bridlington*	C
	Townsend, Cyril: *Bexleyheath*	C
†	Tracey, Richard: *Surbiton*	C
	Trippier, David: *Rossendale and Darwen*	C
	Trotter, Neville: *Tynemouth*	C
†	Twinn, Ian: *Edmonton*	C

V

	van Straubenzee, Sir William: *Wokingham*	C
*	Varley, Eric: *Chesterfield*	Lab
	Vaughan, Dr Gerard: *Reading East*	C
	Viggers, Peter: *Gosport*	C

W

	Waddington, David: *Ribble Valley*	C
	Wainwright, Richard: *Colne Valley*	L
	Wakeham, John: *Colchester South and Maldon*	C
	Waldegrave, William: *Bristol West*	C
†	Walden, George: *Buckingham*	C
†	Walker, Cecil: *Belfast North*	OUP
	Walker, Harold: *Doncaster Central*	Lab
	Walker, Peter: *Worcester*	C
	Walker, William: *Tayside North*	C
	Wall, Sir Patrick: *Beverley*	C
†	Wallace, James: *Orkney and Shetland*	L
	Waller, Gary: *Keighley*	C
	Walters, Dennis: *Westbury*	C
	Ward, John: *Poole*	C
	Wardell, Gareth: *Gower*	Lab
†	Wardle, Charles: *Bexhill and Battle*	C
†	Wareing, Robert: *Liverpool, West Derby*	Lab
	Warren, Kenneth: *Hastings and Rye*	C
	Watson, John: *Skipton and Ripon*	C
†	Watts, John: *Slough*	C
	Wells, Sir John: *Maidstone*	C

* Mr Eric Varley announced in Nov 1983 that he was resigning his seat at Chesterfield.

Weatherill, Bernard: *Croydon North East*	C
Weetch, Kenneth: *Ipswich*	Lab
Wells, John: *Maidstone*	C
Wells, Bowen: *Hertford and Stortford*	C
Welsh, Michael: *Doncaster North*	Lab
Wheeler, John: *Westminster North*	C
White, James: *Glasgow, Pollok*	Lab
* Whitelaw, William: *Penrith and the Border*	C
† Whitfield, John: *Dewsbury*	C
Whitney, Raymond: *Wycombe*	C
Wiggin, Jerry: *Weston-super-Mare*	C
Wigley, Dafydd: *Caernarfon*	Pl C
Wilkinson, John: *Ruislip–Northwood*	C
Williams, Alan: *Swansea West*	Lab
Wilson, Gordon: *Dundee East*	SNP
Winnick, David: *Walsall North*	Lab
† Winterton, Mrs Ann: *Congleton*	C
Winterton, Nicholas: *Macclesfield*	C
Wolfson, Mark: *Sevenoaks*	C
† Wood, Timothy: *Stevenage*	C
Woodall, Alec: *Hemsworth*	Lab
† Woodcock, Michael: *Ellesmere Port and Neston*	C
Wrigglesworth, Ian: *Stockton South*	SDP

Y

† Yeo, Timothy: *Suffolk South*	C
Young, David: *Bolton South East*	Lab
Young, Sir George: *Ealing, Acton*	C
Younger, George: *Ayr*	C

* Mr William Whitelaw, Home Secretary since May 1979, received immediately after the election, an hereditary peerage, and as Viscount Whitelaw, became Lord President of the Council and Leader of the House of Lords. His elevation created a vacancy in Penrith and the Border, where a by-election was held on July 28, 1983.

The General Election 1983

The general election of June 9, 1983 gave a landslide victory to Mrs Margaret Thatcher, the Prime Minister, and the Conservative Party. She was returned to power with a majority of 144 over all other parties, and a majority over the Labour Party of 188.

Within 72 hours of victory, Mrs Thatcher had removed two Cabinet ministers and nine junior ministers from her Government, and demoted the only other woman from her Cabinet; Mr Michael Foot had announced he would not seek re-election as Leader of the Labour Party, and Mr Roy Jenkins had said he would stand down as Leader of the SDP. Dr David Owen became the new leader of the SDP on June 21, 1983.

The Liberal/SDP Alliance polled 7,781,082 votes but won only 23 seats in the new Commons.

The state of the parties compared with the compositions of the Commons at dissolution and after the general election in May, 1979 was:

	June 1983	Dissolution	May 1979
Conservative	397	334	339
Labour	209	239	268
Liberal	17	13	11
SDP	6	29	–
Scottish National	2	2	2
Plaid Cymru	2	2	2
Official Unionist	11	5	5
Democratic Unionist	3	3	3
Ulster Popular Unionist	1	1	–
Social Democratic and Labour	1	–	1
Provisional Sinn Fein	1	–	–
United Ulster Unionist	–	1	1
Socialist	–	1	–
Anti H-Block	–	1	–
Labour Independent	–	1	–
Independent Ulster Unionist	–	–	1
Independent	–	–	1
The Speaker	–	1	1
Vacant	–	2	–
Total	650	635	635

Following the boundary changes, most gains and losses were based on the BBC/ITN estimates of what the 1979 election results might have been had the boundaries been operating then. Under this it was calculated that the Conservatives gained 51 seats and lost 10; Labour gained 13 and lost 55; the Alliance gained 8 and lost none; and others gained six and lost six.

The June 1983 Election Campaign

Conservative lead was never challenged

by Julian Haviland
Political Editor of *The Times*

The announcement of the election on May 9 1983 left exactly one calendar month for campaigning. To the opposition parties, this seemed precious little time to weaken the Conservatives' formidably strong position. But they were ready to fight.

Labour and Alliance leaders, who thought they understood Mrs Margaret Thatcher's make-up, had assumed for several weeks that she would not miss the June opening when so many omens were favourable.

Among Conservatives, June factions and October factions had argued long, with the occasional voice raised for an election in 1984. But by Sunday, May 8, when the Prime Minister gathered senior ministers, party officials and advisers at Chequers, those who had urged delay—notably Mr William Whitelaw, the Home Secretary, and Mr John Biffen, Leader of the Commons—had fallen silent. The opportunists held the field and had no difficulty in equating the national interest with their insistence that the party should go while the going was good.

And it looked very good. Four opinion polls taken over the previous four days gave the Conservatives a lead over Labour of between 11 and 18 per cent, with Conservative supporters more determined than others to vote. The English and Welsh district elections three days earlier had shown that compared with 1979, the Tories had lost support in the North, gained a little in the South, and overall—though with no evidence from London or Scotland—had a lead over Labour of not much less than in 1979. The Alliance performance was rather weaker than before.

The timing made it likely that regular indicators of economic performance due for publication before polling day, notably the retail prices index for April, would supply more ammunition to the Government than to its opponents.

There were two potentially awkward foreign engagements in the Prime Minister's diary. She was to visit Washington and then Williamsburg at the end of May, for the economic summit conference of the western powers, and Stuttgart just three days before polling day for the European Council, where she had staked her credit on securing yet another large rebate of Britain's budget payments. With some careful diplomacy, it was agreed at Chequers, the Stuttgart meeting could be delayed and the American visit shortened and turned to advantage, with the Prime Minister displayed as a world figure on British television screens; and so it turned out.

The leadership of the Labour Party and of the big trade unions had also assembled on May 6–7 as guests of Mr David Basnett and the municipal workers at Woodstock College, Kingston upon Thames. This gathering was first mooted with the intention of restoring the party's unity and morale after the bruising loss of the Bermondsey by-election in February.

The sense that the general election was imminent turned it into a timely council of war and the unions' good will took the solid form of £2.5m pledged to Labour's campaign funds and a promise of up to 300 helpers, including full-time officials to work in marginal seats.

The Social Democrats had to cancel a meeting of their policy-making Council for Social Democracy, planned for Birmingham the following weekend. But the drafting of their joint manifesto with the Liberals was far advanced and candidates were chosen for all but a handful of seats. The delicate business of dividing constituencies between the two Alliance parties had been done with less ill-will than had seemed likely a year before, and in the end only three local Liberal associations defied the national agreement and ran their own candidates against Social Democrats who bore the Alliance seal of approval.

The election announcement hastened the choice of Labour and Conservative candidates for the few seats where matters were not already settled. One minister, Mr Jock Bruce-

Gardyne, Economic Secretary to the Treasury, had already been squeezed out and on the Labour side Mr Joel Barnett, former Chief Secretary to the Treasury, was among those left without a seat.

The election announcement drew Labour's scorn. 'Our resolute Prime Minister', Mr Michael Foot said, 'has been pushed, pulled and panicked even faster than expected. Here we are with a cut and run election a year before this Parliament needs to be dissolved. If the recovery is on the way, why the rush?'

Mrs Thatcher pleaded the national interest and made use of the uncertainty which, her critics said, she had deliberately allowed to develop. It was becoming intolerable, she said, and everyone was growing obsessed with the election date. It was bad for Britain and bad for people who were wondering whether to invest.

Mr Roy Jenkins, the putative leader of an Alliance government, careful not to appear a reluctant fighter, welcomed the election and agreed it was time to end the uncertainty. The Alliance was 'going in with victory as our aim', he said.

Then followed some days of phoney war. The defending Conservatives, in no hurry to open hostilities, did not produce a manifesto until May 18, two days after Labour officially launched theirs. The Alliance, with more ground to make up, went public first on May 12.

On May 10, the Stock Market suffered a momentary loss of nerve. Share values fell by £3,400m before lunch, then partly recovered.

That night Labour had an early taste of Tory blood. In negotiations over the passage of a truncated Finance Bill they forced Treasury ministers to drop all the concessions to higher rate taxpayers, including the raising to £30,000 of the limit for tax relief on mortgage interest.

Mr James Mortimer, Labour's general secretary, told *The Times* that a Conservative victory was unthinkable. But the bookmakers reported that the gambling fraternity thought of little else: all their money was on a Conservative win.

On May 11 Labour agreed its manifesto at record speed. The joint meeting of the Shadow Cabinet and the National Executive Committee, in just over an hour, simply adopted the campaign document published the previous March. It was a patchwork of painfully-made compromises, notably on incomes, nuclear weapons and the European Community, and both left and right realised that to change a single stitch would risk unravelling the entire garment.

The Labour manifesto offered an emergency programme 'to create jobs and give a new urgency to the struggle for peace', and on those two items, in that order, Mr Foot was to concentrate most of his oratory to the end of the campaign and beyond.

Labour promised a 'massive programme for expansion', through public investment, funded initially by borrowing, with the aim of reducing unemployment to below one million within five years. It was an enormous task, they acknowledged, but 'spending money creates jobs'.

At the heart of the programme was a new partnership with the unions with whom an annual 'national economic assessment' would be agreed covering 'the distribution of income between profits, earnings from employment, rents, social benefits and other incomes.' That phrase, hallowed by repetition in many statements by the party and the TUC, was the tenuous link between those who wanted incomes to be planned and those who clung to unfettered collective bargaining.

The Alliance manifesto, grandiosely entitled *A joint programme for government*, offered less rapid expansion with a target of reducing unemployment by one million over two years. They proposed to increase public borrowing by £3,000m for spending on public works, on jobs for the long-term unemployed and in the labour-intensive health service and personal social services. Uniquely, the Alliance offered a statutory incomes policy, with an annual norm, agreed or imposed, and a counter-inflation tax on employers who paid more.

On May 13, the old Parliament was dissolved and Mrs Thatcher, by a happy accident, had an engagement that night at the Scottish Conservatives' annual conference in Perth. She gave it all she had. 'Tonight we go forth to battle,' she cried. 'Great things are expected of us.'

All the Conservatives' chosen themes were tried out on the Scottish Tories and all were cheered. The Labour programme was 'the most extreme and damaging' ever placed before the electorate. Here was the chance to banish 'the dark, divisive clouds of Marxist Socialism.' Labour stood for 'the renunciation of national self-defence.'

There was also, to the disgust and uneasiness of the Labour Party, the briefest of references to 'our young men in the South Atlantic'. There was ample evidence that Margaret Thatcher's reputation rested on the Falklands war. How much did she mean to exploit it?

Michael Foot opened Labour's campaign in Carmarthen that same Friday night and warned his audience that 'Tory brainwashers' were working overtime to present the Government's disastrous record as a success. Another four years of such success would mean the end of Britain as a great industrial nation.

'The Tories promised us jobs, prosperity, tax cuts, industrial peace and law and order,' he said. But the country had suffered 'torments and evils almost unimaginable in 1979,' and had foisted on it the idea that, in difficult economic circumstances there could not be jobs but must be inadequate health and education services. If Labour had remained in office in 1979, Mr Foot lamented, 'we could have become one of the most prosperous nations in the world.'

Mrs Thatcher, before the election decision was taken, had made it known that she would not appear in televised debate with Mr Foot or any other challenger. Her staff put forward the argument used in 1979, when for once it was the incumbent Prime Minister, Mr James Callaghan, who was eager to debate, and the aspirant Mrs Thatcher who would not risk taking him on. 'We are not electing a president', she said then, and repeated now 'We are choosing a government'.

By May 1983 she had no fear of Mr Foot, who had scored few falls in their twice weekly jousts in the Commons. But she preferred not to share with a rival whom the polls said was less popular than her, the limelight which her appearances in radio or television interviews now attracted. Immediately before and after the election advertisement, however, she suddenly gave interviews to newspapers and broadcasters with the greatest readiness.

On May 16, the day that Labour's manifesto was launched, Mrs Thatcher was still not officially campaigning. But she obliged ITN with an interview which enabled her to say that Labour would 'change the whole basis of our society,' and that the election offered 'the choice between a society that is coerced and a society that is free.'

An hour later, on BBC television's *Newsnight* the first hole in Labour's manifesto began to appear. Mr Denis Healey, Labour's deputy leader, questioned by Mr Michael Heseltine and Dr David Owen, revealed that, for him at least, the manifesto promise to 'carry through in the lifetime of the next Parliament our non-nuclear defence policy' had a strictly limited meaning. A policy of 'no first use' of nuclear weapons was a non-nuclear policy, he said, 'because it meant a conventional deterrent against conventional attack'.

The next day Mr Healey further qualified the manifesto by saying that Britain's Polaris nuclear force would be disposed of only if there were 'adequate concessions' from the Soviet Union. Mrs Joan Ruddock, chairman of CND, spoke for many in the Labour Party when she commented that this did not amount to a non-nuclear policy.

The argument thus began was to do Labour great damage. While Labour shot itself in the foot, the Conservatives still kept their powder dry. Next day, when their manifesto at last saw the light, it looked insubstantial. The proposed legislation seemed no more than enough to fill the 12 months by which the last Parliament had been curtailed. The metropolitan county councils were to go, there would be a third attempt to legislate to restrict rates increases and a third Bill to curb the powers of trade unions.

The Conservatives would limit the immunity of unions to call strikes without first ballotting their members; would increase the power of union members to seek regular election of their leaders by ballot; and would threaten the Labour Party's finances by making it easier for trade unions to withhold payments to political funds.

All this had been foreshadowed. The bulk of the manifesto was a brightly painted picture of the Government past performance. The Conservatives claimed that they had laid the foundations for a prosperous future and that rewards were beginning to appear.

'What it really means is more of the same or even worse,' Mr Foot commented. It was a manifesto of 'miserable complacency'. Mrs Shirley Williams, president of the SDP, said the 'lie at the heart of the manifesto' was that the Government's monetarist policies had made the country stronger.

But the next three weeks proved that the country was willing to give the Conservatives the benefit of the doubt. The opinion polls which adduced the only objective evidence found many voters moving in and out of each party camp. But the Conservatives' lead was never challenged.

Nothing Labour tried could make any impression. As a leader Mrs Thatcher personally continued to attract more than twice as much support as Mr Foot, who also lagged behind Mr David Steel. Opposition spokesmen, by attacking her in every speech, seemed determined to help the Conservatives exploit what was clearly a major asset for them—the Thatcher name and reputation.

On the major issues of inflation, defence, law and order, the polls reported that Conservatives policies were preferred. Only on unemployment did Labour have the edge, but a Marplan poll for *The Guardian* eight days before polling day showed the Conservatives gaining ground on that question, too.

Labour were resourceful in finding and publishing private documents which, they claimed, revealed the Government's real plans. They developed, and the Alliance also took up, the theme of the 'secret manifesto' which they said the Tories' published manifesto, unspecific and reasonable in tone, was designed to conceal.

Mr Healey, an uninhibited pugilist, cited leaked documents from the Think Tank and the No 10 policy unit as evidence that Mrs Thatcher had lied about the trend of unemployment. Mr Neil Kinnock published a report by the National Economic Development Council which he said ministers had suppressed to hide the truth about the country's economic performance.

An official discussion paper about cooperation between public and private medicine was produced as proof, Mr Foot said, that the Conservatives planned a serious attack on the National Health Service. There was indeed evidence from the polls that voters were anxious about Conservative attitudes to the NHS.

Although the grimmest construction was put on ministers' most tentative notions, none of Labour's grenades seemed to breach the Tory defences. Sir Geoffrey Howe was able to maintain that there were 'no intentions that are not disclosed in the manifesto' for raising taxes or cutting public expenditure.

Both sides had their misfortunes. The Conservatives found they had a candidate in Stockton South who had concealed his recent past in the National Front until it was too late to disown him. In mid-campaign a report was suddenly published by a Commons committee which, in the name of Mr Edward du Cann, chairman of the Conservative backbenchers, blamed the Government's tight monetary policy rather than the world recession for most of the rise in unemployment.

Mr Edward Heath was critical of the Williamsburg summit. Mr James Prior was critical of his Cabinet colleagues' language. Mrs Thatcher twice took issue with the Foreign Secretary, Mr Francis Pym, for sounding irresolute over the Falklands and then for expressing doubts about landslide majorities. 'I think I could handle a landslide,' she said.

But the Conservatives recovered from their mistakes, while Labour's, magnified by a largely hostile press, lingered in the memory. The *Daily Mirror*, which supported Labour, chose to 'splash' reported remarks by Mr Foot's wife, Jill, that, win or lose, she did not expect him to stay long as party leader.

Mr Kinnock, without consulting his colleagues, introduced the taboo subject of the Falklands, accusing the Cabinet of ordering the sinking of the Argentine cruiser Belgrano to prevent a peaceful settlement. Within hours Mr Healey went one worse by accusing Mrs Thatcher of 'glorying in slaughter'—a remark which caused such offence that he withdrew it next day.

But Labour's internal differences over defence overshadowed everything. Not since 1935 had defence figured so prominently in an election. Mr Foot, a lifelong opponent of nuclear weapons and a unilateralist, wished it so and yet, in deference to Mr Healey and the Shadow Cabinet majority, he had subscribed to a compromising manifesto which meant everything and therefore nothing.

Labour canvassers learnt early that unilateralism was unpopular. A survey by Marplan for *The Guardian* towards the end of May showed that, although a clear majority agreed with Labour in opposing the purchase of Trident and the deployment of cruise, more Labour voters wanted Britain's nuclear capability maintained or improved (53 per cent) than abandoned (38 per cent). Among all voters the ratio was 74 per cent to 19 per cent and on defence and nuclear weapons policies in general the Conservatives had twice as much support as Labour.

The manifesto commitment to a non-nuclear policy was plain enough for the Conservative and Alliance speakers to attack it from start to end of the campaign; and yet ambiguous enough for the Labour leaders to sound evasive when challenged. In particular, Mr Foot could or would not say whether Polaris would be phased out within a single Parliament.

On May 24 Mr Foot, in a delicately drafted speech in Birmingham, put his own gloss on the manifesto. Labour, he now said, would 'move towards' a non-nuclear defence policy and would 'move to' the removal of nuclear bases. The commitment had become an aspiration. The new formula was approved in advance by Mr Healey whose earlier utterance had made it necessary.

But next day, in Cardiff, Mr James Callaghan, with all the authority of a former Prime Minister, stripped the careful dressing from the wound. Polaris had at least 12 years' effective life, he said, and should not be unilaterally given up. Labour's Left was outraged. Mr Sam McCluskie, the party chairman, rebuked Mr Callaghan. Mr Alex Kitson, a former chairman, said the speech might have cost Labour the election.

While Labour's troubles grew, the Alliance at first made little impact. By the halfway stage, in spite of a far greater share of broadcasting time than they normally received—they were allotted four minutes for every five given to Labour and the Conservatives—there was no evidence that they were gaining support. Their policies appeared least known and least favoured by the voters.

On Sunday, May 29, Mr David Steel, as campaign leader, summoned Mr Jenkins and the leading campaigners of both parties to his home in the Borders. They decided to push Mr Steel, whom the polls showed to be more popular than Mr Jenkins, into the television glare for the last 10 days, but not to de-throne the experienced Mr Jenkins as their Prime Minister designate. All the same, an Alliance Prime Minister looked a more mythical figure with every passing day.

As they met, the polls showed the first upward movement in support for the Alliance. One week later three polls were published which put them within reach of Labour, between three and six points behind, and a fourth put them half a point ahead. That night, in the Alliance's final election broadcast, Mr Steel stated boldly but inaccurately that they had overtaken Labour.

In the closing days Alliance spokesmen, whether to boost their own courage or the voters' credulousness, piled claim upon claim. Labour was 'busted' Dr David Owen said. People need no longer vote Conservative for fear of a Left-wing Labour government. Better vote Alliance to prevent a Conservative landslide and an unbridled Mrs Thatcher.

Mrs Thatcher herself seemed momentarily anxious about the Alliance challenge. In a BBC interview she suddenly chastised 'some of those SDP people' for not having had 'the guts' to stay in the Labour Party and fight. The Labour Party would never die, she said, and the only good opposition would be a reformed Labour Party which had shed its 'state socialism'.

'She's worried,' Dr Owen observed. Mr Steel said the Prime Minister was trying to give Labour the kiss of life. But the Alliance tide came only so far up the shore. They gave Labour an unprecedented shock but their hope of overtaking them proved vain.

By June 5 there was no possible doubt that the Conservatives would win. William Hill, the bookmakers, announced that they would take no more bets on a Tory victory. On June 6 Ladbroke's also closed their book.

Mr Foot on *Panorama* again modified Labour's manifesto, speaking of extra defence spending to strengthen conventional forces. Mr Kinnock was provoked by a heckler into an accidental crudeness about the Falklands fighting which appalled his colleagues. But nothing mattered. Labour by now were beyond any helping or harming.

An hour after the polls closed, a smiling Mrs Thatcher was questioned as she left 10 Downing Street with her husband for her declaration at Finchley. 'We think this will be our home for the next five years,' she said. It was hard to believe that she could ever have doubted it.

One lady who was not for turning

by Anthony Bevins
Political Correspondent of *The Times*

On October 10, 1980, Mrs Margaret Thatcher told the Conservative Party Conference at Brighton: 'You turn if you want to; the lady's not for turning.'

Throughout the Parliament, she was to remark later, commentators had wondered when or whether the U-turn would come. By the time she had called the election, they had ceased to wonder; Britian's first woman Prime Minister had convinced friend and foe alike, both at home and abroad, that it was not in her nature to break for cover.

Unemployment had reached record levels, there had been full-scale riots in Brixton and Toxteth, the Liberals had formed an electoral alliance with Labour's breakaway Social Democrats, and the Falkland Islands had been invaded and recaptured. She gave little sign of flinching in the face of such adversity; she gave no ground, and expected no quarter.

More than that, she also succeeded where others had failed before her; providing a settlement to the running constitutional sore of Rhodesia, with Zimbabwe independence, and even winning rebates, worth £2,400m, from the European Community budget.

But it was the domestic economy which was to prove the more testing, and more inconclusive, battleground.

From the very outset, the Conservative administration had been pledged to cut public spending and borrowing, to reduce inflation and taxation, to create the climate for enterprise and a framework for economic growth.

Certainly, public expenditure was curbed, at a price, although the planned target for the final year of the Parliament, as a proportion of gross domestic product (GDP), remained significantly above the level which had been forced on the previous Labour administration by the International Monetary Fund.

The public sector borrowing requirement, another sacred benchmark for the new brand of Conservative economics, showed greater signs of Treasury success. After some initial difficulty, it fell from an out-turn of £13,200m in 1980–81, 5.7 per cent of GDP, to a target of £8,000m, 2.75 per cent of GDP, in the final year of the four-year Parliament.

Inflation, too, fell during the course of the Parliament. From an initial rate of 10.4 per cent, the Retail Price Index (RPI) shot up to 21.9 per cent one year after the Tories had taken office, with pay indices showing similarly high increases, particularly in the public sector. But by the end of the Parliament, the RPI had fallen to 4 per cent, the lowest level for just over 15 years.

Undoubtedly, the sqeeze on inflation and on pay increases had come from unemployment, which rose inexorably, topping the two million mark, for the first time since 1935, in August 1980, and exceeding three million, for the first time since 1933, in January 1982.

There were those, Mr Edward Heath, the former Conservative Prime Minister included, who called for a change of direction, with lower interest rates, a return to exchange controls, abolished within six months of Sir Geoffrey Howe taking over as Chancellor of the Exchequer, and a return to consensus politics, abolished as soon as Mrs Thatcher went through the door of Number 10.

Minimum lending rate, before it, too, was wiped out in favour of more subtle means of interest rate control, was set at the all-time high of 17 per cent in November 1979, helping to push mortgage interest rates to 15 per cent. Such high-level inducements and the inbuilt advantage of North Sea oil helped to keep the pound buoyant, peaking at $2.40 over the winter of 1980–81.

All business interests felt the pinch, but exporters were particularly hard-hit. Sir Terence Beckett, the Director General of the Confederation of British Industry, even went so far as to suggest that the country's industrialists should take their gloves off and get into a 'bare-knuckle fight' to defend their interests against government. He later retracted.

But if industry was hit and the unemployed were finding it increasingly difficult to find work, a fact underlined by the mounting numbers of long-term unemployed, those who maintained their jobs did not fare much better.

The Conservatives had taken office with a promise to reduce the burden of taxation, to make a switch from direct to indirect taxes, so that individuals could choose how to spend their hard-earned money.

Sir Geoffrey's first Budget did indeed cut the basic rate of tax from 33p in the pound to 30p, and lower the top rate, as promised, from 83p in the pound to 60p. Overall, those and other direct tax concessions were estimated to be worth as much as £4,500m in a full year. But, then, so too, were the indirect tax increases, including a rise from 8 per cent and 12.5 per cent to the single rate of 15 per cent value added tax.

The Conservatives were to admit by the end of their term of office that 'given the recession and the need to bring down government borrowing, the burden of taxation has inevitably risen since 1979.'

By the beginning of 1981, Mrs Thatcher felt strong enough to take preemptive action against those who were known to be critical of the hardline economic measures which were being pursued.

Mr Norman St John Stevas, the Leader of the Commons, who had created the powerful new squad of departmental select committees, a significant parliamentary reform, was the first to be sacked, in January. But Mrs Thatcher also took the opportunity to make new dispositions in her team.

Mr Francis Pym, who, as Secretary of State for Defence, had rebelled over spending cuts demanded by the Treasury the previous autumn, was put into the political backwater of the Commons leadership. Three ministers known to subscribe to the spirit of Mrs Thatcher's line were then promoted: Mr John Nott, as Secretary of State for Defence, Mr John Biffen, as Secretary of State for Trade, and Mr Leon Brittan as Chief Secretary to the Treasury.

Later in that same year, before the party conference, Mrs Thatcher further consolidated her grip on cabinet, wringing out the men of consensus politics, the so-called 'wets' of traditional Conservatism. Two peers, Lord Thornycroft, the party chairman, and Lord Soames, Leader of the Lords, were put out to grass; Sir Ian Gilmour, Lord Privy Seal and deputy Foreign Secretary, and Mr Mark Carlisle, Secretary of State for Education and Science, were dismissed.

But perhaps most controversial of all, Mr James Prior, Secretary of State for Employment, was removed to Northern Ireland, to be replaced by Mr Norman Tebbit, the man who delighted the Tory conference at Blackpool the following month by saying that his father, when unemployed, had not rioted. 'He got on his bike and looked for work,' Mr Tebbit declared.

As the Parliament progressed, there was less and less doubt, more and more confidence, about the political direction in which Mrs Thatcher intended to take her party. She had said, in 1980, that she wanted to create one of the truly radical ministries of post-war Britain. One minister described the government's political purpose more graphically; as a mirror image of left-wing Labour policies, predicting that Mrs Thatcher planned to bring about an irreversible shift in the balance of power and wealth towards the private sector.

Remorseless trade union reform, Civil Service cutbacks, privatization of nationalized industry and the repeated, if internal, Whitehall reviews of the welfare state, all indicated the will and the determination of the Government to seek fundamental change.

The 1980 Employment Act made secondary picketing illegal, provided that all new, closed shops should be approved by 80 per cent of those affected, and made public funds available as an encouragement for union postal ballots.

The 1982 Employment Act, the second of a biennial, slow-but-steady approach to industrial relations reform, provided for regular review of existing closed shops by secret ballot, enabled the Government to pay compensation to people dismissed from closed shops, and made unions liable to civil action for damages if they caused unlawful industrial action.

Yet more industrial relations reform was presaged in a Green Paper, a discussion document, which considered secret ballots for the election of union leaders, the feasibility of holding secret ballots before strike action, and a change in the method by which union members contracted to pay their unions' political levy; the source of Labour Party fighting funds.

When the Tories took office, the Civil Service was 732,000-strong. The target for April 1984 was put at 630,000, the smallest bureaucracy since the war, and ministers were well on course for this aim by the spring of 1983.

British Aerospace, Britoil, the National Freight Corporation, Amersham International, Cable and Wireless, and the British Transport Docks Board, were all subjected to the process which became known as privatization, and although asset sales raised an estimated

£2,000m during the Parliament, criticism was provoked by the multiple oversubscription for shares in Amersham International, Cable and Wireless and British Aerospace.

Further privatization, for British Airways, British Telecom, and British Shipbuilders, was also proposed before the dissolution of the Parliament.

But the sale of public assets was not confined to the corporate sector. Tenants of local authorities, new towns and some housing associations were given the right to buy their own homes, and during the Parliament it was estimated that as many as 500,000 people completed purchase, while a further 500,000 staked a claim with two-year options to buy.

Less resolve appeared to have been shown in dealing with the politically sensitive expenditure problems of the welfare state.

There had been much public discussion about the merits of an education voucher scheme, under which parents would be given tokens or vouchers to the value of their children's state education, to be exchanged at schools of their own choice, as well as replacement of students' grants with some form of loan scheme.

Then, in September 1982, the substance of a leaked document from the Central Policy Review Staff (CPRS), the so-called Downing Street 'Think Tank', indicated that Treasury ministers, at the very least, had questioned the organization and financing of the National Health Service, the very shrine of the welfare state. The political hostility to revolutionary review of the state education and health service systems was so strong that all ideas of radical reform eventually ran into the ground. The Prime Minister herself was forced to publicly distance herself from the CPRS proposals at the 1982 party conference.

The sea-change in political direction was not confined to the government benches in the Commons. If it was not part of Mrs Thatcher's nature to perform somersaults, there were those in the Labour Party, too, who were incapable of bowing to the increasing influence of the left-wing.

In October 1979, the Labour Party conference carried resolutions for the compulsory reselection of Labour MPs, once every Parliament, national executive committee control of the manifesto, and the creation of an electoral college, which would give the unions and the constituency parties, as well as the parliamentary party, the right to choose party leader and deputy.

The first suggestion of a possible backlash was delivered by Mr Roy Jenkins, the former Labour deputy leader, who had become president of the European Commission. On November 22, he spoke publicly of the need for a radical centre in British politics.

The divergence between Labour left and right continued into the following year, 1980, as the left, led by Mr Anthony Wedgwood Benn, pursued their policy aims of unilateral nuclear disarmament and Common Market withdrawal, along with their constitutional demands; winning confirmation at the annual party conference of changes in MPs' reselection procedures and the principle of the electoral college.

However, before the leadership election college had been created, Mr James Callaghan resigned the leadership, on October 15. On November 11, Mr Michael Foot, then aged 67, beat Mr Denis Healey for the party leadership by 139 votes to 129 under the old system of parliamentary contest.

Dr David Owen, the former Foreign Secretary, announced 10 days later that he was not going to stand for re-election to the shadow cabinet, and Mrs Shirley Williams, another former cabinet minister and a non-parliamentary member of the national executive committee, announced that she would not be standing as a candidate at the next General Election because of the changes in party policy.

The breaking point came in 1981. At a special one-day party conference, held at Wembley on January 24, Mr Foot was defeated in his efforts to win at least 50 per cent of the electoral college votes for his fellow MPs. The result of the card vote gave the unions 40 per cent, the constituency parties 30 per cent and the MPs 30 per cent.

The very next day, on January 25, the so-called Gang of Four, Mr Jenkins, Dr Owen, Mrs Williams and Mr William Rodgers, another former Labour minister, formed a Council of Social Democracy. On March 2, Dr Owen, Mr Rodgers, 10 other Labour MPs and 9 Labour peers renounced the party whip at Westminster.

The Social Democratic Party was launched on March 26, and by the end of the year, in alliance with the Liberals, led by Mr David Steel, they had notched up more than 50 per cent support in public opinion polls, a number of famous by-election results, including a near-miss for Mr Jenkins in the Labour stronghold of Warrington, Cheshire, and a gain from the Conservatives, by Mrs Williams, in the true-blue constituency of Crosby, Lancashire.

Meanwhile, Labour's turmoil continued apace. Mr Benn challenged Mr Healey for the deputy leadership of the Labour Party under the new electoral college procedures, and at Brighton on September 27 Mr Healey scraped through to victory by just 0.852 per cent of the electoral college vote.

So, within a year of taking office as Labour leader, Mr Foot had failed to halt the right-wing breakaway and a Bennite challenge to the authority of the leadership, and in spite of continuing efforts to curb Mr Benn and the left, by concession and by threat, he never managed to re-establish his lost authority.

But the unrest was not confined to the ranks of senior industrialists and the political parties. On April 11, 1981, the Brixton riots broke, and there were further large-scale disturbances in the Toxteth district of Liverpool and the Moss Side area of Manchester, in July.

Following an official inquiry, Lord Scarman reported in November that there were conditions which created a climate for violent protest, and he called for remedial action which would ameliorate conditions of racial disadvantage.

Yet the external events of the Parliament – from the trial and acquittal of Mr Jeremy Thorpe, the former Liberal leader, on a charge of conspiracy to murder, in June 1979; the assassination of Lord Mountbatten at Mullaghmore, and the Warrenpoint slaughter of 18 British servicemen by Irish terrorists in August 1979; the exposure, by the Prime Minister, of Sir Anthony Blunt, the Queen's own art adviser, as the fourth man in the Burgess-Maclean-Philby Soviet spy ring, in November 1979; and the Soviet invasion of Afghanistan, over Christmas 1979; to the Iranian Embassy siege, broken by a spectacular Special Air Service raid, in May 1980; the Maze hunger strikes of 1980–81; and the marriage of the Prince of Wales to Lady Diana Spencer, in July 1981 – were all completely eclipsed by the April 2 invasion of the Falkland Islands by the Argentines in 1982.

Earlier, in March, one opinion poll had put the Alliance of Liberals and Social Democrats level-pegging with Labour at 33 per cent, while the Conservatives trailed behind with 31.5 per cent support. That same month Mr Jenkins had won the Glasgow, Hillhead, constituency from the Conservatives in another by-election coup for the Alliance.

But the eventual recapture of the Falklands, with an Argentine surrender on June 15, appeared to bolster the Prime Minister's reputation for pursuing the 'resolute approach' to the country's domestic and international problems.

One month after the surrender of Port Stanley, Conservative fortunes had revived, with the opinion polls showing 46.5 per cent support for the Tories, compared with 27.5 per cent for Labour and 24 per cent for the Alliance.

In the year that followed the Falklands, a long time, if not an eternity, in politics, much could have happened to alter that delicate balance.

But Labour, somehow, managed to hang on to its bedrock support, winning the Birmingham, Northfield, by-election in October 1982, its first by-election gain from the Conservatives in 11 long years; losing Southwark, Bermondsey, a rock-solid Labour seat, in February 1983, but then, critically, clinging on to its credibility and Mr Foot's leadership at Darlington in a March by-election.

Four years after she had been elected, all doubt had been erased; no one had any remaining illusion that the lady was for turning. She could only go forward. There appeared to be no one and nothing strong enough to stop her. Parliament was dissolved on Friday, May 13.

Constituency results and biographies

House of Commons, June 1983

The parliamentary constituencies of the United Kingdom (England, Scotland, Wales and Northern Ireland) for election to the House of Commons are set out in alphabetical order. Constituencies in cities or towns (for example, Liverpool, Manchester, Glasgow, Cardiff, Belfast, etc) are listed under that city or town.

Abbreviations used to designate the principal political parties contesting the election are: C – Conservative; Lab – Labour; All – Alliance; L – Liberal; SDP – Social Democratic Party; SNP – Scottish National Party; Pl C – Plaid Cymru; OUP – Official Unionist Party; DUP – Democratic Unionist Party; SDLP – Social Democratic and Labour Party; NF – National Front; Eco – Ecology Party; Com – Communist Party. Abbreviations of minor parties are given at the end of this constituency analysis followed by abbreviations of union and other organizations mentioned in biographical details.

The percentage of the votes cast for each candidate and the majority in relation to the total poll in each constituency are calculated to the nearest decimal place, as is the percentage turnout.

The electoral register came into effect on February 16, 1983, and the electorate figures for each constituency consist of those eligible to vote when the register came into force plus the relevant proportion of those registered as becoming 18 years of age during the year. The relevant proportion used was 113/364th—the number of days the register was in force until polling day. Ministers resign their directorships while holding office. *Denotes member of the last Parliament.

Mr John Morris

ABERAVON Electorate 53 443

*Morris, J. (Lab)	23 745	58.8%
Cutts, Mrs S. (L/All)	8 206	20.3%
Bailey, G. (C)	6 605	16.3%
Phillips, G. (Pl C)	1 859	4.6%
Lab majority	15 539	38.5%
Total vote 40 415	Turnout 75.6%	

Mr John Morris, QC, who was Secretary of State for Wales 1974–79, returned to back benches in 1981 after a spell as spokesman on Wales and then on legal affairs. Opposition spokesman on defence, 1970–74; Minister for Defence for Equipment, 1968–70; Parliamentary Secretary, Ministry of Transport, 1966–68; Parliamentary Secretary, Ministry of Power, 1964–66. Elected in 1959. Barrister. Born Nov 1931; educ. University College of Wales, Aberystwyth, Gonville and Caius College, Cambridge, and the Academy of International Law, The Hague. Chairman, Welsh Labour group, 1970–71, and Welsh parliamentary power, 1972–73.

Mrs Sheila Cutts, flower farmer. Born Nov 3 1928; educ. convent and school in Exeter, Exeter University, City of Bath Teacher Training College. Contested seat, 1979, and Oct, 1974.

Dr George Bailey, research director. Born Dec 14 1944; educ. Allhallows School and Edinburgh and Exeter universities. GLC member for Hounslow, Brentford and Isleworth, since 1977; Member, Surrey Heath Borough Council.

Mr Glenn Phillips, unemployed teacher, is secretary of the National Organization of Plaid Trades Unionists. Educ. University College of Wales, Aberystwyth.

Mr Robert Hughes

ABERDEEN NORTH Electorate 63 049

*Hughes, R. (Lab)	19 262	47.0%
Deans, C. S. (SDP/All)	10 118	24.7%
Scanlan, Mrs G. (C)	7 426	18.1%
McCugan, J. A. (SNP)	3 790	9.3%
Harty, Ms M. (Eco)	367	0.9%
Lab majority	9 144	22.3%
Total vote 40 963	Turnout 65.0%	

Mr Robert Hughes, an Opposition spokesman on transport since 1981, and chairman, Select Committee on Scottish Affairs 1981–82; member since 1979; Under-Secretary of State for Scotland, 1974–75. Engineering draughtsman. Elected in 1970; contested North Angus and Mearns 1959. Born Jan 3 1932; educ. Benoni High School, Transvaal and Pietermaritzburg Technical College, Natal. Chairman, Anti-Apartheid Movement. Member, Aberdeen Town Council 1962–71. Sponsored by AUEW.

Mr Colin Deans, engineering consultant. Born 1941; educ. in Canada. Executive director of his own company, acting for international oil and petrochemical companies.

Mrs Gay Scanlan runs an employment agency. Aged 31; educ. Westbourne School and Strathclyde University. Member, Citizens Advice Bureau. Contested district council elections, 1977 and 1980.

Mr James McGugan, agricultural seedsman, contested North Angus and Mearns, 1970, and North Aberdeen, 1974. Born Jul 1937; educ. Doune School, Angus and Forfar Academy. Member, Arbroath Town Council, 1968–71.

Mr Gerald Malone

ABERDEEN SOUTH Electorate 57540

Malone, G. (C)	15393	38.9%
Middleton, R. (Lab)	11812	29.9%
Philip, I. G. (SDP/All)	10372	26.2%
Coull, S. (SNP)	1974	5.0%
C majority	3581	9.1%
Total vote 39551		Turnout 68.7%

Mr Gerald Malone, solicitor, was elected in 1983; contested Glasgow Provan Feb 1974, Glasgow Pollok Oct 1974, Roxburgh, Selkirk and Peebles 1979, and Glasgow Hillhead 1982 by-election. Born Jul 1950; educ. St Aloysius' College, Glasgow, and Glasgow University.

Mr Robert Middleton, assistant executive engineer with British Telecom, has been Labour leader on Grampian Council since 1978 and a member since 1975. Born July 7 1932; educ. Aberdeen Grammar School. Former Aberdeen councillor. Member, Labour Co-ordinating Committee and CND. Member, Society of Post Office Executives.

Mr Ian Philip, chartered accountant and director of horticultural, engineering, wind energy and oil, and employee consultancy companies, contested South Angus, 1979. Born 1937; educ. Oxford and Edinburgh universities. Member, Council for Social Democracy.

Mr Samuel Coull, postman and former trade union branch secretary. Born 1940; educ. Peterhead Academy. Member, District and Regional Council, Peterhead.

Mr Julian Critchley

ALDERSHOT Electorate 77593

*Critchley, J. (C)	31288	55.5%
Westbrook, N. (L/All)	19070	33.8%
Crawford, A. (Lab)	6070	10.8%
C majority	12218	21.7%
Total vote 56428		Turnout 72.7%

Mr Julian Critchley, writer, journalist and public affairs adviser, was returned in 1970. MP for Rochester and Chatham 1959–64: contested seat 1966. Born Dec 8 1930; educ. Shrewsbury, Sorbonne, and Pembroke College, Oxford. Chairman, Bow Group, 1966–67; vice-chairman, Conservative defence committee since 1976; Chairman, Conservative Media Committee, 1976–80. Chairman, WEU defence committee, 1974–77. Delegate to WEU and Council of Europe; North Atlantic Assembly; president, Atlantic Association of Young Political Leaders, 1968–70.

Mr Nicholas Westbrook, chief executive, Youth Training Resources Ltd, contested Plymouth, Devonport, Oct 1974, and Aldershot, 1979. Born May 26 1948; educ. Peter Symonds School, Winchester; Framlingham College, Suffolk, and Heriot-Watt University. Member, MSC young persons forum and CBI/YTS working party; ASTMS national advisory commitee on industrial relations.

Mr Alexander Crawford, journalist. Born Jan 15 1944; educ. Queen Mary's School, Basingstoke; Imperial College of Science and Technology, and Chelsea College of Science and Technology. Member, Rushmoor Borough Council, since 1976; Hampshire County Council 1981–82. NUJ.

Mr Richard Shepherd

ALDRIDGE-BROWNHILLS Electorate 60803

*Shepherd, R. (C)	24148	50.7%
Burford, R. T. (Lab)	11864	24.9%
Gunn, P. (SDP/All)	11599	24.4%
C majority	12284	25.8%
Total vote 47611		Turnout 78.3%

Mr Richard Shepherd, director of a retail food business in London, won the seat in 1979; contested Nottingham, East, in Feb 1974. Born Dec 6 1942; educ. LSE and the School of Advanced International Studies. Underwriting member of Lloyd's since 1974. Member, Select Committee on Treasury and Civil Service, since 1979; Secretary, Conservative backbench European Affairs and Industry Committees 1980–81; member, South East Economic Planning Council, 1970–74.

Mr Raymond Burford, barrister, has been a member of Walsall Metropolitan District Council since 1979. Born Jan 29 1954; educ. Brownhills Central Secondary School, University College, London, College of Law, London. TGWU.

Mr Peter Gunn, marketing director in the automotive industry. Born 1946. Independent council member, Shelfield/High Heath/Walsall Wood ward, 1975–79. Chairman, Walsall Area Party. Established first consultative committee to unite industry and the community to find ways to co-exist in heavily populated urban areas.

Mr Fergus Montgomery

ALTRINCHAM AND SALE Electorate 65984

*Montgomery, F. (C)	25321	52.5%
Clancy, B (L/All)	14410	29.9%
Erwin, A. (Lab)	7684	15.9%
Marsh, Mrs. C. (Eco)	629	1.3%
Wolstenholme, I. J. (Ind)	152	0.3%
C majority	10911	22.6%
Total vote 48196		Turnout 73.0%

Mr Fergus Montgomery, has been a member of the Select Committees on Environment, since 1979, and House of Commons Services and its catering sub committee since 1979. Elected in Oct 1974; MP for Brierley Hill from the by-election in 1967 until Feb 1974, when he unsuccessfully contested Dudley West. Represented Newcastle upon Tyne, East 1959–64; contested Consett 1955. Born Nov 25 1927; educ. Jarrow Grammar School and Bede College, Durham, Member Hebburn UDC, 1950–58. National chairman, Young Conservatives 1957–58. PPS to Mrs Thatcher as Secretary of State for Education and Science, 1973–74, and as Leader of the Opposition, 1975–76. NAS.

Mr Brian Clancy, chartered civil and structural engineer. Born Jun 30 1940; educ. St Benedict's School, Ealing, and University College, London. Member, Sale Borough Council and Trafford Borough Council (Liberal group leader). Senior partner in consultancy partnership and managing director, company of software designers to engineering industry.

Mr Alexander Erwin, college lecturer. Aged 39. Active trade union member and a member of NATFHE.

Mr Barry Jones

ALYN AND DEESIDE Electorate 56618

*Jones S. B. (Lab)	17806	40.3%
Burns, S. (C)	16438	37.2%
Owen, E. C. (SDP/All)	9535	21.6%
Shore, A. (Pl C)	413	0.9%
Lab majority	1368	3.1%
Total vote 44192		Turnout 78.1%

Mr Barry Jones has been an Opposition spokesman on employment since 1981; Under Secretary of State for Wales, 1974–79. Elected in 1983; MP for East Flint 1970–83, contested Northwich, 1966; Member, Select Committee on Public Accounts 1979–82. Teacher and former regional organizer, NUT. Born Jun 1938; educ. Hawarden Grammar School and University of Wales, Bangor College of Education. Former UK delegate to Council of Europe and WEU. Parliamentary consultant to NUT Former executive member, Wales Regional Labour Party; PPS to Mr Dennis Healey, 1972–74.

Mr Simon Burns, journalist, company director and company secretary. Personal and research assistant to Mrs Sally Oppenheim MP 1975–80. Born Sep 6 1952; educ. Christ the King School, Accra, Stamford School and Worcester College, Oxford. Secretary of Oxford University Conservative Association 1972–75; founded Young Conservatives in Rutland and Stamford, 1970.

Mr Eric Owen, laywer, is chairman, Wrexham SDP. Born 1946; educ. Grove Park Grammar School, Wrexham and Liverpool University. Chairman, North Wales SDP steering committee; vice-chairman, Wales SDP; drafted constitution for Wales SDP. Licensed lay reader, Church in Wales; co-organizer, SDP Christian Forum.

Dr Alan Shore, a co-author of Plaid Cymru's energy policy, is a lecturer in electronics at Liverpool University. Former member, Rhymni Valley District Council.

Mr Phillip Oppenheim

AMBER VALLEY Electorate 66720

Oppenheim P. (C)	21502	41.7%
Bookbinder, D. M. (Lab)	18184	35.3%
Johnson, B. (L/All)	10989	21.3%
Griffiths, P. (Ind)	856	1.7%
C majority	3318	6.4%
Total vote 51531		Turnout 77.2%

Mr Phillip Oppenheim, author, journalist, editor and farmer. Elected in 1983. Born 1956; educ. Harrow and Oriel College, Oxford. Son of Mrs Sally Oppenheim, who retained her seat at Gloucester. Joint founder of business consumer magazine covering high technology business products.

Mr David Bookbinder, confectionery distributor, contested High Peak in 1974 and 1979. Born Mar 1941; educ. secondary modern school and technical college. Member, Derbyshire County Council since 1973. TGWU.

Mr Brian Johnson, printer. Born Jan 23 1935; educ. state schools. NGA.

Mr Peter Fraser

ANGUS EAST Electorate 59 359

*Fraser, P. L. (C)	19 218	44.1%
Welsh, A. (SNP)	15 691	36.0%
Hammond, Miss P. (SDP/All)	4 978	11.4%
McConnell C. (Lab)	3 497	8.0%
Ross, Mrs P. (Eco)	239	0.6%
C majority	3 527	8.1%
Total vote 43 623	Turnout 73.5%	

Mr Peter Fraser, QC, became Solicitor General for Scotland in 1982. An advocate, he was elected to Angus East in 1983; MP Angus South 1979–83, having fought Aberdeen North in Oct 1974. Born May 29 1945; educ. Loretto School, Gonville and Caius, Cambridge and Edinburgh University. Former lecturer in constitutional law, Heriot-Watt University 1971–75. Chairman, Scottish Conservative Lawyers Law Reform Group, 1976.

Mr Andrew Welsh, college lecturer, was MP for Angus South, Oct 1974–79. SNP chief whip 1978–79; spokesman on housing, 1974–78; also spokesman on the self employed, small businesses and agriculture; contested Dunbartonshire, Central, Feb 1974. Born Apr 1944; educ. Govan High School and Glasgow University, National vice-chairman, SNP: former Stirling district councillor.

Miss Pauline Hammond became senior adviser to Secretary of State for Scotland, 1969. Now retired. Born 1922; educ. at Reading. Taught in London during war. Qualified as social worker, 1953; joined staff of National Institute for Social Work; appointed to University of Aberdeen to start new postgraduate course in applied social studies. Member, Council for Social Democracy.

Mr Charles McConnell, lecturer at a college of education. Born 1951; educ. St Peter's School, Harrogate; Huyton Hill School Ambleside; Granby Park School, Harrogate; College of Further Education, Harrogate; City of Birmingham Polytechnic; Paisley College of Technology.

Mr Roy Beggs

ANTRIM EAST Electorate 58 863

Beggs R. (OUP)	14 293	37.4%
Allister, J. (DUP)	13 926	36.5%
Neeson S. (All)	7 620	20.0%
O'Cleary, M. (SDLP)	1 047	2.7%
Cunning, W. (Ind)	741	1.9%
Kelly, A. (WP)	581	1.5%
OUP majority	367	1.0%
Total vote 38 208	Turnout 64.9%	

Mr Roy Beggs a farmer, elected in 1983, has been a member of the Northern Ireland Assembly for North Antrim since Oct 1982. Mayor of Larne for last five years; Larne district councillor for 9 years. Vice-chairman, North Eastern Education and Library Board. Second vice president, Assoc. of Education and Library Boards for Northern Ireland. Chairman, Larne Industrial Development Assoc. Ulster Farmers Union.

Mr James Allister is a barrister. Aged 30; educ. Regent House Grammar School, Newtownards, Co Down, Queen's University, Belfast. European assistant to the Rev Ian Paisley, 1980–82. DUP party press officer. Elected Northern Ireland Assembly, 1982. Vice-chairman assembly's personnel and finance committee; party chief whip.

The Rev Ian Paisley

ANTRIM NORTH Electorate 63 254

*Paisley, Rev I. (DUP)	23 922	54.2%
Coulter, Rev R. (OUP)	10 749	24.3%
Farren, S. (SDLP)	6 193	14.0%
McMahon, P. (PSF)	2 860	6.5%
Samuel, M. H. (Eco)	451	1.0%
DUP majority	13 173	29.8%
Total vote 44 175	Turnout 69.8%	

The Rev Ian Paisley, leader of the Ulster Democratic Unionist Party, has represented North Antrim since 1970. Elected as a Northern Ireland member of the European Parliament in 1979 and to the Northern Ireland Assembly in 1982. Moderator of the Free Presbyterian Church. Founded Protestant Unionist Party and sat as Protestant Unionist MP, 1970–74. Born Apr 6 1926; educ. Model School, Ballymena, and Ballymena Technical College and Reformed Presbyterian Theological Hall, Belfast. Ordained 1946. Won Bannside in 1970 and was a Stormont MP until 1972. Democratic Unionist member for North Antrim of Northern Ireland Assembly 1973–75, and UUUC member in the NI Constitutional Convention, 1975–76.

Mr Clifford Forsythe

ANTRIM SOUTH Electorate 59 321

Forsythe, C. (OUP)	17 727	45.7%
Thompson, R. (DUP)	10 935	28.2%
Mawhinney, G. (All)	4 612	11.9%
Maginness, A. (SDLP)	3 377	8.7%
Laverty, S. (PSF)	1 629	4.2%
Smyth, K. (WP)	549	1.4%
OUP majority	6 792	17.5%
Total vote 38 829		Turnout 65.5%

Mr Clifford Forsythe, a plumbing and heating contractor, aged 54; educ. Gengormley public elementary school. Elected in 1983. Mayor of Newtownabbey. Chairman South Antrim constituency assocn; member, party executive. Former professional footballer with Linfield and Derry City. Elected Northern Ireland Assembly, 1982.

Mr Roy Thompson, aged 37, farmer. Educ. Everton secondary school, Belfast; Belfast College of Technology, Shaftesbury House Tutorial College Belfast. Member, Antrim borough council, since 1981. Elected Northern Ireland assembly, 1982, for South Antrim; member of agriculture and economic development committees. Member of the Orange Order, Royal Black Preceptory, and Apprentice Boys of Derry.

Mr John MacKay

ARGYLL AND BUTE Electorate 47 497

*MacKay, J. (C)	13 380	38.6%
Michie, Mrs J. R. (L/All)	9 536	27.5%
Smith, I. (SNP)	8 514	24.6%
McCafferty, C. (Lab)	3 204	9.3%
Con majority	3 844	11.1%
Total vote 34 634		Turnout 72.9%

Mr John MacKay was appointed Under Secretary of State for Scotland in Apr 1982. Elected in 1983; MP for Argyll, 1979–83; contested the seat in Oct 1974 and Western Isles in Feb 1974. Former principal teacher of mathematics. Oban High School. Born Nov 15 1938; educ. Dunoon and Campbeltown Grammar Schools, Glasgow University and Jordanhill College of Education. Former chairman, Scottish Conservatives education policy committee; member, Scottish Secondary Teachers Association. Secretary, Scottish Conservative backbench MPs committee.

Mrs Ray Michie, area speech therapist for Argyll and Clyde Health Board, contested Argyll 1979. Born Feb 4 1934; educ. Lansdowne House School, Edinburgh, and School of Speech Therapy, Edinburgh. Member, Liberal/SDP Commission on Constitutional Reform.

Mr Ian Smith, managing director, contested Kinross and West Perthshire, 1979. Born Jan 1937; educ. Nicholson Institute, Stornoway. Member, SNP national executive committee and the national council; former chairman, SNP health policy committee.

Mr Charles McCafferty, further education lecturer at Glasgow College of Nautical Studies. Born Jun 10 1937; educ. Strathclyde University.

Mr Michael Marshall

ARUNDEL Electorate 74 849

*Marshall, R. M. (C)	31 096	59.6%
Walsh, J. (L/All)	15 391	29.5%
Rees, G. C. (Lab)	4 302	8.2%
Wadman, J. (CFCP)	1 399	2.7%
C majority	15 705	30.1%
Total vote 52 188		Turnout 69.7%

Mr Michael Marshall, Under Secretary of State for Industry 1979–81. Elected in Feb 1974; contested the Hartlepools, 1970. Writer, broadcaster and company chairman. Born Jun 21 1930; educ. Bradfield College, Harvard and Stanford universities. Member, Select Committee on Overseas Development 1974–76, Nationalized Industries, 1976–79 and Defence 1982–83. Vice-chairman, Conservative Industry Committee 1975–79. Vice-chairman, Parliamentary Information, Technology Committee. Chairman Marshall Consultants Ltd. Member, Equity.

Dr James Walsh, general practitioner, contested Hove, Oct, 1974 and 1979 and Sussex, West, in Euro-election, 1979. Born Jan 11 1943; educ. Wimbledon College and University of London (The London Hospital Medical College). Member, Arun District Council, since 1976; Worthing District Health Authority, since 1982. On board of directors of Arundel Festival. Member, European Movement. BMA. Surgeon Commander in RNR.

Mr Gareth Rees, company executive. Born April 4 1944; educ. Barry Comprehensive School and Polytechnic of Wales. Hotel and Catering Workers Union.

Mr Frank Haynes

ASHFIELD Electorate 69 791

*Haynes, D. F. (Lab)	21 859	42.5%
Seligman, R. (C)	15 772	30.7%
Stein, Mrs F. (L/All)	13 812	26.9%
Lab majority	6 087	11.8%
Total vote 51 443		Turnout 73.7%

Mr Frank Haynes, Opposition whip for the East Midlands, was elected in 1979. Member, Select Committee on Parliamentary Commission for Administration (Ombudsman), since 1979. NUM branch official for 20 years; a member of the union for 34 years. Born Mar 8, 1926; educ. secondary schools in London. Member, Nottinghamshire County Council since 1965, and district council for 12 years. Sponsored by NUM.

Mr Roderick Seligman, consultant and chartered accountant. Born Nov 16 1954; educ. Harrow and Trinity College, Oxford. Economics secretary, Bow Group, and treasurer, British Atlantic Group of Young Politicians, since 1982. Chairman, Bayswater Conservatives, 1981–83.

Mrs Frances Stein, state registered nurse. Born Jun 18 1941; educ. Northampton Girls' School, Wingsthorpe. Member, Ashfield District Council.

Mr Keith Speed

ASHFORD Electorate 65 442 1979: 61 460 same

*Speed, K. (C)	27 230	56.8%
Hawkes, Mrs J. (SDP/All)	13 319	27.8%
Lewis, P. (Lab)	6 167	12.9%
Porter, C. A. (Eco)	569	1.2%
King, J. W. (Nat Lab)	456	1.0%
Lockwood, R. E. (BNP)	195	0.4%
C majority	13 911	0.4%
Total vote 47 936		Turnout 73.3%

1979: Total vote 47 119 (76.9%); C 26 224 (55.7%); Lab 12 586 (26.7%); L 7 631 (16.2% NF 678 (1.4%). C maj 13 638 (29.0%); swing 7.6% to C.

Mr Keith Speed, company director and marketing consultant, was Under Secretary of Defence for the Royal Navy 1979–81. Opposition spokesman on environment and local government. 1975–79. Elected in Oct 1974; MP for Meriden, Mar 1968 to Feb 1974. Regular naval officer, 1947–56. Under Secretary of State for Environment, 1972–74; assistant Government whip, 1979–72. Born Mar 11 1934; educated at Greenhill School, Evesham, Bedford Modern School, and Royal Naval Colleges, Dartmouth and Greenwich. Member Select Committee on Procedure (Finance) 1982–83. Served in Conservative Research Department, 1965–68. Parliamentary adviser to Professional Assoc. of Teachers.

Mrs Jo Hawkes is a publisher specialising in press releases for Latin America. Born 1944; educ. Westfield College, London.

Mr Paul Lewis, deputy director, National Council for One Parent Families. Born Apr 22 1948; educ. Maidstone Grammar School and Stirling University. Maidstone borough councillor since 1976.

Mr Robert Sheldon

ASHTON–UNDER–LYNE Electorate 58 963 1979: 58 588 minor

*Sheldon, R. (Lab)	20 987	49.7%
Spring, R. (C)	13 290	31.5%
Adler, J. (SDP/All)	7 521	17.8%
Hallsworth, D. (Ind)	407	1.0%
Lab majority	7 697	18.2%
Total vote 42 205		Turnout 71.6%

1979: Total vote 44 876 (76.6%); Lab 24 535 (54.7%); C 16 156 (36.0%); L 3 699 (8.2%); NF 486 (1.1%). Lab maj 8 379 (18.7%); swing 2.9% to C.

Mr Robert Sheldon, an Opposition spokesman on Treasury and economic affairs 1979–83; Financial Secretary to the Treasury, 1975–79; Minister of State, Treasury, 1974–75; Minister of State, Civil Service Department, 1974. Former Opposition spokesman on the Civil Service and machinery of government and Treasury matters. Member, Treasury and Civil Service Select Committee, 1979–81 and Chairman of its sub-committee, 1979–81. Chairman, Public Accounts Committee 1965–70, 1975–79, since 1983; member, Public Expenditure Committee, and chairman of subcommittee, 1972–74; member, Fulton Committee on Civil Service, 1966–68. Elected in 1964; contested Manchester, Withington, 1959. Former company director. Born Sep 13 1923; educ. grammar school and technical colleges; external graduate, London University.

Mr Richard Spring, international financial adviser. Born 1946; educ. Rondebosch, Cape Town, South Africa and Magdalene College, Cambridge. Vice-chairman, Eccleston Committee.

Mr John Adler is a lecturer in management and economics. Born 1937; educ Nuneaton and Coventry colleges of technology and the Open University.

Mr Timothy Raison

AYLESBURY Electorate 72 792

*Raison, T. H. (C)	30 230	58.1%
Soole, M. (SDP/All)	15 308	29.4%
Moran, M. P. (Lab)	6 354	12.2%
Chapman, T. (Ind)	166	0.3%
C majority	14 922	28.7%
Total vote 52 058	Turnout	71.5%

Mr Timothy Raison, appointed Minister for Overseas Development in Jan 1983; Minister of State, Home Office from May 1979; chief Opposition spokesman on the environment and member of the Shadow Cabinet 1974–77; spokesman on prices and consumer affairs 1974–75 and on social services and education during 1974. Under Secretary of State for Education and Science 1973–74. Journalist and magazine publisher. Elected in 1970. Born Nov 3 1929; educ. Dragon School, Oxford; Eton and Christ Church, Oxford. Senior fellow, Centre for Studies in Social Policy. Former director, Private Patients Plan. Member, Richmond upon Thames Borough Council 1967–71.

Mr Michael Soole, barrister. Born Jul 18 1954; educ. Berkhamsted School and University College, Oxford.

Mr Michael Moran, technical college lecturer. Born Aug 6 1945; educ. Forest County Secondary School, Horsham; Croydon Technical College, Garnett College, University of Manchester. Member, Chesham Town Council, since May 1983. NATFHE.

Mr George Younger

AYR Electorate 65 010

*Younger, G.K. (C)	21 325	42.8%
MacDonald, K. (Lab)	13 338	26.8%
Brodie, C. (L/All)	12 740	25.6%
Goldie. I. (SNP)	2 431	4.9%
C majority	7 987	16.0%
Total vote 49 834	Turnout	76.7%

Mr George Younger, who became Secretary of State for Scotland in May 1979, had been an Opposition spokesman on Scottish Office matters; chief Opposition spokesman on defence and member of Shadow Cabinet 1975–76; a spokesman on defence, 1974–75. Minister of State for Defence 1974; Under Secretary for Development Scottish Office, 1970–73. Elected in 1964; contested North Lanarkshire 1959. Scottish Conservative whip 1965–67. Eldest son of Viscount Younger of Leckie. Born 22 Sep 1931, educ. Cargilfield School, Edinburgh, Winchester College and New College, Oxford. Governor, Royal Scottish Academy. Former director, Tennant Caledonian Breweries Ltd, Glasgow. Chairman, Scottish Conservative Party, 1974–75. Former member, Select Committee on Procedure.

Mr Keith MacDonald, a representative and former teacher and bookseller. Born Feb 21 1953; educ. Stirling University. Member, Kyle and Garrick District Council, since 1980. TGWU.

Mr Charles Brodie, a European business manager in electronics. Born May 8, 1944; educ. Morgan Academy, Dundee, and St Andrew's University. Contested Dundee, East, 1979 and Oct 1974. Vice-chairman, Scottish Liberal Party.

Mr Ian Goldie, principal teacher of modern languages. Born 1941; educ. Hutchesons School, Glasgow and the universities of Glasgow and Paris.

Mr Tony Baldry

BANBURY Electorate 65 324

Baldry, A. (C)	26 225	53.4%
Fitchett, K. (SDP/All)	13 200	26.9%
Hodgson, J. B. (Lab)	9 343	19.0%
Brough, D. N. (Ind)	383	0.8%
C majority	13 025	26.5%
Total vote 49 151	Turnout	75.2%

Mr Tony Baldry, barrister, publisher and company director, elected in 1983; contested Thurrock, 1979. Born Jul 10 1950, educ. Leighton Park and Sussex University. Personal aide to Mrs Thatcher in Oct 1974 election; served in Leader of the Opposition's office, 1975. Member, executive committee, European Union of Conservative and Christian Democrat Students, 1971–72; NEC, British Council of the European Movement, 1973–74. Founder member, Students for a United Europe; first national chairman, Young European Democrats, 1974. Awarded Robert Schumann Silver Medal, 1978, for contributions to European politics. Member, Carlton Club political committee.

Mr Keith Fitchett, accountant, born Feb 21 1946; educ. Coventry College of Technology and New College, Oxford. Member, Lewisham Borough Council 1981–82. APEX.

Mr James Hodgson, a college of further education lecturer, contested Banbury in 1979. Born Oct 1938; educ. Bradfield College, Berkshire and King's College, Newcastle. Member, National Council for Civil Liberties; Fabian Society; CASE; SEA. NATFHE.

Mr Albert McQuarrie

BANFF AND BUCHAN Electorate 60 403

*McQuarrie, A. (C)	16 072	39.7%
Henderson, D. (SNP)	15 135	37.4%
Needham, E. (SDP/All)	6 084	15.0%
Lloyd, I.F.R. (Lab)	3 150	7.8%
C majority	937	2.3%
Total vote 40 441		Turnout 67.0%

Mr Albert McQuarrie, secretary, Conservative backbench fisheries committee, 1981–82, and vice-chairman since 1982, was MP for East Aberdeenshire 1979–83. Professional civil engineer and company director, he contested Kilmarnock, 1966 and Caithness and Sutherland. Oct 1974. Born Jan 1 1918; educ. Greenock High School and Royal College of Science and Technology. Member, Select Committee on Scottish Affairs since 1979. Dean of Guild, Town Council, Burgh of Gourock, Renfrewshire 1949–52. Chairman, British-Gibraltar Group.

Mr Douglas Henderson, management consultant, was MP for East Aberdeenshire, Feb 1974–79. SNP spokesman on employment 1974–79; Chief Whip, 1974–78. Previously spokesman on finance, trade and industry. Senior vice-chairman, SNP, until 1972. Born Jul 1935; educ. Royal High School, Edinburgh and Edinburgh University.

Mr Edward Needham, self-employed fisheries consultant. Born 1943; educ. London and Edinburgh universities. Worked on fish farming team, Unilever research in Aberdeen. In 1979 became consultant retained by several commercial concerns, the Ministry of Agriculture, Fisheries and Food and the Highlands and Islands Development Board.

Mr Ian Lloyd, personnel officer with the National Health Service. Born Aug 29 1955; educ. Aberdeen University. Branch secretary, Nalgo, 1982; NUPE shop steward; secretary, Grampian health unions strike committee, 1982.

Ms Jo Richardson

BARKING Electorate 52 362

*Richardson, Ms J. (Lab)	14 415	42.1%
Summerson, H. (C)	10 389	30.4%
Gibb, J. (L/All)	8 770	25.6%
Newport, I. (NF)	646	1.9%
Lab majority	4 026	11.8%
Total vote 34 220		Turnout 65.4%

Ms Jo Richardson, member of Labour Party National Executive Committee since 1979, was elected in Feb 1974; contested Harrow East 1964; Hornchurch 1959, and Monmouth 1955 and 1951. Born Aug 28 1923: educ. Southend High School for Girls. Former member, select committees on home affairs, nationalized industries and expenditure procedure. Vice President, CND. Chairman, PLP Civil Liberties Group 1975–79; executive council, National Council for Civil Liberties. APEX and ASTMS.

Mr Hugo Summerson chartered surveyor and company director. Born Jul 1950; educ. Harrow; Royal Agricultural College.

Mr John Gibb, company director, contested Ince Oct 1974 and 1979, and West Lancashire in the Euro-election 1979. Born Sep 13 1926; educ. King George V Grammar School, Southport; St Egberts College, Chingford, and Dolcoath Technical College.

Mr Roy Mason

BARNSLEY CENTRAL Electorate 55 115

*Mason, R. (Lab)	21 847	59.8%
Oldfield, H. (C)	7 674	21.0%
Reid, Rev. G. (L/All)	7 011	19.2%
Lab majority	14 173	38.8%
Total vote 36 532		Turnout 66.3%

Mr Roy Mason was chief Opposition spokesman on agriculture, fisheries and food 1979–81; Secretary of State for Northern Ireland 1976–79; Secretary of State for Defence 1974–76. Opposition spokesman on trade and civil aviation 1970–74. Former chairman of the PLP miners' group. President of the Board of Trade 1969–70; Minister of Trade, 1969–70; Minister of Power 1968–69; Postmaster-General Apr–Jun 1968; Minister of Defence (Equipment) 1967–68; Minister of State, Board of Trade 1964–67. Elected in 1983; MP for Barnsley 1953–83. Born Apr 18 1924; educ. elementary schools and LSE. Miner, 1938–53. Sponsored by NUM.

Mr Howard Oldfield, engaged in hotel and catering and food manufacturing.. Born 1942; educ. Barnsley Grammar School. Chairman, Conservative Assoc; vice-president, Barnsley Market Traders' Federation.

Rev Geoffrey Reid, Methodist minister, contested Rother Valley, Oct, 1974. Born Sep 5 1946; educ. Heaton Grammar School, Newcastle; Newcastle University and Wesley House, Cambridge. Former secretary, Alliance of Radical Methodists.

Mr Terry Patchett

BARNSLEY EAST Electorate 53 611

Patchett, T. (Lab)	23 505	65.9%
Tomlinson, P. (L/All)	6413	18.0%
England, G. (C)	5749	16.1%
Lab majority	17 092	47.9%
Total vote 35 667		Turnout 66.5%

Mr Terry Patchett, miner. Elected in 1983. Born July 11 1940. NUM sponsored.
Mr Peter Tomlinson, a self employed chiropodist, contested Barnsley Oct 1974. Born May 1945; educ. Longcroft School, Beverley and Salford College of Chiropody.
Mr George England, barrister, contested Barnsley, 1974 and 1979. Born 1947; educ. Barnsley Holgate Grammar School and Sheffield University. Former chairman, Barnsley Young Conservatives; former officer, Barnsley constituency Conservative Assoc.

Mr Allen McKay

BARNSLEY WEST AND PENISTONE Electorate 60 648

*McKay, A. (Lab)	22 560	50.8%
Hartley, T. (C)	12 218	27.5%
Evans, J. (SDP/All)	9624	21.7%
Lab majority	10 342	23.3%
Total vote 44 402		Turnout 73.2%

Mr Allen McKay, an Opposition whip 1981–83, was elected in 1983; MP for Penistone, 1978–83. Mining electrical engineer 1947–65; industrial relations officer with the National Coal Board 1966–78. Born Feb 5 1927; educ. Hoyland Kirk Balk School; Extra-Mural Department of University of Sheffield. Served on Hoyland Nether UDC 1965–74; chairman 1973–74. Member, Barnsley Metropolitan Borough Council 1974–78. Committee member and branch president NUM.
Mr Timothy Hartley, barrister and former law school lecturer. Born 1947; educ. King's School, Canterbury; Bristol University, and Gray's Inn.
Mr John Evans, mechanical engineer, was elected to Barnsley Metropolitan Council in 1975. Deputy leader of the opposition 1979–81. Educ Barnsley College of Technology and Sheffield Polytechnic. Member, Darton Youth Advisory Committee which he represents on West Barnsley Community Education Governing Body.

Mr Cecil Franks

BARROW AND FURNESS Electorate 67 896

Franks, C. (C)	22 284	43.6%
*Booth, A. E. (Lab)	17 707	34.7%
Cottier, D. (SDP/All)	11 079	21.7%
C majority	4577	9.0%
Total vote 51 070		Turnout 75.2%

Mr Cecil Franks, a solicitor, elected in 1983, is leader of the Conservative Group on Manchester City Council. Born Jul 1 1935; educ. Manchester Grammar School and Manchester University.
Mr Albert Booth chief Opposition spokesman on transport 1979–83. Former member of the Shadow Cabinet. Secretary of State for Employment 1976–79. Minister of State for Employment 1974–76. Chairman Select Committee on Statutory Instruments 1970–74. An Opposition spokesman on trade and industry, 1973–74. Elected in 1966; contested Tynemouth 1964. Born May 28 1928; educ. St Thomas's Winchester, South Shields Marine School, Rutherford College of Technology. Member Tynemouth Borough Council, 1961–65. Sponsored by AUEW (TASS).
Mr David Cottier is a local government officer. Born Feb 9 1946; educ. Workington Technical College; Workington and Carlisle Colleges of Further Education and Liverpool Polytechnic.

Mr David Amess

BASILDON Electorate 69 604

Amess, D. (C)	17 516	38.7%
Fulbrook, J. G. H. (Lab)	16 137	35.6%
Slipman, Ms S. (SDP/All)	11 634	25.7%
C majority	1 379	3.1%
Total vote 45 287		Turnout 65.1%

Mr David Amess, senior partner in specialist employment consultancy was elected in 1983. Born 1952; educ. St Bonaventures grammar school and Bournemouth College of Technology Contested Newham North West 1979. Member Redbridge Council and vice-chairman housing committee. Member, Redbridge community health council and arts council. Member, Beacon youth management centre committee and Mayfield youth centre; school governor.

Mr Julian Fulbrook, lecturer in law at LSE; barrister, contested Huntingdonshire 1979. Born May 10 1948; educ. Eltham College, Redruth County Grammar School, Exeter and Cambridge universities, Harvard Law School. Member, Camden Borough Council, since 1978; chairman, housing management, 1981–83. TGWU.

Ms Sue Slipman is former president of the National Union of Students. Now an official of NUPE. Born Aug 1949; educ. Stockwell Manor School, University of Wales, University of Leeds.

Mr Andrew Hunter

BASINGSTOKE Electorate 71 975

Hunter, A. (C)	28 381	51.3%
*Hudson Davies, G. E (SDP/All)	15 931	28.8%
McAllister, J. (Lab)	10 646	19.3%
Wilson, I. (BNP)	344	0.6%
C majority	12 450	22.5%
Total vote 55 302		Turnout 76.8%

Mr Andrew Hunter, teacher, elected in 1983, contested Southampton, Itchen 1979. Born Jan 1943; educ. St George's School, Harpenden, Durham University and Jesus College, Cambridge. Member, Durham University Liberal Party, 1962–65; Cambridge University Conservative Association, 1966–68. Major in Territorial Army.

Mr Ednyfed Hudson Davies was elected Labour MP for Caerphilly in 1979; resigned party and joined SDP in 1981, MP for Conway 1966–70. Lecturer, barrister and journalist. Born Dec 4 1929; educ. Dynevor Grammar School, Swansea, University College of Wales. Swansea and Balliol College, Oxford. Member, Select Committee on Energy 1980–83. Secretary, All-Party Tourism Committee 1979–83. Member, Select Committee on Agriculture, 1966–70. Former chairman, Welsh Tourist Board. TGWU. NUS.

Mr James McAllister, university lecturer. Born Apr 30 1949; educ. Ruskin College, Oxford, and Sussex and Reading universities. Hants county councillor; member, Hants health authority, and school governor, TGWU.

Mr Joe Ashton

BASSETLAW Electorate 65 721

*Ashton, J. (Lab)	22 231	45.6%
Cleasby, M. (C)	18 400	37.7%
Withnall, B. (SDP/All)	8 124	16.7%
Lab majority	3 831	7.9%
Total vote 48 755		Turnout: 74.2%

Mr Joe Ashton, formerly a design engineer and now a journalist, novelist and playwright, was returned at a by-election in Oct 1968. Opposition spokesman on energy, 1979–81. Member Select Committee on Members' Interests since 1979 and Select Committee on Members' Salaries 1981–82. Government whip 1976–77; PPS to Mr Benn, 1974–76. Born Oct 9 1933; educ. High Storrs Grammar School, Sheffield and Rotherham Technical College. Member Select Committee on nationalized industries, 1974–76. Sponsored by AUEW (TASS).

Mr Martyn Cleasby, schoolmaster. Born Jul 9 1939; educ. Barnsley Grammar School, Durham University. Member, Bassetlaw District Council since 1976. NAS.

Mr Brian Withnall, head of special education at Joseph Whitaker's School, Rainworth, Nottingham. Born 1944; educ. Durham university. Former Labour district councillor.

Mr Christopher Patten

BATH

Electorate 64 325 1979: 63 575 same

*Patten, C. F. (C)	22 544	47.1%
Dean, J. M. (SDP/All)	17 240	36.0%
Pott, A. J. (Lab)	7 259	15.2%
Grimes, D. (Eco)	441	0.9%
Wandle, R. S. (Prog L)	319	0.7%
Young, G. S. (Wrld Gv)	67	0.1%
C majority	5 304	11.1%
Total vote 47 870		Turnout 74.4%

Mr Christopher Patten, became an Under-Secretary of State for Northern Ireland, Jun 1983. Director of the Conservative Research Department, 1974–79, elected in 1979; contested Lambeth Central in Feb 1974. Director and consultant. Born May 12 1944; educ. St Benedict's School, Ealing; Balliol College, Oxford. Parliamentary Private Secretary to the Leader of the House 1979–81 and to the Secretary of State for Social Services 1981. Member, Select Committee on Defence, Select Committee on Procedure (Finance). Personal assistant and political secretary to Lord Carrington when he was chairman of party, 1972–74. Former secretary of the Shadow Cabinet. Senior Fellow, 1983, the Policy Studies Institute.

Mr Malcolm Dean, journalist on staff of *The Guardian*, specialising in social policy. Special adviser to Secretary of State for Social Services, 1978–79. Member of advisory committees on dangerous offenders, machinery of government, ECT and community medicine. Born June 11 1939; educ. Macclesfield Grammar School; Ruskin College, Oxford, and University of Chicago. NUJ.

Mr Andrew Pott, accountant for a co-operatively organised housing association. Born 1947. Member and leader-elect, Avon County Council. APEX.

Mrs Elizabeth Peacock

BATLEY AND SPEN

Electorate 73 798

Peacock, Mrs E. J. (C)	21 433	39.6%
*Woolmer, K. J. (Lab)	20 563	38.0%
Woollery, D. S. (SDP/All)	11 678	21.6%
Lord, C. (Eco)	493	0.9%
C majority	870	1.6%
Total vote 54 167		Turnout 73.4%

Mrs Elizabeth Peacock, assistant to the executive director, York Community Council Ltd. was elected in 1983. Born Sep 4 1937; educ. Skipton, Yorkshire. Magistrate. Member, North Yorkshire County Council.

Mr Kenneth Woolmer became an Opposition spokesman on trade in 1981. University lecturer. MP for Batley and Morley, 1979–83; contested Leeds, North-West, 1970. Born Apr 1940; educ. Kettering Grammar School and Leeds University. Member, Leeds County Borough Council 1970–74; West Yorkshire Metropolitan County Council 1973–79 (leader of Labour Group 1975–79 and of Council 1975–77). Parliamentary adviser, Inland Revenue Staff Federation. PLP Finance and Economics Group chairman 1980–81, vice-chairman, 1981–83. AUT and GMBATU.

Mr Stephen Woollery, journalist specialising in education matters. Aged 35; educ. grammar school and university. Vice-chairman of Kirklees SDP since 1982.

Mr Alfred Dubs

BATTERSEA

Electorate 65 938

*Dubs, A. (Lab)	19 248	43.8%
Allason, R. (C)	15 972	36.4%
Harris, M. (SDP/All)	7 675	17.5%
Salt, M. J. (NF)	539	1.2%
Willington, Mrs S. (Eco)	377	0.9%
Jackson, T. (CBWU)	86	0.2%
Purie-Harwell, Mrs K. (Com)	22	0.1%
Lab majority	3 276	7.5%
Total vote 43 919		Turnout 66.6%

Mr Alfred Dubs, a local government officer, represented Battersea South, 1979–83; contested Cities of London and Westminster 1970, and South Hertfordshire in both 1974 elections. Member, Select Committee on Home Affairs and its sub-committee on Race Relations and Immigration since 1979. Born Dec 1932; educ. London School of Economics. Member, Westminster City Council 1971–78; chairman, Westminster Community Relations Council 1972–77. Nalgo. Vice-chairman, PLP home affairs and Northern Ireland groups.

Mr Rupert Allason, researcher and author, contested Kettering 1979. Born Nov 1951; educ. Downside School, Grenoble University, and London University. Father, Mr James Allason, was Conservative MP for Hemel Hempstead 1959–74.

Mr Michael Harris, barrister. Born Jan 11 1942; educ. Newbury Grammar School and Merton College, Oxford.

Mr Timothy Smith

BEACONSFIELD Electorate 66186

*Smith, T. J. (C)	30552	63.8%
Ive, D. (L/All)	12252	25.6%
Smith, J. S. (Lab)	5107	10.7%
C majority	18300	38.2%
Total vote 47911	Turnout	72.4%

Mr Timothy Smith, held the seat for the Conservatives at the by-election in May 1982; MP for Ashfield 1977–79. Chartered accountant. Born Oct 1947; educ. Harrow School and St Peter's College, Oxford. Secretary, Conservative health and social services committee and of Conservative small business committee since 1982. Member, Select Committee on Health and Social Services, since 1982. Parliamentary consultant, consultative committee of accountancy bodies. Editorial consultant of *Accountancy Age*.

Mr David Ive, solicitor. Aged 33; educ. Birmingham University. Contested Barnet, Chipping Barnet, 1979.

Mr Sherwin Smith, lecturer and former accountant. Born Mar 2 1935; educ. Durham University. NATFHE.

Sir Philip Goodhart

BECKENHAM Electorate 58719 1979: 57939 minor

*Goodhart, Sir P. C. (C)	23606	57.4%
Forrest, Mrs C. (L/All)	10936	26.6%
Dowd, J. P. (Lab)	6386	15.5%
Younger, G. W. (BNP)	203	0.5%
C majority	12670	30.8%
Total vote 41131	Turnout	70.1%

1979: Total votes 43281 (74.7%); C 24 607 (56.9%); Lab 10856 (25.1%); L 6450 (14.9%); Eco 762 (1.8%) NF 606 (1.4%). C Maj 13751 (31.8%); swing 5.4% to C.

Sir Philip Goodhart was Under Secretary of State for Defence 1981; Under-Secretary of State for Northern Ireland 1979–81. Author and Journalist 1952–56, *Daily Telegraph* and *Sunday Times*. Returned for Beckenham at by-election, in Mar 1957; contested Consett 1950. Born Nov 3 1925; educ. Hotchkiss School, United States, and Trinity College, Cambridge. Joint secretary, 1922 Committee, 1960–79. Secretary. Conservative Parliamentary Defence Committee, 1967–72, chairman 1972–74, vice-chairman 1974–79. Chairman, Conservative Parliamentary Northern Ireland Committee 1976–79. Advisory Council on Public Records, 1970–79; Executive Committee, British Council, 1974–79. Member, Council, Consumers' Association 1959–68 and 1970–79, UK delegation to UN General Assembly 1963, and North Atlantic Assembly 1964–79.

Mrs Christina Forrest contested the seat in 1979. An economist. Born May 1 1950; educ. Hutchesons' Girls' Grammar School, Glasgow; Glasgow University. Formerly a trade union research officer. ASTMS.

Mr James Dowd, service engineer. Born 1951. Chief Labour whip, Lewisham Council. ASTMS.

Mr Nicholas Lyell

BEDFORDSHIRE MID Electorate 75558

*Lyell, N. W. (C)	33042	56.9%
Howes, Mrs. M. (L/All)	15661	26.9%
Tizard, J. (Lab)	9420	16.2%
C majority	17381	29.9%
Total vote 58123	Turnout	76.9%

Mr Nicholas Lyell QC, a barrister, was MP for Hemel Hempstead 1979–83; contested Lambeth Central, Oct 1974. Elected for this seat 1983. PPS to the Attorney General since Oct 1979. Secretary, Conservative parliamentary constitutional committee, May–Oct 1979. Born Dec 12 1938; educ. Stowe School and Christ Church, Oxford. Member of Lloyd's. Member, Select Committee on Procedure (Finance), since 1982.

Mrs Monica Howes, course manager in health and social welfare section, Open University. Born Sep 12 1938; educ. Haberdashers' Aske's School, Johannesburg High School for Girls, Polytechnic of Central London. Member, national executive, Liberal Party. AUT.

Mr John Tizard works for the Spastics Society; member, Bedfordshire County Council, since 1981. Born Nov 1954; educ. LSE. TGWU.

Mr Trevor Skeet

BEDFORDSHIRE NORTH Electorate 71 491

*Skeet, T. H. (C)	27 969	52.0%
Gibbons, B. K. (L/All)	14 120	26.3%
Healy, Ms P. (Lab)	11 323	21.1%
Hughes, N. J. (Ind)	344	0.6%
C majority	13 849	25.8%
Total vote 53 756	Turnout	75.2%

Mr Trevor Skeet won this seat in 1983; MP for Bedford 1970–83, and for Willesden East 1959–64; contested Llanelli 1955 and Stoke Newington and Hackney North 1951. Barrister and industrial consultant. Born 28 Jan 1918; educ. King's College, Auckland, and University of New Zealand. Vice-chairman, Conservative power and energy committee, 1959–64; chairman, oil subcommittee, 1959–64; chairman, Conservative trade committee 1971–74; member Select Committee on Wealth Tax, 1975. Secretary, all party group on airships, 1971–78; Chairman, Conservative Middle East Committee 1973–78; member all-party group on minerals since 1971, co-chairman 1979. Vice-chairman, British-Brazilian Group and British-Japanese Group; secretary British-Nigerian Group; Secretary, Parliamentary and Scientific Committee. Consultant to Blue Circle Industries.

Mr Brian Gibbons, manager with British Aerospace. Born Nov 6 1926. County councillor since 1974.

Ms Pat Healy, journalist; social services correspondent of *The Times*. Born May 19 1941; educ. Ursuline High School, Brentwood, and Mid-Essex Technical School, Chelmsford. Labour Government appointee to UK Commission for UNESCO 1974–79. NUJ.

Mr David Madel

BEDFORDSHIRE SOUTH WEST Electorate 76 298

*Madel, W. D. (C)	31 767	55.1%
Byfield, R. (SDP/All)	16 036	27.8%
Cochrane, W. (Lab)	9 899	17.2%
C majority	15 731	27.3%
Total vote 57 702	Turnout	75.6%

Mr David Madel has been a member of the Select Committee on Members' Interests and of the Select Committee on Education, Science and the Arts since 1979; consultant and company director. Elected in 1983; MP for Bedford South, 1970–83, contested Erith and Crayford, 1965 by-election and 1966. Born Aug 6 1938; educ. Uppingham School, Keble College, Oxford. Member, former Expenditure Committee. Secretary, Conservative parliamentary home affairs committee, 1972–73. PPS to Ministry of Defence, 1973–74. Joint vice-chairman (previously joint secretary), Conservative employment committee, 1974–79. Advertising executive, Thomson Organization, 1964–70. Parliamentary consultant to the Banking Insurance and Finance Union. Joint vice-chairman, Conservative backbench education committee, since 1979.

Mr Richard Byfield, college lecturer in government and politics. Born Apr 27 1949; educ. University of Bradford, Huddersfield College of Education (Technical), Hatfield Polytechnic.

Mr William Cochrane, co-ordinator for nationwide education and training programme sponsored by Community Service Volunteers. Born Sep 7 1954; educ. Barrhead High School, Renfrewshire and Salvation Army International Training College. Member, South Bedfordshire District Council.

Mr Peter Robinson

BELFAST EAST Electorate 55 581

*Robinson, P. (DUP)	17 631	45.3%
Burchill, J. (OUP)	9 642	24.8%
Napier, O. (All)	9 373	24.1%
Donaldson, D. (PSF)	682	1.8%
Tang, Mrs M. (Lab & TU)	584	1.5%
Prendiville, P. (SDLP)	519	1.3%
Cullen, F. (WP)	421	1.1%
Boyd, H. (NA)	59	0.2%
DUP majority	7 989	20.5%
Total vote 38 911	Turnout	70.0%

Mr Peter Robinson, who won the seat in 1979, has been general secretary of the Democratic Unionist Party since 1975, having been a member of the party's executive 1973–79, and secretary of the central executive committee 1974–77. Elected to Northern Ireland Assembly, 1982; chairman of Environment Committee. Elected to Castlereagh Borough Council, 1977. Appointed by Council as Deputy Mayor 1978. Born Dec 29 1948; educ. Annadale Grammar School and Castlereagh CFE. Director, Crown Publications, Belfast.

Mr Jeremy Burchell, aged 32, barrister. Ed Campbell College, Belfast, Queens University, Belfast. Elected N Ireland Convention 1975, for South Belfast; N. Ireland Assembly 1982, for East Belfast. Unsuccessfully contested North Antrim in Westminster parliamentary election 1979. Belfast City councillor since 1981.

Mr Cecil Walker

BELFAST NORTH Electorate 61 128

Walker, A. C. (OUP)	15 339	36.2%
Searight, G. (DUP)	8 260	19.5%
Feeny, B. (SDLP)	5 944	14.0%
Austin, J. (PSF)	5 451	12.9%
Maguire, P. (All)	3 879	9.1%
Lynch, S. (WP)	2 412	5.7%
Gault, W. (Ind DUP)	1 134	2.7%
OUP majority	7 079	16.7%
Total vote 42 419	Turnout 69.4%	

Mr Cecil Walker, a sales manager, elected in 1983, contested the seat in 1979. Born 1925; educ. Methodist College, Belfast. Belfast City councillor for six years. Unsuccessfully contested Northern Ireland Assembly 1973.

Mr George Seawright, a shipyard worker, aged 32; educ. Kingsridge Secondary School. Drumchapel, Glasgow. City councillor, Belfast since 1981. Elected Northern Ireland Assembly 1982; member health and social service committee and security committee.

The Rev Martin Smyth

BELFAST SOUTH Electorate 53 694

*Smyth Rev M. (OUP)	18 669	50.0%
Cook, D. (All)	8 945	23.9%
McRae, R. S. (DUP)	4 565	12.2%
McDonnell, A. (SDLP)	3 216	8.6%
McKnight, S. (PSF)	1 107	3.0%
Carr, G. (WP)	856	2.3%
OUP majority	9 724	26.0%
Total vote 37 358	Turnout 69.6%	

The Rev Martin Smyth, held the seat for the Official Unionists at by-election in Mar 1982 caused by the murder of the Rev Robert Bradford. Party spokesman on health, social services and housing. A minister of religion without pastoral charge; vice-chairman all-party committee on Soviet Jewry. Grand Master of the Grand Orange Lodge of Ireland since 1972; Grand Master of World Orange Council 1973–82, honorary past Grand Master, Canada, honorary deputy Grand Master, USA, New Zealand, New South Wales, of Orange Order. Born Jun 15 1931; educ. Methodist College, Belfast, Magee University College, Londonderry, Trinity College, Dublin, Presbyterian College, Belfast. Elected Assembly member for Belfast South Oct 1982.

Mr David Cook, aged 39, solicitor. Educ. Campbell College, Belfast; Pembroke College, Cambridge. Belfast city councillor since 1973, leader of Alliance group 1973–81. Lord Mayor of Belfast 1978–79, was the first non-Unionist to hold the office. Unsuccessfully contested Westminster parliamentary election in Belfast South, Feb 1974 and by-election in Mar 1982. Elected N. Ireland Assembly, 1982, for Belfast South; member of environment committee, deputy leader, Alliance Party.

Mr Gerry Adams

BELFAST WEST Electorate 59 750

Adams, G. (PSF)	16 379	36.9%
Hendron, J. (SDLP)	10 934	24.7%
*Fitt, G. (Ind)	10 326	23.3%
Passmore, T. (OUP)	2 435	5.5%
McMahon, Ms M. (WP)	1 893	4.3%
PSF majority	5 445	12.3%
Total vote 44 366	Turnout 74 3%	

Mr Gerry Adams, a former barman, elected in 1983. Aged 33; educ. St Mary's Grammar School, Belfast. Vice-President, Provisional Sinn Fein since 1978. Elected, Northern Ireland Assembly 1982 for West Belfast. Interned, 1971 released in 1972 and flown to London for secret talks between PIRA and Secretary of State for Northern Ireland. Re-interned 1973. Attempted to escape from the Maze Prison and sentenced to 18 months imprisonment. Released 1976. Feb 1978 charged with membership of Provisional IRA. Spent seven months on remand but freed. Served with exclusion order banning him from entering London for talks with GLC leader Mr Ken Livingstone, Dec 1982.

Dr Joseph Henderson, a general practitioner, aged 50; educ. St Malachy's College Belfast, Queen's University Belfast. Member, Northern Ireland convention 1975 for West Belfast; member Northern Ireland assembly 1982. West Belfast. Chairman of SDLP elected Assembly members 1982. Member Belfast City Council since 1981; leader of SDLP council group.

Mr Gerard Fitt resigned the leadership of the Social Democratic and Labour Party in Northern Ireland in 1979 and sat as a Socialist. Won Belfast West from the Ulster Unionists in 1966 as Republican Labour Leader. Born Apr 9 1926; educ. Christian Brothers School, Belfast. MP for Dock constituency of Belfast from 1962 until Stormont ceased to function in 1972. Member, Northern Ireland Assembly, 1973–75; deputy chief executive, Northern Ireland Executive, 1974. Served in Merchant Navy 1941–53. Member, Belfast City Council, 1958–81.

Mr Andrew MacKay

BERKSHIRE EAST Electorate 81 512

MacKay, A. (C)	33 967	56.8%
O'Sullivan, K. (SDP/All)	17 868	29.9%
Rogers, Ms E. (Lab)	7 953	13.3%
C majority	16 099	26.9%
Total vote 59 788		Turnout 73.4%

Mr Andrew MacKay, estate agent and director of family housing construction business, was elected in 1983; MP for Birmingham, Stechford, from by-election in Mar 1977, but was defeated by Labour in 1979. Member of foreign affairs, industry and environment backbench committees 1977–79. Born Aug 27 1949; educ. Solihull School. Member National Executive, 1979–82. Member Central Council of the National Union, 1971–74; chairman, Britain in Europe campaign in Meriden constituency during 1975 referendum. Member, Conservative Friends of Israel.

Mr Kevin O'Sullivan, company chairman. Born 1938; educ. Cambridge and Yale universities. Member, Council, Royal Anthropological Institute; treasurer, SOS Sahel, a charity working to improve living conditions in poorest parts of Africa. Author of policy papers for study groups on Third World development and House of Lords reform.

Ms Elizabeth Rogers, accountancy recruitment consultant. Born Jan 1957; educ. Slough College of Higher Education and Warwick University. Member, Co-operative Party; TGWU (ACTSS).

Mr Alan Beith

BERWICK-UPON-TWEED Electorate 53 585

*Beith, A. (L/All)	21 958	52.7%
Brazier, J. (C)	13 743	33.0%
Baird, Mrs V. (Lab)	5 975	14.3%
L/All majority	8 215	19.7%
Total vote 41 676		Turnout 77.8%

Mr Alan Beith won the seat in a by-election, 1973, having contested it, 1970. Chief whip since Mar 1976 and education spokesman; previously spokesman on home affairs and Northern Ireland Member, House of Commons Commission. Served on procedure and selection committees. Born Apr 20 1943; educ. King's School, Macclesfield; Balliol and Nuffield Colleges, Oxford. Former university lecturer. Member Council of Europe and WEU since 1976. Member general advisory council, BBC. Former member Tynedale and Hexham councils. Parliamentary adviser to the AUT.

Mr Julian Brazier, secretary to executive committee of board of mining and industrial company. Born 1953; educ. Dragon School, Oxford, Wellington College, Berkshire, and Brasenose College, Oxford. Former president and treasurer, Oxford University Conservative Association; member, Royal Institute of International Affairs and Royal Commonwealth Society.

Mrs Vera Baird, barrister. Aged 33; educ. Oldham Grammar School, Newcastle Polytechnic and Open University. Labour Party member for 12 years. Called to the bar 1975.

Mr Peter Shore

BETHNAL GREEN AND STEPNEY Electorate 55 333

*Shore, P. D. (Lab)	15 740	51.0%
Charters S. (L/All)	9 382	30.4%
Argyropulo, D. (C)	4 323	14.0%
Clark, V. J. (NF)	800	2.6%
Rees, J. (Com)	243	0.8%
Chadhuri, B. (Ind)	214	0.7%
Mahoney, P. (RAP)	36	0.4%
Lab majority	6 358	20.6%
Total vote 30 738		Turnout 55.7%

Mr Peter Shore, member of Shadow Cabinet since 1979, became chief Opposition spokesman on Treasury and economic affairs in 1981; chief spokesman on foreign and Commonwealth affairs 1979–81. Secretary of State for Environment, 1976–79; Secretary of State for Trade 1974–76; spokesman on European affairs 1971–74 with responsibility for prices and consumer protection. Elected in 1983; represented Stepney and Poplar, 1974–83 and Stepney 1964–74; contested St Ives 1950, and Halifax 1959. Born May 20 1924; educ. Quarry Bank High School, Liverpool, and King's College, Cambridge. Minister without Portfolio and Deputy Leader of the House 1969–70; Secretary of State for Economic Affairs 1967–69; Parliamentary Secretary, Ministry of Technology, 1966–67; PPS to Mr Harold Wilson 1965–66. Political economist and head of Labour research department 1959–64. Sponsored by TGWU.

Mr Stephen Charters, trainee solicitor, has been a councillor for the London Borough of Tower Hamlets since 1982. Born Jun 5 1957; educ. King Alfred Grammar School, Wantage and St Edmund Hall, Oxford.

Mr Demitri Argyropulo, education consultant. Born 1950; educ. St John's School, Leatherhead. National vice-chairman, Young Conservatives, 1977–79; member, Surrey County Council 1973–77.

Sir Patrick Wall

BEVERLEY Electorate 75 813

*Wall, Sir P. (C)	31 233	56.3%
Pitts, M. (L/All)	17 364	31.3%
Morley, E. M. (Lab)	6 921	12.5%
C majority	13 869	25.0%
Total vote 55 518		Turnout 73.2%

Sir Patrick Wall was elected in 1983; MP for Haltemprice 1954–83; contested Cleveland, 1951 and 1952 by-election. Born Oct 19 1916; educ. Downside. Member, Select Committee on Defence. Joint vice-chairman, Conservative parliamentary committee on defence, 1965–77; chairman, Conservative sub-committee on fisheries since 1970. Member, Westminster City Council, 1953–62. Chairman, North Atlantic Assembly military committee since 1977; chairman, Conservative-Christian Democrat group, North Atlantic Assembly, since 1977. Treasurer, British group IPU, since 1976. Substitute delegate, Council of Europe and WEU since 1974. Royal Marines, 1935–50. IoJ.

Mr Michael Pitts, a teacher, contested Cleveland and Whitby 1979; Scarborough Feb 1974; Scarborough and Whitby 1970; Cleveland 1966; Warrington 1964. Contested Cleveland in elections for European Parliament 1979. Born Mar 19 1936; educ. Scarborough High School for Boys and Pembroke College, Oxford. Leader, Liberal group and member Scarborough District Council since 1973; Scarborough RDC 1968–74; chairman, health and housing committee. Former county borough councillor. NUT.

Mr Elliot Morley, teacher, is chairman of Hull City Council's public transport committee. Born Jul 6 1952; educ. St Margaret's CE High School, Liverpool. Former president, Hull NUT.

Mr Charles Wardle

BEXHILL AND BATTLE Electorate 61 785

Wardle, C. (C)	30 329	67.3%
Smith, P. (L/All)	10 583	23.5%
Pearson, I. (Lab)	3 587	8.0%
Rix, Ms A. (Eco)	538	1.2%
C majority	19 746	43.8%
Total vote 45 037		Turnout 72.9%

Mr Charles Wardle, chairman of a public engineering company; elected in 1983. Born Aug 23 1939; educ. Tonbridge School; Lincoln College, Oxford, and Harvard Business School. Member, CBI Central Council, CBI West Midlands Council and Chairman's Advisory Committee; Midlands committee, Institute of Directors; economic and finance committee of the Engineering Employers' Federation; and Birmingham Hippodrome fund raising group.

Mr Paul Smith is a company accountant. Born Nov 11 1944; educ. Dacres Road Boys' School, Forest Hill. Member, East Sussex County Council since 1981, chief opposition spokesman on highways and transport; Hastings Borough Council since 1978. Chairman, East Sussex Liberal Party.

Mr Ian Pearson is studying for a master's degree in industrial relations at Warwick University. Born 1959; educ. Prestwood comprehensive school, Brierley Hill; Balliol College, Oxford.

Mr Cyril Townsend

BEXLEYHEATH Electorate 59 263

*Townsend, C.D. (C)	23 411	53.1%
Standen, B. (L/All)	13 153	29.8%
Erlam, A. (LAb)	7 560	17.1%
C majority	10 258	23.3%
Total vote 44 124		Turnout 74.5%

Mr Cyril Townsend was elected in February, 1974. Member, Select Committee on Violence in the Family, 1976–77. Chairman of allparty 'Freedom for Rudolph Hess' Campaign. Vice-chairman, 'Friends of Cyprus'. Member, Select Committee on Foreign Affairs and sub-committee on overseas development. Secretary, Conservative backbench committee on defence. Born Dec 21 1937; educ. Bradfield College, Berkshire, Royal Military Academy. Was employed in Conservative Research Department, 1970–74. A personal assistant to Mr Edward Heath, 1968–70. Chairman, Council for Advancement of Arab-British Understanding.

Mr Barry Standen, a mining export executive. Born Jan 22 1947; educ. SE London Technical School and University of Kent. Member, London Borough of Bexley Council. APEX.

Mr Andrew Erlam, former assistant director, Howard League for Penal Reform. NUJ and GMBATU.

Mr Harvey Proctor

BILLERICAY Electorate 74 779

*Proctor, K. H. (C)	29 635	53.7%
Bonner, E. (L/All)	15 020	27.2%
Sewell C. (Lab)	10 528	19.1%
C majority	14 615	26.5%
Total vote 55 183	Turnout	73.8%

Mr Harvey Proctor, consultant to the British Paper and Board Industry Federation was elected in 1983; represented Basildon, 1979–83; contested Hackney South and Shoreditch, February and October, 1974. Born Jan 15 1947; educ. High School for Boys, Scarborough, and York University (Chairman of University Conservative Association, 1967–69).

Mr Eric Bonner, shop assistant. Born Jan 25 1945; educ. St Mirrens Academy, Paisley. Member, Brentwood District Council, since 1980.

Mr Christopher Sewell, teacher and former member of Richmond Borough Council. Aged 55; educ. Oxford University. Teaches geography at a Peckham comprehensive school. Former army officer on military intelligence duties. Member, TGWU, League Against Cruel Sports, CND and Co-operative Party.

Mr Frank Field

BIRKENHEAD Electorate 67 293

*Field, F. (Lab)	23 249	49.6%
Peet, T. (C)	13 535	28.9%
Lindsay, G. (L/All)	9 782	20.9%
Clarke, Miss H. (Eco)	337	0.7%
Lab majority	9 714	20.7%
Total vote 46 903	Turnout	69.7%

Mr Frank Field, was an Opposition spokesman on education, 1979–81. Elected in 1979. Director of the Child Poverty Action Group, 1969–79, and of the Low Pay Unit, 1974–80. Former teacher. Contested South Buckinghamshire in 1966. Born Jul 16 1942; educ. St Clement Danes Grammar School and Hull University. Parliamentary consultant to the Civil and Public Services Association. Hounslow councillor, 1964–68. TGWU.

Mr Thomas Peet, shift charge engineer (electrical) at Golborne Colliery, contested Wigan 1979. Born Sep 30 1942; educ. All Saints School, Wigan and Wigan and St Helen's Mining and Technical Colleges. Chairman, Wigan Conservative Association trade union group; vice chairman, NW area CTU advisory committee; member, national CTU committee.

Mr Gordon Lindsay, solicitor, contested Birkenhead, Feb and Oct, 1974. Born Jun 28 1933; educ. Loretto and Liverpool University. Member, Birkenhead County Borough Council 1970–74; Merseyside County Council 1973–77; Wirral Metropolitan Borough Council since 1973. Past President, Liverpool Law Society.

Mrs Jill Knight

BIRMINGHAM, EDGBASTON Electorate 55 063

*Knight, Mrs J. C. J. (C)	19 585	53.7%
Binns, J. (SDP/All)	8 167	22.4%
Bilson, P. A. (Lab)	7 647	21.0%
Hurdley, J. (Eco)	516	1.4%
Hardwick, S. T. (Ind C)	293	0.8%
Davies, Ms P. A. (Com)	169	0.5%
Howlett, Miss D. C. (JAHC)	97	0.3%
C majority	11 418	31.3%
Total vote 36 474	Turnout	66.2%

Mrs Jill Knight, chairman, Conservative backbench committee on health and social services since 1982, was elected in 1966; contested Northampton, 1959 and 1964. Housewife, lecturer and broadcaster. Born Jul 9 1927; educ. Fairfield School, Bristol; King Edward VI Grammar School, Birmingham. Member, Northampton Borough Council 1956–66. Member, Council of Europe since 1977, and chairman, Lords and Commons all-party Family and Child Protection Group. Member, Select Committee on Race Relations and Immigration 1969–72. Member, Select Committee on Home Affairs since 1980 and of executive, 1922 Committee. President, West Midlands Conservative Political Centre since 1980.

Mr Joseph Binns, an insurance broker and company director. Contested Bromley 1964 and Gillingham 1966, for Labour. Born May 29 1931. Member, Greenwich Borough Council 1963–65. Member, Council of Institute of Credit Management and chairman, West Midlands branch, Institute of Exports.

Mr Peter Bilson, leading fireman with West Midlands Fire Service. Born Aug 22 1953; educ. Wolverhampton grammar and technical schools. Member, Wolverhampton Metropolitan Borough Council since 1982. West Midlands Secretary, Fire Brigades Union.

Mr Robin Corbett

BIRMINGHAM, ERDINGTON Electorate 56019

Corbett, R. (Lab)	14930	39.8%
Moylan, D. (C)	14699	39.2%
Barber, C. (SDP/All)	7915	21.1%
Lab majority	231	0.6%
Total vote 37544		Turnout 67.0%

Mr Robin Corbett, freelance journalist, elected in 1983, was MP for Hemel Hempstead, Oct 1974–79; contested the seat Feb 1974 and 1966; and West Derbyshire by-election 1967. Born Dec 1933; educ. Holly Lodge Grammar School, Smethwick. Former chairman, PLP agriculture and food group; former secretary, PLP civil liberties group. Chairman, Farm Animal Welfare Coordinating Executive; Committee for Reform of Animal Experiments, NUJ.

Mr Daniel Moylan, merchant banker. Born 1956; educ. St Philip's Grammar School, Birmingham and Queen's College, Oxford.

Mr Christopher Barber, market research officer, was the first Erdington councillor to join SDP. Born 1930; educ. in Ireland. Served two terms as Erdington councillor, which he represented on the executive committee of the CABs and the Birmingham Council for Old People. President, Castle Vale Association for the Physically and Mentally Handicapped.

Mr Reginald Eyre

BIRMINGHAM, HALL GREEN Electorate 61023

*Eyre, R. E. (C)	21142	49.1%
Willis, M. H. (Lab)	11769	27.3%
Hemming, J. (L/All)	10175	23.6%
C majority	9373	21.8%
Total vote 43086		Turnout 70.6%

Mr Reginald Eyre was appointed Under-Secretary of State for Transport in 1982, having been Under-Secretary of State for Trade since 1979. Vice-chairman, Conservative Party, with responsibility for urban areas, 1975–79. Under-Secretary (Housing and Construction) for Environment 1972–74; Comptroller of Household (Whip), 1970–72; Lord Commissioner of the Treasury, 1970; Opposition Whip, 1966–70. Returned at by-election May 1965; contested Birmingham, Northfield 1959. Solicitor and former company director. Born May 28 1924; educ. King Edward's Camp Hill School. Birmingham and Emmanuel College, Cambridge. Former member, Committee of Selection.

Mr Martin Willis, social worker. Born Jul 19 1950; educ. school, university, home, work, and in trade union and Labour movement. Vice-chairman, Economic Development Committee, West Midlands County Council, member since 1981; with West Midlands Enterprise Board and Warwick University science park.

Mr John Hemming, computer programmer. Born Mar 16 1960; educ. King Edward's School, Birmingham, and Magdalen College, Oxford.

Mr Terence Davis

BIRMINGHAM, HODGE HILL Electorate 61234

*Davis, T. (Lab)	19692	47.6%
Roe, P. (C)	14600	35.3%
Gopsill, G. A. (L/All)	6557	15.9%
Tomkinson, N. (NF)	529	1.3%
Lab majority	5092	12.3%
Total vote 41378		Turnout 67.6%

Mr Terence Davis, an Opposition spokesman on health and social services since 1980 won Birmingham, Stechford in 1979 and Hodge Hill in 1983. He won Bromsgrove for Labour in the 1971 by-election, having contested seat 1970. Defeated at new seat of Bromsgrove and Redditch Feb and Oct 1974 and in 1977 by-election at Birmingham, Stetchford. Was a manager in motor industry. Born Jan 5 1938; educ. King Edward VI Grammar School, Stourbridge, London University, Michigan University. Member, Expenditure Committee, 1973–74; Opposition Whip 1979–80. Yeovil RDC 1967–68. Sponsored by ASTMS.

Mr Peter Roe, a marketing director. Born Aug 21 1941; educ. Pangbourne College; Royal Naval College, Dartmouth; Cranfield Business School. An officer of the Fulham Conservative Association. Director, Through Transport Mutual Services Ltd.

Mr Graham Gopsill, insurance agent, Born Dec 1938; educ. Mosely School of Art. Birmingham City and District Councillor 1969. Contested Birmingham, Stechford in both 1974 elections, by-election 1977 and in 1979. Contested East Midlands in the 1979 European election.

BIRMINGHAM, LADYWOOD Electorate 60 441

Ms Clare Short

Short, Ms C. (Lab)	19 278	51.0%
Le Hunte, Mrs P. (C)	10 248	27.1%
Hardeman, K. (L/All)	7 758	20.5%
Bakhtaura, B. (Stop Dep)	335	0.9%
Atkinson, R. W. (WRP)	198	0.5%
Lab majority	9 030	23.9%
Total vote 37 837	Turnout 62.6%	

Ms Clare Short, elected in 1983. Born Feb 5 1946; educ. Keele and Leeds Universities. Director, Youthaid and the Unemployment Unit. Married to Mr Alexander Lyon, who lost his seat at York. TWGU (ACTSS).

Mrs Pramila Le Hunte, the Conservative Party's first Asian woman parliamentary candidate, was selected from a list of 41 applications. Born 1939; educ. University of Calcutta, Cambridge University. Head of English Department, North London Collegiate School.

Mr Kenneth Hardeman, director of catering company, contested the seat, 1974 and 1979. Born Jan 21 1936.

BIRMINGHAM, NORTHFIELD Electorate 74 326

Mr Roger King

King, R. (C)	22 596	42.7%
*Spellar, J. (Lab)	19 836	37.5%
Webb, D. (L/All)	10 045	19.0%
Shepherd, P. (Com)	420	0.8%
C majority	2 760	5.2%
Total vote 52 897	Turnout 71.2%	

Mr Roger King who runs a business specializing in design, production and marketing of new motoring products. Born Oct 26 1943; educ. Solihull School. Chairman, West Midlands Area Young Conservatives, 1972–74; chairman, Telford New Town Liaison Committee since 1982. Won this seat in 1983; contested Cannock, Feb 1974.

Mr John Spellar won this seat from the Conservatives at a by-election in Oct 1982; contested Bromley 1970. Trade union official. Born Aug 5 1947; educ. Dulwich College and St Edmund Hall, Oxford. Member, Select Committee on Energy. Member Bromley Borough Council, 1970–74. National Officer, EETPU.

Mr David Webb, company director. Born Apr 13 1935; educ. Hitchin Boys' Grammar School, University of London, Cranfield Institute of Technology and Police Staff College, Bramshill. Police officer for 27 years, retired as Superintendent in charge of Handsworth. Fellow of British Institute of Management and Institute of Sales and Marketing Managers.

BIRMINGHAM, PERRY BARR Electorate 74 371

Mr Jeffrey Rooker

*Rooker, J. W. (Lab)	27 061	52.6%
Portillo, M. D. (C)	19 659	38.2%
Williams, C. E. G. (L/All)	4 773	9.3%
Lab majority	7 402	9.3%
Total vote 51 493	Turnout 69.2%	

Mr Jeffrey Rooker, a chartered engineer, has been an Opposition spokesman on social services since 1979. Elected in Feb 1974. Born Jun 5 1941; educ. Handsworth Technical School and College, Acton University and Warwick University. Secretary, Birmingham Labour Group. Co-opted member, Birmingham Educ. Committee, 1972–74. Sponsored by ASTMS.

Mr Michael Portillo, employee with oil company and political researcher with television programme. Born May 26 1953; educ. County School for Boys, Harrow, and Peterhouse, Cambridge. Special adviser to Mr David Howell, when Secretary of State for Energy; previously in Conservative research department. Member, Bow Group and Centre for Policy Studies, and has served in policy unit at 10 Downing Street since 1979 general election.

Mr Gus Williams, director of community development organization, contested Nuneaton 1979 and Birmingham, Sparkbrook 1974. Born Aug 22 1948; educ. Birmingham Polytechnic.

BIRMINGHAM, SELLY OAK Electorate 71 671

*Beaumont-Dark, A. (C)	23 008	44.9%
Turner, J. (Lab)	17 612	34.4%
Wheldall, K. (SDP/All)	10 613	20.7%
C majority	5 396	10.5%
Total vote 51 233	Turnout 71.5%	

Mr Anthony Beaumont-Dark, elected in 1979, is an investment analyser and a senior partner of firm of stockbrokers. Contested Birmingham, Aston in 1964 and 1959. Born Oct 11 1932; educ. Cedarhurst School, Solihull. Birmingham College of Arts and Birmingham University. Member Select Committee on Treasury and Civil Service since 1979, and Select

Mr Anthony Beaumont-Dark

Committee on Procedure (finance) since 1982. Secretary, Conservative Finance Committee. Member Birmingham City Council 1957–67 (alderman from 1967); West Midland Metropolitan County Council 1973–80. Chairman, Birmingham Executive Airways Ltd; director Cope Allman International Ltd and Wigham Poland (Midlands) Ltd.

Mr John Turner, design engineer and furnace specialist. Born Apr 14 1926; secondary schools. District and county councillor; member, area health authority and area manpower board. AUEW (TASS), Regional TUC.

Mr Kevin Wheldall, Director of the Centre for Child Study, is general secretary of the British Psychological Society. Born 1949; educ. Henry Cavendish Secondary Technical School and Manchester University. Lecturer in educational psychology at Birmingham University, 1973. Chairman, Association of Behavioural Approaches with Children. Awarded the education section prize of the British Psychological Society, while working at the Hester Adrian Research Centre.

Mr Denis Howell

BIRMINGHAM, SMALL HEATH

Electorate 59 376

*Howell, D. (Lab)	22 874	63.8%
Nischal, P. (C)	7 262	20.3%
Bostock, A. (SDP/All)	5 722	15.9%
Lab majority	15 612	43.5%
Total vote 35 858		Turnout 60.4%

Mr Denis Howell has been Opposition spokesman on sport and on environment matters since 1979. Minister of State (Sport and Recreation) in the Department of the Environment, 1974–79; Opposition spokesman on housing, local government and sport 1970–74; Minister of State for Housing and Local Government 1969–70; Under Secretary for Education and Science, 1964–69. Returned at a by-election. March 1961; represented the All Saints division, 1955–59; contested Kings Norton, 1951. Born 4 Sep 1923; educ. elementary OSC School, Birmingham. Member, Birmingham City Council, 1946–56. Football referee. President of Apex 1971–83. Sponsored by APEX.

Mr Paul Nischal, estate agent and insurance broker. Born 1944; educ. in India.

Mr Andrew Bostock, personnel and industrial relations manager. Born Jul 13 1953; educ. Herbert Strutt School, Belper, Derby College of Further Education and Aston University.

Mr Roy Hattersley

BIRMINGHAM, SPARKBROOK

Electorate 53 612

*Hattersley, R. (Lab)	19 757	59.9%
Douglas-Osborn, P. (C)	9 209	27.9%
Parmar, O. S. (SDP/All)	3 416	10.4%
Eden, Ms F. (Rev Com)	305	0.9%
Chinn, C. S. A. (Ind)	281	0.9%
Lab majority	10 548	32.0%
Total vote 32 968		Turnout 61.5%

Mr Roy Hattersley was elected Deputy leader of the Labour Party in 1983 and became chief Opposition spokesman on Treasury and economic affairs; chief Opposition spokesman on home affairs 1980–83. Chief Opposition spokesman on the environment, 1979–80. Secretary of State for Prices and Consumer Protection and member of the Cabinet, 1976–79; Minister of State for Foreign and Commonwealth Affairs, 1974–76; Opposition spokesman on education, 1972–74, spokesman for foreign and Commonwealth affairs 1970–72, and defence 1972. Minister of Defence for Administration 1969–70; Under Secretary, Department of Employment and Productivity, 1968–69; Parliamentary Secretary, Ministry of Labour, 1967–68. Elected in 1964; contested Sutton Coldfield 1959. Health service executive. Born Dec 28 1932; educ. Sheffield City Grammar School and Hull University. ASTMS.

Mr Peter Douglas-Osborn, engineering director. Born Oct 20 1949; educ. Wrekin College and University of Newcastle upon Tyne. Member, Dudley Borough Council since 1975; West Midlands County Council 1977–81. West Midlands Police Committee since 1980; Birmingham Airport Committee since 1979.

Mr Omkar Parmar, chartered architect. Born Oct 23 1930; educ. Duke of Gloucester School, Nairobi and Birmingham School of Architecture. Chairman, South East Birmingham SDP; vice-chairman, Social Democratic Campaign for Racial Justice. Member, Birmingham Community Relations Council and of executive committee of Birmingham International Council.

Mr David Bevan

BIRMINGHAM, YARDLEY Electorate 57 707

*Bevan, D. (C)	17 986	43.2%
Godsiff, R. D. (Lab)	15 141	36.3%
Bennett, D. (SDP/All)	8 109	19.5%
Jones, R. (NF)	415	1.0%
C majority	2 845	6.8%
Total vote 41 651	Turnout	72.1%

Mr David Gilroy Bevan, an incorporated auctioneer, estate agent, valuer and surveyor, company director and political and parliamentary adviser, was elected in 1979. Born 10 Apr 1928; educ. Woodrough's School, Moseley, and King Edward's School, Birmingham. Member, Birmingham City Council 1959–74 and West Midlands CC, 1974–81. Vice-chairman, tourism sub-committee of Conservative trade and industry committee since 1982. Secretary, Conservative urban affairs and new towns committee. Fellow and past chairman (Midlands) and council member of the Incorporated Association of Architects and Surveyors; past chairman and fellow of the West Midlands branch of the Incorporated Society of Valuers and auctioneers and a fellow of the Rating and Valuation Association, President, Moseley and Sheldon Conservative Association.

Mr Roger Godsiff, trade union official. Educ. Catford Comprehensive School. Member, Lewisham Council since 1971, Mayor 1977–78, chief whip 1974–77. Apex.

Mr David Bennett, an economist. Born Oct 4 1948; educ. Harold Malley Grammar School, Solihull, Portsmouth Polytechnic and John Hopkins University. GMBATU.

Mr Derek Foster

BISHOP AUCKLAND Electorate 71 142

*Foster, D. (Lab)	22 850	44.4%
Legg, B. (C)	18 444	36.0%
Collinge, A. (L/All)	10 070	19.6%
Lab majority	4 406	8.6%
Total vote 51 364	Turnout	72.1%

Mr Derek Foster an Opposition spokesman on social security since 1982 and a member of the Select Committee on Industry and Trade, 1980–83, was an assistant director of education in Sunderland. Elected in 1979. Born Jun 25 1937; educ. Bede Grammar School, Sunderland and Oxford University. Chairman, PLP Finance and Economic group. Former chairman, North of England Development Council and of economic development committee, Tyne and Wear County Council. NUT. Member of Salvation Army.

Mr Barry Legg is a company secretary and director of a foods groups; accountant and tax specialist. Born 1949; educ. Manchester University. Member, Westminster City Council since 1978; management committee, community housing association.

Mr Arthur Collinge, senior lecturer in management studies. Born Jul 6 1939; educ. Queen Elizabeth's Grammar School, Blackburn, and universities of Wales and Durham. NATFHE.

Mr Nigel Lawson

BLABY Electorate 71 930 1979: 68 576 same

*Lawson, N. (C)	32 689	58.7%
Lustig, R. (L/All)	15 573	28.0%
Wrigley, C. (Lab)	6 838	12.3%
Gegan, P. (NF)	568	1.0%
C majority	17 116	30.8%
Total vote 55 668	Turnout	77.4%

1979: Total vote 57 135 (83.3%) – C 33 221 (58.1%); Lab 12 581 (22.0%); L 9 277 (16.2%); NF 2 056 (3.6%). C maj 20 640 (36.1%); swing 6.1% to C.

Mr Nigel Lawson became Chancellor of the Exchequer in June 1983; Secretary of State for Energy, 1981–83; Financial Secretary to the Treasury, 1979–81 An Opposition spokesman on Treasury affairs 1977–79, was elected in February, 1974. Contested Eton and Slough, 1970. Born Mar 11 1932; educ. Westminster School, Christ Church, Oxford. An Opposition whip 1976–77. Special assistant to Prime Minister (Sir Alec Douglas-Home) 1963–64; special political adviser, Conservative Party, 1973–74. Former member, Public Expenditure Committee; Select Committee on Wealth Tax. Editorial staff, *Financial Times* 1956–60; City Editor, *The Sunday Telegraph* 1961–63; Editor of *The Spectator* 1966–70. Fellow, Nuffield College, Oxford, 1972–73.

Mr Richard Lustig, a management consultant, contested Derbyshire South East for the Liberals in 1979. Born Dec 1931; educ. Salford Grammar School and LSE. Has held office in NALGO and IPCS.

Mr Christopher Wrigley, university teacher and author. Born Aug 18 1947; educ. Kingston Grammar School, University of East Anglia and Birkbeck College, London. Member, Leicestershire County Council; member, Charnwood Borough Council, deputy leader of Labour group and housing spokesman. Executive member, Loughborough Trades Council. AUT.

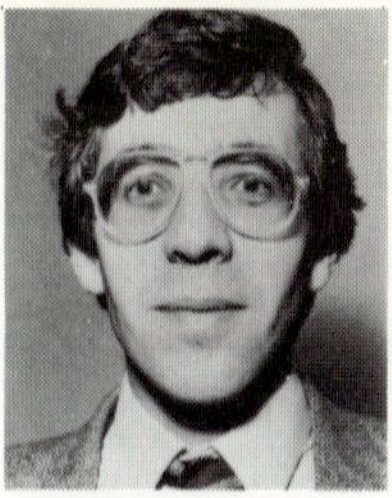

Mr Jack Straw

BLACKBURN Electorate 76078

*Straw, J. W. (Lab)	25400	44.7%
Mather, G. (C)	22345	39.4%
Fairbrother, E. (SDP/All)	8174	14.4%
Riley, D. A. (NF)	864	1.5%
Lab majority	3055	5.3%
Total vote 56783	Turnout 74.6%	

Mr Jack Straw, an Opposition spokesman on Treasury and economic affairs since 1980, was elected in 1979. Special adviser to Mrs Barbara Castle as Secretary of State for Social Services, 1974–76 and to Mr Peter Shore, Secretary of State for the Environment, 1976–77. On staff of Granada TV (World in Action) 1977–79. Barrister. Contested Tonbridge and Malling, Feb 1974. Born Aug 3 1946; educ. Brentwood School, Essex; Leeds University and Inns of Court School of Law. President, National Union of Students, 1969–71. Member, Islington Borough Council, 1971–78; Inner London Educ. Authority, 1971–74; Deputy leader, 1973–74. GMBATU: ACTT (member, shop committee).

Mr Graham Mather, head of policy unit, Institute of Directors, solicitor to the Supreme Court. Member, Centre for Policy Studies, and 'Think Tank', and trade union reform and nationalized industry committees. Member of team that produced Conservative Party manifesto for 1983 election. Born Oct 23 1954; educ. Hutton Grammar School, Preston, New College, Oxford. Elected to Westminster City Council 1982.

Mr Eric Fairbrother, manager of a Boots branch in Blackpool, is a member of the Lancashire Pharmaceutical Committee and chairman of the Blackpool Major Retailers Consortium. Born 1942; educ. Liverpool Bluecoat School and Liverpool School of Pharmacy. Member, Blackpool District Hospital Pharmaceutical Committee.

Mr Norman Miscampbell

BLACKPOOL NORTH Electorate 57576 1979: 59557 same

*Miscampbell, N. A. (C)	20592	51.1%
Heyworth, C. (L/All)	10440	25.9%
Hindley, M. J. (Lab)	8730	21.7%
Hanson, A. S. (NF)	514	1.3%
C majority	10152	25.2%
Total vote 40276	Turnout 70.0%	

1979: Total vote 43259 (72.6%) – C 23209 (53.7%): Lab 12980 (30.0%); L 6127 (14.2%); NF 943 (2.2%). C maj 10229 (23.7%); swing 5.2 to C.

Mr Norman Miscampbell, barrister and recorder of the Crown Court, was returned at a by-election in Mar 1962. Member. Select Committee on the Environment, since 1979. Contested Newton in 1955 and 1959. Born Feb 20 1925; educ. St Edward's School, Oxford and Trinity College, Oxford. Member, Hoylake UDC, 1955–61.

Mr Christopher Heyworth, lecturer in academic studies. Born Jul 5 1946.

Mr Michael Hindley, lecturer. Born Apr 11 1947; educ. Clitheroe Royal Grammar School and London and Lancaster universities. Member, Hyndburn District Council since 1979; leader of council since Oct 1981. Former shop steward. GMBATU.

Sir Peter Blaker

BLACKPOOL SOUTH Electorate 56201 1979: 58615 same

*Blaker, P. (C)	19852	50.6%
Jackson, F. J. (Lab)	9714	24.8%
Cox, A. (SDP/All)	9417	24.0%
Smith, W. (NF)	263	0.7%
C majority	10138	25.8%
Total vote 39246	Turnout 69.8%	

1979: Total vote 42257 (72.1%) – C 21762 (51.5%) Lab 12914 (30.6%); L 7057 (16.7%); NF 524 (1.2%). C maj 8848 (20.9%); swing 4.0% to C.

Sir Peter Blaker was Minister of State for the Armed Forces 1981–83; Minister of State for Foreign and Commonwealth Affairs 1979–81. Under-Secretary for Foreign and Commonwealth Affairs 1974, and Under-Secretary for Defence for the Army 1972–74. An Opposition whip 1966–67. Vice-chairman of the Conservative Parliamentary Foreign and Commonwealth Affairs Committee 1974–79. Elected in 1964. Born Oct 4 1922; educ. Shrewsbury School, Toronto University, and New College, Oxford (president of the union and University Law society). Barrister and solicitor. In the foreign service 1953–64. On executive committee of 1922 Committee 1967–70. Secretary, Conservative parliamentary trade committee 1967–70. Member of Lloyd's.

Mr Frederick Jackson is a process worker at UKAEA. Born Jan 17 1938; educ. Hawes Side Primary School and Highfield Secondary Modern School, Blackpool. Methodist lay preacher. Member, Blackpool Borough Council 1971–74; Lancashire County Council since 1981; Bakers' Union 1953–79; TGWU.

Mr Michael Foot

BLAENAU GWENT Electorate 55948

*Foot, M. M. (Lab)	30113	71.6%
Atkinson, G. (L/All)	6 488	15.4%
Morgan, T. (C)	4816	11.5%
Morgan, S. (Pl C)	1624	3.9%
Lab majority	23 625	56.2%
Total vote 42 041	Turnout	75.1%

Mr Michael Foot who became Leader of the Opposition in 1980, announced three days after polling day that he was standing down as leader of the Labour Party. In 1980, in the leadership election, he defeated Mr Denis Healey; Deputy Leader, 1976–80. He was Lord President of the Council and Leader of the Commons 1976–79; Secretary of State for Employment 1974–76. Opposition spokesman on the power and steel industries 1970–71; shadow Leader of the House principally concerned with Common Market legislation 1971–72; from 1972–74 concerned with EEC only. Unsuccessfully contested Deputy Leadership of PLP in Jul 1970, and Nov 1971. Elected for this seat, 1983; MP for Ebbw Vale 1960–83; MP for Plymouth Devonport, 1945–55, he contested the seat in 1959, and Monmouth, 1935. Journalist and author, former managing director of *Tribune*. Born July 23 1913; educ. Forres School, Swanage, Leighton Park School, Reading and Wadham College, Oxford; president of Union, 1933. Member, Committee of Privileges; Labour Party National Executive 1947–50, and since 1972.

Mr Gareth Atkinson, who is 21, joined the Liberal Party at the age of 16 and was branch secretary at 17, Ebbw Vale constituency secretary at 19 and prospective parliamentary candidate at 20. Educ. Mid Gwent College of Further Education, Pontypool.

Mr Talmai Morgan, barrister and company director. Born Jan 7 1953; educ. Gowerton School, Emmanuel College, Cambridge.

Mr Stephen Morgan, an electrician at Panteg Steelworks, is a member of Brynmawr Town Council.

Mr John McWilliam

BLAYDON Electorate 65481

*McWilliam, J. D. (Lab)	21285	44.4%
Williams, A. (C)	14063	29.3%
Carr, M. (SDP/All)	12607	26.3%
Lab majority	7222	15.1%
Total vote 47955	Turnout	73.2%

Mr John McWilliam was elected in 1979. Member of the Select Committee on Education, Science and the Arts, since 1979; select committees on procedure and finance. Member, Parliamentary committees on information technology and on freedom of information. Former Post Office engineer. Born May 1941; educ. Leith Academy, Herriot Watt College and Napier College of Science and Technology. Contested Edinburgh, Pentlands, February, 1974. Member, Edinburgh Corporation, 1970–75. Commissioner for local authority accounts in Scotland, 1974–78. Member Post Office Engineering Union since 1957; branch secretary, 1966–72. Appointed Deputy Shadow Leader of Commons, Jun 1983. Sponsored by POEU.

Mr Andrew Williams, merchant banker. Born Apr 27 1952; educ. Christ Church, Oxford. Called to the bar by Middle Temple, 1975.

Mr Maurice Carr, barrister. Born Aug 14 1937; educ. Hookergate Grammar School, LSE and Harvard Law School. Gateshead Borough Council 1978–82.

Mr John Ryman

BLYTH VALLEY Electorate 57639

*Ryman, J. (Lab)	16583	39.5%
Brownlow, Ms R. (SDP/All)	13340	31.8%
Hargreaves, A. (C)	11657	27.8%
Robinson, S. (Ind)	406	1.0%
Lab majority	3243	7.7%
Total vote 41986	Turnout	72.8%

Mr John Ryman, a barrister was elected for Blyth in Oct 1974 and for Blyth Valley in 1983. Born Nov 7 1930; educ. Leighton Park School, Reading, and Pembroke College, Oxford. Harmsworth law scholar. Contested Derbyshire South East 1970, and Gillingham 1964.

Mrs Rosemary Brownlow is a deputy headmistress. Aged 35; educ. Convent of the Sacred Heart, Newcastle and Leeds University.

Mr Andrew Hargreaves, merchant banker. From 1977–81 he was a fine art auctioneer and valuer with Christies. Born May 15 1955; educ. Eton and St Edmund Hall, Oxford. Vice-chairman, Battersea Conservative Association. Representative on Wandsworth Council Community Relations Committee; member, executive committee, Wandsworth Volunteer Bureau.

Mr Dennis Skinner

BOLSOVER Electorate 64 769

*Skinner, D. E. (Lab)	26 514	56.3%
Roberts, S. (C)	12 666	26.9%
Reddish, S. (SDP/All)	7 886	16.8%
Lab majority	13 848	29.4%
Total vote 47 066		Turnout 72.7%

Mr Dennis Skinner, former miner, chairman of the Miners Group of Labour MPs 1977–78. Elected in 1970. Member, Labour Party national executive committee, since October, 1978. Born Feb 11 1932; educ. Tupton Hall Grammar School and Ruskin College Oxford. President, Derbyshire Miners (NUM), 1966–70, and NE Derbyshire Constituency Labour Party 1968–71. Former member, Clay Cross UDC and Derbyshire County Council. Chairman, Tribune Group, 1973–74. Spnsored by NUM.

Mr Samuel Roberts, company director. Born Apr 16 1948; educ. Harrow School, Sheffield University and Manchester Business School. Founder and director of Curzon Steels Ltd of Staveley, Derbyshire.

Mr Stuart Reddish, a self-employed newsagent, contested Beeston, Feb and Oct 1974. Born May 3 1948; educ. High Pavement Grammar School. Member, Ashfield District Council since 1983; National Council for Social Democracy; Association of Social Democrats.

Mr Peter Thurnham

BOLTON NORTH EAST Electorate 58 918

Thurnham, P. (C)	19 632	43.2%
*Taylor, Mrs W. A. (Lab)	17 189	37.8%
Alcock, J. (SDP/All)	8 311	18.3%
Ball, D. P. (BNP)	186	0.4%
Keen, T. L. (Ind)	104	0.2%
C majority	2 443	5.4%
Total vote 45 422		Turnout 77.1%

Mr Peter Thurnham, professional engineer running his own business. Elected in 1983. Born Aug 1938; educ. Oundle School, Peterhouse, Cambridge, and Harvard Business School. Member, South Lakeland District Council.

Mrs Ann Taylor an Opposition spokesman on environment 1980–83, and education 1979–80. An assistant Government whip 1977–79; PPS to Secretary of State for Education and Science 1975–76, and to Secretary of State for Defence 1976–77. Contested Bolton West Feb 1974, won it in Oct 1974 from Conservatives. Teacher. Born Jul 2 1947; educ. Bolton schools and Bradford and Sheffield Universities. Member, Select Committee on Violence in Marriage 1975–76; on Wealth Tax 1975–77, and on Sound Broadcasting 1976–77. AUT, APEX.

Mr John Alcock is a solicitor. Born 1947. Member, Stoke-on-Trent Council 1973–75.

Mr David Young

BOLTON SOUTH EAST Electorate 67 527

*Young D. (Lab)	23 984	48.3%
Walsh, J. (Con)	15 231	30.7%
Rothwell, Mrs M. (L/All)	10 157	20.5%
Keen, T. L. (Ind)	296	0.6%
Lab majority	8 753	17.6%
Total vote 49 668		Turnout 73.6%

Mr David Young, a teacher, was MP for Bolton East Feb 1974–83; won this seat, 1983; contested Bath 1970, Banbury 1966, and Worcestershire South 1959. Born Oct 1930; educ. Greenock Academy, Glasgow University and St Paul's College, Cheltenham. PPS to Secretary of State for Defence 1977–79. Former alderman, Nuneaton Borough Council, and councillor, Nuneaton District Council, Chairman, Coventry East Labour Party, 1964–68. TGWU.

Mr John Walsh, management consultant. Born Nov 7 1951; educ. Bolton School. Member, Bolton Metropolitan District Council, 1975–79. School manager and governor; founder-secretary, Moss Bank Football Club in 1973.

Mrs Margaret Rothwell, deputy head-teacher, contested Farnworth Feb and Oct 1974 and 1979. Born Jun 23 1931; educ. Farnworth Grammar School and Manchester College of Housecraft. Kearsley Urban District Council 1965–74, chairman 1971–72. NUT.

Mr Thomas Sackville

BOLTON WEST Electorate 67 354

Sackville, T. (C)	23 731	45.1%
Green, D. (Lab)	16 579	31.5%
Baker, R. (SDP/All)	12 321	23.4%
C majority	7 512	13.6%
Total vote 52 631	Turnout	78.1%

Mr Thomas Sackville, elected in 1983, fought Pontypool, 1979. Divisional sales manager with a firm of international bullion and metal brokers. Formerly in banking. Born 1950; educ. Eton College; Oxford University.

Mr Denis Green, aged 33, a sheet metal worker at Horwich locomotive works. TUC and WEA lecturer.

Mr Ronald Baker, lecturer in business and management. Born Dec 24 1935; educ. St Edward's Grammar School, Liverpool, York University, Ontario and Keele University. NATFHE.

Sir Paul Bryan

BOOTHFERRY Electorate 72 370

*Bryan, Sir P. (C)	30 536	57.7%
Ellis, A. (L/All)	13 116	24.8%
Geraghty, T. (Lab)	9 271	17.5%
C majority	17 420	32.9%
Total vote 52 923	Turnout	73.1%

Sir Paul Bryan, Minister of State for Employment, 1970–72, was chairman Conservative employment committee 1973–74; vice-chairman, 1974. Member Select Committee on Sound Broadcasting. Elected in 1983; MP for Howden 1955–83. Born Aug 3 1913; educ. St John's School, Leatherhead, and Gonville and Caius College, Cambridge. Assistant whip, 1956; a Lord Commissioner of the Treasury (whip), 1958–61. Contested Sowerby, 1951, 1950 and 1949 (by-election). Director Granada Television since 1972, Granada Theatres Ltd since 1973, Greater Manchester Independent Radio since 1972 and Furness Withy & Co Ltd since 1983. Vice-chairman 1922 Committee; chairman all-party Hongkong group.

Mr Andrew Ellis, self-employed printer and election organizer, contested Newcastle upon Tyne Central Oct 1974; by-election Nov 1976 and 1979. National Liberal Party vice-chairman since 1980. Born May 19 1952; educ. Trinity College, Cambridge, and University of Newcastle upon Tyne. Member, Tyne and Wear County Council 1977–81, leader of the Liberal Group.

Mr Terence Geraghty is an unemployed registered dock worker. Aged 46; elementary education in Hull. Member, Hull City Council 1959–77; Humberside County Council since 1977, chairman, leisure services committee. TGWU.

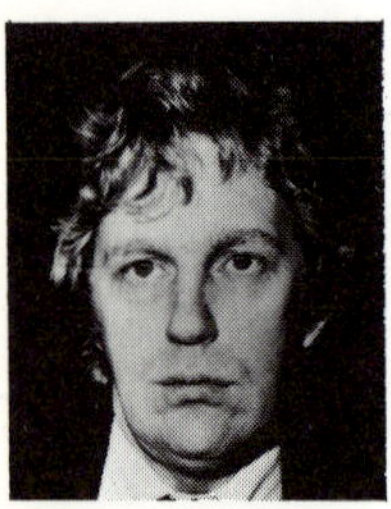

Mr Allan Roberts

BOOTLE Electorate 75 354

*Roberts, A. (Lab)	27 282	53.0%
Watson, R. (C)	12 143	23.6%
Wall, J. (SDP/All)	12 068	23.4%
Lab majority	15 139	29.4%
Total vote 51 493	Turnout	68.3%

Mr Allan Roberts was a City of Manchester councillor and housing chairman. Born Oct 28 1943; educ. Droylesden Littlemoss County Secondary School, Aston-under-Lyne College of Education, Didsbury College of Education and Manchester University. Principal officer (child care) of the City of Salford Social Services Department, 1976–79. Member of TGWU and Co-operative Party. MP for Bootle since May 1979; contested Hazel Grove Feb and Oct 1974. Former teacher, social worker and training officer. Chairman, PLP environment group.

Mr Ronald Watson, manager of a travel company, fought Bootle 1979. Leader, Sefton Borough Council; member since 1973. Elected Southport County Borough Council, 1969. Member, Association of Metropolitan Authorities policy committee. Born May 1945; educ. South Shields Grammar Technical School and Waterloo Grammar School. Has been President, Southport Chamber of Trade and Commerce.

Mr John Wall, company director. Born Apr 13 1938; educ. Bootle Grammar School and Sheffield College.

Mr Adam Butler

BOSWORTH Electorate 73097

*Butler, A. C. (C)	31663	55.4%
Fox, M. (SDP/All)	14369	25.1%
Janner, D. J. M. (Lab)	11120	19.5%
C majority	17294	19.5%
Total vote 57152		Turnout 78.2%

Mr Adam Butler has been Minister of State for Northern Ireland since 1981; Minister of State for Industry, 1979–81. Won the seat for the Conservatives in 1970. An assistant Government whip, 1974 and an Opposition whip 1974–75. Born Oct 11 1931; educ. Eton and Pembroke College, Cambridge. Second son of late Lord Butler. Courtaulds Ltd, 1955–73; director, Aristoc Ltd 1966–73; Kayser Bondor Ltd 1971–73. Capital and Counties Property Co Ltd 1973–79. PPS to Mrs Thatcher as Leader of the Opposition 1975–79. Member of Lloyd's; NFU; Fellow, Royal Society of Arts.

Mr Malcolm Fox, electronics company director and polytechnic lecturer. Contested Blaby Oct 1974, and Holland with Boston 1979, for Labour. Born May 5 1939; educ. Wilsons GS, London; Kings College, London University; and Hatfield Polytechnic. Leicester city councillor 1979–83. NATFHE.

Mr Daniel Janner, barrister, formerly a researcher for ASTMS. Son of Mr Greville Janner, MP for Leicester West since 1970. Born Apr 27 1957; educ. University College School and Trinity Hall, Cambridge. Member, Fabians; Society of Labour Lawyers; Labour Friends of Israel; Labour Industry Group; ASTMS.

Mr David Atkinson

BOURNEMOUTH EAST Electorate 70 771

*Atkinson, D. A. (C)	25176	53.5%
Millward, J. (L/All)	13760	29.2%
Shutler, M. J. (Lab)	4026	8.6%
Hogarth, Mrs M. (Ind Con)	3644	7.7%
Dykes, T. (Eco)	273	0.6%
Stooks, J. (LM)	225	0.5%
C majority	11416	24.2%
Total vote 47104		Turnout 66.6%

Mr David Atkinson, managing director of a printing and marketing company which he founded in 1971, was elected at the Nov 1977, by-election. Contested Newham North-West Feb 1974, and Basildon in Oct 1974. Born Mar 24 1940; educ. St George's College, Weybridge, Southend College of Technology, and the College of Automobile and Aeronautical Engineering, Chelsea. National Young Conservative chairman, 1970–71. Member, Essex County Council 1973–78; Southend County Borough Council, 1969–72. Member, Council of Europe and WEU. President Christian Solidarity International UK. PPS to Mr Paul Channon, Minister for the Civil Service 1979–81, Minister for the Arts 1981–83. Director Modus Politicus.

Dr John Millward, medical practitioner. Born June 22 1933; educ. Dudley Grammar School, Keble College, Oxford and St Bartholomew's Hospital. Member, Dorset County Council.

Mr Michael Shutler, council manual worker. Born Aug 27 1937; educ. Harbridge county primary and Ringwood secondary modern schools. Member, Ringwood council for seven years; district committee, Southern Co-op Retail Service Ltd.

Mr John Butterfill

BOURNEMOUTH WEST Electorate 72297

Butterfill, J. (C)	28466	56.9%
James, M. (L/All)	15135	30.3%
Horrocks, K. (Lab)	6243	12.5%
Morse, J. H. (BNP)	180	0.4%
C majority	13331	26.7%
Total vote 50024		Turnout 69.2%

Mr John Butterfill, senior partner in a firm of chartered surveyors, was elected in 1983; contested Croydon North-West Oct 1981 by-election; also contested London South Inner in elections to European Parliament, 1979. Born 1941; educ. Caterham School and College of Estate Management, London, Vice-chairman, Guildford Conservative Association and chairman of Conservative Political Centre. Member, Conservative Group for Europe and a national council member, European Movement. Committee member, London Europe Society, European Democrat Forum, and Foreign Affairs Forum. Member, management advisory committee, Nuffield Hospital, Woking.

Mr Michael James, legal assistant. Born Mar 8 1935; educ. Cardiff Technical College, University of Wales. Contested Plymouth, Devonport 1979, and Cardiff West twice in 1974.

Mr Kelvin Horrocks is a classified advertisement sales manager for a London newspaper group and former bingo caller and film extra. Born May 19 1930. Sogat.

Mr Ian Mikardo

BOW AND POPLAR Electorate 57 768

*Mikardo, I. (Lab)	15 878	49.6%
Flounders, E. (L/All)	10 017	31.3%
Eyres, S. (C)	5 129	16.0%
Bartlett, Ms S. (NF)	596	1.9%
Snooks, A. J. L. (Lab Ind)	266	0.8%
Scotcher, K. R. (WRP)	117	0.4%
Lab majority	5 861	18.3%
Total vote 32 003		Turnout 55.4%

Mr Ian Mikardo elected in 1983; represented Bethnal Green and Bow Feb 1974–83; MP for Poplar 1964–74; for Reading 1945–50; Reading South 1950–55, and Reading 1955–59. Born Jul 1908; educ. Portsmouth Southern Secondary School and Portsmouth Municipal College. Chairman of Labour Party 1970–71; member, party national executive committee 1950–59 and 1960–78. Chairman, Select Committee on Nationalized Industries, 1966–70; President, ASTMS, 1968–73; member, Committee of Privileges, since 1974; Select Committee on Industry and Trade, since 1979. Chairman of PLP and PLP Liaison Committee, 1974. Hon chairman of Tower Hamlets Centre for Small Business Ltd. Sponsored by ASTMS.

Mr Eric Flounders, company manager. Born Aug 27 1947; educ. Scarborough High School for Boys and Westminster College, Oxford. Contested Tower Hamlets, Bethnal Green and Bow 1979. Member, Council of London Borough of Tower Hamlets since 1978.

Mr Stephen Eyres, journalist. Born Dec 1948; educ. Portsmouth, University of St Andrews. Secretary, Selsdon Group 1974–79. Contested Fife Central Feb 1974 and Waltham Forest, Walthamstow 1979. Former tutor, Swinton Conservative College and editor, *Swinton Journal*.

Mr Geoffrey Lawler

BRADFORD NORTH Electorate 66 349

Lawler, G. (C)	16 094	34.3%
Wall, C. P. (Lab)	14 492	30.9%
Birkby, P. (SDP/All)	11 962	25.5%
*Ford, B. T. (Lab Ind)	4 018	8.6%
Howarth, A. (Loony Socy)	194	0.4%
Easter, M. (BNP)	193	0.4%
C majority	1 602	3.4%
Total vote 46 953		Turnout 70.8%

Mr Geoffrey Lawler, a public relations executive won the seat in 1983. Born Oct 30 1954; educ. Colchester Royal Grammar School; Richmond School, North York. Hull University. NUJ.

Mr Patrick Wall, hardware buyer for mail order firm and previously stock controller and laboratory assistant. Founder-member, Militant Tendency. Born May 6 1933; educ. Liverpool Institute Grammar School. Elected secretary, Liverpool Garston Constituency Labour Party, at age of 16. Former member, Liverpool City Council and Bingley UDC. President, Bradford Trades Council since 1973. ASTMS.

Mr Peter Birkby, founder organizer of SDP in Yorkshire, was chairman of Bradford Labour Party and in 1979 agent to Mr Edward Lyons, Labour MP for Bradford West. Faculty head at Wyke Manor Upper School, Bradford. Born Feb 8 1946; educ. Hanson Boys' Grammar School, Manchester University, Sheffield City College of Education, Sheffield Polytechnic.

Mr Benjamin Ford was elected for Labour in 1964 but was not reselected for this election. Engineer and industrial relations consultant. Born April 1 1925; educ. Rowan Road Central School, Surrey. Chairman, Inter-Parliamentary Union (British Branch). Chairman, all-party wool textile group. Member, British Shooting Sports Council.

Mr Thomas Torney

BRADFORD SOUTH Electorate 69 588

*Torney, T. W. (Lab)	18 542	37.5%
Hall, G. T. (C)	18 432	37.3%
Pearl, D. A. (SDP/All)	12 143	24.6%
Adset, R. (Eco)	308	0.6%
Lab majority	110	0.2%
Total vote 49 425		Turnout 71.0%

Mr Thomas Torney, elected in 1970, was Derby and district area organizer USDAW, 1946–70; member, Select Committee on Agriculture since 1979. Born July 2 1915; ed elementary school. Chairman, PLP Agriculture and Food Groups since 1981. Member, former Select Committee on Race Relations and Immigration Secretary, wine and spirit industry liason committee. Sponsored by USDAW.

Mr Graham Hall is a businessman. Born Jun 30 1953; educ. Crossley and Porter Grammar School, Percival Whitley Ccllege. Partner in family firm. Former councillor for Shelf area of Bradford South.

Mr David Pearl, university lecturer in law. Born 1954; educ. Westminster City School, University of Birmingham and Queen's College, Cambridge. Member, Cambridge City Council 1972–73; Cambridgeshire County Council since 1973.

Mr Max Madden

BRADFORD WEST Electorate 71 296

Madden, M. (Lab)	19 499	39.7%
Day, S. (C)	16 162	32.9%
*Lyons, E. (SDP/All)	13 301	27.1%
Slaughter, Ms B. (WRP)	139	0.3%
Lab majority	3 337	6.8%
Total vote 49 101		Turnout 68.9%

Mr Max Madden, former Labour Party director of publicity, was elected in 1983; MP for Sowerby 1974–79; contested Sudbury and Woodbridge 1966. Born Oct 1941; educ. Pinner Grammar School and secondary modern school, Harrow. Former chairman, PLP employment group and vice-chairman, textile group. Former member, Wandsworth Borough Council. Now engaged in Nalgo publicity. TGWU sponsored.

Mr Stephen Day, sales representative. Born 1948; educ. Otley Secondary School; Park Lane College of Further Education, Leeds; Leeds Polytechnic. Member, Otley Town Council. Former member, Leeds City Council. Member, West Riding branch, Institute of Export.

Mr Edward Lyons, QC, was elected for Labour in February 1974; represented Bradford, East 1966–74. Resigned from party and joined SDP in March 1981, becoming their spokesman on legal affairs. Crown court recorder since 1972. Born May 17 1926; educ. elementary and secondary schools in Leeds and Leeds University. Russian interpreter with Control Commission, Germany 1946–48. Former chairman PLP Home Office group. Member Select Committee on European Legislation, since 1979. PPS to Treasury, 1969–70. Member Executive of Justice.

Mr Antony Newton

BRAINTREE Electorate 73 548

minor

*Newton A. (C)	29 462	52.6%
Bing, I. (SDP/All)	16 021	28.6%
Dyson, Mrs J. M. (Lab)	10 551	18.8%
C majority	13 441	24.0%
Total vote 56 034		Turnout 76.2%

1979: Total vote 60 783 (80.9%). C 31 593 (52.0%); Lab 19 075 (31.4%); L 10,115 (16.6%). C Maj 12 518 (20.6%); swing 9.2%

Mr Antony Newton has been Under Secretary of State, Department of Health and Social Security, since 1982; Assistant Government whip, 1979–82. Elected in Feb 1974; contested Sheffield, Brightside 1970. Economist B Aug 29, 1937; educ. Friends' School, Saffron Walden and Trinity College, Oxford. (President of Union, 1959). Joint secretary, Conservative backbench health and social security committee, 1976–79. Assistant director, Conservative research department, 1970–74; head of economic section 1965–70; research secretary, Bow Group, 1964–65.

Mr Inigo Bing is a barrister. Born 1944 Member, Lambeth Borough Council 1971–78; chairman of the finance committee.

Ms Janet Dyson, a teacher of music and religious studies. Born Nov 9 1947; educ. Kidderminster High School, Goldsmiths College, University of London. NUT.

Mr Tom Hooson

BRECON AND RADNOR Electorate 47 277

*Hooson, T. E. (C)	18 255	48.2%
Morris, D. (Lab)	9 471	25.0%
Livsey, R. (L/All)	9 226	24.4%
Meredudd, Ms S. (PLC)	640	1.7%
Booth, R. (Ind)	278	0.7%
C majority	8 784	23.2%
Total vote 37 870		Turnout 80.1%

Mr Tom Hooson, a publishing director, is former chairman of the Bow Group and *Crossbow*. Elected in 1979; fought Caernarvon, 1959. Born Mar 16 1933, educ. Rhyl Grammar School and University College, Oxford. Lived in United States and France during business career. Conservative Party Director of Communications 1976–78. Member, Select Committee on Welsh Affairs, since 1979.

The Rev David Morris is education advisor to Gwent County Council. Born 1930. Former member, Newport Borough Council.

Mr Richard Livsey, a smallholder, is senior lecturer in farm management at Welsh Agricultural College, Aberystwyth. Born May 2 1935; educ. Bedales School, Seale-Hayne Agricultural College, Reading University. Contested Perth and East Perthsire 1970, and Pembroke 1979.

Mrs Sian Meredudd, a teacher and member of Llandrindod Town Council. Educ. University of Bristol. Active in peace movement and Welsh Anti-Nuclear Alliance.

Mr Reginald Freeson

BRENT EAST Electorate 61 489

*Freeson, R. (Lab)	18 363	47.0%
Lacey, R. (C)	13 529	34.6%
Rosen, M. (SDP/All)	6 598	16.9%
O'Leary, J. (Ind)	289	0.7%
Downing, G. (WRP)	222	0.6%
Radclyffe, K (Ind)	88	0.2%
Lab majority	4 834	12.4%
Total vote 39 089		Turnout 63.6%

Mr Reginald Freeson became chairman of the Select Committee on Environment in 1982, member since 1979; Minister for Housing and Construction, Department of the Environment, 1974–79; Parliamentary Secretary, Ministry of Housing and Local Government, 1969–70; Parliamentary Secretary, Ministry of Power, 1967–69. B 24 Feb 1926; educ. Jewish Orphange, West Norwood. Returned for Brent East Feb 1974; MP for Willesden East 1964–74. Opposition spokesman on housing and construction, 1970–74. Willesden Borough Council member, 1952–65; leader, 1958–65. Member, Brent Council, 1964–68; chairman, 1964–65. Member, Natsopa 1942–55; NUJ since 1956; TGNU, 1980.

Mr Robert Lacey, assistant bank manager. Born 1943; educ. Westminster City School. Leader, Conservative group, Brent Borough Council; member since 1974, and formerly 1968–71. Member, Foreign Affairs Forum; Institute of Economic Affairs; Freedom Association.

Dr Maurice Rosen, general practitioner. Born Mar 3 1939; educ. St Mary's Hospital and London University. Contested Brentwood and Ongar, 1974 for Labour. Brent borough councillor 1974–82. Member, NW Thames RHA, since 1980. ASTMS/MPU.

Dr Rhodes Boyson

BRENT NORTH Electorate 62 679

*Boyson, R. (C)	24 842	56.3%
Jackson, Ms S. (Lab)	10 191	23.1%
Mann, T. (SDP/All)	9 082	20.6%
C majority	14 651	33.2%
Total vote 44 115		Turnout 70.4%

Dr. Rhodes Boyson became Minister of State for Social Security in 1983: Under-Secretary of State for Education and Science 1979–83; an Opposition spokesman on education 1976–79. Elected in Feb 1974; contested Eccles 1970. Former headmaster Highbury Grove School. Born May 1925; educ. Haslingden Grammar School, University College, Cardiff. Manchester University. LSE and Corpus Christi College, Cambridge. Former chairman National Council for Educational Standards. Member Waltham Forest Borough Council. 1968–74.

Mrs Sandra Jackson, lecturer. Born Dec 7 1939; educ. state schools and University of Nottingham. London Borough of Ealing Council, co-opted member of education committee. Ealing Borough secretary of the National Association of Teachers in Further and Higher Education.

Dr Thomas Mann, general practitioner. Born Dec 4 1954; educ. Kerela and Bombay, St Anne's Cricklewood, Finchley Catholic Grammar School and London University.

Mr Laurie Pavitt

BRENT SOUTH Electorate 62 783

*Pavitt, L. A. (Lab)	21 259	53.3%
Smedley, C. (C)	10 740	26.9%
Billins, R. (L/All)	7 557	18.9%
Sawh, R. (Eth Min)	356	0.9%
Lab majority	10 519	26.4%
Total vote 39 912		Turnout 63.6%

Mr Laurie Pavitt was an Assistant Government Whip 1974–76. MP for Willesden West, 1959–74; returned for Brent South in Feb 1974. National organizer of the Medical Practitioners' Union, 1956–59. Born Feb 11 1914; educ. elementary and central schools. Member, Medical Research Council, 1969–72; Hearing Aid Council 1968–74; Chairman PlP health group, 1964–77, vice-chairman since 1977. Vice-president, British association for the hard of hearing; chairman, British China all party group. NUPE. Sponsored by Co-operative Party.

Mr Charles Smedley, stockbroker. Born Apr 18 1951; educ. Monkton Comb School, Bath. Member, Kensington and Chelsea Borough Council.

Mr Roger Billins, solicitor. Born Sept 1954; educ. St Olave's Grammar School and University College, London.

Mr Barney Hayhoe

BRENTFORD AND ISLEWORTH

Electorate 69 170 same

*Hayhoe, B. J. (C)	24 515	47.4%
Rowlands, P. (Lab)	15 128	29.3%
Wilks, M. (SDP/All)	11 438	22.1%
Andrews, P. (NF)	427	0.8%
Simmerson, R. (Oth)	179	0.4%
C majority	9 387	18.2%
Total vote 51 687		Turnout 74.7%

1979: Total vote 55 717 (78.1%) – C 27 527 (49.4%); Lab 22 533 (40.4%); L 4 208 (7.6%); NF 738 (1.3%); Other 257 (0.5%). C maj 4 994 (9.0%); swing 4.2% to C.

Mr Barney Hayhoe, Minister of State, Treasury, with responsibilities for Civil Service since 1981; Minister of State, Civil Service Department, 1981; Under Secretary of Defence for the Army, 1979–81. An Opposition spokesman on employment, 1974–79. Returned for Hounslow, Brentford and Isleworth in Feb 1974; MP for Heston and Isleworth 1970–74; contested Lewisham South, 1964. Member of Lloyds. Born Aug 1925; educ. elementary school and Stanley Technical School, South Norwood, Croydon and Borough Polytechnics. Former vice-chairman, Conservative Group for Europe, and sec. European Movement. Former vice-chairman, Conservative Party International office. IPCS.

Mr Peter Rowlands, college lecturer. Born Feb 10 1944; educ. King Edward VI Grammar School, Chelmsford, and LSE. Secretary, Hounslow Trades Union Council, 1972–82. NATFHE.

Dr Michael Wilks, general practitioner. Born May 26 1949; educ. St John's School, Leatherhead, St Mary's Hospital Medical School, London University. Member, BMA, General Medical Services Committee, Acheson report on inner London general practice. Former member, BMA Central Ethical Committee.

Mr Robert McCrindle

BRENTWOOD AND ONGAR

Electorate 65 976

*McCrindle, R. (C)	29 484	58.4%
Amor, N. (L/All)	15 282	30.3%
Orpe, J. W. (Lab)	5 739	11.4%
C majority	14 202	28.1%
Total vote 50 505		Turnout 76.6%

Mr Robert McCrindle, an insurance broker, has been a member of the Select Committee on Energy since 1979. Elected in Feb, 1974; MP for Billericay 1970–74; contested Thurrock 1964, and Dundee East 1959. Born Sep 19 1929; educ. Allen Glen's College, Glasgow. Associate of the Chartered Insurance Institute. Parliamentary consultant to British Insurance Brokers' Association and British Transport Police Federation. Joint vice-chairman, Conservative back-bench health and social services committee, since 1982. Chairman, Economic Committee of the North Atlantic Assembly since 1980. Chairman of the All-Party Aviation Group.

Mr Nicholas Amor, trainee solicitor. Born Sep 26 1958; educ. Great Baddow School; Magdalen College, Oxford; Guildford College of Law. Member, Brentwood District Council since 1982.

Mr James Orpe. Born Sep 27 1951; educ. Colchester Grammar School and Institute of Further Education. Member, Colchester Borough Council 1978–82. NUS.

Mr Peter Hubbard-Miles

BRIDGEND

Electorate 53 918

Hubbard-Miles, P. (C)	15 950	38.4%
Fellows, J. A. (Lab)	14 623	35.2%
Smart, R. (SDP/All)	9 630	23.2%
Bush, K. (PLC)	1 312	3.2%
C majority	1 327	3.2%
Total vote 41 515		Turnout 77.0%

Mr Peter Hubbard-Miles, self-employed businessman, was elected in 1983; contested Aberavon, Feb 1974. Born May 9 1927; educ. Lewis' School, Pengam. Member, Mid-Glamorgan county and Ogwr borough councils for 16 years.

Mr Alan Fellows, sales account manager with British Steel Corporation. Born 1936.

Mr Russel Smart, civil servant and senior lecturer in economics, Polytechnic of Wales, Treforest. Born 1931; educ. Rhondda Technical School, Coleg Harlech and University College, Cardiff. Former toolmaker.

Mr Keith Bush, barrister, contested Cardiff South East for Pl Cymru, in Feb and Oct 1974. Born May 1948; educ. County School, Tregaron and Imperial College, London.

Mr Tom King

BRIDGWATER Electorate 64 225

*King T. J. (C)	25 107	52.3%
Farley, Mrs R. (SDP/All)	14 410	30.0%
May, A. J. (Lab)	8 524	17.7%
C majority	10 697	17.7%
Total vote 48 041	Turnout 74.8%	

Mr Tom King became Secretary of State for Employment in Oct 1983; Secretary of State for Transport June–Oct 1983; Secretary of State for the Environment 1983; Minister for Local Government and Environmental Services at the Department of Environment, 1979–83. Opposition spokesman on energy, 1976–79, and formerly on industry. Vice-chairman, Conservative industry committee, 1974–75. Won seat in Mar 1970 by-election. Born 13 Jun 1933; educ. Rugby and Emmanuel College, Cambridge. Former chairman Sale, Tilney and Co Ltd; former general manager, E. S. and A. Robinson, Bristol.

Mrs Rosemary Farley, farmer. Born June 6 1933; educ. Rosemead School, Littlehampton and Brighton Technical College.

Mr Andrew May, lecturer in further education. Born 1939; educ. Grammar school and Selwyn College, Cambridge. Member, Bristol City Council since 1979. Former secretary, Bristol West Constituency Labour Party; former chairman, Bristol Tribune Group; former vice-chairman, Bristol CND. NATFHE.

Mr John Townend

BRIDLINGTON Electorate 76 718

*Townend, J. (C)	31 284	57.8%
Martin, Mrs. E. (SDP/All)	14 675	27.1%
Craven, M. (Lab)	7 370	13.6%
Tooke, S (Eco)	803	1.5%
C majority	16 609	30.7%
Total vote 54 132	Turnout 70.6%	

Mr John Townend, a wine merchant and chartered accountant, was elected in 1979; contested Kingston upon Hull North 1970. Born Jun 12 1934; educ. Hymers College, Hull. Leader, Humberside County Council, 1977–70. Hull City councillor, 1966–74. Director, J Townend and Sons (Hull) Ltd and associated companies. Director, Merchant Vintners Ltd. Member of Lloyd's Divisional chairman, Haltemprice and Beverley Young Conservatives 1952–54. Governor, Hymers College. PPS to Mr Hugh Rossi, Minister for the Disabled, from 1981.

Mrs Elaine Martin, housewife, author and former consular assistant at the British Embassy in Venezuela. Born May 31 1952; educ. University of Essex, Latin American Institute, London, and King's College, London. National recruitment officer SDP. Organised local elections in Sutton, Surrey, 1983.

Mr Michael Craven, information and research assistant to Humberside Council Council leader. Born Feb 1 1959; educ. Marist College, Hull and Hull University. T&GWU.

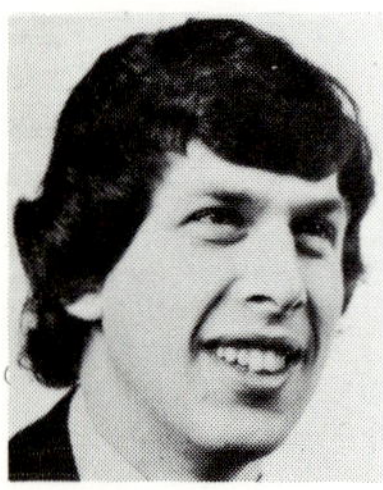

Mr Michael Brown

BRIGG AND CLEETHORPES Electorate 77 471

*Brown, M. R. (C)	28 893	50.7%
Wigginton, G. (L/All)	16 704	29.3%
Hough, J. D. (Lab)	11 404	20.0%
C majority	12 189	21.4%
Total vote 57 001	Turnout 73.6%	

Mr Michael Brown elected in 1983, was MP for Brigg and Scunthorpe 1979–83. Company director, Parliamentary assistant to MPs, 1976–70. Born Jul 3 1951; educ. Andrew Cairns County Secondary Modern School, Littlehampton, and York University. Vice-president York University Students' Union 1971–72. Vice-chairman York University Conservative Association 1971–72. Lecturer and tutor Swinton Conservative College 1974–75. Joint secretary Conservative backbench Northern Ireland committee. Parliamentary consultant to Michael Forsyth Associates, public relations company.

Mr Gavin Wigginton, personnel executive. Born Nov 7 1945; educ. Nottingham High School, University of Wales and University of Hull. Member, Grimsby Borough Council 1974–77.

Mr John Hough is a member of a workers' co-operative. Born 1946. Member, East Midland regional executive committee, Labour Party. Has worked for VSO, some years in Africa on a government overseas aid programme.

Mr Andrew Bowden

BRIGHTON, KEMPTOWN Electorate 60 877

*Bowden, A (C)	22 265	51.1%
Fitch, R. (Lab)	12 887	29.6%
Burke, T. (SDP/All)	8 098	18.6%
Budden, E. (NF)	290	0.7%
C majority	9 378	21.5%
Total vote 43 540	Turnout	71.5%

Mr Andrew Bowden, a personnel consultant, won the seat in 1970; contested the seat in 1966; Kensington North 1964; Hammersmith North 1955. Member Select Committee on Employment since 1979. Joint chairman all-party group for pensioners, 1972–74. Born Apr 8 1930; educ. Ardingly College, Sussex. Member Select Committee on Expenditure, 1973–74; Select Committee on Abortion (Amendment) Bill, 1975–76. National chairman Young Conservatives, 1960–61. Member Wandsworth Borough Council, 1956–62.

Mr Roderick Fitch, a bricklayer, is a member of the TGWU. Born Oct 6 1947; educ. Bevendean First and Middle Schools, Moulsecoomb Secondary School. Governor, Fairlight Middle School. Vice-president, Sussex Christmas Island Veterans Group.

Mr David Burke, environmentalist. B Jan 5 1947; educ. St Boniface's College, Plymouth and Liverpool University.

Mr Julian Amery

BRIGHTON, PAVILION Electorate 59 769

*Amery, H. J. (C)	21 323	51.5%
Neves, M. (SDP/All)	10 191	24.6%
Spillman, H. (Lab)	9 879	23.9%
C majority	11 132	26.9%
Total vote 41 393	Turnout	69.3%

Mr Julian Amery, Minister of State, Foreign and Commonwealth Office, 1972–74; Minister for Housing and Construction 1970–72. Minister of Public Building and Works 1970. Returned at by-election in 1969. Minister of Aviation, 1962–64. Secretary of State for Air from Oct 1960. Under-Secretary, Colonial Office from 1958. Under-Secretary War Office, from 1957. MP for Preston North 1950–66. Contested the two-member Preston seat in 1945. Author, journalist and company director. Born Mar 27 1919; educ. Eton and Balliol College, Oxford. Consultant to Sedgwick Forbes Overseas Group Ltd. Adviser to Bank of Credit and Commerce International.

Mr Michael Neves, senior lecturer, contested Worthing, Feb and Oct 1974. Born Sep 12 1933; educ. Brighton Technical College, Brighton College of Technology and Garnett College of Education. Member, Brighton Borough Council 1973–76 and 1980–83. SE Regional Chairman of NATFHE.

Mr Harold Spillman, teacher, has been an East Sussex councillor since 1981. Born Jun 10 1947; educ. grammar school and New College, Oxford. NUT.

Mr Jonathan Sayeed

BRISTOL EAST Electorate 66 296

Sayeed, J. (C)	19 844	40.5%
*Benn, A. N. W. (Lab)	18 055	36.9%
Tyrer, P. (L/All)	10 404	21.3%
Andrews, E. (NF)	343	0.7%
Dorey, G. (Eco)	311	0.6%
C Majority	1 789	3.7%
Total vote 48 957	Turnout	73.9%

Mr Jonathan Sayeed is a shipping and insurance consultant, won the seat in 1983. Born Mar 20 1948; educ. primary school in Hampstead, London; Woolverstone Hall, Suffolk; Royal Naval College, Dartmouth; Royal Naval Engineering College, Manadon. Former trainee manager for Marks and Spencer. Has unsuccessfully fought GLC elections for East Lewisham and North Islington.

Mr Tony Benn opted for the backbenches after the 1979 election and then unsuccessfully contested Deputy Leadership of Labour Party in 1981 against Mr Healey. Secretary of State for Energy, 1975–79; Secretary of State for Industry 1974–75; Minister for Posts and Telecommunications 1974. Chief Opposition spokesman on Trade and Industry 1970–74; Minister of Technology 1966–70; Postmaster General 1964–66. MP for Bristol South-East 1950–83. Debarred from the Commons on the death of his father, Viscount Stansgate in Nov 1960, he won the by-election in May 1961, but an Election Court declared his Conservative opponent elected. He renounced his title under the Peerage Act and was reelected in Aug 1963. Member Labour Party Executive 1959–60 and since 1962; chairman 1971–72. Journalist. Born Apr 3 1925; educ. Westminster and New College, Oxford. NUJ.

Mr Peter Tyrer, teacher, school counsellor, and area organiser for Oxfam, contested Wallasey, Feb and Oct 1974. Born Feb 12 1947; educ. Bishop Court Prep School, Freshfield; Austin Friars School, Carlisle; De La Salle College of Education, Manchester; Exeter University, and the Open University.

Mr Michael Stern

BRISTOL NORTH WEST Electorate 72 996

Stern, M. (C)	24 617	43.9%
Palmer, Dr S. (Lab)	18 290	32.6%
Long, Mrs H. (SDP/All)	13 228	23.6%
C majority	6 327	11.3%
Total vote 56 135	Turnout	76.9%

Mr Michael Stern, partner in firm of chartered accountants was elected in 1983; contested Derby South 1979. Born Aug 3 1942; educ. Christ's College Grammar School, Finchley. Co-opted member, London Borough of Ealing education committee, 1981–83. Chairman Bow Group, 1977–78; treasurer, Finchley Conservative Association, 1972–76.

Dr Sarah Palmer is a lecturer. Born Sep 16 1943; educ. Wimbledon High School, Durham University, Indiana University and the LSE. Former member, Maidstone Council. Member of and sponsored by Co-operative Party.

Mrs Hilary Long is a teacher at Clifton High School, Bristol. Born November 19 1936. Member, Gas Consumer Council.

Mr Michael Cocks

BRISTOL SOUTH Electorate 72 067

*Cocks, M. F. (Lab)	21 824	44.0%
Gammell, A. (C)	17 405	35.1%
Stanbury, D. (SDP/All)	9 674	19.5%
Collard, G. (Eco)	352	0.7%
Chester, A. (Com)	224	0.5%
Byrne, Mrs L. (WRP)	113	0.2%
Lab majority	4 419	8.9%
Total vote 49 592	Turnout	68.8%

Mr Michael Cocks has been chief Opposition whip since 1979; Parliamentary Secretary to the Treasury (Government Chief Whip) 1976–79; Assistant Government Whip 1974–76. Elected for Bristol South in 1970; contested South Gloucestershire 1964 and 1966, and Bristol West, 1959. Lecturer. Born Aug 19 1929; educ. Bristol University, President Bristol Borough Labour Party, 1961–63. Sponsored by GMWBU.

Mr Alistair Gammell, head of international affairs for Royal Society for the Protection of Birds. Born Jul 28 1949; educ. Clifton College, Bristol; High Wycombe College of Art and Technology. Member, Mid Bedfordshire County Council since 1976; Sandy Town Council, 1976–83 (Chairman 1981–82).

Mr David Stanbury, industrial buyer. Born 1941; educ. grammar school and Oxford University. Member, Council for Social Democracy. Former member, Staffordshire County Council; former chairman, Stafford Co-operative Party; former treasurer, Stafford Constituency Labour Party.

Mr William Waldegrave

BRISTOL WEST Electorate 73 190

*Waldegrave, W. A. (C)	25 400	49.1%
Ferguson, G. (L/All)	15 222	29.4%
Tatlow, Mrs P. (Lab)	10 094	19.5%
Scott, J. (Eco)	872	1.7%
Boyle, S. (Ind)	142	0.3%
C majority	10 178	19.7%
Total vote 51 730	Turnout	70.7%

Mr William Waldegrave, Under Secretary of State for the Environment since 1983 (also Government spokesman on the Arts in the Commons); Under Secretary of State for Education and Science, 1981–83. Elected in 1979. Member of the Central Policy Review Staff, Cabinet Office, 1971–73 and on the Political Staff at No 10 Downing Street, 1973–74. He was head of Mr Edward Heath's political office, 1974–75. With GEC Ltd from 1975 to 1981. Born Aug 15 1946; educ. Eton, Corpus Christi, Oxford (President of the Union) and Harvard (Kennedy Fellow in Politics). Fellow of All Souls College, Oxford. Published book on future of Conservatism, 1978.

Mr George Ferguson, architect. Born Mar 22 1947; educ. Bristol University. Member, Bristol City Council 1973–79. Director of Proscenium Publications.

Ms Pam Tatlow, part-time TUC tutor. Born Jul 13 1950; educ. Tynemouth and Nottingham University. Member, Bristol City Council since May 1983. Member, CND; Bristol South East Co-operative Party; Labour Party Race Action Group; NATFHE and NUT.

Mr Hal Miller

BROMSGROVE Electorate 66 146

*Miller, H. D. (C)	27 911	56.2%
Milligan, J. (SDP/All)	10 736	21.6%
Titley, G. (Lab)	10 280	20.7%
Churchman, J. (Eco)	716	1.4%
C majority	17 175	34.6%
Total vote 49 643		Turnout 75.1%

Mr Hal Miller, a company director and consultant, elected in 1983 was MP for Bromsgrove and Redditch, Feb 1974–83. Contested Bromsgrove in a 1971 by-election, and Barrow-in-Furness, 1970. Born Mar 6 1929; educ. Eton, Merton College, Oxford, and London University. Joint chairman, all-party motor industry group since 1979. With the Colonial Service in Hongkong 1955–68. Fellow of the Economic Development Institute of the World Bank. PPS to Secretary of State for Defence 1979–81, and to Chancellor of the Duchy of Lancaster 1981. Member, UK delegation to Council of Europe, 1974–76.

Mr James Milligan, lecturer, was elected to Hereford–Worcester County Council 1981. Born 1935; educ. Stourport Secondary School, Kidderminster Grammar School and Bristol University. Lectures in modern history at Warley College of Technology, Smethwick. Member, Worcestershire County Council, 1958–61; Council for Social Democracy.

Mr Gary Titley, teacher aged 33. Member, West Midlands County Council since 1981; vice-chairman, economic development committee. Chairman, Halesowen and Stourbridge Constituency Labour Party.

Mrs Marion Roe

BROXBOURNE Electorate 67 387

Roe, Mrs M. (C)	29 328	58.8%
Pollock, B. (L/All)	11 862	23.8%
Stears, M. J. (Lab)	8 159	16.4%
Smith, J. R. (BNP)	502	1.0%
C majority	17 466	35.0%
Total vote 49 851		Turnout 74.0%

Mrs Marion Roe elected in 1983, contested Barking, 1979. Born 1936; educ. Bromley High School, Croydon High School, and English School of Languages, Vevey. Bromley borough councillor, 1975–78; GLC member since 1977; Conservative spokesman on police committee and former deputy chief whip. Member, Independent Broadcasting Authority London advisory committee 1978–81; member, South East Thames Regional Health Authority and Greater London area local government advisory committee. Freeman of the City of London.

Mr Brian Pollock is a teacher. Born May 8 1950; educ. Central Foundation Boys' Grammar School, London, Padgate College of Education, Warrington and Manchester University. NUT.

Mr Martin Stears, a computer programmer, analyst and researcher for ICL. Born May 11 1950; educ. London University. North Hertfordshire councillor since 1979. Chairman, North Herts and Stevenage Co-operative Development Agency. ASTMS, Co-operative Party, Fabian Society, Institute for Workers Control.

Mr James Lester

BROXTOWE Electorate 69 760

*Lester, J. T. (C)	28 522	53.5%
Melton, K. (L/All)	13 444	25.2%
Warner, M. (Lab)	11 368	21.3%
C majority	15 078	28.3
Total vote 53 334		Turnout 76.5%

Mr James Lester elected in 1983, was an Under Secretary of State for Employment 1979–81. Former director of footwear distributing company. MP for Beeston 1974–83. Opposition whip 1975–79. Born May 23 1932; educ. Nottingham High School. Contested Bassetlaw, 1968 by-election and 1970. Member, Nottinghamshire County Council 1967–74. Delegate, Council of Europe and WEU, 1974. Member, Select Committee on Foreign Affairs 1982–83; chairman, party committee on employment, 1983.

Mr Keith Melton, a senior lecturer in management, contested Lincoln 1979. Born Jun 10 1947; educ. North Kesteven Grammar School and University of Manchester Institute of Science and Technology.

Mr Michael Warner, maintenance fitter, aged 33. Member, Nottinghamshire County Council since 1981; Broxtowe Borough Council 1976–79.

Mr George Walden

BUCKINGHAM Electorate 62758

Walden, G. (C)	27552	56.9%
Ryder, R. (L/All)	13584	28.1%
Groucutt, M. (Lab)	7272	15.0%
C majority	13968	28.9%
Total vote 48408	Turnout	77.1%

Mr George Walden, former diplomat and ex-principal private secretary to Lord Carrington, served in China, France and worked in USSR. Elected in 1983. Born Sep 15 1939; educ. Latymer Upper School and Cambridge University. Was head of the planning department in Foreign and Commonwealth Office.

Mr Richard Ryder, psychologist and animal rights campaigner, was RSPCA national chairman 1977–79. Born Jul 3 1940; educ. Sherborne and Cambridge, Columbia and Edinburgh universities. Broadcaster and author of *Victims of Science*.

Mr Martyn Groucutt, teacher, aged 33; educ. West Bromwich Grammar School and the universities of Wales and Durham. Member, National Trust and Naturalist Trust. NUT.

Mr Peter Pike

BURNLEY Electorate 66542

Pike, P. L. (Lab)	20178	39.7%
Bruce, I. (C)	19391	38.2%
Steed, M. (L/All)	11191	22.1%
Lab majority	787	1.6%
Total vote 50760	Turnout	76.3%

Mr Peter Pike, factory inspector was elected in 1983. Born June 26 1937; educ. Hinchley Wood county secondary school and Kingston Technical College, Burnley councillor since 1976 and Labour group leader, May 1980–83. GMBATU (shop steward).

Mr Ian Bruce, company chairman. Born Mar 14 1947; educ. Chelmsford Technical High School, Mid-Essex Technical College, Bradford University.

Mr Michael Steed, senior lecturer in government at University of Manchester, contested Manchester Exchange 1973, Manchester Central Feb 1974, Burnley 1979 and Greater Manchester North in the Euro election 1979. Born Jan 25 1940; educ. Corpus Christi Cambridge and Nuffield, Oxford. Member, Fisher Commission on constitutional reform. President of the Liberal Party 1978–79. AUT.

Mr Ivan Lawrence

BURTON Electorate 71849 1979: 70130 same

*Lawrence, I. J. (C)	27874	51.1%
Slater, R. E. G. (Lab)	16227	29.8%
Garner, Mrs J. (L/All)	10420	19.1%
C majority	11647	21.4%
Total vote 54521	Turnout	75.9%

1979: Total vote 55224 (78.7%); C 29821 (54.0%); Lab 20020 (36.3%); L 5383 (9.7%). C maj 9801 (17.7%); swing 6.9% to C.

Mr Ivan Lawrence, QC, became MP for Burton in Feb, 1974; contested Peckham 1966 and 1970. Born Dec 24 1936; educ. Brighton, Hove and Sussex Grammar School; Christ Church, Oxford. Member, Select Committee on Social Services and Employment 1974–79; Select Committee on Foreign Affairs 1983. Member, Joint Select Committee on Consolidation of Statutes since 1979. Vice-chairman, Conservative parliamentary home affairs committee and of legal committee. Chairman, all-party anti-fluoridation committee. Secretary, all-party committee for release of Soviet Jewry. Member, council of Justice. Vice President, Federation of Conservative Students 1981–83. Hon. President, National Association of Approved Driving Instructors.

Mr Robert Slater, college lecturer. Born Dec 13 1948; educ. Leicester University. Leicester councillor since 1979; chairman, employment committee. Member, Amnesty International. NATFHE.

Mrs June Garner, senior lecturer. Born Nov 9 1930.

Mr Alistair Burt

BURY NORTH Electorate 66065

Burt, A. (C)	23923	45.5%
*White, F. R. (Lab)	21131	40.2%
Wilson, Mrs E. (L/All)	7550	14.4%
C majority	2792	5.3%
Total vote 52604		Turnout 79.6%

Mr Alistair Burt, solicitor, was elected in 1983. Born May 25 1955; educ. Bury Grammar School, St John's College, Oxford. Member, Haringey Borough Council and Conservative spokesman on community affairs.

Mr Frank White, industrial relations manager, was an Opposition whip 1980–81. He was an assistant Government whip, 1976–78. MP for Bury and Radcliffe 1974–83; contested it in Feb 1974. Born Nov 11 1939; educ. Bolton Technical College. Chairman, all-party paper industry group and of north-west Labour group. Member, Select Committee on Employment since 1979. Member, Bolton County Borough Council 1963–74 and of Greater Manchester County Council 1963–74 and of Greater Manchester County Council 1973–75. Sponsored by GMWU.

Mrs Elisabeth Wilson, senior hospital social worker. Born Jan 24 1948; educ. Mount School, York, and East Anglia and Manchester universities. Member, Calderdale Health Authority 1977–83, West Yorkshire Metropolitan County Council, Todmorden Town Council, National Childbirth Trust, National Council for Civil Liberties. Nalgo.

Mr David Sumberg

BURY SOUTH Electorate 64827

Sumberg, D. (C)	21718	44.0%
Boden, D. (Lab)	17998	36.5%
Evans, K. (SDP/All)	9628	19.5%
C majority	3720	7.5%
Total vote 49344		Turnout 76.1%

Mr David Sumberg, a solicitor, was elected in 1983; contested Manchester, Wythenshawe 1979. Born Jun 20 1941; educ. Tettenhall College, Wolverhampton, and College of Law, London. Member, Manchester City Council; executive and council, Manchester Youth and Community Service. Chairman, research committee, Greater Manchester Conservative co-ordinating committee.

Mr Derek Boden, engineer, aged 46. Member, Whitefield Urban District Council, 1972–74 and Bury Metropolitan Borough Council since 1973 (deputy leader, Labour group). Member, National Council for Civil Liberties and CND. ASTMS.

Mr Keith Evans, economist, Born Apr 1 1956; educ. Greenmore College, Edgbaston, Coleshill School, and Polytechnic, Wolverhampton. Elected Greater Manchester County Council, 1981; former member of police authority. Chairman, USDAW Manchester central branch 1981–83, and divisional councillor of USDAW 1981–83.

Mr Eldon Griffiths

BURY ST EDMUNDS Electorate 72875

*Griffiths, E. W. (C)	31081	59.0%
Harland, Sir R. (SDP/All)	14959	28.4%
Mosczynski, W. (Lab)	6666	12.7%
C majority	16122	30.6%
Total vote 52706		Turnout 72.3%

Mr Eldon Griffiths was Opposition spokesman on Europe 1975–76; a spokesman on trade and industry 1974–75, Under Secretary for the Environment with special responsibilities for sport 1970–74. Returned at a by-election in May 1964. Parliamentary Secretary, Ministry of Housing and Local Government, 1970. Company director. Parliamentary adviser to the Police Federation of England and Wales, 1966–70 and since 1974, and Northern Ireland since 1981. Born May 25 1925; educ. Ashton Grammar School; Emmanuel College, Cambridge. Chairman, Anglo-Iranian Parliamentary Group; Anglo-Polish Parliamentary Group. Served in the Conservative Research Department. Chief European Correspondent of *Washington Post* 1961–63. Director of several engineering companies. Member, Select Committee on Foreign Affairs, since 1979.

Sir Reginald Harland, Air Marshal. Born May 30 1920; educ. Summer Fields, Oxford, Stowe and Trinity College, Cambridge. President, Society of Environmental Engineers, 1974–78. With WS Atkins and Partners, Epsom, since 1977.

Mr Wiktor Mosczynski, departmental section leader with an export company. Member, Ipswich Borough Council since 1979; was vice-chairman, planning and transportation committee. Born 1946; educ. Catholic grammar school and Sussex University. APEX.

Mr Dafydd Wigley

CAERNARFON Electorate 44 147 1979: 43 041 same

*Wigley, D. W. (Pl C)	18 308	52.7%
Jones, D (C)	7 319	21.1%
Williams, Mrs B. H. (Lab)	6 736	19.4%
Griffiths, O. G. (L/All)	2 356	6.8%
Pl C majority	10 989	31.7%
Total vote 34 719	Turnout	78.6%

1979: Total vote 35 083 (81.5%) – Pl Cymru 17 420 (49.7%); Lab 8 696 (24.8%); C 6 968 (19.9%); L 1 999 (5.7%). Pl Cymru maj 8 724 (24.9%).

Mr Dafydd Wigley has been president of Plaid Cymru since 1981. Won the seat, February, 1974; contested Merioneth, 1970. Member, All-Party Disablement Group; Sponsor, Disabled Persons Act 1981. Awarded Grimshaw Memorial Award (1982) by Nat. Fed. of the Blind. An industrial economist; financial controller, Hoover Ltd 1971–74; chief cost accountant and financial planning manager, Mars Ltd 1967–71; on finance staff, Ford Motor Company 1964–67. Served on Merthyr Borough Council, 1972–74. Born Apr 1 1943; educ. Caernarvon Grammar School, Rydal School, Colwyn Bay, and Manchester University.

Mr Dennis Jones, college lecturer. Born Aug 16 1949; educ. Bala Boys' Grammar School, Denbighshire Technical College, University of Essex, Huddersfield College of Education.

Mrs Betty Williams, housewife Born Jul 31 1944; educ. Ysgol Dyffryn Nantlle. Member, Gwynedd County Council.

Mr Gwyn Griffiths, solicitor, is a former secretary of the Welsh Liberal Party and member, WLP executive for the last seven years. Age 26. Member, Court of Governors, University of Wales, Standing Conference of the Welsh Centre for International Affairs.

Mr Ronald Davies

CAERPHILLY Electorate 63 479

Davies, R. (Lab)	21 570	45.6%
Lambert, A. (L/All)	10 017	21.2%
Welby, C. (C)	9 295	19.7%
Whittle, L. (Pl C)	6 414	13.6%
Lab majority	11 553	24.4%
Total vote 47 296	Turnout	74.5%

Mr Ronald Davies, an education officer, elected in 1983. Born Aug 6 1946; educ. grammar school, Portsmouth Polytechnic, University of Wales. District councillor since 1969. NUPE.

Mr Anthony Lambert, Post Office senior manager, contested Gloucestershire South 1970, Staffordshire South West Oct 1974, and Newport 1979. Born Sep 30 1943; educ. Hitchin Grammar School and Oxford University. Elected, Thornbury town council 1970. Former national executive member, Post Office Management Staffs Association. SCPS.

Mr Charles Welby, farmer. Born May 6 1953; educ. Eton and Royal Agricultural College, Cirencester.

Mr Lindsay Whittle, welfare assistant, is a member of Rhymni Valley District Council.

Mr Robert Maclennan

CAITHNESS AND SUTHERLAND Electorate 30 871 1979: 29 564 minor

*Maclennan, R. (SDP/All)	12 119	52.0%
Scouller, A. (C)	5 276	22.7%
Carrigan, D. (Lab)	3 325	14.3%
Ingram, J. (SNP)	2 568	11.0%
SDP/All majority	6 843	29.4%
Total vote 23 288	Turnout	75.4%

1979: Total vote 23 174 (78.4%); Lab 9613 (41.5%); C 7074 (30.5%); SNP 6487 (28.0%). Lab Maj 2539 (11.0%); swing 2.7%.

Mr Robert Maclennan won the seat for Labour in March 1966; resigned party in 1981 and joined SDP. Member, Public Accounts Committee, since 1979. SDP spokesman on Scotland and agriculture and fisheries since 1981. Labour Under Secretary for Prices and Consumer Protection, 1974–79. Opposition spokesman on Scottish Affairs, 1970–72, and defence, 1972 to 1974. An Opposition spokesman on Foreign Affairs 1980–81. Barrister. Born 26 Jun 1936; educ. Glasgow Academy, Balliol College, Oxford, Trinity College, Cambridge and Columbia University, New York.

Mr Alastair Scouller, freelance conference interpreter, contested Glasgow, Craigton Feb 1974. Former auxiliary staff interpreter with EEC Commission. Born May 1950; educ. Jordanhill College School, Glasgow; Glasgow University; University of Besancon, France; University of Zurich.

Mr Daniel Carrigan, full-time union official. Born 1948; educ. senior secondary, night school and university. Member, Fabian Society, since 1981.

Mr James Ingram, advertising agency proprietor. Born 1939; educ. Keith Grammar School. Member, Peterhead District and Regional Council.

Mr Donald Thompson

CALDER VALLEY Electorate 71 309

*Thompson, D. (C)	24 439	43.7%
Shutt, D. (L/All)	16 440	29.4%
Holmes, Ms A. (Lab)	15 108	27.0%
C majority	7 999	14.3%
Total vote 55 987		Turnout 78.5%

Mr Donald Thompson, became a Lord Commissioner of the Treasury (Government Whip) 1983; assistant Government whip 1981–83. MP for Sowerby 1979–83; elected for this seat in 1983; contested Sowerby in both 1974 elections and Batley and Morley in 1970. Former farmer and owner of contract butchering firm. Born Nov 13 1931; educ. Hipperholme Grammar School. Member, West Riding County Council 1967–74; West Yorkshire County Council 1974–75; Calderdale District Council 1975–79. Chairman, Conservative Candidates' Association 1972–74.

Mr David Shutt, chartered accountant. Born Mar 16 1942; educ. Pudsey Grammar School. Contested Sowerby 1979, 1970 and twice in 1974. Member, Calderdale Metropolitan Council since 1973; mayor of Calderdale 1982–83. Trustee, Joseph Rowntree Social Service Trust Ltd.

Ms Ann Holmes, research and development officer and sociologist, contested Kensington and Chelsea 1979. Born Jul 22 1946; educ. Whitcliffe Mount Grammar School, West Yorkshire, and Hull University. Member, Islington Council 1974–78. TGWU.

Mr Robert Rhodes James

CAMBRIDGE Electorate 67 018

*Rhodes James, R. V. (C)	20 931	41.5%
Oakeshott, M. (SPD/All)	14 963	29.7%
Jones, Ms J. (Lab)	14 240	28.2%
Dougrez-Lewis, J. (Loony Socy)	286	0.6%
C majority	5 968	11.8%
Total vote 50 420		Turnout 75.2%

Mr Robert Rhodes James, author, publisher and business consultant, was elected in a December 1976 by-election. Born Apr 10 1933; educ. Sedbergh School, Yorkshire and Worcester College, Oxford. Senior clerk, House of Commons 1961–64; Fellow of All Souls College, Oxford, 1964–68; Director of Institute for the Study of International Organization, University of Sussex, 1968–73; principal officer, executive office of the Secretary General of the United Nations, 1973–76. PPS Foreign and Commonwealth Office 1979–82; Conservative liaison officer for Higher and Further Education since 1979; vice-chairman, Home Affairs and Constitutional committees; member, Advisory Council on Public Records.

Mr Matthew Oakeshott, investment manager, contested Horsham and Crawley Oct 1974 for Labour. Special advisor to Mr Roy Jenkins MP, 1972–76. Born Jan 10 1947; educ. Charterhouse, University College, Oxford, and Nuffield College, Oxford. Member, Oxford City Council 1972–76; national steering committee SDP 1981–82. APEX.

Ms Janet Jones, a single parent mother, was a full-time member of Cambridgeshire County Council for 12 years. Born 1940; educ. Blyth Grammar School, Norwich. Former chairman, Labour Party Young Socialists; elected to national committee when 17. Member, Labour Party national executive subcommittees on local government and social policy.

Mr Clement Freud

CAMBRIDGESHIRE NORTH EAST Electorate 69 894

*Freud, C. R. (L/All)	26 936	50.5%
Duval, N. (C)	21 741	40.8%
Harris, R. J. (Lab)	4 625	8.7%
L / All majority	5 195	9.8%
Total vote 53 306		Turnout 76.3%

Mr Clement Freud, Liberal spokesman on social services, broadcasting, the arts and sport, was elected in 1983: MP for Isle of Ely 1973–83. Writer and broadcaster. Rector of Dundee University. Born Apr 24 1924; educ. Dartington Hall and St Paul's School. Party spokesman on education, 1973–76. Former member, Select Committee on Broadcasting, NUJ, Equity. Sponsored Official Information Bill in 1978–79 session.

Mr Nicholas Duval, television journalist and farmer. Born Jul 22 1946; educ. Gresham's School, Holt, and Norfolk College of Agriculture. Former branch chairman, South Norfolk Conservative Assoc; member, Eastern Region Conservative agricultural advisory council; parish council chairman. Founder member and director of East Anglia independent radio station, Saxon Radio; producer with Anglia Television. ACTT, NUJ and NFU.

Mr Ronald Harris, social worker. Born July 12 1934; educ. John Clare Secondary Modern school, Northampton. Member, Fenland District Council. Nalgo.

Mr Francis Pym

CAMBRIDGESHIRE SOUTH EAST Electorate 66885

*Pym F. L. (C)	28555	57.6%
Slee, C. (SDP/All)	14791	29.8%
Jackson, Ms M. E. (Lab)	6261	12.6%
C majority	13764	27.8%
Total vote 49607		Turnout 74.2%

Mr Francis Pym, was asked to resign as Secretary of State for Foreign and Commonwealth Affairs within 48 hours of the election result. Appointed to that post in 1982; Lord President of the Council and Leader of the Commons 1981–82; Chancellor of the Duchy of Lancaster, Paymaster General and Leader of Commons 1981; Secretary of State for Defence, 1979–81. Was chief Opposition spokesman on devolution and House of Commons Affairs until Nov 1978, when appointed spokesman on foreign and Commonwealth affairs, and previously on agriculture, fisheries and food and Northern Ireland, 1973–74. Represented Cambridgeshire, 1961–83; he was elected to this seat, 1983. Parliamentary Secretary to the Treasury and Government Chief Whip 1970–73. Contested Rhondda West 1959. Partner in farm; former company director; member of Lloyd's. Born Feb 13 1922; educ. Eton and Magdalene College, Cambridge. Assistant Government Whip 1962–64. Opposition Whip 1964–67; Opposition Deputy Chief Whip 1967–70. Chairman, Conservative constitutional backbench committee, 1976–79. Member, Herefordshire County Council, 1958–61. Hon. Felllow, Magdalene College.

Mr Christopher Slee, consultant editor and writer. Born May 10 1948; educ. Bristol Aeroplane Technical College and Imperial College, London. Lieutenant in the Royal Engineers 1972–75.

Ms Mary Jackson is an unemployed teacher. Aged 38. Educ. Lincoln High School and Girton College, Cambridge. Active member of Epping Labour Party. NUT.

Sir Anthony Grant

CAMBRIDGESHIRE SOUTH WEST Electorate 76228

*Grant, Sir A. (C)	32521	56.2%
Nicholls, D. (L/All)	18654	32.2%
Gluza, J. (Lab)	6703	11.6%
C majority	13867	24.0%
Total vote 57878		Turnout 75.9%

Sir Anthony Grant was MP for Harrow Central 1964–83; contested Hayes and Harlington 1959. Elected for this seat, 1983. Vice-chairman of the Conservative Party with responsibilities for candidates, 1974–76. Under-Secretary for Trade and Industry 1972–74; Parliamentary Secretary, Board of Trade 1970–72. Solicitor and company director. Born May 29 1925; educ. St Paul's School and Brasenose College, Oxford. Freeman, City of London; member, Court of Guild of Freemen. Member, executive, 1922 Committee, and chairman, backbench trade committee, since 1979. Opposition whip, 1966–70. Deputy Leader, Conservative delegation to Council of Europe and chairman of Economic Committee since 1980. Member, Select Committee on Foreign Affairs since 1980. Consultant to Guild of British Travel Agents.

Dr Derek Nicholls, lecturer in land economy at Cambridge University. Born Apr 8 1939; educ. Helston Grammar School and St John's College, Cambridge. AUT.

Mr Joseph Gluza is a computer officer at Cambridge University. Born Jan 12 1945; educ. St Cuthbert's Grammar School, Newcastle upon Tyne, Newcastle University and Churchill College, Cambridge. Member, Cambridgeshire County Council since 1981; SDP chief whip. ASTMS, former branch vice-chairman; AUT, former branch secretary; CND; Socialist Educational Assoc.

Mr Gerald Howarth

CANNOCK AND BURNTWOOD Electorate 66188

Howarth, G. (C)	20976	40.9%
*Roberts, G. E. (Lab)	18931	36.9%
Withnall, J. W. (SDP/All)	11336	22.1%
C majority	2045	4.0%
Total vote 51243		Turnout 77.4%

Mr Gerald Howarth, international banker, was elected in 1983. Born Sep 12 1947; educ. Haileybury and ISC Junior School, Bloxham School, Banbury, University of Southampton. Member, Hounslow Borough Council since 1982; shadow vice-chairman, Environmental Planning Committee.

Mr Gwilym Roberts was returned for Cannock in Feb 1974; MP for Bedfordshire South, 1966–70. Contested Conway, 1964, and Ormskirk, 1959. Born Aug 7 1928; educ. Brynefaie Grammar School and University of Wales. Principal lecturer, Polytechnic and University. Industrial consultant

on computer methods, market and industrial research. Vice-President, Institute of Statisticians. PPS, Department of Industry 1976–79. Adviser to National Association of Teachers in Further and Higher Education.
Mr William Withnall, deputy head teacher. Born 1941; educ. St Mary's Grammar School and St Paul's College, Cheltenham, and University of Birmingham. Member, Walsall Council, 1970–80; former chairman, education committee. Founder member, SDP; secretary, Walsall area party and its representative on Council for Social Democracy.

Mr David Crouch

CANTERBURY Electorate 73 464

*Crouch, D. L. (C)	29 029	56.5%
Purchese, J. (L/All)	13 287	25.9%
Gould, Ms J. (Lab)	7 906	15.4%
Conder, D. (Eco)	962	1.9%
White, J. (Ind)	226	0.4%
C majority	15 742	30.6%
Total vote 51 410	Turnout	70.0%

Mr David Crouch, company director, public relations and marketing consultant. Elected in 1966; contested Leeds West 1959. Born June 23 1919; educ. University College School, London. Chairman, Anglo-Egyptian parliamentary group; all-party group for the chemical industry; all-party group for energy studies. Vice-Chairman, Conservative Middle East Council. Member, select committee on Nationalized Industries 1966–74; public accounts, 1974–79 and Social Services, 1983. Vice-chairman, Conservative industry committee 1972–75. Member, South East Thames Regional Health Authority. Member, Council of University of Kent. Director, Foster Crouch (Consultants) Ltd, Pfizer Ltd and David Crouch and Co Ltd. Deputy chairman, Theatres Trust.
Mr John Purchese runs a printing business. Contested Canterbury 1979. Born Feb 21 1925; educ. Steyning Grammar School and Ardingly College, Sussex. Member, Canterbury City Council, 1976; member, Kent County Council, 1977.
Ms Jeannette Gould is a research assistant to Mr Stanley Orme, MP for Salford. Born 1953; educ. Essex University and the Polytechnic of North London.

Mr Ian Grist

CARDIFF CENTRAL Electorate 53 815

*Grist, I. (C)	16 090	41.5%
German, M. (L/All)	12 638	32.6%
Davies, R. T. (Lab)	9 387	24.2%
Morgan, P. (PLC)	704	1.8%
C majority	3 452	8.9%
Total vote 38 819	Turnout	72.1%

Mr Ian Grist, elected in 1983 was MP for Cardiff North Feb 1974–83. PPS, Secretary of State for Wales 1979–81 and member, Select Committee on Welsh Affairs since 1981. Information officer, Welsh Conservative Party office 1963–74. Contested Aberavon, 1970. Born Dec 5 1938; ed Repton and Jesus College, Oxford. Chairman, Conservative West African Affairs Committee, since 1977. Vice chairman, Association of Conservative Clubs since 1978–82.
Mr Michael German, teacher, contested Cardiff North, Oct 1974 and 1979. Born May 8 1945; educ. Open University, Bristol Polytechnic and St Mary's College. Member, Cardiff City Council since 1983.
Mr Raymond Davies has worked as a miner and steelworker. Sings with Caerphilly male voice choir. Born 1930.
Mr Paul Morgan, teacher; secretary, Pl Cymru's constituency committee.

Mr Gwilym Jones

CARDIFF NORTH Electorate 53 377

Jones, G. (C)	19 433	47.1%
Jeremy, A. (SDP/All)	12 585	30.5%
Hutt, Ms J. (Lab)	8 256	20.0%
Huws, Dr D. (PlC)	974	2.4%
C majority	6 848	16.6%
Total vote 41 248	Turnout	77.3%

Mr Gwilym Jones, insurance broker was elected in 1983. Member, Cardiff City Council 1973–83, 1969–72. Born 1947. Former chairman, South Wales Public Passenger Transport Operators. Parliamentary election agent, Cardiff South East, Feb and Oct 1974.
Mr Anthony Jeremy, lawyer, is a member of the Council for Social Democracy. Born 1937; educ. Cardiff High School and Fitzwilliam College, Cambridge. Lecturered in law at UWIST, Cardiff, before establishing law firm in 1964.
Ms Jane Hutt, social worker, co-ordinator of Welsh Women's Aid. Born Dec 15 1949; educ. Kenya; Rosemead School, Littlehampton; University of Kent; LSE. Member, South Glamorgan County Council since 1981.
Dr Dafydd Huws, consultant psychiatrist, is Plaid Cymru's spokesman on health. Aged 47. Contested Cardigan 1979.

Mr James Callaghan

CARDIFF SOUTH AND PENARTH Electorate 59 520

*Callaghan, L.J. (Lab)	17 448	41.3%
Tredinnick, D. (C)	15 172	35.9%
Roddick, W. (L/All)	8 816	20.9%
Edwards, Ms S. (PlC)	673	1.6%
Lewis, B. T. (FWD)	165	0.4%
Lab majority	2 276	5.4%
Total vote 42 274	Turnout 71.0%	

Mr James Callaghan was Prime Minister from Apr 5, 1976, upon election as Leader of the Labour Party in succession to Sir Harold Wilson, to May 1979, and Leader of the Opposition until his resignation in 1980. Secretary of State for Foreign and Commonwealth Affairs, 1974–76. Was chief Opposition spokesman on foreign and Commonwealth affairs 1972–74; employment 1971–72; Home Office matters 1970–71. Home Secretary 1967–70 and Chancellor of the Exchequer 1964–67. Chairman of the Labour Party 1973–74, member national executive 1957–67, and party treasurer 1967–76. Parliamentary Secretary Admiralty 1950–51, after three years as Parliamentary Secretary, Ministry of Transport. Labour spokesman on Treasury affairs 1961–64, won this seat in 1983. Elected for Cardiff South, 1945 and represented Cardiff South-East 1950–83. Born Mar 27 1912; educ. Portsmouth Northern elementary and secondary schools.

Mr David Tredinnick, manager of family property company. Born Jan 19 1950; educ. Eton, Mons Officer Cadet School, Graduate School of Business, University of Cape Town, and St John's College, Oxford.

Mr Winston Roddick, a barrister and assistant recorder. Chairman of the Welsh Liberal Party and spokesman on home affairs and the law. Born 1940; educ. University College, London. Contested Anglesey 1970.

Ms Sian Edwards, freelance translator, is a founder member of the Welsh Campaign for Civil and Political Liberties. Active in peace movement.

Mr Stefan Terlezki

CARDIFF WEST Electorate 58 538

Terlezki, S. (C)	15 472	38.0%
Seligman, D. (Lab)	13 698	33.6%
*Thomas, J. (SDP/All)	10 388	25.5%
Parri, M. (PlC)	848	2.1%
Jones, G. (Eco)	352	0.9%
C majority	1 774	4.4%
Total vote 40 758	Turnout 69.6%	

Mr Stefan Terlezki, management consultant, elected in 1983. Born Oct 29 1927; educ. Cardiff College of Food Technology and Commerce. Contested Cardiff South-East Feb and Oct 1974, and South Wales in Euro elections 1979. Member, Cardiff City Council since 1968; South Glamorgan County Council since 1973.

Mr David Seligman, a solicitor. Born Apr 21 1928; educ. Aberystwyth and London Universities, and Hebrew University, Jerusalem. Member, Cardiff City Council since 1973.

Mr Jeffrey Thomas, QC, was elected as Labour MP for Abertillery in 1970, but joined the SDP in Dec 1981. SDP spokesman on the Civil Service. Former Opposition spokesman on legal affairs. Recorder, Crown Court, since 1975. Contested Barry in 1966. Born Nov 12 1933; educ. Abertillery Grammar School, King's College, London.

Mr Meurig Parri, accountant, is a former organizer for Plaid Cymru in the Pontypridd constituency and for Oxfam. Works for Chapter Arts Centre, Canton, Cardiff.

Mr Ronald Lewis

CARLISLE Electorate 54 515 1979: 53 703 same

*Lewis, R. (Lab)	15 618	37.5%
Sowler, R. (C)	15 547	37.3%
Hunt, R. (SDP/All)	10 471	25.2%
Lab majority	71	0.2%
Total vote 41 636	Turnout 76.4%	

1979: Total vote 42 949 (80.0%) – Lab 21 343 (49.7%); C 16 777 (39.1%); L 4 829 (11.2%). Lab maj 4 566 (10.6%); swing 2.3% to C.

Mr Ronald Lewis, a former British Rail employee and former miner, was elected in 1964; contested West Derbyshire 1951; South Northants 1955; Darlington 1959. Member, Select Committee on Social Services, since 1979. Born Jul 1909; educ. elementary school and Cliff Methodist College. Sponsored by NUR. Former President, Pleasley Cooperative Society Ltd. Member, Derbyshire County Council since 1949 and Blackwell RDC since 1940. Local Methodist preacher.

Mr Richard Sowler, a barrister. Born Apr 1943; educ. Harrow and University College, Oxford.

Mr Richard Hunt, senior careers officer with Cumbria LEA. Born Mar 30 1942; educ. Montreal, Vancouver, Canberra and City of Birmingham Polytechnic. Local government officer for 11 years. Member, Nalgo.

Dr Roger Thomas

CARMARTHEN Electorate 63468

*Thomas, R. G. (Lab)	16459	31.6%
Thomas N. M. (C)	15305	29.4%
Evans, G. (PlC)	14099	27.1%
Colin, Mrs J. (SDP/All)	5737	11.0%
Kingzett, B. (Eco)	374	0.7%
Grice, C (BNP)	154	0.3%
Lab majority	1154	2.2%
Total vote 52128	Turnout 82.1%	

Dr Roger Thomas, a general practitioner, elected May 1979. A former Opposition spokesman on Wales. Born Nov 14 1925; educ. Ammanford Grammar School and London Hospital Medical College. Member, Dyfed County Council since 1977. Member Select Committee on Welsh Affairs since 1979.

Mr Nigel Thomas, barrister and tutor in land law at University College, London. Contested Carmarthen 1979. Born 1952; educ. Whitland Grammar School, Carmarthen, the University College of Wales, Aberystwyth and Emmanuel College, Cambridge. Assistant secretary, Society of Conservative Lawyers since 1978. Editor of the Encyclopedia of Capital Taxation.

Mr Gwynfor Evans, farmer and market gardener, was president of Plaid Cymru 1945–81; now party's honorary president. MP for Carmarthen 1966–70, and Oct 1974–79. Born Sep 1912; educ. Barry County School, University College of Wales, Aberystwyth, and St John's College, Oxford.

Mrs Joan Colin, teacher, is a founder member of the Disablement Income Group and co-ordinator of the (Wales) 300 Group. Born Jun 22 1928.

Mr George Foulkes

CARRICK, CUMNOCK AND DOON VALLEY Electorate 55925

*Foulkes, G. (Lab)	21394	51.5%
McInnes, J. (C)	10024	24.1%
Logan, R. (SDP/All)	7421	17.9%
Wyllie, R. (SNP)	2694	6.5%
Lab majority	11370	27.4%
Total vote 41533	Turnout 74.3%	

Mr George Foulkes, Director of Age Concern, Scotland 1973–79, represented South Ayrshire 1979–83; won this seat in 1983; contested Edinburgh Pentlands in Oct 1974, and Edinburgh West 1970. Born January 21 1942; educ. Keith Grammar School, Bannffshire, Haberdashers' Aske School and Edinburgh University. Member, Select Committee on Foreign Affairs since 1979; secretary-treasurer, all-party pensioners' group; treasurer, UK-Benelux and UK-Spanish Committees. Member, Edinburgh Corporation, 1970–75; Lothian Regional Council 1974–79.

Mr James McInnes, managing director of firm of steel stockholders; vice-chairman, West of Scotland Area Council, Scottish Conservative and Unionist Association. Born 1935; educ. Edinburgh Academy, Nottingham Technical College and Scottish College of Commerce. Member, Cumnock and Doon Valley District Council 1977–80; Strathclyde Regional Council since 1982.

Mr Robert Logan, solicitor, is a member of the West of Scotland SDP committee. Born 1954; educ. Ayr Grammar School, Ayr Academy and Glasgow University.

Mr Ronald Wyllie, lay preacher and writer, contested Coatbridge and Airdrie at the by-election 1982. Born 1955; educ. Glasgow University.

Mr Nigel Forman

CARSHALTON & WALLINGTON Electorate 68682 1979: 67255 same

*Forman, F. N. (C)	25396	51.3%
Ensor, J. (SDP/All)	14641	29.6%
Baker, Mrs J. (Lab)	8655	17.5%
Steel, R. (Eco)	784	1.6%
C majority	10755	21.7%
Total vote 49476	Turnout 72.0%	

1979: Total vote 51644 (76.8%) – C 26492 (51.3%); Lab 16121 (31.2%); L 8112 (15.7%); NF 919 (1.8%). C maj 10.371 (20.1%); swing 6.3% to C.

Mr Nigel Forman represented Sutton, Carshalton, 1976–83; won this seat in 1983. Former assistant director, Conservative Research Department. Contested Coventry North East, Feb 1974. Born March 25 1943; educ. Shrewsbury School, New College, Oxford, College of Europe, Bruges, Harvard and Sussex Universities. Member, Select Committee on Science and Technology, 1976–79. Secretary, Conservative backbench committees on education 1976–79 and energy 1977–79. PPS to Mr Douglas Hurd, Minister of State, Foreign and Commonwealth Office, 1979–83.

Mr James Ensor, management consultant. Born Aug 10 1943; educ. Dragon School, King's School, Canterbury, King's College, Cambridge.

Mrs Joan Baker, housewife and former clerk. Born May 29 1932; educ. grammar school. Wandsworth councillor 1962–65; Lambeth councillor 1964–68.

Sir Bernard Braine

CASTLE POINT Electorate 64023

*Braine, Sir B. (C)	26730	58.5%
Bastow, Ms A. (SDP / All)	11313	24.8%
Cunningham, Ms L. (Lab)	7621	16.7%
C majority	15417	33.8%
Total vote 45664		Turnout 71.3%

Sir Bernard Braine was MP for Essex, South-East, until 1983, chairman of Select Committee on Overseas Aid and Development 1970–74. Conservative spokesman on foreign and commonwealth affairs and overseas development 1967–70; Parliamentary Secretary, Ministry of Health 1962–64; Under-Secretary, Commonwealth Relations Office 1961–62; Parliamentary Secretary, Ministry of Pensions and National Insurance 1960–61. Consultant. Won this seat in 1983; represented Essex South East 1955–83; Billericay 1950–55; contested Leyton East 1945. Born Jun 1914; educ. Hendon County School. A governor Commonwealth Institute 1968–81, trustee since 1981. Chairman National Council on Alcoholism 1975–82. Chairman, British-German parliamentary group since 1970 and British-Greek parliamentary group 1979, and UK chapter, Society of International Development since 1976. President, Society for the Defence of the Unjustly Prosecuted and British Solidarity with Poland Campaign.

Ms Anne Bastow, teacher. Born Aug 20 1951; educ. Carleton University, Canada and Durham University.

Ms Lynne Cunningham, local government officer. Born Sep 2 1946; educ. Frome Grammar School, Hull University. Head of Neighbourhood Support Services, Basildon Council.

Mr Geraint Howells

CEREDIGION AND PEMBROKE NORTH Electorate 60523

*Howells, G. (L/All)	19677	41.8%
Raw-Rees, T. (C)	14038	29.8%
Hughes, G.E. (Lab)	6840	14.5%
Dafis, C. (PlC)	6072	12.9%
Smith, Miss M. (Eco)	431	0.9%
L/All majority	5639	12.0%
Total vote 47058		Turnout 77.8%

Mr Geraint Howells is leader of the Welsh Liberal Party. MP for Cardigan 1974–83; won this seat in 1983; contested Brecon and Radnor 1970. Liberal spokesman on agriculture and Wales since 1976. Member Select Committee on Welsh Affairs since 1979. Born April 15 1925; educ. Ardwyn Grammar School. Member, Cardiganshire County Council since 1952. Vice-chairman, British Wool Marketing Board since 1971. Managing director, Wilkinson and Stanier Ltd, meat wholesalers, Manchester; chairman, Wool Producers of Wales Ltd; Secretary, Ponterwyd Eisteddfod. President, International Sheep Dog Society, 1983; president, Royal Welsh Agricultural Society.

Mr Tom Raw-Rees has been chairman, Dyfed branch, Council for the Protection of Rural Wales since 1979. Member, Development Board for Rural Wales since 1981, and of Ceredigion District Council since 1974. Former member, Aberystwyth Rural District Council.

Mr Griffith Hughes, postman. Born Sep 24 1935; educ. Cardigan Grammar School. Member, Dyfed County Council since 1974. UPOW.

Mr Cynog Dafis, teacher at Aberaeron, is editor of Plaid Cymru's Welsh language monthly paper. Member, Teifiside Housing Association.

Mr Tom Normanton

CHEADLE Electorate 66474

*Normanton, T. (C)	28452	55.7%
Clark, P. (L/All)	19072	37.3%
Parker, K. (Lab)	3553	7.0%
C majority	9380	18.4%
Total vote 51077		Turnout 76.8%

Mr Tom Normanton won the seat for the Conservatives in 1970; contested Rochdale 1964 and 1959. Industrialist; a director of Commercial Union Assurance Co. Council member, CBI since 1964. Member, European Parliament since 1973. Born Mar 12 1917; educ. Manchester Grammar School and Manchester University. Past president, British Textile Employers' Assoc. and International Federation of Textile Industries, Consultant to Midland Bank on EEC affairs. Former member, Textile Industrial Training Board. Member, Rochdale County Borough Council 1950–53.

Mr Paul Clark, solicitor, contested Liverpool and Bootle in the Euro-election, 1979. Born May 7 1953; educ. St Mary's College, Crosby and Liverpool University. Member, Liverpool City Council since 1976; chairman of the social services committee 1980–83.

Mr Kenneth Parker is an insurance manager. Aged 54, elementary education.

Mr Norman St John-Stevas

CHELMSFORD Electorate 78 849

*St John-Stevas, N. A. (C)	29 824	47.6%
Mole, S. (L / All)	29 446	47.0%
Playford, C. (Lab)	3 208	5.1%
Waite, P.D.P. (Ind)	127	0.2%
C majority	378	0.6%
Total vote 62 605	Turnout 79.4%	

Mr Norman St John-Stevas was Chancellor of the Duchy of Lancaster, Leader of the House of Commons and Minister for the Arts 1979–81. Author, barrister and journalist, he was elected in 1964; contested Dagenham, 1950. Opposition spokesman on education, science and the arts 1974–78. Member of the shadow Cabinet 1974–79. Appointed spokesman on constitutional and Commons affairs and arts, Nov 1978. Minister of State for Education and Science with responsibility for arts 1973–74; Under Secretary for Education and Science 1972–73. Born May 18 1929; educ. Radcliffe College; Fitzwilliam College, Cambridge; Christ Church, Oxford; Yale. Former member, 1922 Committee executive. Member, Select Committee on Race Relations and Immigration, 1970–72.

Mr Stuart Mole, personal assistant to Mr David Steel, the Liberal leader, contested the seat in Feb and Oct 1974, and 1979. Born Jan 15 1949; educ. St Paul's Cathedral Choir School, St John's School, Leatherhead and the universities of Nottingham, Oxford and London. Member, Chelmsford Borough Council since 1972.

Mr Clive Playford, social researcher. Born Jan 24 1953; educ. Highbury Grove School, Essex University and LSE. Researcher with the Docklands Forum in London and formerly with Low Pay Unit. TGWU (ACTSS).

Mr Nicholas Scott

CHELSEA Electorate 53 864 1979: 57 515 minor

*Scott, N. P. (C)	19 122	63.2%
Fryer, J. (L / All)	7 101	23.5%
Palmer, N. (Lab)	3 876	12.8%
Fielding, Ms. A (Ind)	139	0.5%
C majority	12 021	39.8%
Total vote 30 238	Turnout 56.1%	

1979: Total Vote 32 955 (57.3%); C 21 782 (66.1%); Lab 6 092 (18.5%); L 4 544 (13.8%); NF 342 (1.0%). C maj 15 690 (47.6%); swing 3.4% to C.

Mr Nicholas Scott, appointed Under Secretary of State for Northern Ireland. Former member Shadow Cabinet and chief Opposition spokesman on housing. Returned in Oct 1974; represented Paddington South 1966–74; contested Cities of London and Westminster, Paddington, Feb 1974; Islington South West 1964 and 1959. Under Secretary for Employment, Jan–Feb 1974. Born Aug 5 1933; educ. Clapham College. Chairman, Conservative backbench committee on employment 1979–81. Member 1922 executive commitee 1978–81. Former director of printing and publishing and other companies. National chairman, Young Conservatives 1963, and president Greater London YCs.

Mr Jonathan Fryer, writer and journalist on international affairs, contested London South East as Euro candidate in 1979. Born Jun 5 1950; educ. Manchester Grammar School and St Edmund Hall, Oxford.

Mr Nicholas Palmer is a researcher in medical computing and author of two books on conflict simulation games. Born Feb 5 1950; educ. at international schools in Vienna and Denmark and at the universities of Copenhagen and London.

Mr Charles Irving

CHELTENHAM Electorate 76 068

*Irving, C. G. (C)	29 187	50.6%
Holme, R. (L/All)	23 669	41.0%
James, Mrs J. M. (Lab)	4 390	7.6%
Swindley, D. (Eco)	479	0.8%
C majority	5 518	9.6%
Total vote 57 725	Turnout 75.9%	

Mr Charles Irving, a director of the Dowty Group of companies and other companies including hotels, won the seat, Oct 1974; contested Bilston 1970, and Kingswood Feb 1974. Member, Cheltenham Borough and District Council since 1974, and Gloucestershire County Council since 1948; Mayor of Cheltenham 1958–60 and 1971–72. Born May 1926; educ. Glengarth School, Cheltenham, and Lucton School, Herefordshire. Chairman, House of Commons catering subcommittee of Services Committee.

Mr Richard Holme, director, Campaign for Electoral Reform, contested East Grinstead 1964 and 1965, Braintree Oct 1974. Born May 27 1936; educ. Royal Masonic School, St John's College, Oxford, and Harvard Business School.

Mrs Judith James, supervisor on community project for young unemployed. Born Feb 2 1946; educ. at teacher training college. Member, Newport Council since 1979.

Mr Geoffrey Pattie

CHERTSEY AND WALTON Electorate 70210 1979: 68749 same

*Pattie, G. E. (C)	29679	58.3%
de St Croix, R. (SDP/All)	13980	27.5%
Green, D. (Lab)	6902	13.6%
Barrett, F. (FAMP)	318	0.6%
C majority	15699	30.9%
Total vote 50879	Turnout	72.5%

1979: Total vote 52626 (76.5%) – C 25810 (49.0%); L 13786 (26.2%); Lab 12211 (23.2%); NF 819 (1.6%). C maj 12024 (22.8%); swing 2.5% to C.

Mr Geoffrey Pattie appointed Minister of State for Defence Procurement in 1983; Under Secretary of State for Defence Procurement 1981–83; Under-Secretary of State for the RAF 1979–81. Elected in 1974; contested Barking 1966 and 1970. Born Jan 17 1936; educ. Durham and St Catherine's College, Cambridge. Barrister, GLC member for Lambeth 1968–70. Former member, Public Accounts Committee, former vice-chairman, Conservative aviation committee; former joint secretary, Conservative defence committee. Former director, advertising agency.

Mr Richard de St Croix, solicitor. Born 1947; educ. Oxford University. Specialist in law relating to building, the engineering industry and employment. Former volunteer solicitor, Paddington Citizens Advice Bureau and Law Centre.

Mr David Green, solicitor. Born 1956. Member, Amnesty International, Haldane Society, Society of Labour Lawyers, ASTMS, Weybridge CND.

Sir Ian Gilmour

CHESHAM AND AMERSHAM Electorate 69980

*Gilmour, Sir I. (C)	32 425	61.0%
Bradnock, R (L/All)	16556	31.2%
Duncan, C. (Lab)	4150	7.8%
C majority	15 869	29.9%
Total vote 53 131	Turnout	75.9%

Sir Ian Gilmour was Lord Privy Seal and principal spokesman on foreign and Commonwealth affairs in the Commons 1979–81. Chief Opposition spokesman on defence 1975–79; spokesman on Northern Ireland 1974–75. Secretary of State for Defence 1972–74; Minister of State for Defence Procurement 1971–72; Under Secretary of State for Defence for the Army, 1970–71. Former chairman, Conservative Research Department. Returned Feb 1974; MP for Norfolk Central 1962–74. Journalist and barrister. Former editor, *Spectator*. Born July 8 1926; educ. Eton and Balliol College, Oxford.

Dr Robert Bradnock, university lecturer, fought the seat in 1979. Born Dec 9 1943; educ. Eltham College and Fitzwilliam College, Cambridge. Elder, United Reformed Church. AUT.

Mr Clive Duncan, teacher. Born Aug 12 1950; educ. Douai School, St John's College, Oxford, and Nottingham University. NUT, divisional president.

Mr Peter Morrison

CHESTER, CITY OF Electorate 64508

*Morrison, P. H. (C)	22645	47.1%
Robertson, D. E. (Lab)	13546	28.2%
Stunell, A. (L/All)	11874	24.7%
C majority	9099	18.9%
Total vote 48065	Turnout	74.5%

Mr Peter Morrison, Minister of State for Employment 1983; Under Secretary of State for Employment 1981–83; Lord Commissioner of the Treasury (Government whip) 1979–81; Opposition whip 1976–79. Elected Feb 1974. Secretary, North-West group of Conservative MPs 1975–76. Former director of farming and hotel companies. Born Jun 2 1944; educ. Eton College and Keble College, Oxford. Personal assistant to Mr Peter Walker 1966–67 and investment manager with Slater Walker Securities Ltd 1968–70. Younger brother of Mr Charles Morrison, Conservative MP for Devizes.

Dr David Robertson, former general practitioner, now a community physician. Born Feb 27 1944; educ. Liverpool University. Member, Frodsham Council since 1976. Member, Labour Co-ordinating committee; Co-operative Party; Fabians. ASTMS.

Mr Andrew Stunell, freelance architectural assistant, is leader of the Liberal group, Cheshire County Council. Born Nov 24 1942; educ. Surbiton Grammar School, Manchester University, Liverpool Polytechnic. Member, Chester City Council since 1979; Cheshire County Council since 1981. Contested Chester 1979. Nalgo 1967–81; Staff Side, Whitley Council (new towns) 1977–80. Baptist lay preacher.

Mr Eric Varley

CHESTERFIELD Electorate 68 486 By-election Mar 1 1984

*Varley, E. G. (Lab)	23 881	48.1%
Bourne, N. (C)	16 118	32.4%
Payne, M. (L/All)	9 705	19.5%
Lab majority	7 763	15.6%
Total vote 49 704	Turnout	72.6%

Mr Eric Varley, who was elected Treasurer of the Labour Party in 1981, was Chief Opposition spokesman on employment 1981–83 and on industry 1979–81. Elected to shadow cabinet in 1979, Secretary of State for Industry 1975–79; Secretary of State for Energy 1974–75. An Opposition spokesman on regional policy 1970–72; chief spokesman on fuel and power, 1972–74. Chairman, PLP trade union group 1972–74. Minister of State Technology and Power 1969–70; assistant Government whip 1967–69. Elected in 1964. Craftsman in mining industry. Born Aug 11 1932; educ. secondary school, technical college, and Ruskin College, Oxford. Member, Derbyshire area executive NUM 1955–64. Sponsored by NUM. *See page 366 for by-election result.*

Mr Nicholas Bourne, barrister, is supervisor in law at St Catherine's and Corpus Christi Colleges, Cambridge. Born 1952; educ. King Edward VI School, Chelmsford, University College of Wales, Aberystwyth, Trinity College, Cambridge.

Mr Max Payne, polytechnic lecturer, contested Carlton 1964 and 1966, and Chesterfield 1979. Born Jan 1 1930; educ. Heanor Grammar School and Manchester University. Chairman, NATFHE, Sheffield City Polytechnic, 1981; vice-chairman since 1982.

Mr Anthony Nelson

CHICHESTER Electorate 77 259 1979: 73 720 same

*Nelson, R. A. (C)	35 482	63.7%
Gibson, H. (SDP/All)	15 365	27.6%
Rhodes, R. H. (Lab)	3 995	7.2%
Sherlock, J. (Eco)	838	1.5%
C majority	20 117	36.1%
Total vote 55 680	Turnout	72.1%

1979: Total vote 55 704 (75.6%) – C 34 696 (62.3%); L 10 920 (19.6%); Lab 8 569 (15.4%); other 863 (1.5%); Eco 656 (1.2%). C maj 23 776 (42.7%); swing 5.7% to C.

Mr Anthony Nelson, former merchant banker, was elected in Oct 1974; contested Leeds East, Feb 1974. Born Jun 11 1948; educ. Harrow and Christ's College, Cambridge. Founder member, National Victims Association; member, Howard League Council, since 1977; and of Bow Group Council 1973. PPS to Minister for Housing and Construction since 83. Member, Select Committee on Science and Technology 1975–79; secretary of Conservative industry committee 1974–77. Secretary, British Jordanian parliamentary group. Fellow of Royal Society of Arts.

Mr Howard Gibson, personnel manager. Born Jul 7 1933; educ. Ryhope Grammar School and University College, Durham. Chairman south coast branch Institute of Personnel Management; governor Chichester High School for Boys.

Mr Robert Rhodes, social worker. Born May 4 1949; educ. Cheltenham Grammar School and Birmingham Polytechnic. Member, Warwickshire County Council and North Warwickshire Health Authority.

Mr Norman Tebbit

CHINGFORD Electorate 56 228 1979: 56 061 minor

*Tebbit, N. B. (C)	22 541	55.1%
Hoskins, R. (L/All)	10 127	24.8%
Shepherd, W. (Lab)	7 239	17.7%
Morgan, J. (Eco)	479	1.2%
Cheetham, B. (NF)	380	0.9%
Neighbour, J. (Ind)	104	0.3%
Barklem, S. (Ind)	34	0.1%
C majority	12 414	30.4%
Total vote 40 904	Turnout	72.8%

1979: Total vote 43 928 (78.4%) – C 24 640 (56.1%); Lab 12 257 (27.9%); L 5 225 (11.9%); NF 1 157 (2.6%); Eco 649 (1.5%). C maj 12 383 (28.2%); swing 8.5%. to C.

Mr Norman Tebbit, Secretary of State for Trade and Industry 1983; Secretary of State for Employment 1981–83; Minister of State for Industry 1981; Under Secretary of State for Trade 1979–81. PPS to Minister of State for Employment 1972–73. Elected for the constituency Feb 1974; represented Epping 1970–74. Born Mar 29 1931; educ. Edmonton County Grammar School. Served on former Select Committee on Science and Technology; ex-chairman, Conservative aviation committee. Former vice-chairman and secretary, Conservative housing and construction committee; former secretary, New Town MPs. Former airline pilot; member, Balpa (former elected official).

Mr Richard Hoskins, training manager, contested Wanstead and Woodford 1970. Born Sep 28 1938; educ. Ebbw Vale Grammar School. Former constituency chairman.

Mr William Shepherd, personnel manager. Born 1942.

Mr Sydney Chapman

CHIPPING BARNET Electorate 58 423 1979: 58 254 same

*Chapman, S. B. (C)	23 164	56.1%
Perkin, C. (L/All)	10 771	26.1%
Smith, N. J. M. (Lab)	6 599	16.0%
Parry, E. (Eco)	552	1.3%
Hopkins, J. (Ind)	195	0.5%
C majority	12 393	30.0%
Total vote 41 281	Turnout	70.7%

1979: Total vote 44 033 (75.6%) – C 24 154 (57.1%); Lab 11 147 (25.3%); L 6 867 (15.6%); NF 865 (2.0%). C maj 14 007 (31.8%); swing 6.4% to C.

Mr Sydney Chapman, a chartered architect and town planning consultant, was returned for this seat in 1979; MP for Birmingham, Handsworth, 1970 – Feb 1974; contested Stalybridge and Hyde, 1964. Member, Council of Royal Institute of British Architects 1972–77; vice-president, 1974–75. Born Oct 17 1935; educ. Rugby School and Manchester University. Member executive committee. National Union of Conservative and Unionist Associations 1961–70. National Chairman, Young Conservatives 1964–66. Originator of National Tree Planning Year 1973. Non-executive director of Capital and Counties plc and Lovell Construction Ltd. PPS, Secretary of State for Transport 1979–81, and Secretary of State for Social Services since 1981. Chairman, Parliamentary Consultants Group since 1980.

Mr Christopher Perkin, photographer and photo-librarian for a container leasing company.

Mr Nigel Smith, teacher, contested South-East Essex 1979 and Chichester in Feb and Oct 1974. Born Oct 1947; educ. Chichester High School, Manchester Polytechnic, Kent State University, USA, and Oxford, Member, Basildon District Council since 1975. NUT.

Mr Roger Sims

CHISLEHURST Electorate 54 567 1979: 54 024 minor

*Sims, R. E. (C)	22 108	55.7%
Lingard, P. (L/All)	10 047	25.3%
McDonald, A. H. (Lab)	7 320	18.5%
Waite, A (BNP)	201	0.5%
C majority	12 061	30.4%
Total vote 39 676	Turnout	72.7%

1979: Total vote 42 652 (79.0%); C 23 259 (54.5%); Lab 13 494 (31.6%) L 5 335 (12.5%); NF 564 (1.3%). C maj 9 765 (22.9%); swing 6.7% to C.

Mr Roger Sims, an export manager, was elected in Feb 1974; contested Shoreditch and Finsbury 1966 and 1970. Born Jan 27 1930; educ. City Boys' Grammar School, Leicester, and St Olave's Grammar School, London. PPS to Home Secretary since 1979–83. Joint secretary, Conservative parliamentary home affairs committee 1976–1979. Vice-chairman, all-party paper industry committee, parliamentary adviser to the Alcohol Research and Education Committee of the Scotch Whisky Association. Former member, Select committee on Race Relations and Immigration. Member, Choral Society. Member, Chislehurst and Sidcup UDC, 1956–62. Member Central Exec. Committee, NSPCC.

Mr Philip Lingard, chartered accountant. Born April 28 1956; educ. Queen Elizabeth's Grammar School, Blackburn and Hull University. Honorary auditor of anti-nuclear campaign.

Mr Alistair Macdonald, a credit analyst, MP for Chislehurst 1966–70; contested Beckenham 1964. Born May 18 1925; educ. Dulwich College, Enfield Technical College and Corpus Christi College, Cambridge. Member, Chislehurst and Sidcup Council 1958–62; Bromley Council 1964–68 and since 1971. Alderman, London Borough of Bromley 1964–68. Deputy company secretary and branch chairman of the Banking Insurance and Finance Union 1960; branch treasurer 1961.

Mr Den Dover

CHORLEY Electorate 72 841

*Dover, D. (C)	27 861	48.3%
Taylor, I. (Lab)	17 586	30.5%
O'Neill, P. (SDP/All)	11 691	20.3%
Holgate, S. (Eco)	451	0.8%
Rokas, Mrs E. (Ind)	114	0.2%
C majority	10 275	17.8%
Total vote 57 703	Turnout	79.2%

Mr Den Dover was elected in May 1979. A civil engineer and member of the Institution of Civil Engineers. Born Apr 4 1938; educ. Manchester Grammar School and Manchester University. Contested Caerphilly Oct 1974. Member, Barnet Council 1968–71; Member, Select Committee on Transport; director of housing construction. GLC, 1977–79. Parliamentary consultant to George Wimpey plc. Secretary, Conservative backbenchers environment, urban affairs and new towns committees.

Mr Ivan Taylor, an engineer with British Aerospace, contested Blackpool North in both 1974 elections.

Born Jul 1939. Member, Blackpool District Council; Blackpool Borough Council 1966–73.
Mr Peter O'Neill, a freelance journalist, contested London East in the Euro-Elections 1979. Aged 37; educ. at the Universities of Bradford (President of the Union), Moscow and New Dehli. Member, national executive NUJ; Diplomatic and Commonwealth Writers' Assoc. Former chairman, London agency branch, NUJ.

Mr Robert Adley

CHRISTCHURCH Electorate 65 489

*Adley, R. (C)	31 722	67.1%
Alexander, S. (SDP/All)	11 984	25.3%
Mitchell, J. R. (Lab)	3 590	7.6%
C majority	19 738	41.7%
Total vote 47 296		Turnout 72.2%

Mr Robert Adley, marketing consultant of international hotel company, was elected for Christchurch and Lymington in Feb 1974; MP for Bristol North-East 1970–74; contested Birkenhead 1966. Born Mar 2 1935; educ. Falconbury and Uppingham. Chairman, all-party tourism committee. First chairman and founder member Brunel Society. Member steering committee. SS Great Britain project. Trustee, Brunel Engineering Centre Trust; member committee, National Railway Museum. Chairman, Anglo-Chinese parliamentary group. Vice-chairman, Conservative parliamentary transport committee. Member, National Council of British Hotels, Restaurants and Caterers' Assoc. Director, General and Wholesale Representation Ltd. Member Select Committee on Members' Interests since 1979.
Mr Stephen Alexander, barrister. Born 1947; educ. New Zealand University and University College, London. Chairman, East Dorset area party; member, Council for Social Democracy.

Mr Nicholas Ridley

CIRENCESTER AND TEWKESBURY Electorate 80 067

*Ridley, N. (C)	34 282	57.2%
Beckerlegge, P. (L/All)	20 455	34.1%
Penny, T. J. R. (Lab)	5 243	8.7%
C majority	13 827	23.1%
Total vote 59 980		Turnout 74.9%

Mr Nicholas Ridley, Secretary of State for Transport 1983; Financial Secretary to the Treasury 1981–83. Minister of State for Foreign and Commonwealth Affairs 1979–81; Under Secretary of State for Trade 1970–72; Under-Secretary, Ministry of Technology 1970. Chairman, Conservative parliamentary finance committee 1972–73, and joint vice-chairman 1974–79. Former member, expenditure committee. An Opposition spokesman on technology and trade 1969–70, and on defence 1965–66. Elected 1959; contested Blyth 1955. Civil engineer. Born Feb 17 1929; educ. Eton and Balliol College, Oxford.
Mr Philip Beckerlegge, solicitor. Born Dec 20 1942; educ. Tapton House Grammar School, Chesterfield. Contested the seat in 1979. Member, Cotswold District Council, 1977–83.
Mr Terence Penny is a skilled machinist; former merchant seaman. Age 34; educ. secondary modern school. GMBATU.

Mr Peter Brooke

CITY OF LONDON AND WESTMINSTER SOUTH Electorate 67 773

*Brooke, P. L. (C)	20 754	59.1%
Walker-Smith, A. (L/All)	7 367	21.0%
Jones, S. (Lab)	6 013	17.1%
Shorter, R. (Eco)	419	1.2%
Reeve, A. (NF)	258	0.7%
Spence, A. (Com)	161	0.5%
Litvin, W. (Ind)	147	0.4%
C majority	13 387	38.1%
Total vote 35 119		Turnout 51.8%

Mr Peter Brooke, elected at a by-election in Feb 1977, was appointed Under Secretary of State for Education and Science in Jun 1983; a Government whip 1979–83. Contested Bedwellty Oct 1974. Born Mar 1934; educ. Marlborough, Balliol College, Oxford, and Harvard Business School. Vice-president National Union of Students 1955–56; president Oxford Union 1957. Member Camden Borough Council 1968–69. Former Swiss correspondent of *Financial Times*. Former chairman of London firm of international management consultants; underwriting member of Lloyd's.
Mr Adrian Walker-Smith, manager in firm of mail order publishers. Born Oct 22 1947; educ. London University. Former member, British Actors Equity.
Mr Stephen Jones, building society trainee manager. Aged 25; educ. Kent University. Son of Mr Barry Jones MP for Alyn and Deeside. Director of Westminster Homes Ltd, a charitable housing assoc. for the elderly. Member, Co-operative movement.

Mr Martin O'Neill

CLACKMANNAN Electorate 47 642

*O'Neill, M. (Lab)	16 478	45.8%
Jones, Mrs J. (SNP)	6 839	19.0%
Hendry, C. (C)	6 490	18.0%
Campbell, Mrs H. (SDP/All)	6 205	17.2%
Lab majority	9 639	26.8%
Total vote 36 012		Turnout 75.6%

Mr Martin O'Neill represented Stirlingshire East and Clackmannan 1979–83. Won this seat in 1983. An Opposition spokesman on Scotland in 1981. Teacher. Born January 6 1945; educ. Wardie Primary School, Trinity Academy, Heriot Watt University and Moray House College of Education, Edinburgh. GMWU/MATSA. Sponsored by SLADE.

Mrs Janette Jones, housewife, contested West Stirlingshire Feb 1974. Born August 1931; educ. Kilsyth Academy. A vice-president of the SNP; formerly a vice-chairman (publicity). Former member, Kilsyth Burgh Council.

Mr Charles Hendry, public relations executive, is a former vice-chairman, Federation of Conservative Students for Scotland. Aged 24; educ. Rugby, Edinburgh University, University of Vienna. Former research officer, Bow Group and former research assisant to Mr Michael Ancram and Mr Peter Fraser.

Mrs Hilary Campbell, part-time tutor. Born 1952; educ. Barr's Hill Grammar School, Coventry, Middlesex Polytechnic, Accra, Ghana and University of Western Ontario. Member, Council for Social Democracy, SDP Council for Scotland, and Women for Social Democracy.

Sir Anthony Meyer

CLWYD NORTH WEST Electorate 62 503

*Meyer, Sir A. (C)	23 283	51.0%
Lewis, J. (L / All)	13 294	29.1%
Campbell, I. (Lab)	7 433	16.3%
Rhys, Mrs M. (PlC)	1 669	3.7%
C majority	9 989	21.9%
Total vote 45 679		Turnout 73.1%

Sir Anthony Meyer, former diplomat, represented Flint West 1970–83; Eton and Slough 1964–66. Underwriter at Lloyd's. Chairman of the Franco-British Parliamentary Relations Committee since 1979. Member, Select Committee on Welsh Affairs, since 1979. Joint vice-chairman of the Conservative backbench European affairs committee; Vice-chairman, Welsh Conservative MPs; PPS to Chief Secretary to the Treasury 1970–72, and to Secretary of State for Employment 1972–74. A trustee of the Shakespeare Memorial National Theatre. Born Oct 27 1920; educ. Eton and New College, Oxford.

Mr James Lewis, northern chief reporter for *The Guardian*, was formerly newspaper/journalism consultant to the Indian and Sudanese governments. Lecturer in journalism. Born Jun 30 1932; educ. Liverpool College of Art, Bradford College of Advanced Technology. NUJ.

Mr Ian Campbell teacher. Born 1936. Board of Trade yachtmaster and crew member, RNLI.

Mrs Manon Rhys, freelance researcher, is an active member of CND. Member of the Council of CND in Wales.

Mr Robert Harvey

CLWYD SOUTH WEST Electorate 55 792

Harvey, R. (C)	14 575	33.8%
*Ellis, R. T. (SDP/All)	13 024	30.2%
Carter, D. B. (Lab)	11 829	27.4%
Schiavone, T. (PlC)	3 684	8.6%
C majority	1 551	3.6%
Total vote 43 112		Turnout 77.3%

Mr Robert Harvey, journalist, elected in 1983, contested Caernarvon in Oct 1974, and Merioneth 1979. Born Aug 8 1953; educ. Eton and Christ Church, Oxford. Assistant editor of *The Economist*; broadcaster and interviewer for BBC. Member, Bow Group's economic, foreign affairs and parliamentary standing committees; Royal Institute of International Affairs. NUJ.

Mr Tom Ellis was elected as Labour MP for Wrexham in 1970 and joined the SDP in 1981; becoming its spokesman on Wales. Contested West Flintshire 1966. Member, European Parliament 1975–79. Mining engineer. Born Mar 15 1924; educ. Ruabon Grammar School and Universities of Wales and Nottingham. Former president, Wrexham Fabian Society.

Mr Dennis Carter, head teacher at Taliesin Junior School, Sholton, Clwyd. Educ. Preston secondary modern, Birkenhead Technical School, Chester College of Education, London and Exeter universities. Member, Socialist Education Association, CND and NUT.

Mr Toni Schiavone, Plaid Cymru spokesman on the Welsh language, is head of geography department at Ysgol Dyffryn Conwy, Llanrwst. Party representative on CND Cymru.

Mr Hugh McCartney

CLYDEBANK AND MILNGAVIE Electorate 50 831 1979: 49 381 minor

*McCartney, H. (Lab)	17 288	44.8%
Gourlay, J. (SDP/All)	9 573	24.8%
Graham, R. (C)	7 852	20.4%
Aitken, A. (SNP)	3 566	9.2%
Bollan, J. (Com)	308	0.8%
Lab majority	7 715	20.0%
Total vote 38 587		Turnout 75.9:

1979: Total vote 39 510 (80.0%); Lab 20 515 (51.9%); C 8 512 (21.5%); SNP 6 055 (15.3%); L 3 099 (7.8%); Com 1 017 (2.6%); other 312 (0.8%); Lab maj 12 003 (31.4%); swing 3.7% to Lab.

Mr Hugh McCartney, former sales representative, was MP for Central Dunbartonshire February 1974–83 and; for Dunbartonshire East 1970–74. Born Jan 3 1920; educ. John Street Secondary School, Glasgow and Royal Technical College, Glasgow. Secretary, Scottish Labour Group of MPs. Member, Dunbarton County Council 1965–70; burgh councillor 1955–70. Sponsored by TGWU.

Mr James Gourlay, college lecturer, former engine driver and industrial relations officer on British Railways Board. Born 1923; educ. Ruskin College, Strathclyde University and Dundee Teacher Training College. Contested Angus North for Labour 1970, and Dundee West as independent, Feb 1974. Former member, Dundee Labour executive committee.

Mr Robert Graham, university administrator, is a former Army officer and diplomat. Aged 46. Member, Western Area Council, Scottish Conservative and Unionist Association. Member, Strathclyde West Europe Council.

Mr Cameron Aitken, company director, contested Glasgow, Maryhill 1970, and Central Dunbartonshire Oct 1974. Born 1947; educ. at universities of Glasgow, Strathclyde and Western Ontario.

Dame Judith Hart

CLYDESDALE Electorate 60 240

*Hart, Dame J. (Lab)	17 873	38.8%
Bainbridge, P. (C)	13 007	28.2%
Craig, Miss M. (SDP/All)	9 908	21.5%
McAlpine, T. (SNP)	5 271	11.4%
Lab majority	4 866	10.6%
Total vote 46 059		Turnout 76.5%

Dame Judith Hart was chairman of the Labour Party 1981–82; a member of the National executive 1969–83. Opposition spokesman on overseas development 1979–80; Minister for Overseas Development 1977–79; also from Mar 1974, but resigned in Jun 1975. Opposition spokesman on overseas development 1970–74. Minister of Overseas Development 1969–70, Paymaster General 1968–69, with seat in Cabinet 1967–68; Minister off State, Commonwealth Office 1966–67; Under Secretary, Scottish Office 1964–66. Won this seat in 1983; MP for Lanark 1959–83; contested Bournemouth West 1951; Aberdeen South 1955. Born Sep 1924; educ. Royal Grammar School, Clitheroe; London School of Economics and London University. President, International Institute for Resource Development, Vienna.

Mr Peter Bainbridge, graduate marketing trainee with ICI. Born 1956; educ. George Heriot's school, Edinburgh and St Andrew's University. President, St Andrew's University Conservative Association 1976–77; member, East Fife Conservative Association executive committee.

Miss Moira Craig, educational psychologist. Born 1929; educ. Glasgow University. Employed by Lanarkshire Child Guidance Service since 1971; deputy principal psychologist since 1974. Founder member of Scottish Association of Local Government and Educational Psychologists 1974; its president for first three years.

Mr Thomas McAlpine, managing director. Born 1929; educ. Dalziel High School, Motherwell and Glasgow University. SNP spokesman on industry and an executive member of the Scottish Council; formerly a vice-chairman and a vice-president of the party.

Sir Antony Buck

COLCHESTER NORTH Electorate 77 292

*Buck, Sir P. A. (C)	29 921	53.0%
Montgomerie, R. (L/All)	14 873	26.3%
Allen, R. C. (Lab)	10 397	18.4%
Wilkinson, D. (Ind C)	784	1.4%
Davies, R. (Ind)	510	0.9%
C majority	15 048	26.6%
Total vote 56 485		Turnout 73.1%

Sir Antony Buck, QC. Under Secretary for Defence for the Royal Navy 1972–74, was MP for Colchester 1961–83. Barrister and non-executive director. Born Dec 19 1928; educ. King's School, Ely, and Trinity Hall, Cambridge. Chairman, Select Committee on Parliamentary Commissioner for Admin. (Ombudsman) since

1977. Chairman, Conservative defence committee since 1979. Chairman, executive committee of Conservative Lawyers 1979. Member, Parliamentary Assembly of the Council of European Union 1975–77. Secretary, Conservative Home Affairs Committee 1964–70. Member, executive, 1922 Committee.

Mr Ronald Montgomerie, solicitor, contested Harrow Central Feb and Oct 1974. Born May 16 1929; educ. Rutherglen Academy, Glasgow; John Lyon School, Harrow, and University College, London. Member, Harrow Borough Council since 1980. Treasurer, Association of Liberal Lawyers.

Mr Raymond Allen, printer and trade union officer. Born Apr 10 1929; educ. elementary schools and Open University. Secretary, Kent Graphical Society. NGA.

Mr John Wakeham

COLCHESTER SOUTH AND MALDON Electorate 79 582

*Wakeham J. (C)	31 296	53.6%
Stevens, J. (SDP/All)	19 131	32.8%
Barnard, H. J. (Lab)	7 932	13.6%
C majority	12 165	20.9%
Total vote 58 359	Turnout 73.3%	

Mr John Wakeham was appointed Parliamentary Secretary to the Treasury, Government Chief Whip, in Jun 1983. Minister of State, Treasury, Apr 1982–83; Under Secretary of State for Industry 1981–82. Government whip 1979–81 and a Lord Commissioner of the Treasury 1981. A chartered accountant and former company director. Represented Maldon Feb 1974–83; won this seat in 1983; contested Putney, Wandsworth 1970, and Coventry East 1966. Born Jun 1932; educ. Charterhouse. Former secretary, Conservative small business committee. Member of Lloyd's.

Mr John Stevens, stamp auctioneer, member of the Council for Social Democracy. Born 1932; educ. Kingsbury Grammar School and Magdalene College, Cambridge. Worked for 10 years for Mobil Oil in the North East, then joined a production engineering group as marketing consultant, moving to Colchester.

Mr Hilary Barnard, trade union researcher. Born Jun 3 1953; educ. St Dunstan's College, Catford; Universities of Kent and Warwick. International vice-chairman, Labour Middle East Council. APEX.

Mr Richard Wainwright

COLNE VALLEY Electorate 69 634

*Wainwright, R. S. (L/All)	21 139	39.8%
Holt, J. (C)	17 993	33.9%
Williams, A. (Lab)	13 668	25.8%
Keen, T. L. (Ind)	260	0.5%
L / All majority	3 146	5.9%
Total vote 53 060	Turnout 76.2%	

Mr Richard Wainwright won the seat for the Liberals in 1966 after contesting it in 1964, in the 1963 by-election and in 1959. He lost it in 1970 and regained it in 1974. Liberal parliamentary spokesman on Treasury affairs. Former spokesman on trade and industry and previously spokesman on economic and industrial affairs. Chartered accountant and company director. Born Apr 11 1918; educ. Shrewsbury School and Clare College, Cambridge, Chairman of Liberal Party, 1971–72; vice-president 1959–66. Director, Rowntree Social Service Trust. Member, Select Committee on Treasury and Civil Service since 1979.

Mr John Holt, textile agent and company director, is Conservative leader of Kirklees Council. Born 1939; educ. Silcoates School, Wakefield and Huddersfield Technical College. Conservative whip, Kirklees Council 1974–82; deputy leader, West Yorkshire County Council 1981–82. Contested Huddersfield East 1970.

Mr Arthur Williams, lecturer in public administration and former scrapyard labourer and British Rail waiter. Born May 1 1949; educ. Newcastle and Manchester universities and Bolton College of Education. Rochdale councillor 1979–83. NATFHE.

Mrs Ann Winterton

CONGLETON Electorate 63 897

Winterton, Mrs A. (C)	23 895	48.7%
Smedley, C. (L/All)	15 436	31.4%
Gill, E. (Lab)	9 783	19.9%
C majority	8 459	17.2%
Total vote 49 114	Turnout 76.9%	

Mrs Ann Winterton, elected in 1983, wife of Mr Nicholas Winterton, who was returned for the adjoining Macclesfield constituency. Born Mar 6 1941; educ. Erdington Grammar School for Girls. Member, West Midlands Conservative Women's Advisory Committee 1969–71. Joint Master, South Staffordshire Hunt 1959–64.

Mr Clive Smedley, an employee relations manager, contested Stoke-on-Trent North 1979. He was an agent in the 1979 Euro-Elections. Born Aug

1945; educ. Leicester Polytechnic, Vaughan College, Leicester and Northern Counties Radio School, Preston.

Mr Eric Gill, retired NCB scientist. Born 1925. Labour group leader, Congleton Borough Council and Cheshire county councillor.

Mr Wyn Roberts

CONWY Electorate 51 567

*Roberts, I. W. (C)	16 413	41.7%
Roberts, Rev J. R. (L/All)	12 145	30.8%
Walters, I. (Lab)	6 731	17.1%
Iwan, D. (PlC)	4 105	10.4%
C majority	4 268	10.8%
Total vote 39 394		Turnout 76.4%

Mr Wyn Roberts, an Under-Secretary of State for Wales since 1979, was Opposition spokesman on Welsh affairs 1974–79. Television executive and journalist. Won the seat for Conservatives in 1970. Born Jul 10 1930; educ. Beaumaris County School, Harrow, and University College, Oxford, Formerly Welsh Controller, TWW, and a former executive of Harlech Television. Joint secretary, Conservative Broadcasting Committee 1974–79.

The Rev Roger Roberts, Methodist minister, contested the seat in 1979. Born Oct 1935; educ. John Bright Grammar School, Llandudno; University College, Bangor; Handsworth College, Birmingham.

Mrs Ira Walters has been a research officer for EETPU since 1981. Born Feb 15 1960; educ. University College of Wales. Fabians. Welsh speaker.

Mr Dafydd Iwan, national chairman of Plaid Cymru since 1982. Graduated in architecture from the Welsh School of Architecture. Organizer of Cymdeithas Tai Gwynedd, a Gwynedd housing association. Co-founder of Sain Cyf, a Welsh record company.

Dr John Cunningham

COPELAND Electorate 54 208 1979: 52 787 same

*Cunningham, J. A. (Lab)	18 756	44.2%
Wilson, Mrs V. (C)	16 919	39.9%
Beasley, J. (SDP/All)	6 722	15.9%
Lab majority	1 837	4.3%
Total vote 42 397		Turnout 78.2%

1979 (as Whitehaven): Total vote 43 146 (81.7%); Lab 22 626 (52.4%); C 17 171 (39.8%); L 2 559 (5.9%) Ind 790 (1.8%). Lab maj 5 455 (12.6%); swing 6.3% to C.

Dr John Cunningham, Opposition front bench spokesman on industry since 1979; Under Secretary of State for Energy 1976–79. Elected for this seat in 1983; MP for Whitehaven 1970–83. Research scientist. Appointed PPS to Mr James Callaghan 1972. Born Aug 4 1939; educ. Jarrow Grammar School and Bede College, Durham University. Member, Select Committee on Science and Technology 1970–76. Full time officer GMWU 1965–70. Member, Chester-le-Street UDC 1969–73; chairman, finance committee. GMWU.

Mrs Veronica Wilson, solicitor. Born Aug 27 1942; educ. secondary school, college of further education and Preston Polytechnic.

Mr John Beasley is a teacher of modern languages. Aged 35; educ. Leeds University.

Mr William Powell

CORBY Electorate 63 067

Powell, W. (C)	20 827	42.6%
*Homewood, W. D. (Lab)	17 659	36.1%
Whittington, T. G. (L/All)	9 905	20.3%
Stanning, Miss R. (Eco)	505	1.0%
C majority	3 168	6.5%
Total vote 48 896		Turnout 77.5%

Mr William Powell, barrister and businessman, elected in 1983. Born Aug 3 1948; educ. Woolpit School, Surrey, Lancing College and Emmanuel College, Cambridge. Member, Eastern Area CPC Committee. Researching book about American elections.

Mr William Homewood represented Kettering, 1979–83. Former full-time organizer of the Iron and Steel Trades Confederation; previously branch secretary and district committee secretary. Born Mar 17 1920; educ. elementary school and Ruskin College, Oxford. Rural district councillor for seven years. A former constituency party secretary and agent. Sponsored by Iron and Steel Trades Confederation.

Mr Glynn Whittington, sociology teacher. Born Feb 20 1943; educ. grammar school in Gloucestershire and London University. Brass bandmaster. NAS.

Mr Gerrard Neale

CORNWALL NORTH Electorate 66 813

*Neale, G. A. (C)	28 146	52.4%
Chambers, D. (L/All)	23 087	43.0%
Hayday, J. (Lab)	2 096	3.9%
Whetter, J. C. A. (Cor Nat)	364	0.7%
C majority	5 059	9.4%
Total vote 53 693		Turnout 80.4%

Mr Gerrard Neale, elected 1979, contested the seat in Oct 1974. PPS to former Minister for Trade (Mr Peter Rees). Solicitor and company director. Born Jun 25 1941; educ. Bedford School. Chairman, Buckingham Constituency Conservative Association 1974–76. Milton Keynes borough councillor 1973–79; mayor 1976–77. Former Milton Keynes City Forum 1977. Chairman, area crime prevention panel 1978. Director of Telephone Rentals Ltd.

Mr David Chambers, a chiropodist, contested Mansfield in both 1974 elections and in 1979. Born Feb 15 1947; educ. Great Yarmouth Grammar School, City of Norwich School, Chelsea School of Chiropody. Member, Notts County Council; Society of Chiropodists.

Mr James Hayday is a science teacher in a Bude school. Born 1932. Served with the RAF leaving with the rank of Flight Lieutenant.

Mr Robert Hicks

CORNWALL SOUTH EAST Electorate 65 166

*Hicks, R. A. (C)	28 326	55.3%
Blunt, D. (L/All)	19 972	39.0%
Bebb, A. J. (Lab)	2 507	4.9%
Chadwick, J. (Eco)	337	0.2%
Dent, Mrs J. (Ind)	94	0.2%
C majority	8 354	16.3%
Total vote 51 236		Turnout 78.6%

Mr Robert Hicks, lecturer and consultant, was elected in 1983; MP for Bodmin 1970-Feb 1974 and Oct 1974–83; contested Aberavon, 1966. Assistant Government whip 1973–74. Born Jan 18 1938; educ. Queen Elizabeth Grammar School, Crediton, University College, London, and Exeter University. Chairman, West Country group of Conservative MPs 1976–77; vice-chairman, Conservative parliamentary committee on agriculture 1972–73 (chairman, horticultural subcommittee) and of committee on European affairs 1979–80. Member, Select Committee on European Legislation since 1979.

Mr David Blunt, barrister and writer, contested Lambeth Central at by-election in 1978 and in 1979. Born Oct 25 1944; educ. Farnham Grammar School and Trinity Hall, Cambridge.

Mr Andrew Bebb, principal lecturer in religious studies. Born Dec 9 1930; educ. St Michael's College, Leeds; Ushaw College, Durham; Nottingham University. NATFHE.

Mr George Park

COVENTRY NORTH EAST Electorate 67 037

*Park, G. M. (Lab)	22 190	47.8%
Weeks, D. (C)	13 415	28.9%
Simmons, D. (SDP/All)	10 251	22.1%
Prince, R. (WRP)	342	0.7%
Meacham, J. (Com)	193	0.4%
Lab majority	8 775	18.9%
Total vote 46 391		Turnout 69.2%

Mr George Park, elected in Feb 1974, has been joint chairman, all-party motor industry group since 1979. Chairman, PLP industry group since 1981. Member, Public Accounts Committee since 1981. Senior AEU shop steward at Chrysler (UK) Ltd 1968–73; Coventry city councillor 1961–74; Coventry district councillor 1973–74; leader of council Labour group 1967–74, and West Midlands Metropolitan County Council 1973–77; leader, Coventry City and District Councils 1972–74 Born Sep 27 1914; educ. Onslow Drive Secondary School, Glasgow, Whitehill Grammar School, Glasgow, and Coventry Technical College. Sponsored by AUEW.

Mr David Weeks, businessman. Born Mar 26 1946; educ. Brentwood School and Bristol University. Member, Westminster City Council since 1974 (Deputy Leader 1983, chairman of housing committee since 1979).

Mr David Simmons, director for Industrial Projects, was formerly with the Diplomatic Service. Served in New Dehli as immigration officer; in Hanoi as political-economic analyst during the Vietnam war; in Rio de Janeiro as commercial attaché. Born 1945; educ. Loughborough Grammar School and Polytechnic of Central London.

Mr Geoffrey Robinson

COVENTRY NORTH WEST Electorate 52072

*Robinson G. (Lab)	17239	44.3%
Coombs, A. (C)	14201	36.5%
Talbot, W. (L/All)	7479	19.2%
Lab majority	3038	7.8%
Total vote 38919		Turnout 74.7%

Mr Geoffrey Robinson won by-election Mar 1976. Former financial controller, British Leyland;managing director, Leyland Innocenti, Italy, 1972–73; chief executive Jaguar Cars, Coventry, 1974–75. Consultant to Meriden Cooperative. Research assistant, Labour Party, 1965–68. Born May 25 1939; educ. Emanuel School, Cambridge University, and Yale. Unpaid chief executive, Triumph Motorcycles (Meriden) Ltd 1977–80 and director, West Midlands Enterprise Board. TGWU.

Mr Anthony Coombs is a director of various companies. Born Nov 18 1952; educ. Bilton Grange School, near Rugby; Charterhouse; Worcester College, Oxford. Member, Birmingham City Council since 1978 (vice-chairman, education committee); executive committee, Conservative City Councillors; West Midlands Advisory Council for Sport and Recreation. Governor, Birmingham Polytechnic and Handsworth Technical College. Vice-chairman, Bourneville School of Art.

Mr William Talbot, managing director, Pathfinder Technology Ltd. Born May 8 1929.

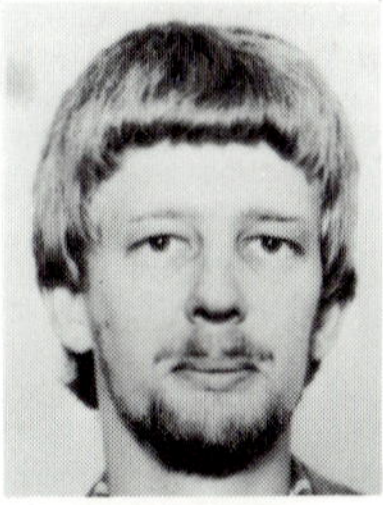

Mr David Nellist

COVENTRY SOUTH EAST Electorate 52538

Nellist, D. (Lab)	15307	41.1%
Arnold, J. (C)	12625	33.9%
Kilby, G. (L/All)	9323	25.0%
Lab majority	2682	7.2%
Total vote 37255		Turnout 70.9%

Mr David Nellist is a council building services division worker, elected in 1983. Born Jul 1952. County councillor since 1982. Nalgo.

Mr Jacques Arnold, international banker. Born Aug 27 1947; educ. schools in Brazil and LSE. Member, Northamptonshire County Council since 1981. Regional director, Thomas Cook.

Mr Gordon Kilby is a teacher. Born Nov 6 1940; educ. Guildhall School of Music and Drama, Open University and the University of Wales. Executive chairman, Rugby divisional executive Liberal Assoc. 1979–82; chairman, Rugby and Kenilworth Liberal Assoc. since 1982.

Mr John Butcher

COVENTRY SOUTH WEST Electorate 65077

*Butcher, J. P. (C)	22223	45.0%
Edwards, D. (Lab)	15776	31.9%
Lyle, Mrs M. (SDP/All)	11174	22.6%
Williamson, Mrs M. (Oth)	214	0.4%
C majority	6447	13.1%
Total vote 49387		Turnout 75.9%

Mr John Butcher appointed Under-Secretary of State for Industry Apr 1982 and Industry and Trade, Jun 1983. PPS to Mr Leon Brittan, Chief Secretary to the Treasury 1981–82. Elected in 1979; contested Birmingham Northfield Feb 1974. Former director of a computer services company. Born Feb 13 1946; educ. Huntingdon Grammar School, Birmingham University. At the Institute of Strategic Studies in London he did research into guerrilla warfare and Nato. Former member Birmingham City Council and district council; former parliamentary adviser to Professional Association of Teachers.

Mr David Edwards, car worker. Born Aug 9 1934; educ. Barker Butts Secondary Modern School. Member, Coventry City Council 1966–68 and since 1980. Member TGWU; 28 years, convenor and former shop steward.

Mrs Marjorie Lyle, education officer, Canterbury Archaeological Trust. Born 1926; educ. Ashford School and St Hugh's College, Oxford. East Kent Education Adviser for Historical Assoc. Member, Urban Studies Society. Member, Council for Social Democracy.

Mr Nicholas Soames

CRAWLEY Electorate 70713

Soames, N. (C)	25963	48.1%
Allan, L. (Lab)	14149	26.2%
Forester, T. (SDP/All)	13900	25.7%
C majority	11814	21.9%
Total vote 54012	Turnout	76.4%

Mr Nicholas Soames, executive director with KCA International Ltd, an oil services company, was elected in 1983; contested Central Dumbartonshire 1979. Son of Lord Soames and grandson of Sir Winston Churchill. Born 1948; educ. St Aubyns, Sussex, and Eton College. Former legislative assistant to an American senator, then associate director with a firm of Lloyd's brokers.

Dr Leslie Allen, reader in experimental physics at Sussex University. Born Oct 22 1935; educ. Haberdashers' Aske's School, Hatcham School, and Imperial College, London. AUT (President Sussex branch 1970–72).

Mr Thomas Forester, author and journalist. Born 1949; educ. grammar school, Sussex University and Balliol, Oxford. Industry and employment correspondent, *New Society*, 1976–80; has also written for *The Times*, *The Sunday Times*, *The Guardian* and *New Statesman*. Press aide and literature organizer, McGovern campaign, USA, 1972. Member, Brighton Council, 1976 (Labour), and 1981 (SDP).

Mrs Gwyneth Dunwoody

CREWE AND NANTWICH Electorate 71787

*Dunwoody, Mrs G. P. (Lab)	22031	41.1%
Rock, P. (C)	21741	40.6%
Pollard, J. (SDP/All)	9820	18.3%
Lab majority	290	0.5%
Total vote 53592	Turnout	74.7%

Mrs Gwyneth Dunwoody, Opposition spokesman on Health 1981–83; previously front bench spokesman on foreign affairs. Elected to Shadow Cabinet and Labour NEC, 1981. Won this seat 1983. MP for Crewe, Feb 1974–83; Exeter, 1966–70; contested seat 1964. Member, European Parliament 1975–79. Parliamentary Secretary, Board of Trade 1967–70. Born Dec 12 1930; educ. Fulham County Secondary School and the Convent of Notre Dame. Director, Film Producers' Assoc. of Great Britain 1970–74. Parliamentary adviser to Assoc. of Independent Cinemas.

Mr Patrick Rock, director of oil company research department, contested Greenwich, Woolwich East 1979. Born 1951; educ. Beaumont College, Windsor, Stonyhurst College, Blackburn, and Worcester College, Oxford. Member, Conservative Research Department 1974–79; Prime Minister's political correspondence secretary 1979–80. Board member, Hanover Housing Assoc. 1976–79.

Mr John Pollard, solicitor and an assistant deputy coroner. Born Jan 4 1952; educ. Kings School, Macclesfield, Hymers College, Kingston-upon-Hull, Leeds University. Nalgo.

Mr Malcolm Thornton

CROSBY Electorate 83274

*Thornton, G. M. (C)	30604	47.2%
*Williams, Mrs S. V. (SDP/All)	27203	42.0%
Waring, R. (Lab)	6611	10.2%
Hussey, P. (Eco)	415	0.6%
C majority	3401	5.3%
Total vote 64833	Turnout	77.9%

Mr Malcolm Thornton, a River Mersey pilot was MP for Liverpool, Garston 1979–83. Won this seat in 1983. Born Apr 3 1939; educ. Wallasey Grammar School and Liverpool Nautical College. Member, Wallasey County Borough Council 1965–74; Wirral Metropolitan Council, 1973–79 (leader, 1974–77) Chairman, Merseyside Districts liaison committee 1975–77; chairman, education committee, AMA, 1978–79, and of CLEA, 1978–79. Member, Select Committee on Environment 1979–81, PPS to Secretary of State for Industry (Mr Patrick Jenkin) 1981–83. Member Burnham Committee 1978–79. Secretary, Conservative parliamentary education committee and of shipping and shipbuilding committee since 1979. Parliamentary Consultant to Nalgo. TGWU.

Mrs Shirley Williams, a joint leader of the Social Democratic Party since its formation in 1981 and President since 1982; became the first SDP candidate to win a seat backed by the Alliance with the Liberals by gaining Crosby from the Conservatives in the 1981 by-election. Labour Secretary of State for Education and Science 1976–79; Secretary of State for Prices and Consumer Protection 1974–76 and additionally Paymaster General from Apr 1976; Labour MP for Hertford and Stevenage, Feb 1974–79; MP for Hitchin 1964–74. Chief Opposition spokesman on social services 1970–71, when elected to the Shadow Cabinet, Spokesman on Home Office affairs 1971–73, and on prices 1973–74. Minister of State, Home Office, 1969–70;

Minister of Education and Science 1967–69; Parliamentary Secretary, Ministry of Labour, 1966–67. Born Jul 27 1930; educ. Summit School, Minnesota, St Paul's School, Hammersmith, Somerville College, Oxford, and Columbia University, New York. Member, Labour Party NEC, 1970–80 when she resigned from party.

Mr Robert Waring is a psychiatric social worker. Born 1950. Member, Merseyside County Council since 1981. Chairman, Merseyside County Council Social Security Benefits Campaign.

Mr John Moore

CROYDON CENTRAL Electorate 56 531

*Moore, J. E. M. (C)	20 866	53.8%
McKinley, A. S. (Lab)	9 045	23.3%
Burgess, T. (SDP/All)	8 864	22.9%
C majority	11 821	30.5
Total vote 38 775	Turnout 68.6%	

Mr John Moore was appointed Economic Secretary to the Treasury June 1983 and then Financial Secretary later in 1983; Under Secretary of State for Energy 1979–83. Elected in Feb 1974. An investment banker, stockbroker and former company director; vice-chairman of the Conservative Party with responsibility for youth 1975–79. Born Nov 26 1937; educ. Licensed Victuallers' School, Slough; London School of Economics, (Chairman, Conservative Assoc; President of the Union 1959–60). Councillor, London borough of Merton 1971–74. Member, Public Accounts Committee 1974–75. Lived in United States 1961–65 where he was Precinct Captain (1962) and Ward Chairman (1964) Democratic Party. Underwriting member of Lloyd's.

Mr Andrew MacKinlay, Nalgo trade union official, contested Surbiton in Feb and Oct 1974. Born Apr 24 1949; educ. Catholic primary schools in Wembley and Tolworth and Salesian College, Chertsey. Member, Kingston upon Thames Council 1971–78. TGWU.

Mr Tyrrell Burgess, reader in North-East London Polytechnic, was a Labour candidate at Croydon 1964. Chairman, Croydon SDP; member, policy working group on education. Born 1931. Has contributed to *The Guardian*, *The Times Educational Supplement* and *New Society*.

Mr Bernard Weatherill

CROYDON NORTH EAST Electorate 62 923

*Weatherill, B. B. (C)	22 292	52.5%
Goldie, J. (SDP/All)	10 665	25.1%
Riley, Ms K. (Lab)	9 503	22.4%
C majority	11 627	27.4%
Total vote 42 460	Turnout 67.5%	

Mr Bernard Weatherill became Speaker of the Commons Jun 1983; Deputy Speaker and Chairman of Ways and Means 1979–83. Deputy Chief Opposition Whip 1974–79; Government Deputy Chief Whip 1973–74; Comptroller of the Household (Whip) 1972–73; Vice-Chamberlain of the Household (Whip) 1971–72. Lord Commissioner of the Treasury (Whip) 1970–72; Opposition Whip 1967–70. Elected 1964. Master tailor and director of family business. Member of Lloyd's. Freeman of City of London. Born Nov 25 1920; Educ. Malvern College. Member, National Union of Conservative Party, 1963–64. Vice-President, Clothing and Textile Institute. Member, House of Commons Services Committee 1970–79.

Mr Julian Goldie, sales representative in life assurance. Born Aug 3 1931; educ. Clapham College, London.

Ms Kathryn Riley, teacher. Born 1950. Married to Mr John Tilley, Labour candidate at Southwark, Bermondsey.

Mr Humfrey Malins

CROYDON NORTH WEST Electorate 58 333

Malins, H. (C)	16 674	42.3%
*Pitt, W. H. (L/All)	12 582	31.9%
Smedley, I. (Lab)	9 561	24.2%
Griffin, N. (NF)	336	0.9%
Rowe, R. (Eco)	286	0.7%
C majority	4 092	10.4%
Total vote 39 439	Turnout 67.6%	

Mr Humfrey Malins, solicitor, elected in 1983, contested Liverpool, Toxteth in both 1974 elections and Lewisham East in 1979. Born Jul 31, 1945; educ. St John's School, Leatherhead and Brasenose College, Oxford. Member, Mole Valley district council since 1974; chairman, housing committee 1980–82.

Mr William Pitt, a lighting engineer, won the by-election in 1981. Liberal spokesman on home affairs 1982–83; contested the seat in 1979 and in both 1974 elections. Born Jul 1937; educ. Heath Clark School, Croydon, London Nautical School, and Polytechnic of the South Bank. Former chairman. London Liberal Party. Joint vice-chairman, all-party committee against racialism. Nalgo.

Mr Ian Smedley, teacher. Born Nov 13 1949; educ. Philippa Fawcett College of Education. Ex-Croydon councillor.

Sir William Clark

CROYDON SOUTH Electorate 64482 1979: 62022 minor

*Clark, Sir W. G. (C)	29842	65.1%
Forrest, J. (L/All)	12402	27.1%
Brooks, R. C. E. (Lab)	3568	7.8%
C majority	17440	38.1%
Total vote 45812	Turnout	71.1%

1979: Total vote 47598 (76.7%); C 30874 (64.9%); L 10006 (21.0%); Lab 6249 (13.1%); NF 469 (1.0%). C maj 20868 (3.9%); swing 5.0% to C.

Sir William Clark was returned in Feb 1974. MP for Surrey East 1970–74 and for Nottingham South 1959–66. Contested Northampton 1955. Born Oct 18 1917; educ. London secondary school. Chairman, Conservative back-bench finance committee since 1979. Joint deputy chairman, Conservative Party, 1975–77; joint treasurer 1974–75. Chairman, Select Committee on Taxation 1973, and member of the former Select Committee on Wealth Tax. Opposition spokesman on Treasury affairs 1964–66. Accountant, company director and consultant to Commercial Union Assurance.

Mr James Forrest, journalist, is an NUJ chapel official. Born Feb 25 1947; educ. Allan Glen's School, Glasgow and Glasgow University. Contested Lewisham East 1979.

Mr Robert Brooks, photographer with Medical Research Council. Born May 27 1952. Croydon councillor 1981–82. ASTMS.

Mr Norman Hogg

CUMBERNAULD AND KILSYTH Electorate 44190

*Hogg, N. (Lab)	16629	49.2%
Herbison, D. (SDP/All)	6701	19.8%
Murray, G. (SNP)	5875	17.4%
Thompson, Mrs A. (C)	4590	13.6%
Lab majority	9928	29.4%
Total vote 33795	Turnout	76.5%

Mr Norman Hogg, elected in 1983, was MP for East Dunbartonshire, 1979–83. District officer, National and Local Government Officers Assoc. 1967–79. Member, Transport Users' Consultative Committee for Scotland 1977–79; Select Committee on Scottish Affairs 1979–82. Born Mar 12 1938; educ. Ruthrieston Secondary School, Aberdeen. Parliamentary consultant to National and Local Government Officers Assoc; adviser to Scottish Institute of Housing. Scottish Labour whip since 1982.

Mr Douglas Herbison is a representative for a trade organisation in the European Economic Community. Aged 32.

Mr Gordon Murray, civil engineer and part-time crofter. Born 1927; educ. Aberdeen Grammar School. A vice-chairman (local government) of the SNP. Member, District and Regional Council in Cumbernauld. Provost of Cumbernauld and Kilsyth District Council 1967–80. Local branch chairman, Nalgo.

Mrs Ann Thompson, teacher for mentally handicapped and adult education tutor for Youth Opportunities Programme. Aged 40. Member, Strathclyde East European Constituency Council; former community councillor.

Mr John Corrie

CUNNINGHAME NORTH Electorate 53126

*Corrie, J. (C)	15 559	38.7%
Carson, J. N. (Lab)	13920	34.6%
Leishman, R. (SDP/All)	7268	18.1%
Cameron, C. (SNP)	3460	8.6%
C majority	1 639	4.1%
Total vote 40 207	Turnout	75.7%

Mr John Corrie, a farmer, was MP for Ayrshire North and Bute Feb 1974–83; won this seat in 1983; contested Ayrshire Central 1966 and Lanark North 1964. Chairman, Scottish Conservative MPs since 1982. Treasurer, Scottish Conservative Committee 1975–80. Member, Select Committee on Scottish Affairs since 1979. Member European Parliament 1975–76 and 1977–79. Opposition whip 1976–79. Born Jul 29 1935; educ. George Watson's College, Edinburgh, and Lincoln Agricultural College, New Zealand. Past President, Scottish Young Conservatives and Kirkcudbright Unionist Assoc. Nuffield Agricultural Scholar 1972–73.

Mr John Carson is a maintenance fitter with ICI. Member, Saltcoats Town Council 1971–74. Born Jun 4 1945; educ. Saltcoats primary and secondary schools. AUEW.

Mr Ralph Leishman, computer audit specialist in firm of chartered accountants. Born 1957; educ. Hillhead High School, Glasgow Academy, Glasgow University, Glasgow College of Technology. Former community councillor, Glasgow North Kelvin.

Mr Colin Cameron, solicitor, contested South Ayrshire, 1979. Born Aug 1933; educ. Uddingston Grammar School and Glasgow University.

Mr David Lambie

CUNNINGHAME SOUTH Electorate 48 552

*Lambie, D. (Lab)	19 344	54.1%
Gallie, P. (C)	7 576	21.2%
Boss, J. (L/All)	6 370	17.8%
Ullrich, Mrs K. (SNP)	2 451	6.9%
Lab majority	11 768	32.9%
Total vote 35 741	Turnout 73.6%	

Mr David Lambie has been chairman of the Select Committee on Scottish Affairs since 1982; member from 1979. MP for Central Ayrshire, 1970–83; won this seat 1983; contested Ayrshire North and Bute 1966, 1964 and 1959. Former teacher. Born Jul 13 1925; educ. Ardrossan Academy, Glasgow, and Glasgow and Geneva universities. Chairman, Scottish Labour Party 1964. Member, Select Committee on Parliamentary Commissioner for Administration since 1974. Chairman, Scottish parliamentary Labour group 1980; secretary, all-party parliamentary group for energy studies.

Mr Phillip Gallie, electrical engineer. Aged. 43. Elder of the Church of Scotland.

Mr John Boss, a personnel officer. Born Dec 31,1940; educ. Reading School; Dublin University; LSE. Secretary, Central Ayrshire Liberal Assoc. Chairman, Irvine new town branch, Central Ayrshire Liberal Party.

Mrs Kay Ullrich, social work student at Queen's College, Glasgow. Born 1943; educ. Ayr Academcy. Press officer, Cunninghame South SNP. Worked in the USA as a swimming coach. Former chairman, Dreghorn Youth Band.

Mr Ioan Evans

CYNON VALLEY Electorate 50 284 By-election May 3 1984

*Evans, I. L. (Lab)	20 668	56.0%
Aubel, F. (SDP/All)	7 594	20.6%
Arbuthnot, J. (C)	5 240	14.2%
Jarman, Mrs P. (PlC)	3 421	9.3%
Lab majority	13 074	35.4%
Total vote 36 923	Turnout 73.4%	

Mr Ioan Evans, a member of the Select Committee on Welsh Affairs 1981–82. An Opposition spokesman on European and Community affairs since 1982. Won this seat in 1983; MP for Aberdare Feb 1974–83; Birmingham Yardley 1964–70. Comptroller of the Household (Whip) 1968–70; assistant Government Whip 1966–68. Born Jul 1927; educ. Llanelli Grammar School and Swansea University College. Director, International Defence and Aid Fund 1970–74; Secretary Welsh Group of Labour MPs 1974 and since 1977; PLP Foreign Affairs Group since 1981. Chairman, PLP trade group 1977–78, vice-chairman 1980–81. Vice-chairman, disablement group and prices and consumer protection group since 1974. Member, Commons Services Committee since 1979 and previously. Sponsored by Co-operative Party. *See page 366 for by-election result.*

Mr Felix Aubel, student at University College, Cardiff and lay preacher. Born Sep 21 1960; educ. in Aberdare and Rhydyfelin Welsh School, and University College, Lampeter. Founder member SDP. Worked for Keep Britain in Europe campaign, 1975.

Mr James Arbuthnot, a barrister. Born Aug 4 1952; educ. Eton; Trinity College, Cambridge; College of Law, London. Deputy chairman, Chelsea Conservative Assoc. 1980–82. Member, Kensington and Chelsea borough council since 1978; chairman, works committee since 1982; chairman, joint works committee 1983.

Mrs Pauline Jarman, a shopkeeper, is a member of Mid-Glamorgan County Council and Cynon Valley District Council.

Mr Bryan Gould

DAGENHAM Electorate 62 960

Gould, B. C. (Lab)	15 665	39.3%
Neill R. (C)	12 668	31.8%
Horne, Mrs J. (SDP/All)	10 769	27.0%
Pearce, J. A. (NF)	645	1.6%
Walshe, D. (Com)	141	0.4%
Lab majority	2 997	7.5%
Total vote 39 888	Turnout 63.4%	

Mr Bryan Gould, television journalist, elected in 1983, was MP for Southampton, Test Oct 1974 to 1979; contested seat, Feb 1974. Born Feb 11 1939; educ. Dannevirke High School, Auckland University, New Zealand and Balliol College, Oxford. Formerly member, Select Committee on European Legislation, and chairman, Safeguard Britain Campaign.

Mr Robert Neill, barrister. Born Jun 24 1952; educ. Abbs Cross School, Hornchurch and LSE. Member, Havering London Borough Council, since 1974; chief whip and chairman, environmental services committee.

Mrs Jacqueline Horne, a senior lecturer and freelance journalist. Born Nov 2 1935; educ. University of London. Chairman, Central Essex Area SDP. Member, Chelmsford Council since May 1983, leader of the SDP group.

Mr Michael Fallon

DARLINGTON Electorate 65233 1979: 63218 same

Fallon, M. (C)	22434	44.6%
*O'Brien, O. (Lab)	18996	37.8%
Dutton, R. (SDP/All)	8737	17.4%
Clark, A. (CD)	108	0.2%
C majority	3438	6.8%
Total vote 50275	Turnout	77.1%

C gain from Lab.
1979: Total vote 49576 (78.4%); Lab 22565 (45.5%); C 21513 (43.4%); L 5054 (10.2%); NF 444 (0.9%). Lab maj 1052 (2.1%); swing 2.9% to C.
1983 by-election: Total vote 52001 (80.2%); Lab 20544 (39.5%); C 18132 (34.9%); SDP/All 12735 (24.5%); others 590 (1.1%). Lab maj 2412 (4.6%).

Mr Michael Fallon, political researcher and writer, elected in 1983, contested Darlington by-election, 1983. Born 1952; educ. St Andrews University. Political assistant and adviser to Lord Carrington, 1974–77; EEC adviser, Conservative Research Department, 1977–79.

Mr Oswald O'Brien was returned at a by-election in Mar 1983. Former director of studies at Co-operative College. Aged 51; educ. local schools and Fircroft College, Birmingham. Member, Darlington Borough Council 1955–61 and Darlington District Council 1973–76. Co-operative Society sponsored. NATFHE.

Mr Raymond Dutton is an investment analyst. Born Oct 25 1948; educ. George Dixon Grammar School, Birmingham, Hall Green Technical College, and the universities of Keele and City of London.

Mr Robert Dunn

DARTFORD Electorate 71622

*Dunn, R. (C)	28199	41.6%
Townsend, D. (Lab)	14 630	26.8%
Mills, J. (L/All)	11204	20.5%
Crockford, A. (FDP)	374	0.7%
Nye, G. E. (NF)	282	0.5%
C majority	13 569	24.8%
Total vote 54 689	Turnout	76.4%

Mr Robert Dunn was appointed an Under Secretary of State for Education and Science Jun 1983. Elected in 1979; contested Eccles in Feb and Oct 1974. Chairman, Eccles Young Conservatives 1965–68; deputy chairman, Eccles Conservative Association 1971–72 and vice-chairman 1972–73. Southwark borough councillor 1974–78. Joint secretary, Conservative backbenchers' education committee 1980–83. Born July 1946; educ. Manchester Polytechnic, Brighton Polytechnic, and Salford University. Senior buyer, J. Sainsbury 1973–79; adviser to company till June 1983. Former parliamentary adviser to Professional Assoc. of Teachers.

Mr David Townsend, director of social services, London Borough of Harringey, was a special adviser to the Secretary of State for Social Services 1976–78. Born Jan 8 1944; educ. Kingston High School, Hull; Manchester and Hull Universities, and LSE. Contested West Derbyshire Oct 1974. Member, Lewisham Borough Council 1978–81; member and finance chairman, Lambeth, Southwark and Lewisham Area Health Authority. NUPE.

Mr John Mills is a surveyor. Born Jun 17 1950; educ. at a Catholic School in Croydon. Writes for local and Liberal papers.

Mr Reg Prentice

DAVENTRY Electorate 64314

*Prentice, R. (C)	26357	53.3%
Collins, D. (SDP/All)	13221	26.8%
Middleton, D. (Lab)	9840	19.9%
C majority	13.136	26.6%
Total vote 49418	Turnout	76.8%

Mr Reg Prentice was elected Conservative MP for Daventry in 1979 and was Minister of State for Social Security with responsibility for disabled 1979–81. Member of Labour Governments from 1966–76; resigned from the Labour Party and continued to sit for Newham North-East, as Conservative. Resigned from the Government in 1976 when Minister of Overseas Development, to which he was appointed in 1975. Secretary of State for Education and Science 1974–75; Labour Opposition spokesman on employment 1971–74. Minister of Overseas Development 1967–69; Minister of Public Building and Works 1966–67; Minister of State, Education and Science, 1964–66. Represented Newham North-East 1974–79; East Ham North 1959–74; contested Streatham 1955 and Croydon North in 1950 and 1951. Born Jul 16 1923; educ. Whitgift School and London School of Economics. President, Assoc. of Business Executives; consultant and advisory tutor.

Mr David Collins, management consultant. Born Jul 10 1943; educ. Sir Joseph Williamson's Mathematical School, Rochester, and Hull Univer-

sity. Contested Rye 1966. Local government officer for 18 years.
Mr David Middleton is a probation officer. Born Aug 31 1954. Member, Leicester City Council since 1979; chairman of the works, and policy and resources committees. Former chairman, Leicester South Constituency Labour Party. Member, Phoenix Theatres Board of Management. Deputy area representative NAPO 1979–80. TGWU.

Mr Winston Churchill

DAVYHULME Electorate 64 363

*Churchill, W. (C)	22 055	46.0%
Wrigley, D. (L/All)	13 041	27.2%
Rogers, S. (Lab)	12 887	26.9%
C majority	9014	18.8%
Total vote 47 983	Turnout	74.6%

Mr Winston Churchill author, journalist and member of Lloyd's, was an Opposition spokesman on defence from 1976–78. Won this seat 1983; represented Stretford 1970–83; contested Manchester Gorton by-election 1967. Born Oct 10 1940; educ. Eton and Christ Church, Oxford. Secretary, Conservative backbench foreign affairs committee 1973–76, Vice-chairman, Conservative defence committee since 1979. Member, executive 1922 Committee since 1979. Trustee, National Benevolent Fund for the Aged 1973; Governor, English Speaking Union 1975–80. Chairman Gatwick Air Taxis Ltd.
Mr Dennis Wrigley, management consultant, contested Stretford Feb and Oct 1974 and 1979; High Peak 1970, 1966, 1964 and 1961 by-election and Oldham East 1959. Born Jan 9 1930; educ. Manchester Grammar School and Manchester Regional School of Architecture.
Mr Sean Rogers is a local government officer. Aged 29. Member, Rochdale Council for Voluntary Services. Nalgo.

Mr Keith Raffan

DELYN Electorate 62 483

Raffan, K. (C)	20 242	41.6%
Colbert, J. J. (Lab)	14 298	29.4%
Parry, J. H. (L/All)	12 545	25.8%
Huws, H. (PlC)	1 558	3.2%
C majority	5 944	12.2%
Total vote 48 643	Turnout	77.9%

Mr Keith Raffan, former parliamentary correspondent of the *Daily Express*, elected in 1983, contested Dulwich Feb 1974 and East Aberdeenshire Oct 1974. Born Jun 1947; educ. Robert Gordon's College, Aberdeen, Trinity College, Glenalmond, Perth, and Corpus Christi College, Cambridge. National chairman, PEST, 1970–74. Conservative Party representative on national campaign for the homeless since 1980. Executive committee member, British Atlantic Group of Young Political Leaders since 1970. NUJ.
Mr James Colbert, material blender. Born Jan 30 1936; Member, Wrexham Maelor Borough Council since 1979. TGWU.
Mr John Parry, solicitor, contested Flint West 1979. Born Mar 1934; educ. Clifton College and Bristol University. Constituency Organizer, West Flint Assoc. Editor, *West Flint Bulletin*. Member, Flint Male Voice Choir; Board of Management, CAB.
Mr Haydn Huws, Plaid Cymru spokesman on home affairs, is a solicitor in Caernarfon. Member, Gwynedd County Council.

Mr Andrew Bennett

DENTON AND REDDISH Electorate 68 661

*Bennett, A. (Lab)	22 123	44.3%
Snadden, J. (C)	16 998	34.0%
Begg, J. (SDP/All)	10 869	21.7%
Lab majority	5 125	10.3%
Total vote 49 990	Turnout	72.8%

Mr Andrew Bennett, a teacher represented Stockport North Feb 1974–83; won this seat 1983; contested Knutsford 1970. Member, Select Committee on Members' Interests since 1979; Select Committee on Social Services since 1979; joint Select Committee on Statutory Instruments and former Select Committee on Violence in the Family. Oldham borough councillor 1964–74. Born Mar 9 1939; educ. Birmingham University. NUT. Chairman PLP Health and Social Services group; secretary, PLP Civil Liberties group.
Mr John Snadden, solicitor. Born Apr 5 1954; educ. Buxton College and Brunel University.
Mr John Begg, teacher, North Manchester High School for Girls. Born 1946; educ. Oakham Public School, Aston Technical College and Leeds University.

Mr Gregory Knight

DERBY NORTH Electorate 70 374

Knight, G. (C)	22 303	43.7%
*Whitehead, P. (Lab)	18 797	36.8%
Connolly, S. (L/All)	9 924	19.5%
C majority	3 506	6.9%
Total vote 51 024		Turnout 72.5%

Mr Gregory Knight, solicitor, managing director of music publishing company and proprietor of recording studio in Leicestershire. Elected in 1983. Born Apr 4 1949; educ. Alderman Newton's Grammar School, Leicester and College of Law, Guildford. Has served on Leicester City Council and Leicestershire County Council. Author of pamphlets and articles for law publications and has written broadcast scripts on politics, consumer law, comedy and satire. A director of Leicester Theatre Trust Ltd and former chairman of its finance committee.

Mr Phillip Whitehead, an Opposition spokesman on education 1981–83 and on Arts 1982–83, was elected in 1970; contested West Derbyshire 1966. Writer and television producer. Born May 30 1937; educ. Lady Manners School, Bakewell, and Exeter College, Oxford. Member of Annan Committee on future of broadcasting. Chairman, Fabian Society 1978–79; national executive, RSPCA; a founder of 76 Group for Broadcasting Reform 1969; Member, Select Committee on Home Affairs 1979–81; Council of Europe Assembly 1975–80. NUR.

Mr Stephen Connolly, lodging scheme assistant with Derby Probation Service. Born Oct 4, 1954; educ. Bemrose Grammar School. County councillor for Derwent Ward, Derby.

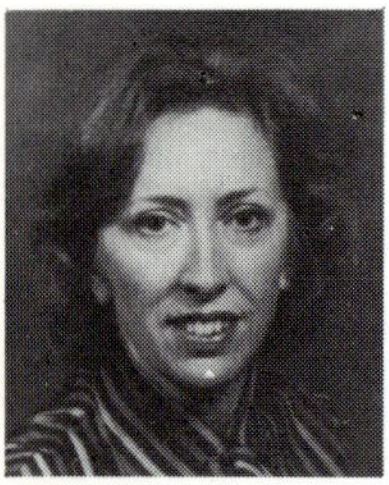
Mrs Margaret Beckett

DERBY SOUTH Electorate 68 578

Beckett, Mrs M. (Lab)	18 169	39.3%
Hales, G. (C)	17 748	38.4%
Smith, I. (SDP/All)	9 976	21.6%
Wall, E. (Eco)	297	0.6%
Lab majority	421	0.9%
Total vote 46 190		Turnout 67.4%

Mrs Margaret Beckett was, as Miss Margaret Jackson, MP for Lincoln Oct 1974–79; contested the seat Feb 1974. Elected for this seat in 1983. Under Secretary for Education and Science 1976–79 and assistant Government whip 1975–76. Former metallurgist, now principal researcher, Granada TV. Born Jan 15 1943; educ. Notre Dame High School and Manchester College of Science and Technology. Member, Labour Party NEC 1980–81; member, Tribune Group, CND and Fabian Society. TGWU sponsored.

Dr Gerald Hales, psychologist. Born May 24 1944; educ. Battersea Grammar School and London and Open Universities. Member, Convocation of London University; member, Senate of the Open University; visiting examiner to the Associated Examining Board. Member, Oxford Diocesan Synod and is on its Council for Education. Member, governing council and executive, National Bureau for Handicapped Students. Former director of music at two secondary schools in Surrey. Research officer at the Open University 1972–78. AUT.

Mr Ivor Smith, personnel manager. Born Mar 27 1937; educ. Hornchurch Grammar School and Wadham College, Oxford.

Mr Raymond Ellis

DERBYSHIRE NORTH EAST Electorate 68 273

*Ellis, R. (Lab)	21 094	40.8%
Bridge, I. (C)	19 088	36.9%
Hardy, S. (SDP / All)	11 494	22.2%
Lab majority	2 006	3.9%
Total vote 51 676		Turnout 75.7%

Mr Raymond Ellis was President of the Derbyshire area NUM, 1972; former branch secretary. Member, Select Committee on European Legislation since 1979. Elected in 1979. Born Dec 17 1923; educ. elementary schools, Sheffield University and Ruskin College. Member, South Yorkshire County Council 1976–79. Sponsored by NUM.

Mr Ian Bridge, wine bar proprietor. Born Jul 3 1952; educ. Bushmead Secondary Modern School, St Neots, Hunts, and Durham University. Former police officer. ASTMS.

Mr Stephen Hardy, solicitor. Born 1948; educ. Jesus College, Cambridge and the University of Brussels.

Mrs Edwina Currie

DERBYSHIRE SOUTH Electorate 75 391

Currie, Mrs. E. (C)	25 909	43.8%
Kent, P. (Lab)	17 296	29.2%
MacFarquhar, R. (SDP / All)	15 959	27.0%
C majority	8 613	14.6%
Total vote 59 164	Turnout 78.5%	

Mrs Edwina Currie, teacher. Born Oct 13 1946; educ. Liverpool Institute, St Anne's College, Oxford, and LSE. Elected in 1983. City councillor, Birmingham, being chairman, social services 1979–80, and housing 1982–83. NATFHE.

Mr Peter Kent, computer projects officer, British Rail, contested Shrewsbury, 1970 and Northwich, Oct, 1974. Born Jul 12 1943; educ. Crewe Grammar School. Member, Crewe and Nantwich Borough Council since 1971. TSSA.

Mr Roderick MacFarquhar, research scholar. Labour MP for Belper 1974–79. Contested Ealing South 1966, Meriden 1968. He was a former member of Select Committee on Science and Technology; former vice-chairman, Labour foreign affairs group. Born Dec 2 1930; educ. Fettes, Oxford, Harvard and LSE. NUJ.

Mr Matthew Parris

DERBYSHIRE WEST Electorate 68 668

*Parris, M. (C)	29 695	55.9%
Bingham, V. (L/All)	14 370	27.1%
March, J. S. (Lab)	9 060	17.1%
C majority	15 325	28.9%
Total vote 53 125	Turnout 77.4%	

Mr Matthew Parris was a member of the private office of Mrs Thatcher when she was leader of the Opposition. Elected in 1979. Born Aug 7 1949; educ. Waterford School, Swaziland; Clare College, Cambridge; and Yale University. Served in Foreign Office 1974–76; Conservative Research Department 1976–79. Secretary, Conservative backbench transport committee, and sports committee.

Mr Vivian Bingham, management consultant and managing director of own company, contested Heywood and Royton Feb and Oct 1974, Hazel Grove 1979, and East Cheshire in Euro-elections 1979. Born April 11 1932; educ. Duke's School, Alnwick; King Edward's School, Birmingham, and New College, Oxford. National president of the Liberal Party 1981–82.

Mr John March, teacher. Born Feb 18 1947; educ. Heanor Grammar School, and universities of Warwick, San Francisco and Hull. NUT.

Mr Charles Morrison

DEVIZES Electorate 83 211 1979: 80 028 minor

*Morrison, C. (C)	33 644	54.0%
Palmer, Mrs E. (SDP/All)	18 020	28.9%
Hulme, D. (Lab)	10 468	16.8%
Ewen, Mrs G. (W Reg)	234	0.4%
C majority	15 624	25.1%
Total vote 62 366	Turnout 75.0%	

1979: Total vote 63 704 (79.6%); C 32 439 (50.9%); Lab 16 351 (25.7%); L 14 059 (22.1%); Eco 713 (1.1%); Other 142 (0.2%). C maj 16 088 (25.2%); swing 6.6% to C.

Mr Charles Morrison, farmer and company director, was returned at the 1964 by-election. Member of Lloyd's. Born June 25 1932; educ. Eton and Royal Agricultural College, Cirencester. Chairman, trustees of Young Volunteer Force Foundation 1971–74. Elder brother of Mr Peter Morrison, Conservative MP for City of Chester. Joint-vice-chairman, 1922 Committee from 1974, chairman, Conservative backbench constitutional committee 1982; joint-vice-chairman, Conservative countryside conservation committee since 1982. President of the British Trust for Conservation Volunteers, 1978–83.

Mrs Elizabeth Palmer, lecturer. Born Nov 17 1933; educ. Bishop Fox's Grammar School, Taunton and Exeter University. NATFHE.

Mr David Hulme is a teacher. Born Jul 22 1952; educ. public school and St John's College, Oxford. Member, Thamesdown Council since 1976, chairman of housing and health committee; Swindon District Health Authority since 1982. NUT.

Mr Tony Speller

DEVON NORTH Electorate 63638

*Speller, A. (C)	28066	55.1%
Blackmore, R. (L/All)	19339	37.9%
James, P. E. (Lab)	2893	5.7%
Jones, R. (Eco)	669	1.3%
C majority	8727	17.1%
Total vote 50967	Turnout	80.1%

Mr Tony Speller was elected in 1979; contested the seat in Oct 1974. Holds controlling interest in The Copyshops of SW England; non-executive director. Born Jun 12 1929; educ. Exeter School, Universities of London and Exeter. Exeter city councillor 1964–74 (chairman, education committee). Chairman, parliamentary liaison group for Alternative Energy Strategies; vice-chairman, Conservative backbench energy committee; member, Select Committee on Energy; council member, Parliamentary Information Technology Committee. Hon. parliamentary adviser to The Caravan Club; the National Federation of Retail Newsagents; the Hotel, Catering and Institutional Management Association; and the British Association of Quick Printers.

Mr Roger Blackmore, senior lecturer in government and politics, contested Gainsborough in 1970, Feb and Oct 1974 and 1979. Born Dec 30 1941; educ. Shebbear College, North Devon and Leicester University. NATFHE.

Mr Peter James, operating department assistant in the NHS. Born Sep 29 1953; educ. West Bridgford Grammar School. NUPE branch secretary.

Sir Peter Mills

DEVON WEST AND TORRIDGE Electorate 70648

*Mills, Sir P. (C)	31156	58.0%
Howell, V. (L/All)	18805	35.0%
Tupman, W. A. (Lab)	3531	6.6%
Beale, M. J. (Ind)	116	0.2%
Rous, Miss H. E. (W Reg)	113	0.2%
C majority	12351	23.0%
Total vote 53721	Turnout	76.0%

Sir Peter Mills was Under Secretary, Northern Ireland Office 1972–74. Parliamentary Secretary, Agriculture, Fisheries and Food Apr to Nov 1972. Elected in 1983; represented Devon West Feb 1974–83 and Torrington, 1964–74. Born Sep 22 1921; educ. Epsom College and Wye College. Farmer and company director, insurance and agricultural consultant. Chairman, Conservative agriculture committee, and member, Select Committee on European Secondary Legislation 1974–79. Member, Select Committee on Foreign Affairs 1979–82. Deputy chairman, Commonwealth Parliamentary Assoc. since 1982.

Mr Victor Howell, master builder, contested Honiton Feb and Oct 1974 and West Devon 1979. Born Sep 20 1945; educ. Kelly College, Tavistock, Whitelands Teacher Training College, Putney, and Exeter Technical College. Exeter councillor 1970–76.

Mr William Tupman, university lecturer. Born Apr 10 1948; educ. grammar school and Exeter and Birmingham universities. ASTMS.

Mr John Whitfield

DEWSBURY Electorate 69734

Whitfield J. (C)	20297	39.4%
Ripley, D. (Lab)	18211	35.3%
*Ginsburg, D. (SDP/All)	13065	25.3%
C majority	2086	4.0%
Total vote 51573	Turnout	74.0%

Mr John Whitfield, solicitor and company director, elected in 1983; contested Hemsworth 1979. Born Oct 31 1941; educ. Sedbergh School and Leeds University. Specialist in taxation and company law.

Mr Denis Ripley. Born Dec 1932; educ. Dewsbury Technical College. Member Kirkless Council since 1979; chairman, Kirkless arts council and Huddersfield contemporary music festival. ASTMS.

Mr David Ginsburg, SDP spokesman on trade, was elected as Labour MP for Dewsbury in 1959 and joined new party from Labour in 1981. Consultant to various companies in IMS International Group. Born Mar 18 1921; educ. University College School, Hampstead, and Balliol College, Oxford. Member, Select Committee on Science and Technology 1967–81; chairman, Parliamentary and Scientific Committee 1968–71. Member, Select Committee on Parliamentary Commissioner for Administration since 1979.

Mr Harold Walker

DONCASTER CENTRAL Electorate 71 039

*Walker, H. (Lab)	21 154	42.0%
Somers, J. (C)	18 646	37.1%
Stables, T. (SDP/All)	10 524	20.9%
Lab majority	2 508	5.0%
Total vote 50 324		Turnout 70.8%

Mr Harold Walker was elected Chairman of Ways and Means and Deputy Speaker in Jun 1983. An Opposition spokesman on employment 1979–83; Minister of State, Department of Employment 1976–79; Under Secretary for Employment 1974–76; a spokesman on employment 1970–74. Under Secretary, Department of Employment and Productivity, 1968–70. Assistant Government Whip 1967–68. Elected for this seat 1983; MP for Doncaster 1964–83. Engineer. Born July 12 1927; educ. at council school and Manchester College of Technology. Sponsored by AUEW.

Mr John Somers, management accountant, contested Whitehaven 1979. Born 1955; educ. Valley Comprehensive School and Manchester University (chairman, Conservative Assoc. 1974–76). Chairman, North West Federation of Conservative Students 1975–76; Stockport Young Conservatives 1976.

Mr Trevor Stables is a charge nurse. Member, Doncaster Borough Council 1978–82. Born Feb 6 1957; educ. Edlington Comprehensive School and Doncaster School of Nursing.

Mr Michael Welsh

DONCASTER NORTH Electorate 72 184

*Welsh, M.C. (Lab)	26 626	52.8%
Stephen, B.M.L. (C)	13 915	27.6%
Orford, D. (SDP / All)	9 916	19.7%
Lab majority	12 711	25.2%
Total vote 50 457		Turnout 69.9%

Mr Michael Welsh, a miner, elected for this seat in 1983 represented Don Valley 1979–83; local councillor since 1962. Born Nov 23 1926; educ. at elementary schools, Sheffield University and Ruskin College. Sponsored by NUM.

Mr Michael Stephen, barrister. Born Sep 25 1942; educ. Stanford and Harvard Universities.

Mr Dennis Orford, company director. Born 1938; educ. secondary modern school. Member, European Movement; founder member, Campaign against Racial Prejudice.

Mr Martin Redmond

DON VALLEY Electorate 73 112

Redmond, M. (Lab)	23 036	45.1%
Utting, Mrs B. (C)	16 570	32.4%
Lange, D. (L/All)	11 482	22.5%
Lab majority	6 466	12.7%
Total vote 51 088		Turnout 69.9%

Mr Martin Redmond, elected in 1983, is a heavy goods vehicle driver. Born Aug 15 1937; educ. Woodlands Roman Catholic School and day release at Sheffield University. Member, Doncaster Town Council, since 1975; leader since 1982; chairman of the Labour Group since 1982; NUM delegate for 17 years. Panel chairman for Doncaster pits since 1975. Vice-chairman, Doncaster Area Health Authority. Member, CND.

Mrs Brenda Utting, accountant with Portsmouth City Council. Born 1939; educ. Southern Grammar School for Girls. Member, national executive council, Nalgo, since 1981; finance committee since 1982.

Mr Donald Lange, quantity surveyor, contested Carlton Feb and Oct 1974. Born Sep 24 1942; educ. Sir Percy Jackson Grammar School and Doncaster Technical College.

Mr Nicholas Baker

DORSET NORTH Electorate 67 524

*Baker. N (C)	30 058	58.1%
Tapper, G. (L/All)	18 678	36.1%
Fox, Ms J. (Lab)	2 710	5.2%
Fox, D. (W Reg)	294	0.6%
C majority	11 380	22.0%
Total vote 51 740		Turnout 76.6%

Mr Nicholas Baker was elected in 1979; contested Southwark, Peckham in both 1974 elections. Solicitor specializing in company and commercial law. Born Nov 23 1938; educ. St Neot's School, Hampshire, and Clifton College and Exeter College. Oxford. Former executive officer, Oxford University Conservative Association and editor of *Oxford Tory*; president, Oxford Carlton Club and member, consultative committee, Union Society. Has held various offices in Bow Group: secretary 1970–71 and political officer 1971–72. Former advertising manager and member of editorial board, *Crossbow*. Member, Select Committee on Consolidated Bills and Select Committee on Statutory Instruments 1979–1983. Secretary, Conservative backbench media committee 1980–81 and of legal committee 1979–81. PPS to Minister of State for Armed Forces since 1981.

Dr Geoffrey Tapper is a general practitioner. Born Oct 4 1931; educ. Kingswood School, Bath, and Middlesex Hospital Medical School. Liberal borough councillor for 15 years, Liberal district councillor, North Dorset, eight years.

Ms Jennifer Fox, student of naturopathic medicine. Born 1943. Member, Fabian Society; CND; Amnesty International; Co-operative Party; and the Labour Parliamentary Assoc.

Viscount Cranborne

DORSET SOUTH Electorate 68 998

*Cranborne, Viscount (C)	28 631	57.1%
Head, S. (SDP / All)	13 533	27.0%
Hewitt, D. (Lab)	7 831	15.6%
Smith, Mrs B. (Ind)	151	0.3%
C majority	15 098	30.1%
Total vote 50 146		Turnout 72.7%

Viscount Cranborne, a director of Gascoyne-Cecil Farms and other companies, is heir to the sixth Marquess of Salisbury. Elected in 1979. Born Sep 30 1946; educ. Eton and Christ Church, Oxford. President, Hatfield and Welwyn Garden City Society for the Mentally Handicapped. Chairman, Afghanistan Support Committee.

Mr Simon Head, journalist. Born 1944; educ. Oxford and University of California. Member, SDP working party on East-West relations and consultant on SDP policy on defence in Europe. Covered Vietnam war as journalist. Chairman, permanent university seminar on war and peace, Columbia University, New York; member, Institute of International Affairs.

Mr David Hewitt, buyer in computer industry. Born Dec 15 1952; educ. Claverham County Secondary School, Battle; Longmead County Secondary School, Epsom; Glyn Grammar School, Epsom; King Alfred's College of Education, Winchester and Portsmouth Polytechnic. ASTMS.

Mr James Spicer

DORSET WEST Electorate 60 997

*Spicer, J. (C)	27 030	59.7%
Jones, T. (L / All)	13 078	28.9%
Cash, D. (Lab)	5 168	11.4%
C majority	13 952	30.8%
Total vote 45 276		Turnout 74.2%

Mr James Spicer, company director. Born Oct 4 1925; educ. Latymer. Elected in Feb 1974, contested Southampton, Itchen by-election in 1971. Member, European Parliament 1975–78 and since 1979 for Wessex. Member, Select Committee on European Secondary Legislation 1974–75; chairman, Conservative Group for Europe 1975–78; Chief Whip of Conservatives Group in European Parliament 1976–80. National chairman, Conservative Political Centre 1969–71; chairman British-Turkish Parliamentary Group since 1978; former chairman, Wessex Area CPC; chairman, National CPC Advisory Committee, 1969–72. Member, S W Sports Council. Secretary, House of Commons gymnasium.

Mr Trevor Jones, shopkeeper, contested Preston North 1970 and West Dorset 1979. Born Jun 21 1944; educ. LSE. National chairman, Assoc. of Liberal Councillors since 1976. Member, West Dorset District Council since 1973; Mayor of Dorchester 1982–83.

Mr Derek Cash is a journalist. Born 1954. Member, West Dorset District Council, Bridport Trades Council; Youth Centre Management Committee. NUJ.

Mr Peter Rees

DOVER Electorate 67922

*Rees, P. (C)	25454	48.3%
Love, S. (Lab)	16234	30.8%
Nice, G. (SDP / All)	10601	20.1%
Potter, M. (Eco)	404	0.8%
C majority	9220	17.5%
Total vote 52693		Turnout 77.6%

Mr Peter Rees QC, was appointed to the Cabinet as Chief Secretary to the Treasury in June 1983. Minister for Trade 1981–83; Minister of State, Treasury, 1979–81. Elected for Dover in 1983; MP for Dover and Deal 1970–83; fought Liverpool, West Derby 1966, and Abertillery in 1965 by-election and 1964. Born Dec 9 1926; educ. Stowe and Christ Church, Oxford. Member, former Select committee on Wealth Tax and Company Taxation. A former Opposition spokesman on Treasury affairs. Former member, executive of 1922 Committee. Joint secretary, Conservative finance committee 1974–79, and officer of legal committee. Member, Institute of Taxation and Inns of Court Conservative and Unionist Society.

Mr Stephen Love, headmaster of a comprehensive school. Contested Gillingham 1979. Born Aug 13 1934; educ. University College, Oxford. Chairman, Disabled Housing Trust, Lancing Youth Centre. Member, West Sussex Education Committee. Educational adviser to IBA. NUT.

Mr Geoffrey Nice, a barrister. Born Oct 21 1945; educ. St Dunstan's College, Catford, and Keble College, Oxford.

Mr James Kilfedder

DOWN NORTH Electorate 61574

*Kilfedder, J. (UPUP)	22861	56.1%
Cushnahan, J. (All)	9015	22.1%
McCartney, R. (OUP)	8261	20.3%
O'Baoill, C. (SDLP)	645	1.6%
UPUP majority	13846	34.0%
Total vote 40782		Turnout 66.2%

Mr James Kilfedder, leader of the Ulster Popular Unionist Party since 1980, became Speaker, Northern Ireland Assembly, in 1982. Official Unionist MP for North Down 1970–79; resigned from the party to stand as Ulster Unionist in 1979 election. Represented Belfast West 1964–66. Former Secretary and Chief Whip, Official Unionist Parliamentary Party. Member of Northern Ireland Assembly 1973–75 and Northern Ireland Constitutional Convention 1975–76. Barrister. Born Jul 16 1928; educ. Portora Royal School, Enniskillen and Trinity College, Dublin.

Mr Enoch Powell

DOWN SOUTH Electorate 66968

*Powell, J.E. (OUP)	20693	40.3%
McGrady, E. (SDLP)	20145	39.3%
Fitzsimmons P. (SF)	4074	7.9%
Harvey, C. (DUP)	3743	7.3%
Forde, P.M.D. (All)	1823	3.6%
Magee, Ms M (WP)	851	1.7%
OUP majority	458	1.1%
Total vote 51329		Turnout 76.6%

Mr Enoch Powell was returned for the seat in Oct 1974. In Feb of that year he had refused to stand as a Conservative in his former seat of Wolverhampton South-West, denouncing the general election as 'fraudulent'. He was dismissed as defence spokesman for the Opposition by Mr Heath in 1968 following a speech on immigration. Unsuccessful candidate for Conservative leadership in 1965. Minister of Health 1960–63; Financial Secretary to Treasury 1957–58 when he resigned in protest at Government spending. Parliamentary Secretary, Ministry of Housing and Local Government 1955–57. Represented Wolverhampton South-West 1950–74. Born Jun 16 1912; educ. King Edward's School, Birmingham and Trinity College, Cambridge. Professor of Greek, Sydney University, 1937–39. Army 1939–46, private to brigadier.

Mr Edward McGrady, a chartered accountant, contested the seat in 1979. Born 1943; educ. St Patrick's Grammar School, Downpatrick, Belfast College of Technology. Founder-member SDLP. Member, Northern Ireland Assembly 1973, Convention 1975, and Assembly 1982.

Dr John Gilbert

DUDLEY EAST Electorate 74 765

*Gilbert, J. (Lab)	24 441	45.8%
Gillies, Mrs. S. (C)	18 625	34.9%
Simon, C. (SDP/All)	10 272	19.3%
Lab majority	5 816	10.9%
Total vote 53 338		Turnout 71.3%

Dr John Gilbert, a member of Select Committee on defence since 1979, was Minister of State for Defence, 1976–79; Financial Secretary to Treasury 1974–75; Minister for Transport, Department of Environment, 1975–76. Elected Feb 1974; MP for Dudley 1970–74, contested by-election Dudley 1968 and Ludlow 1966. Opposition spokesman on Treasury matters 1972–74. Born Apr 1927; educ. Merchant Taylors' School, Northwood; St John's College, Oxford and New York University. Chartered accountant and economist. Chairman PLP Defence Group and vice-chairman Labour Finance and Industry Group. Member, Council for Arms Control. GMBATU.

Mrs Susan Gillies, management consultant, contested Nuneaton and Bedworth 1970, and Warley East Feb 1974. Born 1938; educ. The Downs, Seaford, Ashridge College and Lausanne University, Switzerland.

Mr Crispin Simon, economic forecaster for merchant bank. Born Mar 25 1958; educ. Westminster and Lincoln College, Oxford.

Mr John Blackburn

DUDLEY WEST Electorate 77 795

*Blackburn, J. (C)	27 250	46.2%
Price, W. (Lab)	18 527	31.4%
Lewis, G. (L/All)	13 251	22.5%
C majority	8 723	14.8%
Total vote 59 028		Turnout 75.9%

Mr John Blackburn, formerly regional sales manager with an international engineering company, is parliamentary adviser to the Armitage Shanks Group of Engineering Companies and to the National Association of Retired Police Officers. Member Select Committee on Home Affairs. Joint Secretary Conservative backbench committee on arts and heritage. Elected in 1979. Former member of Royal Military Police and former detective sergeant in Liverpool. Born Sep 2 1933; educ. Liverpool Collegiate School and Liverpool University. Member Institute of Sales Engineers and Institute of Commercial and Technical Representatives. Member Wolverhampton Council, 1972–80. Member Post Office Users' National Council 1972–80.

Mr William Price, a journalist, was MP for Rugby 1966–79. Born Jun 1934; educ. Forest of Dean Technical College. Parliamentary Secretary to Privy Council Office 1974–79; Parliamentary Secretary, Overseas Development 1974; PPS to Deputy Leader of the Opposition 1972–74; NUJ.

Mr Gerald Lewis, a student counsellor, contested Dudley East 1979. Born Mar 17 1926; educ. at Aberdeen, Belfast and Aston, Birmingham, universities. President, students' union at Queen's University, Belfast. Treasurer of NATFHE branch at Dudley College of Technology.

Mr Gerald Bowden

DULWICH Electorate 56 596

Bowden, G. (C)	15 424	40.6%
Huey, Ms C. (Lab)	13 565	35.7%
Taverne, D. (SDP/All)	8 376	22.0%
Barker, R. (NF)	338	0.9%
Baker, R. (Eco)	237	0.6%
Vero, R. (Loony Soc)	99	0.3%
C majority	1 859	4.9%
Total vote 38 039		Turnout 67.2%

Mr Gerald Bowden, principal lecturer in Department of Estate Management, South Bank Polytechnic, and barrister and chartered surveyor, was elected in 1983. Born Aug 26 1935; educ. Battersea Grammar School; Magdalen College, Oxford; Gray's Inn, and College of Estate Management, London. GLC member for Dulwich 1977–81. Active member of TA serving with rank of Lt-Colonel. Co-opted member, ILEA. Chairman, Lambeth and Southwark Housing Soc.

Ms Catherine Huey, lecturer and educational adviser to London football clubs. Born Jun 21 1948; educ. Belfast Royal Academy, Ulster College of Physical Education and City of London College. Member, Hackney Borough Council, 1978–82.

Mr Dick Taverne QC, contested Southwark, Peckham for the SDP at the Oct 1982 by-election. Became Labour MP for Lincoln at by-election in 1962. Financial Secretary to the Treasury 1969–70; Minister of State, Treasury 1968–69; Under-Secretary, Home Office 1966–68. Re-elected as a Democratic MP at a by-election in 1973 after resigning from the Labour Party over policy towards the EEC. Born Oct 18 1928; educ. Charterhouse and Balliol College, Oxford. Chairman, Institute for Fiscal Studies since 1981.

Mr Ian Campbell

DUMBARTON Electorate 57 373 1979: 54 509 minor

*Campbell, I. (Lab)	15 810	36.7%
Lawson, I. (C)	13 695	31.8%
Sawyer, R. (SDP/All)	9 813	22.8%
Bayne, I. (SNP)	3 768	8.8%
Lab majority	2 115	4.9%
Total vote 43 086	Turnout 75.1%	

1979 (as Dunbartonshire West): Total vote 43 710 (80.2%); Lab 21 666 (48.4%); C 14 709 (33.7%); SNP 7 835 (17.9%)Lab maj 6 457 (14.7%); swing 0.1% to C.

Mr Ian Campbell, chairman of the all-party Scotch whisky industry group, represented Dumbartonshire West 1970–83. Former secretary, Scottish Labour group. Electrical power engineer with South of Scotland Electricity Board, 1953–70. Born Apr 26 1926; educ. Dumbarton Academy, Royal Technical College. Member Dumbarton town and county councils 1958–70; Provost of Dumbarton 1962–70. PPS to Secretary of State for Scotland 1976–79. Member Chairmen's Panel, Unopposed Bills Panel since 1981.

Mr Iain Lawson, proprietor of a pest control company, contested Glasgow, Garscadden at the by-election 1978 and in 1979. Born 1952; educ. Clydebank High School.

Mr Robert Sawyer, educational technologist in Scottish Central Institution. Born Mar 15 1936; educ. Wyggeston School, Leicester, and LSE.

Mr Ian Bayne, lecturer at college of further education, contested Rutherglen, Oct, 1974 and Glasgow, Kelvingrove, 1979. Born 1940; educ. at universities of Edinburgh and Glasgow.

Sir Hector Monro

DUMFRIES Electorate 57 594

*Monro, Sir H. (C)	18 730	44.5%
McCall, J. (SDP/All)	10 036	23.9%
McAughtrie, T. (Lab)	8 764	20.8%
Gibson, E. (SNP)	4 527	10.8%
C majority	8 694	20.7%
Total vote 42 057	Turnout 73.0%	

Sir Hector Monro was Under Secretary of State for Environment with special responsibilities for sport 1979–81; Opposition spokesman on sport 1974–79, on Scotland, 1974–75; Under Secretary of State for Health and Education, Scottish Office, 1971–74; Lord Commissioner of the Treasury (whip) 1970–71; Opposition whip 1967–70. Elected in 1964. Farmer. Born Oct 4 1922; educ. Canford School and King's College, Cambridge. Member, Dumfries County Council 1952–67. Manager, Scottish rugby XV during tour of Australia. Member, Scottish Advisory Board, Abbey National Building Society. President, Scottish Rugby Union 1976–77. Royal Air Force 1941–46 (pilot). Hon Air Commodore, Royal Auxiliary Air Force.

Mr James McCall, publishing director. Born Jan 3 1948; educ. Ayr Academy and Glasgow University. Board member, Educational Publishers Council. Director, Blackie Publishing Group.

Mr Thomas McAughtrie, process worker. Born Apr 9 1951; educ. Locharbriggs Primary School and Dumfries Academy. District councillor since 1980; regional councillor since 1982.

Mr Ernest Gibson, teacher, contested Dumfries 1979. Born Nov 1928; educ. Portobelloe High School, Edinburgh and the University of Glasgow.

Mr Gordon Wilson

DUNDEE EAST Electorate 62 752 1979: 64 330 minor

*Wilson, G. (SNP)	20 276	43.8%
Bowman, C. (Lab)	15 260	33.0%
Vaughan, Mrs B. (C)	7 172	15.5%
Rottger, S. (L/All)	3 546	7.7%
SNP majority	5 016	10.8%
Total vote 46 254	Turnout 73.7%	

1979: Total vote 49 959 (77.7%); SNP 20 497 (41.0%); Lab 17 978 (36.0%); C 9 072 (18.2%); L 2 317 (4.6%); WRP 95 (0.2%). SNP maj 2 519 (5.0%).

Mr Gordon Wilson, SNP chairman since 1979 and the party's spokesman on economic affairs, won the seat in Feb 1974; contested it in the by-election of Mar 1973. Partner in a law practice. Born Apr 16 1938; educ. Douglas High School and Edinburgh University. Senior vice-chairman SNP 1973–74; spokesman on energy 1974; home affairs 1975–76; and devolution 1976–79. National Secretary SNP 1963–71; Deputy leader, SNP Parliamentary Party 1974–79. Rector of University of Dundee. Member, Law Society of Scotland.

Mr Charles Bowman, senior instructor, BR training school. Born Nov 15 1924; educ. secondary modern school. Dundee councillor and deputy group leader. Sponsored by ASLEF.

Mrs Barbara Vaughan, an economics lecturer, contested City of Glasgow in the Euro-elections 1979. Aged 43. Member, Tayside Regional Council since 1980; ASTMS executive.

Mr Stephen Rottger, Univ. of Dundee housing officer. Born Jan 19 1950; educ. Royal Belfast Academical Institution, City of London Polytechnic.

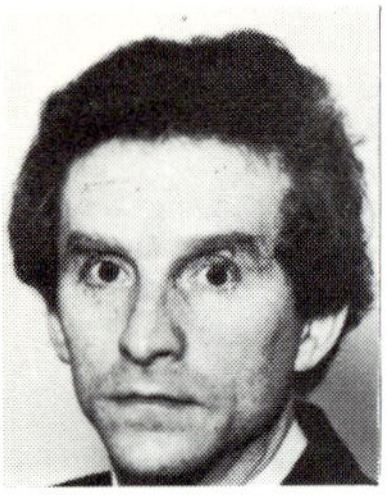

Mr Ernest Ross

DUNDEE WEST

Electorate 62 703 1979: 63 883 minor

*Ross, E. (Lab)	20 288	43.5%
Senior, D. (C)	10 138	21.7%
Dick, Mrs E. (SDP/All)	7 976	17.1%
Lynch, J. (SNP)	7 973	17.1%
Marks, P. (Eco)	302	0.7%
Lab majority	10 150	21.8%
Total vote 46 677		Turnout 74.4%

1979: Total vote 50 059 (78.4%); Lab 23 654 (47.3%); SNP 13 197 (26.4%); C 12 892 (25.8%); Com 316 (0.6%). Lab maj 10 457 (20.9%); swing 0.5% to C.

Mr Ernest Ross has been member of Unopposed Bills Panel and Select Committee on Standing Orders since 1981. Elected 1979. Quality control engineer with Timex. Born Jul 1942; educ. St Joseph's and St Mary's Primary School, St John's Junior Secondary School. Sponsored by AUEW (TASS).

Mr David Senior, former political researcher. Former member, Macclesfield District Council. Aged 24; educ. King's School, Macclesfield; Jesus College, Cambridge.

Mrs Elizabeth Dick is an economic research assistant. Aged 47.

Mr James Lynch, chartered accountant, contested Edinburgh North Feb and Oct 1974, and Fife Central 1979. Born Oct 1934; educ. Lawside Academy, Dundee. Has held a number of local SNP offices.

Mr Gordon Brown

DUNFERMLINE EAST

Electorate 49 881

Brown, G. (Lab)	18 515	51.5%
Harcus, D. (L/All)	7 214	20.1%
Shenton, C. (C)	6 764	18.8%
Hunter, G. (SNP)	2 573	7.2%
Maxwell, A. (Com)	864	2.4%
Lab majority	11 301	31.5%
Total vote 35 930		Turnout 72.0%

Mr Gordon Brown is chairman of the Scottish Labour Party; member of its executive committee since 1977. Elected in 1983. Journalist with Scottish TV. Born Feb 20 1951; educ. Kirkcaldy High School. Was second student rector at Edinburgh University.

Mr David Harcus, solicitor and company director. Born Dec 8 1939; educ. Nairn Primary School, George Watsons Boys' College and Edinburgh University.

Mr Clive Shenton, advocate. Aged 36; educ. Edinburgh University. Army officer 1966–70.

Mr George Hunter, telecommunications engineer. Born 1929; educ. George Heriot's School and Heriot Watt College. Has held a number of local SNP offices.

Mr Richard Douglas

DUNFERMLINE WEST

Electorate 49 075

*Douglas, R. (Lab)	12 998	36.0%
Davison, Dr P. (C)	10 524	29.2%
Moyes, F. (SDP / All)	9 434	26.2%
Fairlie, J. (SNP)	2 798	7.8%
Dobson, S. (Eco)	321	0.9%
Lab majority	2 474	6.9%
Total vote 36 075		Turnout 73.5%

Mr Richard Douglas elected in 1983, was MP for Dunfermline 1979–83; MP for Stirlingshire East and Clackmannan 1970 to Feb 1974; unsuccessfully contested that seat in Oct 1974; contested Glasgow, Pollock in 1967 by-election; Edinburgh West in 1966 and South Angus in 1964. Member, Public Accounts Committee 1979–83 and of Select Committee on Defence. Economic consultant. Born Jan 4 1932; educ. Govan High School, Co-operative College, Stanford Hall, Loughborough, and University of Strathclyde. Hon Lecturer, Strathclyde since 1980. AUEW. Sponsored by Co-op Party.

Dr Peter Davison, has been member, Fife Regional Council, since 1979, contested Hamilton 1979. Born Jan 1930; educ. George Watson's Boys College, Edinburgh University. Organic chemist.

Mr Frank Moyes, a member of the Council for Social Democracy. Born 1942; educ. West Africa and Manchester University. Technical manager of team of navigation systems consultants to Royal Navy at Rosyth dockyard.

Mr James Fairlie, teacher, contested Dundee West Feb and Oct 1974, and 1979. Born May 1940; educ. Perth Academy and Dundee University. Former vice-chairman (policy) of the SNP, now senior vice-chairman.

Dr Mark Hughes

DURHAM, CITY OF Electorate 66925

*Hughes, M. (Lab)	18163	36.5%
Stoker, D. (SDP / All)	16190	32.5%
Lavis, M. (C)	15438	31.0%
Lab majority	1973	4.0%
Total vote 49791	Turnout	74.4%

Dr Mark Hughes, an Opposition spokesman on agriculture, fisheries and food since 1981, was elected MP for Durham in 1970 and for City of Durham in 1983: member, European Parliament, 1975–79. Lecturer in economic history at Durham University, 1964–70. Born Dec 18 1932; educ. Shincliffe School, Durham School, Balliol College, Oxford, and Durham University. Served on Durham Rural Council. Member, Select Committee on European Legislation since 1979. Former member, Select Committee on Parliamentary Commissioner for Administration and of Public Expenditure Committee.

Mr David Stoker, research associate at the Centre for Urban and Regional Development Studies, University of Newcastle. Born 1952; educ. King Edward VI School, Morpeth and Manchester University.

Mr Matthew Lavis, university assistant registrar. Born Dec 6 1944; educ. Cheltenham Grammar School, St John's College, Durham. Contested Durham 1979. Chairman, Durham Conservative Association, 1972–76 and since 1980.

Mr Giles Radice

DURHAM NORTH Electorate 71256

*Radice, G. (Lab)	26404	51.0%
Howarth D. (L / All)	12967	25.0%
Popat, S. (C)	12418	24.0%
Lab majority	13437	26.0%
Total vote 51789	Turnout	72.7%

Mr Giles Radice was elected in 1983; MP for Chester-le-Street 1973–83; contested Chippenham 1964 and 1966. An Opposition spokesman on employment; former spokesman on foreign affairs. Head of research department GMBATU 1966–73. Chairman, Fabian Society 1976–77. Born Oct 4 1936; educ. Winchester and Magdalen College, Oxford. Sponsored by GMBATU.

Mr David Howarth, building society office manager. Born Mar 23 1955; educ. Newcastle Polytechnic, Rochdale College of Art, and Queen Elizabeth's High School, Middleton.

Mr Andrew Popat, barrister. Born 1943; educ. at the universities of London and California. Vice-president, Berkeley Young Republican Party 1969–70, the first non-American to be elected an officer of the Republican Party. Associate Attorney to a Wall Street law firm 1970–75. Member, executive committee of the Society of Conservative Lawyers since 1980; Roehampton, Putney and Barnes Community Health Council 1978–81.

Mr Ernest Armstrong

DURHAM NORTH WEST Electorate 60747

*Armstrong, E. (Lab)	19135	44.6%
Middleton, T. (C)	12779	29.8%
Foote Wood, C. (L/All)	11008	25.7%
Lab majority	6356	14.8%
Total vote 42922	Turnout	70.7%

Mr Ernest Armstrong has been first Deputy Chairman of Ways and Means since 1982; second Deputy Chairman 1979–82. Under-Secretary for Environment 1975–79, and for Education and Science 1974–75; Member, Unopposed Bills Panel, 1981. Opposition spokesman on education and science 1973–74; Opposition whip 1970–73; Lord Commissioner of the Treasury (Government whip) 1969–70; Assistant Government whip 1967–69. Elected in 1964; contested Sunderland South 1955 and 1959. Schoolmaster. Born Jan 12 1915; educ. Wolsingham Grammar School and Leeds City Teacher Training College. NUT and NUGM. Vice-President Methodist Conference 1974–75. Managing trustee, Municipal Mutual Insurance Ltd.

Mr Terence Middleton, sub-postmaster and former bank employee. Born 1944; educ. St Cuthbert's Grammar School, Newcastle-upon-Tyne, and Ushaw College, Durham. Member, Gateshead Council since 1975, Conservative group secretary 1976–82.

Mr Christopher Foote Wood, journalist running press agency, contested Newcastle upon Tyne North Feb 1974, Teeside, Middlesborough Oct 1974, Durham 1979 and County Durham in the Euro-elections, 1979. Born Dec 15 1940; educ. Bury Grammar School, Durham University and the Open University. Member, Wear Valley District Council since 1967 (chairman, 1976–77); Durham County Council 1973–77. Nalgo and NUJ.

Sir George Young

EALING, ACTON Electorate 62078

*Young, Sir G. (C)	22051	49.2%
Daniel, G. J. (Lab)	11959	26.7%
Mitchell, P. (SDP/All)	10593	23.7%
Pulley, S. (Com)	192	0.4%
C majority	10092	22.5%
Total vote 44795	Turnout 72.2%	

Sir George Young, Under Secretary of State for Environment since 1981; Under Secretary of State for Health and Social Security 1979–81. Opposition whip 1976–79. Economist. Elected Feb 1974. Born Jul 16 1941; educ. Eton and Christ Church, Oxford. Chairman, Acton Housing Assoc. 1972–79. Member, Select Committee on Violence in Marriage 1975. Member GLC 1967–70; Lambeth Borough Council 1968–71. Economic adviser, Post Office Corporation 1969–74.

Mr Gareth Daniel is full-time Greater London councillor for Ealing North. Fought Worcestershire South in 1979. Born Mar 30 1954; educ. St Edward's College, Liverpool; Jesus College, Oxford. Nalgo.

Mr Parry Mitchell, company director. Born May 6 1943; educ. Christ's College Grammar School, Ealing Technical College and Columbia University Graduate School of Business, New York. Chairman, United Leasing Group.

Mr Harry Greenway

EALING NORTH Electorate 68538

*Greenway, H. (C)	23128	45.1%
Benn, H. J. (Lab)	16837	32.8%
Miller, A. (L/All)	11021	21.5%
Shaw, J. (BNP)	306	0.6%
C majority	6291	12.3%
Total vote 51292	Turnout 74.8%	

Mr Harry Greenway won Ealing North for the Conservatives in 1979. Part-time lecturer; examiner, the London Regional Examination Board; former deputy headmaster at a London school. Contested Stepney 1970; Stepney and Poplar Feb and Oct 1974. Born Oct 1934; educ. Warwick School, College of St Mark and St John, London and Caen University. Chairman, All-Party Adult Education Committee, and member, Select Committee on Education, Science and the Arts, since 1979. Member, Council of British Horse Society since 1973. Vice-chairman, Conservative backbench committee of Greater London MPs. Secretary, Conservative Education Committee since 1981; of the National Advisory Committee on Education since 1980; president Conservative Trade Unionist Teachers 1982–83; chairman, British Atlantic Committee's education committee since 1970; member, council, Open University since 1980; vice-president, England schoolboys' hockey assoc. and captain, Lords and Commons hockey XI. AMMA.

Mr Hilary Benn, trade union research officer, ASTMS. Born Nov 26 1953; educ. Holland Park Comprehensive School and Sussex University. Member, London Borough of Ealing Council since 1979, Labour education spokesman. APEX. Son of Tony Benn. Member, Co-operative Party and founder member, Labour Common Market Safeguards Committee. APEX.

Mr Anthony Miller, personnel adviser, contested Streatham 1964, and Harrow Central 1966 and 1970. Born Dec 27 1934; educ. various schools in India; Wells Cathedral School; Dulwich College, and St John's College. Has own consultancy.

Mr Sydney Bidwell

EALING, SOUTHALL Electorate 71441 1979: 73146 same

*Bidwell, S. (Lab)	26664	52.3%
Linacre, N. (C)	15548	30.5%
Nadeen, M. (L / All)	8059	15.8%
Pendrous, E. (NF)	555	1.1%
Paul, S. (Ind)	150	0.3
Lab majority	11116	21.8%
Total vote 50976	Turnout 71.4%	

1979: Total vote 52412 (71.7%); Lab 28498 (54.4%); C 17220 (32.9%); L 3920 (7.5%); NF 1545 (2.9%); Ind 637 (1.2%); Soc Unity 477 (0.9%); other 115 (0.2%). Lab maj 11278 (21.5%); swing 0.3% to C.

Mr Sydney Bidwell was elected in 1966. Born Jan 14 1917; educ. elementary school and evening classes and trade union movement. Contested Hertfordshire South West 1964; Hertfordshire East 1959. Former member, Select Committee on Race Relations and Immigration. Member Select Committee on Transport since 1979. Lecturer; former tutor and organizer for National Council of Labour Colleges. Previously railway worker. Former NUR and now TGWU. Chairman Tribune Group 1975. Vice-chairman PLP transport group 1977. Sponsored by TGWU.

Mr Nigel Linacre, account manager with an advertising agency. Born 1957; educ. Imberhorne School, East Grinstead, and George Heriot's School, Edinburgh.
Mr Mahmud Nadeen, solicitor. Born Aug 10 1931. Member of Liberal Party community relations panel.

Mr Jack Dormand

EASINGTON Electorate 65 732

*Dormand, J. D. (Lab)	25 912	58.4%
Patterson, F. E. (L/All)	11 120	25.1%
Coulson-Thomas, C. J. (C)	7 342	16.6%
Lab majority	14 792	33.3%
Total vote 44 374		Turnout 67.5%

Mr Jack Dormand was elected chairman of the PLP in 1981. Lord Commissioner of the Treasury (Government Whip) 1974–79; assistant Government Whip 1974. Elected in 1970. Born Aug 27 1919; educ. Wellfield Grammar School, Bede College, Durham, Loughborough College and Oxford and Harvard Universities. Former member, Select Committee on Nationalized Industries. Secretary, Northern Group of Labour MPs 1973–81. Member, Easington RDC 1949–52; education officer for Easington RDC 1963–70. APEX, formerly Nalgo, and NUT.
Mr Frank Patterson, senior lecturer in management, contested Gateshead West 1979. Born Jul 29 1944; educ. local schools and Durham University. District councillor since 1976; town councillor since 1979. NATFHE.
Mr Colin Coulson-Thomas, publishing director and chartered accountant. Born Apr 26 1949; educ. LSE, London Business School, universities of Chicago and Southern California. Chairman, Bow Group 1982–83; deputy chairman, London Electricity Consultative Council since 1980. Member, Greenwich Borough Council 1977–82; Council for Professions Supplementary to Medicine since 1982. Governor, Moorfields Eye Hospital since 1978.

Mr Ian Gow

EASTBOURNE Electorate 72 980

*Gow, I. (C)	31 501	59.1%
Driver, P. (L/All)	18 015	33.8%
Clark, C. (Lab)	3 790	7.1%
C majority	13 486	25.3%
Total vote 53 306		Turnout 73.0%

Mr Ian Gow was appointed Minister for Housing and Construction in Jun 1983 having been PPS to Mrs Thatcher since 1979. Solicitor. Elected in Feb 1974; contested Coventry East 1964, and Clapham 1966. Born Feb 11 1937; educ. Winchester. Former member, Select Committee on Wealth Tax and Select Committee on Parliamentary Commissioner for Administration. Secretary, Conservative Party backbench committees on Northern Ireland 1976–79 and Constitutional Committee 1977–79.
Mr Peter Driver, sales manager with Esso, contested Chelsea 1979. Born Dec 9 1934; educ. Epsom College.
Mr Charles Clark, painter and decorator. Born Aug 11 1947; educ. Rye Secondary Modern School. Worked for Sue Ryder Foundation in Poland for Voluntary Service Overseas 1972–74. UCATT.

Dr Maurice Miller

EAST KILBRIDE Electorate 61 420

*Miller, Dr M. S. (Lab)	17 545	37.1%
Sullivan, D. (SDP/All)	13 199	27.9%
Dalkeith, R. (C)	11 483	24.3%
Urquhart, D. (SNP)	4 795	10.1%
Doolan, W. (Com)	256	0.5%
Lab majority	4 346	9.2%
Total vote 47 278		Turnout 77.0%

Dr Maurice Miller won the seat in Feb 1974; MP for Glasgow, Kelvingrove 1964–74. Government whip 1968–69. Medical practitioner and company director. Born Aug 16 1920; educ. Shawlands Academy, Glasgow and Glasgow University. Member, Glasgow Corporation, 1950–64; Bailie 1954–57. Chairman, Glasgow and West of Scotland Socialist Medical Assoc. Member, former Commons Expenditure Committee, Select Committee on Abortion (Amendment) Bill 1975–76. Chairman, PLP health group. Sponsored by ASTMS.
Mr Denis Sullivan is secretary and a founder of the SDP in Scotland. Chairman, Dumbarton SDP. Born Mar 1 1945; educ. schools in Glasgow; Glasgow School of Art; Jordanhill College of Education. EIS official.
Mr Richard Dalkeith, charity worker. Aged 29; educ. Eton, Christ Church, Oxford. Heir to the Duke of Buccleuch. Father was MP for Edinburgh North 1960–73.
Mr David Urquhart, Church of Scotland Minister. Born 1946; educ. Glasgow Academy and Glasgow University.

Sir David Price

EASTLEIGH Electorate 82 447

*Price, Sir D. (C)	32 393	51.0%
Kyrle, M. (L/All)	19 385	30.5%
Hallman, P. (Lab)	11 736	18.5%
C majority	13 008	20.5%
Total vote 63 514		Turnout 77.0%

Sir David Price, an industrial consultant, was Under Secretary of State for Aerospace, Department of Trade and Industry 1971–72; Parliamentary Secretary, Ministry of Aviation Supply 1970–71; Parliamentary Secretary, Ministry of Technology, Jun to Oct 1970; Opposition spokesman on technology and science 1964–70. Parliamentary Secretary, Board of Trade, 1962–64. Member, Select Committee on Transport since 1979; vice-chairman, Conservative Shipping and Ship-Building Committee. Elected 1955. Born Nov 20 1924; educ. Eton, Trinity College, Cambridge, and Yale University (Research Fellow); President, Cambridge Union, 1948. Vice-President, Institution of Industrial Managers; Deputy Lieutenant, County of Hampshire.

Mr Martin Kyrle, teacher, contested Christchurch and Lymington, Feb 1974 and New Forest 1979. Born Mar 16 1933; educ. Southampton and Sussex universities. Member, Eastleigh Borough Council since 1980. Executive member, Eastleigh Trades Council. NAS/UWT.

Mr Peter Hallman is a teacher at a comprehensive school. Born 1954. Was vice-chairman, Eastleigh Labour Party.

Mr John Home Robertson

EAST LOTHIAN Electorate 62 581

*Home Robertson, J. (Lab)	20 934	43.9%
Fry, M. (C)	14 693	30.8%
Kibby, M. (L/All)	9 950	20.9%
Knox, R. (SNP)	2 083	4.4%
Lab majority	6 241	13.1%
Total vote 47 660		Turnout 76.2%

Mr John Home Robertson, elected in 1983, was MP for Berwick and East Lothian Oct 1978–83. Farmer. Born Dec 5 1948; educ. Ampleforth and West of Scotland Agricultural College. Member, Select Committee on Scottish Affairs since 1979; chairman, Socttish group of Labour MPs 1983 and of Rural Affairs Group, Scottish PLP; member, Berwickshire Council 1974–78; member, Borders Health Board 1975–78. TGWU (farm workers section) and NUPE.

Mr Michael Fry, journalist. Born 1947; educ. Owen's School, Pembroke College, Oxford, and the University of Hamburg. Member, Scottish Economic Society; Scottish History Society. NUJ, former father of the chapel.

Dr Michael Kibby, senior lecturer in biochemistry. Born Apr 22 1938; educ. Whitgift School, Croydon, Trinity College, Cambridge, St Mary's Hospital Medical School, London. District councillor in Glasgow. Contested Glasgow, Garscadden Oct 1974. AUT.

Mr Roger Knox, lecturer in computer education, contested Kirkcaldy Feb 1974. Born 1942; educ. universities of St Andrew's and Heriot-Watt.

Mr Allan Stewart

EASTWOOD Electorate 59 378

*Stewart, A. (C)	21 072	46.6%
Pickett, J. (SDP/All)	12 477	27.6%
McGuire, J. (Lab)	9 083	20.1%
Herriot, Ms J. (SNP)	2 618	5.8%
C majority	8 595	19.0%
Total vote 45 250		Turnout 76.2%

Mr Allan Stewart was appointed Under Secretary of State for Scotland in 1981. A university lecturer, he was elected for this seat in 1983; MP for East Renfrewshire 1979–83; contested Dundee East in 1970. PPS to Minister of State for Energy 1981. Member, Select Committee on Scottish Affairs 1979–81. Born Jun 1 1942; educ. Bell Baxter High School, Cupar; St Andrews University and Harvard. Councillor, London Borough of Bromley 1974–76. Head of Regional Development Department, Confederation of British Industry 1971–73; Deputy Director (Economics) 1973–76; Scottish Section 1976–78; Scottish Director 1978–79.

Mr James Pickett, director of David Livingstone Inst of Overseas Development Studies at Strathclyde University. Born 1929; educ. Greenock Acad. and Edinburgh, Glasgow and Paris universities. Member, Council for Social Democracy.

Mr James McGuire has worked for Barrhead Co-op Society. Ass. manager and fleshing manager. Born 1929. Elected to Barrhead Town Council 1963; leader of Lab group 1973–75. Provost 1970–73. Renfrew County Council 1968. Chairman, Barrhead branch, Lab Party. USDAW.

Ms Jenny Herriott, radiographer. Born 1944; educ. Kirkcaldy High School and Glasgow Royal Infirmary. Member, ASTMS.

Mr Lewis Carter-Jones

ECCLES Electorate 67 230

*Carter-Jones, L. (Lab)	21 644	45.9%
Philp, D. (C)	15 639	33.2%
Hemsley, K. A. (L/All)	9 392	19.9%
Cottam, B. (Com)	485	1.0%
Lab majority	6 005	12.7%
Total vote 47 160		Turnout 70.2%

Mr Lewis Carter-Jones, elected in 1964, contested City of Chester 1956 by-election and in 1959. Teacher, lecturer and industrial training adviser. Born Nov 17 1920; educ. Bridgend County School and University College of Wales, Aberystwyth. Chairman Committee for Research for Apparatus for Disabled and of PLP disablement group. Vice-chairman PLP aviation group; disabled income group. Secretary all-party BLESMA group. Unpaid director, Possum Controls Ltd. Sponsored by TGWU.

Mr David Philp, barrister. Born Dec 20 1947; educ. Lancaster Royal Grammar School; Keble College, Oxford, and Inns of Court School of Law. Adviser to northern editions of a national newspaper group.

Mr Kenneth Hemsley, retired senior lecturer, temporary post as senior development officer with Youth Training Scheme. Born Feb 24 1926; educ. Bridgnorth Grammar School, Kirkby College of Education, University of Manchester. Member, Congleton Borough Council and Town Council; executive, Cheshire Association of Parish Councils. NUT.

Mr Alastair Goodlad

EDDISBURY Electorate 71 506

*Goodlad, A. (C)	28 407	53.5%
Fletcher, R. (L/All)	13 561	25.5%
Hanson, D. G. (Lab)	11 169	21.0%
C majority	14 846	27.9%
Total vote 53 137		Turnout 74.3%

Mr Alastair Goodlad became a Lord Commissioner of the Teasury (Government Whip) in 1983; an assistant Government whip 1981–83. Elected in 1983; MP for Northwich Feb 1974–83; contested Crewe 1970. Born Jul 4 1943; educ. St Faith's School, Cambridge, Marlborough College and King's College, Cambridge. Underwriting member of Lloyd's, Personal assistant to Mr Peter Walker when Opposition spokesman on Transport. Joint secretary, Conservative parliamentary trade committee 1978–79, joint vice-chairman 1979–81; joint secretary, Northern Ireland committee 1979–81; secretary, all-party heritage group 1979–81; member select committee on agriculture 1979–81.

Mr Roderick Fletcher, controller, British Rail. Born Jul 10 1943; educ. King's School, Macclesfield. Member, Alsager Town Council since 1979; member, Congleton Borough Council since 1980; deputy leader of Liberal Group since 1981. TSSA.

Mr David Hanson, North West regional officer of The Spastics Society. Member, Vale Royal District Council. Born Jul 5 1957; educ. Verdin Comprehensive School, Winsford; Hull University. AUEW (TASS).

Mr Alexander Fletcher

EDINBURGH CENTRAL Electorate 57 064

*Fletcher, A. (C)	14 095	38.0%
Kelley, R. (Lab)	11 529	31.1%
Macleod, Dr M. (SDP/All)	9 498	25.6%
Halliday, R. (SNP)	1 810	4.9%
Carson, D. (Com)	119	03%
C majority	2 566	6.9%
Total vote 37 051		Turnout 64.9%

Mr Alexander Fletcher became an Under-Secretary of State for Trade and Industry in Jun 1983; Under Secretary of State for Scotland 1979–83; previously an Opposition spokesman on Scotland. Elected in 1983; represented Edinburgh North 1973–83. Chartered accountant and company director. Born Aug 26 1929; educ. Greenock High School. Contested West Renfrewshire 1970. Member, East Kilbride Development Corporation 1971–73. Elder of Church of Scotland. Member, Select Committee on Science and Technology 1974–76. Member, European Parliament 1976–77.

Mr Richard Kelley, community education worker. Branch chairman of Labour Party CLP. Nalgo and NUPE. Shop steward and convenor. District councillor since 1980.

Dr Marion Macleod, scientist. Born Oct 10 1930; educ. Heaton High School, Newcastle upon Tyne; King's College, University of Durham, and University of Glasgow.

Mr Ronald Halliday, college administrator. Born 1949; educ. Edinburgh University and Aberdeen College of Education. SNP spokesman on employment and a member of the SNP national council. Nalgo shop steward.

Mr Gavin Strang

EDINBURGH EAST Electorate 51156

*Strang, G. (Lab)	16169	44.9%
Martin, P. (C)	10303	28.6%
Macleod, R. (L/All)	7570	21.0%
Scott, P. (SNP)	1976	5.5%
Lab majority	5866	16.3%
Total vote 36018		Turnout 70.4%

Mr Gavin Strang was an Opposition spokesman on agriculture, fisheries and food 1979–82. Parliamentary Secretary, Ministry of Agriculture, Fisheries and Food 1974–79 Under-Secretary for Oil, Department of Energy, 1974. Elected in 1970. Member, Select Committee on Science and Technology 1970–74. An Opposition spokesman on trade and industry 1973–74. Agricultural scientist. Born Jul 10 1943; educ. Morrison's Academy, Edinburgh University, and Churchill College, Cambridge. Sponsored by TGWU.

Mr Paul Martin, insurance executive. Born 1958; educ. Royal High School, Edinburgh, and Edinburgh University. Member, Edinburgh District Council since 1980; Edinburgh Festival Council; Edinburgh Health Council. Former member, executive committee of Edinburgh and District Spastic Association. NUPE and ASTMS.

Mr Roderick MacLeod, solicitor, is a member of Liberal assocs of Invernessshire, Hillhead and Edinburgh South. Born Dec 7 1952; educ. Portree High School, Edinburgh Univ.

Mr Paul Scott, freelance writer. Born 1920; educ. Royal High School, Edinburgh University, and at European universities. Former diplomat, Foreign Office. Works with organizations connected with Scottish heritage.

Mr Ronald Brown

EDINBURGH, LEITH Electorate 60562

*Brown, R. (Lab)	16177	39.7%
Graham, D. (SDP/All)	11204	27.5%
Cooklin, B. (C)	10706	26.3%
Young, J. (SNP)	2646	6.5%
Lab majority	4973	12.2%
Total vote 40733		Turnout 67.3%

Mr Ronald Brown was elected in 1979. Chairman, Pilton branch, AUEW; former fitter. Born Jun 1940; educ. Ainslie Park High School, Edinburgh. Member Lothian Regional Council 1974–79. AUEW.

Mr David Graham is a school teacher. Aged 32.

Mr Brian Cooklin, teacher, Aged 29. County councillor. Chairman, Scottish Young Conservatives, 1977–80.

Mr John Young, educational researcher at Moray House College. Born 1942; educ. Broughton Hill School and Edinburgh University. Chairman, Newhaven SNP.

Mr Malcolm Rifkind

EDINBURGH, PENTLANDS Electorate 59295

*Rifkind, M. (C)	17051	39.2%
Smith, K. (SDP/All)	12742	29.3%
Milligan, E. (Lab)	10390	23.9%
MacCormick, N. (SNP)	2642	6.1%
Nicol-Smith, A. (Eco)	687	1.6%
C majority	4309	9.9%
Total vote 43512		Turnout 73.4%

Mr Malcolm Rifkind was appointed Minister of State for Foreign and Commonwealth Affairs in Jun 1983; Under Secretary of State for Foreign and Commonwealth Affairs 1982–83; Under-Secretary of State for Scotland 1979–82; Opposition spokesman on Scotland from 1975 until he resigned in 1977 over devolution. Elected 1974; contested Edinburgh Central 1970. An advocate Born Jun 21 1946; educ. George Watson's College, Edinburgh and Edinburgh University. Former member, Select Committee on Overseas Development, and former member, Select Committee on European Secondary Legislation. Edinburgh Council 1970–74. Joint Secretary, Conservative Parliamentary Foreign and Commonwealth Affairs Committee 1977–79. Hon President, Scottish Young Conservatives 1976–77; hon secretary, Federation of Conservative Students 1977–79. Lecturer in politics, University College of Rhodesia 1967–69.

Mr Keith Smith, soil scientist, lecturer and researcher. Born Feb 9 1940; educ. King Alfred's School, Wantage, Durham and Reading universities Member, Berkshire County Council 1964–67; Wantage urban district council 1972–73. IPCS.

Mr Eric Milligan, printer. Born Jan 27 1951; educ. Tynecastle School. Member, Edinburgh District Council 1974–78; Lothian Region Council since 1978. SOGAT.

Mr Neil MacCormick, Regius Professor of Public Law at Edinburgh University and former Dean of the Faculty, contested Edinburgh North 1979. Born 1941; educ. Glasgow High School and the universities of Glasgow and Oxford. Former President, Oxford Union.

Mr Michael Ancram

EDINBURGH SOUTH Electorate 62 517

*Ancram, M. (C)	16 485	36.8%
Godfrey, J. (SDP/All)	12 830	28.6%
McCreadie, R. (Lab)	12 824	28.6%
MacCallum, N. (SNP)	2 256	5.0%
Hendry, Mrs L. (Eco)	450	1.0%
C majority	3 655	8.2%
Total vote 44 845		Turnout 71.7%

Mr Michael Ancram became an Under Secretary of State for Scotland in Jun 1983. Advocate and former company director; is heir to the Marquess of Lothian. Elected in 1979; MP for Berwick and East Lothian Feb to Oct 1974; contested West Lothian in 1970. Born Jul 7 1945; educ. Ampleforth and Oxford and Edinburgh Universities. Member Select Committee on Energy 1979–83. Vice-chairman Scottish Conservative Party 1975–80, and chairman since 1980. First chairman, Thistle group.

Mr John Godfrey, university teacher. Born Jun 13 1931; educ. Penzance Grammar School, University College, London, and Edinburgh University.

Mr Robert McCreadie, university lecturer. Born Aug 17 1948; educ. Madras College, St Andrews; University of Edinburgh, and Christ's College, Cambridge. AUT.

Mr Neil MacCallum, health service administrator. Born 1954; educ. Firrhill High School and Napier College. National Secretary, SNP. Member, City of Edinburgh District Council, 1977–80. Former Nalgo shop steward.

Lord James Douglas-Hamilton

EDINBURGH WEST Electorate 61 050

*Douglas-Hamilton, Lord J. (C)	17 646	38.2%
King, D. (L/All)	17 148	37.1%
Wood, A. (Lab)	9 313	20.1%
Nicoll, J. (SNP)	2 126	4.6%
C majority	498	1.1%
Total vote 46 233		Turnout 75.7%

Lord James Douglas-Hamilton, advocate, second son of the Duke of Hamilton, Lord Commissioner of the Treasury (Government Whip) 1979–81; formerly an Opposition Whip. Elected in Oct 1974; contested Hamilton Feb 1974. Born Jul 31 1942; educ. Strathavon, Eton, Balliol College, Oxford (president of the union, 1964), and Edinburgh University. Boxing Blue. Hon. President, Scottish Amateur Boxing Association 1975. President Royal Commonwealth Society in Scotland 1979. Member of Select Committee on Scottish Affairs since 1981. President, Scottish Council UNA 1981.

Mr Derek King, university management consultant. Born Jul 27 1949; educ. Harrow County Grammar School, Middlesex, and Lancaster University. Member, Edinburgh District Council since 1980.

Mr Alex Wood, principal teacher, remedial education, Craigroyston High School, Edinburgh; contested Dumfries 1979. Born Nov 11 1950; educ. Paisley Grammar School, New University of Ulster, Moray House College of Education and the University of Stirling. Member, Edinburgh District Council since 1980. EIS.

Mr John Nicol, project manager. Born 1939; educ. North Kelvinside Senior Secondary School and Strathclyde University.

Dr Ian Twinn

EDMONTON Electorate 64 809

Twinn, I. (C)	18 968	42.5%
*Graham, T. E. (Lab)	17 775	39.8%
Brass, L. (L/All)	7 523	16.9%
Bruce, D. J. (BNP)	372	0.8%
C majority	1 193	2.7%
Total vote 44 638		Turnout 68.9%

Dr Ian Twinn, senior lecturer in planning, Polytechnic of South Bank was elected in 1983. Born Apr 26 1950; educ. Netherhall Sec Mod School, Cambridge; Cambridge Grammar School for Boys; University College of Wales, Aberystwyth; Reading University. NATFHE.

Mr Edward Graham, an Opposition spokesman on environment since 1979, was Lord Commissioner of the Treasury (Government Whip) 1976–79. Elected for Enfield, Edmonton in Feb 1974. National Secretary of the Co-operative Party until Apr 1974. Contested Enfield West 1966. Born Mar 26 1925; educ. WEA Co-operative College, Open University. Member, National Assoc. of Co-operative Officials; Expenditure Committee 1974–75. Life peer 1983.

Mr Laurence Brass, solicitor, contested Hornsey 1970, and Finchley Feb and Oct 1974; also 1979 European parliamentary election for London North. Born Jul 26 1947; educ. Clifton College, Bristol, and University College, London. Member, Hertsmere Borough Council 1972–81. Former executive member, London Liberal Party Council Member, Board of Deputies of British and Commonwealth Jews and of Association of Liberal Lawyers.

Mr Michael Woodcock

ELLESMERE PORT AND NESTON Electorate 69 992

Woodcock, M. (C)	24 371	45.9%
Davies, A. (Lab)	17 284	32.6%
George, L. (L/All)	11 413	21.5%
C majority	7 087	13.4%
Total vote 53 068	Turnout 75.8%	

Mr Michael Woodcock, managing director of four companies which he founded, was formerly senior consultant with an industrial training board. Elected in 1983. Aged 39. Former member, dairy industry training and education committee. City and Guilds of London Institute, council, Distributive Trading Education and Training Council, and manpower advisory committee NEDC. A magistrate, he is a member of local licensing committee, Nottinghamshire Compensation Authority and deputy chairman, domestic court panel.

Mr Andrew Davies, trade union research and legal officer. Born Feb 17 1952; educ. St Anselms, Birkenhead, Cambridge and LSE. Leader of Labour Group, Wirral Metropolitan Council since 1980. Sponsored by GMBATU.

Mr Lester George, managing director, Ferranti Instrumentation Ltd, contested Bromsgrove as Labour candidate 1955. Born Aug 10 1924; educ. elementary and junior technical schools. Former member AUEW and Draughtsmen's Union.

Mr Spencer Batiste

ELMET Electorate 67 008

Batiste, S. (C)	23 909	47.3%
Wilson, R. (Lab)	16 053	31.8%
Paterson, Mrs G. (L/All)	10 589	21.0%
C majority	7 856	15.5%
Total vote 50 551	Turnout 75.4%	

Mr Spencer Batiste, solicitor and company director. Born Jun 5 1945; educ. Carmel College, Sorbonne and Cambridge University. Elected in 1983; contested constituency of Sheffield in 1979 European elections. Member, national board, Small Business Bureau; council of Sheffield Chamber of Commerce, council of Sheffield University.

Mr Ray Wilson, civil engineer. Born 1934.

Mrs Gillian Paterson, teacher and former journalist. Member, Council for Social Democracy, and press officer for Leeds area SDP. Born Aug 17 1938; educ. St Helen's School, Northwood, Middlesex, and King's College, London University (secretary of the Union).

Mr Peter Bottomley

ELTHAM Electorate 55 062

*Bottomley, P. J. (C)	19 530	47.9%
Moore, C. P. (Lab)	11 938	29.3%
Randall, E. (L/All)	9 030	22.2%
Banks, P. (BNP)	276	0.7%
C majority	7 592	18.6%
Total vote 40 774	Turnout 74.1%	

Mr Peter Bottomley, an industrial economist and personnel adviser, was elected in 1983; represented Woolwich West Jun 1975–83. Contested that seat in Feb and Oct 1974. Born Jul 30 1944; educ. Westminster School and Trinity College, Cambridge. Secretary, Conservative health and social services committee 1977–79; foreign and Commonwealth affairs committee, 1979–81. Member Select Committee on Violence in the Family 1976, and former member Select Committee on Overseas Development. President Conservative Trade Unionists 1978–80. Chairman British Union of Family Organizations. 1973–80. Chairman, Church of England Children's Society. Member council of Mind since 1981. TGWU.

Mr Colin Moore, town planner, contested Kingston upon Thames, Surbiton 1979. Born May 11 1950; educ. King George V Grammar School, Southport and The Queen's College, Oxford. Wandsworth branch chairman of Nalgo.

Mr Edward Randall, university lecturer. Born Jul 13 1951; educ. Durham University, LSE, St Thomas Hospital. Councillor, London Borough of Greenwich, since 1982. NATFHE.

Mr Timothy Eggar

ENFIELD NORTH Electorate 67 980

*Eggar, T. (C)	25 456	51.7%
Grayson, B. G. (Lab)	13 740	27.9%
Daly, J. (L/All)	9 452	19.2%
Persighetti, Miss T. (Eco)	320	0.7%
Billingham, J. (BNP)	268	0.5%
C majority	11 716	23.8%
Total vote 49 236	Turnout 72.4%	

Mr Timothy Eggar was a member of the Select Committee on the Treasury and Civil Service 1979–82. Elected in 1979. Merchant banker. Born Dec 19 1951; educ. Winchester college, and Magdalene College, Cambridge. Chairman, Cambridge University Conservative Assoc. 1972. Vice-chairman, Federation of Conservative Students 1973–74. Personal assistant to Mr William Whitelaw in Oct 1974 general election. Secretary, Conservative backbench committee on finance 1980–82. PPS to Mr Timothy Raison, Minister for Overseas Development.

Mr Brian Grayson, printing sales representative. Member, Enfield Borough Council 1962–64; London Borough of Enfield 1964–68 and 1971–78. Born Jun 23 1938; educ. Bush Hill Park Secondary Modern School, Enfield. ASTMS.

Mr James Daly, senior lecturer at NE London Polytechnic. Born Oct 9 1936; educ. University of Nottingham, Co-operative College, Loughborough. Contested Maidstone, 1964; West London European election, 1979. Member, GLC, 1973–77 (chairman, Transport Committee). Former press officer, AUEW and NUT. Director, Galleon World Travel Ltd and JGA Advertising and Marketing.

Sir Anthony Berry

ENFIELD, SOUTHGATE Electorate 65 438

*Berry, Sir A. G. (C)	26 451	58.1%
Morgan, D. (L/All)	10 652	23.4%
Honeyball, Ms M. (Lab)	8 132	17.9%
Braithwaite, M. (BNP)	318	0.7%
C majority	15 799	34.7%
Total vote 45 553	Turnout 69.6%	

Sir Antony Berry, Treasurer of the Household; Comptroller, 1981–83; and Vice-Chamberlain 1979–81. Opposition whip 1975–79. Elected in 1964. Former deputy chairman, Leopold Joseph and Sons Ltd; formerly assistant editor of *The Sunday Times* and director of Kemsley Newspapers Ltd 1954–59. Born Feb 12 1925; educ Eton and Christ Church, Oxford. PPS to Mr Peter Walker 1970–74. Former vice-chairman Conservative transport industries committee. Former joint vice-chairman and joint secretary Conservative London members' committee.

Mr David Morgan, international banker and adviser to a foreign bank in the City. Born May 28 1921; educ. St Dunstan's College, Watford, and Llandovery College.

Ms Mary Honeyball. Born 1952. Political organiser, RACS.

Sir John Biggs-Davison

EPPING FOREST Electorate 66 578 1979: 66 723 minor

*Biggs-Davison, Sir J. (C)	27 373	56.5%
Pettman, M. (SDP/All)	11 995	24.8%
Bryan, Ms H. J. (Lab)	8 289	17.1%
Boenke, R. (Eco)	452	0.9%
Smith, S. (Brit Nat)	330	0.7%
C majority	15 378	31.8%
Total vote 48 439	Turnout 72.8%	

1979: Total vote 51 079 (76.6%); C 29 447 (57.6%); Lab 13 994 (27.4%); L 6 528 (12.8%); NF 1 110 (2.2%). C maj 15 453 (30.2%); swing 7.9% to C.

Sir John Biggs-Davison, an Opposition spokesman on Northern Ireland 1974–78, was elected for the seat in Feb 1974; MP for Chigwell 1955–74; contested Coventry South 1951. Member executive 1922 Committee. Author, journalist and broadcaster. Born Jun 7 1918; educ. Clifton College and Magdalene College, Oxford. Served Royal Marines and Pakistan administration. Chairman (previously vice-chairman) Conservative parliamentary Northern Ireland Committee. Former joint chairman, UK Falkland Islands parliamentary group 1977. Vice-chairman Conservative backbench foreign and Commonwealth affairs committee since 1982. IOJ.

Mr Michael Pettman, partner in London firm of solicitors associated with an American law firm specialising in international corporate and commercial law. Born 1950; educ. Gravesend Grammar School and Magdalene College, Oxford. Elected to Epping Forest Council as a Labour candidate in 1979, re-elected 1980 and joined SDP as sole party member until May 1982.

Ms Hilary Bryan has been a member of Essex County Council since 1981. Born Apr 25 1956; educ. Essex University. President, NUS. A clerk; former Labour Party agent in Braintree. NUR since 1980. Formerly ASTMS.

Mr Archibald Hamilton

EPSOM AND EWELL Electorate 70 630

*Hamilton, A. (C)	30 737	60.4%
Anderson, M. (L/All)	13 542	26.6%
Carpenter, W. R. (Lab)	6 587	13.0%
C majority	17 195	33.8%
Total vote 50 866		Turnout 72.0%

Mr Archibald Hamilton, an assistant Government whip since 1982, became MP at the by-election in Apr 1978; contested Dagenham, Feb and Oct 1974. Farmer. Born 30 Dec 1941; educ. Eton. Member, Council of Royal Borough of Kensington and Chelsea 1968–71. PPS to Secretary of State for Energy 1979–81 and Secretary of State for Transport 1981–82.

Mr Michael Anderson, personnel adviser with Shell UK Ltd; contested Epsom and Ewell 1978 by-election and 1979. Born Sep 4 1930; educ. Perse School, Cambridge, and Emmanuel College, Cambridge. Member, Mid Surrey District Health Authority; Governor, Epsom High School.

Mr William Carpenter has retired as education officer with Surrey County Council. Born Sep 4 1916. Member, Epsom and Ewell Council since 1967, mayor 1982–83, deputy mayor 1983–84. Member, Epsom Protection Society; Nonsuch Antiquarian Society. Former member, Fabians. Nalgo, former member of the executive.

Mr Peter Rost

EREWASH Electorate 73 355

*Rost, P. L. (C)	25 167	45.3%
Moore, W. (Lab)	13 848	25.0%
Corbett, J. (SDP/All)	12 331	22.2%
Camm, W. G. (Ind Lab)	4 158	7.5%
C majority	11 319	20.4%
Total vote 55 504		Turnout 75.7%

Mr Peter Rost, former stockbroker, was elected in 1983; MP for Derbyshire North-East 1970–83; contested Sunderland North 1966. Born Sep 19 1930; educ. Aylesbury Grammar School and Birmingham University. Former teacher and financial journalist. Joint secretary, Conservative parliamentary committee on trade 1972–74 joint secretary, energy committee 1974–77. Member, Select Committee on Energy since 1979. Treasurer. Anglo-German Parliamentary Group since 1974. Grand Cross, Order of Merit, Germany, 1979. FRGS (member of council since 1980). Company director, investment adviser and energy consultant.

Mr William Moore, an unemployed polytechnic lecturer; contested West Derbyshire 1979. Born Aug 1933; educ. Birmingham College of Commerce and Sheffield University. Member, Derbyshire County Council. ATTI.

Mr James Corbett. Born 1952; educ. grammar school, Exeter University. Practises law in Nottingham. Leicester University tutor specialising in EEC law, 1975–77.

Mr David Evennett

ERITH AND CRAYFORD Electorate 56 066

Evennett, D. (C)	15 289	37.1%
*Wellbeloved, A. J. (SDP/All)	14 369	34.9%
Smart, M. G. (Lab)	11 260	27.3%
Hawke, O. (BNP)	272	9.7%
C majority	920	2.2%
Total vote 41 190		Turnout 73.5%

Mr David Evennett, Lloyds underwriter, was elected in 1983. Born Jun 3 1949; educ. Buckhurst Hill County High School and LSE. Contested Hackney South and Shoreditch 1979. Member, Redbridge Borough Council, 1974–78.

Mr James Wellbeloved, was elected for Labour in this seat in the 1965 by-election. Resigned from party and joined SDP in 1981, became spokesman on parliamentary affairs. Under Secretary of State for Defence for the RAF, 1976–79. Commercial consultant. Born Jul 19 1926; educ. elementary school and South East London Technical College Member, Erith Borough Council 1956–65. Former vice-chairman, PLP Defence and Services Group. Former leader of the Council of the London borough of Bexley. Opposition whip 1972–73. Chairman, London parliamentary group of camping and caravanning group. Former joint vice-chairman, Manifesto Group. TGWU.

Mr Malcolm Smart, executive secretary. Born Feb 4 1943; educ. state schools and London College of Divinity. Church of England vicar at Greenford until adopted as candidate in May 1982. ASTMS.

Mr Carol Mather

ESHER Electorate 61 745

*Mather, D. C. (C)	28 577	63.3%
Wheatley, C. (L/All)	12 665	28.1%
Plaskow, Ms D. (Lab)	3 250	7.2%
Wellie, W. (LS)	664	1.5%
C majority	15 912	35.2%
Total vote 45 156		Turnout 73.1%

Mr Carol Mather was appointed Comptroller of the Household in Feb 1983; Lord Commissioner of the Treasury 1979–81; Vice-Chamberlain of the Household 1981–83. Elected in 1970. An Opposition whip 1975–79. Member, Conservative Research Department 1962–70. Contested Leicester North-West 1966. Born Jan 3 1919; educ. Harrow and Trinity College, Cambridge. Member of Lloyd's Joint secretary, Conservative home affairs committee 1974–76 and of Foreign and Commonwealth Affairs committee 1972–74. Joint vice-chairman, Northern Ireland Committee 1974–76, joint secretary 1972–74. Served with the Welsh Guards 1940–62, and was a liaison officer to General Montgomery in the Western Desert campaign, the Normandy landings and the advance into Europe.

Mr Colin Wheatley, trainee solicitor. Born Oct 5 1940; educ. Cranleigh School and College of Law, Guildford. Member, Elmbridge Borough Council since 1976.

Ms Daphne Plaskow, radio journalist. Born May 6 1936; educ. Royal Free Hospital, London and London University. Member, Elmbridge Borough Council since 1974.

Mr John Hannam

EXETER Electorate 73 441 1979: 68 825 same

*Hannam, J. (C)	26 660	46.5%
Mennell, S. (SDP/All)	16 780	29.3%
Evans, R. (Lab)	13 085	22.8%
Frings, P. (Eco)	779	1.4%
C majority	9 880	17.2%
Total vote 57 304		Turnout 78.0%

1979: Total vote 56 128 (81.6%); C 27 173 (48.4%); Lab 19 146 (34.1%); L 8 756 (15.6%); Eco 1 053 (1.9%). C maj 8 027 (14.3%); swing 5.0% to C.

Mr John Hannam, secretary of the all-party disablement group, won the seat in 1970. Parliamentary adviser to Pharmaceutical Society of Great Britain; non-executive company director. Born Aug 2 1929; educ. Yeovil Grammar School. President, British Motels Federation 1964–80. Chairman, Conservative energy committee since 1979; vice-chairman, arts and heritage committee 1974–79. Chairman Bow Group Standing Committee on Arts and Leisure since 1977. Vice-chairman of British Branch of Rehabilitation International. Member of Council of Action Research for the Crippled Child. Somerset county councillor 1967–69. Captain, Lords and Commons tennis club since 1975; ski club 1977–81. Member, Glyndebourne Festival Opera society. Board of National Theatre.

Mr Stephen Mennell, senior lecturer in sociology, Exeter University. Born May 1 1944; educ. Huddersfield New College, St Catharine's College, Cambridge, and Harvard University.

Mr Richard Evans, self-employed marquee hirer and caterer, contested St Ives 1979. Born Aug 12 1945; educ. in Canada. Chairman, SW Regional TUC/Labour Party Liaison Committee. Member, Labour Party Regional Executive Committee.

Mr Harry Ewing

FALKIRK EAST Electorate 52 045

*Ewing, H. (Lab)	17 956	47.7%
Masterton, D. (C)	7 895	21.0%
Wedderburn, A. (SDP/All)	6 967	18.5%
MacGregor, J. (SNP)	4 490	11.9%
McGregor, Miss F. (Com)	344	0.9%
Lab majority	10 061	26.7%
Total vote 37 652		Turnout 72.3%

Mr Harry Ewing, an Opposition spokesman on Scotland since 1979, was an Under-Secretary of State for Scotland with responsibility for devolution and home affairs, 1974–79. Elected in 1983; represented Stirling, Falkirk and Grangemouth Feb 1974–83; MP for Stirling and Falkirk 1971–74. Post Office worker. Born Jan 20 1931; educ. Beath High School, Cowdenbeath. Fought Fife East 1970.

Mr Donald Masterton, marine engineer, contested Glasgow Provan, 1970. Member, Strathclyde Regional Council. Born Sep 1934; educ. Renfrew High School, Oakshaw Technical College and Paisley Technical College.

Mr Alexander Wedderburn, senior lecturer in psychology, Department of Business Organization at Heriot Watt University. Labour Party member 1951–81. Born 1935; educ. Exeter College, Oxford.

Mr John MacGregor, self-employed, promoting travel in Scotland. Born 1941; educ. Inverness. Assistant National Secretary of SNP. Worked 20 years in National Health Service.

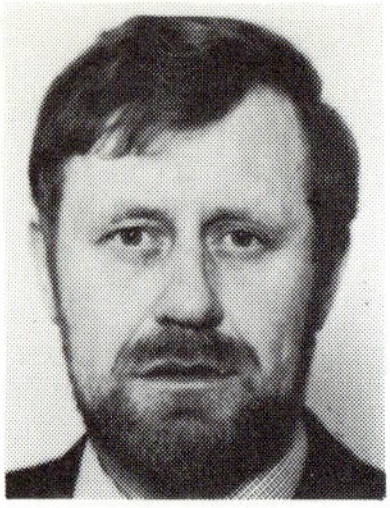
Mr Dennis Canavan

FALKIRK WEST Electorate 49 402

*Canavan, D. (Lab)	16 668	45.6%
Mitchell, I. (C)	7 690	21.0%
Harris, M. (L/All)	7 477	20.4%
Cochrane, B. (SNP)	4 739	13.0%
Lab majority	8 978	24.6%
Total vote 36 574	Turnout	74.0%

Mr Dennis Canavan, elected for West Stirlingshire Oct 1974 and for this seat in 1983. Chairman, Scottish parliamentary labour group 1980–81. Convenor of group's education subcommittee since 1976, and parliamentary spokesman for Scottish committee on mobility for the disabled since 1977. Member Select Committee on Foreign Affairs since 1982. Former Assistant headmaster. Leader of Labour Group, Sitrling District Council 1974. Born Aug 8 1942; educ. St Columba's High School, Cowdenbeath and Edinburgh University. NUPE; EIS.

Mr Iain Mitchell, vice-chairman, Edinburgh West Conservative Association. Born 1951; educ. Perth Academy and Edinburgh University. Advocate, part-time tutor in mercantile law at Edinburgh University, writer and partner in firm of dyers and cleaners. Member, Faculty of Advocates Standing Committee on European Affairs, Scotland in Europe, European Movement and Lothians Euro-Constituency Council.

Mr Marshall Harris, Scottish national officer and secretary of the Scottish National Council, United Nations Assoc. Born 1929; educ. Armadale Secondary School, Edinburgh and Glasgow universities. Former president, Hillhead Liberal Assoc. Member, international committee, Scottish Liberal Party, and working group on international affairs. Contested Glasgow, Hillhead 1979.

Mr Brian Cochrane, employed in sales and marketing. Born 1941; educ. Morpeth College. Member, children's panel, SNP.

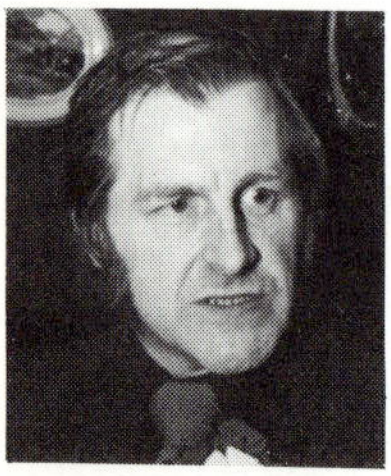
Mr David Mudd

FALMOUTH AND CAMBORNE Electorate 65 624

*Mudd, W. D. (C)	24 614	50.0%
Fieldsend, D. (SDP/All)	13 589	27.6%
Bunt, A. (Lab)	10 446	21.2%
Jenkin, R. (MK)	582	1.2%
C majority	11 025	22.4%
Total vote 49 231	Turnout	75.0%

Mr David Mudd, a member of the Unopposed Bills Panel since 1981; Transport Select Committee since 1982; secretary of the Fisheries subcommittee of the Conservative backbench Agricultural and Fisheries Committee. Won the seat in 1970. Freelance journalist, broadcaster and author. PPS to Minister of State for Energy 1979–81. Parliamentary consultant to the National Federation of Fruit and Potato Trades Ltd and to the National Federation of Site Operators. Born Jun 2 1933; educ. Truro Cathedral School; Member, Tavistock Urban Council 1959–61. Secretary, West Country Group of Conservative MPs 1973–76. NUJ.

Mr David Fieldsend, freelance town and country planning consultant. Born Oct 15 1950; educ. The Leys School, Cambridge; Newcastle University; Trinity Theological College, Bristol. Senior planning assistant, Somerset County Council 1975–81. Member, RTPI and IAAS.

Mr Anthony Bunt, postman. Born Sep 12 1948; educ. Redruth Grammar School, St Luke's College of Education, Exeter, and Queen Elizabeth College, London University. Former Kerrier district councillor and Cornwall county councillor. UCW.

Mr Peter Lloyd

FAREHAM Electorate 71 901

Lloyd, P. (C)	32 762	61.8%
Yolland, S. (L/All)	16 446	31.0%
Sommerville, D. (Lab)	3 808	7.2%
C majority	16 316	30.8%
Total vote 53 016	Turnout	73.7%

Mr Peter Lloyd, former marketing manager of United Biscuits Ltd, was elected May 1979; contested Nottingham, West, Feb and Oct 1974. Born Nov 12 1937; educ. Tonbridge School and Pembroke College, Cambridge. Chairman, Bow Group 1972–73, research secretary 1970–72, and editor of *Crossbow* until 1976. Vice-chairman, Conservative European Affairs Committee 1980–82; Secretary, Conservative Employer Committee 1979–81; Member, Select Committee for Employment 1983. PPS to Minister of State for Northern Ireland 1982–83. Member of Lloyd's.

Mr Stephen Yolland, computer systems adviser. Born Jun 18 1957; educ. Lord Wandsworth College, Long Sutton, and University of Southampton.

Mr Dennis Somerville, royalty accountant, contested Aldershot, 1979. Born May 1930; educ. North Paddington Central School and Paddington Technical College. Rushmoor councillor 1974–76. Secretary, Racial Unity Movement. ASTMS, Co-operative Party.

Mr Roger Moate

FAVERSHAM Electorate 76 467

*Moate, R. (C)	29 849	53.1%
Goyder, M. (SDP/All)	15 252	27.1%
Bromley, C. M. (Lab)	11 130	19.8%
C majority	14 597	26.0%
Total vote 56 231		Turnout 73.5%

Mr Roger Moate, insurance broker, won the seat in 1970; contested it in 1966. Member, Statutory Instruments Committee. Joint vice-chairman, Conservative transport committee. Director of Alexander Howden Insurance Brokers Ltd. Born May 12 1938; educ. Latymer Upper School, Hammersmith. Vice-chairman, Greater London area Young Conservatives 1964–66. Hon secretary, British-American parliamentary group.

Mr Edward Goyder, distribution manager and author. Born Jun 11 1953; educ. Rugby School and Trinity College, Cambridge.

Mr Christopher Bromley, divisional director, Greater London Enterprise Board. Born Jul 7 1943; educ. Felsted School, University College, London. Councillor, London Borough of Islington; chairman of development and planning committee 1982; deputy chairman of housing committee since May 1983. ASTMS.

Mr Patrick Ground

FELTHAM AND HESTON Electorate 78 366 1979: 79 873 same

Ground, P. (C)	23 724	43.4%
*Kerr, R. W. (Lab)	21 576	39.4%
Alagappa, A. (L/All)	8 706	15.9%
Glass, S. (NF)	696	1.3%
C majority	2 148	3.9%
Total vote 54 702		Turnout 69.8%

C gain from Lab

1979: Total vote 59 362 (74.3%); Lab 28 675 (48.3%); C 24 570 (41.4%); L 5 051 (8.5%); NF 898 (1.5%); WRP 168 (0.3%). Lab maj 4 105 (6.9%); swing 5.0% to C.

Mr Patrick Ground, Q.C., won the seat in 1983; contested Hounslow, Feltham and Heston in both 1974 elections and in 1979. Born Aug 9 1932; educ. Beckenham and Penge County Grammar School, Lycee Guy Lussac, Limoges, Selwyn College, Cambridge and Magdalen College, Oxford. President, Oxford University Conservative Assoc. 1958. Member, Hammersmith Borough Council 1968–71. Chairman of the Fulham Society.

Mr Russell Kerr, an air charter executive, was a member of the Select Committee on Industry and Trade 1979–83. Returned for the seat in Feb 1974; MP for Feltham 1966–74; contested Horsham 1951, Merton and Morden 1959 and Preston North 1964. Chairman, Select Committee on Nationalized Industries 1974–79, vice-chairman 1970–74, member from 1967. Chairman, Tribune Group 1969–70. Sponsored by ASTMS, and member, national executive 1964–78. Born Feb 1921; educ. Shore School, Sydney, and Sydney University.

Mr Alex Alagappa, company director and solicitor. Born Jul 19 1944; educ. in Penang, Malaysia; Lincoln's Inn, and London University, College of Law. Chairman, Ruislip-Northwood constituency Liberal Association, 1981–83. IPCS.

Mr Kenneth Maginnis

FERMANAGH AND SOUTH TYRONE Electorate 67 880

Maginnis, K. (OUP)	28 630	47.6%
Carron, O. (PSF)	20 954	34.8%
Flanagan, Mrs R. (SDLP)	9 923	16.5%
Kettyles, D. (WP)	649	1.1%
OUP majority	7 676	12.8%
Total vote 60 156		Turnout 88.6%

Mr Kenneth Maginnis, a teacher, won the seat in 1983; contested it in the 1981 by-election. Aged 45; educ. Royal School, Dungannon, Co Tyrone, Stranmillis College of Further Education, Belfast. Member, Dungannon district council since 1982; Northern Ireland Assembly since 1982, being chairman of security committee, vice-chairman, finance and personnel committee. Party spokesman on security.

Mr Owen Carron, an Anti-H Block candidate, won by-election in Aug 1981, following the death of Mr Robert Sands on H Block hunger strike one month after his election as MP to succeed Mr Frank Maguire who had held the seat since Oct 1974. Up to the time of the general election, Mr Carron had not taken his seat.

Mr William Hamilton

FIFE CENTRAL Electorate 54 389

*Hamilton, W. W. (Lab)	17 008	43.1%
Little, Mrs T. (L/All)	9 214	23.4%
Mason, D. (C)	8 863	22.5%
Taggart, J. (SNP)	4 039	10.3%
Allison, D. (Eco)	297	0.8%
Lab majority	7 794	19.8%
Total vote 39 421	Turnout	72.5%

Mr William Hamilton was returned in Feb 1974; MP for West Fife 1950–74; contested that seat in 1945. Teacher. Born Jun 26 1917; educ. Washington Grammar School, County Durham, and Sheffield University. Member, Select Committees on Procedure (Finance) from 1982, Public Accounts from 1979. Chairman Estimates Committee 1964–70. Vice-chairman, Parliamentary Labour Party 1966–70. Member, European Parliament 1975–79. Chairman, Scottish PLP group on health and social services. NUT. Sponsored by Cohse.

Mrs Teresa Little, former teacher, was elected to Fife Regional Council, 1982. Born 1949; educ. St Joseph's Convent, Girvan and Edinburgh University.

Mr Douglas Mason, freelance journalist. Born 1941; educ. Bradford Grammar School and St Andrew's University.

Mr James Taggart, market manager with the Scottish Milk Marketing Board. Born 1943; educ. St Mungo's Academy and Glasgow and Strathclyde universities.

Mr Barry Henderson

FIFE NORTH EAST Electorate 50 476

*Henderson, J. S. B. (C)	17 129	46.1%
Campbell, M. (L/All)	14 944	40.2%
Hulbert, Dr J. K. M. (SNP)	2 442	6.6%
Caldwell, D. (Lab)	2 429	6.5%
Flinn, T. G. (Eco)	242	0.6%
C majority	2 185	5.9%
Total vote 37 186	Turnout	73.7%

Mr Barry Henderson, management and systems consultant, was elected for Fife East in 1979; MP for East Dumbartonshire Feb to Oct 1974; contested that seat in 1970, and Edinburgh East 1966. Born Apr 29 1936; educ. Lathallan School and Stowe. Member, Commons Chairman's Panel since 1981; Select Committee for Scottish Affairs since 1979. Vice-chairman, Scottish Conservative backbench committee since 1979. Member, Council of the Parliamentary Information Technology Comm. since 1980.

Mr Menzies Campbell, QC., contested Greenock and Port Glasgow Feb and Oct 1974, and East Fife 1979. Born May 22 1941; educ. Hillhead High School, Glasgow; Glasgow University and Stanford University, California.

Dr John Hulbert, general practitioner, contested West Aberdeenshire 1979. Born March 1939; educ. Madras College and the universities of St Andrew's and Edinburgh.

Mr David Caldwell, university administrator. Born Feb 25 1944; educ. George Watson's College, St Andrew's University, Glasgow University.

Mrs Margaret Thatcher

FINCHLEY Electorate 55 638 1979: 55 468 same

*Thatcher, Mrs M. H. (C)	19 616	51.1%
Spigel, L. G. (Lab)	10 302	26.8%
Joachim, Dr M. (L/All)	7 763	20.2%
Wilkinson, Ms S. (WFLOE)	279	0.7%
Sutch, D. (Loony Soc)	235	0.6%
Noonan, A. J. (BELLS)	75	0.2%
Anscomb, Miss H. (Ind)	42	0.1%
Whitehead, A. P. (LAO)	37	0.1%
Webb, D. A. (Anti-Cen)	28	0.1%
Wareham, B. C. (PAL)	27	0.1%
Wedmore, B. (Belgrano)	13	0.0%
C majority	9 314	24.2%
Total vote 38 417	Turnout	69.1%

1979: Total vote 39 832 (71.8%); C 20 918 (52.5%); Lab 13 040 (32.7%); L 5 254 (13.2%); NF 534 (1.3%); other 86 (0.2%). C mag 7 878 (19.8%); swing 4.7% to C.

Mrs Margaret Thatcher, the first woman Prime Minister. took office on May 4 1979. She was elected as Leader of the Conservative Party and Leader of the Opposition in Feb 1975. Member of the shadow Cabinet and chief Opposition spokesman on the environment 1974–75; Secretary of State for Education and Science 1970–74. Chief Opposition spokesman on education 1969–70; previously spokesman on transport, power, Treasury matters, housing, and pensions, Member, Shadow Cabinet 1967–70. Returned for Finchley in 1959; contested Dartford in 1950 and 1951. Parliamentary Secretary, Ministry of Pensions and National Insurance 1961–64. Barrister and formerly a research chemist. Born Oct 1925; educ. Grantham High School and Somerville College, Oxford.

Mr Laurence Spigel, social worker. Born Aug. 11 1952; educ. Christ's College, Finchley, and UMIST. Member, London Borough of Barnet Council since 1982.

Dr Margaret Joachim, computer consultant, contested West Gloucestershire 1979. Born Jun 25 1949; educ. Brighton and Hove High School; St Hugh's College, Oxford; West Midlands College of Education, Walsall, and Birmingham University.

Mr Michael Howard

FOLKESTONE AND HYTHE Electorate 67 802 1979: 66 297 same

Howard, M. (C)	27 261	57.0%
MacDonald, J. (L/All)	15 591	32.6%
Lawrie, L. (Lab)	4 700	9.8%
Todd, P. A. (Ind)	318	0.7%
C majority	11 670	24.4%
Total vote 47 870	Turnout	70.6%

1979: Total vote 48 147 (72.6%); C 26 837 (55.7%); L 10 817 (22.5%); Lab 10 015 (20.8%); NF 478 (1.0%). C maj 16 020 (33.2%); swing 7.2% to C.

Mr Michael Howard, QC, specialising in employment law and town and county planning. Contested Liverpool, Edge Hill 1966 and 1970. Born Jul 7 1941; educ. Llanelli Grammar School and Peterhouse, Cambridge. (President of the Union, 1962). Chairman, Bow Group, 1970–71; chairman, Coningsby Club, 1972–72; member, committee Conservative Group of Europe and executive committee of European Movement, 1970–73.

Mr John Macdonald, QC, human rights lawyer. Appeared for the Banabans of Ocean Island and defended Yuri Orlov, chairman of Moscow Helsinki group; represented Canadian Indians against UK Gov. Born Sep 26 1931; educ. St Edward's School, Oxford, and Queens' College, Cambridge.

Mr Leslie Lawrie, teacher. Born Dec 15 1947; educ. Ashford Grammar School and Borough Road College, Isleworth. Member, Ashford Borough Council since 1976.

Mr John Hume

FOYLE Electorate 67 432

Hume, J. (SDLP)	24 071	46.0%
Campbell, G. (DUP)	15 923	30.5%
McGuiness, M. (PSF)	10 607	20.3%
O'Grady, G. (All)	1 108	2.1%
Melaugh, E. (WP)	582	1.1%
SDLP majority	8 184	15.6%
Total vote 52 291	Turnout	77.6%

Mr John Hume a former teacher, won the seat in 1983. Aged 46, educ. St Columb's College Londonderry, national University of Ireland. Associate Fellow, Centre for International Affairs Harvard 1976. Research fellow in European studies Trinity College Dublin 1976–77. Member, European Parliament since 1979. Returned as independent MP for Foyle in the 1969 election to Stormont. Founder member, SDLP; deputy leader 1970–79; leader since 1979. Elected, Northern Ireland Assembly 1973, Convention 1975, and Assembly 1982. Contested Londonderry Oct 1974. Minister for Commerce in Northern Ireland power sharing executive Jan to May 1974.

Mr Martin Stevens

FULHAM Electorate 51 833 1979: 57 018 same

*Stevens, M. (C)	18 204	46.2%
Powell, A. (Lab)	13 415	34.0%
Rendel, D. (L/All)	7 194	18.3%
Grimes, Ms J. (Eco)	277	0.7%
Pearce, R. (NF)	229	0.6%
Keats, J. (Ind L)	102	0.3%
C majority	4 789	12.2%
Total vote 39 421	Turnout	76.1%

1979: Total vote 43,380 (76.1%); C 20 249 (46.7%); Lab 18 750 (43.2%); L 3 882 (8.9%); NF 499 (1.2%). C maj 1 499 (3.5%); swing 8.2% to C. C gain from Lab.

Mr Martin Stevens, a partner in a marketing consultancy group, gained the seat for the Conservatives in 1979. Contested the seat in both 1974 elections and Dulwich 1966 and 1964. Joint secretary, Greater London Conservative MPs since 1981. Member, Select Committee on Members' Salaries since 1982 and Select Committee on Industry and Trade since 1981. Chairman, All Party Committee for Lead-Free Air. Born Jul 31 1929; educ. Bradfield and Trinity College, Oxford. Member LCC (Dulwich) 1955–58; Camberwell Borough Council 1959–65. Member, National Appeals Committee, Cancer Research Campaign since 1956 (chairman 1968). APEX. Parliamentary consultant to British Gas Corporation; F. W. Woolworth; Society of Company and Commercial Accountants; National Assoc. of Probation Officers.

Mr Anthony Powell, senior legal executive for London Borough of Southwark; Hammersmith councillor since 1971 and leader of opposition 1978–82. Member, ILEA. Born Jan 29 1939; educ. grammar school.

Mr David Rendel, business analyst, contested Hammersmith, Fulham 1979. Born Apr 15 1949; educ. Eton, Magdalen College, Oxford and St Cross College, Oxford.

Sir Edward Gardner

FYLDE Electorate 62 238

*Gardner, Sir E. (C)	27 879	62.9%
Smith, Mrs E. A. (L/All)	10 777	24.3%
King, D. J. (Lab)	4 821	10.9%
Fowler, H. (Ind)	863	2.0%
C majority	17 102	38.6%
Total vote 44 340	Turnout	71.2%

Sir Edward Gardner, QC, a crown court recorder, elected in 1983, represented Fylde South from 1970–83; MP for Billericay 1959–66; contested Erith and Crayford in 1955. Called to the Bar (Gray's Inn) in 1947, admitted to the Nigerian and British Guianan Bars 1962, and became a Master of the Bench of Gray's Inn in 1968. Born May 10 1912; educ. Hutton Grammar School. Committee Chairman, Society of Conservative Lawyers 1975 (chairman, executive committee, since 1969). Steward, British Boxing Board of Control since 1975. Chairman, Conservative backbench home affairs committee since 1982. Governor of Thomas Coram Foundation for Children since 1962. Commonwealth War Graves Commission since 1971. Chairman, Conservative Study Group on British Nationality Law 1978–80.

Mrs Anne Smith is a civil servant. Born Mar 30 1929; educ. Layton Hill Convent, Blackpool. Member, Lancashire County Council since 1982, leader of the Liberal group; Fylde Borough Council since 1979.

Mr David King, wine consultant. Born Aug 11 1944; educ. Holmer Green County Secondary School, Slough Polytechnic, Polytechnic of the South Bank, Open University. USDAW.

Mr Edward Leigh

GAINSBOROUGH AND HORNCASTLE Electorate 67 115

Leigh, E. (C)	25 625	50.9%
Phillips, A. (L/All)	20 558	40.8%
James, C. (Lab)	3 886	7.7%
Dixon, G. (Eco)	279	0.6%
C majority	5 067	10.1%
Total vote 50 348	Turnout	75.0%

Mr Edward Leigh, barrister, elected in 1983, is chairman of the National Council for Civil Defence and director of the Coalition for Peace through Security. Born 1950; educ. Durham University. Former president of Durham Union Society and chairman of Durham University Conservative Association. Member of Richmond Borough Council and GLC, 1974–81. Member, Conservative Research Department 1973–75. Member of Mrs Thatcher's private office in charge of correspondence 1976–77.

Mr Andrew Phillips, solicitor, contested Harwich 1970, for Labour; Saffron Walden by-election 1977, and general election 1979 for Liberals; also fought North East Essex election for European Parliament 1979. Born Mar 15 1939; educ. Culford and Uppingham schools. Non-executive chairman of small hotel group.

Mr Carl James, a lecturer working in local government in Leeds, contested Lincolnshire in the 1979 European elections. Aged 34. Formerly a principal local government officer in Tower Hamlets.

Mr Ian Lang

GALLOWAY AND UPPER NITHSDALE Electorate 51 831

*Lang, I. (C)	17 579	44.7%
Thompson, G. (SNP)	12 118	30.8%
Douglas, G. (L/All)	5 129	13.1%
Miller, M. B. (Lab)	4 464	11.4%
C majority	5 461	13.9%
Total vote 39 290	Turnout	75.8%

Mr Ian Lang, a Lord Commissioner of the Treasury (Government whip) from 1983 and assistant Government whip 1981–83, was elected for this seat in Jun 1983. MP for Galloway 1979–83, a gain from SNP; contested Central Ayrshire 1970, and Glasgow, Pollok Feb 1974. Born Jun 1940; educ. Rugby and Sidney Sussex College, Cambridge. Member, Select Committee on Scottish Affairs, 1979–81. Hon-President, Scottish Young Conservatives, 1982.

Mr George Thompson, teacher at Annan Academy, gained Galloway for the SNP in Oct 1974 and held it until 1979; was spokesman on home affairs and on health. Born Sep 1928; educ. Kirkcudbright Academy and Edinburgh University. Former SNP assistant secretary.

Mr Gerald Douglas, secretary of a council of social service. Born Nov 16 1925; educ. Dalbeattie High School and Dumfries Academy.

Dr Barry Miller, teacher. Born Sep 15 1947; educ. Garlieston Primary School, Douglas Ewart High School, Newton Stewart, and Edinburgh University. EIS.

Mr Bernard Conlan

GATESHEAD EAST Electorate 68 364

*Conlan, B. (Lab)	22 981	48.3%
Rogers, F. (C)	12 659	26.6%
Nunn, P. (SDP/All)	11 920	25.1%
Lab majority	10 322	21.7%
Total vote 47 560		Turnout 69.6%

Mr Bernard Conlan was elected in 1964. Contested High Peak in 1959. Engineer and export sales adviser. Born Oct 24 1923; educ. Manchester secondary school. Member, Select Committee on Expenditure 1971–79; Select Committee on Defence since 1970; and unopposed Bills panel since 1981. Member, Select Committee on Standing Orders since 1981. Member, Manchester City Council 1954–66. Official, Amalgamated Engineering Union 1944–66, and sponsored by AUEW. Former joint vice-chairman, PLP trade union group.

Mr Frank Rogers, teacher. Born Apr 1928; educ. Gateshead Grammar School, Oriel College, Oxford and Durham University. Member, Gateshead Borough Council 1952–65, and North Tyneside Metropolitan Borough Council since 1975. Contested Gateshead East 1979.

Mr Paul Nunn, journalist. Born Aug 28 1948; educ. Woodhouse Grove School, Bradford and Bristol University. Former secretary, policy committee, Gateshead SDP. Member, Council for Social Democracy; national economic policy committee. Chairman, Whickham Residents Assoc. NUJ.

Sir Philip Holland

GEDLING Electorate 66 656

* Holland, Sir P. W. (C)	27 207	54.1%
Berkeley, A. (SDP / All)	12 543	25.0%
Peck, J. (Lab)	10 330	20.6%
Szatter, J. (Ind)	186	0.4%
C majority	14 664	29.2%
Total vote 50 266		Turnout 75.4%

Sir Philip Holland, an employee relations adviser, was elected for this seat in 1983; MP for Carlton, 1966–83; MP for Acton 1959–64; contested Birmingham, Yardley 1955. Born Mar 14 1917; educ. Sir John Deane's Grammar School, Northwich. Chairman, Commons Selection Committee since 1979; vice-chairman, Conservative parliamentary labour committee 1970; member, Public Accounts Committee, 1966–70; president, Conservative trade union national advisory committee, 1971–73; member, Kensington Borough Council, 1955–59.

Mr Adrian Berkeley, freelance photographer and journalist, was member, Nottinghamshire County Council 1977–81. Born 1948; educ. Nottingham University, reading law. Served in photographic intelligence, RAF, 1964–74; intelligence and counter-intelligence in the Army 1974–76. Worked for CBI in East Midlands 1978–81. Member, Council of Nottingham University since 1977.

Mr John Peck, primary school teacher. Born Sep 10 1948; educ. County High School, Arnold, Nottingham, and Cambridge Grammar School. Author of Nottinghamshire County Council education policy manifesto. School governor. NUT.

Mr James Couchman

GILLINGHAM Electorate 69 256 1979: 63 951 minor

Couchman, J. R. (C)	26 381	51.7%
Lewcock, C. (L/All)	15 538	30.5%
West, A. S. (Lab)	9 084	17.8%
C majority	10 843	21.3%
Total vote 51 003		Turnout 73.6%

1979: Total vote 50 423 (78.8%); C 26 791 (53;1%); Lab 16 292 (32.3%); L 6219 (12.3%); NF 528 (1.0%); ECO 501 (1.0%); WRP 92 (0.2%). C maj 10 499 (20.8%); swing 6.1%.

Mr James Couchman, director of a licensed trade company was elected in 1983. Born Feb 11 1942; educ. Cranleigh School, Surrey and King's College, Newcastle upon Tyne. Contested Chester-le-Street, 1979. Councillor, London Borough of Bexley 1974–82; chairman of social services 1975–78 and 1980–82. Chairman, Bexley Health Authority 1981–83. Director of Chiswick Caterers Ltd. Freeman of City of London and Vintner. NULV.

Mr Christopher Lewcock, local government town planner, contested Havering, Hornchurch 1979. Born Jun 6 1953; educ. Woodroffe School, Lyme Regis; Churcher's College, Petersfield; St George's School, Hong Kong, and Lanchester Polytechnic, Coventry. Member, Kent County Council since 1981. Member, Kent Family Practitioner Panel 1980–82; secretary, Kent branch of the Conservation Society 1978–80; board member, Medway Towns Young Unemployed project.

Mr Anthony West, train driver, and London Borough of Bexley councillor 1975–83. Born June 26 1940; educ. St Bonaventures RC School, Forest Gate. Sponsored by Aslef.

Mr Richard Hickmet

GLANFORD AND SCUNTHORPE Electorate 71 962

Hickmet, R. (C)	20 356	38.5%
Ellis, J. (Lab)	19 719	37.3%
Nottingham, C. (SDP/All)	12 821	24.2%
C majority	637	1.2%
Total vote 52 896		Turnout 73.5%

Mr Richard Hickmet, barrister and company secretary of family hotel group, won this seat in 1983. Chairman, leisure and amenities committee, Wandsworth Borough council; member since 1978. School governor. Trustee and member, management committee, Battersea Arts Centre. Born Dec 1 1947; educ. Millfield School; the Sorbonne; Hull University.

Mr John Ellis, steelworker, was MP for Bristol North-West 1966–70 and Brigg and Scunthorpe 1974–79. An assistant Government whip 1974–76. PPS to the late Mr Stephen Swingler at Ministry of Transport, and was member, Select Committee on Nationalized Industries. Born Oct 22 1930; educ. Doncaster Grammar School and Rastrick Grammar School. ISTC, sponsored by TGWU.

Mr Cyril Nottingham, a self-employed master butcher, contested Brigg and Scunthorpe 1979. Member, Scunthorpe Borough Council since 1966.

Mr John Maxton

GLASGOW, CATHCART Electorate 51 055

*Maxton, J. (Lab)	16 037	41.4%
May, D. (C)	11 807	30.5%
Bloomer, K. (SDP/All)	8 710	22.5%
Steven, W. (SNP)	2 151	5.6%
Lab majority	4 230	10.9%
Total vote 38 705		Turnout 75.8%

Mr John Maxton, gained the seat for Labour in 1979. Lecturer in social studies at Hamilton College of Education; national chairman, Assoc. of Lecturers in Colleges of Education, Scotland. Member of Educational Institute of Scotland and Socialist Educational Assoc. Member, Select Committee on Scottish Affairs, 1979–82. Born May 5 1936; educ. Lord William's Grammar School, Thame and Oxford University.

Mr Douglas May, advocate, was chairman of Edinburgh South Conservative Assoc. 1977–80. Born May 1946; educ. George Heriot's School, Edinburgh, and Edinburgh University. Vice-chairman, Lothians Euro-constituency Council, 1979–81; former vice-chairman, Federation of Conservative Students, and of Scottish Young Conservatives; former president, Edinburgh University Conservatives. Contested Edinburgh East Feb 1974.

Mr Keir Bloomer, trade union official, contested Ross and Cromarty 1979, as Labour candidate. Born Jul 1 1947; educ. Greenock Academy and Cambridge University.

Mr William Steven, science technician. Born 1955; educ. Glenwood Secondary School and David Dale College, Glasgow. Has held a number of local SNP offices. Nalgo.

Mr Robert McTaggart

GLASGOW CENTRAL Electorate 51 217

*McTaggart, R. (Lab)	17 066	53.0%
Harvey, W. (C)	6 104	19.0%
Nelson, Mrs I. (L/All)	5 366	16.7%
Mallan, P. (SNP)	3 300	10.3%
McGoldrick, J. (Com)	347	1.1%
Lab Majority	10 962	34.1%
Total vote 32 183		Turnout 62.8%

Mr Robert McTaggart won the by-election in 1980. Born Nov 2 1945; educ. St Constantine's, St Bartholomew's and Holyrood. Marine plumber and trigonometrical calculator. EETPU shop steward 1971–77; Glasgow Corporation councillor 1974–75; district councillor 1977–80. Sponsored by EETPU.

Mr William Harvey, assistant manager of a building society, is chairman of the City of Glasgow Conservative Assoc. Born 1955; educ. Woodside Secondary School, Glasgow, Central College of Commerce, Glasgow, and Glasgow College of Technoloyg. Chairman, Glasgow Central Conservative Assoc. since 1978. Member, Glasgow Chamber of Commerce.

Mrs Isabel Nelson was vice-chairman of the Glasgow anti-dampness campaign for two years before resigning to take up a research assistant's post at University of Strathclyde investigating dampness-related problems in council housing. Born 1940; educ. Langside College and Glasgow University. Contested Toryglen/Rutherglen at 1982 regional election as Liberal/Alliance candidate.

Mr Peter Mallan, principal music teacher, contested Glasgow, Queen's Park by-election 1982. Born 1934; educ. Royal Academy of Music, London. Regular host of radio and television programmes. Member, Glasgow children's panel.

Mr Donald Dewar

GLASGOW, GARSCADDEN Electorate 50589 1979: 52440 minor

*Dewar, D. (Lab)	19635	56.2%
Lyden, W. (SDP/All)	6161	17.6%
Macleod, K. (C)	5368	15.4%
MacLeod, N. (SNP)	3566	10.2%
Barr, S. A. (Com)	218	0.6%
Lab majority	13474	38.6%
Total vote 34948	Turnout	69.1%

1979: Total vote 38370 (73.2%); Lab 23591 (61.5%); C 8393 (21.9%); SNP 6012 (15.7%); Com 374 (1.0%). Lab maj 15198 (39.6%); swing 0.8%.

Mr Donald Dewar has been an Opposition spokesman on Scotland since 1980; chairman, Select Committee on Scottish Affairs, 1979–81. Returned at the Apr 1978 by-election. MP for Aberdeen South 1966–70; contested the seat, 1964 and 1970. Solicitor. Born Aug 21 1937; educ. Glasgow Academy and Glasgow University (president of the Union 1961–62). PPS to President of Board of Trade, 1967. Member, Expenditure Committee 1978–79.

Mr William Lyden is a hospital engineer. Aged 53.

Mr Kenneth Macleod, former regular soldier turned businessman, contested Dunfermline Oct 1974. Born 1926; educ. Royal High School, Edinburgh and Musselburgh Grammar School.

Mr Norman MacLeod, office manager. Born 1951; educ. Jordanhill College School. Chairman, Glasgow Dist SNP.

Mr Bruce Millan

GLASGOW, GOVAN Electorate 51754

*Millan, B. (Lab)	20370	55.0%
McDonald, I. (SDP/All)	7313	19.7%
Mackenzie A. (C)	7180	19.4%
Kindlen, P. (SNP)	2207	6.0%
Lab majority	13057	35.2%
Total vote 37070	Turnout	71.6%

Mr Bruce Millan was chief Opposition spokesman on Scotland 1979–83; member shadow cabinet 1981–83. Secretary of State for Scotland 1976–79 Minister of State for Scotland, responsible for Scottish Economic Planning Department and aid for development, 1974–76. An Opposition spokesman on Scottish affairs, 1973–74, and on industry, 1970–73. Under Secretary for Scotland, 1966–70; Under Secretary of Defence for the RAF 1964–66. Elected for this seat 1983; MP for Glasgow, Craigton 1959–83; contested the seat 1955, and West Renfrewshire 1951. Chartered Accountant. Born Oct 5 1927; educ. Harris Academy, Dundee.

Mr Ian McDonald is an assistant head teacher. Aged 36.

Mr Alastair Mackenzie, a former member of Glasgow District Council, is an Elder of the Church of Scotland.

Mr Peter Kindlen, plant services manager. Educ. Morgan Academy, Dundee and Jordanhill College of Education.

Mr Roy Jenkins

GLASGOW, HILLHEAD Electorate 57016

*Jenkins, R. (SDP/All)	14856	36.2%
*Carmichael, N. (Lab)	13692	33.4%
Tosh, M. (C)	9678	23.5%
Leslie, G. (SNP)	2203	5.4%
Davidson, J. (Ind C)	249	0.6%
Whitelaw, A. (Eco)	239	0.6%
Robins, J. (AV)	139	0.3%
SDP/All majority	1164	2.8%
Total vote 41 056	Turnout	71.9%

Mr Roy Jenkins, who was elected leader of the SDP in 1982, having defeated Dr David Owen, indicated shortly after the Jun 1983 election that he would be standing down from the post. He is one of the four original leaders of the party which was formed Mar 1981, from the Council for Social Democracy, established in Jan 1981. He was returned for the seat in 1982 having failed to win Warrington in 1981. President, EEC Commission 1977–81. Deputy leader, Parliamentary Labour Party 1970–72; Home Secretary 1974–76 and 1965–67; Chancellor of the Exchequer 1967–70; Minister of Aviation 1964–65. MP for Birmingham, Stechford 1950–76 and Central Southwark 1948–50; contested Solihull 1945. Born Nov 11 1920; educ. Abersychan Grammar School; Balliol College, Oxford.

Mr Neil Carmichael, Under-Secretary, Department of Environment 1974–75, and Under-Secretary, Department of Industry 1975–76. An Opposition spokesman on Scottish affairs 1970–74. Parliamentary Secretary Ministry of Technology 1969–70, and Ministry of Transport 1967–69. MP for Glasgow Kelvingrove Feb 1974–83; MP for Glasgow Woodside 1962–74. Engineer. Born Oct 10 1921; educ. Estbank Academy and Royal College of Science and Technology, Glasgow.

Mr Murray Tosh, principal history teacher at Kilwinning Academy, contested Ayr as a Liberal candidate in Oct 1974.

Mr George Leslie, veterinary surgeon, contested the Hillhead by-election in Mar 1982. Born 1936; educ. Hillhead High School and Glasgow University.

Mr Jim Craigen

GLASGOW, MARYHILL Electorate 51 847

*Craigen, J. (Lab)	18 724	55.2%
Attwooll, Ms E. (L/All)	7 521	22.2%
Gibbs, J. (C)	5 014	14.8%
Morrison, I. (SNP)	2 408	7.1%
Smith, P. (Com)	274	0.8%
Lab majority	11 203	33.0%
Total vote 33 941		Turnout 65.5%

Mr Jim Craigen, industrial liaison officer, was elected in Feb 1974; contested Ayr 1970. Born Aug 2 1938; educ. Shawlands Academy, Glasgow; University of Strathclyde and Heriot-Watt University. PPS to Secretary of State for Scotland, 1974–76. Chairman, Scottish Labour Group of MPs 1978–79. Chairman, Co-operative Parliamentary Group 1978–79; PLP Employment Group since 1981. Member, UK delegation to Council of Europe and WEU 1976–80. Member, Select Committee on Employment, and chairman since 1982. Member, Glasgow City Council 1965–68; Secretary, all-party group on management since 1975; chairman, all-party group on housing assocs in Scotland since 1980. GMBU. Sponsored by Co-operative Party.

Ms Elspeth Attwooll, university lecturer. Born Feb 1 1943; educ. Tiffin Girls Grammar School; Queen's College, St Andrews University. Contested the seat 1979 and Oct 1974. Fought Glasgow in European Parliament election 1979. AUT.

Mr Joseph Gibbs, former antique dealer and journalist; now public relations executive. Aged 26; educ. Eton and Highbury Tech. Coll., Portsmouth.

Mr Iain Morrison, chief engineer. Born 1922; educ. Glasgow College of Marine Engineering.

Mr James White

GLASGOW, POLLOK Electorate 53 217

*White, J. (Lab)	18 973	52.3%
Carlaw, J. (C)	7 441	20.5%
McKell, G. (L/All)	6 308	17.4%
Hannigan, F. (SNP)	3 585	9.9%
Lab majority	11 532	31.8%
Total vote 36 307		Turnout 68.2%

Mr James White won the seat for Labour in 1970. Member, Select Committee on Abortion (Amendment) Bill 1975, which he sponsored. Born Apr 10 1922; educ. Knightswood Senior Secondary School. Managing director, Glasgow Car Collection Ltd. TGWU. Member, Commonwealth Parliamentary Assoc. delegation, Bangladesh 1973, and Nepal 1981.

Mr Jackson Carlaw, company manager in the Scottish motor trade, contested Glasgow Queen's Park at Dec 1982 by-election. Born 1959; educ. Glasgow Academy. Chairman, East Renfrewshire Young Conservatives 1979; chairman, West of Scotland Area Young Conservatives 1980; national vice-chairman, Scottish Young Conservatives 1982.

Mr George McKell contested the seat 1979. Family greengrocer. Chairman, Pollock Liberal Assoc. since 1978. Contested elections for Pollokshields/Shawlands Regional Council 1982, and for Pollokshields District Council 1980 and 1977. Born May 8 1939; educ. The Abbey, Birmingham, and St Joseph's, Salop.

Mr Frank Hannigan, insurance agent. Born 1940; educ. St Conval's School, Pollokshaws. Was a Glasgow district councillor for four years and held office at Baillie.

Mr Hugh Brown

GLASGOW, PROVAN Electorate 47 706 1979: 52 482 minor

*Brown, H. D. (Lab)	20 040	64.4%
Heron, A. (SDP/All)	4 655	15.0%
Gordon, Miss S. (C)	3 374	10.9%
Kennedy, Ms P. (SNP)	2 737	8.8%
Jackson, I. (Com)	294	1.0%
Lab majority	15 385	49.5%
Total vote 31 100		Turnout 65.2%

1979: Total vote 34 659 (66.0%); Lab 24 083 (69.5%); C 5 239 (15.1%); SNP 4 767 (13.8%); Com 377 (1.1%); WRP 193 (0.6%). Lab maj 18 844 (54.4%); swing 2.8%.

Mr Hugh Brown was a member of the Select Committee on Members' Salaries 1981–82. Under-Secretary of State for Scotland with responsibilities for housing and agriculture and fisheries 1974–79. Elected in 1964. Company director; former civil servant, Ministry of Pensions and National Insurance. Born May 1919; educ. Allan Glen's School and Whitehill Secondary School, Glasgow. Member Glasgow Corporation 1954–64. TGWU.

Mr Allan Heron is an employee benefit consultant. Aged 26.

Miss Sheenagh Gordon, former chairman of Federation of Conservative Students in Scotland. Aged 26; educ. Great Yarmouth and Aberdeen University.

Ms Pat Kennedy. Born 1947; educ. Carntyne Primary and Wellshot Secondary schools. Member, Glasgow District Council, 1977–80.

Mr Gregor Mackenzie

GLASGOW, RUTHERGLEN Electorate 59 209

*Mackenzie, J. G. (Lab)	21 510	48.3%
Brown, R. (L/All)	12 384	27.8%
Hodgins, Mrs H. (C)	8 017	18.0%
Fee, K. (SNP)	2 438	5.5%
Corrigan, C. (WRP)	148	0.3%
Lab majority	9 126	20.5%
Total vote 44 497		Turnout 75.2%

Mr Gregor Mackenzie was Minister of State, Scottish Office 1976–79; Minister of State for Industry 1975–76; Under Secretary for Industry 1974–75. Previously Opposition spokesman on broadcasting and communications. Won Rutherglen in the 1964 by-election; contested Kinross and West Perth 1959, and East Aberdeenshire 1950. Sales manager. Born Nov 15 1927; educ. Queens Park School and School of Social Studies, Glasgow University. PPS to Mr James Callaghan, 1965–70. Chairman, all-party media group. Sponsored by TGWU.

Mr Robert Brown, solicitor, contested Rutherglen Oct 1974 and 1979. Born Dec 25 1947; educ. Gordon Schools, Huntly, Aberdeenshire, and Aberdeen University. First Liberal councillor on Glasgow District Council, 1977, leader of Liberal Group. Member, Scottish Liberal Party, since 1966, and of its national executive and agenda committee. Chairman, Rutherglen Citizens' Advice Bureau.

Mrs Helen Hodgins, regional councillor, Strathclyde. Aged 38; educ. Strathclyde University and Jordanhill.

Mr Kenneth Fee, teacher. Born 1931; educ. Hamilton Academy and Glasgow University. Convenor, SNP consumer affairs committee; former member, national executive committee.

Mr David Marshall

GLASGOW, SHETTLESTON Electorate 51 955

*Marshall, D. (Lab)	19 203	54.2%
Henderson, I. (C)	6 787	19.1%
Strachen, S. (L/All)	6 568	18.5%
Hood, D. (SNP)	2 801	7.9%
Hill, K. (BNP)	103	0.3%
Lab majority	12 416	35.0%
Total vote 35 462		Turnout 68.3%

Mr David Marshall, a member of Select Committee on Scottish Affairs, was elected for the seat in 1979. Put the Solvent Abuse (Scotland) Bill through Parliament May 1983. Secretary, Scottish Group of Labour MPs. Born May 7 1941; educ. Larbert High School, Denny High School, Falkirk High School, and Woodside Senior Secondary School. Member, Glasgow Corporation 1972–75; Strathclyde Regional Council 1974–79. (Chairman, Manpower Committee). Chairman COSLA Manpower Committee. Former transport worker and shop steward. Sponsored by T&GWU.

Mr Iain Henderson, public relations and marketing consultant and director of a tourist business, served in the Queen's Own Highlanders, 1964–72. Born 1945; educ. Sedbergh School, Yorks. Member, Scottish Committee of RSPB.

Mr Simon Strachan, political researcher. Born Mar 21 1959; educ. Uddington Grammar School, Glasgow; Strathclyde University and McMaster University Hamilton, Ontario. Formerly parliamentary election agent; former member, Canadian Union of Educational Workers.

Mr Daniel Hood, retired barrister. Born 1926; educ. Whitehill School and Glasgow University. Chairman, local community council. Former trade union president.

Mr Michael Martin

GLASGOW, SPRINGBURN Electorate 53 373

*Martin, M. J. (Lab)	22 481	64.7%
Kelly, J. (L/All)	4 882	14.1%
Tweedie, D. (C)	4 565	13.1%
McLaughlin, J. (SNP)	2 804	8.1%
Lab majority	17 599	50.7%
Total vote 34 732		Turnout 65.1%

Mr Michael Martin, a former trade union officer, and sheet metal worker, elected for Glasgow, Springburn 1979. Served on Glasgow Corporation, 1973–75 and Glasgow District Council since 1975. Born Jul 3 1945; educ. St Patrick's School, Glasgow. Nat Union of Sheet Metal Workers (1962), AUEW (1970) and NUPE (1976). Chairman, PLP Industry and Economic Group sub-committee. PPS to Mr Dennis Healey.

Mr James Kelly, engineer. Born 1943. Chairman, Milton and Ruchill Liberal Assoc; founder member and chairman, Milton Community Council. Former chairman, Maryhill Liberal Party; member, Maryhill Citizen's Advice Bureau steering committee.

Mr David Tweedie, solicitor, is a councillor for Hammersmith and Fulham. Born 1941; educ. Eton and New College, Oxford. Member, Society of Conservative Lawyers.

Mr John McLaughlin, traffic official. Born 1936; educ. St Mungo's Academy. Former member, Glasgow Corporation. ACTSS.

Mrs Sally Oppenheim

GLOUCESTER Electorate 74 268

*Oppenheim, Mrs S. (C)	27 235	48.5%
Hinds, C. W. V. (Lab)	14 698	26.2%
Golder, M. (SDP/All)	13 499	24.0%
Waters, J. (Eco)	479	0.9%
Rhodes, R. (BNP)	260	0.5%
C majority	12 537	22.3%
Total vote 56 171	Turnout	75.6%

Mrs Sally Oppenheim was Minister for Consumer Affairs 1979–82. Joined the shadow Cabinet in Feb 1975, as chief Opposition spokesman on consumer affairs for which she had been a spokesman since 1974. Won the seat in 1970. Born Jul 26 1930; educ. Sheffield High School, Lowther College, North Wales and the Royal Academy of Dramatic Art. Member, BBC Advisory Council, 1971–79. National vice-president, Royal Society for Prevention of Accidents, the Assoc. of Townswomen's Guilds and the National Mobile Homes Residents' Assoc. Vice-President, Assoc. of District Councils. Director, Boots Co. Ltd.

Mr Charles Hinds, engineer. Born May 6 1945; educ. Bauynulme County Junior School and Welacre Secondary Modern School, Manchester. AUEW.

Mr Michael Golder, chief executive of a group of travel and catering companies, is founder chairman of the *Democrat*, the SDP monthly political magazine. Born 1945; educ. Witney Grammar School and LSE. Contested Windsor and Maidenhead in both 1974 elections and Gloucester in 1979, as Labour candidate. Member for Gloucester on the Council for Social Democracy.

Mr Paul Marland

GLOUCESTERSHIRE WEST Electorate 74 266 1979: 70 104 same

*Marland, P. (C)	27 092	45.8%
Watkinson, J. (SDP/All)	17 440	29.5%
Hodkinson, M. J. (Lab)	14 572	24.7%
C majority	9 652	16.3%
Total vote 59 104	Turnout	79.6%

1979: Total vote 58 832 (83.9%); C 28 183 (47.9%); Lab 24 009 (40.8%); L 6 370 (10.8%); NF 270 (0.5%). C maj 4 174 (7.1%); swing 3.9% to C. C gain from Lab.

Mr Paul Marland, a farmer and company director, was elected in 1979; contested the seat Feb and Oct 1974, and Bedwellty 1970. Born Mar 19 1940; educ. Gordonstoun School and Trinity College, Dublin. Former secretary Conservative Agriculture, Fisheries and Food Committee. Former member, North Cotswold RDC. Member, Lloyd's, NFU.

Mr John Watkinson, TV reporter, barrister and former teacher, was Labour MP for West Gloucestershire Oct 1974–79. Born Jan 1941; educ. Bristol Grammar School and Oxford University. Former member, Public Accounts Committee and WEU; PPS in the Home Office. Taught economics and politics at Repton and Rugby Schools 1964–71. Since leaving Parliament worked mainly as TV reporter for BBC's *Money Programme*. Member, Council for Social Democracy and SDP International Committee. Contested Warwick and Leamington 1970.

Mr Michael Hodkinson, lecturer at Bristol Polytechnic. Born Sep 4 1946; educ. Blackpool Grammar School, Liverpool College of Commerce, and Essex University. Former member, AUT; NATFHE.

Mr Malcolm Bruce

GORDON Electorate 65 537

Bruce M. (L/All)	20 134	43.8%
Cran, J. (C)	19 284	42.0%
Grant, G. (Lab)	3 899	8.5%
Guild, K. (SNP)	2 636	5.7%
L/All majority	850	1.9%
Total vote 45 953	Turnout	70.1%

Mr Malcolm Bruce, publisher, was elected in 1983; contested North Angus and Mearns Oct 1974 and West Aberdeenshire 1979. Born Nov 17 1944; educ. Wrekin College, Shropshire; St Andrew's and Strathclyde universities.

Mr James Cran, Northern Director of the CBI, was chief executive of the National Assoc. of Pension Funds 1971–79. Born Jan 1944; educ. Ruthrieston School, Aberdeen, Aberdeen Grammar School, Aberdeen College of Commerce and Kings College, University of Aberdeen. Contested Glasgow Shettleston, Oct 1974. Member, Conservative Research Department 1970–71.

Mr George Grant, scientific officer, contested Aberdeenshire West 1979. Born 1951. Grampian regional councillor since 1978. IPCS.

Mr Kenneth Guild, college lecturer. Born 1946; educ. Harris Academy and Dundee University. Held various offices in SNP locally. EIS.

Mr Peter Viggers

GOSPORT Electorate 64 877

*Viggers, P. J. (C)	28 179	60.6%
Chegwyn, P. (L/All)	13 728	29.5%
Bond, B. B. (Lab)	4 319	9.3%
McMillan, R. A. (Ind)	241	0.5%
C majority	14 451	31.1%
Total vote 46 467		Turnout 71.6%

Mr Peter Viggers, solicitor and company director, was elected in Feb 1974. Born Mar 13 1938; educ. Portsmouth Grammar School and Trinity Hall, Cambridge. Delegate to North Atlantic Assembly since 1980. Joint secretary 1975–76 and vice-chairman, Conservative energy committee 1977–79; Secretary Wessex group of Conservative MPs. Taxation adviser to NFBTE. PPS to Solicitor General since 1979; Member, National Committee of RNLI.

Mr Peter Chegwyn, parliamentary consultant and agent. Born Apr 9 1956; educ. Worthing High School for Boys and Worthing Sixth Form College. Former deputy leader, Medina Borough Council, Isle of Wight; member, Gosport Borough Council.

Mr Bernard Bond is a watch and clock repairer. Born Aug 17 1931; educ. primary schools and through trades unions. Former town councillor. Member, Labour Party Parliamentary Assoc. Formerly on Manpower Services Commission in South East Hants. AUEW; Portsmouth district committee for 17 years. Has been shop steward in MOD.

Mr Gareth Wardell

GOWER Electorate 56 693

*Wardell, G. (Lab)	16 972	38.0%
Kenyon, T. (C)	15 767	35.3%
Jones, G. (SDP/All)	10 416	23.4%
Williams, N. (PlC)	1 444	3.2%
Lab majority	1 205	2.7%
Total vote 44 599		Turnout 78.7%

Mr Gareth Wardell, geography lecturer, won Gower by-election Sep 1982. Member, Welsh Select Committee. Born Nov 29 1944; educ. Gwendraeth Grammar School and LSE. NATFHE and APEX.

Dr Tom Kenyon, general practitioner. Born Jun 22 1937; educ. Cranleigh School and St Bartholomew's Hospital. Contested Glasgow, Kelvingrove Feb 1974.

Mr Gwynoro Jones, assistant education officer on West Glamorgan County Council, was Labour MP for Carmarthen 1970 to Oct 1974. Born Nov 1942; educ. Gwendraeth Grammar School and Cardiff University. PPS to Mr Roy Jenkins as Home Secretary 1970–74; former member, Consultative Assembly of Council of Europe and Assembly's agriculture committee. Member, SDP national committee.

Mr Nigel Williams, a native of Llandysul, is a development manager.

Mr Douglas Hogg

GRANTHAM Electorate 75 047

*Hogg, D. M. (C)	31 692	57.5%
Titley, S. (L/All)	12 781	23.2%
Savage, T. E. (Lab)	10 677	19.4%
C majority	18 911	34.3%
Total vote 55 150		Turnout 73.5%

Mr Douglas Hogg, elder son of Lord Hailsham of St Marylebone, the Lord Chancellor, became an assistant Government whip in 1983. Elected in 1979. Barrister. Born Feb 5 1945; educ. Eton, Christ Church, Oxford, and Lincolns Inn. Member, legal research committee, Assoc. of Conservative Lawyers, and part author of several publications. Member, Select Committee on Agriculture, 1979–83; PPS to Chief Secretary to the Treasury 1982–83.

Mr Simon Titley, a research and information officer at Liberal Party HQ in London. Born May 27 1957; educ. City School, Lincoln and Keele University. Member, Liberal Party National executive and council since 1977; national chairman, Union of Liberal Students 1978–79; secretary general, Young Liberal Movement 1979–80; vice-chairman, National League of Young Liberals 1980–81; member, national executive, British Youth Council 1980–81. APEX.

Mr Terence Savage is an area organizer with USDAW. Born Jan 1948. Founder member, North Nottinghamshire District Manpower Committee. Served on the Industrial Tribunal Panel 1977, and the Local Appeals Tribunal.

Mr Timothy Brinton

GRAVESHAM Electorate 71 150

*Brinton, T. D. (C)	25 968	47.0%
Ovenden, J. F. (Lab)	17 505	31.7%
Horton, M. (SDP/All)	10 826	19.6%
Sewell, M. (Eco)	495	0.9%
Johnson, P. (NF)	420	0.8%
C majority	8 463	15.3%
Total vote 55 214		Turnout 77.6%

Mr Timothy Brinton won this seat in 1983 and Gravesend in 1979. Broadcasting consultant, freelance commentator and interviewer. Born Dec 24 1929; educ. Summerfields. Oxford, Eton, Geneva University and Central School of Speech and Drama, London. Staff announcer and newsreader, BBC radio 1951–57; head of English programmes, Radio Hong Kong, 1957–59, and newscaster and reporter ITN 1959–62. Member Kent County Council 1974–81. Member Select Committee on Education, Science and Arts since 1979. Vice-chairman, Conservative backbench media committee and of education committee. Equity, ACTT.

Mr John Ovenden, an executive engineer with British Telecom, was MP for Gravesend from Feb 1974–79. Born Aug 17 1942; educ. Chatham House Grammar School, Ramsgate. Contested Sevenoaks 1970. Member Public Accounts Committee 1976–79; vice-chairman PLP Housing Group 1978–79; secretary, all-party committee for widows and one-parent families 1976–79. Member, Gillingham Borough Council, 1966–71.

Mr Austin Mitchell

GREAT GRIMSBY Electorate 68 388 1979: 66 644 same

*Mitchell, A. V. (Lab)	18 330	36.3%
Hancock, C. (C)	17 599	34.9%
Genney, P. (SDP/All)	14 552	28.8%
Lab majority	731	1.5%
Total vote 50 481		Turnout 73.8%

1979 (as Grimsby): Total vote 50 511 (75.8%); Lab 26 282 (52.0%); C 20 041 (39.7%); L 3 837 (7.6%); other 214 (0.4%); NF 137 (0.3%). Lab maj 6 241 (12.3%); swing 1.4% to C.

Mr Austin Mitchell was elected for Grimsby at the Apr 1977 by-election. Journalist, Yorkshire Television 1969–71 and 1973–77; presenter BBC current affairs group 1972–73. Born Sep 19 1934; educ. Woodbottom Council School, Bingley Grammar School, and Manchester and Oxford Universities. Member of Select Committee on Treasury and Civil Service since 1979. Lecturer in history, University of Otago, Dunedin, New Zealand, 1959–63. Senior lecturer in politics, University of Canterbury, Christchurch, New Zealand, 1963–67. Official Fellow, Nuffield College, Oxford, 1967–69. Vice-chairman, PLP economics and finance group. NUJ.

Mr Colin Hancock, director of food distribution and property companies. Born Feb 29 1936; educ. Leamington College. Member, executive committee, Young Conservative Council for London 1961–63 and now chairman, South Suffolk steering committee. Former chairman, Suffolk rate action group; past chairman, business computers users' group. Chairman-elect, Bury St Edmunds Industrialists Assoc. Member, committee, West Suffolk Voluntary Assoc. for the Blind. Parish councillor.

Mr Paul Genney, community dentist and barrister. Born 1941; educ. Bristol University and Middle Temple. Acted as agent to Mr Austin Mitchell, MP for Great Grimsby, in the 1979 election.

Mr Michael Carttiss

GREAT YARMOUTH Electorate 62 809

Carttiss, M. (C)	22 423	50.5%
Lloyd, O. (Lab)	11 223	25.3%
Minett, E. (L/All)	10 803	24.3%
C majority	11 200	25.2%
Total vote 44 449		Turnout 70.8%

Mr Michael Carttiss, former constituency agent for Yarmouth, has been a member of Norfolk County Council since 1966. Won seat in 1983. Born 1938; educ. Great Yarmouth Technical High School, London University and London School of Economics.

Mr Owen Lloyd, a fitter. Born Jun 23 1928; educ. Westfield Secondary Modern School, Hinckley, Leicestershire. Member, Great Yarmouth Borough Council. Former member, Norfolk County Council. President, Lowestoft and Yarmouth District, AUEW (engineering section); secretary, Yarmouth branch; member, national committee for five years.

Mr Eric Minett, a principal lecturer. Born Jul 27 1932; educ. Yarmouth Grammar School, Culham College, Oxon and Open University. Contested Yarmouth 1979. District councillor, Yarmouth Borough Council since 1976 (leader, Liberal group). NATFHE.

Mr Norman Godman

GREENOCK & PORT GLASGOW Electorate 59 437 1979: 61 610 minor

Godman, N. A. (Lab)	20 650	46.8%
Blair, A. (L/All)	16 025	36.3%
Crichton, C. (C)	4 314	9.8%
Clayton, A. (SNP)	2 989	6.8%
McKinlay, G. (WRP)	114	0.3%
Lab majority	4 625	10.5%
Total vote 44 092		Turnout 74.2%

1979: Total vote 45 397 (73.7%); Lab 24 071 (53.0%); L 12 789 (28.2%); C 4 926 (10.9%); SNP 3 435 (7.6%); WRP 176 (0.4%). Lab maj 11 282 (24.8%); swing 2.6% to Lab.

Mr Norman Godman, a teacher and former shipwright, won this seat in 1983. Born Apr 1937; educ. Hull University. Contested Aberdeen South 1979. Joined Labour Party 1962. Sponsored by TGWU; member, TGWU, AUT.

Mr Alan Blair, solicitor. Born Feb 24 1939; educ. Greenock Academy, Glasgow University. Member, Greenock Town Council 1965–75, Inverclyde District Council since 1975.

Mr Charles Crighton, proprietor of a hydro-electric scheme and former company director. Aged 40; educ. Winchester and London Polytechnic. President of an NFU branch.

Mr Alan Clayton, teacher. Born 1936; educ. Notre Dame College of Education and the Open University. Elected member, SNP national council; regional executive member, EIS.

Mr Guy Barnett

GREENWICH Electorate 51 586

*Barnett, N. G. (Lab)	13 361	38.2%
Rolfe, A. (C)	12 150	34.8%
Ford, T. (SDP/All)	8 783	25.1%
Dell, I. (BNP)	259	0.7%
Mallone, R. (Fellowship)	242	0.7%
Hooks, Ms F. (Com)	149	0.4%
Lab majority	1 211	3.5%
Total Vote 34 944		Turnout 67.7%

Mr Guy Barnett, chief Opposition spokesman on overseas development 1982–83, was an Opposition spokesman on European and Community affairs 1981–82; spokesman on overseas development 1979–81. Under-Secretary of State for the Environment 1976–79. Retained the seat for Labour in the Jul 1971 by-election; MP for Dorset South 1962–64; contested Scarborough and Whitby 1959. Member European Parliament 1975–76 and of Council of Get Britain Out (of EEC) Campaign. Teacher; former chief education officer of Commonwealth Institute. Born Aug 23 1928; educ. Highgate School and St Edmund Hall, Oxford. Secretary Oxford Union 1953. Member Select Committee on Race Relations 1972–74. Parliamentary consultant to National Union of Teachers.

Mr Arthur Rolfe, engineering consultant. Born Dec 29 1942; educ. Catford Boys' School and South East London Technical College. Member, London Borough of Greenwich Council 1968–71 and since 1974; GLC since 1980.

Mr Timothy Ford, solicitor and company director. Born 1945; educ. Bancroft's School, Woodford and College of Law, Lancaster Gate, London. Partner in firm of city solicitors; chairman and director, computer consultancy.

Mr David Howell

GUILDFORD Electorate 75 134

*Howell, D. A. (C)	30 016	55.1%
Sharp, Mrs M. (L/All)	18 192	33.4%
Chesterton, K. (Lab)	5 853	10.7%
Farrell, A. (PAL)	425	0.8%
C majority	11 824	21.7%
Total vote 54 486		Turnout 72.5%

Mr David Howell, Secretary of State for Transport, 1981–83, was Secretary of State for Energy, 1979–81. Opposition spokesman on Home Office affairs and previously on Treasury and economic affairs and energy; Minister of State for Energy, 1974; Minister of State for Northern Ireland, Nov 1972–74; and Under Secretary for Northern Ireland 1972; Lord Commissioner of the Treasury (Whip) 1970–71; Parliamentary Secretary, Civil Service Department, 1970–72; and Under-Secretary for Employment, 1971–72. Elected in 1966; contested Dudley 1964. Born Jan 18 1936; educ. Eton and King's College, Cambridge.

Mrs Margaret Sharp, economist and senior research fellow, Sussex University. Born Nov 21 1938; educ. Tonbridge Girls' Grammar School and Newnham College, Cambridge. AUT.

Mr Keith Chesterton, company planner. Born Jan 19 1935; educ. Coleman Road Primary School and Wyggeston Boys' Grammar School, Leicester, and Cambridge University. Member, Northwich District Council since 1981. ASTMS. Ex-chairman of long distance walking association.

Mr Ernest Roberts

HACKNEY NORTH AND STOKE NEWINGTON Electorate 66 754

*Roberts, E. A. C. (Lab)	18 989	52.0%
Hartley-Booth, E. (C)	10 444	28.6%
Ash, D. (L/All)	5 746	15.8%
Fitzpatrick, D. (Eco)	492	1.4%
Goldman, M. (Com)	426	1.2%
Field, J. (NF)	396	1.1%
Lab majority	8 545	23.4%
Total vote 36 493	Turnout	54.7%

Mr Ernest Roberts was Assistant General Secretary of the AUEW for 20 years; member of the union since 1940. Chairman, Labour Parliamentary Assoc. 1979. Elected for Hackney North and Stoke Newington 1979; fought Stockport 1955. Born Apr 20 1912; educ. St Chad's Boys' Elementary School, Shrewsbury. Member, Coventry City Council, 1949–57. Author of books and pamphlets. Founder member of Institute of Workers' Control, Anti-Nazi League and CND. member of Government EDCs and other organizations. Sponsored by AUEW.

Mr Edward Hartley-Booth, is a barrister. Educ. Bristol and Cambridge universities.

Mr David Ash, self-employed cleaning contractor. Born Nov 15 1957; educ. Pretoria Boys' High School, South Africa.

Mr Brian Sedgemore

HACKNEY SOUTH AND SHOREDITCH Electorate 71 304

Sedgemore, B (Lab)	16 721	43.5%
Croft, P. (C)	8 930	23.2%
*Brown, R. W. (SDP/All)	7 025	18.3%
Roberts, J. (IL)	3 724	9.7%
Quilty, S. (LIL)	704	1.8%
Ashton, R. (NF)	593	1.6%
Tyndall, Mrs V. (BNP)	374	1.0%
Green, D. (Com)	246	0.5%
Goldstein, R. (WRP)	141	0.4%
Lab majority	7 791	20.3%
Total vote 38 458	Turnout	53.9%

Mr Brian Sedgemore, a barrister and researcher with Granada Television since 1980, was elected in 1983; represented Luton West Feb 1974–79. Born Mar 17 1937; educ. Heles School, Exeter, Oxford University. PPS to Mr Tony Benn 1977–78. Wandsworth Borough Councillor 1971–74. Member, NUJ, ACTT, Writer's Guild, Fabian Society, Haldane Society.

Mr Peter Croft, direct investment manager, British Rail pension funds. Born 1949. Member, Ealing Borough Council.

Mr Ronald W. Brown was elected as Labour MP for Hackney South and Shoreditch in Feb 1974; resigned party in 1981 and joined SDP. Labour MP for Shoreditch and Finsbury 1964–76. An assistant Government whip 1966–67. Born Sep 1921; educ. elementary school, south London and Borough Polytechnic. Brother of Lord George-Brown. Senior lecturer in electrical engineering; principal of industrial training school; parliamentary adviser to Furniture, Timber and Allied Trades Union. Member European Parliament 1977–79. Former chairman PLP Greater London area group. Former member Select Committee on Science and Technology.

Mr John Stokes

HALESOWEN AND STOURBRIDGE Electorate 76 403

*Stokes, J. H. (C)	28 250	48.4%
Clitheroe, T. (SDP/All)	14 934	25.6%
Ellison, C. (Lab)	14 611	25.0%
Rudd, D. (Eco)	582	1.0%
C majority	13 316	22.8%
Total vote 58 377	Turnout	76.4%

Mr John Stokes, was elected for the constituency Feb 1974; represented Oldbury and Halesowen 1970–74; contested Gloucester 1964. Born Jul 23 1917; educ. Haileybury and Queens College, Oxford. Member, Select Committee on Parliamentary Commissioner for Administration (Ombudsman) since 1979. Member, Conservative parliamentary defence committees and committees on foreign and home affairs. Chairman, general purposes committee, Primrose league. Vice-President, Royal Stuart Society.

Mr Thomas Clitheroe, lecturer. Born Feb 28 1940; educ. grammar school and University of Exeter. Member, Dudley Metropolitan District Council 1973–82, leader of council 1975–76, leader of opposition 1976–80, leader of SDP group 1980–82. NATFHE.

Mr Colin Ellison, lecturer at Stourbridge College of Art. Born 1935; educ. Bradford and Cambridge universities. Member, West Midlands County Council since 1981. NATFHE.

Mr Roy Galley

HALIFAX Electorate 72 747

Galley, R. (C)	22 321	40.9%
*Summerskill, Dr S. (Lab)	20 452	37.4%
Cockroft, F. (SDP/All)	11 868	21.7%
C majority	1 869	3.4%
Total vote 54 641	Turnout 75.1%	

Mr Roy Galley, Post Office manager, won the seat in 1983; contested Dewsbury, 1979. Born Dec 8 1947; educ. King Edward VII Grammar School, Sheffield, and Worcester College, Oxford. Member, Calderdale Metropolitan Borough Council, since 1980. Member, Society of Public and Civil Servants.

Dr Shirley Summerskill, an Opposition spokesman on home affairs 1979–83, represented Halifax 1964–83. Opposition spokesman on health 1970–74; Under-Secretary of State, Home Office, 1974–79. Born Sep 9 1931; educ. St Paul's School, Somerville College, Oxford, St Thomas's Hospital. Medical practitioner. Contested Blackpool North 1962 by-election. Member, Labour Party National Executive Committee 1981–83

Mr F. L. Cockcroft, manager consultancies division, Booker Agriculture International Ltd. Born 1943; educ. Cambridge University.

Mr Gordon Oakes

HALTON Electorate 72 743

*Oakes, G. J. (Lab)	24 752	46.4%
Pedley, P. (C)	17 923	33.6%
Tilling, R. (SDP/All)	10 649	20.0%
Lab majority	6 829	12.8%
Total vote 53 324	Turnout 73.3%	

Mr Gordon Oakes, an Opposition spokesman on environment 1979–83; Minister of State for Education and Science 1976–79; Under Secretary of State for Environment 1974–76; Under Secretary of State for Energy 1976. Returned in 1983; MP for Widnes 1971–83; represented Bolton West 1964–70; contested Bebington 1959, and Manchester, Moss Side 1961. Member, Select Committee on race relations 1968–70. Born Jun 22 1931; educ. Wade Deacon School, Widnes, and Liverpool University, Public affairs consultant to 3M United Kingdom Ltd, the Pharmaceutical Society of Great Britain, and the Caravan Club; solicitor, not in practice. Member Widnes Borough Council 1952–66; Mayor 1964–65. Vice-President, Assoc. of County Councils and Assoc. of District Councils. Sponsored by TGWU.

Mr Philip Pedley, a manager at Ford, is national Young Conservatives chairman (1982–84). Born Nov 2 1957; educ. Calday Grange Grammar, Merseyside and Lancaster University. Member, National Union general purposes committee since 1981, advisory committee on party policy since 1982, and advisory committee on candidates since 1982.

Mr Thomas Tilling, company chairman of Garden Centres of Cheshire. Born Jun 10 1943; educ. Helsby Grammar School and Manchester College of Commerce.

Mr George Robertson

HAMILTON Electorate 61 430

*Robertson, G. (Lab)	24 384	52.4%
Donaldson, S. (L/All)	9 365	20.1%
Scott, Mrs M. (C)	8 940	19.2%
Whitehead, Mrs M. (SNP)	3 816	8.2%
Lab majority	15 019	32.3%
Total vote 46 505	Turnout 75.7%	

Mr George Robertson, an Opposition spokesman on foreign and Commonwealth affairs since 1981, was an Opposition spokesman on defence 1980–81, having been a spokesman on Scotland 1979–80. Won the by-election in May 1978. Scottish organizer for the GMWU 1970–78. Born Apr 12 1946; educ. Dunoon Grammar School and Dundee University, Secretary of Manifesto group of PLP since 1979; chairman, Scottish Council, Labour Party, 1977–78. Board member, Scottish Development Agency 1975–78, and of Scottish Tourist Board 1974–76. Sponsored by GMBATU.

Mr Stewart Donaldson, investment analyst, contested Edinburgh Central 1979. Born Dec 11 1953; educ. Morrisons Academy, Crieff, Perthshire; Edinburgh University; Scottish Business School. Founder member and NEC member, Campaign for a Scottish Assembly.

Mrs Margaret Scott followed her husband, who stood for Hamilton in 1979. Teacher. Educ. Glasgow High School for Girls and Royal Scottish Academy of Music and Drama, and Vienna Conservatoire.

Mrs Maire Whitehead, head teacher. Born 1940; educ. Notre Dame High School and Glasgow University. Executive member, Glasgow Assoc. of Head Teachers.

Mr Clive Soley

HAMMERSMITH

Electorate 46178 1979: 50821 same

*Soley, C. (Lab)	13645	41.6%
Mansfield, N. (C)	11691	35.6%
Starks, M. (SDP/All)	4925	15.0%
Knott, S. (Ind L)	1912	5.8%
Sutherland, Ms D. (Eco)	325	0.7%
Bennett, Mrs L. (NP)	250	0.6%
Dixon Ms C. (WRP)	81	0.3%
Dick, P. (Ind)	73	0.2%
Lab majority	1954	6.0%
Total vote 32 902		Turnout 71.0%

1979 (as Hammersmith North): Total vote 35778 (70.4%); Lab 17241 (48.2%); C 13735 (38.4%); L 4147 (11.6%); NF 462 (1.3%); WRP 193 (0.5%). Lab maj 3506 (9.8%), swing 7.1% to C.

Mr Clive Soley, elected to Hammersmith in 1983, had represented Hammersmith North since 1979. He became an Opposition spokesman on Northern Ireland in 1981. Probation officer. Born May 7 1939; educ. Downshal Ilford, secondary modern school, Newbattle Abbey Adult Education College, and Strathclyde and Southampton universities. Hammersmith councillor 1974–78. Chairman, Alcohol Education Centre. GMBATU.

Mr Nicholas Mansfield, senior partner of property management and estate agents which he founded in 1977. Born Mar 5 1945; educ. St George's College, Weybridge. Chairman, Sutton Young Conservatives 1968, president 1970. Chairman, Epsom and Ewell CPC Committee 1980–81.

Mr Michael Starks, is in broadcasting management. Born Jan 25 1944; educ. King Edward's School, Bath, Glasgow Academy and Gonville and Caius College, Cambridge. Member, Notting Hill Housing Trust (Hammersmith and Fulham area committee chairman).

Mr Michael Mates

HAMPSHIRE EAST

Electorate 79303

*Mates, M. J. (C)	36968	62.8%
Bryan, Ms R. (L/All)	18641	31.7%
Cowan, S. J. (Lab)	3247	5.5%
C majority	18327	31.1%
Total vote 58856		Turnout 74.2%

Mr Michael Mates, a member of the Select Committee on Defence since 1979, and parliamentary adviser to three companies, was elected for this seat in 1983. MP for Petersfield 1974–83, prior to which he was a regular soldier. Born Jun 9 1934; educ. Blundell's and King's College, Cambridge. Served on Staff of Vice Chief of Defence Staff. Former Secretary and vice-chairman Conservative Northern Ireland Committee; vice-chairman, Conservative backbench Home Affairs Committee, since 1979. Chairman, All-Party Anglo-Irish group.

Ms Rebecca Bryan, special assistant to the technical director of GEC. Born Jan 18 1960; educ. St Clements, Toronto; St Martin's Solihull; Solihull Sixth Form College, and LSE. National chairman, Union of Liberal Students, 1980. On BBC South TV advisory board.

Mr Steven Cowan, teacher. Born Sep 6 1951; educ. Secondary school and St Paul's College, Cheltenham. Member, ILEA, NUT.

Mr David Mitchell

HAMPSHIRE NORTH WEST

Electorate 65780

*Mitchell, D. B. (C)	28044	57.3%
Willis, I. (L/All)	15922	32.6%
Davis, M. J. (Lab)	4957	10.1%
C majority	12122	24.8%
Total vote 48923		Turnout 74.4%

Mr David Mitchell became Under Secretary of State for Transport in June 1983; Under Secretary of State for Northern Ireland 1981–83, and for Industry 1979–81. Elected in 1983; MP for Basingstoke 1964–83; contested St Pancras North 1959. Opposition whip 1965–67. Market gardener turned wine merchant. Born Jun 20, 1928; educ. Aldenham. Member, St Pancras Borough Council 1956–59. Secretary, Conservative parliamentary labour committee 1968–70; chairman, Conservative parliamentary small businesses committee 1974–79; founder chairman, Small Businesses Bureau.

Mr Ian Willis, management consultant. Born Jul 7 1946; educ. Harrow, Royal Military Academy, Sandhurst and Christ Church, Oxford.

Mr Michael Davis is a graphic designer for a publishing company. Aged 31. Chairman, Andover Labour Party. Former member, Test Borough Council. Member, Andover and District Sports Association for the Disabled. ASTMS.

Mr Geoffrey Finsberg

HAMPSTEAD AND HIGHGATE

Electorate 66 554

*Finsberg, G. (C)	18 366	41.2%
McDonnell, J. (Lab)	14 996	33.7%
Sofer, Mrs A. (SDP/All)	11 038	24.8%
Stevenson, J. (Poet)	156	0.4%
C majority	3 370	7.6%
Total vote 44 556	Turnout 66.9%	

Mr Geoffrey Finsberg was Under-Secretary of State for Health and Social Security 1981–83; Under-Secretary of State for Environment 1979–81; Opposition spokesman on Greater London 1974–79. Vice-chairman Conservative Party Organization 1975–79. Gained Hampstead for the Conservatives in 1970; contested Islington East 1955. Born Jun 13 1926; educ. City of London School. Member, Hampstead Borough Council 1949–65, Camden Borough Council 1964–74 (leader 1968–70). Vice-chairman, Conservative parliamentary committee on trade 1972–73; member, Expenditure Committee 1974–79; member executive 1922 Committee 1974–79. Chief industrial relations adviser and personnel controller, Great Universal Stores Ltd 1968–79. Member, Post Office Users' National Council 1970–77; Council of CBI 1968–79 (chairman, Post Office Panel).

Mr John McDonnell, GLC councillor and former trade union officer. Born Sep 8 1951; educ. Great Yarmouth Grammar School, Burnley Technical College, Brunel University, University of London. Member, GLC, since 1981; chairman, Finance Comm. NUPE.

Mrs Anne Sofer, full-time GLC councillor. Born Apr 19 1937; educ. college in USA and Somerville College, Oxford. GLC member for St Pancras, North since 1977; chairman of ILEA schools sub-committee, 1978–81.

Sir John Farr

HARBOROUGH

Electorate 72 177 1979: 68 989 same

*Farr, Sir J. A. (C)	32 957	60.1%
Swift, T. (L/All)	14 472	26.4%
Upham, M. (Lab)	6 285	11.5%
Fewster, B. (Eco)	802	1.5%
Taylor, J. (BNP)	280	0.5%
C majority	18 485	33.7%
Total vote 54 796	Turnout 75.9%	

1979: Total vote 55 209 (80.0%); C 33 328 (60.4%); Lab 11 350 (20.6%); L 9 529 (17.3%); NF 1 002 (1.8%). C maj 21 978 (39.8%); swing 6.1% to C.

Sir John Farr, a member of the Select Committee on Standing Orders since 1981, was elected in 1959; contested Ilkeston 1955. Born Sept 25 1922; educ. Harrow. Member of Lloyd's and landowner. Vice-chairman, Conservative Northern Ireland Committee 1974–78. Secretary, party's committee on agriculture 1970–74 and vice-chairman since 1979. Secretary, all-party conservation committee, chairman, Anglo-Irish Parliamentary Group 1977–80; chairman British Zimbabwe parliamentary group since 1980 and chairman all-party knitwear group. Member, United Kingdom delegation to WEU and Council of Europe 1973–78.

Mr Timothy Swift, computer programmer. Born Jul 1 1957; educ. Beauchamp College, Oadby, and Leicester Univ. Member, Leicestershire C C and leader of Alliance group since 1981; Oadby and Wigston Borough Council since 1983. ASTMS.

Mr Martin Upham, a research officer for ISTC. Born Mar 3 1947; educ. Manchester, Bristol and Hull universities.

Mr Jeremy Hayes

HARLOW

Electorate 69 715 1979: 67 494 minor

Hayes, J. (C)	21 924	41.1%
*Newens, A. S. (Lab)	18 250	34.2%
Bastick, J. (L/All)	12 891	24.2%
Ward, J. (Ind)	266	0.5%
C majority	3 674	6.9%
Total vote 53 331	Turnout 76.5%	

C gain from Lab
1979: Total vote 53 133 (78.7%); Lab 22 698 (42.7%); C 21 306 (40.1%); L 8 289 (15.6%); NF 840 (1.6%). Lab maj 1 392 (2.6%); swing 12.9%

Mr Jeremy Hayes, barrister and company director, won the seat in 1983. Born 1953; educ. Oratory School and London University. Vice-president, Eastern Area Young Conservatives and Epping Forest YCs; member, Eastern area executive, Essex Euro constituency Council and area speakers panel.

Mr Stanley Newens, was returned in Feb 1974; MP for Epping, 1964–70. Chairman Tribune Group 1982–83. Member Select Committee on Agriculture since 1979. Former teacher and miner. Born Feb 4 1930; educ. Buckhurst High School, University College, London, and Westminster Teacher Training College.

Mr John Bastick, co-director of an advertising company. Born Apr 12 1942; educ. Malmesbury Grammar School and Regent Street Polytechnic.

Mr Robert Banks

HARROGATE Electorate 72 815

*Banks, R. G. (C)	30 269	60.2%
Burney, J. (SDP/All)	14 381	28.6%
Dixon, J. (Lab)	5 128	10.2%
Kelly, D. (RHCP)	316	0.6%
Vessey, P. (NF)	163	0.3%
C majority	15 888	31.6%
Total vote 50 257		Turnout 69.0%

Mr Robert Banks, a member of Lloyd's and a farmer, was elected in Feb 1974. Paddington councillor 1959–65. Born Jan 18 1937; educ. Haileybury. Member Select-Committee on Foreign Affairs and of sub-committee on Overseas Development since 1982. Joint secretary, Conservative parliamentary defence committee 1976–79. Vice-chairman, all-party tourism group and secretary Anglo-Sudan all-party group. Member Council of Europe and WEU 1977–81. PPS to Ministers of State for Foreign and Commonwealth Affairs, 1979–82. Member, Alcohol Education and Research Council since 1982, North Atlantic Assembly.

Mr John Burney, company director and freelance writer. Owner and co-director of an agricultural market research company. Born Jun 1924; educ. Rugby School. Member SDP national policy group on the arts. Member, Writers' Guild of Great Britain.

Mr John Dixon, vice-principal, Trinity and All Saints College, Leeds University. Born Mar 14 1940; educ. St Michael's College, Leeds; Christ Church, Oxford. Member, Leeds City Council 1972–74. NATFHE. TGWU (ACTSS).

Mr Hugh Dykes

HARROW EAST Electorate 79 926

*Dykes, H. J. (C)	28 834	49.8%
Hains, R. (L/All)	16 166	27.9%
Brough, D. D. (Lab)	12 941	22.3%
C majority	12 668	21.9%
Total vote 57 941		Turnout 72.5%

Mr Hugh Dykes, stockbroker and consultant, won the seat for the Conservatives in 1970; contested Tottenham 1966. Born May 17 1939; educ. Weston-super-Mare Grammar School and Pembroke College, Cambridge (chairman, University Conservative Assoc. 1962). Member, European Parliament, 1974–76. Member of Select Committee on European Legislation since 1979; chairman, Conservative parliamentary European affairs committee, 1979–81; Vice-President Conservative Group for Europe 1981. Member, London Stock Exchange. Governor, North London Collegiate School since 1981.

Mr Richard Hains, principal social worker, contested Ealing, Southall 1979; Birmingham, Northfield Oct 1974; Walsall South Feb 74. Born Jan 25 1945. Harrow councillor and leader of opposition since 1982.

Mr David Brough, local government officer with Hillingdon Council. Born Oct 12 1947. Member, Harrow Council 1971–75. Member, Fabian Society and Socialist Education Assoc. Nalgo.

Sir John Page

HARROW WEST Electorate 73 151

*Page, Sir J. A. (C)	28 056	53.0%
Bayliss, S. (SDP/All)	17 035	32.2%
Toms, K. A. (Lab)	7 811	14.8%
C majority	11 021	20.8%
Total vote 52 902		Turnout 72.3%

Sir John Page, company chairman and director of other companies, was returned in a by-election in Mar 1960; contested Eton and Slough 1959. Born Sep 16 1919; educ. Harrow and Magdalene College, Cambridge. Member Conservative parliamentary labour affairs committee 1970–74; secretary, Conservative broadcasting committee 1974–76 and chairman 1979–81. President, Conservative Trade Unionists National Advisory Council 1967–69, Chairman, British Group, Interparliamentary Union 1979–82; member IPU International Executive 1982. Member, Select Committee on Race Relations and Immigration 1970–71; delegate to Council of Europe and WEU since 1972, and chairman, budget committee, 1973–74, and social and health committee since 1975. President, Independent Schools Assoc. 1971–78; chairman, Council for Independent Education, 1974–80.

Mr Stuart Bayliss, a company director. Born 1955; educ. Nottingham University. Chairman, university sector NUS executive 1977–79; vice-chairman, British Youth Council 1978–80; national chairman, Conservative Students 1979–80; vice-chairman, National Advisory Committee on education. Director of Financial Conferences, Oyez IBC and of companies servicing the accounting profession. SDP council member.

Mr Albert Toms, deputy leader of Lab. group on Harrow Council. Born Apr 1940; educ. Reading and Brunel Univs.

Mr Edward Leadbitter

HARTLEPOOL Electorate 69346 1979: 65732

*Leadbitter, E. L. (Lab)	22048	45.5%
Rodgers, F. (C)	18 959	39.1%
Bertram, N. (SDP/All)	7 422	15.3%
Lab majority	3 089	6.4%
Total vote 48 429	Turnout 69.8%	

1979: Total vote 49109 (74.7%); Lab 27039 (55.1%); C 18877 (38.4%); L 3193 (6.5%). Lab maj 8162 (16.7%)

Mr Edward Leadbitter has been member of the House of Commons Chairmen's Panel since 1980. Successfully sponsored Children's Home Registration Bill, 1981. Elected in 1964. Teacher. Born Jun 18 1919; educ. state schools and Cheltenham Teacher Training College. Member Select Committee on Energy since 1980. President Hartlepool Labour minor Party 1958–62; member West Hartlepool Borough Council 1956–58. Chairman, PLP transport and ports groups. Member Select Committee Science and Technology 1969–73. Sponsored by NUPE.

Mr Frank Rogers, a stationer, bookseller and educational contractor. Born Mar 19 1927; educ. Hartlepool Grammar School. Member, Hartlepool Borough Council since 1967; leader, Conservative Group since 1977. Member, Cleveland County Council since 1973; chairman 1980–81.

Mr Norman Bertram, headmaster of a comprehensive school in Middlesbrough, is chairman of Guiseborough and East Cleveland group, SDP. Born Mar 1 1936; educ. Ryhope Grammar School, and Keele and Leeds universities.

Sir Julian Ridsdale

HARWICH Electorate 72179

*Ridsdale, Sir J. (C)	27422	54.2%
Goodenough, R. (L/All)	14920	29.5%
Knight, R. (Lab)	8302	16.4%
C majority	12502	24.7%
Total vote 50644	Turnout 70.2%	

Sir Julian Ridsdale, CBE, company director, was returned at a by-election in Feb 1954. Contested Paddington North 1951. Under-Secretary of State, Air Ministry, 1962–64; Under-Secretary for Defence for the RAF 1964. Chairman, British-Japanese parliamentary group since 1964; vice-chairman, United Nations Parliamentary Association 1966–80. Chairman, Japanese Society, London, 1976–79. Member, Public Accounts Committee 1970–74; member North Atlantic Assembly since 1979; member Trilateral Commission, EEC, USA and Japan since 1973. Born Jun 8 1915; educ. Tonbridge, the Royal Military College, Sandhurst and London University School of Oriental Languages.

Mr Robert Goodenough, teacher, contested Harwich 1979. Born Jun 16 1948; educ. Gilberd School, Colchester, and Borough Road College. NUT.

Mr Ralph Knight, electrical supervisor with Harwich Dock Co Ltd. Born Sep 22 1934; educ. elementary school. Member, Harwich Borough Council and Essex County Council. NUR.

Mr Kenneth Warren

HASTINGS AND RYE Electorate 69747

*Warren, K. R. (C)	25626	53.3%
Amies, D. (L/All)	14646	30.5%
Knowles, N. (Lab)	7304	15.2%
McNally, G. (Ind)	503	1.1%
C majority	10980	22.8%
Total vote 48079	Turnout 68.9%	

Mr Kenneth Warren, aeronautical engineer and company director, was elected in 1983; MP for Hastings 1970–83; contested St Pancras North 1964. Chairman, Western European Union science, technology and aerospace committee 1977–80. Member, Select Committee on Science and Technology. Chairman, Conservative parliamentary aviation committee 1974–76; chairman, parliamentary committee on offshore technology 1974–75. Born Aug 15 1926; educ. Midsomer Norton Grammar School, Aldenham School, De Havilland Aeronautical Technical School, King's College, London, and London School of Economics. PPS to Secretary of State for Industry, 1979–81 and to Secretary of State for Education and Science from 1981.

Mr David Amies, Barbican manager, contested Havant and Waterloo 1979. Born Feb 16 1942; educ. Robertsbridge Primary School, Bexhill Grammar School and Leeds University. Member, Rother District Council 1974–76; East Sussex County Council since 1981.

Mr Nigel Knowles, trade union education officer, contested Bodmin 1979. Born Dec 5 1946; educ. King Charles I Grammar School, Birmingham Polytechnic, Essex University and Worcester College of Higher Education. Elected Haringey Council 1982.

Mr Ian Lloyd

HAVANT Electorate 73096

*Lloyd, I. S. (C)	29148	55.3%
Cleaver, Mrs E. (SDP/All)	17192	32.6%
Norris, R. J. (Lab)	6335	12.0%
C majority	11956	22.7%
Total vote 52675		Turnout 72.1%

Mr Ian Lloyd, was elected in 1983; MP for Havant and Waterloo Feb 1974–83. Represented Portsmouth, Langstone 1964–74. Company director, group economic adviser, British and Commonwealth Shipping Co. Chairman, Select Committee on Energy since 1979; chairman, all-party committee on information technology since 1979; member, Select Committee on Science and Technology 1971–79. Born May 30 1921; educ. Michaelhouse, Natal, Witwatersrand University, King's College, Cambridge (former president of Union) and Administrative Staff College, Henley. Fellow of Royal Statistical Society. Economic adviser to Central Mining and Investment Corporation 1949–53; member, South African Board of Trade and Industries 1953–56. Member, UK delegation, Council of Europe, Western European Union 1968–72.

Mrs Elizabeth Cleaver, senior lecturer. Born 1935; educ. Portsmouth High School for Girls and LSE. Member, Mid Hants Area Advisory Committee on Education; Council for Social Democracy.

Mr Robert Norris, Assistant Secretary, NUJ. Born Feb 29 1940; educ. Alresford Preparatory School, Peter Symonds' School, Winchester. NUJ official since 1970.

Mr Terence Dicks

HAYES AND HARLINGTON Electorate 57620 1979: 56165 same

Dicks, T. (C)	16451	40.3%
Fagan, P. (Lab)	12217	29.9%
*Sandelson, N. D. (SDP/All)	11842	29.0%
Hill, F. (Freedom)	324	0.8%
C majority	4234	10.4%
Total vote 40834		Turnout 70.9%

1979: Total vote 42129 (75.0%); Lab 20350 (48.3%); C 17048 (40.5%); L 3900 (9.3%); NF 582 (1.4%); Com 249 (0.6%). Lab maj 3302 (7.8%); swing 8.2% to C.

Mr Terence Dicks, local government officer, elected in 1983, contested Bristol South 1979. Born Mar 17 1937; educ. Oxford University and LSE. Member, London Borough of Hillingdon Council since 1974, deputy leader since 1982, housing chairman since 1978. Head of Opposition secretariat and personal assistant to leader of the GLC Opposition.

Mr Peter Fagan, shopkeeper, is leader of the London Borough of Hillingdon Labour group. Born Jun 15 1932; educ. Christian Brothers School. Member London Borough of Hillingdon Council since 1976. TGWU.

Mr Neville Sandelson, retained seat for Labour in the 1971 by-election; resigned party in 1981 and joined SDP. SDP spokesman on Northern Ireland since 1981 and recently SDP spokesman on the Arts. Barrister, parliamentary and legal consultant. Born Nov 27 1923; educ. Westminster and Trinity College, Cambridge. Contested Chichester 1970; Leicester South-West by-election 1967; Heston and Isleworth 1966; Rushcliffe 1959; Beckenham by-election 1957, and Ashford 1950, 1951 and 1955. Member of former expenditure committee and defence and external affairs subcommittee. Former vice-chairman PLP foreign and home affairs group. Joint chairman, all-party group on the theatre. Member, LCC 1952–58. GMBATU.

Mr Tom Arnold

HAZEL GROVE Electorate 63630

*Arnold, T. R. (C)	22627	46.1%
Vos, A. (L/All)	20605	41.9%
Comyn-Platt, J. (Lab)	5895	12.0%
C majority	2022	4.1%
Total vote 49127		Turnout 77.2%

Mr Tom Arnold, theatre producer and publisher; won the seat in Oct 1974; contested it Feb 1974 and Manchester, Cheetham Jun 1970. Born Jan 25 1947; educ. Bedales, Le Rosey (Geneva) and Pembroke College, Oxford. Secretary Conservative north-west MPs group since 1976. Parliamentary private secretary to Secretary of State for Northern Ireland May 1979–Sep 1981, and to Lord Privy Seal Sep 1981–Apr 1982. Member Society of West End Theatre. ASTMS.

Mr Andrew Vos, barrister. Born Jul 4 1956; educ. Manchester Grammar School and Jesus College, Cambridge. Member, Stockport Council, since May 1983.

Mr Jonathan Comyn-Platt, a solicitor. Aged 35. Member, Greater Manchester Legal Services Committee.

Mr Alec Woodall

HEMSWORTH Electorate 54 323

*Woodall, A. (Lab)	22 081	59.3%
Woofindin, J. (L/All)	7 891	21.2%
Williamson, D. (C)	7 291	19.6%
Lab majority	14 190	38.1%
Total vote 37 263	Turnout	68.6%

Mr Alec Woodall, a colliery surface foreman, has held the seat since Feb 1974. Born Sep 20 1918; educ. Southmoor Road County School, Hemsworth. Member, Hemsworth Urban District Council 1966–73. Member joint committee on consolidation Bills and on statutory instruments. Member, Select Committee on the Environment. Sponsored by NUM. PPS to Secretary of State for Trade 1976.

Mr John Woofindin is a schoolmaster and Methodist local preacher. Born Mar 4 1941; educ. King James' Grammar School, Huddersfield and Durham University. Member, Wakefield Borough Council since 1982, deputy leader of the Liberal group. AMMA.

Mr David Williamson, stockbroker and investment adviser. Born 1950; educ. King Edward VI School, Lichfield; Southampton University; Birmingham College of Commerce. Member, Lichfield District Council 1976–79; chairman, housing committee 1977–79. Former member, South Staffordshire area Social Services Advisory Committee.

Mr John Gorst

HENDON NORTH Electorate 54 505 1979: 54 036 minor

*Gorst, J. M. (C)	18 449	49.9%
Craig, K. (SDP/All)	9 474	25.6%
Williams, A. M. (Lab)	8 786	23.7%
Franklin, B. (Nat)	194	0.5%
Clayton, R. (Ind)	116	0.3%
C majority	8 975	24.2%
Total vote 37 019	Turnout	68.0%

1979: Total vote 39 891 (73.8%); C 20 766 (52.1%); Lab 14 374 (36.0%); L 4 113 (10.3%); NF 638 (1.6%). C maj 6 392 (16.1%); swing 5.7% to C.

Mr John Gorst, company director and consultant. Elected in 1970; contested Bodmin 1966, and Chester-le-Street 1964. Member, Select Committee on Employment since 1979. Born Jun 28 1928; educ. Ardingly College and Corpus Christi College, Cambridge. Founder and former secretary, Telephone Users' Association; and the Local Radio Association.

Mr Kenneth Craig, barrister. Born Aug 19 1950; educ. Haberdashers' Aske's School, Sussex University and Council of Legal Education.

Mr Tony Williams, accountant. Born Jan 17 1938; educ. local state schools. Former Barnet councillor. NGA.

Mr Peter Thomas

HENDON SOUTH Electorate 53 929 1979: 53 954 minor

*Thomas, P. J. M. (C)	17 115	48.6%
Palmer, M. (L/All)	10 682	30.3%
Neall, Mrs D. N. (Lab)	7 415	21.1%
C majority	6 433	18.3%
Total vote 35 212	Turnout	65.3%

1979: Total vote 37 864 (70.2%); C 19 981 (52.8%); Lab 11 231 (29.7%); L 5 799 (15.3%); Eco 563 (1.5%); NF 290 (0.8%). C maj 8 750 (23.1%); swing 4.7% to C.

Mr Peter Thomas, QC, was a member of the Shadow Cabinet as chief Opposition spokesman on Wales 1974–75. Secretary of State for Wales 1970–74; President, National Union of Conservative and Unionist Associations 1974–76; Chairman Conservative Party organization 1970–72; Minister of State, Foreign Affairs 1963–64; Under Secretary, Foreign Office 1961–63; Parliamentary Secretary, Ministry of Labour 1959–61. Elected for Hendon South 1970, MP for Conway 1951–66. Recorder. Born Jul 31 1920; educ. Epworth College, Rhyl and Jesus College, Oxford. Member, Select Committee on Conduct of Members, 1977. Chairman, Select Committee on Members' Salaries since 1982; chairman, Select Committee on Standing Orders 1983. Member, Select Committee on Procedure (Supply) 1982.

Mr Monroe Palmer, chartered accountant, contested Barnet, Hendon South 1979. Born Nov 30 1938; educ. Orange Hill Grammar School. Joint treasurer, Liberal Party.

Mrs Doreen Neall is a Co-operative councillor in Barnet and West Hendon. Member, TGWU 1951–53; CPSA 1973.

Mr Michael Heseltine

HENLEY Electorate 62120

*Heseltine, M. R. (C)	27039	59.7%
Brook, I. (L/All)	13258	29.3%
Roxburgh, I. (Lab)	4282	9.5%
Johnson, Ms R. (WFLOE)	517	1.1%
Rogers, T. (ONC)	213	0.5%
C majority	13781	30.4%
Total vote 45309		Turnout 72.9%

Mr Michael Heseltine was appointed Secretary of State for Defence in Jan 1983; Secretary of State for Environment 1979–83. Joined the Shadow Cabinet as chief Opposition spokesman on industry 1974–76, and was chief spokesman on environment 1976–79; spokesman on trade Mar–Jun 1974. Minister for Aerospace and Shipping 1972–74; Under Secretary for the Environment 1970–72; Parliamentary Secretary, Ministry of Transport Jun–Oct 1970. Returned in Feb 1974; represented Tavistock 1966–74; contested Coventry North 1964, and Gower 1959. Born Mar 21 1933; educ. Shrewsbury and Pembroke College, Oxford (President of Union 1954). Chairman, Haymarket Press, 1966–70 and 1974–79.

Mr Ian Brook, sales executive. Born Aug 2 1949; educ. Cheney School, Oxford. Mayor of Thame 1981–82 district councillor. ASTMS.

Mr Iain Roxburgh, civil engineer and personnel officer. Born Nov 4 1943; educ. Imperial College, London University. Member, Brent Council 1971–78; Brent Co-operative Party. GLCSA.

Mr Colin Shepherd

HEREFORD Electorate 64051 1979: 61447 same

*Shepherd, C. (C)	23334	48.1%
Green, C. (L/All)	21057	43.4%
Evans, J. (Lab)	3690	7.6%
Murray, Ms V. (Eco)	463	1.0%
C majority	2277	4.7%
Total vote 48544		Turnout 75.8%

1979: Total vote 48204 (78.4%); C 23012 (47.7%); L 18042 (37.4%); Lab 7150 (14.8%). C maj 4907 (10.3%); swing 9.3% to C.

Mr Colin Shepherd was elected in Oct 1974. Marketing director and parliamentary adviser. Born Jan 13 1938; educ. Oundle, Caius College, Cambridge, McGill University, Montreal. Joint vice-chairman, Conservative backbench agricultural committee since 1979; former joint secretary. Member, Select Committee on House of Commons Services and catering subcommittee since 1979.

Mr Christopher Green, arts administrator to the City of London Festival and director of an advertising association, contested Surbiton 1970, Cheadle Feb and Oct 1974, and Hereford 1979. Born May 10 1943; educ. Wrekin College, Shropshire, and King's College, University of London. NUJ.

Mr John Evans is deputy manager, Ebbw Vale adult education centre and leisure centre. Born Aug 6 1941; educ. Lewis Boys' School, Pengam; Cardiff University; London University. President, Ebbw Vale Labour Party, 1982. Member, Rhymney Valley District Council, since 1976; chairman, environmental health committee. NATFHE. NUPE.

Mr Bowen Wells

HERTFORD AND STORTFORD Electorate 68615

*Wells, P. B. (C)	29039	56.0%
Wotherspoon, R. (SDP/All)	16110	31.1%
Carr, J. (Lab)	6203	12.0%
Wiles, G. (BNP)	314	0.6%
Cullen, P. (PFA)	221	0.4%
C majority	12929	24.9%
Total vote 51 887		Turnout 75.6%

Mr Bowen Wells, elected for this seat in 1983, was MP for Hertford and Stevenage 1979–83. Senior executive of the Commonwealth Development Corporation 1961–73. Owner and managing director of Substation Group Services Ltd from 1973. Born Aug 4 1935; educ. St Paul's School, London. PPS to Minister of State for Employment. Secretary, Conservative backbench employment committee 1981–82; vice chairman, trade committee, 1981. Member, Select Committee on Foreign Affairs and Overseas Development 1981–82. Former member, Bow Group research team on overseas aid and development, and former chairman, Westminster for Europe Campaign.

Mr Ronald Wotherspoon, systems liaison manager. Born 1948; educ. St Bonaventure School, Forest Gate, and University College Swansea. A founder and former national political director, Tory Reform Group. Systems liaison manager for Cambridge company, responsible for development of computer systems and their introduction to end users. Founder member, Crisis at Christmas.

Mr John Carr is Hackney Borough Council equal opportunities officer. Aged 33; educ. LSE and Huddersfield Technical College. Member, GLC and ILEA since May 1981 responsible for GLC equal opportunities and formative action policy. Member, Campaign for Labour Party Democracy; Labour Co-ordinating Committee; CND; Fabians. Nalgo and NUPE.

Mr Ian Stewart

HERTFORDSHIRE NORTH Electorate 75 439

*Stewart, I. (C)	29 302	49.0%
Binney, G. (L/All)	19 359	32.4%
Reilly, J. (Lab)	11 104	18.6%
C majority	9 943	16.6%
Total vote 59 765	Turnout	79.2%

Mr Ian Stewart, became Economic Secretary to the Treasury in 1983; Under Secretary of State for Defence Procurement Jan–Nov 1983. Won this seat in 1983; MP for Hitchin 1974–83; contested Hammersmith North 1970. Company director. Born August 10 1935; educated Haileybury and Jesus College, Cambridge. Secretary, Conservative parliamentary finance committee 1977–79. PPS to the Chancellor of the Exchequer 1979–83. County vice-president, St John Ambulance Brigade for Herts since 1977. Trustee, Sir Halley Stewart Trust since 1978. Member, Council British Museum Society 1975–76; life Governor, 1977.

Mr George Binney is an international business consultant. Born Dec 30 1941. Educ. Cambridge University and the European Business School, France. Qualified as a barrister before entering business.

Mr James Reilly, wood machinist. Became member, Hitchin Council 1960, later leader of Labour group, North Herts District Council. Born Nov 18 1926; educ. secondary school. AUEW.

Mr Richard Page

HERTFORDSHIRE SOUTH WEST Electorate 74 371

*Page, R. (C)	30 217	53.6%
Blair, I. (L/All)	18 023	32.0%
Playfair, E. (Lab)	7 818	13.9%
Luton, M. (Ind)	307	0.5%
C majority	12 194	21.6%
Total vote 56 365	Turnout	75.8%

Mr Richard Page was returned at a by-election in Dec 1979. Contested Workington Feb and Oct 1974, and was MP for Workington Nov 1976–May 1979. Director of family company. Born Feb 22 1941; educ. Hurstpierpoint College and Luton Technical College. Banstead UDC councillor 1968–71. PPS to Leader of the House since 1982.

Dr Ian Blair, principal scientific officer, Atomic Energy Research Establishment, Harwell. Born May 9 1936; educ. King George V School, Southport; Oriel College, Oxford; University of Liverpool. Contested Abingdon, 1979. Member, Oxfordshire County Council, since 1981. IPCS. Author of *Taming the Atom*.

Mr Edward Playfair, a science teacher, fought London borough elections in 1982.Born Nov 14, 1960; educ. French Lycée, London; London University. NUT. Fabian Society.

Mr Robert Jones

HERTFORDSHIRE WEST Electorate 76 597

Jones, R. (C)	28 436	46.7%
Hollinghurst, N. (SDP / All)	18 860	31.0%
Boateng, P. (Lab)	13 583	22.3%
C majority	9 576	15.7%
Total vote 60 879	Turnout	79.5%

Mr Robert Jones, civil engineering adviser was elected in 1983. Born Sep 26 1950; educ. Merchant Taylors and St Andrews University. Contested Teesside, Stockton 1979; Kirkcaldy Oct 1974. Member, St Andrews Burgh Council 1972–75, Fife County Council 1973–75, Chiltern District Council since 1979.

Mr Nicholas Hollinghurst, marketing consultant. Born Sep 22 1945; educ. St Anselm's College, Birkenhead, and University of Manchester Institute of Science and Technology. Member, Dacorum District Council since 1981.

Mr Paul Boateng, solicitor. Born 1951. Member, GLC; chairman, police committee.

Mr Cecil Parkinson

HERTSMERE Electorate 72 997

*Parkinson, C. (C)	28 628	53.2%
Gifford, Mrs Z. (L/All)	13 758	25.6%
Reed, I. D. D. (Lab)	10 315	19.2%
Parkinson, R. (Ind Com)	1 116	2.1%
C majority	14 870	27.6%
Total vote 53 817	Turnout	73.7%

Mr Cecil Parkinson, chairman of the Conservative Party 1981–83, when he resigned, was Secretary of State for Trade and Industry Jun–Oct 1983. His party chairmanship coincided with his appointment in 1981 as Paymaster General attending all Cabinet meetings. In 1982 he was appointed to the additional post of Chancellor of the Duchy of Lancaster. Minister of State for Trade, 1979–81; an Opposition spokesman on trade, 1976–79; Opposition whip, 1974–76; assistant Government whip 1974. Elected for Hertsmere 1983; MP for South Hertfordshire Feb 1974–83, and for Enfield West 1970–74; contested Northampton 1970. Chartered accountant; founder and former chairman, Parkinson Hart Securities; former chairman of other companies. Born Sep 1 1931; educ. Royal Grammar School, Lancaster and Emmanuel College, Cambridge.

Mrs Zerbanoo Gifford, housewife. Born May 11 1950; educ. Roedean and Watford College of Technology. Member, Harrow Council.

Mr Derek Reed, economist. Born Nov 23 1950; educ. Letchworth Grammar School, Oxford University and Manchester University. School governor. APEX, Co-operative Party. Head of research, IPCS.

Mr Geoffrey Rippon

HEXHAM Electorate 54 341

*Rippon, G. (C)	21 374	51.5%
Robson, E. (L/All)	13 066	31.5%
Byers, S. J. (Lab)	7 056	17.0%
C majority	8 308	20.0%
Total vote 41 496	Turnout	76.4%

Mr Geoffrey Rippon QC, was leader of the Conservative Group in the European Parliament 1977–79. Appointed to the Shadow Cabinet in Mar 1974 as a spokesman on foreign and Commonwealth affairs and Europe, and Nov 1974–Mar 1975 was chief spokesman. Secretary of State for the Environment 1972–74; Chancellor of the Duchy of Lancaster with responsibility for EEC negotiations 1970–72; Minister of Technology Jun–Jul 1970. Chief Opposition spokesman on housing and local government 1968–70, and Opposition spokesman on defence 1968–70. Minister of Public Buildings and Works 1962–64, joining Cabinet in 1963; Parliamentary Secretary Ministry of Housing and Local Government 1961–62, and Ministry of Aviation 1959–61. Returned in 1966; represented Norwich South 1955–64. Barrister and non-executive company chairman. Born May 28 1924; educ. King's College, Taunton, and Brasenose College, Oxford. Chairman, Conservative parliamentary foreign and Commonwealth affairs committee 1979–82.

Mr Euan Robson, deputy regional secretary of the Northern Gas Consumers' Council. Born Feb 17 1954; educ. Trinity College, Glenalmond; universities of Newcastle, Durham and Strathclyde. Agent, Hexham constituency Liberal Assoc. 1977–81. Member, Northumberland County Council since 1981. Life member, Scottish National Trust. Nalgo.

Mr Stephen Byers, law lecturer. Born Apr 13 1953; educ. Chester College of Further Education; Liverpool Polytechnic. Member, North Tyneside Metropolitan Borough Council; chairman, North Tyneside Education Committee. NATFHE.

Mr Jim Callaghan

HEYWOOD AND MIDDLETON Electorate 59 870

*Callaghan, J. (Lab)	18 111	43.3%
Hodgson, Mrs C. (C)	14 137	33.8%
Rumbelow, A. (SDP/All)	9 262	22.1%
Henderson, K. (BNP)	316	0.8%
Lab majority	3 974	9.5%
Total vote 41 826	Turnout	69.6%

Mr Jim Callaghan, elected in 1983, was MP for Middleton and Prestwich 1974–83. Former lecturer at St John's College, Manchester. Born Jan 1927; educ. Manchester University and London University. Member Commons Standing Orders Committee since 1981. Middleton Borough Council 1971–74. Football coach and referee.

Mrs Christine Hodgson, teacher. Born Dec 10 1941; educ. St Felix School, Southwold, Suffolk, and Cambridge and London universities. Member, Fylde Borough Council since 1972. Company secretary to farming group. NAS, UWT.

Mr Arthur Rumbelow, a barrister and

deputy judge in the Crown Court, has been an SDP member of Rochdale Council since 1982. Born 1943; educ. Cambridge University. Called to the Bar, 1967; practises in Manchester; recently appointed a deputy judge, Crown Court. Member and past president, Middleton Catenian Assoc.

Mr Christopher Hawkins

HIGH PEAK Electorate 67 358

Hawkins, C. (C)	24 534	46.4%
Marquand, D. (SDP / All)	14 594	27.6%
Wilcox, D. J. (Lab)	13 755	26.0%
C majority	9 940	18.8%
Total vote 52 883		Turnout 78.5%

Mr Christopher Hawkins, elected in 1983, is senior lecturer in economics at Southampton University. Born Nov 26 1937; educ. Bristol Grammar School and Bristol University. Former member, Coventry City Council. Author of Conservative policy on council house sales.

Mr David Marquand, professor of contemporary history and politics, Salford University, since 1978, was Labour MP for Ashfield 1966–77, and chief adviser, Secretariat-General, European Commission, 1977–78. Born Sep 20 1934; educ. Emanuel School and Magdalen and St Antony's Colleges, Oxford. PPS to Minister of Overseas Development 1967–69; an Opposition spokesman on economic affairs 1971–72. Member, Select Committee on Estimates 1966–68, Select Committee on Procedure 1968–73, Select Committee on Corporation Tax 1971. British delegate to Council of Europe 1970–73. Member, SDP National Steering Committee since 1981.

Mr David Wilcox aged 36. Member, High Peak District and Derbyshire County Councils; Friends of the Earth.

Mr Frank Dobson

HOLBORN AND ST PANCRAS Electorate 71 604

*Dobson, F. G. (Lab)	20 486	47.5%
Kerpel, A. (C)	13 227	30.7%
Jones, W. (L/All)	9 242	21.4%
Price, R. (WRP)	155	0.4%
Lab majority	7 259	16.8%
Total vote 43 110		Turnout 60.2%

Mr Frank Dobson, an Opposition spokesman on education since 1981, was elected in 1983, having been MP for Holborn and St Pancras South 1979–83. An assistant secretary, local government ombudsman's office 1975–79; member, Camden Borough Council 1971–76, leader 1973–75. Born Mar 15 1940; educ. primary school and Archbishop Holgate Grammar School, York, and LSE. Member, executive, Chile Solidarity Campaign, and of national committee, Anti-Apartheid Movement. NUR sponsored. Member, Select Committee on Environment 1979–81.

Mr Tony Kerpel, senior film examiner, British Board of Film Censors, has led the Conservative opposition on Camden Borough Council since 1981. Born Mar 22 1945; educ. Haberdasher's Aske's School, Elstree; Bath University. Member, Camden Borough Council since 1974. National chairman, Young Conservatives 1975–76. President, European Young Christian Democrats and Young Conservatives 1977–79.

Mr William Jones, television journalist. Born Apr 4 1943; educ. Ling's School, Taunton; Selwyn College, Cambridge; Mannheim University, West Germany, and Brown University, USA. ACTT.

Mr Richard Body

HOLLAND WITH BOSTON Electorate 63 562

*Body, R. (C)	24 962	55.3%
Le Brun, Mrs C. (L / All)	13 226	29.3%
Moore, J. A. (Lab)	6 970	15.4%
C majority	11 736	26.0%
Total vote 45 158		Turnout 71.1%

Mr Richard Body, elected in 1966, has been member of the Select Committee on Agriculture since 1979 and Joint Committee on Consolidation Bills since 1976. Represented Billericay 1955–59; contested Leek 1951, Rotherham 1950, and Abertillery by-election 1950. Barrister, farmer, a member of Lloyd's. Born May 18 1927; educ. Reading School. Former officer of Conservative backbench subcommittee on horticulture. Chairman Open Seas Forum, since 1970. Joint chairman of the council on Get Britain Out (of EEC) Campaign, 1975. A vice-president of Selsdon Group.

Mrs Carole Le Brun, teacher. Born Jan 31 1939; educ. Doncaster Girls' High School, Kenton Lodge Training College, Newcastle upon Tyne, and the Open University. NAS/UWT Lincolnshire Federation, junior vice-president 1983–84.

Mr John Moore, an official of NUPE. Born Jul 5 1938; educ. secondary modern school. Member, Nottinghamshire County Council, Newark Borough Council. NUPE.

Sir Peter Emery

HONITON Electorate 72232

*Emery, Sir P. (C)	32602	60.6%
Sampson, A. (SDP/All)	17833	33.1%
Sharpe, R. A. C. (Lab)	3377	6.3%
C majority	14769	27.5%
Total vote 53812	Turnout	74.5%

Sir Peter Emery was Under-Secretary of State for Energy, 1974; Under-Secretary of State for Trade and Industry, 1972–74, with responsibility for industry. Returned at by-election in 1967; MP for Reading 1959–66; contested Poplar 1951; and Lincoln 1955. An Opposition spokesman on Treasury, economic affairs and trade 1964–65. Member, Select Committee on Industry and Trade since 1979 and Procedure (Finance) since 1982. Joint founder of the Bow Group 1951. Born Feb 27 1926; educ. Scotch Plains, New Jersey, and Oriel College, Oxford. Member, Hornsey Borough Council 1951–58 (deputy mayor 1957–58). Chairman, Shenley Trust Services Ltd and director, Purchasing Management Services Ltd. Chairman, Consultative Council of Professional Management Organisations 1964–72.

Mr Alistair Sampson, antique dealer. Born May 1 1929; educ. Tonbridge School and Cambridge.

Mr Raymond Sharpe, an accountant, contested Surrey North West 1979. Born 1923. Member, CND.

Mr Robin Squire

HORNCHURCH Electorate 61741 1979: 60865 same

*Squire, R. C. (C)	21393	47.0%
Williams, A. R. (Lab)	12209	26.9%
Martin, J. (SDP/All)	11251	24.7%
Joyce, Mrs A. (NF)	402	0.9%
Crowson, M. (Eco)	219	0.5%
C majority	9184	20.2%
Total vote 45474	Turnout	73.7%

1979: Total vote 47562 (78.1%); C 21340 (44.9%); Lab 20571 (43.3%); L 4657 (9.8%); NF 994 (2.1%). C maj 769 (1.6%); swing 8.5% to C; C gain from Lab.

Mr Robin Squire gained Hornchurch for the Conservatives in 1979; contested the seat, Oct 1974. Chartered accountant. Born Jul 12 1944; educ. Tiffin School, Kingston upon Thames. Vice-chairman, Conservative backbench trade and consumer affairs committee 1981–83; member, Select Committee on Environment 1979–83; London borough of Sutton Council 1968–82 (leader 1976–79). Vice-chairman, Conservatives for Electoral Reform 1982–83, and now chairman. National Young Conservatives vice-chairman 1974–75. and director of Shelter since 1982. Appointed PPS to Joint Under Secretaries of State, Transport, June 1983.

Mr Alan Williams, barrister and former schoolteacher, has been GLC member for Hornchurch since 1981. Born Nov 14 1945; educ. Abingdon School, universities of Bradford and Nottingham, Inns of Court School of Law. Vice-chairman, GLC planning committee. Former member, NUT.

Mr John Martin, business consultant and publisher. Born 1936; educ. grammar school and LSE. Former Secretary, Consumer Council.

Sir Hugh Rossi

HORNSEY AND WOOD GREEN Electorate 73870

*Rossi, Sir H.A.L. (C)	22323	42.4%
Veness, Mrs V. (Lab)	18424	35.0%
Burrell, M. (SDP/All)	10995	20.9%
Lang, P. (Eco)	854	1.6%
C majority	3899	7.4%
Total vote 52596	Turnout	71.2%

Sir Hugh Rossi, Minister for Social Security 1981–83; Minister of State for Northern Ireland 1979–81. An Opposition spokesman on housing and land 1974–79. Under Secretary for the Environment 1974; Lord Commissioner of the Treasury (Whip) 1972–74; Assistant Government Whip 1970–72. Elected in 1983, represented Haringey, Hornsey 1966–83. Born Jun 21 1927; educ. Finchley Catholic Grammar School and King's College, London University. Member, Haringey Council 1964–68; Hornsey Council 1956–65 (deputy mayor 1964–65); Middlesex County Council 1961–65. Secretary Conservative housing committee 1967–70; vice-chairman legal committee 1970. Deputy leader Government delegation to Council of Europe and Western European Union 1970–73.

Ms Valerie Veness, deputy leader of the Labour group, Islington council.

Mr Michael Burrell, senior account executive with public relations consultancy; lobby correspondent, Westminster Press, 1973–83. Born Jun 1950; educ. Godalming County Grammar School, St Peter's College, Oxford. NUJ.

Mr Peter Hordern

HORSHAM Electorate 80 407

*Hordern, P. (C)	37 897	63.2%
Archibald, G. (SDP/All)	16 112	26.9%
Ward, G. R. (Lab)	4 999	8.3%
Spurrier, P. (Eco)	925	1.5%
C majority	21 785	36.4%
Total vote 59 933		Turnout 74.5%

Mr Peter Hordern, MP for Horsham 1964–74, was returned for Horsham and Crawley 1974; and for Horsam in 1983. Member of the Public Accounts Committee since 1966. Chairman, Conservative finance committee, 1970–72; member, executive 1922 Committee since 1966. Chairman, Conservative Parliamentary Finance committee, 1970–72. Company director and member, London Stock Exchange, 1957–74. Director, Petrofina (UK) Ltd since 1973, of TR Technology Investment-Trust PLC since 1975 and of Alliance Investment Co since 1978. Born Apr 18 1929; educ. Geelong Grammar School, Australia, and Christ Church, Oxford. Consultant to Fisons Ltd and to House of Fraser. Member of Lloyd's.

Mr Giles Archibald, an actuary. Born Jun 29 1951; educ. Strathallen School, Perthshire, and St Andrew's University. Fellow, Faculty of Actuaries.

Mr Geoffrey Ward, social studies and careers teacher, Warnham Court School, near Horsham. Born 1942. Previously worked as trainee quantity surveyor and estate agent. Member, Christian Socialist Movement, NUT.

Mr Roland Boyes

HOUGHTON AND WASHINGTON Electorate 75 686

Boyes, R. (Lab)	26 168	51.7%
Kenyon, R. (SDP/All)	12 347	24.4%
Vane, R. (C)	12 104	23.9%
Lab majority	13 821	27.3%
Total vote 50 619		Turnout 66.9%

Mr Roland Boyes, MEP for Durham since 1979, was elected in 1983. Born Feb 12 1937. Former teacher and assistant director, Durham County Council. Former district and town councillor for Peterlee, Easington. GMBATU.

Mr Richard Vane, farmer and barrister. Born Jul 31 1951; educ. Eton, Trinity College, Cambridge, Lincoln's Inn, Cumbria College of Agriculture and Forrestry.

Mr Timothy Sainsbury

HOVE Electorate 71 918 1979: 70 318 same

*Sainsbury, T. (C)	28 628	60.5%
Beamish, Mrs T. (L/All)	11 409	24.1%
Wright, C. (Lab)	6 550	13.9%
Layton, T. (SEE)	524	1.1%
Lillie, K. (MDP)	189	0.4%
C majority	17 219	36.4%
Total vote 47 300		Turnout 65.8%

1979: Total vote 50 342 (71.6%); C 30 256 (60.1%); Lab 10 807 (21.5%); L 8 771 (17.4%); NF 508 (1.0%). C maj 19,449 (38.6%); swing 3.4% to C.

Mr Timothy Sainsbury was appointed an assistant Government Whip in Jun 1983; former director of J Sainsbury Ltd and Blackwell Press Ltd. Elected at the 1973 by-election. Born Jun 11 1932; educ. Eton and Worcester College, Oxford. Appointed PPS to the Secretary of State for the Environment 1979. Chairman, all-party group for retail trade since 1979; chairman, all-party parliamentary committee for the release of Soviet Jewry 1976–79, and vice-chairman since 1979; joint honorary treasurer Conservative friends of Israel. Governor, Centre for Environmental Studies 1976–79. Sponsored Indecent Displays (Control) Act 1981.

Mrs Theodora Beamish, housewife. Born Jul 8 1921; educ. Convent of Sacred Heart, London. Member, Liberal Party groups on electoral reform, ecology and CND.

Mr Christopher Wright, lithographic retoucher. Born 1947.

Mr Barry Sheerman

HUDDERSFIELD Electorate 68174

*Sheerman, B. (Lab)	20051	41.4%
Tweddle, J. (C)	16096	33.2%
Hasler, Mrs K. J. L. (L/All)	12027	24.8%
Hirst, H. (Ind)	271	0.6%
Lab majority	3955	8.2%
Total vote 48445		Turnout 71.1%

Mr Barry Sheerman, chairman of the PLP trade group since 1981, represented Huddersfield East 1979–83; contested Taunton, Oct 1974. Born Aug 17 1940; educ. Hampton Grammar School, Kingston Technical College, and LSE. Adviser to Institute for European Studies; member, Public Accounts Committee since 1981; chairman, Parliamentary Advisory Council on Transport Safety; member, Loughor UDC 1972–74, and Lliw Valley Borough Council 1973–78. Sponsored by Co-operative Party. ASTMS.

Mr John Tweddle, electrical engineer. Born 1949; educ. St George's College, Weybridge, and Birmingham and Huddersfield polytechnics. Opposition chief whip and spokesman on traffic and highways and strategic policy, West Yorkshire Metropolitan County Council. Member, Advisory Committee, Rathbone Training Workshops, Leeds; associate member, Institution of Electrical Engineers. Founder member, Barkston Ash Conservative Trade Union Group. EPEA.

Mrs Kathleen Hasler contested Huddersfield West in 1979 and in Feb and Oct 1974. Born Mar 10 1939; educ. Twickenham County School and Exeter University. Kirklees councillor; formerly a teacher.

Mr John Prescott

HULL EAST Electorate 70037

*Prescott, J. (Lab)	23615	49.9%
Leng, D. (C)	13541	28.6%
Grurevitch, Mrs C. (L/All)	10172	21.5%
Lab majority	10074	21.3%
Total vote 47328		Turnout 67.6%

Mr John Prescott became Opposition spokesman on regional affairs in 1981, spokesman on transport 1979–81. Member, European Parliament 1975–79 and leader of the Labour delegation 1976–79. Former official of the National Union of Seamen. Elected in 1970; contested Southport 1966. Born May 31 1938; educ. Grange Secondary Modern School, Ellesmere Port, Ruskin College and Hull University. Sponsored by NUS. Former member, Select Committee on Nationalised Industries, PPS to Mr Peter Shore when Secretary of State for Trade 1974–76.

Mr Dennis Leng, company director; retired managing director, export division, Reckitt and Colman. Born Sep 11 1923; educ. Malet Lambert Grammar School, Hull, and Manchester and Geneva universities. Member, Beverley Borough Council. Fellow, Institute of Marketing.

Mrs Christine Gurevitch, teacher. Born Dec 25 1947.

Mr Kevin McNamara

HULL NORTH Electorate 74543

*McNamara, K. (Lab)	21365	42.5%
Hayward, C. (C)	15337	30.5%
Smith, T. A. (SDP/All)	13381	26.6%
Tenny, R. (Nat)	222	0.4%
Lab majority	6028	12.0%
Total vote 50305		Turnout 67.5%

Mr Kevin McNamara, an Opposition spokesman on defence and disarmament since 1982. Lecturer in law. Represented Kingston-upon-Hull Central Feb 1974–83; returned for this seat in 1983; MP for Kingston-upon-Hull North 1966–74; contested Bridlington 1964. Born Sep 5 1934; educ. St Mary's College, Crosby, and Hull University. Chairman, PLP Northern Ireland group. Former member, UK delegation to Council of Europe. Member of Select Committee on Procedure (Finance), Member, Foreign Affairs Select Committee and chairman, subcommittee on Overseas Aid and Development Secretary, TGWU parliamentary group. Sponsored by TGWU.

Mr Christopher Hayward, employed in his family construction, civil engineering and property companies. Born Aug 13 1959. A former National Young Conservatives vice-chairman and former chairman, Wessex Young Conservatives. Member, Dorset County Council since 1981.

Mr Terence Smith, university administrator. Born Apr 3 1934; educ. Chesterfield School, University of Hull. AUT.

Mr Stuart Randall

HULL WEST Electorate 57702

Randall, S. (Lab)	15361	41.9%
Humphreys, M. (C)	11707	32.0%
Unwin, W. (SDP/All)	9575	26.1%
Lab majority	3654	10.0%
Total vote 36643		Turnout 63.5%

Mr Stuart Randall, elected in 1983, business consultant, contested Worcestershire South Oct 1974, and the European Parliament constituency of Midlands West 1979. Born Jun 22 1938; educ. University of Wales, Cardiff. Sponsored by EETPU.
Mr Martin Humphrys, teacher. Born 1955; educ. Chatham House Grammar School, Ramsgate, and Downing College, Cambridge. Former chairman, Thanet East Young Conservatives, and former research assistant to Mr Jonathan Aitken, MP. Assistant house master, Eastbourne College.
Mr Stephen Unwin, university lecturer and chartered accountant. Councillor, Hammersmith and Fulham 1971–82, deputy leader of opposition. Born Mar 5 1947; educ. Bournemouth School and LSE. AUT, departmental representative.

Mr John Major

HUNTINGDON Electorate 76668

*Major, J. (C)	34254	62.4%
Gatiss, Mrs S. (L/All)	13906	25.3%
Slater, M. (Lab)	6317	11.5%
Eiloart (Eco)	444	0.8%
C majority	20348	37.1%
Total vote 54921		Turnout 71.6%

Mr John Major, who was appointed a Government whip in 1983, was elected for Huntingdonshire in 1979; contested Camden, St Pancras North, in Feb and Oct 1974. Senior Executive of British Overseas Bank, and associate of the Institute of Bankers. Born Mar 29 1943; educ. Rutlish Grammar School. Member, London Borough of Lambeth Council 1968–71. Founded Lambeth Borough Young Conservatives in 1965. Chairman, Brixton Conservative Association 1970–71. Chairman, Beckenham Conservative Association. Member, Board of Warden Housing Association 1975–83. Former secretary, Conservative parliamentary party environment committee, PPS to Ministers of State, Home Office 1981–83.
Mrs Sheila Gatiss, research assistant. Born Dec 1 1937; educ. Streatham Hill and Clapham High School; and Guy's Hospital, London. Member, Cambridgeshire County Council since 1981; chairman, Cambridge Community Health Council; national chairman, National Association for the Welfare of Children in Hospital.
Mr Mark Slater, teacher. Born 1938.

Mr Kenneth Hargreaves

HYNDBURN Electorate 59341

Hargreaves, J. K. (C)	19405	42.2%
*Davidson, A. (Lab)	19384	42.2%
Bridgen, J. (SDP/All)	6716	14.6%
Smith, F. (Eco)	266	0.6%
Gateson, P. (Ind)	169	0.4%
C majority	21	0.0%
Total vote 45940		Turnout 77.4%

Mr Kenneth Hargreaves, an office manager, elected in 1983. Born Mar 1 1939; educ. St Mary's College, Blackburn; Manchester College of Commerce. Member, Oswaldtwistle UDC 1965–74, then Hyndburn Borough Council; Mayor of Hyndburn 1979–80; deputy leader, Conservative Group since 1981. Secretary, Oswaldtwistle Council of Churches.
Mr Arthur Davidson QC, MP for Accrington 1966–83, became Opposituon spokesman on legal affairs in 1981 and chief legal spokesman in Nov 1982. A spokesman on defence 1979–81; Parliamentary Secretary to the Law Officers 1974–79. Contested Preston North 1959 and Blackpool South 1955. Born Nov 1928; educ. Liverpool College, King George V School, Southport, and Trinity College, Cambridge. Chairman, home affairs group, PLP, 1971–74. Member, Council of Consumers' Association 1970–74; Executive Committee, Soc of Labour Lawyers since 1981; Nat Exec Fabian Society. Chairman, House of Commons Jazz Club 1973. Council member, National Jazz Youth Orchestra. GMBATU.
Mr John Bridgen, principal lecturer at Preston Polytechnic. Educ. Wallington County School and Emmanuel College, Cambridge. Secretary, International Higher Education Standing Conference; executive committee member responsible for public relations. Alternate to director on Inter-University and Polytechnic Council.

Mr Vivian Bendall

ILFORD NORTH Electorate 60248

*Bendall, V. W. H. (C)	22042	51.3%
Gapes, M. J. (Lab)	10841	25.3%
Roxburgh, I. (SDP/All)	10052	23.4%
C majority	11201	26.1%
Total vote 42935	Turnout	71.3%

Mr Vivian Bendall won the seat for the Conservatives in Mar 1978 by-election; contested Hertford and Stevenage Feb and Oct 1974. Born Dec 14 1938; educ. Coombe Hill House, Croydon, and Broad Green College, Croydon. Member Croydon Borough Council, 1964–78, and GLC 1970–73. Chairman Greater London Young Conservatives 1967–68. Principal of firm of surveyors and valuers. Vice-chairman Conservative Transport Committee; secretary foreign and Commonwealth Affairs and Employment Committees.

Mr Michael Gapes is a research officer in the Labour Party international department. Born Sep 4 1952; educ. Buckhurst Hill County High School, Cambridge University, and Middlesex Polytechnic. Sponsored by TGWU (ACTS).

Mr Ian Roxburgh, member SDP national working group on energy. Born 1939; educ. King Edward VII Grammar School and Nottingham and Cambridge universities. Professor of applied mathematics; adviser consultant, Science and Engineering Research Council, Ministry of Defence, European Space Agency; partner, Micro-Main Computing Services.

Mr Neil Thorne

ILFORD SOUTH Electorate 58208

*Thorne, N. G. (C)	18672	45.4%
Hogben, J. H. (Lab)	14106	34.3%
Scott, R. (L/All)	7999	19.5%
Martin, R. A. (BNP)	316	0.8%
C majority	4566	11.1%
Total vote 41093	Turnout	70.6%

Mr Neil Thorne, chartered surveyor, company director, and Lloyd's underwriter, gained Redbridge, Ilford South for Conservatives in 1979; contested the seat in Oct 1974. Born Aug 8 1932; educ. City of London School and London University. Member, Select Committee on Consolidation Bills since 1979. Vice-chairman, Conservative backbench committee of Greater London MPs. Member, County of London Territorial Assoc., vice-president, British Legion. Member, Redbridge Borough Council 1966–68, and alderman 1976–78, GLC 1967–73; member, Statutory Committee for Dockland Development; freeman and liveryman, City of London. Chairman, National Council for Civil Defence since 1982.

Mr John Hogben, industrial engineer. Born Feb 22 1925; educ. technical college and college of further education. Member, Redbridge Borough Council since 1971.

Mr Ralph Scott fought Redbridge, Ilford South 1979, and Waltham Forest, Leyton Oct 1974. Born Jan 10 1939; educ. South East Essex County Technical School, Barking and North East London Polytechnic. Contracts officer.

Mr Russell Johnston

INVERNESS, NAIRN AND LOCHABER Electorate 63645

*Johnston, R. (L/All)	20671	46.1%
Maclean, D. G. (C)	13373	29.8%
MacMillan, D. (Lab)	6448	14.4%
Vernal, H. (SNP)	4395	9.8%
L/All majority	7298	16.3%
Total vote 44887	Turnout	70.5%

Mr Russell Johnston has been leader of the Scottish Liberal Party since 1974. Elected for Inverness in 1964 and for this seat in 1983. First United Kingdom Liberal member of European Parliament (1973–75, 1976–79) and Vice-President, Political Committee 1976–79; unsuccessfully contested first European direct elections 1979. Liberal spokesman on foreign affairs and Scotland since 1981 and a former spokesman on defence. Former member, Select Committee on EEC secondary legislation. Born Jul 28 1932; educ. Portree High School, Isle of Skye, and Edinburgh University, and Moray House College of Education. Former teacher and party research assistant. Chairman, Scottish Liberal Party 1970–74; vice-chairman 1965–70. Member, Royal Commission on Local Government in Scotland, 1966–69.

Mr David Maclean, security training consultant. Born 1953; educ. Fortrose Academy and Aberdeen University.

Mr Duncan MacMillan, technical officer with British Telecom, contested Argyll 1964. Born Dec 16 1929; educ. Campbeltown Grammar School. Provost of Campbeltown 1965–68.

Mr Hamish Vernal, primary school headteacher. Born 1945; educ. Paisley College of Education and Durham University. Member, SNP national organization committee. EIS.

Mr Kenneth Weetch

IPSWICH Electorate 67 292

*Weetch, K. (Lab)	22 191	43.7%
Cottrell, Dr E. (C)	21 114	41.6%
Miernik, Mrs P. (L/All)	7 220	14.2%
Pearson, A. (BNP)	235	0.5%
Lab majority	1 077	2.1%
Total vote 50 760		Turnout 75.4%

Mr Kenneth Weetch, lecturer in economic history, was elected in Oct 1974, after contesting the seat in Feb 1974, and Saffron Walden 1970. Born Sep 17 1933; educ. Newbridge Grammar School and LSE. Head of history dept. Hockerill College of Education, Bishop's Stortford, 1964–74. President National Houseowners Soc. 1975–78; parliamentary adviser, Home Owners Mutual Enterprise since 1980. Member, Home Affairs Committee, since 1983. PPS Department of Transport 1976–77. TWGU.

Dr Elizabeth Cottrell, head of research centre for policy studies and freelance writer and broadcaster, contested Teesside, Redcar 1979. Born Mar 8 1941; educ. Grove Park Girls' Grammar School, Wrexham; New Hall, Cambridge; and Nottingham University. Partner in family business.

Mrs Pat Miernik is a housewife. Born Jul 13 1950; educ. Notre Dame Grammar School, Manchester and Hollings College, Manchester, where she studied fashion design.

Mr Stephen Ross

ISLE OF WIGHT Electorate 94 226 1979: 90 961 same

*Ross, S. (L/All)	38 407	51.0%
Bottomley, Mrs V. (C)	34 904	46.3%
Wilson, Mrs C (Lab)	1 828	2.4%
McDermott, B. (IWPP)	208	0.3%
L/All majority	3 503	4.7%
Total vote 75,347		Turnout 80%

1979: Total vote 74 440 (81.8%); L 35 889 (48.2%); C 35 537 (47.7%); Lab 3 014 (4.0%). L maj 352 (0.5%)

Mr Stephen Ross won the seat for the Liberals in Feb 1974 having contested it in 1966 and 1970. Currently party spokesman on transport, Northern Ireland and environmental subjects. Chartered Surveyor, ex-farmer. Born July 6 1926; educ. Bedford School. Member, IOW County Council 1967–74 and since 1981. Non-executive company director and retailer. IOW chairman, local enterprise agency.

Mrs Virginia Bottomley, magistrate and social worker. Born 1948; educ. Essex University and LSE. Chairman, Lambeth Juvenile Court. Member, Conservative Women's National Committee. Part-time psychiatric social worker in a child guidance unit. Vice-chairman, National Council of Carers and their Elderly Dependants. Executive member, Church of England Children's Society.

Mrs Catherine Wilson, housewife. Born Jun 17 1943; educ. St Mary's Elementary School, Liverpool. Contested constituency, 1979. TGWU.

Mr Jeremy Corbyn

ISLINGTON NORTH Electorate 59 984

Corbyn, J. (Lab)	14 951	40.5%
Coleman, D. (C)	9 344	25.3%
*Grant, J. (SDP/All)	8 268	22.4%
*O'Halloran, M. (Ind Lab)	4 091	11.1%
Bearsford-Walker, L. (BNP)	176	0.5%
Lincoln, R. (CUI)	134	0.4%
Lab majority	5 607	15.2%
Total vote 36 964		Turnout 61.6%

Mr Jeremy Corbyn, area officer for NUPE: previously researcher for Tailor and Garment Workers Union and for AUEW (Engineering Section). Elected in 1983. Born May 1949; educ. Adams Grammar School, Newport, Shropshire. Member, Haringey Borough Council since 1974. Apex.

Mr David Coleman, lecturer in demography at Oxford University. Born 1946; educ. St Benedict's School, Ealing, Queen's College, Oxford, LSE. Member, Bow Group, Education Standing Committee.

Mr John Grant, SDP spokesman on industry, was Labour Under Secretary of State for Employment 1976–79. Resigned from party in Oct 1981. In Nov 1981 joined SDP. Under Secretary of State, Overseas Development 1974–76; Parliamentary Secretary, Civil Service Department, Mar to Oct 1974. MP for Islington East 1970–74, Islington Central Feb 1974–83. Born Oct 16 1932; educ. Stationers Company's School, Hornsey. Chairman SDP Trade Unionists Assoc.

Mr Michael O'Halloran was returned as Labour MP at a by-election in Oct 1969, but resigned from party in 1981 and joined the SDP. Later resigned and fought as Ind. Lab. Builder, railwayman and office manager. Born Aug 20 1928; educ. Clohanes National School, Eire. Member, Islington Borough Council 1967–71. NUR.

Mr Christopher Smith

ISLINGTON SOUTH AND FINSBURY Electorate 59 795

Smith, C. (Lab)	13 460	36.3%
*Cunningham, G. (SDP/All)	13 097	35.3%
Johnston, A. (C)	9 894	26.7%
Donegan, J. (NF)	341	0.9%
Murphy, J. (IFP)	102	0.3%
Stentiford, D. (BNP)	94	0.3%
Slapper, C. (SPGB)	85	0.2%
Lab majority	363	1.0%
Total vote 37 073		Turnout 62.0%

Mr Christopher Smith, housing development worker, was elected in 1983; contested Epsom and Ewell 1979. Born Jul 24 1951; educ. Cassiobury Primary School, Watford; George Watson's College, Edinburgh, Pembroke College, Cambridge, and Harvard University. Member, London Borough of Islington 1978–83; chief whip 1978–79, chairman of housing 1981 and 1982–83. Member, Council for National Parks; ASTMS, branch sec. 1978–80, branch chairman 1980–83.

Mr George Cunningham, was a Labour spokesman on home affairs 1979 to Nov 1981, when he resigned from party and became Independent Labour before joining the SDP in Jun 1982. Returned in Feb 1974. MP for Islington South-West 1970–74, contested Henley 1966. Born Jun 10 1931; educ. Dunfermline High School, Blackpool Grammar School and Manchester and London Universities.

Mr Arthur Johnston, consultant surveyor, contested Luton East Oct 1974. Born 1932; educ. Winchester and Magdalene College, Cambridge.

Mr Neil Kinnock

ISLWYN Electorate 50 259

*Kinnock, N. (Lab)	23 183	59.3%
Johnson, D. (SDP/All)	8 803	22.5%
Bevan, M. (C)	5 511	14.1%
Richards, A. (PlC)	1 574	4.0%
Lab majority	14 380	36.8%
Total vote 39 071		Turnout 77.7%

Mr Neil Kinnock became Leader of the Opposition in Oct 1983 following his election as Leader of the Labour Party. Chief Opposition spokesman on education 1979–83. Represented Bedwelty 1970–83. Elected to Labour Party National Executive Committee, 1978. Born Mar 28 1942; educ. Lewis School, Pengam, Glamorgan, and University College, Cardiff. PPS to Secretary of State for Employment 1974–75; Member BBC General Advisory Council since 1977. Former chairman, PLP Welsh group. Former member, select committees on European secondary legislation and nationalized industries. Member Tribune Group; member, editorial board, Labour Research Dept since 1974; executive member Anti-Apartheid Movement; council member, 'Get Britain Out' of EEC Campaign. Sponsored by TGWU.

Mr David Johnson, head of English department at Cwmcarn Comprehensive School. Born 1947; educ. Lewis' School, Pengam; University College of Wales, Aberystwyth, and Cardiff University. Joined SDP at its formation. SDP councillor Islwyn Borough Council since 1981.

Mr Michael Bevan, sales and marketing administrator. Born Aug 6 1944; educ. primary and secondary schools. Member, Milborne Port parish council.

Mr Aneurin Richards, former official with the National Coal Board, is a member of Islwyn Borough Council.

Mr Donald Dixon

JARROW Electorate 63 770

*Dixon, D. (Lab)	25 151	55.3%
Copland, Miss S. (C)	11 274	24.8%
Lennox, J. A. (L/All)	9 094	20.0%
Lab majority	13 877	30.5%
Total vote 45 519		Turnout 71.4%

Mr Donald Dixon, a trade union official, was elected in 1979. Member, Services Committee since 1979. Chairman PLP shipbuilding committee; vice-chairman, PLP industry committee. Born Mar 6 1929; educ. Ellison Street Church of England School, Jarrow. Member, Jarrow Borough Council 1963–74; leader 1969–74. Member, South Tyneside District Council since 1974; chairman, Labour group and housing committee. Vice-president, Jarrow and Hebburn Trades Council. Member, GMBATU regional council. Sponsored by GMBATU.

Miss Sonia Copland, is manager, domicillary services, Central Brixton, Lambeth Borough Council; formerly an advertising executive. Born 1946; educ. at a convent in Liverpool. Member, Croydon Borough Council, 1968–71; GLC, Lewisham East, 1977–81; and Sutton since 1981.

Mr John Lennox, economics teacher, contested Sunderland North Feb and Oct 1974, and 1979. Born Jun 17 1946; educ. St Aidan's Grammar School, De La Salle College of Education, Durham University and Sunderland Polytechnic. NAS/UWT.

Mr Gary Waller

KEIGHLEY Electorate 63,678

*Waller, G.P.A. (C)	21370	42.6%
*Cryer, R. (Lab)	18596	37.0%
Wells, J. (L/All)	9951	19.8%
Penney, M. (Eco)	302	0.6%
C majority	2774	5.5%
Total vote 50219	Turnout 78.9%	

Mr Gary Waller, elected in 1983; MP for Brighouse and Spenborough 1979–83. Born Jun 24 1945; educ. Rugby School and Lancaster University. Contested Rother Valley Feb and Oct 1974. Member, Transport Select Committee 1979–82; Joint Committee on Consolidation Bills since 1982. Secretary, all-party wool textiles group since 1979. Treasurer, Parliamentary Information Technology Committee since 1981. Secretary, Yorkshire Conservative MPs committee since 1979. PPS to Mr David Howell, Secretary of State for Transport May 1982–83.

Mr Robert Cryer won the seat in Feb 1974. Chairman of the joint select committee on Statutory Instruments 1979–83. Contested Darwen, 1964. Resigned in Nov 1978 as Under-Secretary for Industry, to which he was appointed in 1976, in protest at a decision to cut off public funds to a Merseyside workers' cooperative. Former technical college lecturer. Member, Keighley Borough Council 1971–74. Born Dec 3 1934; educ. Salt High School, Shipley and Hull University.

Mr John Wells, educational psychologist. Born Feb 26 1948; educ. Colfe's Grammar School, West Ham College of Technology, North East London Polytechnic. Member, West Yorkshire County Council since 1981.

Sir Brandon Rhys Williams

KENSINGTON Electorate 49 854 1979: 52396 minor

*Rhys Williams, Sir B. (C)	14274	46.0%
Bousquet, B. T. (Lab)	9173	29.5%
Goodhart, W. (SDP / All)	6873	22.1%
Porritt, J. (Eco)	649	2.1%
Knight, T. (Ind)	86	0.3%
C majority	5101	16.4%
Total vote 31055	Turnout 62.3%	

1979: Total vote 33850 (64.6%); C 17361 (51.3%); Lab 11898 (35.1%); L 3537 (10.4%); Eco 698 (2.1%); NF 356 (1.1%). C maj 5463 (16.2%); swing 5.3% to C.

Sir Brandon Rhys Williams has been a member, Select Committee on Social Services since 1979. Industrial consultant. Represented Kensington since Feb 1974; represented Kensington South 1968–74. Member, European Parliament since 1974, being elected as MEP for London South-East in first direct elections in 1979. Contested Pontypridd 1959 and Ebbw Vale in 1960 by-election and 1964. Born Nov 14 1927; educ. Eton. Chairman National Birthday Trust. Assistant director (appeals) Spastics Society 1962–63. Formerly with ICI Ltd. Former vice-chairman, parliamentary health and social security parliamentary finance committees.

Mr Benjamin Bousquet, housing advice officer. Born Nov 18 1938; educ. Fircroft College, Birmingham. Kensington and Chelsea councillor; former shop steward. Nalgo.

Mr William Goodhart, barrister, is brother of Mr Philip Goodhart, Conservative MP for Beckenham; his wife Celia was SDP candidate for Kettering. He helped produce the original SDP constitution. A trustee, Campden Charities; chairman, local residents' assoc., Campden Hill.

Mr Andrew Rowe

KENT MID Electorate 66510

Rowe, A. (C)	25400	53.5%
Wainman, Mrs A. (L/All)	12857	27.1%
Hull, V. (Lab)	8928	18.8%
Delderfield, D. (New Brit)	324	0.7%
C majority	12543	26.4%
Total vote 47509	Turnout 71.4%	

Mr Andrew Rowe, journalist and consultant in government affairs, elected in 1983. Born Sep 11 1935; educ. Eton and Merton College, Oxford. Director of Community Affairs at Conservative Central Office, responsible for students, Young Conservatives and trade unionists, 1975–79; founded and directed the Conservative Small Business Bureau and editor of Small Business newspaper. IoJ.

Mrs Allison Wainman, director of a typesetting and origination firm. Born Jul 30 1940; educ. Priory School, Jamaica. Contested Ashford 1979. Member, Kent County Council.

Mr Vernon Hull, South-East district secretary, WEA. Aged 35; educ. Keele and Lancaster universities. Chairman, Medway constituency Labour Party; member, Rochester-upon-Medway City Council. Former further education college lecturer.

Mr Roger Freeman

KETTERING Electorate 62 819

Freeman, R. (C)	23 223	48.4%
Goodhart, Mrs C. (SDP/All)	14 637	30.5%
Gordon, A. (Lab)	10 119	21.5%
C majority	8 586	17.9%
Total vote 47 979	Turnout	76.4%

Mr Roger Freeman contested Don Valley in 1979. Elected in 1983. Managing director in London of an American merchant bank. Chartered accountant. Born May 1942; educ. Whitgift School; Balliol College, Oxford. President, Oxford University Conservative Assoc. 1964. Former treasurer and council member. Bow Group and managing director Bow Publications 1968. Lecturer and conference chairman, Institute of Chartered Accountants; Founder member Hundred Group of UK Chartered Accountant Finance Directors; member, Institute of Fiscal Studies.

Mrs Celia Goodhart, former civil servant, now an SDP regional organizer, fund raiser and membership officer at party HQ. Born Jul 7 1939; educ. at Church Missionary Society schools and St Hilda's College, Oxford.

Mr Alex Gordon, a lecturer at a technical college, is leader of the Labour group on Kettering District Council. Fought European Parliament elections for Northants in 1979. Director, Leicestershire Co-operative Society.

Mr William McKelvey

KILMARNOCK AND LOUDOUN Electorate 61 394 1979: 60 351 same

*McKelvey, W. (Lab)	20 250	43.6%
Leckie, R. (C)	11 450	24.7%
Ross, A. (SDP/All)	10 545	22.7%
Calman, C. (SNP)	4 165	19.0%
Lab majority	8 800	19.0%
Total vote 46 410	Turnout	75.6%

1979 (as Kilmarnock): Total vote 48 932 (81.1%); Lab 25 718 (52.6%); C 14 251 (29.1%); SNP 8 963 (18.3%). Lab maj 11 467 (23.5%); swing 1.6% to C.

Mr William McKelvey is a member of the Select Committee on Scottish Affairs, and of the Select Committee on Standing Orders. He was elected for Kilmarnock in 1979. Former full-time Labour Party and union official. Born Jul 1934; educ. Dundee Academy College of Technology. Sponsored by AUEW engineering section. Member, executive, Scottish Labour MPs. Labour group leader, Dundee District Council.

Mr Ross Leckie, teacher and agriculturalist. Born 1957; educ. Fettes College, Edinburgh, Corpus Christi College, Oxford, Royal Agricultural College, Cirencester. Chairman, Strathearn Young Conservatives and Glenalmond and Buchanty branch. Iain Macleod Memorial Travelling Scholarship holder, 1975; taught English in Kenya, 1975–76.

Mr Aubrey Ross, senior lecturer in law and community relations at the Metropolitan Police College, Hendon, and director of a fine art company. Born 1935.

Mr Charles Calman, teacher. Born 1928; educ. Robert Douglas School and Craigie College of Education, Ayr.

Mr Alick Buchanan-Smith

KINCARDINE AND DEESIDE Electorate 59 552

*Buchanan-Smith, A. (C)	20 293	47.7%
Waugh, S. (L/All)	12 497	29.4%
Morell, Mrs M. (Lab)	6 472	15.2%
Tuttle, A. (SNP)	3 297	7.8%
C majority	7 796	18.3%
Total vote 42 559	Turnout	71.5%

Mr Alick Buchanan-Smith appointed Minister of State for Energy Jun 1983; Minister of State for Agriculture, Fisheries and Food 1979–83; Under-Secretary of State, Scottish Office 1970–74. Former Opposition spokesman on Scottish affairs, and member of Shadow Cabinet from which he resigned in 1977, over devolution. Elected for this seat in 1983; represented Angus North and Mearns 1964–83; contested West Fife 1959. Farmer. Born Apr 8 1932; educ. Edinburgh Academy, Glenalmond, Pembroke College, Cambridge, and Edinburgh University. Member, Select Committee on Agriculture 1968–69; vice-chairman, Conservative agricultural committee 1965–66.

Mr Alexander Waugh, personnel manager. Born Nov 13 1934; educ. The High School of Glasgow, Scottish College of Commerce (University of Strathclyde) and London University. Former member, Scottish Liberal Party Executive. Ordained Elder, Church of Scotland.

Mrs Morag Morrell is a freelance journalist. Aged 51; educ. Arbroath High School. Regional councillor, Grampian Region. Member, Labour Campaign for a Scottish Assembly.

Mr Austin Tuttle, teacher at Mackie Academy. Born 1947; educ. MackieAcademy, Stonehaven and Aberdeen University. EIS.

Mr Norman Lamont

KINGSTON UPON THAMES
Electorate 56 794 1979: 57 572 minor

*Lamont, N. S. H. (C)	22 094	54.1%
Hayes, R. (L/All)	13 222	32.4%
Smith, P. J. (Lab)	4 977	12.2%
Presant-Collins, Miss A. (Eco)	290	0.7%
Dodd, P. (LS)	259	0.6%
C majority	8 872	21.7%
Total vote 40 842	Turnout	71.9%

1979: Total vote 43 115 (74.9%); C 24 944 (57.9%); Lab 11 400 (26.4%); L 6 771 (15.7%). C maj 13 544 (31.5%); swing 5.8% to C.

Mr Norman Lamont, Minister of State for Industry from 1981–83 and for Trade and Industry since Jun 1983; Under Secretary of State for Energy 1979–81. An Opposition spokesman on industry 1976–79, and on consumer affairs and prices 1975–76. Merchant banker. Returned at a by-election in 1972; contested Kingston-upon-Hull East 1970. Secretary, Conservative parliamentary health and social security committee 1972–74. Born May 8 1942; educ. Loretto School and Fitzwilliam College, Cambridge. (President of Union 1964). Chairman Bow Group 1971–72. Joint secretary conservative finance committee 1976. Former member Select Committee on Procedure.

Mr Roger Hayes, local government trainer, Born Jun 23 1953; educ. Faraday Comprehensive, Acton, and Isleworth Polytechnic. Member, Medina Borough Council, Isle of Wight, 1977–81; Royal Borough of Kingston upon Thames Council since 1982. Nalgo.

Mr Peter Smith, teacher in further education. Born Jul 10 1949; educ. LSE and Birkbeck College, London. Hounslow councillor since 1982. Member, ATTI/NATFHE and branch chairman of SEA.

Mr Robert Hayward

KINGSWOOD
Electorate 72 159

Hayward, R. (C)	22 573	40.4%
Walker, T. (Lab)	20 776	37.1%
Gilbert, M. (SDP/All)	12 591	22.5%
C majority	1 797	3.2%
Total vote 55 940	Turnout	77.5%

Mr Robert Hayward, group personnel manager, was elected in 1983; contested Carmarthen, Oct 1974. Born 1949; educ. Abingdon School, Maidenhead Grammar School and University of Rhodesia. Vice-chairman, National Young Conservatives, 1976–77; Coventry City councillor, 1976–78. Qualified rugby referee.

Mr Terence Walker, an accountant, was MP for the constituency Feb 1974–79. Born Oct 26 1935; educ. Clarks Grammar School, Bristol, and Bristol College of Further Education Second Church Estates Commissioner 1974–79. Sponsored by TGWU.

Mr Martyn Gilbert, vice-chairman of his area party and chairman, Bristol East group. Born 1952; educ. Lawrence Weston Comprehensive School. After three years in banking joined liaison/public relations department, Avon Ambulance Service.

Mr Harry Gourlay

KIRKCALDY
Electorate 53 078

*Gourlay, H. (Lab)	15 380	40.3%
Walker, I. (C)	10 049	26.3%
Black, M. (SDP/All)	9 274	24.3%
Wood, D. (SNP)	3 452	9.1%
Lab majority	5 331	14.0%
Total vote 38 155	Turnout	71.9%

Mr Harry Gourlay, elected in 1959, contested South Angus 1955. Chairman, Scottish parliamentary Labour group 1975–77. Deputy Speaker and Deputy Chairman Ways and Means, Oct 1968–70; assistant Government whip Nov 1964–66, and a Lord Commissioner of the Treasury (whip) 1966–68. Chairman, Scottish Grand and Scottish Standing Committees 1979–81. A vehicle examiner. Born Jul 10 1916; educ. Sinclairtown Public School and Kirkcaldy High School. Member, Kirkcaldy Town Council 1946–60 and of Fife County Council 1947–60. Sponsored by TGWU.

Mr Iain Walker, consultant and actuary. Born 1942; educ. Rutherglen Academy and Glasgow University. Member, Westminster City Council, Carlton Club political committee, City of Westminster Arts Council executive committee. Fellow, Faculty of Actuaries; Associate, Institute of Actuaries and of Pensions Management Institute.

Mr Malcolm Black is a principal lecturer in economics. Aged 41.

Mr David Wood, partner in firm of solicitors. Born 1937; educ. Edinburgh University. Chairman, Fife Legal Aid Committee and Freuchie Community Council.

Mr Robert Kilroy-Silk

KNOWSLEY NORTH Electorate 55 606

*Kilroy-Silk, R. (Lab)	24 949	64.5%
Birch, A. (C)	7 758	20.1%
McColgan, B. (SDP / All)	5 715	14.8%
Simons, J. (WRP)	246	0.6%
Lab majority	17 191	44.5%
Total vote 38 668		Turnout 69.5%

Mr Robert Kilroy-Silk, a former university lecturer and author, was elected in 1983; represented Ormskirk, Feb 1974–83 and contested that seat 1970. Born May 19 1942; educ. Saltley Grammar School, Birmingham, LSE, London University. Member, Select Committee on Home Affairs since 1979. Chairman, parliamentary all-party penal affairs group since 1979, and of PLP civil liberties group since 1979. Member, council of Howard League for Penal Reform since 1979, and sponsor of Radical Alternatives to Prison since 1977. Member, Public Accounts Committee 1975–77; Select Committee on Wealth Tax 1974–75; Select Committee on Race Relations and Immigration 1975.

Mr Albert Birch, company director. Born 1931; educ. Upholland Grammar School. Deputy leader, Conservative group, Merseyside County Council (chairman, personnel, appeals and superannuation committees; vice-chairman, policy, planning and resources committee; deputy leader of council 1980–81).

Mr Barry McColgan, chartered accountant, was chairman of the Manchester Blackley Labour Party 1971–72. Founder member of the SDP. Born 1946; educ. St Thomas of Canterbury Secondary Modern School, Salford, Salford Technical College, Hull and Manchester Universities and Manchester Business School. Contested Knutsford Feb 1974 and Clitheroe Oct 1974 both for Labour. Vice-chairman, North Manchester SDP 1981–82.

Mr Sean Hughes

KNOWSLEY SOUTH Electorate 68 114

Hughes, S. (Lab)	25 727	53.8%
Lamont, Miss E. (C)	13 958	29.2%
Smith, I. (L / All)	8 173	17.1%
Lab majority	11 769	24.6%
Total vote 47 858		Turnout 70.3%

Mr Sean Hughes, teacher, won the seat in 1983. Born May 8 1946; educ. grammar school and Liverpool and Manchester universities. Contested Crosby Feb 1974. Member, Huyton District Council (chairman of housing committee); Merseyside County Council.

Miss Elizabeth Lamont, teacher. Born Mar 10 1956; educ. Huyton College, Huyton. Secretary, Ainsdale ward committee, Southport Conservative Assoc. AMMA.

Mr Ian Smith, a teacher, contested St Helens 1979. Born Jul 15 1951; educ. Huyton Hey Secondary School and Liverpool College of Art. Member, Whiston Town Council and Prescot Town Council. NAS.

Mr James Molyneaux

LAGAN VALLEY Electorate 60 099

*Molyneaux, J. (OUP)	24 017	59.2%
Beattie, Rev W. (DUP)	6 801	16.8%
Close, S. (All)	4 593	11.3%
Boomer, C. (SDLP)	2 603	6.4%
McAuley, R. (PSF)	1 751	4.3%
Loughlin, G. (WP)	809	2.0%
OUP majority	17 216	42.4%
Total vote 40 574		Turnout 67.5%

Mr James Molyneaux has been leader of the Offical Ulster Unionist Parliamentary Party since 1977 and leader of the Ulster Unionist Party since 1979. Leader UUUC 1974–77. Elected for this seat Jun 1983. Represented South Antrim 1970–83. Partner in the family firm of letterpress printers. Born Aug 27 1920; educ. Aldergrove School, co Antrim. Deputy Grand Master, Orange Order Sovereign Grand Master, Commonwealth Royal Black Institution, 1971. Member, Antrim County Council 1964–73. Vice-presdient, Ulster Unionist Council 1974. Chairman, Monday Club of Ulster. Vice-chairman, Eastern Special Care Hospital Committee 1966–73. Secretary, South Antrim Unionist Assoc. 1964–70. Chairman, Antrim Division Unionist Assoc.

The Rev William Beattie, former deputy leader, Democratic Unionist Party, has been Minister of Dunmurry Free Presbyterian Church since 1966. Aged 40; educ. Ballymeana Academy, Free Presbyterian Theological Hall, Ravenhill Road, Belfast. Elected to Stormont as Protestant Unionist Party MP for South Antrim 1970; Northern Ireland Assembly 1973; Convention 1975; Assembly 1982, vice-chairman, Economic Development Committee and DUP spokesman on economics. Member, Lisburn Council since 1977.

Mr Kenneth Hind

LANCASHIRE WEST Electorate 73 980

Hind, K. (C)	25 458	46.3%
Farrington, Ms J. (Lab)	18 600	33.8%
Sackville, A. (SDP/All)	10 983	20.0%
C majority	6 858	12.5%
Total vote 55 041	Turnout	74.4%

Mr Kenneth Hind is a barrister. Elected in 1983. Born Sept 15 1949; educ. Woodhouse Grove School, Yorkshire and Leeds University (President of the Union, 1971–72). Secretary, Roundhay Conservative Assoc. Member, North East Leeds constituency executive; Assoc. of Conservative Lawyers; Justice. Vice-president, Headingley Rugby Club.

Ms Josie Farrington is chairman of Lancashire County Council Education Committee and Labour leader, education group, Assoc. of County Councils. Born 1940. Member, Labour Party regional executive.

Mr Andrew Sackville is a senior lecturer at Edge Hill College of Further Education. Born Aug 15 1943; educ. Keele University and University College, Swansea.

Mrs Elaine Kellett-Bowman

LANCASTER Electorate 56 040

*Kellett-Bowman, Mrs E. (C)	21 050	50.3%
Harkins, C. (Lab)	10 414	24.9%
Booth, W. (L/All)	10 214	24.4%
Leach, S. R. (Ind)	179	0.4%
C majority	10 636	25.4%
Total vote 41 857	Turnout	74.7%

Mrs Elaine Kellett-Bowman won the seat in 1970. Barrister, farmer and social worker. Contested Buckingham 1966 and 1964, Norfolk South West 1959 and the 1959 by-election, and Nelson and Colne 1955. Member, European Parliament since 1975; MEP for Cumbria since first European direct elections in 1979. Born Jul 8 1924; educ. Queen Mary's School, Lytham; The Mount, York, and St Anne's College, Oxford. Alderman of Borough of Camden 1968–71. Member of Press Council 1964–68.

Mr Colin Harkins is a research assistant at Preston Polytechnic and a former ship-yard worker. Born 1941; educ. Lancaster University. Former member, Barrow Borough Council. Sponsored by AUEW.

Mr William Booth, radio journalist; duty editor, BBC External Services News, was a member of the Liberal Party National Council 1964–66. Born Nov 30 1930; educ. North Manchester Grammar School, Ashville and Manchester University. NUJ.

Mr Richard Holt

LANGBAURGH Electorate 77 387

Holt, R. (C)	24 239	41.7%
Johnson, Mrs G. (Lab)	18 215	31.4%
Ashby, R. (L / All)	15 615	26.9%
C majority	6 024	10.4%
Total vote 58 069	Turnout	75.0%

Mr Richard Holt, personnel executive, was elected in 1983; contested Brent, South, Feb 1974. Born 1931; educ. Wembley County Grammar School and Hendon and Harrow technical colleges. Former Royal Navy seaman. Member, Wycombe Borough Council since 1976. Fellow, Institute of Personnel Management and member, British Institute of Management.

Mrs Gaye Johnson, principal social services training officer. Born Dec 13 1943; educ. Ackworth School; Bristol, Liverpool and Leeds universities.

Mr Robin Ashby, public relations and marketing consultant. Former steel worker. Born Jun 21 1947; educ. Birmingham University. Member, Middlesbrough Borough Council since 1982. Deputy chairman, Northern Liberal Party 1982–83. Former treasurer, Middlesbrough Liberal Assoc. Former member, Steel Industry Management Assoc.

Mr Derek Fatchett

LEEDS CENTRAL Electorate 63 299

Fatchett, D. (Lab)	18 706	47.9%
Wrigley, P. (L/All)	10 484	26.9%
Ashley-Brown, M. (C)	9 192	23.6%
Cummins, G. (BNP)	331	0.9%
Rogers, J. M. (Com)	314	0.8%
Lab majority	8 222	21.1%
Total vote 39 027		Turnout 61.7%

Mr Derek Fatchett, university lecturer, was elected in 1983; contested Bosworth 1979. Born Aug 8 1945; educ. Lincoln school, Birmingham University and LSE. Wakefield metropolitan borough councillor. ASTMS.

Mr Peter Wrigley, teacher, contested Batley and Morley 1970 and Feb 1974. Born Sep 4 1937; educ. Batley Grammar School and London and Bradford universities. AMMA.

Mr Michael Ashley-Brown, solicitor. Born May 28 1948; educ. Cranleigh School, Surrey, Millbrook School, New York, and College of Law, London. Member, North Yorkshire County Council and York District Council since 1977. Member, York Citizens Advice Bureau management committee; officer of Court of York University.

Mr Denis Healey

LEEDS EAST Electorate 63 611

*Healey, D. (Lab)	18 450	43.8%
Bell, A. (C)	12 355	29.3%
Clay, Mrs M. (L/All)	10 884	25.8%
Brons, A. H. (NF)	475	1.1%
Lab majority	6 095	14.5%
Total vote 42 164		Turnout 66.3%

Mr Denis Healey was Deputy Leader of the Labour Party 1980–83. Unsuccessfully contested the party leadership in 1980, a contest he had also failed in 1976. Won Deputy Leadership against Mr Tony Benn in 1981. Chief Opposition spokesman on foreign and Commonwealth affairs since 1981; chief spokesman on Treasury and economics affairs 1979–81. Chancellor of the Exchequer 1974–79; Chief Opposition spokesman on Treasury matters 1972–74; Chief Opposition spokesman on foreign and Commonwealth affairs 1970–72; Secretary of State for Defence 1964–70. Elected for Leeds South-East at a by-election in 1952, and for Leeds East in 1955; contested Pudsey and Otley 1945. Born Aug 30 1917; educ. Bradford Grammar School and Balliol College, Oxford. Member, Labour Party national executive committee 1970–75 and since being Deputy Leader.

Mr Andrew Bell, stockbroker. Born 1955; educ. Eton College and Christ Church, Oxford. Secretary, Oxford Carlton Club; President, Oxford University Monday Club; and meetings secretary and executive member, Selsdon Group. Formerly an investment analyst and manager of a unit trust fund. Son of the late Sir Ronald Bell who was MP for Beaconsfield.

Miss Margaret Clay, political secretary, contested Leeds South East Feb and Oct 1974 and 1979. Born Apr 13 1947; educ. County Grammar School for Girls, Lewes, and universities of Sheffield and Leeds. Member, Leeds City Council 1978–80, and since 1982; member, West Yorkshire County Council since 1981.

Sir Keith Joseph

LEEDS NORTH EAST Electorate 65 226

*Joseph, Sir K. (C)	21 940	47.6%
Crystal, P. (SDP/All)	12 945	28.1%
Sedler, R. (Lab)	10 951	23.8%
Tibbitts, E. (A Corr)	128	0.3%
Holton, P. (ACIE)	123	0.3%
C majority	8 995	19.5%
Total vote 46 087		Turnout 70.7%

Sir Keith Joseph has been Secretary of State for Education and Science since 1981; Secretary of State for Industry 1979–81. Chief Opposition spokesman on industry with overall responsibility for Conservative Party policy and research 1974–79. Chief Opposition spokesman on home affairs 1974–75. Secretary of State for Social Services 1970–74; Minister of Housing and Local Government and Minister of State, Board of Trade 1961–62. Returned at a by-election in Feb 1956; contested Barons Court 1955. Born Jan 17 1918; educ. Harrow and Magdalen College, Oxford. Barrister. Fellow of All Souls, 1946–60, and since 1972. Former company director. Founder and chairman of management committee of Centre for Policy Studies.

Mr Peter Crystal, solicitor. Born 1948; educ. Leeds Grammar School and St Edmund Hall, Oxford; studied international and comparative law at McGill University, Montreal. Former Labour election agent in Leeds North East.

Mr Ronald Sedler, solicitor. Born Apr 6 1926; educ. Parmiter's School, Bethnal Green, and Leeds University. Contested the seat 1979. Member, Leeds City Council 1957–60 and 1972–82. APEX and Society of Labour Lawyers.

Dr Keith Hampson

LEEDS NORTH WEST Electorate 68 004

*Hampson, K. (C)	22 579	46.6%
Jones, N. (SDP/All)	14 042	29.0%
Battle, J. (Lab)	10 757	22.2%
Laurence, A. (Eco)	673	1.4%
Haygreen, C. (Ind C)	437	0.9%
C majority	8 537	17.6%
Total vote 48 488	Turnout	71.3%

Dr Keith Hampson represented Ripon 1974–83 which he first contested at by-elected Jul 1973. PPS to Mr Tom King 1979–83. Chairman Youthaid since 1979; vice-president WEA since 1979. Consultant to Library Assoc. and Electrical Contractors Assoc. Former vice-chairman, Conservative education committee 1975–79. Personal assistant to Mr Heath in the 1966 general election and assisted him in the Bexley contest in 1970. Born Aug 14 1943; educ. King James I Grammar School, Bishop Auckland, and at Bristol and Harvard Universities. Former chairman, Bristol University Conservative Assoc. Lecturer in American history, Edinburgh University 1968–74.

Mr Norman Jones, barrister; member, SDP national committee. Born 1941; educ. Bideford Grammar School, North Devon Technical College and Leeds University. Leeds member, Council for Social Democracy.

Mr John Battle, research officer. Born Apr 26 1951; educ. Leeds University. Member, Leeds City Council since 1980; housing committee chairman, 1983.

Mr Merlyn Rees

LEEDS SOUTH AND MORLEY Electorate 60 864

*Rees, M. (Lab)	18 995	45.9%
Hyde W. (C)	13 141	31.8%
Burley, P. (SDP/All)	9 216	22.3%
Lab majority	5 854	14.2%
Total vote 41 352	Turnout	67.9%

Mr Merlyn Rees, a member of the Shadow Cabinet 1979–83, was opposition industry and employment policy coordinator 1982–83; chief Opposition spokesman on energy 1981–82; after being chief spokesman on home affairs. Home Secretary 1976–79 and Secretary of State for Northern Ireland 1974–76. Chief Opposition spokesman on Northern Ireland 1972–74; an Opposition spokesman on the Home Office 1970–72; Under-Secretary, Home Office, 1968–70; Under-Secretary for Defence for the RAF 1966–68; Under-Secretary for Defence for the Army 1965–66. Elected for this seat in 1983; MP for Leeds South 1963–83; contested Harrow East 1955 and 1959. Economics lecturer. Born Dec 18 1920; educ. Harrow Weald Grammar School, Goldsmith's College and London School of Economics. Member, Franks Committee on Falklands War 1982–83, and Franks Committee on Official Secrets Act 1972. NUT and GMWBU.

Mr William Hyde, newsagent. Member, Leeds City Council, since 1973; Sheffield City Council, 1967–68. Chairman, Halton Ward Conservative Assoc. Born Oct 12 1933; educ. City of Leeds High School. Chairman, Bridewell (Leeds District) Ltd.

Dr Peter Burley, lecturer in psychology at University College, London and senior psychologist, National Hospital for Nervous Diseases. Born 1947; educ. University of New South Wales and Jesus College, Oxford.

Mr Michael Meadowcroft

LEEDS WEST Electorate 67 538

Meadowcroft, M. (L/All)	17 908	38.4%
*Dean, J. (Lab)	15 860	34.0%
Keeble, Miss J. (C)	12 515	26.9%
Braithwaite, A. (BNP)	334	0.7%
L/All majority	2 048	4.4%
Total vote 46 617	Turnout	69.0%

Mr Michael Meadowcroft, general secretary, Bradford Metropolitan Council for Voluntary Service, won the seat in 1983; contested Leeds West, Feb and Oct 1974. Born Mar 6 1942; educ. King George V School, Southport and University of Bradford. Member, Leeds City Council, since 1968; member, West Yorkshire Metropolitan County Council, 1973–76 and since 1981. Director, Leeds Grand Theatre and Opera House Ltd.

Mr Joseph Dean, an engineer, represented the seat Feb 1974–83. Born Jun 3 1923; educ. St Anne's Roman Catholic School, Manchester. Former leader, Manchester City Council and of Leeds District Council. Former secretary, AUEW group of MPs. Member, Commons Services Committee. Assistant Government whip 1978–79; Opposition whip 1982–83. Life peer 1983.

Miss Jocelyn Keeble, area head of adult education in Wetherby. Born 1943; educ. Allerton Grange County Secondary School, Thoresby High School, City of Portsmouth College of Education, Leeds University, College of Music and Drama and Leeds Polytechnic. Vice-chairman, Yorkshire area advisory committee on education and secretary, Yorkshire area Conservative trade unionists' council.

Mr Peter Bruinvels

LEICESTER EAST Electorate 67 071 1979: 67 269 minor

Bruinvels, P. (C)	19 117	38.9%
Hewitt, Ms P. (Lab)	18 184	37.0%
*Bradley, T. (SDP/All)	10 362	21.1%
Ganatra, R. V. (Ind)	970	2.0%
Sutton, R. L. (BNP)	459	0.9%
C majority	933	1.9%
Total vote 49 092	Turnout	73.2%

1979: Total vote 50 840 (75.6%); Lab 23 844 (46.9%); C 20 988 (41.3%); L 4 623 (9.1%); NF 1 385 (2.7%). Lab maj 2 856 (5.6%); swing 1.3% to C.

Mr Peter Bruinvels, management and parliamentary research consultant. Elected in 1983. Born Mar 30 1950; educ. St John's School, Leatherhead; London University, Council of Legal Education. Chairman, south eastern area Young Conservatives, National Union executive committee, 1977–79. Freeman of City of London. Member, British Institute of Management, Institute of Public Relations, Society of Conservative Lawyers, Guildford Diocesan Synod.

Ms Patricia Hewitt, General Secretary, National Council for Civil Liberties, 1974–83. Born Dec 2 1948; educ. Girls' Grammar School, Canberra, and Newnham College, Cambridge. NCCL's first women's rights officer 1973–74; public relations officer, Age Concern, 1971–73. Columnist, *Daily Star* 1980–82; radio and TV broadcaster. Member, Labour National Women's Committee 1979–83, Secretary of State's advisory committee on the Employment of women.

Mr Tom Bradley, SDP spokesman on transport and industrial relations 1981–83; Labour spokesman on transport 1970–74. Chairman of Select Committee on Transport 1979–83. Elected as Labour MP for Leicester East in Jul 1962 by-election; resigned in 1981 and joined SDP. Director European League for Economic Co-operation (British section) and public affairs adviser; former railway clerk. Born Apr 1926; educ. Kettering Central School, President Transport Salaried Staffs' Assoc. 1964–77. Chairman Labour Party 1975–76; Kettering Town Football Club.

Mr Derek Spencer

LEICESTER SOUTH Electorate 73 573 1979: 70 714 minor

Spencer, D. (C)	21 424	40.3%
*Marshall, J. (Lab)	21 417	40.3%
Renold, R. (L/All)	9 410	17.7%
Davis, C. (Eco)	495	0.9%
Pickard, C. (BNP)	280	0.5%
Roberts, D. P. (WPWS)	161	0.3%
C majority	7	0.0%
Total vote 53 187	Turnout	72.3%

1979: Total vote 52 894 (74.8%); Lab 24 548 (46.4%); C 22 550 (42.6%); L 4 856 (9.2%); NF 940 (1.8%). Lab maj 1 998 (3.8%); swing 0.8% to Lab.

Mr Derek Spencer, QC, won the seat in 1983. Born Mar 31 1936; educ. Clitheroe Royal Grammar School and Keeble College, Oxford. Member, London Borough of Camden Council since 1978 (deputy leader, Conservative group 1980–82).

Mr James Marshall an Opposition spokesman on home affairs 1982–83; elected in Oct 1974; contested the seat in Feb 1974; Harborough 1970. An assistant Government whip 1977–79. Born Mar 13 1941; educ. Sheffield City Grammar School and Leeds University. Member, Leeds City Council 1965–68 and of Leicester City Council 1971–76 (leader 1974).

Mr Robert Renold, design engineer with GEC. Born Apr 20 1952; educ. Gordonstoun and Birmingham University. AUEW (TASS).

Mr Greville Janner

LEICESTER WEST Electorate 67 691 1979: 67 209 minor

*Janner, G. (Lab)	20 837	44.8%
Meacham, R. (C)	19 125	41.1%
Fernando, S. (SDP/All)	5 935	12.8%
Hill, R. (BNP)	469	1.0%
Prangle, B. J. (WRP)	176	0.4%
Lab majority	1 712	3.7%
Total vote 46 542	Turnout	68.8%

1979: Total vote 48 566 (72.3%); Lab 26 032 (53.6%); C 17 194 (35.4%); L 4 032 (8.3%); NF 1 308 (2.7%). Lab maj 8 838 (18.2%); swing 2.1%

Mr Greville Janner QC, a barrister and writer, was elected in 1970; contested Wimbledon 1955. Born Jul 11 1928; educ. Bishop's College School, Quebec; St Paul's School, London; Trinity Hall, Cambridge, and Harvard Law School. Member, Employment Committee. President, Board of Deputies of British Jews since 1979; president Commonwealth Jewish Council since 1982; vice-president, Assoc. of Jewish Ex-Servicemen and of Assoc. for Jewish Youth; vice-chairman, all-party parliamentary committee for release of Soviet Jewry. President retired Executives' Action Clearing House; chairman, all-party parliamentary industrial safety group. NUJ.

Mr Robert Meacham, company

director. Born Feb 28 1937; educ. Coventry Preparatory School and Warwick School. Member of Solihull Metropolitan Borough Council, since 1975, now leader.
Mr Sumal Fernando, solicitor. Born Nov 16 1942; educ. Sri Lanka. Member, Leicester Community Relations Council, Leicester; Charnwood Lions Club; Giants International. Founder member SDP and its first Asian parliamentary candidate.

Mr David Ashby

LEICESTERSHIRE NORTH WEST Electorate 68 510

Ashby, D. (C)	24 760	44.6%
Read, Mrs I (Lab)	18 098	32.6%
Cort, G. (L/All)	12 043	21.7%
Freer, Mrs D. (Eco)	637	1.2%
C majority	6 662	12.0%
Total vote 55 538		Turnout 81.1%

Mr David Ashby, barrister and company director was elected in 1983. Born May 14 1940; educ. Royal Grammar School, High Wycombe; Bristol University. Member, Hammersmith Borough Council 1968–71 (chairman of housing committee); GLC 1977–81 (chairman, legal and parliamentary committee and of housing committee, and member of ILEA); board of London and Quadrant Housing Assoc.
Mrs Imelda Read, lecturer and researcher, contested Melton 1979. Born Jan 8 1939; educ. Bishopshalt Grammar School and Nottingham University. Member, National Executive Council of ASTMS since 1975.
Mr Geoffrey Cort, export sales manager. Born May 31 1943; educ. City of Leicester Boys' School. Member, Ashby-de-la-Zouch Town Council; Alliance group leader, North West Leicestershire District Council.

Mr Lawrence Cunliffe

LEIGH Electorate 68 063

*Cunliffe, L. (Lab)	25 477	51.9%
Johnston, P. (C)	13 163	26.8%
Eccles, D. (SDP/All)	10 468	21.3%
Lab majority	12 314	25.1%
Total vote 49 108		Turnout 72.2%

Mr Lawrence Cunliffe was elected in 1979; contested Rochdale, Oct 1972 and Feb 1974; member Commons Services Committee since 1981; member catering subcommittee. Born Mar 25 1929; educ. St Edmund's RC school Worsley. Manchester. Former engineer with the National Coal Board; councillor, Bolton MDC, 1974–79; magistrate 1967–79. Sponsored by NUM.
Mr Paul Johnston, head of history, law and government and political studies at London Oratory School. Educ. Catholic College, Preston and Lancaster and Manchester universities. Chairman, Lancaster Young Conservatives 1964–67; vice-chairman, North Lancashire and Westmorland Young Conservatives 1965–67. Elected to Wansdyke District Council, Avon, 1976; leader, Conservative group, 1977–78.
Mr David Eccles, barrister. Born Mar 22 1953; educ. grammar school and Clare College, Cambridge. Chairman, Tameside SDP; member, Council for Social Democracy, Greater Manchester regional committee. Former member, Labour Party; local election candidate, 1979 and 1982.

Mr Peter Temple-Morris

LEOMINSTER Electorate 66 286

*Temple-Morris, P. (C)	29 276	57.0%
Pincham, R. (L/All)	19 490	37.9%
Wilcox, D. (Lab)	1 932	3.8%
Norman, Miss F. (Eco)	668	1.3%
C majority	9 786	19.1%
Total vote 51 366		Turnout 77.5%

Mr Peter Temple-Morris, barrister, company director and consultant, was elected in Feb 1974; contested Lambeth, Norwood 1970, and Newport 1964 and 1966. Born Feb 12 1938; educ. Malvern and St Catherine's College, Cambridge. Joint secretary, Conservative back-bench foreign affairs committee, 1979–82 and joint vice-chairman 1982–83. Secretary Conservative transport committee 1976–79; and of Conservative parliamentary legal committee 1977–78. Secretary, Anglo-Iranian parliamentary group and treasurer, Anglo-Lebanese parliamentary group. Chairman, Bow Group standing committee on home affairs 1975–80, and of British Group, IPU since 1982.
Mr Roger Pincham, member of the Stock Exchange and project consultant, was chairman of the Liberal Party 1979–82. Born Oct 19 1935; educ. Wimbledon Park County Primary School, Kingston Grammar School. Former member, Liberal Party central policy-making committee and of national executive. Contested Leominster 1970, both 1974 elections, and 1979. TGWU (farmworkers' section.)
Mr Donald Wilcox, lecturer. Aged 47.

Mr John Rathbone

LEWES Electorate 67 366

*Rathbone, J. (C)	29 261	58.4%
Bellotti, D. (L/All)	15 357	30.7%
Sander, Ms S. (Lab)	4 244	8.5%
Mutter, R. (Eco)	1 221	2.4%
C majority	13 904	27.8%
Total vote 50 083		Turnout 74.3%

Mr John R (Tim) Rathbone was elected in Feb 1974. Born Mar 17 1933; educ. Eton and Christ Church, Oxford, and Harvard Business School. Director, Charles Barker Group Ltd and other companies. Chief publicity and public relations officer, Conservative Central Office, 1966–68. Member, national committee for electoral reform. Former secretary, Conservative media committee. PPS to Minister for Health 1979–82 and to Minister for Consumer Affairs since 1982.

Mr David Bellotti is a community and youth worker who contested Eastbourne 1979. Born Aug 13 1943; educ. Exeter School and YMCA National College. Member, Lewes District Council since 1979; East Sussex County Council since 1981.

Ms Deborah Sander, education officer, Commonwealth Institute. Born Mar 20 1952; educ. Chichester High School for Girls and Somerville College, Oxford. Formerly teacher in Nigeria. Member, NEC subcommittee on Africa.

Mr John Silkin

LEWISHAM DEPTFORD Electorate 58 663

*Silkin, J. (Lab)	17 360	48.3%
Wheatley, R. (C)	11 328	31.5%
Abbott, Miss D. (SDP/All)	6 734	18.8%
Wilson, P. (BNP)	317	0.9%
Housego, S. B. (AB)	173	0.5%
Lab majority	6 032	16.8%
Total vote 35 912		Turnout 61.2%

Mr John Silkin has been in the Shadow Cabinet since 1979. Chief spokesman on House of Commons matters 1980–83, having been spokesman on industry; chief Opposition spokesman on defence and disarmament since 1981. Minister of Agriculture, Fisheries and Food 1976–79. Minister for Planning and Local Government, Department of Environment, 1974–76, with a seat in the Cabinet from Oct 1974. Opposition spokesman on social services 1972–74, and on local government and development 1970–72. Returned at a by-election in 1963. Minister of Public Building and Works 1969–70; Parliamentary Secretary to the Treasury, Deputy Leader of the House and Government Chief Whip 1966–69; Treasurer of the Household and Deputy Chief Whip, Apr–Jul 1966; Lord Commissioner of the Treasury (whip), 1966; Government whip 1964–66. Contested St Marylebone 1950; Woolwich West 1951, and Nottingham South 1959. Solicitor. Born Mar 18 1923; educ. Dulwich College, University of Wales, and Trinity Hall, Cambridge. Member, Select Committee on Privileges since 1979.

Mr Robin Wheatley, barrister and director, South Western Industrial Gases Ltd, Exeter. Born May 23 1949; educ. The Leys School, Cambridge, Inns of Court School of Law.

Miss Denise Abbott, senior executive officer for education and services with the Commission for Racial Equality. Born 1946; educ. High School for Girls, Wolverhampton and York University. Member, SDP national urban policy committee.

Mr Colin Moynihan

LEWISHAM EAST Electorate 61 216

Moynihan, C. (C)	17 168	40.4%
*Moyle, R. (Lab)	15 259	35.9%
Toynbee, Ms P. (SDP/All)	9 351	22.0%
Edmonds, R. (BNP)	288	0.7%
Hassard, A. (Eco)	270	0.6%
Roberts, G. (Com)	135	0.3%
Gibson, P. (WRP)	71	0.2%
C majority	1 909	4.5%
Total vote 42 542		Turnout 69.5%

Mr Colin Moynihan, chief executive, Ridgway's Tea and Coffee Co (Tate and Lyle group) was elected in 1983. Born Sep 13 1955; educ. Monmouth School and University College, Oxford. Member, industry committee, Bow Group. Coxed British lightweight rowing eight 1978, won world gold medal, British Olympic eight 1980, won silver medal, British eight 1981, won world silver medal. Director, British Boxing Board of Control and board's representative on World Boxing Assoc. Governor, Sports Aid Foundation.

Mr Roland Moyle appointed Opposition spokesman on defence Apr 1983; spokesman on foreign and Commonwealth affairs 1981–83 and on health 1979–81; Minister of State for Health 1976–79, Minister of State for Northern Ireland 1974–76, and Parliamentary Secretary, Ministry of Agriculture, Fisheries and Food 1974. Elected for Lewisham East in Feb 1974; MP for Lewisham North

1966–74. Barrister. Born May 12 1928; educ. elementary schools in Bexleyheath, Kent; county school Llanidloes, Montgomeryshire; Univ. College of Wales, Aberystwyth, Trinity Hall, Cambridge and Gray's Inn.

Ms Polly Toynbee is a writer and journalist on *The Guardian*. Born Dec 27 1946; educ. Holland Park Comprehensive and St Anne's College, Oxford. Member, Williams Committee on obscenity and film censorship.

Mr John Maples

LEWISHAM WEST Electorate 63 043

Maples, J. (C)	19 521	44.0%
*Price, C. (Lab)	17 015	38.4%
Mooney, H. (L/All)	7 470	16.9%
Hoy, R.F. (BNP)	336	0.8%
C majority	2 506	5.7%
Total vote 44 342	Turnout	70.3%

Mr John Maples, lawyer and businessman was returned in 1983. Born Apr 22 1943; educ. Cambridge University, Harvard Business School. Contested GLC by-election at Vauxhall, 1980.

Mr Christopher Price, was chairman, Select Committee on Education, Science and Arts 1979–83. Parliamentary adviser (unpaid) to National Graphical Association. Freelance journalist and broadcaster. Returned in Feb 1974; represented Birmingham, Perry Barr 1966–70; contested Shipley 1964. Member, European Parliament 1977–78. Born Jan 26 1932; educ. Leeds Grammar School and Queen's College, Oxford (secretary, Labour Club 1953). Member, Sheffield City Council 1962–66. Editor *New Education* 1967–68; education correspondent *New Statesman* 1968–74. NUJ.

Mr Hugh Mooney, journalist and barrister. Born Sep 1 1936; educ. Worthing High School for Boys, Merton College, Oxford, Dublin University and London University. NUJ.

Mr Harry Cohen

LEYTON Electorate 57 770 1979: 59 176 minor

Cohen, H. (Lab)	16 504	43.5%
Neilson-Hansen, W. (C)	11 988	31.6%
*Magee, B. (SDP/All)	9 448	24.9%
Lab majority	4 516	11.9%
Total vote 37 940	Turnout	65.7%

1979: Total vote 41 060 (69.4%); Lab 21 095 (51.4%); C 15 361 (37.4%); L 3 425 (8.3%); NF 1 179 (2.9%). Lab maj 5 734 (14.0%); swing 7.3% to C.

Mr Harry Cohen is a local council employee, elected in 1983. Born Dec 10 1949; educ. secondary modern school and part-time further education. Member, Waltham Forest Borough Council, since 1972; former chairman planning committee, and secretary, Labour group. Member, Chartered Institute of Public Finance and Accountancy. Nalgo.

Mr Wally Neilson-Hansen, engineer. Born 1918. GLC member for Leyton 1977–81; served as a whip to the planning and communications group; member, northern area, planning and communications committee, finance and establishment committee and general management committee.

Mr Bryan Magee, writer and broadcaster, was elected as Labour MP in Feb 1974 but resigned party to join SDP. Born Apr 12 1930; educ. Christ's Hospital, Lycée Hoche (Versailles), Keble College, Oxford. (President of Union 1953), Yale. Contested Mid Bedfordshire 1959 and 1960 by-election.

Mr Kenneth Carlisle

LINCOLN Electorate 72 887

*Carlisle, K. (C)	25 244	46.4%
Withers, M. (Lab)	14 958	27.5%
Stockdale, F. (SDP/All)	13 631	25.1%
Blades, G. (Ind)	523	1.0%
C majority	10 286	18.9%
Total vote 54 356	Turnout	74.6%

Mr Kenneth Carlisle, a barrister and former farmer, was elected in 1979. Member of the Bow Group. Member Select Committee on European legislation since 1979. Born Mar 21 1941; educ. Harrow, Magdalen College, Oxford. Former chairman Stanton branch of Bury St Edmunds Conservative Assoc. and chairman Conservative Political Centre Committee. NFU.

Mr Malcolm Withers, financial journalist, contested Rutland and Stamford 1974 and 1979. Born Mar 1936; educ. St Clement Danes Grammar School, Leicester University. Member, Rutland District Council since 1973. NUJ.

Mr Frederick Stockdale, farmer, contested Lincoln 1979 for the Lincoln Democratic Labour Assoc. Born May 20 1947; educ. Eton and Jesus College, Cambridge. Member Lincolnshire County Council 1977–81; Trent Regional Health Authority since 1978. NFU.

Mr Peter Tapsell

LINDSEY EAST Electorate 69 715

*Tapsell, P. (C)	27 151	53.2%
Sellick, J. (L/All)	19 634	38.5%
Lowis, G. R. (Lab)	4 229	8.3%
C majority	7 517	14.7%
Total vote 51 014		Turnout 73.2%

Mr Peter Tapsell, elected for this seat in 1983; MP for Horncastle 1966–83; and for Nottingham West, 1959–64; contested Wednesbury 1957. Head of international department of James Capel and Co, stockbrokers. Front bench spokesman on Treasury and economic affairs, 1977–78, and on foreign and Commonwealth affairs 1976–77. Born Feb 1 1930; educ. Tonbridge School and Merton College, Oxford. Personal assistant to Sir Anthony Eden, Prime Minister, during the 1955 general election campaign. Adviser to central banks on management of international reserves.

Mr Geoffrey Lowis, accounts clerk. Born Sep 29 1950; educ. Louth Grammar School and Leeds University. ASTMS.

Mr Tam Dalyell

LINLITHGOW Electorate 58 111

*Dalyell, T. (Lab)	19 694	45.1%
Jones, C. (C)	8 333	19.1%
Ramsay, D. (SNP)	8 026	18.4%
Cockcroft, P. (SDP/All)	7 432	17.0%
Parnell, Dr M. (Com)	199	0.5%
Lab majority	11 361	26.0%
Total vote 43 684		Turnout 75.2%

Mr Tam Dalyell elected to this seat in 1983; was Opposition spokesman on science 1980–82. MP for West Lothian 1962–83; contested Roxburgh, Selkirk and Peebles 1959. Teacher and author. Born Aug 9 1932; educ. Edinburgh Academy, Eton and King's College, Cambridge. Member, European Parliament 1975–79. Member, Public Accounts Committee 1963–65; Select Committee on Science and Technology 1965–68; PLP Liaison Committee 1974–75. Vice-chairman PLP 1975–76. Member, Select Committee on European Secondary Legislation 1974–75. Sponsored by NUR.

Mr Colin Jones, lecturer on taxation and accountancy. Aged 50. Worthsop Rural District councillor 1964–68; elected to Altrick and Lauderdale District Council 1982.

Mr David Ramsay, manufacturer's agent. Born 1936; educ. Harris Academy. Regional councillor in Lothian since 1977.

Mr Paul Cockcroft, tutor in philosophy and political theory at Newbattle Abbey College, Dalkeith. Born 1953; educ. Dundee and Oxford universities.

Mr Geoffrey Dickens

LITTLEBOROUGH AND SADDLEWORTH Electorate 64 018

*Dickens, G. (C)	20 510	42.8%
Knowles, R. (L / All)	14 860	31.0%
Moore, S. (Lab)	12 106	25.3%
Barry, R. (RCCP)	398	0.8%
C majority	5 650	11.8%
Total vote 47 874		Turnout 74.8%

Mr Geoffrey Dickens, elected in 1983; was MP for Huddersfield West 1979–83; contested Ealing North Oct 1974 and Teesside, Middlesbrough, Feb 1974. Company director. Born Aug 26 1931; educ. Harrow and Acton Technical College. Member, Hertfordshire County Council 1970–74; St Albans District Council 1967–73 (chairman 1970–71).

Mr Richard Knowles, lecturer in geography at Salford University. Born Jul 26 1947; educ. Abbeydale Boys' Grammar School, Sheffield, and Newcastle University. Member, Oldham Borough Council 1973–79, and since 1982. AUT.

Mr Stephen Moore is a teacher at Fitton Hill School, Oldham. Aged 34. Former leader, Labour group on Rochdale District Council. Member, Co-operative Party and CND.

Mr Terence Fields

LIVERPOOL, BROADGREEN Electorate 63 826

Fields, T. (Lab)	18 802	40.9%
Dougherty, D. (C)	15 002	32.6%
Pine, R. (Ind L.)	7 021	15.3%
*Crawshaw, R. (SDP / All)	5 169	11.2%
Lab majority	3 800	8.3%
Total vote 45 994	Turnout 72.1%	

Mr Terence Fields, elected in 1983, was a fireman with Merseyside Co. fire brigade 1957–83. Born Mar 8 1937. Vice chairman, Bootle Constituency Labour Party. Former member, North West Regional Executive Committee, Labour Party. Member, National Executive Committee, FBU.

Mr Daniel Dougherty, bank security officer. Born Jan 16 1948; educ. St Oswald's School, Liverpool and Bankfield. Merseyside County Councillor 1977–81. A national vice-chairman of the Conservative Trade Unionists.

Mr Richard Crawshaw, a barrister was Second Deputy Chairman of Ways and Means 1979–80 and a member of the Speaker's panel of chairmen for many years. Elected as Labour MP for Liverpool Toxteth in 1964; resigned and joined SDP in 1981, becoming its spokesman on defence. Member, Select Committee on Defence, since Dec 1982. Born Sep 25 1917; educ. Pendleton Grammar School, Pembroke College, Cambridge, and London University. Member, Liverpool City Council 1958–64. In 1972 established world record for non-stop walking of 255.8 miles.

Mr Edward Loyden

LIVERPOOL, GARSTON Electorate 64 326

Loyden, E. (Lab)	21 450	46.6%
Ross, J. (C)	17 448	37.9%
Cooper, Miss R. (L / All)	7 153	15.5%
Lab majority	4 002	8.7%
Total vote 46 051	Turnout 71.6%	

Mr Edward Loyden, elected in 1983, was MP for the constituency, Feb 1974–79. Former port worker. Born May 1923; educ. Friary School, Liverpool. Liverpool City councillor (deputy leader). TGWU sponsored.

Mr James Ross, chairman and managing director. Born Sep 9 1922; educ. Toxteth Technical College. Lord Mayor of Liverpool 1980–81 and 1981–82; Deputy Lord Mayor May to Nov 1981, and 1982–83; member, Liverpool City Council, for approximately 30 years.

Miss Rosemary Cooper is a management trainee. Born 1950. She has been a local councillor since 1973. Has acted as local election agent.

Mr David Alton

LIVERPOOL, MOSSLEY HILL Electorate 62 789

*Alton, D. (L / All)	18 845	40.9%
Keefe, B. (C)	14 650	31.8%
Snowden, A. C. (Lab)	12 352	26.8%
Erikson-Rohrer, M. (NF)	212	0.5%
L / All majority	4 195	9.1%
Total vote 46 059	Turnout 73.4%	

Mr David Alton, a former teacher, was elected for this seat in 1983. He won Liverpool, Edge Hill for the Liberals in the Mar 1979 by-election. Served for six days until dissolution and was re-elected in general election. Contested that seat Feb and Oct 1974. Appointed political aide to Mr David Steel in Nov 1982 and spokesman on inner cities. Previously spokesman on environment and race relations. Elected to Merseyside County Council 1973. Born Mar 15 1951; educ. Campion School, Hornchurch, and Christ's College of Education Liverpool. Elected Liverpool City Council 1972, Housing chairman and Deputy Leader of City Council 1978.

Mr Brian Keefe, lecturer, contested Ormskirk 1979 and 1974; Liverpool, Toxteth 1970 and 1966; Liverpool, Scotland twice in 1964, by election and general election. Born Jan 1 1934; educ. St Margaret's High School, Liverpool; Chester College of Education; Sheffield University; Rutgers and Michigan Universities, United States. APT.

Mr Andrew Snowden is an officer with a Liverpool housing assoc. aged 32. Member, CND, ASTMS.

Mr Robert Parry

LIVERPOOL, RIVERSIDE Electorate 61 638

*Parry, R. (Lab)	24 978	65.0%
Morrison, T. (C)	7 600	19.8%
Zentner, P. (SDP / All)	5 381	14.0%
Blevin, J. (Com)	261	0.7%
Latchford, D. (WRP)	234	0.6%
Lab majority	17 378	45.2%
Total vote 38 454	Turnout	62.4%

Mr Robert Parry, a building trade worker and former full-time organizer for NUPE, was elected for this seat in 1983; represented Liverpool, Scotland Exchange Feb 1974–83 and Liverpool Exchange, 1970–74. Born Jan 8 1933; educ. Bishop Goss Roman Catholic School, Liverpool. Chairman, Merseyside group of Labour MPs since 1975. Member, Liverpool County Council 1963–74. President, Assoc. for Democracy in Hongkong since 1980. President Kids in Need and Distress since 1981. Sponsored by TGWU.

Mr Thomas Morrison, barristers' clerk. Elected Liverpool City councillor 1982. Member, Garston Conservative Assoc. since 1977 and has held office at county level in Young Conservatives. Educ. Holt High School, Speke Comprehensive School and Cartrefle College, Wrexham.

Mr Paul Zetner is an export management consultant and author. Born 1932; educ. Manchester Grammar School and Gonville and Cauis Colleges, Cambridge.

Mr Eric Heffer

LIVERPOOL, WALTON Electorate 73 532

*Heffer, E. (Lab)	26 980	52.7%
Maddox, A. (C)	12 865	25.2%
Croft, D. (L / All)	10 970	21.4%
McKechnie, D. J. M. (BNP)	343	0.7%
Lab majority	14 115	27.6%
Total vote 51 158	Turnout	69.6%

Mr Eric Heffer, Labour Party Chairman 1983–84 and vice-chairman 1982–83, became Opposition spokesman on European and Community Affairs in 1981 after his election to Shadow Cabinet. Appointed Minister of State for Industry Mar 1974 and left office in 1975. In Opposition Front Bench team on Industrial Relations Bill 1970–71. Opposition spokesman on employment 1971–73. Member, Shadow Cabinet 1972. Elected in 1964. Carpenter-joiner and journalist. Born Jan 12 1922; elementary education. Member, Labour Party national executive committee since 1975. Member and sponsored by UCATT, formerly ASW. Vice-chairman, League Against Cruel Sports.

Mr Alan Maddox, solicitor. Born Aug 30 1945; educ. Epsom College, Birkenhead School and Liverpool University. Member Wirral Borough Council 1976–83.

Mr David Croft is manager of a national freight company. Born Jan 2 1955; educ. Magdalen College, Oxford. Member, Liverpool City Council since 1977; chairman of the highways and environment committee and the performance review and financial control committee. Vice-chairman, Young Liberals, 1976–77.

Mr Robert Wareing

LIVERPOOL, WEST DERBY Electorate 63 088

Wareing, R. (Lab)	23 905	54.5%
Trelawney, W. (C)	12 062	27.5%
*Ogden, E. (SDP/All)	7 871	18.0%
Lab majority	11 843	27.0%
Total vote 43 838	Turnout	69.5%

Mr Robert Wareing, college lecturer, won the seat in 1983; contested Berwick-upon-Tweed 1970, and Liverpool, Edge Hill Mar 1979 by-election, and 1979 general election. Born Aug 20 1930; educ. Ranworth Square School, Liverpool, Alsop High School, Liverpool, and Bolton College of Education. Merseyside county councillor and chief whip of Labour group since 1981. Chairman, Merseyside Economic Development Co Ltd. NATFKE and ASTMS.

Mr William Trelawny, stockbroker. Born Jul 21 1954; educ. Truro School Cornwall, and Essex University. Chairman, Essex University Conservative Assoc. 1975–76, and vice-chairman, Eastern area federation of Conservative students. Chairman, Chelsea Young Conservatives, 1979–80; now vice-chairman, Vauxhall Conservative Assoc.

Mr Eric Ogden, a former miner, was elected as Labour MP for Liverpool, West Derby in 1964; resigned party in 1981 and joined SDP. Born Aug 23 1923; educ. Queen Elizabeth's Grammar School, Middleton, Leigh Technical College and Wigan Mining College. Member, Middleton Borough Council 1958–64. Parliamentary adviser to Council of the Pharmaceutical Society of Great Britain. Joint chairman, all-party Channel tunnel group. Member, Select Committee on House of Commons Services since 1979.

Mr Robin Cook

LIVINGSTON Electorate 53 284

*Cook, R. (Lab)	14 255	37.3%
Henderson, A. (L/All)	9 704	25.4%
Campbell, J. (C)	9 129	23.9%
MacAskill, K. (SNP)	5 090	13.4%
Lab majority	4 551	11.9%
Total vote 38 178	Turnout	71.7%

Mr Robin Cook, elected for this seat in 1983, has been an Opposition spokesman on Treasury and economic affairs since 1980. MP for Edinburgh, Central Feb 1974–83; contested Edinburgh North 1970. Tutor and organizer in adult education. Born Feb 28 1946; educ. Aberdeen Grammar School, Royal High School, Edinburgh and Edinburgh University. Former vice-chairman, PLP defence group, ex-chairman housing sub-committee, Scottish Labour Group, and all-party group on penal reform in Scotland. Former member, advisory panel on arms control and disarmament. Sponsored by NUR.

Mr Alexander Henderson, life assurance salesman. Born Apr 24 1945; educ. Dunoon Grammar School.

Mr John Campbell, chartered surveyor. Born 1944; educ. George Watson's School, Edinburgh, Gordonstoun School, Royal Military Academy, Sandhurst, and College of Estate Management.

Mr Kenneth MacAskill, solicitor. Born 1958; educ. Linlithgow Academy and Edinburgh University. Associated with tenant's rights and shop stewards' groups.

Mr Denzil Davies

LLANELLI Electorate 63 826

*Davies, D. (Lab)	23 207	48.2%
Kennedy, N. (C)	9 601	20.0%
Rees, K. (L/All)	9 076	18.9%
Edwards, H. T. (PlC)	5 880	12.2%
Hitchon, R. E. (Com)	371	0.8%
Lab majority	13 606	28.3%
Total vote 48 135	Turnout	75.4%

Mr Denzil Davies, became in 1983 chief Opposition spokesman on Wales, was an Opposition spokesman on defence and disarmament 1981–83; a spokesman on foreign and Commonwealth affairs 1979–81. Minister of State. Treasury 1975–79. Barrister. Elected in 1970. Born Oct 9 1938; educ. Carmarthen Grammar School and Pembroke College, Oxford. Lectured at Chicago and Leeds Universities. Member, European Secondary Legislation Committee 1974–75; Select Committee on Wealth Tax 1974–75. Also served on Public Accounts Committee, Select Committee on Corporation Tax and Joint Select Committee on Delegated Legislation.

Mr Nicholas Kennedy, merchant banker – corporate finance executive previously head of investment research. Born Oct 6 1946; educ. Christ's Hospital, Horsham; St John's College, Oxford, and Sidney Sussex College, Cambridge. Member, Elmbridge Borough Council 1980–83; Bow Group. Chairman, Cobham Conservative Assoc. 1981–83.

Mr Kenneth Rees, planning engineer, contested the seat, 1979. Born May 1944; educ. Coleshill Secondary Technical School, Llanelli, and Llanelli Technical College. AUEW.

Mr Hywel Edwards, lecturer at the Extra-mural Department, University College of Wales, Swansea. Member, Dyfed County Council.

Mr William Ross

LONDONDERRY EAST Electorate 67 365

*Ross, W. (OUP)	19 469	37.9%
McClure, J. (DUP)	12 207	23.8%
Doherty, A. (SDLP)	9 397	18.3%
Davey, J. (PSF)	7 073	13.8%
McGrath, Mrs M. (All)	2 401	4.7%
Donnelley, F. (WP)	819	1.6%
OUP majority	7 262	14.1%
Total vote 51 366	Turnout	76.3%

Mr William Ross, farmer, was elected in Feb 1974. Party's spokesman on agriculture and fisheries, and local government. Member, Apprentice Boys of Derry, the Orange and Black Institutions; former secretary, Mid-Londonderry Constituency Unionist Party. Born Feb 4 1936 Educ. Dungiven Primary School. Served on Limavady District Council for four years.

Mr James McClure, aged 57, is a company director. Educ. Eden School, Ballymoney. Elected Northern Ireland Convention 1975, for Londonderry; Northern Ireland Assembly 1982, Londonderry deputy chairman, health and social services committee. DUP councillor, Coleraine, since 1977; deputy mayor, Coleraine since 1981. Chairman of the DUP in Northern Ireland. Member, Independent Orange Order, Apprentice Boys of Derry.

Mr Stephen Dorrell

LOUGHBOROUGH Electorate 70668

*Dorrell, S. (C)	29056	52.9%
Jones, M. (Lab)	12876	23.4%
Frears, J. (SDP/All)	12189	22.2%
Whitebread, D. (Eco)	591	1.1%
Peacock, J. A. (BNP)	228	0.4%
C majority	16180	29.5%
Total vote 54940	Turnout	77.7%

Mr Stephen Dorrell, company director, won the seat for the Conservatives in 1979; contested Kingston-upon-Hull East Oct 1974. Born Mar 25 1952; educ. Uppingham and Brasenose College, Oxford. Member, Select Committee on Transport since 1979. Secretary, Conservative backbench committee on Trade and Consumer Affairs. Officer cadet RAF volunteer reserve, 1971–73. Personal assistant to Mr Peter Walker in Feb 1974 general election. Owns share of Tiger Moth aircraft.

Mr Michael Jones, procedures officer. Born Oct 18 1942; educ. Loughborough College School and Loughborough Technical College. Borough councillor for 12 years and county councillor for 13 years. Successfully contested 14 local elections. AUEW(TASS).

Mr John Frears, writer and university lecturer. Contested Melton 1966, for Labour. Born Nov 26 1936; educ. Gresham's School, Holt, and Trinity College, Cambridge. Member, Leicestershire County Council 1973–81. AUT.

Mr Eric Cockeram

LUDLOW Electorate 63256

*Cockeram, E. (C)	26278	55.7%
Lane, D. (SDP/All)	14975	31.7%
Davis, P. M. (Lab)	5949	12.6%
C majority	11303	24.0%
Total vote 47202	Turnout	74.6%

Mr Eric Cockeram, returned in 1979, was MP for Bebington 1970–74; contested Bebington and Ellesmere Port Feb and Oct 1974. Born Jul 4 1924; educ. The Leys School, Cambridge. Member Commons Select Committee on Corporation Tax 1971–72. PPS to minister of industry 1970–72. PPS to Chancellor of the Exchequer 1972–74. Member, Select Committee on Industry and Trade since 1979. Director, Midshires Building Society. Director TSB (NW) since 1968. Chairman, all-party TSB parliamentary committee.

Mr David Lane, founder and managing director of Bridgnorth Engineering Ltd, manufacturing water pumps for the motor industry. Member, SDP financial advisory committee. Born 1948; educ. Stretford Grammar School, Manchester, Bablake School, Coventry and Sheffield University.

Mr Philip Davis is a full time trade union official. Age 29. Member, The Wrekin District Council since 1979; vice-chairman, employment committee, and former chairman of housing committee. Member, Fabian Society, Christian Socialist Movement, Anti Apartheid Movement, National Council for Civil Liberties; Amnesty International, Co-operative Party. GMBATU.

Mr John Carlisle

LUTON NORTH Electorate 69805

*Carlisle, J. (C)	26115	48.3%
Hopkins, K. P. (Lab)	14134	26.2%
Stephen, D. (SDP/All)	13769	25.5%
C majority	11981	22.2%
Total vote 54018	Turnout	77.4%

Mr John Carlisle elected for this seat in 1983, represented Luton West 1979–83. Commodity trader, director of Granfin Agriculture and consultant to Granfin Trading Ltd. Member of the London Corn Exchange, 1970–79. Born Aug 28 1942; educ. Bedford School, St Lawrence College and London University. Chairman Conservative backbench sport and recreation committee since 1982. Secretary, Africa Committee; treasurer, British–Gibraltar group, 1981–82. Chairman Mid-Bedfordshire Conservative Assoc. 1974–76.

Mr Kelvin Hopkins, trade union research officer with Nalgo since 1977. Born Aug 22 1941; educ. Nottingham University. Member, Luton County Borough Council 1972–74, Luton Borough Council, 1973–76. Formerly worked in economic department, TUC. Apex.

Mr David Stephen was special adviser to Dr David Owen at Foreign and Commonwealth Office, 1977–79. Born 1942; educ. Luton Grammar School, King's College, Cambridge, Essex University. Director, Runnymede Trust, 1975–77. Vice-chairman, SDP Urban Policy Committee.

Mr Graham Bright

LUTON SOUTH Electorate 71015

*Bright, G. (C)	22531	41.9%
Clemitson, I. M. (Lab)	17910	33.3%
Franks, D. (L/All)	13395	24.9%
C majority	4621	8.6%
Total vote 53836		Turnout 75.8%

Mr Graham Bright, managing director of a food company, was elected in 1983; gained Luton East for Conservatives in 1979; contested Dartford Oct 1974, and Thurrock 1970 and Feb 1974. Born Apr 2 1942; educ. Hassenbrook County School and Thurrock Technical College. Served on Thurrock UDC and Essex County Council. Former treasurer, deputy chairman and CPC chairman, Thurrock Conservative Assoc. Former vice-chairman Conservative backbench aviation committee and Conservative backbench committee on smaller businesses. Member Select Committee on House of Commons Services since 1982. Former Secretary of Conservative food and drink sub-committee and space committee. PPS to Home Office Ministers, 1983.

Mr Ivor Clemitson represented Luton East Feb 1974–79. Former secretary, all-party industrial common ownership group and member, Select Committee on Parliamentary Commissioner for Administration. Born Dec 1931; educ. Luton Grammar School, London School of Economics and Bishop's Theological College. Research Officer, National Graphical Assoc. 1971–74; Director, Singapore Ind Mission 1969–70; industrial chaplain, diocese of St Albans 1964–69.

Mr David Franks, sales office manager, contested Luton East 1979. Born Oct 29 1944; educ. locally. Member, Luton Borough Council. ASTMS.

Mr Nicholas Winterton

MACCLESFIELD Electorate 73082

*Winterton, N. (C)	32538	59.4%
Coleman, Mrs R. (L/All)	11859	21.6%
Kelly, P. B. (Lab)	9923	18.1%
Reeman, M. (Ind)	488	0.9%
C majority	20679	37.7%
Total vote 54808		Turnout 75%

Mr Nicholas Winterton was elected in 1971 by-election; contested Newcastle-under-Lyme Oct 1969 and 1970. Born Mar 31 1938; educ. Bilton Grange Preparatory School and Rugby. Member, Social Services select committee since 1979. Vice-chairman Anglo-Danish and British Austrian Parliamentry groups; treasurer, British-Indonesia parliamentary group; secretary, British-South Africa parliamentary group; chairman, British-Namibian and treasurer, British Bahamas parliamentary groups; vice-chairman, Conservative parliamentary sport and recreation committee. Member, Select Committee on Standing Orders, since 1981. Non-executive Chairman, Camra (Real Ale) Investments. Parliamentary adviser to Construction Plant Hire Assoc. and to Baird Textile Holdings Ltd. Freeman of the City of London; member, Worshipful Company of Weavers. Was secretary/treasurer, UK Falkland Islands Group. His wife, Ann, is MP for Congleton.

Mrs Ruth Coleman, mathematics teacher, contested Liverpool, Toxteth, 1979. Born Jan 21 1947; educ. Manchester High School for Girls and York and Manchester universities. NATFHE.

Mr Peter Kelly, customs officer. Born 1953. Member, Labour regional executive and Labour NEC local government sub-committee.

Sir John Wells

MAIDSTONE Electorate 70357

*Wells, Sir J. (C)	26420	50.9%
Burnett, J. (L/All)	19194	37.0%
Carey, G. T. (Lab)	6280	12.1%
C majority	7226	13.9%
Total vote 51894		Turnout 73.8%

Sir John Wells was elected in 1959; contested Smethwick 1955. Born Mar 30 1925; educ. Heath Mount School, Hertford, Eton and Corpus Christi College, Oxford. Chairman, Conservative horticulture commiteee, 1965–71 and vice-chairman, Conservative agriculture committee, 1970–71, Member of the Commons chairmen's panel since 1974. Master of the Fruiterers Company, 1979. Joint chairman, all-party Channel tunnel group. Chairman, Anglo-Finnish and Anglo-Spanish parliamentary groups. Horticulturist, company director,

Mr John Burnett, chartered accountant, contested the seat 1979 and Oct 1974. Born Oct 7 1931; educ. Liverpool Collegiate School, and Colfe's Grammar School, Lewisham. Member, Maidstone Borough Council since 1973.

Mr Gordon Carey, teacher. Born 1954; educ. secondary modern school, Newport Grammar School, LSE, and Oxford. Chairman, Maidstone Co-operative Party. NUT.

Mr Michael McGuire

MAKERFIELD Electorate 69 176

*McGuire, M. (Lab)	25 114	49.3%
Hay, E. (C)	14 238	27.9%
Grayson, R. (L/All)	11 633	22.8%
Lab majority	10 876	21.3%
Total vote 50 985	Turnout	73.7%

Mr Michael McGuire, a former coal miner and fulltime NUM official from 1957–64, was elected in 1983; represented Ince 1964–83. Born May 3 1926; elementary education. Member, former Select Committee on Nationalized Industries. PPS to Minister for Sport and Recreation 1974. Member, Council of Europe and of WEU since 1977. Former member, PLP trade union group executive. Sponsored by NUM.

Mr Edward Hay, sales manager in timber industry. Born Dec 1949; educ. Harrow School. Member, Bow Group. Short service commission, Grenadier Guards, 1972–75.

Mr Robin Grayson is a lecturer at Wigan Technical College. Born Jan 29 1949; educ. De La Salle School and Manchester University. Member, Greater Manchester County Council, since 1981. Member, CND; Wigan Civic Trust; campaign for renovation of Wigan Pier. NATFHE.

Mr Kenneth Eastham

MANCHESTER, BLACKLEY Electorate 60 106

*Eastham, K. (Lab)	20 132	48.1%
Ridgway, P. (C)	13 676	32.7%
Cookson, J. (L/All)	8 081	19.3%
Lab majority	6 456	15.4%
Total vote 41 889	Turnout	69.7%

Mr Kenneth Eastham, former planning engineer with GEC, Trafford Park, was elected in 1979. Born Aug 11 1927; educ. Openshaw Technical College. Member, Manchester City Council 1962–80; former deputy leader of council and chairman of education committee. Member, North-West Economic Planning Council 1975–79. Member, Select Committee on Employment. Sponsored by AUEW.

Mr Peter Ridgway, bank securities clerk. Born Jun 24 1951; educ. Langdale Junior School, Seabridge Secondary School and Caulden College of Further Education. Member, Lloyds Bank Group staff union.

Mr John Cookson is a printer. Aged 35. Educ. Manchester Grammar School and Manchester University.

Mr Robert Litherland

MANCHESTER CENTRAL Electorate 69 188

*Litherland, R. (Lab)	27 353	65.3%
Eager, D. (C)	8 868	21.2%
Ahmed, A. (SDP/All)	4 956	11.8%
Coles, A. (NF)	729	1.7%
Lab majority	18 485	44.1%
Total vote 41 906	Turnout	60.6%

Mr Robert Litherland, former sales representative for a printing firm, has represented the seat since Sep 1979. Born 1930; educ. North Manchester High School for Boys. Member, Manchester City Council; deputy chairman, housing committee; former chairman, Manchester Direct Works Committee. Deputy Chairman, Public Works Committee, Association of Municipal Authorities.

Mr David Eager, disc jockey, actor and educational lecturer. Born Sep 26 1946; educ. North Manchester Grammar School and Edge Hill Teachers Training College, Ormskirk. Secretary and vice-chairman, Manchester Central Conservative Assoc. Branch secretary, Equity 1975–80, and member of executive, Equity 1980–82. President, Animals in Distress charity.

Mr Altaf Ahmed, counsellor with special interest in Islamic jurisprudence, immigration and nationality law. Born Dec 27 1937; educ. government college in Pakistan, and Manchester Central Polytechnic.

Mr Gerald Kaufman

MANCHESTER, GORTON Electorate 64 645

*Kaufman, G. B. (Lab)	22 460	51.2%
Kershaw, J. (C)	12 495	28.5%
Whitmore, K. (L/All)	8 348	19.0%
Cowle, M. (Com)	333	0.8%
Andrews, L. C. (BNP)	231	0.5%
Lab majority	9 965	22.7%
Total vote 43 867	Turnout	67.9%

Mr Gerald Kaufman, elected for this seat in 1983, became chief Opposition spokesman on the environment in 1980 after election to shadow cabinet; previously spokesman on housing. Minister of State, Department of Industry 1975–79; formerly Under-Secretary in same department; Under-Secretary, Department of Environment

1974–75. Former parliamentary press liaison officer for the Labour Party. MP for Manchester, Ardwick, 1970–83; contested Gillingham 1959, and Bromley 1955. Born Jun 21 1930; educ. Leeds Grammar School and Queen's College, Oxford. Assistant secretary, Fabian Society 1954–55. Political correspondent, *New Statesman* 1964–65; political staff, *Daily Mirror* 1955–64. Sponsored by GMBATU.

Mr John Kershaw, lecturer. Born 1950; educ. Audenshaw Grammar School, Manchester Polytechnic and Padgate College of Education.

Mr Keith Whitmore is leader, Liberal group, Greater Manchester Council; member since 1981. Member, Manchester City Council since 1979. Born Jun 15 1955; educ. Chorlton High School.

Mr Frederick Silvester

MANCHESTER, WITHINGTON Electorate 64 606

*Silvester, F. (C)	18 329	39.3%
Done, Mrs F. W. (Lab)	15 956	34.2%
Lever, B. (SDP/All)	12 231	26.2%
Gibson, M. G. (Freedom)	184	0.4%
C majority	2 373	5.1%
Total vote 46 700		Turnout 72.3%

Mr Frederick Silvester was elected in Feb 1974; held Walthamstow West for the Conservatives 1967–70, contesting the seat 1966. Advertising executive, barrister and political education officer, Conservative Political Centre 1957–60. Opposition whip 1974–76. Vice-chairman, Conservative employment committee 1976–79. PPS to Secretary of State for Employment 1979–81 and to Secretary of State for Northern Ireland since 1981. Member, select committee on Procedure (Finance). Born Sep 20 1933; educ. Sir George Monoux Grammar School, Walthamstow, and Sidney Sussex College, Cambridge. Company director.

Mrs Frances Done, chartered accountant. Born May 6 1950; educ. Manchester University. Contested Cheadle 1979. Member, Manchester City Council for eight years. ASTMS.

Mr Bernard Lever, barrister. Born Feb 1 1951; educ. Clifton College, Queen's College, Oxford.

Mr Alfed Morris

MANCHESTER, WYTHENSHAWE Electorate 60 995 1979: 60 602 minor

*Morris, A. (Lab)	23 172	54.6%
Jacobs, Mrs I. (C)	12 488	29.4%
Sandiford, D. (L/All)	6 766	16.0%
Lab majority	10 684	25.2%
Total vote 42 426		Turnout 69.6%

1979: Total vote 45 460 (75.0%); Lab 26 860 (59.1%); C 14 747 (32.4%); L 3 853 (8.5%). Lab maj 12 113 (26.7%); swing 2.5% to C..

Mr Alfred Morris, Opposition spokesman on the disabled since 1979, was Under Secretary of State for Health and Social Security with special responsibility for the disabled, 1974–79. Chairman of World Planning Group appointed to draft *Charter for the 1980s* for disabled people world-wide, a document presented to all heads of government in the International year of Disabled People 1981. Elected in 1964; contested seat in 1959, and Liverpool, Garston 1951. Chairman, parliamentary cooperative group 1970–71; Opposition spokesman on social services 1970–74. Promoted Chronically Sick and Disabled Persons Act 1970. Born Mar 23 1928; educ. Manchester elementary schools, Ruskin College and St Catherine's College, Oxford; post-graduate studies at Manchester University. Former chairman, food and agriculture group, Parliamentary Labour Party. Member, General Advisory Council, BBC, 1968–74. Parliamentary adviser to Police Federation 1971–74. Promoted Police Act 1972 and Food and Drugs (Milk) Act 1970.

Mrs Joan Jacobs, banker. Born Apr 12 1945; educ. St Joseph's Convent High School, Manchester. Member, Manchester City Council. Patron, Manchester Conservative Assoc. Member, executive of a civic society and of a self-help group. President of a residents' group.

Dr David Sandiford, university senior lecturer in physics. Born Aug 9 1933; educ. Royal Liberty School, Romford; Downing College, Cambridge; Yale University. Member, Manchester City Council 1979–82; and from 1983; leader, Liberal group. AUT.

Mr Don Concannon

MANSFIELD Electorate 65 277

*Concannon, J. D. (Lab)	18 670	40.5%
Wrenn, R. (C)	16 432	35.7%
Taylor, S. (SDP/All)	11 036	23.9%
Lab majority	2 238	4.8%
Total vote 46 138	Turnout 70.7%	

Mr Don Conconnan, chief Opposition spokesman on Northern Ireland 1980–83, was an Opposition spokesman on defence 1979–80. Minister of State for Northern Ireland 1976–79, and Under Secretary Jun 1974–76. Vice Chamberlain of the Household (whip) Mar–Jun 1974; Opposition whip 1970–74; assistant Government whip 1968–70. Returned in 1966. Miner, former NUM official, sponsored by NUM. Born May 1930; educ. Rossington Secondary School, Doncaster Technical School, WEA, and Nottingham University. Member, Mansfield Council 1962–68.

Mr Richard Wrenn, senior partner in firm of solicitors, is clerk to the General Commissioners of the Inland Revenue, Wellingborough district. Born Nov 12 1943; educ. Wellingborough Grammar School and Gonville and Caius, Cambridge. Former chairman, Wellingborough and East Northants Conservative Assoc; member, Wellingborough District Council since 1976.

Mr Stephen Taylor, manager of motor repair business. Born 1952. Assistant secretary, Mansfield SDP; Mansfield district councillor.

Mrs Peggy Fenner

MEDWAY Electorate 63 387

*Fenner, Mrs P. (C)	22 507	48.9%
Bean, R. E. (Lab)	13 851	30.1%
Winckless, F. (SDP/All)	9 658	21.0%
C majority	8 656	18.8%
Total vote 46 016	Turnout 72.6%	

Mrs Peggy Fenner, elected in 1983, has been Parliamentary Secretary, Ministry of Agriculture, Fisheries and Food since 1981. MP for Rochester and Chatham 1979–83, 1970–Oct 1974. She has served on the Select Committee for the Civil List and the Select Committee on Public Expenditure; Parliamentary Secretary to the Ministry of Agriculture, Fisheries and Food 1972–73. Born Nov 12 1922; educ. LCC elementary school. Brockley and Ide Hill School, Kent. Chairman, Sevenoaks UDC, 1962–63, on which she served for 15 years. Member, executive of Kent Borough and Urban District Councils Assoc. 1967–71. Member, West Kent Divisional Executive Education Committee 1962–72. Member European Parliament 1974–75.

Mr Robert Bean, a polytechnic lecturer and former construction site agent, was MP for Rochester and Chatham Oct 1974–79. Born Sep 1935; educ. Sir Joseph Williamson's Mathematical School, Rochester, and Medway College of Technology. Member, Chatham Borough Council 1958–74; Medway Borough Council 1974–76; Kent County Council 1973–76.

Mr Frederick Winckless, senior lecturer in social work and probation practice, contested Stepney in 1955 as a Liberal. Born Mar 18 1925; educ. Pitman's College and University of London. NATHFE.

Mr Dafydd Thomas

MEIRIONNYDD NANT CONWY Electorate 30 459

*Thomas, D. E. (Pl C)	9 709	39.2%
Lloyd, D. (C)	7 066	28.5%
Roberts, D. (SDP/All)	4 254	17.2%
Williams, G. (Lab)	3 735	15.1%
PlC majority	2 643	10.7%
Total vote 24 764	Turnout 81.3%	

Mr Dafydd Thomas, elected in 1983. Adult education tutor, broadcaster and writer; represented Merioneth Feb 1974–83; contested Conway, 1970. Born Oct 18 1946; educ. University College of North Wales. Became Plaid Cymru parliamentary spokesman on social, educational and cultural policy in 1975; party spokesman on agricultural and rural development, 1974. Vice-president Plaid Cymru 1979–81. Honorary secretary, all-party mental health group, Mind, Institute for Workers Control and Shelter. Member, selected Committee on Education Science and the Arts since 1979. TGWU.

Mr David Lloyd, journalist and broadcaster. Born Sep 25 1932; educ. Llangollen Grammar School. Contested European constituency of Mid and West Wales 1979. NUJ.

Mr David Roberts. Born 1957; educ. Tywyn School, King's College, London, College of Law, Lancaster Gate. Youth leader; member, Campaign for Preservation of Rural Wales.

Mr Glyn Williams, senior lecturer in industrial studies. Born Apr 8 1939; educ. Wrexham Technical College and Goldsmith's College, University of London. Greenwich councillor since 1980.

Mr Iain Mills

MERIDEN Electorate 74161

*Mills, I. C. (C)	28474	53.7%
*Sever, E. J. (Lab)	13456	25.4%
Dunbar, Mrs P. M. (SDP/All)	10674	20.1%
Collins, C. L. (NF)	460	0.9%
C majority	15018	28.3%
Total vote 53064		Turnout 71.6%

Mr Iain Mills, a member of the Select Committee on European legislation since 1981, gained the seat for the Conservatives in 1979. Marketing planning manager with Dunlop, responsible for marketing new tyre projects was responsible for all racing tyre development, 1966–70. Born Apr 21 1940; educ. Prince Edward School, Bulawayo, Rhodesia, and Cape Town University. Member, Lichfield District Council 1974–76. Burgess of the City of Glasgow. Adviser to the National Tyre Distributors Assoc. Secretary, Conservative transport committee since 1979; PPS to Norman Tebbit since 1981.

Mr John Sever, represented Birmingham, Ladywood Aug 1977–83; contested Birmingham, Edgbaston, 1970. PPS to Solicitor General 1978–79. Born Apr 1 1943; educ. Sparkhill Commercial School. Member, Select Committee on Environment since 1979; member, Labour home affairs, foreign affairs and housing groups. Former member, Birmingham City Council. Member and former branch chairman, Apex. Travel executive with tour operator.

Dr Pamela Dunbar, university lecturer and author. Born Dec 15 1944; educ. University of Canterbury, New Zealand, and Girton College, Cambridge. AUT.

Mr Edward Rowlands

MERTHYR TYDFIL AND RHYMNEY Electorate 59486

*Rowlands, E. (Lab)	29053	67.4%
Owen, P. (L/All)	6323	14.7%
Blausten, R. (C)	5449	12.6%
Howells, G. (Pl C)	2058	4.8%
Gould, T. (WRP)	256	0.6%
Lab majority	22730	52.7%
Total vote 43139		Turnout 72.5%

Mr Edward Rowlands an Opposition spokesman on energy since 1980; an Opposition spokesman on foreign affairs 1979–80. Minister of State, Foreign and Commonwealth Office 1976–79; Under Secretary of State 1975–76. Under Secretary of State, Welsh Office 1974–75. Elected in 1983; represented Merthyr Tydfil 1972–83; MP for Cardiff North 1966–70. Under Secretary of State, Welsh Office, 1969–70. Former lecturer, Welsh College of Advanced Technology. Born Jan 23 1940; educ. Rhondda Grammar School, Wirral Grammar School, and King's College, London. ASTMS.

Mr Philip Owen, business manager. Aged 31; educ. Builth Wells, Christ College, Brecon, and Durham University. Co-founder, Durham University Liberal Club; founder, Rugby Young Liberals; Brecon area organizer 1979–82. Duke of Edinburgh Award winner.

Mr Richard Blausten, editor of *Insurance Mail*. Born Dec 18 1948; educ. Clifton College, Bristol, Sheffield University. Member, Barnet Borough Council 1974–82 (vice-chairman, education committee). Chairman, English-Speaking Union Debating Society 1979–81;

Mr Gerald Howells, is Plaid Cymru's national field organizer. Former member, Rhymni Valley District Council.

Mr Stuart Bell

MIDDLESBROUGH Electorate 62950

Bell, S. (Lab)	21220	50.7%
Campey, Mrs L. (C)	11551	27.6%
Sanders, D. (L/All)	8871	21.2%
Simpson, M. (WRP)	207	0.5%
Lab majority	9669	23.1%
Total vote 41849		Turnout 66.5%

Mr Stuart Bell, a barrister was elected in 1983; contested Hexham 1979. Born May 16 1938; educ. Hookergate Grammar School, Durham. Former journalist. Member, Society of Labour Lawyers. Fabian.

Mrs Lucille Campey, researcher. Born Aug 24 1941; educ. Ottawa University and Leeds University.

The Rev David Sanders is a Methodist Superintendent minister. Born Dec 17 1934; educ. Kingswood School, Bath, Balliol College, Oxford. Contested Runcorn 1974 and North Somerset 1979, and European seat of Central Lancashire 1979.

Mr Alexander Eadie

MIDLOTHIAN Electorate 60 496

*Eadie, A. (Lab)	19 401	42.7%
Dewar, A. (SDP/All)	13 245	29.2%
Menzies, D. (C)	9 922	21.9%
Hird, Mrs M. (SNP)	2 826	6.2%
Lab majority	6 156	13.6%
Total vote 45 394		Turnout 75.0%

Mr Alexander Eadie, was the Opposition spokesman on energy 1979–83. Under-Secretary of State for Energy 1974–79. Former Opposition spokesman on energy and former chairman of PLP miners' group and of parliamentary power and steel group. Elected in 1966, contested Ayr 1959 and 1964. Former miners' agent. Born Jun 23 1920; educ. Buckhaven Senior Secondary School, Fife and technical college. Sponsored by NUM.

Mr Alan Dewar, solicitor. Born 1956; sity. Captained Scottish schools basketball team. Part-time tutor in criminal law, Edinburgh University.

Mr Duncan Menzies, advocate, is district chairman of Edinburgh North Conservative Assoc. Born 1953; educ. Edinburgh Academy, Cargilfield School, Trinity College, Glenalmond, Trinity College School, Ontario, Wadham College, Oxford, and Edinburgh University. Chairman, Humbie District Conservative Assoc.

Mrs Marjory Hird, secretary. Born 1935; educ. Macduff High School; Dalkeith College of Further Education.

Mr William Benyon

MILTON KEYNES Electorate 79 229

*Benyon, W. (C)	28 181	48.0%
Nightingale, Mrs J. (SDP/All)	16 659	28.4%
Thakoordin, J. (Lab)	13 045	22.2%
Francis, A. (Eco)	494	0.8%
Rickcord, R. (BNP)	290	0.5%
C majority	11 522	19.6%
Total vote 58 669		Turnout 74.1%

Mr William Benyon, an Opposition whip 1974–76, was elected in 1983; MP for Buckingham 1970–83. Farmer and landowner; Born Jan 17 1930; educ. Royal Naval College, Dartmouth. Member executive 1922 Committee. Member, Berkshire County Council 1964–74; Bradfield Rural Council 1960–62; Council of Reading University; Council of Bradfield College; Royal Agricultural Society of England. Governor, Dominion Students Hall Trust and Peabody Trust. Vice-chairman, Conservative backbench Northern Ireland committee and constitutional committee.

Mrs Janet Nightingale, teacher. Born Jun 21 1939; educ. Altrincham Grammar School, Immarsh College of Physical Education, Liverpool and Newnham College, Cambridge.

Mr James Thakoordin joined Labour Party in 1964. Born Aug 6 1943 in Guyana; parents field workers on sugar plantation.

Mrs Angela Rumbold

MITCHAM AND MORDEN Electorate 63 535 1979: 62 365 same

*Rumbold, Mrs A. (C)	19 827	42.7%
Nicholas, D. (Lab)	13 376	28.8%
Douglas-Mann, B. (SDP / All)	12 720	27.4%
Perryman, J. (NF)	539	1.2%
C majority	6 451	13.9%
Total vote 46 462		Turnout 73.1%

1979: Total vote 47 942 (76.9%); Lab 21 668 (45.2%); C 21 050 (43.9%); L 4 258 (8.9%); NF 966 (2.0%); Lab maj 618 (1.3%); swing 6.0% to C.

1982 by-election: Total vote 30 673 (48.5%); C 13 306 (34.4%); Ind SDP 9 032 (29.5%); Lab 7 475 (24.4%); others 860 (2.8%). C maj 4 274 (13.9%). C gain from Ind SDP.

Mrs Angela Rumbold was returned at by-election in Jun 1982. Educ. Notting Hill and Ealing High School; Perse School for Girls, Cambridge; and King's College, London. Member Select Committee for Social Services; secretary to backbench small businesses committee; vice-chairman, Campaign for Defence and Multilateral Disarmament. Elected to Kingston Council in 1974 and became chairman, education committee. Former member of Burnham Management Committee and Assessment of Performance Unit for Department of Education.

Mr David Nicholas, head teacher, contested Hove 1970 and Mitcham and Morden by-election 1982. Born Oct 17 1945; educ. Bec Grammar School, Tooting, and Exeter University.

Mr Bruce Douglas-Mann, a solicitor, was elected Labour MP for Merton, Mitcham and Morden Feb 1974; MP for Kensington North 1970–74; contested Maldon 1966 and St Albans 1964, as a Labour candidate. Joined the SDP 1982 resigned seat but lost by-election in Jun 1982. Born Jun 1927; educ. in Canada and Jesus College, Oxford.

Mr Kenneth Baker

MOLE VALLEY Electorate 65 067

*Baker, K. (C)	29 691	60.8%
Thomas Ms S. (L/All)	14 973	30.7%
Lines Ms F. (Lab)	4 147	8.5%
C majority	14 718	30.2%
Total vote 48 811		Turnout 75.0%

Mr Kenneth Baker, Minister for Information Technology at the Department of Trade and Industry since 1981, was Parliamentary Secretary, Civil Service Department 1972–74. Elected for this seat in 1983; MP for City of Westminster, St Marylebone, 1970–83, and for Acton 1968–70; contested Acton 1966 and Poplar 1964. Worked in industry. Former member, 1922 Committee executive. Born Nov 3 1934; educ. St Paul's School and Magdalen College, Oxford. Member, Twickenham Borough Council 1961–63. Former member, Public Accounts and Procedure Committees, PPS to Mr Edward Heath 1974.

Ms Susan Thomas, researcher, trade assoc. director and housewife. Born Dec 20 1935; educ. Cranborne Chase School and Lady Margaret Hall, Oxford. Former chairman and treasurer, Richmond Liberals. Former member, London Liberal Party Council; Liberal Party Council. British Clothing Industries Council for Europe chief executive 1974–78. Member, Kew Assoc. for the Control of Aircraft Noise since 1966.

Ms Fanny Lines, industrial chemist. Born May 4 1929; educ. London University. TGWU.

Mr John Smith

MONKLANDS EAST Electorate 49 030

*Smith, J. (Lab)	18 358	51.3%
Love, J. (C)	8 559	23.9%
Rennie, A. (L/All)	5 721	16.0%
Johnston, T. (SNP)	3 185	8.9%
Lab majority	9 799	27.4%
Total vote 35 823		Turnout 73.1%

Mr John Smith, member of Shadow Cabinet and chief Opposition spokesman on energy since 1982 and trade 1979–82; Secretary of State for Trade, 1978–79; Minister of State, Privy Council Office 1976–78; Minister of State, Department of Energy 1975–76; Under Secretary, Department of Energy 1974–75. Elected for this seat in 1983; MP for North Lanarkshire 1970–83; contested East Fife by-election 1961 and in 1964. Advocate. Born Sept 13 1938; educ. Dunoon Grammar School and Glasgow University. Sponsored by Amalgamated Society of Boilermakers.

Mr John Love, accountant, has been a Monklands district councillor for 10 years. Born Aug 1941; educ. Airdrie Academy. Contested Coatbridge and Airdrie Oct 1974 and 1979. Elder of the Church of Scotland.

Dr Alan Rennie, general practitioner. Born Mar 4 1940; educ. Moray School, Glasgow; Glasgow Academy; Glasgow University. Member, Mearns Community Council; Eastwood District Council 1967–74. Former chairman, Eastwood Liberal Assoc. and chairman, Mearns Ratepayers Assoc.

Mr Thomas Johnston, principal history teacher. Born 1947; educ. Bellahouston Academy; Glasgow and London universities.

Mr Thomas Clarke

MONKLANDS WEST Electorate 50 345

*Clarke, T. (Lab)	20 642	54.2%
Cameron, L. (C)	8 378	22.0%
Ackland, R. (SDP/All)	6 605	17.3%
Lyon, A. (SNP)	2 473	6.5%
Lab majority	12 264	32.2%
Total vote 38 098		Turnout 75.7%

Mr Thomas Clarke, was elected for this seat in 1983. MP for Coatbridge and Airdrie 1982–83. Was formerly assistant director, Scottish Film Council. Born Jan 1941; educ. Columba High School and Coatbridge and Scottish College of Commerce. Member, Coatbridge Council, 1964–74; Provost of Monklands District Council 1974–82. President, Convention of Scottish Local Authorities 1978–80; vice president 1976–78. Member, Select Committee on Scottish Affairs and of standing committee on British Telecom. GMWU.

Mr Laurence Cameron, is a chief electrical engineer. Aged 53. Chairman, Monklands East Conservative Assoc; former chairman, Coatbridge and Airdrie Assoc. Member, Airdrie Town Council 1972–74; Monklands District Council, since 1978.

Mr Rodney Ackland is a tutor for the Open University. Born 1945; educ. Eastbourne College School and Sussex and Oxford universities. Former engineer with Lucas Aerospace.

Mr Angus Lyon is Parliamentary Assistant to SNP group at Westminster. Chairman, House of Commons branch of APEX. Born 1956; educ. Lenzie Academy; Strathclyde and Glasgow universities.

Mr John Stradling-Thomas

MONMOUTH Electorate 56 112

*Stradling-Thomas, J. (C)	21 746	49.2%
Lindley, C. (SDP/All)	12 403	28.0%
Short, C. (Lab)	9 593	21.7%
Williams, G. (Pl C)	493	1.1%
C majority	9 343	21.1%
Total vote 44 235	Turnout	78.8%

Mr John Stradling-Thomas was appointed Minister of State, Welsh Office 1983; Treasurer of HM Household and Deputy Chief Whip 1979–83. Member House of Commons Service Committee since 1979. An Opposition whip 1974–79. Won the seat for the Conservatives in 1970. Assistant Government whip 1971–72; Lord Commissioner of the Treasury (whip) 1973–74. Contested Cardiganshire 1966; Aberavon 1964. Farmer, Born Jun 10 1925; educ. Rugby and London University. Member, Carmarthen Borough Council, 1961–64. Chairman, Carmarthenshire NFU 1964; NFU council, 1963–70.

Mr Clive Lindley, chairman of companies, contested Leominster, Feb 1974. Born Sep 22 1934; educ. King Edward VII School, Lytham.

Mr Christopher Short is a solicitor. Born 1947. Governor of South Glamorgan Institute of Higher Education. APEX.

Mr Gwyn Williams, head of geography at Ebbw Vale, senior comprehensive school. Aged 46; educ. Brynmawr Grammar School and University College, Aberystwyth. Contested the seat 1979.

Mr Alex Carlile

MONTGOMERY Electorate 37 474 1979: 35 786 same

Carlile, A. (L/All)	12 863	43.3%
*Williams, D. (C)	12 195	41.1%
Wilson, J. (Lab)	2 550	8.6%
Clowes, C. (Pl C)	1 585	5.3%
Rowlands, D. W. (Ind)	487	1.6%
L/All majority	668	2.3%
Total vote 29 680	Turnout	79.2%

1979: Total vote 29 134 (81.4%); C 11 751 (40.3%); L 10 158 (34.9%); Lab & Labcoop 4 751 (16.3%); Pl Cymru 2 474 (8.5%). C maj 1 593 (5.4%). C gain from L.

Mr Alex Carlile, barrister, won the seat in 1983, contested Flint East 1979 and Feb 1974. Former chairman, Welsh Liberal Party. Born Feb 12 1948; educ. Epsom College, Surrey; London University. Inns of Court School of Law.

Mr Delwyn Williams, a solicitor, a member of the Select Committee on Welsh Affairs since 1979, gained the seat for Conservatives in 1979. Secretary, Welsh Conservative MPs group since 1982. Born Nov 1 1938; educ. Welshpool Grammar School and University College of Wales, Aberystwyth. Fought Cardigan Oct 1974 and Montgomery 1970.

Mr Joe Wilson, lecturer at North Wales Institute of Higher Education. Born Jul 6 1937; educ. Loughborough College, University of Wales.

Dr Carl Clowes, former GP, is a health administrator with Gwynedd Health Authority. Founder member of Antur Aelhaearn, the first village co-operative in Britain.

Mr Alexander Pollock

MORAY Electorate 60 804

*Pollock, A. (C)	16 944	39.2%
Watt, H. (SNP)	15 231	35.2%
Burnett, M. (L/All)	7 901	18.3%
Kiddie, J. (Lab)	3 139	7.3%
C majority	1 713	4.0%
Total vote 43 215	Turnout	71.1%

Mr Alexander Pollock was a member of the Select Committee on Scottish Affairs 1979–82. An advocate, Scottish Bar. Represented Moray and Nairn 1979–83; elected for this seat in 1983, contested it Oct 1974 and West Lothian Feb 1974. Born Jul 27 1944; educ. Glasgow Academy, Brasenose College, Oxford, and Edinburgh University. Former counsellor for Edinburgh marriage guidance council; former treasurer, Order of Christian Unity, founder member, Thistle Group. Parliamentary adviser to Institute of Professional Investigators. PPS to Sec. of State for Scotland since 1982.

Mr Hamish Watt was MP for Banffshire Feb 1974 to 1979. Was spokesman on agriculture, forestry and fisheries; former SNP chief whip. Contested Banffshire 1970, and Caithness and Sutherland 1966 (as a Conservative). Farmer. Chairman, local NFU; Past branch president. Born Dec 1925; educ. Keith Grammar School and St Andrew's University.

Mr Michael Burnett contested Caithness and Sutherland Feb and Oct 1974. Farmer. Born Jul 1935; educ. Morrison's Academy, Crieff, and Edinburgh University. Past President, NFU of Scotland.

Mr James Kiddie is a district personnel officer for the Grampian Health Board. Aged 38; educ. Kirkcaldy High School and Edinburgh University.

Mr Mark Lennox-Boyd

MORECAMBE AND LUNESDALE Electorate 53 238

*Lennox-Boyd, M. (C)	21 968	56.6%
Clare, T. (SDP/All)	9 774	25.2%
Bryning, A. C. (Lab)	6 882	17.7%
Woods, Mrs I. (Ind)	208	0.5%
C majority	12 194	31.4%
Total vote 38 832		Turnout 72.9%

Mr Mark Lennox-Boyd, a barrister and company director was elected in 1983; represented Morecambe and Lonesdale 1979–83; contested Brent South Oct 1974. Born May 4 1943; educ. Eton and Christ Church Oxford. Former member, Select Committee on Energy. PPS to Financial Secretary to the Treasury 1980–81; PPS to Secretary of State for Energy since 1981.

Mr Thomas Clare, a lecturer with university extra mural departments and the WEA, was previously Cumbria County Archeological Officer. Born Jun 1946; educ. Morecambe Grammar School and the universities of Exeter and Liverpool. Nalgo.

Mr Abbott Bryning, senior economics lecturer, Lancaster and Morecambe College of Further Education. Born Mar 17 1932; educ. Morecambe High School, Sheffield University. Mayor of Lancaster 1980–81; Leader Labour Group, Lancaster City Council since 1974; Member since 1967. NATFHE, NUPE.

Mr James Hamilton

MOTHERWELL NORTH Electorate 56 512

*Hamilton, J. (Lab)	24 483	57.8%
Hargrave, R. (C)	6 589	15.6%
Whitelaw, G. (L/All)	5 970	14.1%
Lyle, R. (SNP)	5 333	12.6%
Lab majority	17 894	42.2%
Total vote 42 375		Turnout 75.0%

Mr James Hamilton, a member of the Select Committee on Selection was Vice-Chamberlain of the Household 1974–78. Comptroller 1978–79. Lord Commissioner of the Treasury (Government whip) 1974. Former chairman PLP trade union group. Assistant Government whip 1969–70. Opposition whip 1970–74. Elected in 1983; MP for Bothwell 1964–83. Born Mar 11 1918; educ. senior secondary schools. Member, Lanarkshire County Council 1955–65. President, Constructional Engineering Union 1968–70; member of its national executive 1958–70. Sponsored by AUEW, constructional section.

Mr Robert Hargrave, managing director of an engineering firm. Born 1939; educ. Dalziel High School.

Mr Gordon Whitelaw, sales representative. Born Aug 5 1950; educ. Onslow Drive School, Glasgow. Contested Dunfermline 1979.

Mr Richard Lyle, supervisor in retail trade. SNP group leader on Motherwell District Council. Born 1950; educ. Bellshill Academy.

Dr Jeremy Bray

MOTHERWELL SOUTH Electorate 52 183 1979: 50 317 minor

*Bray, J. (Lab)	19 939	52.4%
Walker, P. (C)	7 590	20.0%
Ashley, B. (L/All)	6 754	17.8%
Wright, J. (SNP)	3 743	9.8%
Lab majority	12 349	32.4%
Total vote 38 026		Turnout 72.9%

1979 (as Motherwell and Wishaw): Total vote 39 146 (77.8%); Lab 22 263 (56.9%); C 11 326 (28.9%); SNP 4 817 (12.3%); Com 740 (1.9%). Lab maj 10 937 (28.0%) swing 0.8% to Lab.

Dr Jeremy Bray, a member of Select Committee on Treasury and Civil Service since 1979 being chairman of its sub-committee, was elected in 1983 having represented Motherwell and Wishaw Oct 1974–83; MP for Middlesbrough West 1962 (by-election) to 1970; contested Thirsk and Malton 1959. Parliamentary Secretary, Ministry of Technology 1967–69; Parliamentary Secretary, Ministry of Power Apr 1966 to Jan 1967. Member, Nationalized Industries Select Committee 1962–64; Estimates Committee (chairman sub-committee) 1964–66; Select Committee on Wealth Tax 1974; Expenditure Committee 1978–79. Chairman Fabian Society 1971. Born June 1930; educ. Aberystwyth Grammar School, Kingswood School, Bath; Jesus College, Cambridge. Choate Fellow, Harvard.

Mr Paul Walker, vice-chairman, Conservative trade unionists in Scotland. Aged 22. Former civil servant. Candidate, 1982 regional elections, Scotland. TA officer cadet.

Mr Brian Ashley was director of school of community studies, Moray House College of Education until he retired to become a freelance consultant on educational research and training. Born May 30 1927; educ. University College, Hull. Vice-chairman, Unicef in Scotland. Member, Commission of Racial Equality.

Mr James Wright, a business management consultant, led the local SNP campaign against the proposed closure of Ravenscraig and in favour of a separate Scottish steel corporation. Born 1942.

Mr Donald Coleman

NEATH Electorate 55 272

*Coleman, D. (Lab)	22 670	53.6%
Davies, K. (SDP/All)	9 066	21.4%
Buckley, R. (C)	7 350	17.4%
Owen, I (Pl C)	3 046	7.2%
Donavon, J. (Comp Dem)	150	0.4%
Lab majority	13 604	32.2%
Total vote 42 282		Turnout 76.5%

Mr Donald Coleman, an Opposition spokesman on Wales 1981–83 was elected in 1964. Opposition whip 1979–81 and 1970–74. Lord Commissioner of the Treasury (Government whip) 1974–78; Vice-Chamberlain of Royal Household 1978–79. Member, Select Committee on Overseas Aid 1969–74, and delegate, Council of Europe and Western European Union 1968–74. Metallurgist; sponsored by Iron and Steel Trades Confederation. Born Sep 19 1925; educ. Cadoxton School, Barry, and Cardiff Technical College. Tenor soloist and former member, Welsh National Opera Company. Parliamentary adviser to Institute of Medical Laboratory Sciences. Sponsored by ISTC.

Mr Keith Davies, a plant fitter at BP Chemicals, Port Talbot. Born 1946. Former shop steward, deputy convenor (AUEW) and chairman, joint shop stewards' committee.

Mr Richard Buckley, design consultant, was member Brent Council 1974–76. Born Sep 7 1947; educ. Harrow County School for Boys, Watford College of Technology, Manchester Polytechnic.

Mr Ieuan Owen, a shopkeeper, contested Gower in the 1982 by-election. Educ. University College of Wales, Swansea. Represents West Glamorgan on Plaid Cymru's national executive committee.

Mr Richard Alexander

NEWARK Electorate 64 008

*Alexander, R. (C)	26 334	53.8%
McGuiggan, J. (Lab)	12 051	24.6%
Thompstone, S. (SDP/All)	10 076	20.6%
Hewis, Mrs P. (Eco)	463	1.0%
C majority	14 283	29.2%
Total vote 48 924		Turnout 76.4%

Mr Richard Alexander, solicitor and company director, gained this seat for the Conservatives in 1979; contested Lincoln 1966 and 1970. Born Jun 29 1934; educ. Eastbourne Grammar School, Dewsbury Grammar School. University College London and Institute of Advanced Legal Studies, University of London. Member Bassetlaw District Council since 1975; Retford Borough Council 1965–74, Nottinghamshire County Council 1967–74. Member Select Committee on Statutory Instruments since 1979. Secretary Conservative backbench arts and heritage committee. Former member East Midland Regional Economic Planning Council and East Midlands Transport Users' Consultative Committee. Director Ice Pick Ltd, Almawahe Ltd and Alexander (Investments) Ltd.

Mr John McGuiggan is an organizer for NUPE; former army photographer. Aged 36; educ. Ruskin College, Oxford.

Mr Stuart Thompstone, lecturer in Russian and Eastern European economic history at Nottingham University since 1973. Born 1941; educ. London University and LSE. Secretary, Notts and North Notts area parties.

Mr Michael McNair-Wilson

NEWBURY Electorate 71 343

*McNair-Wilson, M. (C)	31 836	59.3%
Richards, A. (L/All)	18 798	35.0%
Knight, R. C. (Lab)	3 027	5.6%
C majority	13 038	24.3%
Total vote 53 661		Turnout 75.2%

Mr Michael McNair-Wilson was returned for Newbury in Feb 1974. Member, Select Committee on Nationalized Industries 1974–79. Won Walthamstow East 1969 by-election and held it in 1970; contested Lincoln 1964. Born Oct 12 1930; educ. Eton. Brother of MP for New Forest. Chairman, Conservative Aviation Committee 1972–74; Joint Secretary, United Nations Parliamentary Group 1970–72, and to Greater London Conservative MPs' Committee 1969–70. NUJ 1962–68. PPS to Minister of Agriculture since 1979. Public relations adviser, Exchange Telegraph P.R. and Advertising Ltd.

Mr Anthony Richards, membership relations adviser for London Chamber of Commerce and Industry, contested Newbury 1979. Born May 4 1947; educ. Friars School, Bangor, University of Sheffield and University of Essex. Vice chairman, British Atlantic Group of Young Politicians. NUJ.

Mr Richard Knight is a turkey processor and former accounts clerk. Aged 25.

Mr John Golding

NEWCASTLE-UNDER-LYME Electorate 65 400

*Golding, J. (Lab)	21 210	42.0%
Lawrence, L. (C)	18 406	36.4%
Thomas, A. (L/All)	10 916	21.6%
Lab majority	2 804	5.6%
Total vote 50 532		Turnout 77.3%

Mr John Golding, Assistant Secretary, Post Office Engineering Union; chairman of the Select Committee on Employment 1979–82. Under Secretary of State, Employment 1976–79; member of the Labour Party National Executive committee 1978–83; chairman, Home Policy subcommittee 1982–83. Lord Commissioner of the Treasury (Government whip) Feb–Oct 1974; Opposition whip 1970–74. Elected at the 1969 by-election. Born Mar 9 1931; educ. City Grammar School, Chester, University College of North Staffordshire and London School of Economics. Member, Select Committee on Statutory Instruments 1969–70. Sponsored by POEU.

Mr Leslie Lawrence, a software engineer in the computer industry, has been chairman, Conservative national advisory committee on education since 1982. Born Jan 30 1947; educ. St Peter's Grammar School, Bournemouth; Bournemouth College of Technology and Birmingham Polytechnic. Member, Lichfield District Council and Brentwood Town Council 1976–79; Birmingham City Council since 1982. Member, national executive, Conservative Party. Vice-chairman, Birmingham North Conservative Euro-Committee; chairman, North Birmingham Community Health Council.

Mr Alan Thomas, teacher. Born Dec 1 1939; educ. Wallasey Grammar School, Hull University and Keele University. Contested Stoke-on-Trent Central Oct 1974 and 1979. Member, Staffordshire County Council and Newcastle-under-Lyme Borough Council. Member, ASTMS, 1970–81; NAS/UWT since 1983.

Mr Piers Merchant

NEWCASTLE UPON TYNE CENTRAL Electorate 62 687

Merchant, P. (C)	18 161	40.8%
Todd, N. (Lab)	15 933	35.8%
*Horam, J. (SDP/All)	9 923	22.3%
Jacques, D. N. (Eco)	478	1.1%
C majority	2 228	5.0%
Total vote 44 495		Turnout 71.0%

Mr Piers Merchant, journalist, was elected in 1983; contested the seat in 1979. Born Jan 2 1951; educ. Nottingham High School and Durham University. NUJ, former FOC of Newcastle chapel.

Mr Nigel Todd, relations officer for the North-East Co-operative Society and member, Newcastle City Council. Born Sep 1947; educ. Ruskin College and Lancaster University. NACO.

Mr John Horam, SDP spokesman on Treasury affairs since 1981, was Labour Under Secretary of State for Transport 1976–79, and a former Labour spokesman on economic affairs. He was MP for Gateshead West 1970–83; left Labour in 1981 to help found the SDP. Contested Folkestone and Hythe 1966. Economist. Born Mar 7 1939; educ. Silcoates School, Wakefield, and St Catherine's College, Cambridge. Founder, Commodities Research Ltd, managing director 1968–70, and now a director.

Mr Nicholas Brown

NEWCASTLE UPON TYNE EAST Electorate 59 587

Brown, N. H. (Lab)	19 247	45.5%
Barnes, A. (C)	11 755	27.8%
*Thomas, M. (SDP/All)	11 293	26.7%
Lab majority	7 492	17.7%
Total vote 42 295		Turnout 71.0%

Mr Nicholas Brown is legal adviser, northern region of GMBATU. Elected in 1983. Member, Newcastle upon Tyne City Council since 1980. Has served on housing sub-committee on slum clearance in east end of Newcastle. Aged 32; educ. Tunbridge Wells Technical High School; Manchester University.

Mr Arthur Barnes, a structural designer and partner in his own firm. Member, Newcastle District Council, since 1977; Conservative housing spokesman. Born Jun 12 1942; educ. Heaton Technical School, Newcastle, and Rutherford College of Technology, Newcastle.

Mr Mike Thomas, SDP spokesman on social services and chairman of the SDP organization committee, resigned from the Labour Party in 1981 and joined the SDP. Elected as a Labour MP in Oct 1974; contested Hertfordshire East 1970. Member, Select Committee on Members' Salaries since 1981. Born May 24 1944; educ. Latymer Upper School, Hammersmith, King's School, Macclesfield and Liverpool University.

Mr Robert Brown

NEWCASTLE UPON TYNE NORTH Electorate 69 432

*Brown, R. (Lab)	18 985	37.6%
Straw, P. (C)	16 429	32.5%
Shipley, J. (L/All)	15 136	29.9%
Lab majority	2 556	5.1%
Total vote 50 550		Turnout 72.8%

Mr Robert Brown, Under-Secretary for Defence for the Army 1974–79; Under-Secretary for Social Security 1974; an Opposition spokesman on environment until 1974. Member, Speaker's conference; vice-chairman employment committee; chairman, northern group 1983. Former vice-chairman Parliamentary Labour Party trade union group. Parliamentary Secretary, Ministry of Transport 1968–70. Elected in 1983; MP for Newcastle upon Tyne West 1966–83. Born May 1921; educ. Rutherford Technical College. Secretary of constituency Labour Party and election agent 1950–66. Councillor and alderman Newcastle City Council for 10 years. Sponsored by GMWU. Secretary, GM parliamentary group since 1966.

Mr Philip Straw, barrister, contested Houghton-le-Spring 1979. Born Nov 1 1945; educ. Newcastle Royal Grammar School and Inns of Court School of Law. Sunderland borough councillor 1980–83.

Mr John Shipley, university administrator, contested Blyth Feb and Oct 1974 and Hexham 1979. Born Jul 1946; educ. Whitby Grammar School and University College London (President of the Union 1968–69). Newcastle City Council since 1975. AUT.

Mr Patrick McNair-Wilson

NEW FOREST Electorate 70 033

*McNair-Wilson, P. (C)	34 157	66.4%
Harrison, R. (L/All)	13 262	25.7%
James, D. T. (Lab)	4 075	7.9%
C majority	20 895	40.7%
Total vote 51 494		Turnout 73.5%

Mr Patrick McNair-Wilson was an Opposition spokesman on energy 1974–76, and previously on the private steel sector. Vice-chairman, Conservative fuel and power committee 1968–70. elected at 1968 by-election; represented Lewisham West 1964–66. Director of the London Municipal Society 1960–63. Company director and consultant. Born May 28 1929; educ. Hall School, Hampstead and Eton. Member, Select Committee on Nationalized Industries 1974, and Select Committee on Science and Technology 1968–70. Brother of MP for Newbury. PPS to Minister for Transport Industries 1970–74.

Mr Robin Harrison, research scientist, contested Christchurch and Lymington 1979. Born Jul 31 1934; educ. Kingswood School, Bath, and Balliol College, Oxford. EPEA.

Mr David James is a senior lecturer in valuation and former chartered surveyor. Born May 7 1945; educ. locally. NATFHE.

Mr Ronald Leighton

NEWHAM NORTH EAST Electorate 62 463 1979: 66 371 same

*Leighton, R. (Lab)	19 286	49.7%
Gardener, Mrs H. (C)	10 773	27.8%
Winfield, Mrs A. (L/All)	7 943	20.5%
Adams, F. (NF)	796	2.1%
Lab majority	8 513	21.9%
Total vote 38 798		Turnout 62.1%

1979: Total vote 41 872 (63.1%); Lab 22 818 (54.5%); C 12 778 (30.5%); L 4 027 (9.6%); NF 1 769 (4.2%); Ind 208 (0.5%); WRP 154 (0.4%); DMPSWR 118 (0.3%). Lab maj 10 040 (24.0%). Lab gain from C.

Mr Ronald Leighton, a printer, regained the seat for Labour in 1979. Chairman, Labour's Common Market Safeguards Committee which he founded in 1970. An Opposition whip. Born Jan 24 1930; educ. elementary and Ruskin College, Oxford. Contested Horsham and Crawley Feb 1974, and Middleton and Prestwich 1964. National organizer of referendum campaign for 'No' vote 1975. Sponsored by Sogat '82.

Mrs Helen Gardener, Secondary School mathematics teacher. Born Nov 22 1936; educ. Dr Graham's School, Kalimpong, India; St Mary's Girls' High School, Poona, India; Avery Hill Coll., Eltham; and Open University. Secretary, Conservative trade unionists teachers' group. Member, Greenwich Council since 1978. NAS/UWT, Bromley branch committee member.

Mrs Ann Winfield, full-time councillor. Born Jun 27 1951; educ. City Road Girls' School, Birmingham, and Brooklyn Technical College. Member, Newham London Borough Council since 1982; leader of Liberal group.

Mr Tony Banks

NEWHAM NORTH WEST

Electorate 49814 1979: 54030 same

Banks, T. (Lab)	13042	46.6%
Irons, K. D. (C)	6124	21.9%
Kellaway, A. (SDP/All)	5204	18.6%
*Lewis, A. (Ind Lab)	3074	11.0%
Hipperson, M. (NF)	525	1.9%
Lab majority	6918	24.7%
Total vote 27969	Turnout 56.2%	

1979: Total vote 29923 (55.4%); Lab 18392 (61.5%); C 7937 (26.5%); L 2377 (7.9%); NF 1217 (4.1%). Lab maj 10455 (35.0%); swing 6.7% to C.

Mr Tony Banks, assistant general secretary, Assoc. of Broadcasting Staff, was elected in 1983; contested East Grinstead 1970; Newcastle upon Tyne North Oct 1974; Watford 1979. Chairman, GLC arts committee since 1981, and of general purposes committee 1975–77; GLC member 1970–77 and since 1981. Born Apr 8 1943; educ. state schools, York University, LSE. Former political adviser to Dame Judith Hart and former head of research, AUEW. Sponsored by TGWU.

Mr Keith Irons, journalist and public affairs executive. Born Nov 16 1941; educ. Beal Grammar School, Ilford, and Peter Symonds School, Winchester. Head of public affairs division of Blue Circle Industries PLC.

Mr Alec Kellaway, economist. Born May 31 1953; educ. East Ham Grammar School and Christ Church, Oxford. APEX.

Mr Arthur Lewis was Labour MP for this seat from Feb 1974–83, representing West Ham North 1950–74. Returned at Upton 1945. Born Feb 21 1917; educ. elementary school and Borough Polytechnic, National Council of Labour Colleges and WEA.

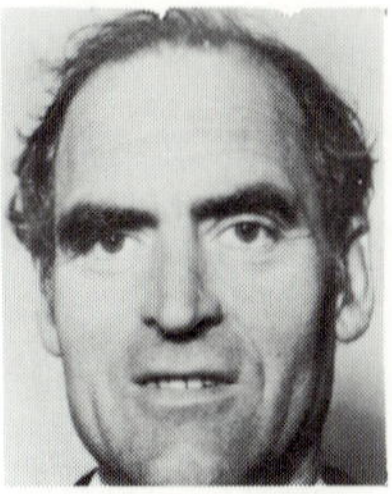

Mr Nigel Spearing

NEWHAM SOUTH

Electorate 50362 1979: 53431 same

*Spearing, N. (Lab)	13561	50.2%
Reilly, A. (SDP/All)	6250	23.1%
Thompson, N. (C)	6212	23.0%
Anderson, I. (NF)	993	3.7%
Lab majority	7311	27.1%
Total vote 27016	Turnout 53.6%	

1979: Total vote 30483 (57.1%); Lab 19636 (64.4%); C 6863 (22.5%)] L 2085 (6.8%); NF 1899 (6.2%). Lab maj 12773 (41.9%); swing 8.1% to C.

Mr Nigel Spearing a teacher, re-elected in by-election May 1974. Born Oct 8 1930; educ. Latymer Upper School, Hammersmith and St Catharine's College, Cambridge. Regained Acton for Labour in 1970, lost it in Feb 1974; contested Warwick and Leamington 1964. Member, Select Committee on European Legislation since 1979; Select Committee on Sound Broadcasting since 1978; Select Committee on Foreign Affairs and its subcommittee on overseas development since 1979; Select Committee on Overseas Development 1977–79; and Select Committee on Procedure 1975–79. Chairman, British Anti-Common Market Campaign since Oct 1977. President Socialist Environment and Resources Assoc. since 1977. NUT.

Mr Andrew Reilly, editor with the publishing division of the Open University and a freelance editor of the International Journal of Vehicle Design. Born Oct 18 1955; educ. St Bonaventure's School, Newham, Worthing Sixth Form College, Sussex. AUT.

Mr Nicholas Thompson, solicitor. Born Mar 19 1947; educ. King's School, Canterbury; University of Kent. Member, Westminster City Council since 1978.

Mr Roy Hughes

NEWPORT EAST

Electorate 52503

*Hughes, R. J. (Lab)	15931	39.6%
Thomason, R. (C)	13301	33.1%
David, Ms F. (SDP/All)	10293	25.6%
Thomas, D. (Pl C)	697	1.7%
Lab majority	2630	6.5%
Total vote 40222	Turnout 76.6%	

Mr Roy Hughes was elected in 1983; MP for Newport 1966–83. Former administrative officer in a Coventry car firm and officer in Transport and General Workers' Union 1959–66. Born Jun 9 1925; educ. Pontllanfraith County Grammar School and Ruskin College, Oxford. Member, Coventry City Council, and secretary, Coventry Labour Party, 1962–66. Chairman, PLP steel group since 1978 and sports group since 1974. Member of Speaker's Panel and chairman of Welsh Grand Committee. Sponsored by TGWU.

Mr Roy Thomason, solicitor. Born Dec 14 1944; educ. Cheney School, Oxford and London University. Member Bournemouth Borough Council since 1970; leader 1974–82; political leader Assoc. of District Councils since 1981.

Mrs Frances David, deputy head teacher of comprehensive school. Born Feb 4 1933; educ. Sherborne School for Girls and St Hugh's College, Oxford.

Mr David Thomas, steelworker, is a former chairman of Ebbw Vale Trades Council.

Mr Mark Robinson

NEWPORT WEST Electorate 54 125

Robinson, M. (C)	15 948	38.0%
Davies, B. (Lab)	15 367	36.6%
Jones, W. (L/All)	10 163	24.2%
Watkins, D. (Pl C)	477	1.1%
C majority	581	1.4%
Total vote 41 955	Turnout	77.5%

Mr Mark Robinson, assistant director, Commonwealth Secretariat, was elected in 1983. Born 1948; educ. Harrow, Christ Church, Oxford and Middle Temple. Non-practising barrister. Personal and political assistant to the UN Secretary-General, Kurt Waldheim, 1974–77. Chairman, Oxford University Conservative Assoc. 1967; chairman, Lambeth Central Conservative Assoc. 1980–81. Contested South Yorkshire in European Parliamentary elections, 1979. Member, Game Conservancy, Royal Academy, National Art Collections Fund.

Mr Bryan Davies, former polytechnic lecturer, now secretary of the PLP, represented Enfield North, Feb 1974–79. Lord Commissioner to the Treasury (Government whip) 1979. Contested Norfolk Central 1966. Member, Select Committee on Overseas Development and of Expenditure Committee 1974–79. Born Nov 1939; educ. Redditch High School and University College, London.

Dr. Whitney Jones, retired lecturer, director of historical studies and secretary, faculty board, Gwent College of Higher Education. Aged 58. Former chairman and vice-chairman, Rhymney Valley Liberals, and rate and rent-payer community councillor. Currently engaged in research.

Mr Dennis Watkins, optician, is chairman of Pontypridd Trades Council.

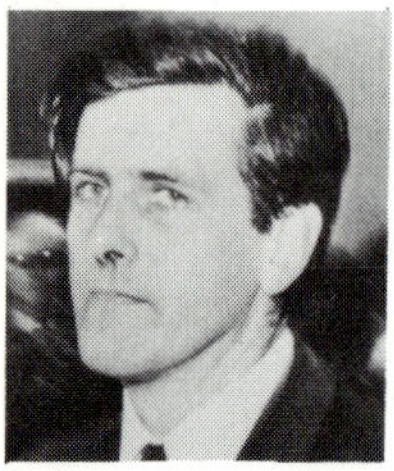

Mr James Nicholson

NEWRY AND ARMAGH Electorate 62 387

Nicholson, J. (OUP)	18 988	40.0%
Mallon, S. (SDLP)	17 434	36.8%
McAllister, J. (PSF)	9 928	20.9%
Moore, T. (WP)	1 070	2.3%
OUP majority	1 554	3.3%
Total vote 47 420	Turnout	76.0%

Mr James Nicholson, a farmer and member of the Northern Ireland Assembly for Armagh since Oct 1982, became MP for this seat in 1983. Member, Armagh District Council for seven years. Former chairman, North West Armagh district, Ulster Farmers' Union. Has been secretary and organiser of Mid and South Armagh Unionist Assoc. for nine years. Member, Southern Health and Social Services Board (Ulster).

Mr Seamus Mallon, a teacher, contested the seat in Oct 1974 and 1979. Born 1939; educ. Christian Brothers Grammar School, Newry, St Mary's College of Education, Belfast. Councillor, Armagh District since 1973. Elected, Northern Ireland Assembly 1973, Convention 1975 and Assembly 1982. Disqualified from Northern Ireland assembly while a member of the Republic's senate. Appointed to the Republic's senate by Mr Charles Haughey 1982 but not reappointed when Dr Garrett Fitzgerald returned to office Dec 1982. Deputy leader SDLP.

Mr Richard Ryder

NORFOLK MID Electorate 68 953

Ryder, R. (C)	29 032	55.9%
Cargill, D. (SDP/All)	13 517	26.0%
Potter, L. J. (Lab)	8 950	17.2%
McNee, M. (Ind Pow)	405	0.8%
C majority	15 515	29.9%
Total vote 51 904	Turnout	75.3%

Mr Richard Ryder, journalist and director of a family farming business, was political secretary to Mrs Margaret Thatcher 1975–81. Elected in 1983. Born 1949; educ. Radley and Magdalene College, Cambridge. Contested Gateshead East in both 1974 elections. Vice-chairman of the Eastern Region Council for Sport and Recreation.

Mr David Cargill, farmer, contested Newark Feb 1974 and Normanton 1970 for the Conservatives; left that party 1974. SDP eastern area regional organizer. Former chairman, Norfolk European Movement; governor, Norwich Art School; vice-chairman, Eastern Arts Assoc; former district councillor. Born 1937; educ. Gresham's School, Holt and Royal Agricultural College.

Mr Leslie Potter has been in local government for 30 years. Represents Dereham on Norfolk County Council. Serves on education, land and estates, and agricultural committees. Member, governing body, Norfolk College of Agriculture. Age 59.

Mr Ralph Howell

NORFOLK NORTH Electorate 65 101

*Howell, R. (C)	26 230	54.0%
Elworthy, J. (SDP/All)	13 007	26.8%
Barber, E. A. (Lab)	9 317	19.2%
C majority	13 223	27.2%
Total vote 48 554	Turnout	74.6%

Mr Ralph Howell, a member of the Select Committee on the Treasury and Civil Service, was a member, European Parliament 1974–79. Farmer and member of Lloyd's. Vice-chairman, Conservative backbench finance committee since 1979. Was joint vice-chairman, backbench committee on agriculture and employment. Won seat for the Conservatives in 1970; contested it 1966. Born May 25 1923; educ. Diss Grammar School. Former local NFU chairman. Member, Mitford and Launditch Rural Council 1961–74. Member, Council of Europe 1981.

Mr John Elworthy, weekly newspaper editor and broadcaster. Former British press representative for Dr Billy Graham. Born 1951; educ. Hamonds Grammar School, Swaffham, and Wycliffe Hall Theological College. Trustee and founder, of Oxford centre for the young unemployed; governor, Oxford area arts council.

Mr Edward Barber, retired headmaster. Born Apr 22 1923; educ. Stowmarket Grammar School, Suffolk, Borough Road College, London and London University. Chairman, Norfolk branch of National Assoc. of Head Teachers. NUT.

Mr Henry Bellingham

NORFOLK NORTH WEST Electorate 69 181

Bellingham, H. (C)	23 358	43.5%
*Brocklebank-Fowler, C. (SDP/All)	20 211	37.6%
Tilbury, M. (Lab)	10 139	18.9%
C majority	3 147	5.9%
Total vote 53 708	Turnout	77.6%

Mr Henry Bellingham, barrister, was elected in 1983. Born Mar 29 1955; educ. Eton; Magdalene College, Cambridge; Council of Legal Education, London. Partner in farming business and haulage company. Former amateur steeplechase jockey.

Mr Christopher Brocklebank-Fowler, marketing and international trade consultant, was elected as Conservative MP for this seat in Feb 1974; resigned the party in 1981 and joined the SDP becoming its spokesman on foreign and Commonwealth affairs and overseas aid. Member, SDP national committee; chairman, SDP Third World policy committee, and vice-chairman, SDP agricultural policy committee. Chairman, UN parliamentary group. Conservative MP for King's Lynn 1970–74, contested West Ham North 1964. Born Jan 13 1934; educ. Perse School, Cambridge. Former chairman, Conservative horticultural and overseas development committees. Former vice-chairman, Conservative agriculture, trade and foreign affairs committees. Member, Select Committee on Overseas Development 1973–79; member, Select Committee on Foreign and Commonwealth Affairs 1979–81. ASTMS.

Mr Michael Tilbury, woodworker. Born Mar 30 1936; educ. local schools on the Isle of Wight, Eastbourne College and Keble College, Oxford. Member, Chipping Norton Rural District Council 1965–68; West Norfolk District Council since 1973, leader of Labour group. Member, National Assoc. of Probation Officers 1960–78. UCATT and FBU.

Mr John MacGregor

NORFOLK SOUTH Electorate 73 523

*MacGregor, J. (C)	30 747	54.2%
Carden, R. A. (L/All)	18 612	32.8%
Holzer, H. A. (Lab)	7 408	13.1%
C majority	12 135	21.4%
Total vote 56 767	Turnout	77.2%

Mr John MacGregor appointed Minister of State for Agriculture, Fisheries and Food Jun 1983; Under Secretary of State for Industry in 1981–83; Lord Commissioner of the Treasury (Government whip) 1979–81; Former director, Hill Samuel and Co Ltd and Hill Samuel Registers Ltd. Elected in Feb 1974. An Opposition whip 1977–79. Member, Public Accounts Committee, 1974–75; Expenditure Committee 1975–77. Chairman, Bow Group 1963–64. Secretary, Conservative Finance Committee, 1976–77. Born Feb 14 1937; educ. Merchiston Castle School, Edinburgh, St Andrews University and King's College, London. Former journalist with *New Society*; special assistant to Sir Alec Douglas-Home when Prime Minister and head of Mr Heath's private office 1965–68.

Mr Richard Carden is a systems engineer. Member, Norfolk County Council since 1981; South Oxfordshire District Council 1974–76; Henley-on-Thames Borough Council 1969–74. Born Jan 14 1942; educ. Keble College, Oxford.

Mr Alan Holzer, teacher. Born Sep 16 1937; educ. Rudolf Steiner School, near Gloucester, and University College, London. NUT.

Sir Paul Hawkins

NORFOLK SOUTH WEST Electorate 70 398

*Hawkins, Sir P. (C)	28 632	55.7%
Baxter, B. (L/All)	13 722	26.7%
Rosenberg, A. L. (Lab)	9 072	17.6%
C majority	14 910	29.0%
Total vote 51 426		Turnout 73.1%

Sir Paul Hawkins, a member of the Select Committee on House of Commons (Services), was Vice-Chamberlain of the Household (whip) 1973–74; a Lord Commissioner of the Treasury (whip) 1971–73 and an assistant Government whip 1970–71. Opposition whip, Mar–Oct 1974. Elected 1964. Chartered surveyor. Born Aug 7 1912; educ. Cheltenham College. Member, Norfolk County Council 1949–70; alderman 1968–70. Member, Select Committee on Wealth Tax 1974; Select Committee on Agriculture 1968–69. Member, United Kingdom delegation to Council of Europe since 1976.

Mr Brian Baxter, smallholder, farmer and seedsman, contested Norfolk South West Oct 1974 and 1979. Born Nov 3 1932; educ. Dunoon Grammar School, Scotland, Scottish Hotel School and King's Lynn Technical College. Member, National Liberal Party Agricultural and Related Industries Panel. Baptist church deacon.

Mr Alan Rosenberg, a teacher, contested the seat in 1979. Born Jun 1938; educ. Archbishop Tenison's Grammar School, Kensington, and The Polytechnic, Regent Street. NUT; SERA.

Mr William O'Brien

NORMANTON Electorate 61 249

O'Brien, W. (Lab)	18 783	43.6%
Paul, A. (C)	14 599	33.9%
Pantelli, P. (SDP/All)	9 741	22.6%
Lab majority	4 184	9.7%
Total vote 43 123		Turnout 70.4%

Mr William O'Brien, coalminer, was elected in 1983. Wakefield councillor since 1973 and deputy leader. Born Jan 29 1929; educ. state schools and Leeds University. Member NUM since 1945.

Mr Alan Paul, local government officer, is vice-chairman of the Conservative Trade Unionists National Committee. Born 1941; educ. Normanton Boys Grammar School and Leeds Kitson College of Science and Technology. Nalgo officer.

Mr Antony Marlow

NORTHAMPTON NORTH Electorate 68 370

*Marlow, A. (C)	23 129	47.0%
Offenbach, D. (Lab)	13 269	27.0%
Rounthwaite, A. (L / All)	12 829	26.1%
C majority	9 860	20.0%
Total vote 49 227		Turnout 72.0%

Mr Antony Marlow, development manager with a grain shippers company gained seat for Conservatives in 1979; contested Normanton Feb 1974, and Rugby Oct 1974. Born Jun 17 1940; educ. Wellington College, Royal Military Academy, Sandhurst, and St Catharine's College, Cambridge. Joint secretary, Conservative backbench Trade and Consumer Affairs Committee since 1981. Chairman, UK-Palestine all-party parliamentary affairs group. Member, Steering Committee Conservative European Reform Group. Former chairman, Daventry Conservative Political Centre committee and East Midlands Area CPC working party.

Mr David Offenbach, a solicitor, contested New Forest 1970 and Harrow Central Feb and Oct 1974. Born Aug 1943; educ. St Marylebone Grammar School and London University. Member, Camden Borough Council 1968–79; chairman, finance and general purposes committee and building works and services committees. Secretary, local branch, ASTMS.

Mr Anthony Rounthwaite, general manager. Born Feb 6 1951; educ. King's School, Tynemouth, Newcastle upon Tyne Polytechnic. Contested Northampton North 1979. Leader, Liberal group, Northants County Council; chairman, NCC policy analysis review committee. Member, Northampton Borough Council.

Mr Michael Morris

NORTHAMPTON SOUTH Electorate 68910

*Morris, M. (C)	26824	53.6%
Kyle, K. (SDP/All)	11698	23.4%
Coleman, M. (Lab)	11533	23.0%
C majority	15126	30.2%
Total vote 50055		Turnout 72.6%

Mr Michael Morris, a member of the Public Accounts Committee since 1979 and the Select Committee on Energy since 1982, was elected in Feb 1974. Consultant. Born Nov 25 1936; educ. Bedford School and St Catharine's College, Cambridge. Contested Islington North 1966. Vice-chairman, Conservative energy committee since 1981. Chairman, all-party Anglo-Sri Lanka committee since 1979, and secretary, all-party Singapore and Burma committees since 1981. Alderman, London Borough of Islington 1971–74; member, Islington Council 1968–70.

Mr Keith Kyle, meeting secretary and conference organizer, Institute of International Affairs and a BBC TV journalist. Contested St Albans 1966 and Braintree Feb and Oct 1974. Born Aug 1925; educ. Chafyn Grove School, Salisbury, Bromsgrove School and Magdalen College, Oxford. Former Washington correspondent and political and parliamentary correspondent of *The Economist*.

Mr Martin Coleman, solicitor and lecturer in law. Born Nov 19 1952; educ. Worcester College, Oxford. Leader of Brent Council since 1978. Member, National Council for Civil Liberties; CND: Haldane Society of Socialist Lawyers.

Mr John Cope

NORTHAVON Electorate 73553

*Cope, J. (C)	30790	53.7%
Conrad, G. (L/All)	17807	31.1%
Norris, Mrs N. P. J. (Lab)	8243	14.4%
Radmall, K. (Eco)	499	0.9%
C majority	12983	22.6%
Total vote 57339		Turnout 78.0%

Mr John Cope, a chartered accountant, was elected for this seat in 1983; MP for South Gloucestershire Feb 1974–83. Government whip since 1979. Contested Woolwich East 1970. Born May 13 1937; educ. Oakham School, Rutland. Conservative research department, and Central Office, 1965–70. Special assistant to Secretary of State for Trade and Industry, 1972–74. Former secretary, Conservative smaller businesses committee and finance committee. Former member, Expenditure Committee and Parliamentary Commissioner for Administration Committee.

Dr George Conrad, general practitioner, contested South Gloucestershire May 1979. Born Apr 16 1949; educ. Latimer Upper School, Hammersmith and University of Bristol medical faculty. Leader of Alliance group on Northavon District Council since 1979.

Mrs June Norris is a housewife and part-time pool administrator. Born 1937. Member, Socialist Educational Assoc; National Council for Civil Liberties; and the Co-operative Party. Chairman of Governors of The Ridings School, Winterbourne. NUPE.

Mr Patrick Thompson

NORWICH NORTH Electorate 62781

Thompson, P. (C)	21355	44.7%
*Ennals, D. (Lab)	15476	32.4%
Jones, G. (L/All)	10796	22.6%
Cairns, Ms F. (WRP)	194	0.4%
C majority	5879	12.3%
Total vote 47821		Turnout 76.2%

Mr Patrick Thompson, a teacher, was elected in 1983; contested Bradford North in both 1974 elections and Barrow-in-Furness in 1979. Born 1936; educ. Felsted School, Essex, and Emmanuel College, Cambridge.

Mr David Ennals was Secretary of State for Social Services 1976–79; Minister of State for Foreign and Commonwealth Affairs 1974–76. Member, Select Committee on Social Services 1979–83. Returned in Feb 1974; represented Dover 1964–70. Minister of State for Health and Social Security 1968–70; Under-Secretary, Home Office 1967–68, and Under-Secretary for Defence (Army) 1966–67. Contested Richmond as a Liberal in 1950 and 1951. Born Aug 19 1922; educ. Queen Mary's Grammar School, Walsall, and at Windsor, Connecticut. Campaign director, National Assoc. for Mental Health until 1974. Secretary, United Nations Assoc. 1952–57. Overseas Secretary, Labour Party, 1958–64. Former chairman, all-party committees on refugees and on UN. Vice-chairman, all-party committee on children. ASTMS.

Mr Graham Jones, chief internal auditor of a district council. Born Aug 12 1943.

Mr John Powley

NORWICH SOUTH Electorate 64 100

Powley, J. (C)	18 998	38.8%
*Garrett, J. (Lab)	17 286	35.3%
Hardie, J. (SDP/All)	11 968	24.5%
Carter, A. (Eco)	468	1.0%
Williams, P. (NF)	145	0.3%
Ward, J. (Ind)	91	0.2%
C majority	1 712	3.5%
Total vote 48 956		Turnout 76.4%

Mr John Powley, owner and director of an electrical retail business, was elected in 1983; contested Harlow 1979. Born 1936; educ. Cambridge Grammar School for Boys and Cambridge College of Arts and Technology. Cambridgeshire County Councillor 1967–77 and Cambridge City Councillor 1967–79.

Mr John Garrett, an Opposition spokesman on industry 1981–83; elected in Feb 1974. Management consultant. Born Sep 8 1931; educ. Sir George Monoux School, London; Oxford University; and University of California. Member, Greenwich Borough Council. Former member, Select Committee on Procedure (Finance). TGWU.

Mr Jeremy Hardie, chairman of National Provident Institution and director of other companies, is a member of the SDP industrial policy committee. Deputy chairman, Monopolies and Mergers Commission. Former member, Conservative Party and Bow Group. Born 1938; until 1975 fellow and tutor in economics, Keble College, Oxford.

Mr John Fraser

NORWOOD Electorate 55 663

*Fraser, J. D. (Lab)	16 280	44.6%
Parfitt, J. P. (C)	13 397	36.7%
Noble, M. (SDP/All)	6 371	17.5%
Williams, Miss C. M. (NF)	343	0.9%
Sanderson, J. (Ind)	123	0.3%
Lab majority	2 883	7.9%
Total vote 36 514		Turnout 65.6%

Mr John Fraser has been an Opposition spokesman on trade, prices and consumer protection since 1979, was Minister of State, Department of Prices and Consumer Protection 1976–79, Under Secretary for Employment 1974–76. Opposition spokesman on the Home Office 1972–74. Won the seat in 1966 and contested it 1964. Solicitor. Born Jun 30 1934; educ. Sloane Grammar School and Society College. Former chairman, PLP Greek Democratic Committee; former member, Select Committees on Education and Science and on Broadcasting Proceedings of House of Commons. Former deputy chairman, PLP Environment Group. Member, Lambeth Borough Council 1962–68. GMBU.

Mr John Parfitt, retired naval officer now marketing manager. Born Feb 23 1931; educ. Paulton Central Methodist School, Paulton, Cotham Grammar School, Bristol and Royal Naval Colleges Dartmouth and Greenwich. Member, Croydon Council 1978–82.

Mr Malcolm Noble, teacher, was vice-chairman, Lambeth Central Labour Party for nine years before joining SDP. Born 1946; educ. London University. Senior teacher in economics, Dunraven School, Streatham. Elected to Lambeth Council 1971; chairman, housing committee, 1976. Helped form SDP/Liberal group, Lambeth Council.

Mr Michael Knowles

NOTTINGHAM EAST Electorate 68 638

Knowles, M. (C)	17 641	40.4%
Sloman, M. (Lab)	16 177	37.1%
Bird, M. (SDP/All)	8 385	19.2%
Merrick, D. S. (Ind C)	1 421	3.3%
C majority	1 464	3.4%
Total vote 43 624		Turnout 63.6%

Mr Michael Knowles, sales manager, was elected in 1983; contested Merthyr Tydfil Feb 1974 and Brent East Oct 1974. Born May 21 1942; educ. Clapham College. Member, Kingston Council since 1971; leader of council since 1974. Member, Surbiton Constituency Executive since 1971; member, Kingston Constituency Executive since 1974. Member, London Boroughs Assoc. and AMA.

Mr Martyn Sloman, an industrial economist with the National Coal Board, contested Leominster 1970 and Bosworth Feb and Oct 1974. Born Jul 1946; educ. Hywel DDA School, Cardiff and Lancaster University. Assistant director, Co-operative Development Agency 1979–81. Former Brent councillor. APEX.

Mr Michael Bird, solicitor. Born May 8 1945; educ. Priory School, Kingston, Jamaica, Nottingham High School, University of London, and Trent Polytechnic. Member, Law Society.

Mr Richard Ottaway

NOTTINGHAM NORTH Electorate 71 807

Ottaway, R. (C)	18 730	39.5%
*Whitlock, W. (Lab)	18 368	38.7%
Williams, L. (SDP/All)	9 200	19.4%
Peck, J. (Com)	1 184	2.5%
C majority	362	0.8%
Total vote 47 482		Turnout 66.1%

Mr Richard Ottaway is a solicitor and specialist in international maritime law. Elected in 1983. Born May 24 1945; educ. Backwell Secondary Modern School, Somerset; Bristol University; RNC Dartmouth. Director of retail company. Chairman, research subcommittee of the Society of Conservative Lawyers. Member, International Commission of Jurists. Trustee, Countee of Derby Trust.

Mr William Whitlock, Under-Secretary for Foreign and Commonwealth Affairs 1967–69. Deputy Chief Whip and Lord Commissioner of the Treasury (whip), Mar–Jul 1967; Comptroller of the Household 1966–67. Vice-Chamberlain of the Household 1964–66. Elected 1959. Opposition whip 1962–64. Area organizer, Union of Shop, Distributive and Allied Workers, 1947–59. Born Jun 1918; educ. Itchen Grammar School, Southampton, and Southampton University.

Mr Leighton Williams, lecturer in economics at Trent Polytechnic. Secretary, Nottingham East/Nottingham North constituency party; chairman, area economic policy working party on defence and foreign affairs and home affairs. Born 1955; educ. King Edward VI School, Norwich, and University College, Cardiff.

Mr Martin Brandon-Bravo

NOTTINGHAM SOUTH Electorate 69 059

Brandon-Bravo, M. (C)	22 238	45.9%
Coates, K. S. (Lab)	16 523	34.1%
Poynter, R. (L/All)	9 697	20.0%
C majority	5 715	11.8%
Total vote 48 458		Turnout 70.2%

Mr Martin Brandon-Bravo, managing director of textile company, was elected in 1983; contested Nottingham East 1979. Born Mar 25 1932; educ. Latymer School, Hammersmith. Member, Nottingham City Council. President, Nottinghamshire international regatta and former member, National Council for Rowing and its executive. Holds international umpire's licence and has officiated at World championships. Member, board of Management, National Water Sports Centre.

Mr Ken Coates, reader in adult education at Nottingham University; formerly worked in mining industry. Aged 51. Founder member of Institute of Workers' Control and director of Bertrand Russell Peace Foundation. Active in helping launch the Movement for European Nuclear Disarmament.

Mr Raymond Poynter, software consultant. Born Oct 12 1956; educ. Gedling Secondary Modern, Arnold and Carlton College and Salford and Nottingham universities. Member, Gedling Borough Council.

Mr Lewis Stevens

NUNEATON Electorate 66 072

Stevens, L. (C)	20 666	40.5%
Haynes, J. (Lab)	15 605	30.6%
Levitt, Ms R. (SDP/All)	14 264	28.0%
Davis, G. E. (Ind Lab)	504	1.0%
C majority	5 061	9.9%
Total vote 51 039		Turnout 77.3%

Mr Lewis Stevens, management consultant. Born Apr 13 1936; educ. Oldbury Grammar School, Worcestershire; Liverpool University; Lanchester College, Coventry. Elected in 1983; contested constituency 1979. Member, Nuneaton Borough Council 1966–72.

Mr John Haynes, teacher. Born Dec 19 1932; educ. Nuneaton school. Local councillor since 1958 (former leader). NASUWT and AUEW.

Ms Ruth Levitt, research assistant to Dr David Owen. Born Apr 1 1950; educ. Camden School for Girls, University of Sheffield, LSE.

Mr Raymond Powell

OGMORE Electorate 51378

*Powell, R. (Lab)	23390	59.2%
Parsons, J. (L/All)	6026	15.3%
O'Sullivan, R. (C)	5806	14.7%
Merriman, E. J. (Pl C)	3124	7.9%
Thomas, N. (Eco)	1161	2.9%
Lab majority	17364	44.0%
Total vote 39507		Turnout 76.9%

Mr Raymond Powell, formerly a senior administrative officer with the Welsh Water Authority, was elected in 1979. Born Jun 19 1928; educ. Pentre Grammar School; National Council of Labour Colleges; and LSE. Chairman of Labour Party of Wales 1977–78. Member, Select Committee on Employment and Select Committee on Welsh Affairs, since 1979. Hon secretary, Welsh Parliamentary Committee, Welsh Parliamentary Committee of Labour MPs. Sponsored by USDAW.

Mr John Parsons, solicitor and part-time town clerk to Machynlleth Town Council. Contested Merioneth 1979. Aged 50; educ. Liverpool University.

Mr Richard O'Sullivan, investment analyst and barrister. Member, Lambeth Borough Council since 1982. Born 1956; educ. Bloxham School, Banbury; Christ Church, Oxford, and the Inner Temple.

Mr Edward Merriman, former miner, is a member of Mid-Glamorgan County Council.

Mr Edward Heath

OLD BEXLEY AND SIDCUP Electorate 50255 1979: 49976 same

*Heath, E. R. G. (C)	22422	60.2%
Vickers, P. (L/All)	9704	26.1%
Kiff, C. A. (Lab)	5116	13.7%
C majority	12718	34.2%
Total vote 37242		Turnout 74.1%

1979: Total vote 39682 (79.4%); C 23692 (59.7%); Lab 10236 (25.8%); L 4980 (12.5%); NF 774 (2.0%). C maj 13456 (33.9%); swing 6.9% to C.

Mr Edward Heath resigned as Leader of the Conservative Party and Leader of the Opposition in Feb 1975, when he failed to top the first of two ballots for the Conservative leadership. He had been Leader of the Opposition since Feb 1974. Prime Minister 1970–74, he first became Leader of the Opposition and Leader of the Conservative Party on Aug 2 1965. Secretary of State for Industry, Trade and Regional Development, and President of the Board of Trade, Oct 1963–64. Lord Privy Seal 1960–63 being the principal Foreign Office Spokesman in the Commons and leading the British team in negotiations to join the EEC. Minister of Labour Oct 1959–Jul 1960; Parliamentary Secretary to the Treasury (Chief Whip) 1955–59; Deputy Chief Whip 1952–55. Elected 1950. Born Jul 9 1916; educ. Chatham House School, Ramsgate, and Balliol College, Oxford; president of the Union 1939. Company director; member public review board of Arthur Anderson & Co. Musician; chairman, trustee of London Symphony Orchestra 1963–70; vice-president Bach Choir since 1970. International yachtsman and author. Member of Lloyd's. Member of Brandt Commission on the third world 1977–83.

Mr Peter Vickers, accountant, contested Bexley, Sidcup 1979. Born Nov 9 1954; educ. St Joseph's College, Blackpool.

Mr Christopher Kiff is a principal administration officer, Lewisham Housing Department. Born Apr 3 1953; educ. Gillingham Grammar School, Brunel University and Hammersmith and West London College.

Mr James Lamond

OLDHAM CENTRAL AND ROYTON Electorate 67177

*Lamond, J. (Lab)	18611	41.4%
Farquahar, J. (C)	15299	34.1%
Jackson, M. (SDP/All)	11022	24.5%
Lab majority	3312	7.4%
Total vote 44932		Turnout 66.9%

Mr James Lamond, a design engineer, was MP for Oldham East 1970–83; elected for this seat 1983. Member, Speaker's panel of chairmen and Select Committee on Members' Salaries since 1979. Born Nov 29 1928; educ. Burrelton School, Coupar Angus junior secondary school. Member, Aberdeen Town Council 1958–70; leader, Labour group 1967–70; Lord Provost, 1970–71; Lord Lieutenant of Aberdeen, 1970–71. Former member, Public Accounts Committee. Sponsored by AUEW (TASS) and a member since 1944. Vice-president, World Peace Council. President, Britain-G.D.R. Society; Treasurer, British-Soviet Friendship Society.

Mr Joseph Farquhar, telephone engineer with British Telecom. Born Feb 18 1945; educ. Cowbridge Grammar School, Barnstaple Grammar School, the Derby School, Bury. Member, Greater Manchester Council, 1977–81. POEU.

Mr Martin Jackson, teacher. Born Jan 1947; educ. Hulme Grammar School, Manchester and University College, Aberystwyth.

Mr Michael Meacher

OLDHAM WEST Electorate 57445

*Meacher, M. (Lab)	17690	44.1%
Dickinson, D. (C)	14510	36.2%
Smith, R. A. M. (L/All)	7745	19.3%
Street, J. (WCPPP)	180	0.5%
Lab majority	3180	7.9%
Total vote 40125		Turnout 69.9%

Mr Michael Meacher, was Under-Secretary of Trade, 1976–79; Under-Secretary for Health and Social Security 1975–76; Under-Secretary for Industry 1974–75. Regained seat for Labour in 1970; contested Colchester 1966. Born Nov 4 1939; educ. Berkhamsted School; New College, Oxford; and LSE. Lecturer in social administration. Member, Select Committee on the Treasury and Civil Service, since 1979. Sponsored by COHSE.

Mr David Dickinson, company director. Born Mar 3 1943; educ. Bolton Technical School and St John's College of Further Education, Manchester; Member, Malvern Hills District Council 1975–79, Conservative group leader 1977–79.

Mr Rodney Smith, lecturer, contested Newton 1979, Warley East Oct 74 and Antrim South 1970. Born Apr 1945, educ. Campbell College, Belfast, St John's College, Cambridge, Queen's University, Belfast, Bolton College of Education. NATFHE.

Mr James Wallace

ORKNEY AND SHETLAND Electorate 30087 1979: 28884 same

Wallace, J. (L/All)	9374	45.9%
*Myles, D. (C)	5224	25.6%
Ewing, Mrs W. (SNP)	3147	15.4%
Goodlad, Ms R. (Lab)	2665	13.1%
L/All majority	4150	20.3%
Total vote 20410		Turnout 67.8%

1979: Total vote 19410 (67.2%); L 10950 (56.4%); C 4140 (21.3%); Lab 3385 (17.4%); SNP 935 (4.8%). L maj 6810 (35.1%)

Mr James Wallace, advocate, was elected in 1983; contested Dumfries 1979, Euro-candidate for South Scotland 1979. Born Aug 25 1954; educ. Annan Academy, Dumfriesshire; Downing College, Cambridge and Edinburgh University. Member, Cambridge University Liberal Club; chairman, Edinburgh University Liberal Club 1976–77. Member, Scottish Liberal Party national executive, since 1976; vice-chairman (policy) since 1982. Former party spokesman on agriculture.

Mr David Myles, a hill farmer and former director of an auction company, has been a member of the Select Committees on Agriculture and on European Legislation since 1979. Represented Banff 1979–83. Secretary, Conservative backbench European affairs committee since 1981 and agriculture, fisheries and food committee since 1979. Convenor, Organization and Publicity Committee of NFU of Scotland 1976–79. Born May 30 1925; educ. Edzell Primary School, Brechin High School. Member, Transport Users Consultative Committee for Scotland 1973–79.

Mrs Winifred Ewing, a vice-president of the SNP, has been SNP MEP for the Highlands and Islands since 1979; MP for Moray and Nairn, Feb 1974–79, and for Hamilton 1967–70. Nominated, member of European Parliament 1975–79. Solicitor. Born Jul 1929; educ. Queen's Park Senior Secondary School, Glasgow and Glasgow University.

Ms Robina Goodlad, housing advisor, contested Orkney and Shetland 1979. Born Aug 16 1950; educ. Scalloway Primary School, Anderson High School, Lerwick and Aberdeen and Glasgow universities. TGWU.

Mr Ivor Stanbrook

ORPINGTON Electorate 58759

*Stanbrook, I. R. (C)	25569	57.3%
Cook, J. W. (L/All)	15418	34.5%
Bean, D. M. (Lab)	3439	7.7%
Taylor, L. T. (BNP)	215	0.5%
C majority	10151	22.7%
Total vote 44641		Turnout 76.0%

Mr Ivor Stanbrook, a barrister, won Orpington for the Conservatives in 1970; contested East Ham South 1966. Born Jan 13 1924; educ. Willesden Central School, University College, London, and Pembroke College, Oxford. RAF 1943–46. Colonial district officer in Nigeria 1950–60. Asst. Secretary Council of Ministers, Lagos, 1954. Former joint vice-chairman and secretary Conservative backbench home affairs committee 1974–77; joint vice-chairman 1979–82; joint vice-chairman Conservative Northern Ireland committee 1982–83. Chairman British-Nigerian all-party group. Member Court of Referees.

Mr John Cook. Born Feb 24 1929.

Mr David Bean is a barrister. Born Mar 25 1954; educ. St Paul's School, London and Trinity Hall, Cambridge. Member, London and Home Counties Area Council of APEX; Co-operative Society; Fabian Society. Executive member, Society of Labour Lawyers.

Mr Steven Norris

OXFORD EAST Electorate 63 613

Norris, S. (C)	18 808	40.0%
Smith, A. D. (Lab)	17 541	37.3%
Godden, Mrs M. (L / All)	10 690	22.7%
C majority	1 267	2.7%
Total vote 47 039	Turnout 74.0%	

Mr Steven Norris, chairman of a transport firm, was elected in 1983. Member, Berkshire County Council, since 1977. Born 1945; educ. Liverpool Institute High School and Worcester College, Oxford. Member, Berkshire Area Health Authority and West Berkshire District Health Authority.

Mr Andrew Smith, an Oxford City councillor since 1976, is a member of Oxford and Swindon Co-operative Society. Born Feb 1 1951; educ. Oxford University. Chairman, Oxford City Council recreation committee, 1980–83. USDAW.

Mr John Patten

OXFORD WEST AND ABINGDON Electorate 67 413

*Patten, J. (C)	23 778	47.7%
Luard, D. E. T. (SDP/All)	16 627	33.4%
Jacottet, J. (Lab)	8 440	16.9%
Starmer, Ms S. (Eco)	544	1.1%
Jones, R. (Loony Socy)	267	0.5%
Smith, C. N. (UP)	95	0.2%
Doubleday, P. (Ind)	86	0.2%
Pinder, Ms R (Ind)	26	0.1%
C majority	7 151	14.3%
Total vote 49 863	Turnout 74.0%	

Mr John Patten, became Under Secretary of State for Health and Social Security in Jun 1983. Under Secretary of State for Northern Ireland 1981–83. MP for Oxford 1979–83. Elected for this seat 1983. Born Jul 17 1945; educ. Wimbledon College and Sidney Sussex College, Cambridge. PPS to Ministers of State at Home Office 1980. Member, Oxford City Council 1973–76. Fellow, Hertford College, Oxford.

Mr Evan Luard, was Under-Secretary for Foreign and Commonwealth Affairs 1976–79 and 1969–70. Labour MP for Oxford 1966–70, and Oct 1974–79. Born Oct 31 1926; educ. Felsted and King's College, Cambridge. Fellow, St Antony's College, Oxford. Delegate, UN General Assembly 1967–68. Member, Oxford City Council 1958–61. Charity worker.

Mr Julian Jacottet, freelance writer and former television producer. Aged 50; educ. Oxford University. Member, Oxfordshire County Council; Abingdon Town Council. Former general secretary of Social Democratic and Labour party, Northern Ireland. Former member Council of National Children's Bureau. Former treasurer, Fair Play for Children.

Mr Allen Adams

PAISLEY NORTH Electorate 50 464

*Adams, A. (Lab)	15 782	45.6%
McCartin, Miss A. (SDP/All)	8 195	23.7%
Townsend, B. (C)	7 425	21.4%
Morrell, H. (SNP)	2 783	8.0%
Carlaw, Dr N. (Eco)	439	1.3%
Lab majority	7 587	21.9%
Total vote 34 624	Turnout 68.6%	

Mr Allen Adams gained Paisley for Lab from Scottish Lab in 1979; elected for this seat 1983. Computer analyst. Born Feb 1946; educ. Camphill High School, Paisley, and Reid-Kerr Technical College, Paisley. Vice-chairman, Strathclyde Social Services Council for 10 years. APEX.

Miss Eileen McCartin, local government officer. Born Mar 1952; educ. Queens College, Glasgow and Jordanhill College of Education.

Mr Brian Townsend, a PR manager and former journalist. Aged 29; educ. Aberdeen University.

Mr Hugh Morell, security officer. Born 1942; educ. Strathbungo Secondary School. Member, Renfrew District Council. (General purposes and manpower committees). TGWU.

Mr Norman Buchan

PAISLEY SOUTH Electorate 52 031

*Buchan, N. (Lab)	15 633	41.4%
Buchanan, Mrs E. (L/All)	9 104	24.1%
Knox, J. (C)	7 819	20.7%
Mitchell, J. (SNP)	4 918	13.0%
Mellor, D. (Eco)	271	0.7%
Lab majority	6 529	17.3%
Total vote 37 745		Turnout 72.5%

Mr Norman Buchan was chief Opposition spokesman on agriculture, fisheries and food 1981–83; chief spokesman on social services 1980–81. Minister of State for Agriculture, Fisheries and Food Mar–Oct 1974 (resigned). Opposition spokesman on agriculture 1973–74, and on Scottish affairs 1970–73; Under-Secretary Scottish Office 1967–70. Elected in 1983; MP for West-Renfrewshire 1964–83. Teacher. Born Oct 27 1922; educ. Kirkwall Grammar School and Glasgow University. Member Public Accounts Committee 1975. Chairman PLP Scottish group. Member Council of Poetry Societies since 1977. Sponsored by TGWU.

Mrs Elspeth Buchanan, lecturer at the Central College of Commerce, Glasgow. Born 1931; educ. Glasgow University. Former curator of People's Palace, Glasgow; former lecturer at Glasgow and Edinburgh Universities; former freelance journalist for *Glasgow Herald* and *Scottish Field*.

Mr Joseph Knox, company director, former chairman, Paisley Conservative Assoc. Aged 46. Regional councillor 1978.

Mr James Mitchell, joiner. Born 1942. Leader, SNP group on Renfrew District Council. Shop steward.

Ms Harriet Harman

PECKHAM Electorate 59 128

*Harman, Ms H. (Lab).	16 616	51.6%
Eckersley, T. (C)	7 792	24.2%
Sawden, A. (SDP/All)	7 006	21.8%
Bailey, Mrs M. (NF)	800	2.5%
Lab majority	8 824	27.4%
Total vote 32 214		Turnout 54.5%

Ms Harriet Harman held Southwark, Peckham for Labour at a by-election in Oct 1982. Solicitor and civil rights campaigner. Member, PLP civil liberties group. Born July 30 1950; educ. St Paul's Girls School and York University. Legal officer, National Council for Civil Liberties 1978–82. Sponsored by TGWU. Broadcaster and writer on women's and trade union rights and civil liberties.

Mr Toby Eckersley, Conservative group leader, Southwark Borough Council. Born Jul 22 1941; educ. Charterhouse, St John's College, Oxford. In banking. Founded London Assoc. for saving homes; former secretary, federation of assocs. in redevelopment and rehabilitation areas, Southwark.

Mr Andrew Sawdon, research officer for the British Youth Council. Aged 32. Member, Lambeth Council 1978–82; former chairman of the amenities committee.

Mr Nicholas Edwards

PEMBROKE Electorate 67 885

*Edwards, N. (C)	24 860	46.9%
Griffiths, A. P. (Lab)	15 504	29.2%
Pullin, J. (SDP/All)	10 983	20.7%
Osmond, O. (Pl C)	1 073	2.0%
Hoffman, D. (Eco)	478	0.9%
Phillips, G. S. (Ind)	136	0.3%
C majority	9 356	17.6%
Total vote 53 034		Turnout 78.1%

Mr Nicholas Edwards has been Secretary of State for Wales since 1979. Became a member of the Shadow Cabinet as chief Opposition spokesman on Wales in 1975 having become a spokesman on Welsh affairs in 1974. Won the seat in 1970. Insurance broker. Born Feb 25 1934; educ. Westminster School and Trinity College, Cambridge. Member, Select Committee on members' interests 1976–79. Secretary, Welsh group of Conservative MPs, 1972–74. Member of Lloyd's. Former company director.

Mr Alan Griffiths, fellow and tutor in law at Exeter College, Oxford. Born Sep 21 1953; educ. St David's Primary School, St David's Comprehensive School and Jesus College, Oxford. Member, Oxford City Council since 1980, vice chairman of the finance committee. AUT.

Mr Ozi Osmond, art teacher. Native of Crumlin, Gwent. Active locally in organizing arts exhibitions.

Mr John Pullin, is a Baptist minister, having previously served in Brazil. Educ. University College, Cardiff and South Wales Baptist College.

Mr John Lee

PENDLE Electorate 64 483

*Lee, J. (C)	22 739	44.2%
Rogers, G. (Lab)	16 604	32.3%
Lishman, G. (L/All)	12 056	23.5%
C majority	6135	11.9%
Total vote 51 399	Turnout 79.7%	

Mr John Lee, was appointed Under Secretary of State for Defence Procurement in 1983. Chartered accountant and company director. Elected in 1983; represented Nelson and Colne 1979–83; contested Manchester Moss Side, Oct 1974. Born Jun 21 1942; educ. William Hulme's Grammar School, Manchester. Former group chairman, North West Bow Group. Member, executive council, Manchester Youth and Community Service, and trustee; vice-chairman, North West Conciliation Committee, Race Relations Board 1976–77. Chairman, Council of National Youth Bureau. Joint secretary, Conservative backbench industry committee 1979–81, PPS to Minister of State for Industry (Kenneth Baker) 1981–83 and to Cecil Parkinson in 1983. Parliamentary Consultant to County Bank Ltd and to the National Bedding Federation.

Mr George Rogers was MP for Chorley Feb 1974–79. Engineer. Born Nov 1925; educ. Longview School, Huyton. Member, Huyton UDC 1963–74. Former chairman, north-west group of Labour MPs; former chairman, Huyton Labour Party. AUEW.

Mr Gordon Lishman, head of field work for Age Concern in England, contested Bradford North Feb and Oct 1974. Born Nov 29 1947; educ. Colne Grammar School, Manchester University. Leader, Lib group, Northamptonshire County Council 1981–83.

Mr William Whitelaw

PENRITH AND THE BORDER Electorate 68 164

By-election Jul 28 1983

*Whitelaw, W. (C)	29 304	58.8%
Young, M. (L/All)	13 883	27.9%
Williams, W. (Lab)	6612	13.3%
C majority	15 421	31.0%
Total vote 49 799	Turnout 73.1%	

Mr William Whitelaw, who had been Home Secretary since May 1979, received, immediately after the election, an hereditary peerage and as Viscount Whitelaw, became Leader of the House of Lords. He continues as Mrs Thatcher's deputy in the Cabinet. *See 'Ministers in the House of Lords' for full biographical details and page 366 for by-election result.*

Mr Michael Young, a company director and economist. Born May 11 1945; educ. Wellington Grammar School, Shropshire; University of York. Member CBI company's committee and management committee of Building Materials Producers. Director, Amey Roadstone Construction Ltd.

Mr Lyndsay Williams runs an outdoor pursuit centre at Alston Moor. Aged 37; educ. Cambridge University. Former agent for Mr Joe Ashton, MP for Bassetlaw. Member, Bassetlaw Council since 1979. Former Olympic canoeist.

Mr Nicholas Fairbairn

PERTH AND KINROSS Electorate 61 478

*Fairbairn, N. (C)	17 888	40.2%
Crawford, D. (SNP)	11 155	25.1%
Coutts, B. (L/All)	10 997	24.7%
Stuart, A. J. (Lab)	4414	9.9%
C majority	6733	15.2%
Total vote 44 454	Turnout 72.3%	

Mr Nicholas Fairbairn, QC, was Solicitor General for Scotland 1979–82. MP for Kinross and West Perthshire Oct 1974–83; and for this seat from 1983; contested Edinburgh Central 1964 and 1966. Farmer, company director, advocate, author, painter and poet. Served on Edinburgh Festival Committee. Former member, joint Select Committee on Statutory Instruments. Member, Council of World Population Crisis, 1968–70. Born Dec 24 1933; educ. Loretto and Edinburgh University. Member, Select Committee on Scottish Affairs.

Mr Douglas Crawford, journalist and company director, was MP for Perth and East Perthshire Oct 1974–79; contested seat Feb 1974. Born 1939; educ. Glasgow Academy and Cambridge University. SNP spokesman on finance and industry 1974–79; former vice-chairman (publicity). Member and former director of communications. NUJ.

Mr Benjamin Coutts, farmer and broadcaster. Joined Sussex Yeomanry and was commissioned during the Middle East campaign, being invalided out with the rank of captain in 1944. Chief executive, Aberdeen-Angus Cattle Society, Perth 1971–80. Frequent radio and television presenter on farming affairs.

Mr Alastair Stuart, teacher. Born Oct 18 1948; educ. Aberlour High School, Keith Grammar School and Robert Gordon's Institute of Technology. Member, Perth and Kinross District Council since 1980. NAS/UWT.

Dr Brian Mawhinney

PETERBOROUGH Electorate 78 957

*Mawhinney, B. (C)	27 270	47.1%
Fish, B. (Lab)	16 831	29.1%
Walston, Lady E. (SDP/All)	13 142	22.7%
Callaghan, N. (Eco)	511	0.9%
Hyland, D. (WRP)	155	0.3%
C majority	10 439	18.0%
Total vote 57 909		Turnout 73.3%

Dr Brian Mawhinney, university lecturer, Royal Free Hospital School of Medicine, London, gained seat for Conservatives in 1979; contested Teesside, Stockton Oct 1974. Born Jul 26 1940; educ. Royal Belfast Academical Institution; Queens University, Belfast; University of Michigan; University of London. Member, Medical Research Council since 1980, National Council for Cancer Relief since 1981 and executive of Conservative Medical Society. Member, Select Committee on the Environment 1979–82; has also been an officer of both the health and Northern Ireland Conservative backbench committees. PPS to Ministers of State, Treasury since 1982.

Mr Brian Fish, a computer systems analyst, has been a member of Peterborough City Council since 1978. Born Jul 16 1953; educ. Wyke Hall Secondary Modern, Kelvin Hall Technical Grammar, and Lancaster University.

Lady Elizaeth Walston is a writer. Born 1933; educ. Alerton High School and Ely College.

Dr David Owen

PLYMOUTH, DEVONPORT Electorate 61 813

*Owen, Dr D. A. (SDP/All)	20 843	44.3%
Widdecombe, Miss A. (C)	15 907	33.8%
Priestley, J. (Lab)	9 845	21.0%
Sullivan, J. E. (Ind C)	292	0.6%
Bearsford-Walker, R. (BNP)	72	0.2%
Hill, Mrs F. (CD)	51	0.1%
SDP/All majority	4 936	10.5%
Total vote 47 010		Turnout 76.0%

Dr David Owen, who was Secretary of State for Foreign Affairs in the last Labour Government, 1977–79, resigned from Labour and became one of the joint leaders of the SDP in 1981. Leader of Social Democratic Party, became SDP parliamentary leader in Jun 1983; SDP deputy parliamentary leader 1982–83 with overall responsibility for defence and foreign affairs. Member, Independent Commission on Disarmament and Security issues 1980–; Opposition spokesman on energy, 1979–80; Minister of State, Foreign Office, 1976–77; Minister of State for Health 1974–76; Under-Secretary of State for Health 1974. Returned Feb 1974; represented Plymouth, Sutton 1966–74; contested Torrington 1964; Opposition spokesman on defence 1970–72 but resigned after disagreement on EEC policy. Under-Secretary of State for Defence for the Royal Navy 1968–70. Born Jul 2 1938; educ. Bradford Collge, Berkshire; Sidney Sussex College, Cambridge, and St Thomas's Hospital, London. Medical practitioner. ASTMS(MPU).

Miss Ann Widdecombe, financial administrator at University of London, contested Burnley 1979. Born Oct 4 1947; educ. La Sainte Union Convent, Bath; Birmingham University, and Lady Margaret Hall, Oxford. Vice-chairman, National Assoc. Conservative Graduates 1976–78; vice-chairman, Women for Defence. Member, Runnymede District Council 1976–78; Society for the Protection of Unborn Children. AUT.

Mr Julian Priestley contested Plymouth, Sutton Oct 1974 and 1979. Administrator, European Parliament. Born May 1950; educ. St Boniface's College, Plymouth, and Oxford University (President, Union, 1972).

Miss Janet Fookes

PLYMOUTH, DRAKE Electorate 52 383

*Fookes, Miss J. (C)	19 718	50.6%
Fitzgerald, W. (SDP/All)	11 133	28.6%
Creswell, Ms S. (Lab)	7 921	20.3%
Bradbury, C. (BNP)	163	0.4%
C majority	8 585	22.1%
Total vote 38 935		Turnout 74.3%

Miss Janet Fookes, elected for the seat in 1974, represented Merton and Morden 1970–74. Chairman, RSPCA 1979–81. Teacher. Born Feb 21 1936; educ. Hastings and St Leonards Ladies' College, Hastings High School and Royal Holloway College, University of London. Member, Speakers' Panel of Chairmen; member, former chairman, education and home affairs sub-committee of Expenditure Committee. Hon. Secretary, all-party mental health group and Co-Chairman, all-party equal opportunities group. Member, councils of Stonham Housing Assoc. SSAFA and National Canine Defence League. Member, Hastings County Borough Council 1960–61 and 1963–70.

Mr Will Fitzgerald, warden of Dartington College, is a member of the SDP national committee and chairman, Devon area SDP. Born 1950; educ. Dartford Grammar School, Warwick University and South Bank Polytechnic.

Ms Sally Creswell, became youngest member of Plymouth City Council when elected in May 1983. Born 1957; educ. Burleigh Secondary Modern School; Stoke Damerel High School for Girls, Plymouth, and Lancaster University.

Mr Alan Clark

PLYMOUTH, SUTTON Electorate 59 890

*Clark, A. K. M. (C)	25 203	55.1%
Puttick, A. (L/All)	13 516	29.6%
Holland, Ms F. (Lab)	6 538	14.3%
Shaw, S. (Eco)	470	1.0%
C majority	11 687	25.6%
Total vote 45 727	Turnout	76.4%

Mr Alan Clark, a barrister and historian, was appointed Under Secretary of State for Employment in Jun 1983. Son of the late Lord Clark. Elected in Feb 1974. Born Apr 13 1928; educ. Eton and Christ Church, Oxford. Joint Secretary, Conservative backbench home affairs committee 1982–83; former vice-chairman, Conservative backbench defence committee. Member, Select Committee on Sound Broadcasting since 1979.

Mr Anthony Puttick, a barrister, fought Plymouth, Drake 1979. Former legal advisor to the ruler of Sharjah, United Arab Emirates. Born 1934; educ. Hele's Grammar School, Exeter; Royal Naval College, Dartmouth. Former Commander, Royal Navy.

Ms Frances Holland is a graduate student. Born 1960. Member, CND; NUS.

Mr Geoffrey Lofthouse

PONTEFRACT AND CASTLEFORD Electorate 64 878

*Lofthouse, G. (Lab)	24 990	57.1%
Howell, B. (C)	11 299	25.8%
Dale, D. (L/All)	7 452	17.0%
Lab majority	13 691	31.3%
Total vote 43 741	Turnout	67.4%

Mr Geoffrey Lofthouse, a personnel manager with the NCB, was elected at the by-election in Oct 1978. Born Dec 18 1925; educ. Featherstone primary and secondary schools, and Leeds University. Spent 20 years in local government service and was for 23 years a member of the NUM, BACM, APEX.

Mr Barry Howell, schoolmaster. Born Dec 19 1933; educ. Castleford Grammar School, Dudley Training College. Formerly member Pontefract Borough Council. AMMA.

Mr Douglas Dale is district catering manager for Wakefield Health Authority. Born Nov 28 1929; educ. Thomas Danby College, Leeds. Nalgo.

Mr Brynmor John

PONTYPRIDD Electorate 60 883

*John, B. (Lab)	20 188	45.6%
Langridge, R. (SDP/All)	11 444	25.8%
Evans, R. (C)	10 139	22.9%
Davies, Mrs J. (Pl C)	2 065	4.7%
Jones, A. K. (Eco)	449	1.0%
Lab majority	8 744	19.7%
Total vote 44 285	Turnout	72.7%

Mr Brynmor John was a member of the Shadow Cabinet 1981–83 when he was chief Opposition spokesman on social security. Chief Opposition spokesman on Northern Ireland, 1979–80; on defence, 1980–81; Minister of State, Home Office, 1976–79; Under-Secretary for Defence for the RAF 1974–76. Elected in 1970. Solicitor. Born Apr 18 1934; educ. Pontypridd Grammar School and University College, London. Specialized in industrial accident law. Governor of Pontypridd Secondary Schools. Former member, local trades council.

Mr Richard Langridge. Born 1955; educ. Stowmarket Grammar School, Lancaster University. Post-graduate student, Sherman Theatre, Cardiff, 1979. Member, BBC Programme Executive Department, Wales.

Mr Richard Evans, solicitor. Born Feb 22 1948; educ. Whitchurch Grammar School, University College of Wales, Aberystwyth. Member, South Glamorgan County Council; chairman 1979.

Mrs Janet Davies, Plaid Cymru's spokesman on agriculture, is a mature student at Trinity College, Carmarthen.

Mr John Ward

POOLE Electorate 70731

*Ward, J. (C)	30358	58.3%
Clements, B. (L/All)	15929	30.6%
Castle, M. V. (Lab)	5595	10.8%
Foster, A. (SACA)	177	0.3%
C majority	14429	27.7%
Total vote 52059		Turnout 73.6%

Mr John Ward, a chartered civil engineer and director of a building company, was elected in 1979; contested Portsmouth North in Oct 1974. Born Mar 8 1925; educ. Romford County Technical School and St Andrew's University. Joint secretary, Conservative backbench industry committee since 1982. Member, national union executive, Conservative Party 1965–78 and central board of finance, conservative party, 1969–78. Member Conservative Political Centre National Advisory Committee; European Movement; and Conservative Group for Europe; founder member, Conservative Commonwealth Council; secretary. Mediterranean group 1955–60.

Mr Brian Clements, lecturer.

Mr Michael Castle, teacher, at a school for educationally subnormal children. Born Dec 1949. Member, Rushmoor Borough Council since 1980; president, NE Hampshire Assoc. of NUT, 1979–80.

Mr Peter Griffiths

PORTSMOUTH NORTH Electorate 77923

*Griffiths, P. (C)	31413	55.3%
Luxon, S. (SDP/All)	13414	23.6%
Beard, N. (Lab)	12013	21.1%
C majority	17999	31.7%
Total vote 56840		Turnout 72.9%

Mr Peter Griffiths was returned in 1979. Represented Smethwick 1964–66 and contested Portsmouth North Feb 1974; former headmaster and senior lecturer. Born May 24 1928; educ. West Bromwich Grammar School, City of Leeds Training College, London University and Birmingham University. Member, Smethwick Borough Council 1955–64 and alderman 1964–66; former president, Young Conservatives.

Mr Stuart Luxon, assistant general manager European services division, British Airways; previously area manager in the United States, Canada and Eastern Europe. Born 1944; educ. Maidstone Grammar School, LSE and Manchester Business School.

Mr Nigel Beard, scientist and planner, contested Woking 1979. Born Oct 10 1936; educ. Castleford Grammar School and University College, University of London. Chief planner for strategy, Greater London Council, 1973–74. Member, South West Thames Regional Health Authority; member, board of the Royal Marsden Hospital. GMBATU.

Mr Bonner Pink

PORTSMOUTH SOUTH Electorate 74537 By-election June 14 1984

*Pink, B. (C)	25101	50.0%
Hancock, M. (SDP / All)	12766	25.4%
Thomas, Mrs S. T. (Lab)	11324	22.6%
Evens, A. J. (Ind L)	554	1.1%
Knight, G. A. (NF)	279	0.6%
Fry, D. W. (TEF)	172	0.3%
C majority	12335	24.6%
Total vote 50196		Turnout 67.3%

Mr Bonner Pink, member of the Speaker's panel of chairmen, was elected in 1966. Former company director. Born Sep 30 1912; educ. Oundle. Member, Estimates Committee, 1967–70; former member, Public Expenditure Committee. Member, Portsmouth City Council from 1948 (Alderman, 1961); Lord Mayor of Portsmouth, 1961–2. *See page 367 for by-election result.*

Mr Michael Hancock, engineer. Born 1946. Member, since 1971, Portsmouth City Council and since 1973 of Hampshire County Council where he was leader of Labour councillors for five years. Member, BBC South board; board of management, Salvation Army; governor, College of Art in Portsmouth; and member, International Union of Local Authorities.

Mrs Sally Thomas, teacher, contested Portsmouth South 1979. Born Oct 12 1946; educ. Portsmouth Art College and Brighton Polytechnic. Member, Portsmouth City Council 1976–83. NUT.

Mr Stanley Thorne

PRESTON Electorate 64 969

*Thorne, S. (Lab)	21 810	46.7%
Huntley, T. (C)	14 832	31.8%
Connolly, M. (SDP / All)	10 039	21.5%
Lab majority	6 978	15.0%
Total vote 46 681		Turnout 71.9%

Mr Stanley Thorne, formerly lecturer in industrial sociology. Elected for Preston in 1983; MP for Preston South Feb 1974–83; contested Liverpool, Wavertree 1964. Born Jul 22 1918; educ. Ruskin College, Oxford and Liverpool University. Vice-chairman, health and education groups PLP; member PLP, housing and aviation groups; chairman, Parliamentary Labour CND. Liverpool councillor 1963–66 and 1971–74, former deputy chairman, Liverpool education committee, AUEW (TASS).

Mr Thomas Huntley, consultant engineer and assessor. Born Sep 1 1930; educ. Stopsley Secondary School, Luton, and Luton Technical College. Contested Newton 1979. Member, Rossendale Borough Council 1968–78. Pilot and gliding instructor, ex rally driver, ABA boxing judge. President, NW Federation of Pigeon Clubs.

Mr Giles Shaw

PUDSEY Electorate 70 583

*Shaw, G. (C)	24 455	45.7%
Cummins, J. (L/All)	19 141	35.8%
Price, Ms S. M. (Lab)	9 542	17.8%
Smith, R. (Ind)	387	0.7%
C majority	5 314	9.9%
Total vote 53 525		Turnout 75.8%

Mr Giles Shaw, became Under Secretary of State for Energy in Jun 1983; Under Secretary of State for Environment 1981–83; Under Secretary of State for Northern Ireland 1979–81. Elected in 1974; contested Kingston upon Hull West 1966. Born Nov 16 1931; educ. Sedbergh School and St John's College, Cambridge (President of the Union, 1954). Former vice-chairman, Conservative prices and consumer affairs committee, and all-party wool textile group. Member, Select Committee on Nationalized Industries 1976–79; served on Flaxton RDC 1956–62. Joint secretary, Yorkshire Conservative MPs 1974–79. Former consultant, Rowntree Mackintosh, and Ogilvy, Benson and Mather. Former director, North Riding Motors.

Mr Julian Cummins has been a member of Leeds City Council since 1982. Runs his own marketing business. Born Jan 29 1955; educ. Wellington College and King's College, Cambridge.

Ms Susan Price is a probation officer. Born 1954.

Mr David Mellor

PUTNEY Electorate 63 853 1979: 64 648 same

*Mellor, D. (C)	21 863	46.5%
Hain, P. (Lab)	16 844	35.9%
Welchman, C. (L/All)	7 668	16.3%
Connolly, M. (NF)	290	0.6%
Baillie-Grohman, Mrs R. (Eco)	190	0.4%
Chalk, L. (Oth)	88	0.2%
Williams, W. (Ind)	41	0.1%
C majority	5 019	10.7%
Total vote 46 984		Turnout 73.6%

1979: Total vote 49 200 (76.1%); C 23 044 (46.8%); Lab 20 410 (41.5%); L 5 061 (10.3%); NF 685 (1.4%). C maj 2 634 (5.3%); swing 5.5% to C. C gain from Lab.

Mr David Mellor, who became Under-Secretary of State, Home Office Jan 1983, had been Under-Secretary of State for Energy since 1981. A barrister, he gained the seat for the Conservatives in 1979; contested West Bromwich East Oct 1974. Born Mar 12 1949; educ. Swanage Grammar School, Christ's College, Cambridge. Joint secretary, Conservative backbench legal committee 1980–81; joint vice-chairman, Greater London Conservative MPs 1980–81. Chairman, Cambridge University Conservative Assoc. 1970. Special Trustee, Westminster Hospital 1980. Member of the Council of the National Youth Orchestra 1981. Fellow, Zoologial Society of London 1981.

Mr Peter Hain, trade union research officer. Member of the Labour Party Co-ordinating Committee. Born Feb 16 1950; educ. Queen Mary College, London University and Sussex University. Was twice vice-chairman of the Young Liberals and was President 1975–77. Branch official, APEX; has worked full time for the Union of Communications Workers since 1976.

Mr Charles Welchman, barrister, contested Esher Oct 1974 and 1979. Born Apr 7 1943; educ. Exeter Technical College and University College, London.

Mr John Hunt

RAVENSBOURNE Electorate 58811

*Hunt, J. L. (C)	27143	63.1%
Boston, Mrs C. M. (SDP/All)	11631	27.0%
Holbrook. J. R. (Lab)	4037	9.4%
Shotton, A. T. (BNP)	242	0.6%
C majority	15512	36.0%
Total vote 43053		Turnout 73.2%

Mr John Hunt, a public relations consultant, was elected for Ravensbourne in Feb 1974; MP for Bromley 1964–74; contested Lewisham South 1959. Born Oct 27 1929; educ. Dulwich College. Member, Bromley Borough Council 1953–65; mayor 1963–64. Member, Speaker's panel of chairmen since 1980; member, Select Committee on Home Affairs (race relations and immigration subcommittee) since 1979. Chairman, Greater London Conservative MPs. Chairman, Indo-British parliamentary group. Member, BBC General Advisory Council since 1975; Member, London Stock Exchange 1958–70. Parliamentary adviser to National Hairdressers' Federation.

Mrs Catharine Boston, deputy head, ILEA support unit. Born Jun 25 1938; educ. Trinity Hall, Southport, and London University. Governor of two Bromley youth centres and Centre for Arts and Crafts, Bromley; JP Bromley bench.

Mr John Holbrook, a teacher, contested Bromley, Ravensbourne 1979. Born Jan 18 1945; educ. North-Western Polytechnic and Sheffield City College of Education. Director, League Against Cruel Sports. Member, Co-operative Party. NUT.

Dr Gerard Vaughan

READING EAST Electorate 67511

*Vaughan, G. (C)	24516	51.6%
Huhne, C. (SDP/All)	13008	27.4%
Boyle, K. (Lab)	9218	19.4%
Darnton, G. (Eco)	519	1.1%
Baker, P. (BNP)	147	0.3%
Shone, B. (CMP)	113	0.2%
C majority	11508	24.2%
Total vote 47521		Turnout 70.4%

Dr Gerard Vaughan was Minister of State for Trade (Minister for Consumer Affairs) 1982–83; Minister for Health, with rank of Minister of State, at Department of Health and Social Security, 1979–82. An Opposition spokesman on the social services 1975–79; Opposition whip 1974–7. Elected for this seat in 1983 after being MP for Reading South, Feb 1974–83 and for Reading, 1970–74; contested Poplar 1955. Specialist at Guy's Hospital. Born Jun 11 1923; educ. London University and Guy's Hospital. Alderman, GLC 1967–72, and LCC 1955–64. President, Conservative Medical Society, Liveryman, Worshipful Company of Barbers.

Mr Christopher Huhne, economic journalist. Born Jul 2 1954; educ. Westminster School, Sorbonne, and Magdalen College, Oxford. NUJ.

Mr Kevin Boyle, teacher. Born Oct 25 1947; educ. grammar school in Warrington, Hatfield Polytechnic and Reading University. Member, Berkshire County Council since 1977. NUT.

Mr Anthony Durant

READING WEST Electorate 66080

*Durant, A. (C)	24948	52.1%
Day, R. J. (L/All)	13549	28.3%
Evans, R. (Lab)	9920	19.3%
Lilley, E. (Ind)	161	0.3%
C majority	11399	23.8%
Lotal vote 47878		Turnout 72.5%

Mr Anthony Durant, director and former company secretary of an audio visual aids company, was elected in 1983; represented Reading North Feb 1974–83; contested Rother Valley 1970. Chairman, Conservative environment committee since 1982. Born Jan 9 1928; educ. Dane Court Preparatory School and Bryanston School, Dorset. Member, Select Committee on Parliamentary Commissioner for Administration since 1974. Chairman, all-party committee for widows and single-parent families. Former secretary, all-party committee on inland waterways and Conservative industry committee; treasurer, parliamentary group for world government. Member, Woking Urban Council 1968–74; chairman, Woking education committee,1969–74; Surrey education committee 1969–74. Consultant to Delta Metal Electrical (Holdings) Ltd and to British Film Production Assoc. PPS to Mr Tom King, Secretary of State for Transport, from Jun 1983.

Mr James Day, economist. Born Jan 3 1921; educ. Grammar School and Nottingham University. Member, Berkshire County Council since 1973.

Mr Richard Evans, head of department in comprehensive school, contested Maidstone 1979. Born May 3 1951; educ. Sutton Valence School, John Maron School, Abingdon and Sussex and London universities. Chairman, Camden Borough Council local government committee.

Mr James Tinn

REDCAR Electorate 63 447 1979: 62 511 same

*Tinn, J. (Lab)	18 348	40.6%
Bassett, P. (C)	15 244	33.7%
Nightingale, G. (SDP/All)	11 614	25.7%
Lab majority	3 104	6.9%
Total vote 45 206	Turnout 71.3%	

1979: Total vote 47 445 (75.9%); Lab & Coop 25 470 (53.7%); C 17 417 (36.7%); L 4 225 (8.9%); Ind 333 (0.7%). Lab maj 8 053 (17.0%); swing 3.6% to C.

Mr James Tinn, an Opposition whip since 1979, was returned in Feb 1974. MP for Cleveland 1964–74. Teacher and former steelworker. PPS to Secretary of State for Commonwealth (formerly for Commonwealth Relations) 1965–66; to Minister for Overseas Development 1966–67; an Assistant Government Whip 1976–79. Born Aug 23 1922; educ. Consett Elementary School, Ruskin College and Jesus College, Oxford. Sponsored by National Union of Blastfurnacemen.

Mr Peter Bassett, economist and senior oil analyst. Born Oct 31 1955; educ. Malvern College, Queen's College, Cambridge. Member, Greenwich Council 1978–82; Conservative chief whip 1980–82. GLC candidate for Greenwich 1981.

Mr Glyn Nightingale, department head of sixth form college. Born Mar 18 1943; educ. Ashton under Lyne Grammar School, and York and Manchester universities. Former chairman, Middlesbrough Labour Party; now Cleveland area secretary, SDP. Member, Council for Social Democracy. AMMA.

Mr George Gardiner

REIGATE Electorate 70 320

*Gardiner, G. (C)	29 932	59.0%
Pamplin, Mrs E. (SDP/All)	13 625	26.9%
Symons, B. A. (Lab)	6 114	12.1%
Newell, D. (Eco)	1 029	2.0%
C majority	16 307	32.2%
Total vote 50 700	Turnout 72.1%	

Mr George Gardiner, journalist, Editor, *Conservative News* 1972–79, and author of a biography on Mrs Thatcher. Elected Feb 1974; contested Coventry South 1970. Born Mar 3 1935; educ. Harvey Grammar School, Folkestone, and Balliol College, Oxford. Secretary, Conservative European affairs committee 1976–79; vice-chairman 1979–80; chairman since 1980. Member, Select Committee on Home Affairs and Race Relations and Immigration sub-committee 1979–82. Former member executive, 1922 Committee. Former senior political correspondent for Thomson Newspapers. NUJ.

Mrs Elizabeth Pamplin, local authority employment development officer. Born Apr 13 1940; educ. Rosebery Grammar School Epsom, and St Hugh's College, Oxford.

Mr Bryan Symons, co-ordinator of a council of voluntary service. Born Aug 17 1946; educ. Queen Elizabeth's Grammar School, Barnet, and Keble College, Oxford. TGWU.

Mrs Anna McCurley

RENFREW WEST AND INVERCLYDE Electorate 53 510

McCurley, Mrs A. (C)	13 669	32.7%
*Mabon, J. D. (SDP/All)	12 347	29.5%
Doherty, G. (Lab)	12 139	29.0%
Taylor, W. (SNP)	3 653	8.7%
C majority	1 322	3.2%
Total vote 41 808	Turnout 78.1%	

Mrs Anna McCurley, was elected in 1983. Teacher and lecturer. Born 1943; educ. Glasgow High School for Girls; Glasgow and Strathclyde universities; Jordanhill College of Education. Strathclyde Regional Councillor 1978–82. Contested West Stirlingshire 1979 and Glasgow Central in 1980 by-election.

Dr J. Dickson Mabon who was Labour's Minister of State for Energy, 1976–79, resigned from the party and joined the SDP in 1981 becoming its spokesman on energy. Under Secretary of State for Scotland 1964–67; Minister of State Scottish Office 1967–70; deputy Opposition spokesman on Scotland 1970–72 (resigned in protest at party's Common Market policy). Physician, medical historian and company director. Born Nov 1 1925; educ. state schools and Glasgow University. Represented Greenock and Port Glasgow Feb 1974–83; MP for Greenock 1955–74; contested Bute and North Ayrshire 1951, and West Renfrewshire 1955. Parliamentary adviser to the Royal Society of Chemistry and to the Scotch Whisky Assoc.

Mr George Doherty is an industrial safety officer with British Rail. Active member of NUR for 30 years.

Mr William Taylor, solicitor. Born 1946; educ. Mossvale School and Strathclyde University. Member, Renfrew District Council.

Mr Allan Rogers

RHONDDA Electorate 62587 1979: 63412 minor

Rogers, A. (Lab)	29448	61.7%
Lloyd, A. (SDP/All)	8078	16.9%
Davies, G. (PlC)	4845	10.2%
Meyer, P. C)	3973	8.3%
True, A. (Com)	1350	2.8%
Lab majority	21370	44.8%
Total vote 47694	Turnout 76.2%	

1979 Total vote 50578 (79.8%); Lab 38007 (75.1%); Com 1819 (3.6%). Lab maj 31481 (62.2%); swing 3.7% to C.

Mr Allan Rogers, returned for this seat in 1983, a former miner and geologist for the National Coal Board, was elected to the European Parliament for Rhondda in 1979. Vice-President of the Parliament 1979–81. Aged 50. Former secretary of the Workers Educational Assoc. Member, Rhondda District Council 1965–71; Mid-Glamorgan County Council 1970–79; area health authority; Welsh joint educational committee. Chairman, Polytechnic of Wales. Vice-president of Wales anti-apartheid movement. CND.

Mr Allan Lloyd, senior tutor and head of careers department, Lady Hawkins School, Kington. Born 1936. Chairman, Hereford and Worcester county careers advisory committee; principal, Kington Further Education College; Mayor of Kington; past chairman, Leominster District Council.

Mr Geraint Davies, pharmacist, is a native of Rhondda. Son of ex-conductor of Treorchy Male Voice Choir.

Mr Peter Meyer, a chartered accountant. Born Apr 1936; educ. Cardiff High School; University College, Cardiff. Member, South Glamorgan County Council since 1973; party education spokesman.

Mr David Waddington

RIBBLE VALLEY Electorate 59982

*Waddington, D. C. (C)	29223	63.4%
Carr, M. (SDP/All)	10632	23.1%
Saville, E. A. (Lab)	6214	13.5%
C majority	18591	40.4%
Total vote 46069	Turnout 76.8%	

Mr David Waddington, QC, who was elected for this seat in 1983, became Minister of State, Home Office, in Jan 1983. Under Secretary for State for Employment 1981–83; Government whip 1979–81. MP for Clitheroe Mar 1979–83, and for Nelson and Colne 1968–Oct 1974; contested Heywood and Royton 1966, Nelson and Colne 1964 and Farnworth 1955. Born Aug 2 1929; educ. Sedbergh School and Hertford College, Oxford. Former Director, Padiham Loom and Power Co Ltd; Progress Mill Ltd; J. and J. Roberts Ltd; and Wolstenholme Rink Ltd.

Mr Michael Carr is head of general studies, Blackthorn County Secondary School, Bacup. Former teacher and local government administrative officer. Former Conservative councillor, Ribble Valley Borough Council. Born 1946; educ. St Joseph's College, Blackpool; Catholic College, Preston; McMillan College of Education, Bradford.

Mr Edward Saville is a lecturer in mathematics and computer studies at Accrington and Rossendale College. Born Jul 1947; educ. Bretton Hall College of Education and the Open University. Member, Hyndburn District Council, since 1980; deputy group leader and chairman of the finance and personnel committee. TGWU.

Mr Jeremy Hanley

RICHMOND AND BARNES Electorate 55845

Hanley, J. (C)	20695	46.5%
Watson, A. J. (L/All)	20621	46.4%
Vaz, K. (Lab)	3156	7.1%
C majority	74	0.2%
Total vote 44472	Turnout 79.6%	

Mr Jeremy Hanley, a chartered accountant and senior lecturer in law, taxation and accountancy, was elected in 1983; contested Lambeth Central in Apr 1978 and 1979. Born Nov 17 1945; educ. Rugby. Chairman of the Conservative Candidates Assoc. Vice-president, Lambeth Central Conservative Assoc. since 1981; member, executive committee, Greater London Conservatives, since 1981; Bow Group Commonwealth and Overseas Council.

Mr Alan Watson, company director, contested Richmond upon Thames, Richmond Oct 1974 and 1979. Born Feb 3 1941; educ. Kingswood School, Bath, and Jesus College, Cambridge. Member, Liberal Party Council; member, Liberal Party National Executive. Chairman, Liberal Candidates Assoc.

Mr Keith Vaz, solicitor. Aged 26; educ. Cambridge University. Former chairman, Cambridge Fabian Society; secretary, Richmond and Twickenham peace campaign; vice-president, Richmond and Barnes Labour Party.

Mr Leon Brittan

RICHMOND (YORKS) Electorate 75 196

*Brittan, L. (C)	32 373	62 6%
Raw, D. (L/All)	14 307	27.7%
Hawkins, Mrs B. (Lab)	4 997	9.7%
C majority	18 066	35.0%
Total vote 51 677		Turnout 68.7%

Mr Leon Brittan QC, was appointed Home Secretary in June 1983, having been Chief Secretary to the Treasury with a seat in the Cabinet 1981–83; Minister of State, Home Office 1979–81. Barrister and journalist. Elected for this seat in 1983; MP for Cleveland and Whitby Feb 1974–83; contested Kensington North 1966 and 1970. An Opposition spokesman on devolution and House of Commons affairs 1976–79. In Nov 1978 also appointed as additional employment spokesman. Born Sep 25 1939; educ. Haberdashers' Aske's School, Trinity College, Cambridge (president of Union) and Yale University. Vice-chairman, National Assoc. of School Governors and Managers. Vice-chairman of Conservative Employment Committee 1974–76. Editor of *Crossbow* 1966–68. Chairman, Bow Group 1964–65. Bencher, Inner Temple since 1983.

Mr David Raw, headmaster, Langworthy School. Born Aug 18 1942.

Mrs Barbara Hawkins, a lecturer, is a member of the Labour Party NEC sub-committee on food and agriculture. Born May 12 1944; educ. Highbury Hill High School, London; London University. Member, North Eastern Co-operative Society area committee.

Mr Cyril Smith

ROCHDALE Electorate 66 976 1979: 66 841 minor

*Smith, C. (L/All)	21 858	46.1%
Broon, Ms V. (Lab)	14 271	30.1%
Fearn, A. (C)	10 616	22.4%
Barker, P. (NF)	463	1.0%
Courtney, P. (UP)	204	0.4%
L/All majority	7 587	16.0%
Total vote 47 412		Turnout 70.8%

1979: Total vote 49 234 (73.7%); L 22 172 (45.0%); Lab 16 878 (34.3%); C 9 494 (19.3%); NF 690 (1.4%). L maj 5 294 (10.7%).

Mr Cyril Smith gained the seat for the Liberals in the by-election in Oct 1972; contested the seat in 1970. Party spokesman on employment and formerly on social services. Born Jun 28 1928; educ. Rochdale Grammar School. Managing director, Smith Springs (Rochdale). Mayor of Rochdale 1966–67. Member, Select Committee on House of Commons Services, and catering subcommittee since 1979. Member, Rochdale Borough Council 1952–75. On Parliamentary panel, TGWU 1955–58. A Deputy Pro-Chancellor, Lancaster University since 1978.

Ms Valerie Broon, Nalgo district education officer. Born Apr 29 1950; educ. grammar school and Warwick University, Kent Training College for Youth Employment Service. Former careers officer. Member, Bolton Council 1980–83. APEX.

Mr Alan Fearn, dental surgeon, contested Ashton under Lyne 1970, Accrington Feb 1974, Middleton and Prestwich Oct 1974, and Ashton under Lyne again 1979. Born 1924; educ. Bury Grammar School, Terra Nova School, Southport, Shrewsbury School and Guy's Hospital. Elected Tameside Metropolitan Borough Council 1976; deputy leader 1978, and leader of opposition 1979. Longest serving member General Dental Council.

Dr Michael Clark

ROCHFORD Electorate 69 392

Clark, M. (C)	29 495	57.8%
Boyd, R. (L/All)	16 393	32.2%
Witzer, M. (Lab)	5 105	10.0%
C majority	13 102	25.7%
Total vote 50 993		Turnout 73.5%

Dr Michael Clark, management consultant and industrial chemist, employed by P A Management Consultants Ltd, was elected in 1983. Contested Ilkeston 1979. Born Aug 1935; educ. King Edward VI Grammar School, East Retford, Nottinghamshire; King's College, London; and St. John's College, Cambridge; Fulbright Scholarship 1956–57 to the University of Minnesota, US. Member, Cambridgeshire Conservative Assoc. since 1969; branch chairman 1973–76 constituency treasurer 1975–78; chairman 1980–83; Eastern Area executive committee 1980–83, Cambridgeshire European Council 1980–83.

Mr Richard Boyd is director of three international airport equipment companies. Born May 15 1945; educ. Harrow County Grammar School and the University of Southampton. Member, Rochford District Council, leader of the Liberal opposition; Essex County Council, vice-chairman of the police community liaison committee.

Mr Mark Witzer, computer programmer. Born 1938; educ. Open University, specializing in sociology, economics and politics. Member, Basildon District Council since 1974. ASTMS.

Mr Michael Neubert

ROMFORD Electorate 55758 1979: 55154 same

*Neubert, M. J. (C)	20771	53.4%
Bates, J. (L/All)	10197	26.2%
Hoepelman, J. (Lab)	7494	19.3%
Caine, Mrs M. P. (NF)	432	1.1%
C majority	10574	27.2%
Total vote 38894		Turnout 69.8%

1979: Total vote 42254 (76.6%); C 22714 (53.8%); Lab 13902 (32.9%); L 4818 (11.4%); NF 820 (1.9%). C maj 8812 (20.9%); swing 7.1% to C.

Mr Michael Neubert was appointed an assistant Government whip in Jun 1983; PPS to Lord Cockfield, Secretary of State for Trade 1982–83; previously as PPS to other ministers. Secretary to Conservative trade committee 1975–79, and to Conservative prices and consumer affairs committee 1974–79. Elected in Feb 1974; contested Romford 1970 and Hammersmith North 1966. Travel and industrial consultant. Born Sep 3 1933; educ. Queen Elizabeth's School, Barnet, Bromley Grammar School and Downing College, Cambridge. Leader, Bromley Council 1967–70 and Mayor 1972–73.

Mr John Bates, barrister, contested Havering, Romford 1979. Born May 29 1951; educ. Harrow and Inns of Court School of Law. Chairman, Liberal Party environmental panel. C/Sgt in Territorial Army.

Mr Jack Hoepelman, London Transport bus mechanic. Born Dec 23 1932; educ. Suttons Secondary Modern Boys' School. Member, Havering Borough Council 1971–78 and since 1982. TGWU.

Mr Michael Colvin

ROMSEY AND WATERSIDE Electorate 70782

*Colvin, M. (C)	30361	56.6%
Bloss, A. (SDP/All)	16671	31.1%
Knight, M. (Lab)	6604	12.3%
C majority	13690	25.5%
Total vote 53636		Turnout 75.8%

Mr Michael Colvin won this seat in 1983; MP for Bristol North-West 1979–83. Farmer, landowner, company director and public house licensee. Member, Select Committee on Employment, 1979–83. Part-time member of Conservative Research Department specializing in aviation 1975–78. Secretary, West Country Conservative MPs 1982–83. Qualified pilot and parachutist. Born Sep 27 1932; educ. Eton, RMA Sandhurst, and Royal Agricultural College, Cirencester. Member, Andover Council 1965–73; Test Valley Council 1973–75. Vice-chairman. Southern Sports Council, 1968–73. Church warden. NFU and National Union of Licensed Victuallers. Director, Accrep Ltd. Chairman, Conservative backbench aviation committee; vice-chairman Conservative backbench committee on Smaller Businesses; secretary of shipping and shipbuilding committee, all until 1983. PPS to Ministers of State at F.O. since 1983.

Mr Alan Bloss, interpreter. Born Mar 19 1938; educ. Palmers School, Grays, and London University.

Mr Matthew Knight, personnel manager for Voluntary Service Overseas. Born May 31 1954; educ. Grove Park School, Wrexham and Selwyn College, Cambridge. Chairman, Wessex Co-operative Party; chairman, local community assoc. and member, community health council. ASTMS.

Mr Charles Kennedy

ROSS, CROMARTY AND SKYE Electorate 48401

Kennedy, C. (SDP/All)	13528	38.5%
*Gray, H. (C)	11824	33.7%
Elder, M. (Lab)	4901	14.0%
Matheson, Miss K. (SNP)	4863	13.9%
SDP/All majority	1704	4.9%
Total vote 35116		Turnout 72.6%

Mr Charles Kennedy who won this seat in 1983, was on a Fulbright scholarship teaching speech communication and British politics in Indiana University. Born 1959 in Inverness, educ. Lochaber High School, Fort William, and Glasgow University (president of the union). Following graduation, worked in radio news reporting and broadcasting with BBC Highland in Inverness.

Mr Hamish Gray who was Minister of State for Energy 1979–83, and MP for Ross and Cromarty 1970–83, was, following on his defeat in this election, made a life peer and appointed Minister of State for Scotland. An Opposition spokesman on energy 1975–79; Lord Commissioner of the Treasury (Government whip) 1973–74; assistant Government whip 1971–73. Born Jun 28 1927; educ. Inverness Royal Academy. Former director of a contracting firm. Member, Inverness Town Council and County Council 1965–60. Former member, council Highland Chamber of Commerce and of Highlands and Islands Youth Employment Committee. Member, Select Committee on Scottish Affairs 1971.

Mr Murray Elder is a research assistant to Mr John Smith, former shadow

Secretary of State for Trade. Aged 33; educ. Kirkcaldy High School and Edinburgh University.
Miss Kay Matheson, teacher. Born 1928; educ. Jordanhill College of Education. Teaches Gaelic in the Highlands. Member, Executive Council, An Comunn Gaidhealach. Took part in return of Stone of the Destiny to Scotland in the 1950s.

Mr David Trippier

ROSSENDALE AND DARWEN

Electorate 74 401

*Trippier, D. (C)	27 214	47.0%
Robinson, C. (Lab)	18 393	31.8%
Taylor, M. (L/All)	12 246	21.2%
C majority	8 821	15.3%
Total vote 57 853		Turnout 77.8%

Mr David Trippier, a stockbroker, was appointed an Under Secretary of State for Trade and Industry in Jun 1983. Elected for this seat in 1983, having been MP for Rossendale 1979–83; contested Rochdale in Oct 1972 by-election and Oldham West in Feb and Oct 1974. Born May 15 1945; educ. Bury Grammar School. Member, Rochdale Council 1969–78. Joint secretary Conservative backbench defence committee 1980–82. Secretary, all-party parliamentary footwear committee, 1979–83. PPS to Minister for Health 1982–83. Chairman, Rochdale Young Conservatives 1965 and chairman, South-East Lancashire Young Conservatives 1966. Member, Stock Exchange; former director, financial planning company. Officer in Royal Marines Reserve.
Mr Christopher Robinson, trade union officer. Deputy leader, Labour group, Rossendale Council, since 1982; council member since 1980. District Officer, Nalgo. Secretary, Lancashire Assoc. of Trades Councils 1980–81. Born May 5 1954; educ. Owens School, Islington, London, Sheffield University and LSE. TGWU.
Mr Michael Taylor, teacher. Born 1950. Youngest-ever mayor of local council.

Mr Stanley Crowther

ROTHERHAM

Electorate 61 165 1979: 60 871 minor

*Crowther, J. S. (Lab)	22 236	54.3%
Middleton, C. (C)	10 523	25.7%
Bowler, P. (L/All)	8 192	20.0%
Lab majority	11 713	28.6%
Total vote 40 957		Turnout 67.0%

1979: Total vote 43 901 (72.1%); Lab 26 580 (60.5%); C 13 145 (29.9%); L 3 686 (8.4%); NF 490 (1.1%). Lab maj 13 435 (30.6%); swing 5.9% to C.

Mr Stanley Crowther was elected at a by-election Jun 1976. Member, Select Committees on Industry and Trade and European legislation since 1979. Born May 30 1925; educ. Rotherham Grammar School and Rotherham College of Technology. Journalist. Member, Rotherham Borough Council 1958–59 and 1961–76. Mayor of Rotherham 1971–72 and 1975–76; chairman planning committee 1964–76; chairman, Yorkshire and Humberside Development Assoc. 1973–76. Member, executive, Town and Country Planning Assoc. Parliamentary adviser to British Reclamation Industries Confederation. Sponsored by TGWU.
Mr Christopher Middleton, solicitor. Born Nov 4 1947; educ. Lady Manner School, Bakewell, Lanchester Polytechnic, Coventry.
Mr Peter Bowler, company representative. Aged 30. Member, Amber Valley District Council 1976; Ripley Council, Derby, 1979, Leader of the Liberal Group. Has held office at local and national level with the Liberal Party.

Mr Kevin Barron

ROTHER VALLEY

Electorate 65 127

Barron, K. (Lab)	21 781	46.5%
Derrick, J. (C)	13 156	28.1%
Boddy, J. (SDP/All)	11 903	25.4%
Lab majority	8 625	18.4%
Total vote 46 840		Turnout 71.9%

Mr Kevin Barron, a coal miner, elected in 1983. Born Oct 26 1946. President, Rotherham and District TUC. NUM delegate for Maltby colliery. Had been vice-chairman of the former Rother Valley Labour Party. Joined party nine years ago.
Mr John Derrick, publisher and journalist. Born Feb 24 1957; educ. Westminster School and Christ Church, Oxford. Director, What to Buy Ltd; joint founder and editor, *What to Buy for Business* magazine. Author of two books on telecommunications and office automation. NUJ.
Mr John Boddy, management consultant, certified accountant and chartered secretary. Aged 53; educ. LSE.

Mr Archy Kirkwood

ROXBURGH AND BERWICKSHIRE Electorate 41 702

Kirkwood, A. (L/All)	15 920	50.3%
*Sproat, I. (C)	12 524	39.6%
Briggs, D. A. (Lab)	2 326	7.4%
Shirley, R. (SNP)	852	2.7%
L / All majority	3 396	10.7%
Total vote 31 622		Turnout 75.8%

Mr Archy Kirkwood, solicitor, who won this seat in 1983, was Scottish Liberal Party spokesman on fisheries. Born Apr 22 1946; educ. Cranhill Secondary School, Glasgow, and Heriot-Watt University, Edinburgh. Battlebus tour organizer in Mr David Steel's election campaign, 1979; member, Mr Steel's staff in London 1977–78; youth campaign director, 'Britain in Europe' referendum campaign, 1975; personal aide to Mr Steel, Feb and Oct 1974.

Mr Ian Sproat, Under Secretary of State for Trade 1981–83, was MP for Aberdeen South 1970–83; contested Rutherglen by-election and general election 1964. Born Nov 8 1938; educ. Winchester and Magdalen College, Oxford. Chairman, Scottish Conservative MPs 1980–81; vice-chairman, Conservative fisheries subcommittee 1980–81; former chairman, Conservative foreign affairs committee.

Mr Robert Shirley, an economics lecturer. SNP spokesman on finance and taxation. Born Mar 1928; educ. Bearsden Academy and Glasgow University. Fought Edinburgh South 1979, and in both 1974 elections.

Mr James Pawsey

RUGBY AND KENILWORTH Electorate 74 501

*Pawsey, J. (C)	29 622	50.9%
Owen-Jones, D. (L / All)	15 381	26.4%
Blundell, P. (Lab)	13 180	22.7%
C majority	14 241	24.5%
Total vote 58 183		Turnout 78.1%

Mr James Pawsey, chairman and chief executive of a vending machine group and director of six subsidiaries, gained Rugby for Conservatives in 1979. Elected for this seat in 1983. Member, Select Committee on Environment since 1979. Born Aug 21 1933; educ. Coventry Technical School and Coventry Technical College. Former President Warwickshire Assoc. of Parish Councils. Member, Rugby Rural District Council and Rugby Borough Council 1964–74; Warwickshire County Council 1975–80. Secretary, Conservative backbench health and social services committee. PPS to Department of Education and Science.

Mr David Owen-Jones, barrister, contested Carmarthen in both 1974 elections. Born Mar 16 1949; educ. Llandovery College, University College, London. Contested Wandsworth Borough Council May 1982 election, for Alliance.

Mr Philip Blundell, a teacher, was Mayor of Rugby 1978–79. Born Aug 22 1942; educ. Lawrence Sheriff Grammar School, Rugby. Member, Warwickshire County Council since 1970; former member, Rugby Borough Council.

Mr John Wilkinson

RUISLIP, NORTHWOOD Electorate 56 378 1979: 55 505 same

*Wilkinson, J. (C)	24 498	59.6%
Stephenson, R. (L/All)	11 516	28.0%
O'Brien, M. (Lab)	5 105	12.4%
C majority	12 982	31.6%
Total vote 41 119		Turnout 72.9%

1979: Total vote 43 633 (78.6%); C 26 748 (61.3%); Lab 9 541 (21.9%); L 6 867 (15.7%); NF 477 (1.1%). C maj 17 207 (39.4%); swing 6.9% to C.

Mr John Wilkinson was elected for Hillingdon, Ruislip-Northwood 1979; MP for Bradford West 1970–Feb 1974 and contested that seat in Feb and Oct 1974. Company director and business consultant. Born Sep 1940; educ. Eton, RAF College, Cranwell, and Churchill College, Cambridge. Former flying instructor at Cranwell. ADC to Commander 2nd Allied Tactical Air Force, Germany, 1967. Member, Select Committee on Science and Technology 1972–74, and for Race Relations and Immigration 1972–74. Secretary, Conservative parliamentary aviation committee 1980–81. Chairman, Anglo-Asian Conservative Society, 1979–82; vice-chairman, Conservative aviation committee 1979 and 1983. Vice-chairman Conservative space committee 1983. Delegate to Council of Europe and WEU since 1979. PPS to Minister of State for Industry 1979–80 and PPS to Secretary of State for Defence 1981–82.

Mr Raymond Stephenson, solicitor; contested Hillingdon, Ruislip-Northwood 1979, and Holland with Boston Feb and Oct 1974. Born Jan 20 1925; educ. Horncastle Wesleyan Day School; Horncastle Grammar School; London University.

Mr Michael O'Brien is a lecturer. Born 1954.

Mr Kenneth Clarke

RUSHCLIFFE Electorate 70 333 1979: 67 286 same

*Clarke, K. (C)	33 253	61.5%
Hamilton, J. (L/All)	13 033	24.1%
Coaker, V. R. (Lab)	7 290	13.5%
Pooks, Mrs M. (Eco)	518	1.0%
C majority	20 220	37.4%
Total vote 54 094		Turnout 76.9%

1979: Total vote 54 968 (81.7%); C 34 196 (62.2%); Lab 11 712 (21.3%); L 9 000 (16;5%). C maj 22 484 (40.9%); swing 5.3% to C.

Mr Kenneth Clarke QC was appointed Minister of State for Health and Social Security (Minister for Health) in 1982. Parliamentary Secretary 1979–81 and Under Secretary of State for Transport 1981–82. An Opposition spokesman on industry 1976–79. Won the seat in 1970. An Opposition spokesman on social services 1974–76; Lord Commissioner of the Treasury (Government whip) 1974; assistant whip 1972–74. Contested Mansfield 1964 and 1966. Born Jul 2 1940; educ. Nottingham High School, Gonville and Caius College, Cambridge. Research secretary, Birmingham Bow Group 1966–67. President Cambridge Union 1963.

Mr Julian Hamilton, financial controller, contested the seat 1974 and 1979. Born Aug 29 1939.

Mr Vernon Coaker, a teacher. Aged 29. Member, Rushcliffe Borough Council. Manager of local football team.

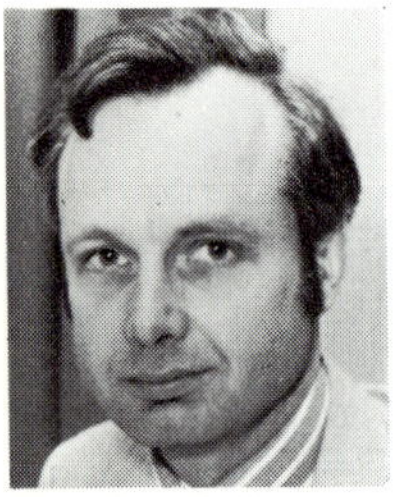

Mr Michael Latham

RUTLAND AND MELTON Electorate 75 180

*Latham, M. (C)	33 262	60.4%
Farrer, D. J. (L/All)	14 909	27.1%
Whitby, J. (Lab)	6 414	11.6%
Goddard, Ms H. A. (Eco)	532	1.0%
C majority	18 353	33.2%
Total vote 55 117		Turnout 73.3%

Mr Michael Latham was elected for Melton in Feb 1974; won this seat in 1983; contested Liverpool, West Derby 1970. Non-executive director of building firm. Born Nov 20 1942; educ. Marlborough College and King's College, Cambridge. Director and chief executive, House Builders' Federation 1971–73; parliamentary liaison officer, National Federation of Building Trades Employers, 1967–73. Vice-chairman, Conservative parliamentary housing committee 1974–76 and of Conservative parliamentary environment committee since 1979. Secretary, Conservative backbench countryside conservation committee since 1977. Vice-president, Building Societies Assoc. since 1981. Westminster city councillor 1968–71. Chairman, Conservative Friends of Israel since 1982, and of British-Israel parliamentary group.

Mr David Farrer, barrister, contested Melton 1979. Born Mar 15 1943; educ. Queen Elizabeth's Grammar School, Barnet and Downing College, Cambridge.

Mr John Whitby, general manager. Born Dec 21 1945; educ. Moat Boys' School, Leicester; Gateway Grammar School, Leicester. Borough councillor since 1980; leader, Labour group. Oadby and Wigston council. National Council for Civil Liberties. Nalgo.

Mr John Spence

RYDALE Electorate 78 388

*Spence, J. (C)	33 312	59.2%
Shields, Mrs E. (L/All)	17 170	30.5%
Bloom, P. (Lab)	5 816	10.3%
C majority	16 142	28.7%
Total vote 56 298		Turnout 71.8%

Mr John Spence has been a member of the Select Committee on Agriculture since 1979; member, Conservative backbench industry committee; former secretary. Member, Speaker's panel of chairmen; vice-chairman (1980–81) and secretary (1972–79) of the Yorkshire group of Conservative MPs. Was returned for Thirsk and Malton in Feb 1974 won this seat in 1983; represented Sheffield, Heeley 1970–74; contested that seat 1966 and Wakefield 1964. Civil engineering contractor with own construction business. Born Dec 7 1920; educ. Queen's University, Belfast. Member, Select Committee on Nationalized Industries 1974–79.

Mrs Elizabeth Shields, teacher, contested Howden 1979. Born Feb 27 1928; educ. Whyteleafe Girls' Grammar School, Avery Hill College of Education and University College, London. Member, Ryedale District Council since 1979.

Mr Philip Bloom, lecturer in law at Hull College of Further Education. Born Oct 28 1953; educ. Hull Grammar School, Newcastle Polytechnic and Hull University. Member, Hull City Council, since 1979; chairman of finance committee.

Mr Alan Haselhurst

SAFFRON WALDEN Electorate 69385 1979: 65034 same

*Haselhurst, A. (C)	30869	57.9%
Torode, J. (SDP/All)	15620	29.3%
Trory, R. P. (Lab)	6078	11.4%
Smedley, W. D. (ACM)	797	1.5%
C majority	15249	28.6%
Total vote 53364		Turnout 76.9%

1979: Total vote 53077 (81.6%); C 28563%); L 13200 (24.9%); Lab 10547 (19.9%); Ind 425 (0.8%); NF 342 (0.6%). C maj 15363 (28.9%); swing 8.1% to C.

Mr Alan Haselhurst was returned at the by-election in Jul 1977. Captured Middleton and Prestwich for Conservatives in 1970 but lost seat to Labour in Feb 1974. Government affairs consultant to Albright & Wilson Ltd. Born Jun 23 1937; educ. King Edward VI School, Birmingham, Cheltenham College and Oriel College, Oxford (President, University Conservative Assoc. and secretary, treasury, and librarian of the Union). Chairman, Young Conservatives National Advisory Committee 1966–68. Member, Select Committee on European Legislation.

Mr John Torode, political journalist, is a founder member of the SDP. Educ. Oxford, Cornell University, New York and Harvard School of Business. Recently worked in India as a UN consultant advising on co-operative dairy farming and marketing. In the 1970s, a member of the Government Committee on Privacy, which advised on press behaviour and the protection of personal files.

Mr Robert Trory, a musician, has been a violinist at the Royal Opera House, Covent Garden, for eight years. Born 1945; educ. in Brighton and Trinity College, London, for which he won a scholarship. Played in the youth side at Brighton and Hove Albion FC.

Mr Peter Lilley

ST ALBANS Electorate 72849

Lilley, P. (C)	29676	52.1%
Walkington, A. S. B. (L / All)	21115	37.0%
Austin, Mrs R. (Lab)	6213	10.9%
C majority	8561	15.0%
Total vote 57004		Turnout 78.3%

Mr Peter Lilley, an investment adviser specialising in North Sea oil and other energy industries, was elected in 1983; contested Haringey, Tottenham, Oct 1974. Born 1946; educ. Dulwich College and Clare College, Cambridge. Twice chairman, Bow Group; cofounder, German Bow Group 1974. Member, Carlton Club. Fellow, Institution of Petroleum since 1978.

Mr Sandy Walkington, press officer in oil industry, and barrister, formerly worked in House of Commons as head of research to the Parliamentary Liberal Party. Born Dec 5 1953; educ. Cheltenham College; Trinity Hall, Cambridge; College of Law, London (Grays Inn); Tulne University, New Orleans. Coordinator, media relations, Texaco Ltd.

Mrs Rita Austin, the Labour Party's first black woman candidate, is the daughter of a Calcutta judge. Director, Development Services, Council for National Academic Awards. Born Nov 19 1940; educ. Universities of Birmingham and Wales. NATFHE.

Mr John Evans

ST HELENS NORTH Electorate 71059

*Evans, J. (Lab)	25334	47.9%
Rhodes, A. (C)	16075	30.4%
Derbyshire, N. (L/All)	11525	21.8%
Lab majority	9259	17.5%
Total vote 52934		Turnout 74.5%

Mr John Evans was elected to the Labour Party National Executive Committee in 1982. PPS to Mr Michael Foot 1980–83. Assistant Government Whip 1979. Elected for this seat 1983; represented Newton Feb 1974–83. Member, European Parliament 1975–79 and chairman of its regional policy and transport committee 1976–79. Former member, Public Accounts Committee. Fitter. Born Oct 19 1930; educ. Jarrow Central School, Member, Hebburn Urban District Council 1962–74, chairman 1972–73, leader 1969–74, and of South Tyneside Metropolitan District Council 1973–74. Sponsored by AUEW.

Mr Anthony Rhodes, technical sales engineer. Born Aug 1 1943; educ. Sale Moor Secondary Modern School and Stretford Technical College. Member, Trafford Borough Council 1975–1979; chairman social services committee 1978–79.

Mr Neil Derbyshire, lecturer. Born Oct 18 1951; educ. Huddersfield and Liverpool Polytechnics.

Mr Gerald Bermingham

ST HELENS SOUTH Electorate 69 172

Bermingham, G. (Lab)	22 906	46.9%
Bull, R. (C)	13 244	27.1%
Briers, P. (SDP/All)	10 939	22.4%
Davies, M. (Ind)	1 780	3.6%
Lab majority	9 662	19.8%
Total vote 48 869	Turnout	70.7%

Mr Gerald Bermingham, a solicitor, was elected in 1983; fought Derbyshire South East 1979. Born Aug 20 1940; educ. Cotton College, Wellingborough Grammar School, Sheffield University. Member, Sheffield City Council 1975–79; 1980–82. APEX. TGWU.

Mr Richard Bull, a chartered accountant. Born Feb 26 1949; educ. grammar school and Kent University. Chairman, Greater London Conservative Political Centre; former chairman, Greater London Young Conservatives.

Mr Philip Briers is an electrical design engineer. Former assistant secretary, St Helens Labour Party. Born May 28 1948. Member, St Helens Metropolitan Borough Council since 1978; former chairman, education committee.

Mr David Harris

ST IVES Electorate 64 012

Harris, D. (C)	24 297	51.4%
Carter, H. (SDP/All)	16 438	34.8%
Crowley, Ms M. (Lab)	5 310	11.2%
Prior, P. (MK)	569	1.2%
Hoptrough, H. (Eco)	439	0.9%
Horner, N. (Ind)	219	0.5%
C majority	7 859	16.6%
Total vote 47 272	Turnout	73.9%

Mr David Harris, journalist and member of European Parliament for Cornwall and Plymouth since 1979. Contested Mitcham and Morden Feb 1974. Born Nov 1 1937; educ. Mount Radford School, Exeter. Conservative spokesman in European Parliament on regional policy. Member, GLC 1968–77, and chairman of council's Thamesmead Committee. Worked for *The Daily Telegraph* at Westminster 1961–79, being chief political correspondent, 1976–79. Founder editor *European Conservative*. NUJ.

Mr Harold Carter, management consultant. Born Feb 6 1952; educ. Caius College, Cambridge (President of the Union 1974), Nuffield College, Oxford and INSEAD, Fontainbleau. Chairman of Wakeham Trust. Vice-chairman, Young Fabians, 1976.

Ms Mary Crowley is a single parent, aged 42. Member, South West Regional Labour Women's Committee; CND; parent-teacher assoc.

Mr Stanley Orme

SALFORD EAST Electorate 63 946

*Orme, S. (Lab)	21 373	53.7%
Cole, S. (C)	11 832	29.7%
Williams, A. (SDP/All)	6 190	15.6%
Carter, S. (WRP)	417	1.1%
Lab majority	9 541	24.0%
Total vote 39 812	Turnout	62.3%

Mr Stanley Orme, member of Shadow Cabinet since 1979. Elected for this seat 1983; represented Salford West 1964–83. Chief Opposition spokesman on industry since 1981, and chief Opposition spokesman on social security, 1979–81. Minister for Social Security, with a seat in the Cabinet, 1976–79; Minister of State, Department of Health and Social Security, 1976; Minister of State for Northern Ireland, 1972–74. Contested Stockport South 1959. Engineer. Born Apr 5 1923; educ. elementary and technical schools, National Councils of Labour Colleges and Workers' Education Assoc. classes. Member, Sale Borough Council 1958–64. Sponsored by AUEW, engineering section; shop steward, branch president for 21 years. Chairman of AUEW parliamentary group of MPs, and of Northern Ireland PLP group.

Mr Simon Cole, teacher and writer. Born Jul 4 1949; educ. Hamonds Grammar School, Swaffham, and Salford University. NUJ.

Mr Adrian Williams, religious education and pastoral care tutor in Moss Side, Manchester. Born Sep 23 1957; educ. Manchester University. Methodist church worker.

Mr Robert Key

SALISBURY Electorate 74 189

Key, R. (C)	28 876	53.5%
Lakeman, J. (L/All)	21 702	40.2%
Lamberth, Mrs C. K. (Lab)	3 139	5.8%
Kemp, Miss M. (W Reg)	182	0.3%
Abbott, T. (Ind)	86	0.2%
C majority	7 174	13.3%
Total vote 53 985		Turnout 72.8%

Mr Robert Key, teacher, was elected in 1983; contested Camden, Holborn and St Pancras South, 1979. Born Apr 22 1945; educ. Sherborne School and Clare College, Cambridge. Former chairman, Harrow Central Conservatives; member, national union executive.
Mr John Lakeman, proprietor of bookshop and printing firm and former teacher; contested Salisbury Feb and Oct 1974 and 1979. Born Dec 17 1947; educ. Bishop Wordsworth School, Salisbury and Exeter University.
Mrs Celia Lamberth, a Wiltshire county and district councillor. Born Nov 22 1946; educ. secondary school.

Sir Michael Shaw

SCARBOROUGH Electorate 72 362

*Shaw, Sir M. (C)	27 977	54.3%
Jordan, Mrs R. (SDP/All)	14 048	27.2%
Battersby, J. (Lab)	9 545	18.5%
C majority	13 929	27.0%
Total vote 51 570		Turnout 71.3%

Sir Michael Shaw, a chartered accountant, was elected in Feb 1974. Member, European Parliament, 1974–79. Represented Scarborough and Whitby, 1966–74, and Brighouse and Spenborough, 1960–64. Contested latter seat in 1959 and Dewsbury, 1955. Born Oct 9 1920; educ. Sedbergh. Member, Select Committees on Members' Salaries, since 1981, Members' Interests, since 1979, and Public Accounts, since 1979; member, Speaker's Panel of Chairman since 1981. Chairman, Yorkshire area Conservatives, 1965–66 and since 1972. Vice-chairman, Conservative trade and industry committee 1967–74.
Mrs Rosamund Jordan, teacher and art dealer. Born Apr 25 1943; educ. Grangefield Grammar School for Girls, Stockton, Darlington College of Education, and Open University. Treasurer, Stockton Young Liberals, 1961–63; independent member Stockton Rural District Council, 1970–74; former organizer South Durham and Cleveland area, National Association for Gifted Children.
Mr John Battersby is an organizer with CAB. Born 1947.

Mr Anthony Blair

SEDGEFIELD Electorate 61 702

Blair, A. C. L. (Lab)	21 401	47.6%
Horton, T. (C)	13 120	29.2%
Shand, D. (SDP/All)	10 183	22.6%
Logan-Salton, M. (Ind)	298	0.7%
Lab majority	8 281	18.4%
Total vote 45 002		Turnout 72.9%

Mr Anthony Blair, barrister, won the seat in 1983. Born May 6 1953; educ. Oxford University. Practising barrister specializing in trade union and industrial law. Contested Beaconsfield by-election, May 1982. TGWU.
Mr Toby Horton, managing director of Radio Tees, farmer and former merchant banker. Born 1947; educ. Christ Church, Oxford. Fellow, British Institute of Management and member of northern board; chairman, finance committee, Assoc. of Independent Radio Contractors. Treasurer, Stockton YMCA. NFU.
Mr David Shand, assistant recreation officer for Easington District Council. Born 1943; educ. Barnsley Holgate Grammar School and Nottingham College of Education. Former chairman, Easington branch of Nalgo and still branch executive member.

Mr Michael Alison

SELBY Electorate 65 365

*Alison, M. (C)	26 712	56.7%
Whitaker, W. (L/All)	10 747	22.8%
Haines, Mrs S. (Lab)	9 687	20.6%
C majority	15 965	33.9%
Total vote 47 146	Turnout 72.1%	

Mr Michael Alison, Minister of State Department of Employment 1981–83; appointed PPS to the Prime Minister Jun 1983. Minister of State for Northern Ireland 1979–81. An Opposition spokesman on environment 1978–79 and on Home Affairs 1975–78. MP for Barkston Ash, 1964–83. Returned for this seat, 1983. Under-Secretary for Health and Social Security 1970–74. Born Jun 1926; educ. Eton, Wadham College, Oxford and Ridley Hall, Cambridge. Member, Expenditure committee, 1974–75; Kensington Borough Council, 1956–59. Research officer, foreign section of Conservative research department 1958–64.

Mr Wilfred Whitaker, lecturer, contested Keighley Feb 1974, Normanton Oct 1974, and Barnsley 1979. Born Jan 1 1946; educ. Morley Grammar School, Hull University and Huddersfield Polytechnic. NATFHE.

Mrs Shirley Haines, health visitor (SRN). Born May 7 1939; educ. Newland High School, Hull; Hammersmith Hospital and Surrey University. Member, North Yorkshire County Council; York City Council, since 1983. NUPE, shop steward for two years.

Mr Mark Wolfson

SEVENOAKS Electorate 71 327

*Wolfson, M. (C)	30 722	58.4%
Jakobi, S. (L/All)	15 016	28.6%
Gooding, R. (Lab)	6 439	12.2%
Burnett, G. L. (NF)	416	0.8%
C majority	15 706	29.9%
Total vote 52 593	Turnout 73.7%	

Mr Mark Wolfson, personnel director with a merchant bank, was elected in 1979, contested Islington North Feb 1974 and City of Westminster, Paddington Oct 1974. Born Apr 7 1934; educ. Eton and Pembroke College, Cambridge. Member, Select Committee on Members' Salaries 1981–82; joint secretary, Conservative backbench committee on employment since 1982. Member, Parliamentary delegation to Nicaragua, 1982. Worked for Canadian Pacific Railway for two years and as a teacher in an Indian reservation in British Columbia. Three years as head of Brathay Hall Centre in the Lake District. London Borough of Wandsworth councillor for three years.

Mr Stephen Jakobi, partner in firm of solicitors, previously contested Battersea North, Windsor and Maidenhead. Born Mar 13 1935. Chairman, Liberal Party's race relations panel.

Mr Roland Gooding is a science teacher at a school for the handicapped at Westerham. Born 1954; educ. Newton Abbott and Rolle College, Exmouth. President, Kent Assoc. NUT.

Mr Patrick Duffy

SHEFFIELD, ATTERCLIFFE Electorate 64 203

*Duffy, A. E. P. (Lab)	23 067	51.5%
Millward, G. (C)	11 455	25.6%
Addison, Ms I. (SDP / All)	10 241	22.9%
Lab majority	11 612	25.9%
Total vote 44 763	Turnout 69.7%	

Mr Patrick Duffy, an Opposition spokesman on defence in 1983 and 1979–81; Under Secretary, Defence (Royal Navy) 1976–79. Returned 1970; MP for Colne Valley 1963–66; contested Tiverton 1955, 1951 and 1950. Economist and consultant. Born Jun 17 1920; educ. London and Columbia Universities. Chairman PLP economic affairs and finance group 1965–66 and in 1974, chairman, trade and industry sub committee; member, Select Committee on Public Expenditure 1970–76 and Vice-Chairman, PLP Northern Ireland Group 1974. PPS to Secretary of State Defence 1974–76. Vice-Chairman PLP Defence Group since 1981; Vice-Chairman PLP Northern Ireland Group since 1982. Sponsored by GMWU.

Mr Gordon Millward, company director. Born Sep 14 1946; educ. Birley Secondary School. Member, South Yorkshire County Council. TGWU.

Ms Irene Addison is a deputy head teacher who has been national coach to the British paraplegic fencing team. Born Mar 3 1943; educ. Glasgow High School for Girls; Elgin Academy; Andrew's University.

Miss Joan Maynard

SHEFFIELD, BRIGHTSIDE Electorate 67 260

*Maynard, Miss J. (Lab)	25 531	58.0%
Butler, F. (L/All)	10 322	23.4%
Grayson, D. (C)	7 888	17.9%
Spinks, P. A. (NF)	286	0.7%
Lab majority	15 209	34.5%
Total vote 44 027		Turnout 65.5%

Miss Joan Maynard, member, Select Committee on Agriculture, since 1979, and of the Labour Party National Executive Committee since 1972. Elected Oct 1974. Yorkshire area secretary, National Union of Agricultural and Allied Workers for 22 years, former president; union's only sponsored MP. Born Jul 5 1921; educ. Ampleforth C of E all-age village school. Member, PLP agricultural and education groups. Vice-president, Rural District Councils Assoc.

Mr Francis Butler, college lecturer. Born May 4 1941; educ. Owler Lane Secondary School and Sheffield Art School.

Mr David Grayson, manager of a local enterprise agency. Born May 26 1955; educ. Mount St Mary's College, Sheffield, Downing College, Cambridge, Free University of Brussels. Secretary-General, Democratic Youth Community of Europe. Former chairman, UK Young European Democrats. Member, Amnesty International and Northern Magic Circle.

Mr Richard Caborn

SHEFFIELD CENTRAL Electorate 66 769

Caborn, R. (Lab)	24 759	60.2%
Major, Miss P. (SDP/All)	7 969	19.4%
Rawlings, Ms P. (C)	7 908	19.2%
Gill, Miss V. (Com)	296	0.7%
Barrett, C. (Rev Com)	226	0.5%
Lab majority	16 790	40.8%
Total vote 41 158		Turnout 61.6%

Mr Richard Caborn, member of European Parliament for Sheffield since 1979, was elected in 1983. Born Oct 6 1943; educ. Hurlfield Comprehensive School, Sheffield, Granville College of Further Education, and Sheffield Polytechnic. Convenor of shop stewards, Firth Brown Ltd, 1967–79; vice-president, Sheffield Trades Council.

Dr Patricia Major, university lecturer in pharmacology. Born Mar 17 1936; educ. Cheadle Hulme School and Sheffield University. AUT.

Ms Patricia Rawlings, director of textile company 1971–82. Born 1939; educ. Oak Hall, Haslemere, and London University.

Sir John Osborn

SHEFFIELD, HALLAM Electorate 72 878

*Osborn, Sir J. (C)	26 851	50.6%
Johnson, M. (L/All)	15 077	28.4%
McCrindle, Ms J. (Lab)	10 463	19.7%
Booler, P. (Ind C)	656	1.2%
C majority	11 774	22.2%
Total vote 53 047		Turnout 72.8%

Sir John Osborn, a former steel works director was elected 1959. Member, European Parliament, 1975–79. Joint Secretary, 1922 Committee since 1968; vice-chairman, Science and Technology Committee, and chairman, joint committee for scientific cooperation of the Council of Europe. Member Education, Science and Arts Select Committee since 1979; member, Science and Technology Select Committee 1970–72; chairman, Conservative transport industries committee 1970–74. Chairman, British Soviet parliamentary group and Anglo-Swiss parliamentary group. Searcher of Cutler's Company since 1951. Born Dec 14 1922; educ. Rugby and Trinity Hall, Cambridge.

Mr Malcolm Johnson, works manager, contested Sheffield, Hallam twice in 1974 and Sheffield, Brightside 1979. Born Jan 3 1928; educ. Aireborough Grammar School and Leeds College of Technology. Member, Sheffield Metropolitan Council.

Ms Jean McCrindle, lecturer. Born Apr 24 1937; educ. Highbury Hill High School, London; St Andrews University. NATFHE and ASTMS.

Mr William Michie

SHEFFIELD, HEELEY Electorate 74 659

Michie, W. (Lab)	24 111	45.8%
Cordle, S. (C)	15 743	29.9%
Day, J. M. (SDP/All)	12 813	24.3%
Lab majority	8 368	15.9%
Total vote 52 667	Turnout 70.5%	

Mr William Michie, unemployed laboratory technician, became redundant in 1981, and was elected for this seat in 1983. Born Nov 24 1935; educ. Abbeydale Secondary School, Sheffield. Sheffield city councillor since 1970 and South Yorkshire county councillor since 1974 (chairman of area planning). As city councillor he was chairman of planning, 1974–81, and chairman of employment 1981–83. AUEW (former shop steward).

Mr Sidney Cordle, insurance agent. Born 1956; educ. Theale Grammar School, Berkshire, and Sheffield University.

Mr John Day, personnel manager. Born Jan 29 1946; educ. Roundhay School, Leeds; Kent and Bradford universities. Worked in management for British Telecom, British Tissues (Yorks) and Brentford Nylons.

Mr Martin Flannery

SHEFFIELD, HILLSBOROUGH Electorate 74 422

*Flannery, M. (Lab)	20 901	37.2%
Chadwick, D. (L/All)	19 355	34.5%
Smith, Mrs C. (C)	15 881	28.3%
Lab majority	1 546	2.8%
Total vote 56 137	Turnout 75.4%	

Mr Martin Flannery, a former head teacher, has been a member of the Select Committee on Education, Science and Arts since 1981. Elected Feb 1974. Born Mar 2 1918; educ. De La Salle Grammar School and Sheffield Teaching Training College. Parliamentary consultant. Chairman PLP education and science group. Former secretary, PLP Chile group. Former chairman, Tribune Group. Sponsored by ASTMS. NUT.

Mr David Chadwick, lecturer, contested Penistone in 1979, 1978 by-election, and twice in 1974; Blackpool South 1970; Nelson and Colne by-election 1968. Born Sep 2 1939; educ. Blackpool College of Art and Technology, Bolton College of Education. Member, South Yorkshire County Council since 1981; Sheffield City Council since 1976. NATFHE, branch chairman at Rotherham.

Mrs Christine Smith, legal secretary. Born Jan 31 1944; educ. Darnall Church of England School, Richmond College of Further Education. Member, North-East Derbyshire District council, 1976–79; Sheffield City Council since 1979. Associate member, CTU.

Mr Andrew Stewart

SHERWOOD Electorate 69 091

Stewart, A. (C)	21 595	41.0%
Bach, W. (Lab)	20 937	39.7%
Cooper, Mrs M. E. (SDP/All)	10 172	19.3%
C majority	658	1.3%
Total vote 52 704	Turnout 76.3%	

Mr Andrew Stewart, was returned for this seat in 1983. Born 1937; educ. Strathaven Academy, Lanark, and West of Scotland Agricultural College. Member, Nottinghamshire County Council since 1974.

Mr William Bach, a barrister, contested Gainsborough in 1979. Born Dec 1946; educ. Oxford University. Former member, Leicester City Council. Member, Co-operative Party.

Mrs Margaret Cooper, housewife. Born Jun 18 1938; educ. Westholme School, Blackburn, and Huyton College, Liverpool.

Mr Marcus Fox

SHIPLEY Electorate 67 584

*Fox, J. M. (C)	25 866	49.7%
Wallace, W. (L/All)	14 421	27.7%
Leathley, M. A. (Lab)	11 218	21.6%
Shepherd, S. (Eco)	521	1.0%
C majority	11 445	22.0%
Total vote 52 026	Turnout 77.0%	

Mr Marcus Fox was Under Secretary of State for the Environment 1979–81; Opposition spokesman on transport 1975–76; on the environment 1974, and on housing 1974–75; assistant whip 1972–73; Lord Commissioner of the Treasury (whip) 1973–74. Elected in 1970; contested Dewsbury 1959 and Huddersfield West 1966. Born Jun 11 1927; educ. Wheelwright Grammar School, Dewsbury. Member, Select Committee on Members' Salaries, 1981–82; Select Committee on Race Relations and Immigration 1970–72. A Conservative Party vice-chairman with responsibility for candidates 1976–79. Company director. Member, executive, 1922 committee.

Mr William Wallace, director of studies, Royal Institute of International Affairs. Born Mar 12 1941. Educ. St Edward's School, Oxford; Cambridge University; Cornell University, US. Contested Huddersfield West 1970, Manchester Moss Side Feb and Oct 1974.

Mr Martin Leathley, teacher. Born Oct 3 1939; educ. Skipton Grammar School, Keighley Technical College, Alnwick College of Education. Member, West Yorkshire County Council. NUT.

Mr Richard Luce

SHOREHAM Electorate 69 720

*Luce, R. (C)	31 679	61.7%
Ingram, J. (L/All)	15 913	31.0%
Hurcombe, Mrs S. J. (Lab)	3 794	7.4%
C majority	15 766	30.7%
Total vote 51 386	Turnout 73.7%	

Mr Richard Luce resigned in Apr 1982 as Minister of State for Foreign and Commonwealth Affairs (a post he had held since 1981) over Argentina's invasion of the Falkland Islands. Reappointed Minister of State, Foreign and Commonwealth Office Jun 1983. Under Secretary of State for Foreign and Commonwealth Affairs 1979–81; an Opposition spokesman on foreign and Commonwealth affairs 1977–79; Opposition whip 1974–75. PPS to Sir G. Howe when Minister for Trade and Consumer Affairs 1972–74. Elected for Arundel and Shoreham at by-election 1971 and for Shoreham in Feb 1974; contested Hitchin 1970. Born Oct 14 1936; educ. Wellington College, Christ's College, Cambridge, and Wadham College, Oxford.

Mr Julian Ingram, advertising executive and former director of travel company. Born Apr 17 1956; educ. Worthing Grammar School, Worthing Sixth Form College and the LSE. Helped research biography on Mr David Steel.

Ms Sylvia Hurcombe is a teacher. Born 1938.

Mr Derek Conway

SHREWSBURY AND ATCHAM Electorate 66 554 1979: 63 236 same

Conway, D. (C)	24 397	49.5%
Bowen, A. (L/All)	15 773	32.0%
Mosley, A. (Lab)	9 080	18.4%
C majority	8 624	17.5%
Total vote 49 250	Turnout 74.0%	

1979 (as Shrewsbury): Total vote 48 470 (76.6%); C 23 548 (48.6%); L 13 364 (27.6%); Lab Co-op 11 558 (23.8%). C maj 10 184 (21.0%); swing 3.8% to C.

Mr Derek Conway, director, was elected in 1983. Born Feb 15 1953; educ. Beacon Hill Boys' School. Contested Newcastle upon Tyne East 1979; Durham Oct 1974. National vice-chairman, Young Conservatives 1973–75; member, Conservative party national executive 1972–81. Member Tyne and Wear Metropolitan County Council 1977–83 (leader 1979–82); borough councillor 1974–77.

Mr Anthony Bowen, teacher. Born May 17 1940; educ. Bradfield and St John's College, Cambridge. Member, Shropshire County Council.

Mr Alan Mosley is a lecturer at Shrewsbury College of Art and Technology. Born Oct 30 1947; educ. Langton High School, Stoke-on-Trent, Salford Univ-ersty and Middlesex and Huddersfield polytechnics. Member, Shrewsbury and Atcham Council since 1978. Branch and county secretary, NATFHE.

Mr John Biffen

SHROPSHIRE NORTH Electorate 73 333

*Biffen, W. J. (C)	28 496	53.4%
Evans, D. (L/All)	16 829	31.6%
Jones, Miss H. (Lab)	7 860	14.7%
Phillimore, J. L. (Oth)	135	0.3%
C majority	11 667	21.9%
Total vote 53 320		Turnout 72.7%

Mr John Biffen, appointed Lord Pivy Seal and Leader of the House of Commons Jun 1983; Lord President of the Council and Leader of the Commons 1982–83; Secretary of State for Trade 1981–82; Chief Secretary to the Treasury, with a seat in the Cabinet 1979–81; chief Opposition spokesman on energy and industry 1976–77. In Nov 1978, appointed spokesman on small businesses and self-employed. Won this seat in 1983; represented Oswestry 1961–83; contested Coventry East 1959. Economist. Born Nov 3 1930; educ. Dr Morgan's Grammar School, Bridgwater; Jesus College, Cambridge. Former member Select Committee on Procedure, Public Accounts Committee; Select Committee on Nationalized Industries. With Economist Intelligence Unit 1960–61; Tube Investments Ltd 1953–60.

Mr David Evans, lecturer, contested Wallasey 1970, and Oswestry Feb and Oct 1974 and 1979. Born Feb 28 1947; educ. Teignmouth Grammar School and Liverpool University. NATFHE.

Miss Helen Jones. Born 1954; educ. Chester College; University College, London; Liverpool University. Fabian Societv. NAS / UWT.

Mr John Watson

SKIPTON AND RIPON Electorate 69 421

*Watson, J. (C)	31 509	60.6%
Brooks, Mrs K. C. (L / All)	16 463	31.7%
Billing, Ms M. A. (Lab)	4 044	7.8%
C majority	15 046	28.0%
Total vote 52 016		Turnout 74.9%

Mr John Watson director of printing and packaging company, also qualified as a solicitor. MP for Skipton 1979–83; won seat in 1983; contested York in Feb and Oct 1974. Born 1943; educ. Bootham School, York and the College of Law, Guildford. Member, Select Committee on Energy, 1979–82. PPS to Secretary of State for Northern Ireland since 1982. Personal assistant to Mr Edward Heath during 1970 election campaign. Joined Young Conservatives in 1961 and has held office at all levels; national chairman in 1971. Member, Law Society, Institute of Arbitrators, and of Lloyd's.

Mrs Claire Brooks, solicitor, contested the seat 1959, 1974 and 1979. Born Jun 20 1931; educ. Settle Girls High School, Skipton Girls High School and University College, London.

Ms Margaret Billing, housewife and former library assistant. Born Jan 20 1938; educ. Manea Primary School, March High School for Girls, and Nottingham University.

Mr John Watts

SLOUGH Electorate 71 907

Watts, J. (C)	22 064	42.9%
*Lestor, Miss J. (Lab)	18 958	36.9%
Bosanquet, N. (SDP / All)	9 519	18.5%
John, G. (NF)	528	1.0%
Flindall, I. (Eco)	325	0.6%
C majority	3 106	6.0%
Total vote 51 394		Turnout 71.5%

Mr John Watts, leader of Hillingdon borough council since 1978; former leader, and deputy leader of the Opposition; council member since 1973. Won the seat for the Conservatives 1983. Chartered accountant. Born Apr 19 1947; educ. Bishopshalt School, Hillingdon; Caius College, Cambridge. Former chairman, Cambridge University Conservative Assoc. Chairman, Uxbridge Conservative Assoc. 1973–76. Member, Council of Brunel University, Uxbridge, and of Hillingdon health authority.

Miss Joan Lestor, Opposition spokesman on women's rights and welfare 1981–83. Chairman Labour Party, 1977–78; vice-chairman, 1976–77; member national executive committee, 1967–82. Under Secretary for Education and Science Oct 1969–70 and 1975–76; resigned in protest at public spending cuts. Under Secretary, Foreign and Commonwealth Office 1974–75. Won the seat for Labour in 1966; contested Lewisham West 1964. Teacher. Born Nov 13 1931; educ. Blaenavon Secondary School, Monmouth, William Morris High School, Walthamstow, and London University. Member, former Select Committee on Race Relations and Immigration; Wandsworth Council 1957–68; LCC 1963–65. Chairman, PLP, Southern Africa subcommittee, 1977–78. NUGMW.

Mr Nicholas Bosanquet is a lecturer at the City University. Born 1942; educ. Winchester, Clare College, Cambridge and the LSE. Member, Camden

Council 1974–82; chairman management committee for a MIND hostel. Former economic adviser to the National Board for Prices and Incomes and to the Royal Commission on the Distribution of Income and Wealth. Member, SDP urban policy and housing working parties.

Mr John M. Taylor

SOLIHULL Electorate 73 677

Taylor, J. M. (C)	31 947	60.8%
Gillett, I. (L/All)	14 553	27.7%
Jamieson, I. (Lab)	6075	11.6%
C majority	17 394	33.1%
Total vote 52 575	Turnout	71.4%

Mr John M. Taylor, solicitor, consultant and company director, has been MEP for the East Midlands since 1979. Elected for this seat in 1983. Deputy Chairman, Conservative group European Parliament 1981–82; Conservative EEC budget spokesman 1979–81. Born Aug 19 1941; educ. Bromsgrove School. Contested Dudley East Feb and Oct 1974. Member, Solihull County Borough Council, 1971–74, and West Midlands County Council since 1973 (Leader, 1977–79).

Mr Ian Gillett, metallurgist, contested the seat 1979. Born Mar 9 1943; educ. at polytechnic. TASS.

Mr Robert Boscawen

SOMERTON AND FROME Electorate 64 695

*Boscawen, R. (C)	26 988	54.4%
Hinton, N. (SDP/All)	17 761	35.8%
Osborn, J. B. (Lab)	4867	9.8%
C majority	9227	18.6%
Total vote 49 616	Turnout	76.7%

Mr Robert Boscawen was MP for Wells 1970–83; won this seat in 1983. Appointed Vice-Chamberlain of Household (whip) 1983; Lord Commissioner of the Treasury (whip) 1981–83; assistant Government whip 1979–81. Contested Falmouth and Camborne 1966 and 1964. Lloyd's underwriter. Born Mar 17 1923; educ. Eton and Trinity College, Cambridge. Former member, Select Committee on Expenditure and its employment and social services subcommittee. Former vice-chairman, Conservative health and social security committee. Member, London Executive Council, National Health Service 1956–65.

Mr Nicholas Hinton, is director of the National Council for Voluntary Organizations. Born 1942; educ. Marlborough College, and the universities of Cambridge and Leeds. Former director of NACRO. Trustee of the Charities Aid Foundation. Member, National Committee Electoral Reform Society. Fellow of the Royal Society of Arts. Member National Urban Policy and Health and Social Services Policy Groups. Chairman, City of London and Westminster South Constituency Group.

Mr Jeffrey Osborn is a lecturer in further education at Trowbridge Technical College. Served with Special Air Service Regiment. Born 1942; educ. elementary, evening classes, Lancaster University and Bolton College of Education. Member, executive committee, Wiltshire Assoc. of Trades Councils. Town councillor. Member, Socialist Environmental Resources Assoc. Civic Society, Trowbridge.

Mr Christopher Chope

SOUTHAMPTON, ITCHEN Electorate 72 233

Chope, C. (C)	21 937	41.5%
*Mitchell, R. (SDP/All)	16 647	31.5%
Denham, J. (Lab)	14 324	27.1%
C majority	5290	10.0%
Total vote 52 908	Turnout	73.3%

Mr Christopher Chope, elected in 1983; has been leader of Wandsworth borough council 1979–83; member since 1974. Barrister. Born May 19 1947; educ. Marlborough College; Dundee and St Andrew's universities.

Mr Richard Mitchell won the seat in the 1971 by-election, being Labour MP until 1981 when he resigned party and joined the SDP. MP for Southampton, Test, 1966–70, having unsuccessfully contested it in 1964, and New Forest 1959. Member, European Parliament 1975–79. Former chairman, PLP education committee. Member, Select Committee on Education and Science, 1968–70. Member, chairman's panel. House of Commons 1979–83. Former deputy headmaster. Born Aug 22 1927; educ. Godalming Grammar School and Southampton University. Member, Southampton City Council 1955–67.

Mr John Denham, youth worker. Born 1953; educ. comprehensive school and Southampton University. Hampshire county councillor since 1981. TGWU (ACTSS).

Mr James Hill

SOUTHAMPTON, TEST   Electorate 74 668

*Hill, J. A. (C)	24 657	45.2%
Whitehead, A. P. V. (Lab)	15 311	28.1%
Vinson, A. (SDP/All)	14 592	26.7%
C majority	9 346	17.1%
Total vote 54 560	Turnout	73.1%

Mr James Hill, a director of two family private companies, regained the seat for Conservatives in 1979; he held seat 1970–Oct 1974. Member, Select Committees on European Legislation and on Industry and Trade, since 1979. Born Dec 1926; educ. Regents Park School, Southampton, North Wales Naval Training College and Southampton University. Member, Select committee on Expenditure 1972–73; secretary, Conservative backbench committee on housing and construction 1971–73. Secretary, industry committee 1979–81 and British Sri Lanka group. Member, European Parliament 1973–75, being chairman of its committee for regional policy and transport. Government whip council of Europe and Western European Union.

Mr Alan Whitehead contested New Forest 1979. Born Sep 1950; educ. Isleworth Grammar school, Southampton University. Deputy director, Outset, a charity assisting disabled. Southampton councillor. ASTMS.

Mr Adrian Vinson, university lecturer in modern history. Born Jan 14 1943; educ. Plymouth College and Gonville and Caius College, Cambridge. AUT.

Mr Edward Taylor

SOUTHEND EAST   Electorate 57 690   1979: 57 037   same

*Taylor, E. M. (C)	21 743	55.8%
George, C. (SDP/All)	11 052	28.4%
O'Brien, C. O. (Lab)	6 188	15.9%
C majority	10 691	27.4%
Total vote 38 983	Turnout	67.6%

1979: Total vote 39 972 (70.1%); C 22 413 (56.1%); Lab 11 639 (29;1%); L 5 244 (13.1%); NF 676 (1.7%). C maj 10 774 (27.0%); swing 7.6% to C.
1980 by-election: Total vote 35 637 (62.5%); C 13 117 (36.8%); Lab 12 687 (35.6%); L 8 939 (25.1%); others 894 (2.5%). C maj 430 (1.2%).

Mr Edward Taylor was elected at the 1980 by-election; MP for Glasgow, Cathcart 1964–79; contested Glasgow, Springburn 1959. Journalist, consultant and company director. Chief Opposition spokesman on Scotland 1977–79; Under Secretary of State (Development) for Scotland 1974, and in 1970–71 when he resigned in disagreement with Government policy on EEC. Born Apr 18 1937; educ. Glasgow High School and Glasgow University. Member, Glasgow City Council 1960–64. Member, Select-Committee on Environment. Adviser to Port of London Police Federation, Northern Engineering Industries, Lawrence Building Company. Vice-chairman, Conservative backbench trade and consumer affairs committee. NUJ.

Mr Colin George, general secretary, Southend Advice Centre, contested Chelmsford Mar 1966 and Southend East Mar 1980. Born May 24 1938; educ. Westcliff High School. Member, Southend Council 1960–69.

Mr Conor O'Brien, teacher, contested Essex North East in European election 1979. Born Jan 31 1931; educ. Farran Cerris, Cork City and St Mary's, Strawberry Hill.

Mr Paul Channon

SOUTHEND WEST   Electorate 67 486   1979: 66 958   same

*Channon, P. (C)	26 360	54.5%
Grant, G. (L/All)	18 327	37.9%
Nisbet, Mrs J. (Lab)	3 675	7.6%
C majority	8 033	16.6%
Total vote 48 362	Turnout	71.7%

1979: Total vote 51 055 (76.2%); C 29 449 (57.7%); L 12 585 (24.6%); Lab 8 341 (16.3%); NF 680 (1.3%). C maj 16 864 (33.1%); swing 6.5% to C.

Mr Paul Channon was appointed Minister for Trade Jun 1983; Minister for the Arts 1981–83; Minister of State, Civil Service Department 1979–81. Chief Opposition spokesman on the environment 1974–75; spokesman on consumer affairs 1974; member of the Shadow Cabinet 1974. Minister for Housing and Construction 1972–74; Minister of State for Northern Ireland Mar–Nov 1972; Under Secretary for the Environment 1970–72; Parliamentary Secretary Ministry of Housing and Local Government, Jun to Oct 1970. Elected at by-election Jan 1959, succeeding his father. Born Oct 9 1935; educ. Lockers Park, Hemel Hempstead, Eton and Christ Church, Oxford. Former director, CSE Aviation, Arthur Guinness and Son.

Mr Gavin Grant, campaigns director of Liberal Party. Born Jun 20 1955; educ. Roan School for Boys, Greenwich, and Reading University.

Mrs Joy Nisbet is an adoption adviser and fostering officer. Born Jan 1930; educ. North London Collegiate School and the LSE.

Mr Anthony Steen

SOUTH HAMS Electorate 74 276

*Steen, A. (C)	31 855	57.2%
Rogers, A. (L/All)	19 454	35.0%
Morris, G. J. (Lab)	3 824	6.9%
Morgan, Ms W. (Eco)	518	0.9%
C majority	12 401	22.3%
Total vote 55 651		Turnout 74.9%

Mr Anthony Steen, community worker and youth leader, barrister, Lloyd's underwriter and company director, won the seat 1983; represented Liverpool, Wavertree 1974–83. Born Jul 22 1940; educ. Westminster School. Chairman, Conservative urban affairs committee since 1979; former vice-chairman, health and social services committee. Founder and first director, Task Force 1964–68 and of Young Volunteers' Force Foundation 1969–74. Chairman, all party friends of cycling group. Secretary parliamentary Caribbean committee. Select committee Race Relations 1975–79. Council member VSO, National Playing Fields Assoc. Trustee task force trust, board member community transport, chairman Outlandos trust; vice-president, Ecology Building Society; international centre for child studies; member council of reference; international Christian relief.

Mr Anthony Rogers, hotelier and company director, contested Totnes Feb and Oct 1974, and 1979. Born Apr 9 1938; educ. Kingsbridge School. Former chairman, South Hams District Council and Kingsbridge urban and rural councils.

Mr Graham Morris, senior lecturer. Born 1946; educ. Essex University. Member, Distributive Industry Training Board 1980–83. NATFHE. Vice-chairman of governors, Stowford Primary School, Ivybridge.

Sir Ian Percival

SOUTHPORT Electorate 70 089 1979: 68 385 same

*Percival, Sir I. (C)	25 612	50.4%
Brodie-Browne, I. B. (L/All)	20 573	40.5%
Brady, F. P. (Lab)	4 233	8.3%
Wood, K. L. (SBILP)	374	0.7%
C majority	5 039	9.9%
Total vote 50 792		Turnout 72.5%

1979: Total vote 51 104 (74.7%); C 25 953 (50.8%); L 19 426 (38.0%); Lab 5 725 (11.2%). C maj 6 527 (12.8%); swing 4.7% to C.

Sir Ian Percival, QC, was Solicitor General in 1979–83; an Opposition spokesman on law 1976–79. Elected in 1959; contested Battersea North 1951 and 1955. Born May 11 1921; educ. Latymer School and St Catharine's College, Cambridge. Chairman, Conservative legal committee, 1970–74; vice-chairman 1974–79. Member, Select Committee on EEC secondary legislation 1974–79. A former recorder.

Mr Ian Brodie-Browne, a charity organizer with MIND, contested Warrington in 1979. Born Jan 16 1953; educ. Blackdown High School.

Mr Francis Brady, lecturer. Born Nov 15 1942; educ. secondary modern and grammar schools, teacher training college, Open University, University of York. Member, Sefton District Council.

Mr Robert Atkins

SOUTH RIBBLE Electorate 72 401

*Atkins, R. (C)	27 625	49.1%
Duffy, F. (Lab)	14 966	26.6%
Walker, R. (L/All)	13 690	24.3%
C majority	12 659	22.5%
Total vote 56 281		Turnout 77.7%

Mr Robert Atkins, a sales executive won this seat in 1983; represented Preston North 1979–83; contested Luton West in Feb and Oct 1974. Born Feb 5 1946; educ. Highgate School. Member Haringey Borough Council 1968–76. Member European Movement; chairman Haringey for Europe Campaign 1975. Chairman Hornsey Young Conservatives, 1967–69; vice-chairman Greater London Young Conservatives 1969–70. Formerly joint secretary, Conservative Defence committee and vice-chairman Conservative aviation committee. National vice-president Conservative trades unionists. PPS to Minister of State Dept of Industry. ASTMS.

Mr Frank Duffy is a works convenor. Aged 52. Member, Stafford Borough Council.

Mr Robert Walker, retired diplomat and university administrator, contested Haltemprice 1979, and twice in 1974; Humberside in the 1979 European elections. Born May 1 1924; educ. local schools and Peterhouse College, Cambridge. Parish councillor and school governor. First Division Assoc. Civil Service and AUT.

Dr David Clark

SOUTH SHIELDS Electorate 61 924

*Clark, D. (Lab)	19 055	46.5%
Groves, P. (C)	12 653	30.9%
Angus, P. (SDP/All)	9 288	22.7%
Lab majority	6 402	15.6%
Total vote 40 996		Turnout 66.2%

Dr David Clark, an Opposition spokesman on environment since 1981 was returned for this seat in 1979; MP for Colne Valley 1970–Feb 1974. Spokesman on agriculture 1972–74, and on defence 1980–81. Born Oct 19 1939; educ. Windermere Grammar School and Manchester and Sheffield universities. Contested Manchester, Withington 1966 and Colne Valley Feb and Oct 1974. Vice-chairman, PLP environment group 1972–74. Sponsored by NUPE.

Mr Peter Groves, solicitor. Born Aug 26 1956; educ. Barnard Castle School, University of Warwick, College of Law, Guildford and City of London Polytechnic.

Mr Peter Angus, industrial development officer with South Tyneside Metropolitan Borough Council. Born Apr 26 1948; educ. Great Yarmouth Grammar School, Thames Polytechnic. Nalgo.

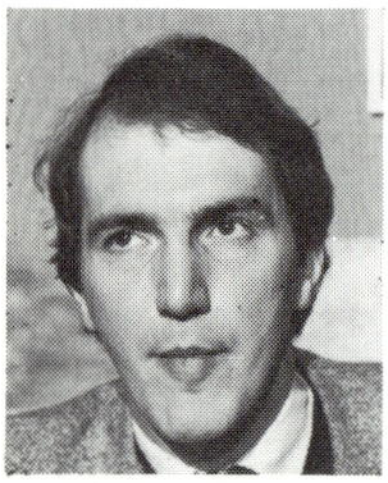

Mr Simon Hughes

SOUTHWARK AND BERMONDSEY Electorate 55 839

*Hughes, S. (L/All)	17 185	49.9%
*Tilley, J. (Lab)	12 021	34.9%
Hughes, R. (C)	4 481	13.0%
Sneath, J. S. (NF)	474	1.4%
Mason, K. T. (New Brit)	154	0.5%
Farehk, A. (Rev Com)	54	0.2%
McKenzie, S. C. (Nat)	50	0.2%
Keen, T. L. (Ind)	50	0.2%
L/All majority	5 164	15.0%
Total vote 34 469		Turnout 61.7%

Mr Simon Hughes, who won the February 1983 by-election is a barrister. Born May 17 1951; educ. Llandaff Cathedral School, Cardiff, Christ College, Brecon, Selwyn College, Cambridge, Inns of Court School of Law and College of Europe, Bruges. GLC candidate, 1981; London Borough of Southwark candidate 1982.

Mr John Tilley was an Opposition spokesman on home affairs 1980–82. Represented Lambeth Central Apr 1978–83; having contested Kensington in both 1974 elections. Journalist, former industrial correspondent. Member, Wandsworth Borough Council 1971–78. Born Jun 1941; Member, NUJ, TGWU, Fabian Society and Co-operative Party, by whom he is sponsored.

Mr Robert Hughes, television news picture editor. Born 1951; educ. Harrow College of Technology and Art. Contested Tower Hamlets, Stepney and Poplar 1979; by-election Bermondsey Feb 1983. GLC member for Croydon Central since 1980. NUJ and ABS.

Mr Humphrey Atkins

SPELTHORNE Electorate 72 236 1979: 70 898 same

*Atkins, H. (C)	26 863	52.4%
Layton, A. (SDP/All)	13 357	26.0%
Rowlands, M. C. (Lab)	7 926	15.5%
Adams, R. (Ind C.)	2 816	5.5%
Butterfield, E. (ACM)	325	0.6%
C majority	13 506	26.3%
Total vote 51 287		Turnout 71.0%

1979: Total vote 54 510 (76.9%); C 31 290 (57.4%); Lab 15 137 (27.8%); L 7 565 (13.9%); NF 518 (1.0%). C maj 16 153 (29.6%); swing 9.0% to C.

Mr Humphrey Atkins was Lord Privy Seal and principal Government spokesman in the Commons for foreign and Commonwealth affairs 1981 to Apr 1982 when he resigned following Argentina's invasion of the Falkland Islands. Secretary of State for Northern Ireland 1979–81. Opposition chief whip 1974–79; Treasurer of the Household (Deputy Chief Whip) 1970–73. Parliamentary Secretary to the Treasury and Government chief whip 1974. Opposition whip 1967–70. Returned for this seat 1970; represented Morden 1955–70; contested West Lothian 1951. Member of Lloyd's. Born Aug 12 1922; educ. Wellington College, Secretary, Conservative parliamentary defence committee 1965–67.

Mr Alexander Layton, barrister. Born Feb 23 1952; educ. Marlborough College, Brasenose College, Oxford; and Munich University.

Mr Murray Rowlands is principal lecturer at Farnborough College and former advisory officer in the New Zealand Civil Service Assoc. Born Mar 1941; educ. Victoria University of Wellington and Liverpool University. Member, Thames Down District Council, 1976–78. ATTI and NATFHE.

Sir Hugh Fraser

STAFFORD Electorate 70 570 By-election May 3 1984

*Fraser, Sir H. (C)	27 639	51.2%
Dunn, D. (SDP/All)	13 362	24.7%
Poulter, M. J. D. (Lab)	12 789	23.7%
Caruso, J. (Gizza Job)	212	0.4%
C majority	14 277	26.4%
Total vote 54 002		Turnout 76.5%

Sir Hugh Fraser, company director, contested the leadership of the Conservative Party in Feb 1975. Appointed Secretary of State for Air Jul 1962; Minister of Defence for RAF 1964; Under-Secretary, Colonial Office 1960–62; War Office 1958–60. President, Assoc. of Conservative Clubs 1975–76. Member for Stone 1945–50, for Stafford and Stone 1950–83; won this seat in 1983. Born Jan 23 1918; educ. Ampleforth, Balliol College, Oxford (President of the Union), and the Sorbonne. Member, Committee of Privileges, Director, Sun Alliance Insurance, Aird Motors, Scottish and Universal Investments Ltd, and other companies. *See page 367 for by-election result.*

Mr David Dunn, senior lecturer in international relations, North Staffordshire Polytechnic. Born 1946; educ. Burnage Grammar School and University College, London. Graduate assistant, University of Pennsylvania 1969–71. Member, British International Studies Assoc. International Institute for Strategic Studies, British Pugwash Group on Science and International Affairs.

Mr Michael Poulter, senior probation officer, Drake Hall Prison, contested Stafford and Stone 1979. Born Nov 29 1942; educ. St Ignatius College, London and English College and Gregorian University, Rome. Member, Staffordshire County Council.

Mr John Heddle

STAFFORDSHIRE MID Electorate 67 425

*Heddle, J. (C)	27 210	52.1%
Jones, T. (L/All)	13 330	25.5%
Lane, P. (Lab)	11 720	22.4%
C majority	13 880	26.6%
Total vote 52 260		Turnout 77.5%

Mr John Heddle, company director, consultant surveyor and Lloyd's underwriter, gained Lichfield and Tamworth for the Conservatives in 1979; won this seat in 1983; contested Bolton East Oct 1974, and Gateshead West Feb 1974. Born Sep 15 1943; educ. Bishop's Stortford College and College of Estate Management (London University). Chairman, Conservative backbench environment committee. Member, environment select committee; Kent County Council 1973–80. Freeman of the City of London; Member, Bow Group. Fellow Rating and Valuation Association; Fellow Institute of Directors; Fellow Royal Society of Arts. Consultant partner Elliottson and Boyton, chartered surveyors.

Mr Timothy Jones, barrister, contested Warwick and Leamington 1974. Born Apr 20 1951; educ. Jesus College, Cambridge, LSE and College of Law. Member, Liberal Party's taxation and social security panel.

Mr Peter Lane is an economist with Shell UK. Born 1946; educ. Croydon Grammar School, LSE and Essex University. Member, Lambeth Borough Council, 1971–81. Member, national executive of the Labour Party. Economic adviser, Treasury, during Callaghan Government.

Mr David Knox

STAFFORDSHIRE MOORLANDS Electorate 72 466

*Knox, D. (C)	30 079	53.8%
Campbell, B. (Lab)	13 513	24.2%
Gubbins, P. (SDP/All)	12 370	22.1%
C majority	16 566	29.6%
Total vote 55 962		Turnout 77.2%

Mr David Knox, economist and management consultant, represented Leek, 1970–83; won this seat in 1983; contested Birmingham, Stechford 1964 and 1966, and Nuneaton by-election 1967. Born May 30 1933; educ. Lockerbie Academy, Dumfries Academy and London University. Vice-chairman, Conservative Party 1974–75. Joint secretary, Conservative finance committee 1972–73; secretary, Conservative trade committee 1974; vice-chairman, Conservative employment committee 1979–80. (Secretary 1976–79). Member, Select Committee on European legislation, since 1976.

Mr Brian Campbell is a senior probation officer and former Baptist minister. Former deputy leader, Newcastle-under-Lyme district council. Member, Staffordshire County Council. Teacher in social and community work for Open University. Born May 27 1935; educ. Blessed Sacrament School, Liverpool; grammar school; Keele University.

Mr Paul Gubbins, journalist in Staffordshire and former teacher. Born 1949; educ. grammar school; Manchester University; fellowship at Queen's University, Canada.

Mr Patrick Cormack

STAFFORDSHIRE SOUTH

Electorate 73 038 1979: 67 838 same

*Cormack, P. (C)	32 764	59.2%
Chambers, J. (L/All)	13 004	23.5%
Cartwright, M. J. (Lab)	9 568	17.3%
C majority	19 760	35.7%
Total vote 55 336	Turnout	75.8%

1979 (as Staffordshire South West): Total vote 53 245 (79.0%); C 32 153 (60.4%); Lab 14 720 (27.6%); L 5 460 (10.3%); NF 912 (1.7%). C maj 17 433 (32.8%); swing 8.2% to C.

Mr Patrick Cormack, writer, company director, consultant and a former teacher, represented Staffordshire South-West, Feb 1974–83; won this seat in 1983; Cannock 1970–74; contested Grimsby 1966; Bolsover 1964. Born May 18 1939; educ. St James Choir and Havelock Schools, Grimsby and Hull University. Member of Select Committee on Education, Science and Arts since 1979. Joint chairman, all-party heritage group and chairman, Conservative arts and heritage committee since 1979. Chairman, council for independent education since 1980; member, Historic Buildings Council since 1979; director, Historic House Hotels Ltd; Consultant, Patrick Cormack and Partners. Chairman, all-party committee for Soviet Jews 1971–75; former member, select committee on anti-discrimination. Chairman, all-party committee for widows and single parent families 1974–77. Member, Royal Commission on Historical Manuscripts and Lord Chancellor's Committee on Public Records; Fellow, Royal Society of Antiquaries since 1977. IOJ.

Mr John Chambers, electrical projects engineer. Born 1947. General election agent, 1979. Councillor and local government agent.

Mr Martin Cartwright is a lecturer in law at Wolverhampton polytechnic. Aged 31; educ. Hull University. Member, Citizens Advice Bureau. Chairman, Wolverhampton Law Centre which he helped establish in 1980. Member, CND

Mr David Lightbown

STAFFORDSHIRE SOUTH EAST

Electorate 63 324

Lightbown, D. (C)	24 556	50.7%
Crawley, Mrs C. M. (Lab)	13 658	28.2%
Lynch, M. (SDP/All)	10 220	21.1%
C majority	10 898	22.5%
Total vote 48 434	Turnout	76.5%

Mr David Lightbown, engineering director, West Midlands plc. was elected in 1983. Born Nov 30 1932. Lichfield District Council, Staffordshire County Council.

Mrs Christine Crawley, a tutor in social skills. Born 1950.

Mr Michael Lynch, lecturer in English and communications, Bilston College of Further Education, Wolverhampton and examiner in English for the Associated Examining Board. Born 1943; educ. William Hulme's Grammar School, Manchester, and St Edmund Hall, Oxford. Qualified lawyer specializing in employment, family and planning law. Member, National Committee for 16–19 Education. AMMA.

Mr Tom Pendry

STALYBRIDGE AND HYDE

Electorate 67 916 1979: 67 772 minor

*Pendry, T. (Lab)	21 798	45.5%
Silvester, B. (C)	17 436	36.4%
Hughes, J. (L/All)	8 339	17.4%
Nylan, B. (NF)	294	0.6%
Lab majority	4 362	9.1%
Total vote 47 867	Turnout	70.5%

1979: Total vote 52 226 (77.1%); Lab 27 082 (51.9%); C 20 502 (39.3%); L 4 642 (8.9%); Lab maj 6 580 (12.6%); swing 3.7% to C.

Mr Tom Pendry, an Opposition spokesman on overseas development since 1981; spokesman on Northern Ireland 1979–81; spokesman on devolution and regional affairs since 1982. Under Secretary of State, Northern Ireland Office 1978–79; Lord Commissioner of the Treasury (Government whip) 1974–77. Opposition whip 1971–74. Former member Public Expenditure Committee. Member, Speaker's Conference on Electoral Reform 1973–74. Full-time official NUPE 1960–70. Elected in 1970. Born Jun 1934; educ. St Augustine's Ramsgate, and Plater Hall, Oxford. Member, Paddington Borough Council, 1962–65. Member, Consultative Assembly, Council of Europe 1973–76. Sponsored by NUPE.

Mr Brian Silvester, self-employed butcher. Born 1952; educ. Nantwich and Acton Grammar School and College of Distributive Trade, Smithfield, London. Former chairman, Nantwich Young Conservatives and of Cheshire Young Conservatives. Vice-chairman, Crewe borough Conservatives; elected to Crewe and Nantwich Borough Council, 1976. Member, Nantwich Young Farmers and

Nantwich Sports Council.
Mr John Hughes, retail consultant. Born Jun 13 1946; educ. King James Grammar School, Huddersfield; Hyde County Grammar School, and Manchester University. Member, National Assoc. of Co-operative Officials.

Sir Kenneth Lewis

STAMFORD AND SPALDING Electorate 65 955

*Lewis, Sir K (C)	27 728	56.5%
Lee, P. (SDP/All)	15 972	32.6%
Mullender, Ms A. (Lab)	5 354	10.9%
C majority	11 756	24.0%
Total vote 49 054		Turnout 74.4%

Sir Kenneth Lewis was MP for Rutland and Stamford 1959–83; won this seat in 1983; contested Ashton-under-Lyne 1951 and Newton 1945 and 1950. Member, Commons Committee of Selection 1964–83 and of Procedure (Finance) Committee 1981–83. Member, Estimates Committee 1962–66. Born Jul 1 1916; educ. Jarrow Central School and Edinburgh University. Former chairman, Conservative parliamentary Employment Committee. Member, Middlesex County Council 1947–50. Chairman, Business and Holiday Travel Ltd. Member of Lloyd's; member, Institute of Travel and Tourism and Institute of Marketing. Deputy Lieutenant of Rutland since 1973.
Mr Peter Lee, head of adult education centre, served as a constituency agent in Oct 1974 election. Born May 16 1940; educ. Latymer Upper School and Keble College, Oxford. AACE.
Ms Audrey Mullender is a lecturer in social work at the University of Nottingham. Aged 31. Chairperson of her local party; held several positions in constituency and county parties. Member, CND and Amnesty International. AUT.

Mr Timothy Wood

STEVENAGE Electorate 67 706

Wood, T. (C)	20 787	39.4%
Stoneham, B. R. M. (SDP / All)	19 032	36.1%
Reeves, Mrs S. (Lab)	12 673	24.0%
Bowmaker, D. R. (BNP)	236	0.5%
C majority	1 755	3.3%
Total vote 52 728		Turnout 77.9%

Mr Timothy Wood, a senior project manager with an international computer firm, won the seat in 1983. Born 1940; educ. Manchester University. Member, Bracknell District Council since 1975. Chairman, Wokingham Conservative Assoc. Vice-chairman, Thames Valley Euro-constituency. Bow Group Member, National Assoc. of Conservative Graduates 1970–79. Former board member, Bracknell Development Corporation.
Mr Benjamin Stoneham contested Saffron Walden for Labour in 1979 and 1977 by-election. Industrial relations executive, Portsmouth and Sunderland Newspaper Group since 1982; with NCB 1975–79. Education officer, National Union of Railwaymen 1979–82. Born Aug 24 1948; educ. Christ's College, Cambridge; Warwick University.
Mrs Susan Reeves, teacher and speech therapist, contested Chelmsford 1979, and South-West Hertfordshire 1979 by-election. Born Mar 31 1943; educ. Dartford Girls' Grammar School and St Mary's College of Education, Twickenham. NUT and TGWU.

Mr Michael Forsyth

STIRLING Electorate 56 302

Forsyth, M. (C)	17 039	40.0%
Connarty, M. (Lab)	11 906	27.9%
Finnie, R. (L/All)	10 174	23.9%
Houston, W. (SNP)	3 488	8.2%
C majority	5 133	12.1%
Total vote 42 607		Turnout 75.7%

Mr Michael Forsyth, public relations consultant, has been a Westminster City Councillor since 1978. Won this seat in 1983. Born 1954; educ. Arbroath High School and St Andrews University. Former national chairman of the Federation of Conservative students.
Mr Michael Connarty, teacher. Born 1947.
Mr Ross Finnie, chartered accountant and merchant bank director, was chairman of the Scottish Liberal Party 1982. Contested Renfrewshire West 1979. Born Feb 11 1947; educ. Greenock Academy. Executive member, Scottish Council for Development and Industry. Inverclyde district councillor since 1977.
Mr William Houston, a senior community worker. Born 1953; educ. Crookston Castle School and Jordanhill College of Education. Joined party 1973. Has fought local elections.

Mr Anthony Favell

STOCKPORT Electorate 58 908

Favell, A. (C)	18 517	42.1%
Ward, P. R. (Lab)	12 731	29.0%
*McNally, T. (SDP / All)	12 129	27.6%
Shipley, M. (Eco)	369	0.8%
Walker, K. (Nat)	194	0.4%
C majority	5 786	13.2%
Total vote 43 940		Turnout 74.6%

Mr Anthony Favell, solicitor, was elected in 1983; contested Bolsover 1979. Born May 29 1939; educ. St Bees, Cumbria and Sheffield University.

Mr Peter Ward contested Shipley 1979; Southport Feb 1974. Born Apr 1934; educ. Wigan College of Further Education. Engineer with British Aerospace. Former member, Preston RDC. AUEW (TASS).

Mr Tom McNally was elected as Labour MP for Stockport South, in 1979, but resigned party in 1981 and joined SDP becoming spokesman on education. Member, Select Committee on Industry and Trade, 1979–83. Political adviser to Mr James Callaghan as Prime Minister 1976–79. Born Feb 20 1943; educ. College of St Joseph, Blackpool and University College, London. Vice-president NUS, 1965–66.

Mr Frank Cook

STOCKTON NORTH Electorate 70 277

Cook, F. (Lab)	18 339	37.1%
Davies, H. (C)	16 469	33.3%
*Rodgers, W. (SDP/All)	14 630	29.6%
Lab majority	1 870	3.8%
Total vote 49 438		Turnout 70.4%

Mr Frank Cook, construction engineer, was elected in 1983. Born Nov 3 1935; educ. Corby School, Sunderland; De La Salle, Manchester; Institute of Education, Leeds, Sponsored by AUEW (TASS).

Mr Harry Davies, head teacher. Born Jun 16 1930; educ. St John's College, Birmingham. Member, Billingham District Council 1958–68; Stockton Borough Council since 1973. National Assoc. of Head Teachers.

Mr William Rodgers, Secretary of State for Transport in the Labour Cabinet 1976–79 and a Labour MP from 1962, resigned from party in 1981 being one of the four joint leaders who formed the SDP. Resigned Shadow Cabinet in 1980 until then being chief Opposition Spokesman on defence. Minister of State for Defence 1974–76. Born Oct 28 1928; educ. Sudley Road Council School, Quarry Bank High School, Liverpool and Magdalen College, Oxford. General Secretary, Fabian Society 1953–60. Contested Bristol West by-election Mar 1957; represented Stockton-on-Tees 1962–75; Teesside, Stockton Feb 1974–83. Opposition spokesman on aviation supply 1970–72; Minister of State, Treasury 1969–70; Minister of State, Board of Trade 1968–69; Under-Secretary of State, Foreign Office 1967–68; Under-Secretary of State, Economic Affairs 1964–67. Consultant to Merke Sharpe and Dohme.

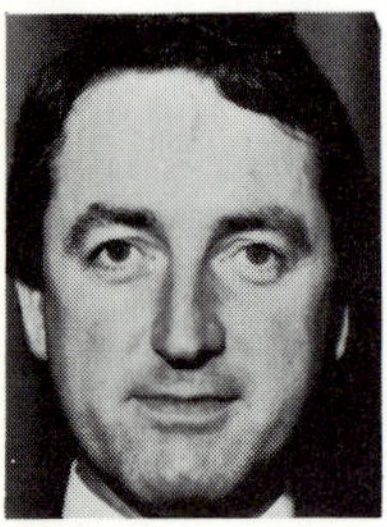

Mr Ian Wrigglesworth

STOCKTON SOUTH Electorate 73 790

*Wrigglesworth, I. (SDP/All)	19 551	36.8%
Finnegan, T. (C)	19 448	36.6%
Griffiths, F. (Lab)	13 998	26.3%
Fern, D. (Ind)	205	0.4%
SDP/All majority	103	0.2%
Total vote 53 202		Turnout 72.1%

Mr Ian Wrigglesworth, SDP spokesman on the Civil Service and on industry, joined the party in 1981 after resigning from the Labour Party. He had been an official opposition spokesman on the Civil Service. Former secretary, Manifesto Group, PLP and former vice-chairman, PLP finance and economic group. Elected as Labour MP for Teeside, Thornaby Feb 1974; won this seat 1983. Director, Galleon World Travel Ltd; divisional director, Smiths Industries Ltd; parliamentary adviser, Civil and Public Services Assoc. Born Dec 1939; educ. Stockton Grammar School, Stockton-Billingham Technical College and College of St Mark and St John, London. Member, General Advisory Council of IBA, 1979–81.

Mr Thomas Finnegan, managing director of vehicle component firm. Born Mar 24 1939; educ. Coleshill Grammar School, Warwickshire, and Brooklyn Technical College, Birmingham. Contested Birmingham, Erdington Feb and Oct 1974 for National Front. Member, Richmond (Yorks) Conservative Assoc; executive member, North of England Employers' Federation.

Mr Francis Griffiths, senior lecturer in health studies. Born Feb 26 1948; educ. Kilmorie Secondary Modern School, London, Teesside Polytechnic and London University. Coopted member, Cleveland Education Committee.

Mr Mark Fisher

STOKE-ON-TRENT CENTRAL

Electorate 66934

Fisher, M. (Lab)	21194	48.1%
Mans, K. (C)	12944	29.4%
Freeman, Ms V. (SDP / All)	9458	21.5%
Cook, C. S. (Loony Socy)	504	1.1%
Lab majority	8250	18.7%
Total vote 44100		Turnout 65.9%

Mr Mark Fisher, former film producer and writer; principal of an education centre 1975–83. Born Oct 1944; educ. Eton and Cambridge. Elected in 1983; contested Leek 1979. Member, Staffordshire County Council, since 1981; chairman, library committee. NUT and Socialist Educational Association.

Mr Keith Mans, retail manager. Born Feb 10 1946; educ. Berkhamsted School, RAF College, Cranwell, Open University. Pilot in RAF Reserve.

Ms Vicki Freeman has been a freelance parliamentary lobbyist. Former social worker with National Council of Voluntary Organizations; general secretary, Women's European Committee 1972–75. Born 1941; educ. Oxford University. Member, Fawcett Society; formerly on executive committee.

Mr John Forrester

STOKE-ON-TRENT NORTH

Electorate 75251

*Forrester, J. (Lab)	24721	46.3%
Ibbs, R. (C)	16518	30.9%
Beswick, T. (SDP/All)	12186	22.8%
Lab majority	8203	15.4%
Total vote 53425		Turnout 71.0%

Mr John Forrester, teacher, was elected in 1966. Member, Select Committee on the Environment. Born Jun 17 1924; educ. Eastwood Council School, City School of Commerce, Stoke-on-Trent, and Alsager Teacher Training College. Member, Chairman's panel of Commons. Member, Stoke-on-Trent city and district councils since 1970. Secretary constituency Labour Party 1961; NUT.

Mr Roger Ibbs, self employed chiropodist and part-time area health authority worker, contested Stoke-on-Trent North 1979. Born Jan 1948; educ. St Alleyne's Grammar School, Stone and Northern College of Chiropody, Salford. Former member, Stoke-on-Trent City Council and former secretary Conservative group. Chairman, Stoke-on-Trent North constituency party 1978–82.

Mr Trevor Beswick, Head of Science, Ryles Park High School, Macclesfield. Born 1935; educ. Bradford Grammar School and Leeds University. Founder member, Macclesfield District Foster Care Assoc. Methodist preacher, youth leader, organist and choirmaster.

Mr Jack Ashley

STOKE-ON-TRENT SOUTH

Electorate 70600

*Ashley, J. (Lab)	23611	48.0%
Maxwell, P. (Con)	16506	33.6%
Walley, W. (L / All)	9050	18.4%
Lab majority	7105	14.5%
Total vote 49167		Turnout 69.6%

Mr Jack Ashley, journalist and broadcaster, is chairman of the all-party Lords and Commons disablement group. Member of the Labour Party national executive committee 1976–78. Elected in 1966; contested Finchley 1951. Born Dec 6 1922; educ. elementary school, Ruskin College, Oxford and Gonville and Caius College, Cambridge (President of the Union). Member, PLP liaison committee 1977–78. Member national executive. Chemical Workers' Union 1946–47; General Advisory Council BBC 1967–69; Widnes Borough Council 1946–47. Sponsored by GMWBU.

Mr Peter Maxwell, a probation officer. Born 1944; educ. Ampleforth College, New College, Oxford and Southampton University. Private secretary and ADC to the Governor of Western Australia 1968–70, while a regular officer in the Grenadier Guards. Member, Winchester City Council since 1979, and chairman of the housing committee; Winchester and Andover constituency executive council; and Wessex Area Council. Secretary, Winchester Constituency Conservative Trade Unionists. Member, National Council for One-Parent Families.

Mr William Walley, chartered civil engineer and university lecturer, Department of Civil Engineering, Aston University. Born Sep 12 1941; educ. Queen Mary College, London, and Birmingham University. Member, Liberal Party's policy panel on planning; Stafford Borough Council. Formerly Senior Engineer, Staffordshire County Council. AUT.

Mr John D Taylor

STRANGFORD Electorate 60 232

Taylor, J. D. (OUP)	19 086	48.8%
Gibson, S. (DUP)	11 716	30.0%
Morrow, A. (All)	6 171	15.8%
Curry, J. (SDLP)	1 713	4.4%
Heath, R. (Ind L)	430	1.1%
OUP majority	7 370	18.8%
Total vote 39 116		Turnout 64.9%

Mr John David Taylor, elected in 1983, chartered engineer, aged 45, educ. Royal School Armagh; Queen's University, Belfast. Member Stormont 1965–72. Elected. Northern Ireland Assembly 1973; convention 1975; Assembly 1982. MEP since 1979, Official IRA attempted to assassinate him in Armagh City in 1972.

Mr Simpson Gibson is a farmer. Vice-chairman of DUP in Northern Ireland. Elected Northern Ireland Assembly 1982. Deputy chairman, agriculture committee. Aged 36; educ. Saintfield Secondary School and Shaftesbury House Tutorial College, Belfast. Member, Ards Borough Council since 1981. Member Orange Order.

Mr Alan Howarth

STRATFORD-ON-AVON Electorate 76 649

Howarth, A. T. (C)	34 041	60.9%
Taylor, W. J. B. (L / All)	16 124	28.9%
*Hooley, F. O. (Lab)	5 731	10.3%
C majority	17 917	32.1%
Total vote 55 896		Turnout 72.9%

Mr Alan Howarth, merchant banker, retained the seat for the Conservatives in 1983. Born Jun 11 1944; educ. Rugby School and King's College, Cambridge. Formerly head of chairman's office at Conservative central office and personal assistant to both Mr William Whitelaw and Lord Thorneycroft during their terms as party chairman; director of Conservative research department 1979–81 and vice-chairman of the party organization 1980–81.

Mr James Taylor, farmer, contested the seat 1979. Born Oct 18 1934; educ. in Bootham, York, and Royal Agricultural College, Cirencester. NFU.

Mr Frank Hooley was MP for Sheffield, Helley Feb 1974–83 and 1966–70 contested it in 1964 and Skipton 1959. Member of Select Committee on Foreign Affairs and chairman of its Overseas Development subcommittee since 1979; member, Select Committee on Procedure (Finance) previously on Select Committees on Public Accounts, Estimates, Science and Technology and on Overseas Development; chairman, PLP parliamentary affairs group 1982–83; chairman, PLP overseas aid group 1977–78. Sponsored by APEX. Born Nov 30 1923; educ. King Edward's School, Birmingham and Birmingham University. Assistant registrar, Sheffield University 1952–65 and senior assistant registrar 1965–66.

Mr Michael Hirst

STRATHKELVIN AND BEARSDEN Electorate 60 500

Hirst, M. (C)	17 501	36.5%
Waddell, R. (L / All)	13 801	28.7%
Ingram, A. P. (Lab)	12 308	25.6%
Bain, Mrs M. (SNP)	4 408	9.2%
C majority	3 700	7.7%
Total vote 48 018		Turnout 79.4%

Mr Michael Hirst contested Dunbartonshire East, 1979; Dunbartonshire Central Feb and Oct 1974. Chartered accountant, partner in Peat Marwick. Born Jan 1946; educ. Glasgow Academy; Glasgow University; Iceland University as an exchange scholar. National vice-chairman, Scottish Young Conservatives 1972–73; chairman, Scottish Conservative Candidates' Assoc. 1978–81. Past President, Glasgow University Conservative Club.

Mr Ronald Waddell, traffic engineer, is organizational vice-chairman, Scottish Liberal Party. Born May 15 1954; educ. Bearsden Academy, Strathclyde and Salford Universities. Chairman Strathclyde University Liberals 1976; chairman Scottish Young Liberals 1981–82. Contested Dunbartonshire East 1979.

Mr Adam Ingram, full time official of Nalgo, former computer programmer. Aged 36. Elected to East Kilbride District Council 1980. Scottish TUC appointee to supplementary benefits appeal tribunal.

Mrs Margaret Bain, an administrator, formerly teacher, was SNP MP for Dunbartonshire East Oct 1974–79; contested seat in Feb 1974. A vice-president of SNP. SNP spokesman on education and social services when an MP. Born Sep 1945: educ. Biggar High School, Glasgow and Strathclyde universities.

Mr William Shelton

STREATHAM Electorate 60 032

*Shelton, W. J. M. (C)	18 264	46.5%
Long, Mrs M. (Lab)	12 362	31.5%
Billenness, P. (L / All)	8 321	21.2%
Handy, K. (NF)	321	0.8%
C majority	5 902	15.0%
Total vote 39 268	Turnout	65.4%

Mr William Shelton Under Secretary for State for Education and Science 1981–83. Elected for Streatham in Feb 1974; MP for Clapham 1970–74. Former chairman of advertising agency. Born Oct 30 1929; educ. Radley College, Worcester College, Oxford, Tabor University, Mass, and Texas University. Member of Lloyd's. GLC councillor, Wandsworth, 1967–70; chief whip, Inner London Education Authority 1968–70. PPS to Mrs Thatcher when Leader of the Opposition 1975–79. Vice-chairman, Conservative education committee and foreign affairs committee 1979–81.

Ms Madeline Long is a lecturer. Born 1949.

Mr Peter Billenness, international marketing consultant. Born May 12 1927; educ. Eastbourne, Cheltenham and University College, London. Contested Hendon South 1959 and 1964; Bromley 1966; Epsom 1970; East Grinstead Feb 1974; Croydon South 1979.

Mr Anthony Lloyd

STRETFORD Electorate 57 448

Lloyd, A. J. (Lab)	18 028	44.9%
Sweeney, W. (C)	13 686	34.1%
Wilks, D. (SDP / All)	8 141	20.3%
Ud-Din, S. A. (Ind Lab)	336	0.8%
Lab majority	4 342	10.8%
Total vote 40 191	Turnout	70.0%

Mr Anthony Lloyd is a university lecturer. Elected in 1983. Born Feb 25 1950; educ. Stretford Grammar School and Nottingham University and Manchester Business School. Member, Trafford Borough Council since 1979; deputy leader Labour group. AUT.

Mr Walter Sweeney, solicitor. Born 1949; educ. Lawrence Sheriff School, Rugby; College of Law, Guildford, and University of Hull. Member, Rugby Borough Council 1976–79; Bedfordshire County Council.

Mr David Wilks, production manager with United Biscuits, Manchester. Born Jun 24 1954; educ. Magdalen College School, Oxford, Oxford College of Further Education and University of Leicester. National chairman, Federation of Conservative Students 1977–78; first Conservative on an NUS political committee for 15 years. Member, Carlisle MSC area board 1979–81.

Sir Anthony Kershaw

STROUD Electorate 77 528

*Kershaw, Sir A. (C)	30 896	51.3%
Fallon, G. (L / All)	19 182	31.9%
Parsons, D. R. (Lab)	10 141	16.8%
C majority	11 714	19.5%
Total vote 60 219	Turnout	77.7%

Sir Anthony Kershaw, a company director, has been chairman of the Select Committee on Foreign Affairs since 1979; was Under Secretary, Defence (RAF) 1973–74; Under Secretary, Foreign and Commonwealth Office 1970–73; Parliamentary Secretary, Ministry of Public Building and Works 1970. Elected in 1955; Contested Gloucester 1950 and 1951. Barrister. Born Dec 14 1915; educ. Eton and Balliol College, Oxford. Member, Defence and External Affairs sub-committee of former Public Expenditure Committee; joint secretary, Conservative defence committee 1964–67. PPS to Mr Heath until 1970. Member, Westminster City Council 1946–50. Vice-chairman British Council since 1975. Adviser to British American Tobacco Co Ltd and to Association of British Machine Tools Marine Ltd.

Mr Gerald Fallon is a college lecturer. Born Apr 17 1938; educ. West Kensington Central, Harlow Technical College, University of London and University of Bath. Member, Harlow District Council 1973–76. NATFHE.

Mr David Parsons is a teacher. Born 1950. Member, Bristol City Council since 1979. NUT. CND.

Mr Michael Lord

SUFFOLK CENTRAL Electorate 75641

Lord, M. (C)	30096	53.5%
Baldwin, N. (L/All)	15365	27.3%
Sierakowski, Mrs M. (Lab)	10828	19.2%
C majority	14731	26.2%
Total vote 56289		Turnout 74.4%

Mr Michael Lord elected in 1983; contested Manchester, Gorton 1979. Arboriculturalist. Born Oct 17 1938; educ. William Hulme's Grammar School, Manchester, and Christ's College, Cambridge. Rugby Blue. Chairman, further education committee, Bedfordshire County Council. Was chairman, policy committee, and deputy leader of Conservative group, North Bedfordshire Borough Council; member 1974–77. Member, Conservative agricultural and countryside forum; foreign affairs forum. NFU.

Mr Nicholas Baldwin, author and lecturer. Born Apr 26 1958; educ. Chulmleigh School and Community College; West Buckland School; Hull and Exeter universities.

Mrs Margaret Sierakowski, research sociologist with Policy Studies Institute. Born Sep 11 1941; educ. LSE and Essex University. Former member, German SPD (Social Democratic Party). Suffolk county councillor since 1981. ASTMS.

Mr John Gummer

SUFFOLK COASTAL Electorate 71521

*Gummer, J. S. (C)	31240	58.2%
Houseley, D. (SDP / All)	15618	29.1%
Ballantyne, D. (Lab)	6780	12.6%
C majority	15622	29.1%
Total vote 53638		Turnout 75.0%

Mr John Selwyn Gummer became chairman of the Conservative Party in Sept 1983. Minister of State for Employment from Nov 1983; Under Secretary of State for Employment Jan to Nov 1983. Assistant Government Whip 1981; Lord Commissioner, Treasury (whip) 1982. MP for Lewisham West 1970 to Feb 1974; for Eye 1979–83; won this seat in 1983; contested Greenwich 1964 and 1966. PPS to Mr James Prior, when Minister of Agriculture, Fisheries and Food. 1971. A vice-chairman of the Conservative Party 1972–74. Born Nov 1939; educ. King's School, Rochester and Selwyn College, Cambridge (President of the Union, 1962). Chairman, Federation of Conservative Students 1961. Coopted member, ILEA 1967–70. Publisher, writer and broadcaster.

Mr David Houseley, travel consultant and company managing director. Born Oct 15 1931; educ. Colchester Royal Grammar School. East Sussex county councillor 1963–77.

Mr Dennis Ballantyne is a scientific adviser, consultant and author. Former reader in electrical engineering at Imperial College, London. Former member, Suffolk Coastal District Council; Felixstowe Town Council. Age 55. Fellow of the Institute of Physics.

Mr Tim Yeo

SUFFOLK SOUTH Electorate 76209

Yeo, T. (C)	29469	50.7%
Kemp, R. (L / All)	18200	31.3%
Billcliffe, S. (Lab)	10516	18.1%
C majority	11269	19.4%
Total vote 58185		Turnout 76.4%

Mr Tim Yeo, director of the Spastics Society and of a building supplies firm. Fought Bedwellty, Feb 1974. Born Mar 1945; educ. Charterhouse; Emmanuel College, Cambridge. Formerly taught agriculture in Tanzania. Treasurer International Voluntary Service 1975–78; trustee of Tanzania Development Trust, since 1980. Campaigned to save Tadworth Court Children's Hospital, Surrey. Member, Independent Development Council on Mental Handicap. Chairman, charities VAT reform group.

Mr Richard Kemp, director of trading and property companies. Born Nov 21 1943; educ. at local schools. Member, Babergh District Council, Long Melford Parish Council, Alpheton Parish Council.

Mr Stephen Billcliffe, National Director of Friends of the Earth. Born Oct 23 1950; educ. Salford College of Technology, Polytechnic of Central London. Former computer operator and regional organizer for Shelter. Member, Socialist Agricultural Society; Labour Housing Group. TGWU.

Mr Robert Clay

SUNDERLAND NORTH Electorate 78 520

Clay, R. A. (Lab)	24 179	46.3%
Lewis, C. (C)	16 983	32.5%
McCourt, D. (L / All)	11 090	21.2%
Lab majority	7 196	13.8%
Total vote 52 252	Turnout 66.6%	

Mr Robert Clay, bus driver, was elected in 1983. Born Oct 2 1946; educ. Bradford School, Gonville and Caius College, Cambridge. Secretary, Sunderland District Labour Party. Member, Co-operative Party and GMBATU branch chairman and member of regional council for six years.

Mr Christopher Lewis, director of a shipping and travel company; son of Sir Kenneth Lewis, MP for Rutland and Stamford 1959–83. Member, Richmond and Barnes Conservative Assoc. chairman, CPC committee. Member, Bow Group and of Conservative Group for Europe. Born 1952; educ. Witham Hall, Lincs; Trent College, Nottingham; College of Distributive Trades.

Mr Douglas McCourt, publican, contested Chester-le-Street, Oct 1974, and 1979. Born Apr 4 1940; educ. Castletown Junior School and Usworth Secondary Modern. Member Tyne and Wear County Council 1974–77.

Mr Gordon Bagier

SUNDERLAND SOUTH Electorate 75 124

*Bagier, G. A. T. (Lab)	22 869	45.7%
Mitchell, A. (C)	17 321	34.6%
Anderson, J. (SDP / All)	9 865	19.7%
Lab majority	5 548	11.1%
Total vote 50 055	Turnout 66.6%	

Mr Gordon Bagier, who won the seat in 1964, was a British Railways signals inspector. Member Select Committee on Transport since 1980. Born Jul 1924; educ. Pendower Secondary Technical School, Newcastle upon Tyne. President Yorkshire District Council NUR 1962–64. Member Keighley Borough Council 1956–60 and Sowerby Bridge Urban Council 1962–65. Member Estimates Committee 1964–66. Sponsored by NUR.

Mr Andrew Mitchell, is a merchant banker. Born 1956; educ. Cambridge (President of the Union). Son of Mr David Mitchell, an Under Secretary of State for Transport. Short service Commission in 1 Royal Tank Regiment 1974–75.

Mr John Anderson, senior administrative officer on Tyne and Wear County Council. Aged 33; educ. Castletown School and a correspondence course leading to a diploma in municipal administration. Acted as SDP agent for Sunderland 1982–83.

Mr Richard Tracey

SURBITON Electorate 46 949 1979: 46 922 minor

Tracey, R. (C)	18 245	54.5%
Nowakowski, C. (SDP/All)	9 496	28.4%
Waskett, N. D. (Lab)	5 173	15.5%
Maclellan, J. (Eco)	551	1.7%
C majority	8 749	26.1%
Total vote 33 465	Turnout 71.3%	

1979: Total vote 35 417 (75.5%); C 20 063 (56.6%); Lab 9 261 (26.1%); L 6 093 (17.2%). C maj 10 802 (30.5%); swing 6.2% to C.

Mr Richard Tracey, public affairs adviser and former BBC current affairs presenter. Born 1943; educ. King Edward VI School, Stratford-upon-Avon and Birmingham University. Presented national rallies for Mrs Thatcher in Apr and Jun 1979. Elected in 1983; contested Northampton North in Oct 1974. Chairman, Putney Conservative Assoc. 1978–79; chairman, London South West Euro Constituency 1979–81; deputy chairman, greater London area Conservative Party 1981–83; member, national union executive committee and policy group for London 1981–83. Member, management board of ISIS and member, Economic Research Council.

Mr Christopher Nowakowski, physics lecturer. Born 1946; educ. Haverstock Comprehensive School, Royal Holloway College (London University), Keele, Garnett College, London. Member, Tawney Society, European Movement. Author.

Dr Nigel Waskett, member Hounslow Borough Council 1978–80. Chairman, North London branch, Medical Practitioners Union (ASTMS) 1982–83. Member, Socialist Health Assoc. and Medical Campaign v Nuclear Weapons. Born Sep 28 1949; educ. Llandovery College, South Wales, St John's College, Cambridge and Westminster Medical School.

Sir Geoffrey Howe

SURREY EAST

Electorate 58485 1979: 57364 same

*Howe, Sir G. (C)	27272	62.9%
Liddell, Mrs S. (L/All)	11836	27.3%
Pincott, H. (Lab)	4249	9.8%
C majority	15436	35.6%
Total vote 43357		Turnout 74.1%

1979: Total vote 44982 (78.4%); C 28266 (62.8%); L 8866 (19.7%); Lab 7398 (16.4%); NF 452 (1.0%). C maj 19400 (43.1%); swing 6.2% to C.

Sir Geoffrey Howe QC, was appointed Secretary of State for Foreign and Commonwealth Affairs Jun 1983; Chancellor of the Exchequer 1979–83. Chief Opposition spokesman on Treasury and Economic affairs 1975–79. Contested the leadership of the Conservative Party 1975. Opposition spokesman on social services 1974–75; Minister for Trade and Consumer Affairs 1972–74; Solicitor General 1970–72. Returned for this seat Feb 1974; represented Reigate 1970–74; and Bebington 1964–66; contested Aberavon 1955 and 1959. Born Dec 20 1926; educ. Winchester and Trinity Hall, Cambridge. Former director of insurance and market research companies. Member, General Council of Bar 1957–61; elected Bencher of Middle Temple 1969.

Mrs Susan Liddell, housewife. Born Jun 28 1923; educ. privately and Newnham College, Cambridge.

Mr Hugh Pincott, chartered chemist and company administrator. Born Oct 11 1941; educ. Pontardawe Grammar School, and St Andrew and Dundee universities. Co-opted member, London Borough Council of Lewisham leisure services committee. TGWU.

Mr Michael Grylls

SURREY NORTH WEST

Electorate 78377 1979: 75197 same

*Grylls, M. (C)	35297	64.1%
Weedon, J. (L/All)	14279	26.0%
Burrow, J. (Lab)	5452	9.9%
C majority	21018	38.2%
Total vote 55028		Turnout 70.2%

1979: Total vote 56815 (75.6%); C 36219 (63.7%); Lab 10763 (18.9%); L 9037 (15.9%); NF 796 (1.4%). C maj 25456 (44.8%); swing 8.5% to C.

Mr Michael Grylls, chairman of the Small Business Bureau, has been chairman of the Conservative backbench industry committee since 1981 and vice-chairman 1975–81. Returned in Feb 1974; MP for Chertsey 1970–74; contested Fulham 1964 and 1966. Company director and consultant to the pharmaceutical industry. Born Feb 21 1934; educ. Royal Naval College, Dartmouth and universities in Paris and Madrid. Member, Select Committee on Overseas Development 1972–77; member, GLC 1967–68; deputy leader of ILEA, 1969–70; St Pancras Borough Council 1959–62. Leader, parliamentary panel. Institute of Directors; consultant to Assoc. of Authorized Public Accountants.

Mr John Weedon, contracts manager in building industry. Born Jul 27 1934; educ. secondary school and technical college. Borough councillor 1975–78.

Mr John Burrow, barrister. Born Jun 19 1950; educ. Bishops Stortford College, Essex University. Member, Society of Labour Lawyers.

Mr Maurice Macmillan

SURREY SOUTH WEST

Electorate 69875 By-election May 3 1984

*Macmillan M. (C)	31067	59.7%
Scott, G. (L/All)	16716	32.1%
Williams, S. E. D. (Lab)	4239	8.2%
C majority	14351	27.6%
Total vote 52022		Turnout 74.5%

Mr Maurice Macmillan, a member of the Select Committee on Privileges since 1979, was Paymaster General attached to the Treasury 1973–74; Secretary of State for Employment 1972–73; Chief Secretary to the Treasury 1970–72. MP for Farnham 1966–83, and for Halifax 1955–64; won this seat in 1983; contested Seaham 1945, Lincoln 1951 and Wakefield (by-election). Economic Secretary to the Treasury 1963–64. Born Jan 27 1921; educ. Eton and Balliol College, Oxford, Chairman, Macmillan and Co Ltd, 1966–70, and since 1974. Son of Mr Harold Macmillan. Formerly director, Yorkshire Television and Monotype Corporation. Executive chairman, Wider Share Ownership Council 1964–70. Member, Shadow Cabinet and a spokesman on Treasury and economic affairs 1974–75. Member, Select Committee on Wealth Tax 1975–6. *By-election result page 367.*

Mr George Scott, author, journalist and broadcaster, is head of UK office of European Commission. Contested Wimbledon 1964, and by-elections at Middlesbrough East Mar 1962, and Middlesbrough West Jun 1962. Born Jun 22 1925; educ. Middlesbrough High School and New College, Oxford. NUJ.

Mr Stephen Williams, teacher. Born Nov 20 1953; educ. Hereford Cathedral School; Christ Church, Oxford and Gloucestershire College of Education. NUT.

Mr Timothy Renton

SUSSEX MID Electorate 77 005

*Renton, T. (C)	35 310	61.4%
Campbell, J. (L/All)	18 566	22.3%
Hawkes, Mrs P. (Lab)	3 470	6.0%
Bray, J. (Ind)	196	0.3%
C majority	16 744	29.1%
Total vote 57 542	Turnout 74.7%	

Mr Timothy Renton, director of building, investment and insurance companies, was elected in Feb 1974; contested Sheffield Park 1970. Born May 28 1932; educ. Eton and Magdalen College, Oxford. National President, Conservative Trade Unionists since 1980. Chairman, Conservative backbench employment committee 1981–82; vice-chairman, Conservative parliamentary trade committee 1974–79. Member Select Committee on Nationalized Industries 1974–79; Fellowship, Industry and Parliament Trust 1977–78. PPS to Chief Secretary to the Treasury 1979–81, to Secretary of State for Trade 1981–82 and Chancellor of the Exchequer 1983. Grower of ornamental amenity trees in partnership with wife. APEX.

Mr Jack Campbell, certified accountant and director of group of engineering companies. Born Aug 16 1930; educ. Allan Glen's School, Glasgow. Contested seat 1979. Member, West Sussex County Council since 1979; leader of Liberal group.

Mrs Patricia Hawkes, teacher. Born Apr 28 1936; educ. Hove County Grammar School for Girls, Brighton College of Education, Sussex University. Brighton borough councillor.

Mr Neil Macfarlane

SUTTON AND CHEAM Electorate 63 099 1979: 63 083 same

*Macfarlane, D. N. (C)	26 782	57.1%
Caswill, C. (L/All)	16 518	35.2%
Dixon, G. S. (Lab)	3 568	7.6%
C majority	10 264	21.9%
Total vote 46 868	Turnout 74.3%	

1979: Total vote 49 697 (78.8%); C 28 842 (58.0%); L 13 136 (26.4%); Lab 7 126 (14.3%); NF 465 (0.9%); Ind 128 (0.3%). C maj 15 706 (31.6%); swing 5.7. to C.

Mr Neil Macfarlane has been Under Secretary of State for the Environment and Minister for Sport since 1981; Minister for Children's Play since 1983 and was Under Secretary of State for Education and Science 1979–81. Former company director and former executive with an oil company. Regained the seat for the Conservatives, Feb 1974; contested East Ham North 1970; Sutton and Cheam by-election 1972. Born May 7 1936; educ. St Aubyns, Woodford Green, and Bancrofts School, Woodford Wells. Member Select Committee on Science and Technology, 1974–79; former secretary, Conservative backbench committees on energy, Greater London and on sport and recreation.

Mr Christopher Caswill, science administrator. Born Jan 20 1944; educ. Cranbrook School, Kent and Queen's College, Cambridge. Contested the seat 1979. Member, Sutton Borough Council since 1982. ASTMS.

Mr Geoffrey Dixon, credit controller. Born Jan 16 1953; educ. Haberdashers' Aske's Hatcham Boys School. SOGAT 82; member, London clerical branch committee 1982.

Mr Norman Fowler

SUTTON COLDFIELD Electorate 67 695 1979: 64 093 same

*Fowler, N. (C)	31 753	65.4%
Jones, A. (L/All)	12 769	26.3%
Gibbons, C. C. (Lab)	4 066	8.4%
C majority	18 984	39.1%
Total vote 48 588	Turnout 71.8%	

1979: Total vote 49 521 (77.3%); C 34 096 (68.9%); Lab 7 989 (16.1%); L 6 511 (13.1%); NF 466 (0.9%); Other 459 (0.9%). C maj 26 107 (52.8%); swing 5.5% to C.

Mr Norman Fowler has been Secretary of State for Social Services since 1981; Secretary of State (1981) and Minister (1979–81) for Transport. Chief Opposition spokesman on transport 1976; chief spokesman on the social services 1975–76; joined shadow cabinet 1975. Spokesman on home affairs 1974–75. Journalist on *The Times* 1961–70; Home Affairs Correspondent 1966–70. Elected for this seat Feb 1974; MP for Nottingham South 1970–74. Born Feb 2 1938; educ. King Edward VI School, Chelmsford and Trinity Hall, Cambridge. Member, Select Committee on Race Relations and Immigration 1970–74. NUJ.

Mr Aubrey Jones, an economist and company director, was MP for Birmingham, Hall Green 1950–65; contested South East Essex 1945; Heywood and Radcliffe by-election 1946. Minister of Fuel and Power 1955–57. Minister of Supply 1957–59. Chairman, National Board for Prices and Incomes 1965–70. Vice-president, Consumers' Assoc. 1967–72. Born Nov 20 1911; educ. Cyfarthfa Castle Secondary School, Merthyr Tydfil.

Mr Christopher Gibbons, barrister. Born 1952; educ. Birmingham University.

Mr Donald Anderson

SWANSEA EAST Electorate 57 285

*Anderson, D. (Lab)	22 297	54.4%
Shrewsbury, M. (L/All)	8 762	21.4%
O'Shaughnessy, N. (C)	8 080	19.7%
Reid, C. (PlC)	1 531	3.7%
Jones, W. R. (Com)	294	0.7%
Lab majority	13 535	33.0%
Total vote 40 964		Turnout 71.5%

Mr Donald Anderson, an Opposition spokesman on foreign affairs since 1983; barrister, formerly a diplomat and university lecturer, was returned in Oct 1974; MP for Monmouth 1966–70. Chairman, Welsh labour Group 1977. Chairman, Select Committee on Welsh Affairs since 1979. Born Jun 17 1939; educ. Swansea Grammar School and University College, Swansea. Member, Kensington and Chelsea Council 1971–75. Chairman, PLP environment committee 1974–76, 1977–79; secretary, Anglo-German and Anglo-French parliamentary groups. Executive member of IPU and CPA. Methodist local preacher. President, Gower Society 1976–78. Sponsored by NUR.

Mr Martyn Shrewsbury, teacher of English as a foreign language. Born Apr 7 1958; educ. Burton Grammar School, Dynevor Comprehensive and Swansea University.

Mr Nicholas O'Shaughnessy, lecturer. Born 1954; educ. Bedford School and London University.

Mr Clive Reid, pharmacist, is a past-chairman of West Glamorgan Pharmaceutical Committee.

Mr Alan Williams

SWANSEA WEST Electorate 58 237

*Williams, A. (Lab)	18 042	42.1%
Lewis, J. (C)	15 692	36.6%
Berry, P. (SDP/All)	8 036	18.8%
Pennar, Ms M. (PlC)	795	1.9%
Oubridge, B. (Eco)	265	0.6%
Lab majority	2 350	5.5%
Total vote 42 830		Turnout 73.5%

Mr Alan Williams, Opposition spokesman on the Civil Service since 1979; Minister of State, Department of Industry, 1976–79; Minister of State, Prices and Consumer Protection 1974–76. Opposition spokesman on education and science 1970–73; consumer affairs 1973–74. Parliamentary Secretary, Ministry of Technology and Power 1969–70; Under Secretary, Department for Economic Affairs 1967–69. Won the seat 1964; contested Poole 1959. Born Oct 14 1930; educ. Cardiff High School, Cardiff College of Technology and University College, Oxford. Director, Job Creation Ltd; Parliamentary adviser to Institution of Plant Engineers; adviser (unpaid) to Assoc. of First Division Civil Servants. Economics lecturer.

Dr Julian Lewis, consultant on defence and international affairs, research director to coalition for peace through security. Born Sep 26 1951; educ. Dynevor Grammar School, Swansea, Balliol and St Antony's Colleges, Oxford.

Mr Peter Berry. Born 1946; educ. Cambridge and London universities. Former teacher, industry consultant, civil servant and Welsh Office adviser on economic and regional policy.

Mrs Meirion Pennar, a native of Swansea, is a lecturer in Welsh at St David's University College, Lampeter.

Mr Simon Coombs

SWINDON Electorate 76 833 1979: 65 761 minor

Coombs, S. C. (C)	22 310	39.2%
*Stoddart, D. (Lab)	20 915	36.7%
Scott, D. J. (SDP/All)	13 743	24.1%
C majority	1 395	2.5%
Total vote 56 968		Turnout 74.2%

1979: Total votes 50 246 (76.4%); Lab 25 218 (50.2%); C 19 319 (38.4%); L 5 709 (11.4%). Lab maj 5 899 (11.8%); swing 5.1% to C.

Mr Simon Coombs, marketing executive, British Telecom, won the seat in 1983. Born Feb 21 1947; educ. Wycliffe College and Reading University. Member, Reading County Borough Council 1969–72; Reading Borough Council since 1973; Society of Post-Office Executives. Chairman, Wessex Area Conservatives, 1980–83 and Wessex Area Young Conservatives, 1973–76. Member, Southern Electricity Consultative Council since 1981.

Mr David Stoddart was an Opposition spokesman on industry 1982–83 and a member, Select Committee on Energy 1979–83. Lord Commissioner of the Treasury (whip) 1976–78, and an Assistant Government Whip 1975–76. Won the seat in 1970 after contesting it at the 1969 by-election. Born May 4 1926; educ. St Clement Danes and Henley Grammar Schools, Bromley Technical College.

Mr Derek Scott, economist, was special adviser to Mr Denis Healey at the Treasury in the last Labour Government; economic adviser to Mr James Callaghan as Leader of the Opposition. Economist in oil industry. Born 1947; educ. Liverpool University; LSE; Birkbeck College, London.

Mr Neil Hamilton

TATTON Electorate 68 747

Hamilton, N. (C)	27 877	54.6%
Levy, D. (SDP/All)	13 917	27.2%
Davies, D. W. (Lab)	9 295	18.2%
C majority	13 960	27.3%
Total vote 51 089		Turnout 74.3%

Mr Neil Hamilton, Director of Institute of Directors (European and parliamentary affairs). Elected in 1983. Born 1950; educ. Amman Valley Grammar School; Aberystwyth University; Corpus Christi, Cambridge. Contested Abertillery 1974 and Bradford North 1979.

Mr David Levy, chartered accountant and co-director of civil engineering company. Born Jun 27 1942; educ. Manchester Grammar School and Manchester University. Liveryman, Worshipful Company of Chartered Accountants.

Mr William Davies, university lecturer, fought East Cheshire in the European elections 1979. Vice-chairman, Oxfam National Council of Management, and director, executive development centre, Manchester Business School. Born 1925.

Mr Edward du Cann

TAUNTON Electorate 70 359 1979: 66 349 minor

*du Cann, E. (C)	28 112	52.9%
Cocks, M. (SDP/All)	15 545	29.2%
Gray, J. (Lab)	9 498	17.9%
C majority	12 567	23.6%
Total vote 53 155		Turnout 75.6%

1979: Total vote 53 573 (80.7%) C 28 483 (53.2%); Lab 15 759 (29.4%); L 7 928 (14.8%); Eco 1 403 (2.6%). C maj 12 724 (23.8%); swing 5.1% to C.

Mr Edward du Cann was chairman Select Committee on the Treasury and Civil Service and Chairman Liaison Committee, of Select Committee Chairman 1979–83; chairman 1922 Committee since 1972. Chairman, Public Accounts Committee, 1974–79. Founder chairman (1971) Select Committee on Public Expenditure. Elected 1956 by-election; contested Barrow-in-Furness 1955, and West Walthamstow 1951. Born May 28 1924; educ. Colet Court, Woodbridge School and St John's College, Oxford. Member Committee of Privileges, since 1974. Admiral, House of Commons Yacht Club since 1973. Founder of the Unicorn Group of Unit Trusts. Chairman of Conservative Party Organization 1956–67; President 1981–82. Minister of State, Board of Trade, 1963–64; Economic Secretary to the Treasury 1962–63. Deputy chairman, Lonrho Ltd.

Mr Michael Cocks, financial consultant. Born Oct 16 1936; educ. Eastwood and Beaufort Lodge preparatory schools, Barnet; Westcliff High School, and Peterhouse, Cambridge.

Mr Jon Gray, systems analyst with Somerset County Council. Born Nov 15 1945; educ. Peterhouse, Cambridge. Chairman, Labour Party regional executive committee.

Mr William Walker

TAYSIDE NORTH Electorate 51 972

*Walker, W. C. (C)	19 269	51.0%
Morgan, A. (SNP)	9 170	24.3%
Skene, D. (L/All)	7 255	19.2%
Wylie, N. (Lab)	2 057	5.5%
C majority	10 099	26.8%
Total vote 37 751		Turnout 72.6%

Mr William Walker, member, Select Committee on Scottish Affairs since 1979, and of Select Committee on Parliamentary Commissioner for Administration since 1979. Joint vice-chairman, Conservative backbench European Affairs committee since 1982; joint secretary, aviation committee. Managing director of his own management, marketing and design consultancy company. Gained Perth and East Perthshire for Conservatives 1979; won this seat 1983; contested Dundee East Oct 1974. Born Feb 20 1929; educ. Logie and Blackness Schools Dundee; Trades College Dundee; College of Arts, Dundee; and College of Distributive Trades, London. Former senior Gliding Instructor Air Cadet Gliding School; former political officer and vice-chairman, Brandwood Branch, Birmingham Hall Green Conservative Assoc; Fellow, British Institute of Management, fellow, Institute of Personnel Management and Royal Society of Arts.

Mr Alasdair Morgan, computer consultant. Born 1945; educ. Breadalbane Academy; Glasgow University; Moray House College.

Mr Danus Skene, teacher, contested Kinross and West Perthsire as Labour candidate Feb and Oct 1974. Born Apr 2 1944; educ. at universities of Sussex, Chicago and Aberdeen. Member, Perth and Kinross District Council.

Mr Noel Wylie is a general dental practitioner. Aged 48; educ. Queen's Park Senior Secondary School, Glasgow and the universities of Glasgow and Dundee. Former chairman, Tayside branch of Medical Campaign against Nuclear Weapons.

Mr Patrick Nicholls

TEIGNBRIDGE Electorate 67 515

Nicholls, P. (C)	28 265	54.0%
Alderson, J. (L / All)	20 047	38.3%
Loughlin, M. (Lab)	3 749	7.2%
Hope, A. (Loony Socy)	241	0.5%
C majority	8 218	15.7%
Total vote 52 302	Turnout	77.5%

Mr Patrick Nicholls, solicitor, won this seat in 1983. Born Nov 14 1948; educ. St Peter's Harefield, Red Rice College, and the College of Law, Guildford. Member, East Devon District Council since 1980; vice-chairman property services committee 1983.

Mr John Alderson, research fellow at Nuffield College, Oxford, writer and broadcaster, and former Chief Constable of Devon and Cornwall. Born May 28 1922; educ. Barnsley Technical College and Inns of Court where he qualified as a barrister. Served 36 years with the police in the provinces and metropolitan area.

Mr Michael Loughlin is a buyer for electrical engineers and contractors. Born Dec 20 1950; educ. Monmouth Grammar School. EETPU.

Mr Roger Gale

THANET NORTH Electorate 66 678

Gale, R. (C)	26 801	58.4%
MacMillan, W. (SDP / All)	12 256	26.7%
Booth, Ms C. (Lab)	6 482	14.1%
Dobing, B. (BNP)	324	0.7%
C majority	14 545	31.7%
Total vote 45 863	Turnout	68.8%

Mr Roger Gale, a producer with Thames Television, elected in 1983; contested Birmingham, Northfield 1982 by-election. Born Aug 20 1943; educ. Southbourne Preparatory School and Hardye's School, Dorchester. Member, British Actors Equity, NUJ, ACTT.

Dr William Macmillan teaches at Kent University. Born 1948; educ. Bristol University. Vice-chairman, East Kent area party; an organizer of SDP third World and Development Assoc.

Ms Cherie Booth, barrister. Born Sep 23 1954; educ. convent, grammar schools, LSE. Member, Society of Labour Lawyers. GMBATU.

Mr Jonathan Aitken

THANET SOUTH Electorate 61 989

*Aitken, J. (C)	24 512	56.5%
Josephs, I. (L/All)	10 461	24.1%
Clark, M. (Lab)	8 429	19.4%
C majority	14 051	32.4%
Total vote 43 402	Turnout	70.0%

Mr Jonathan Aitken, journalist, won the seat in 1983; represented Thanet East Feb 1974–83; contested Meriden 1966. Born Aug 30 1942; educ. Eton and Christ Church, Oxford. Member, Select Committee on Employment since 1979; Chairman, British-Saudi Arabian parliamentary group. Former secretary, Conservative broadcasting and communications committee. Director, TV-am; Aitken Hume plc.

Mr Ian Josephs, principal of school of English, contested Thanet 1970; Dartford Feb 1974, Bexley Sidcup Oct 1974, Dartford 1979. Born Jan 1932; educ. Charterhouse and Pembroke College, Oxford. Member, Kent County Council 1960–66.

Mr Martin Clarke, assistant investment manager for NCB pension fund. Aged 27; educ. Cambridge University. Candidate, local government election, Lewisham, 1982. Member, Fabian Society.

Dr Oonagh McDonald

THURROCK Electorate 66 300

*McDonald, Dr O. (Lab)	17 600	39.2%
Tallon, Miss J. (C)	15 878	35.4%
Benson, D. (SDP/All)	9 761	21.7%
Bibby, M. J. (Ind)	1 220	2.7%
Sinclair, R. W. (BNP)	252	0.6%
Paul, J. (Com)	199	0.4%
Lab majority	1 722	3.8%
Total vote 44 910	Turnout	67.7%

Dr Oonagh McDonald has been an Opposition spokesman on defence and disarmament since 1981. Elected at a by-election in 1976; contested Gloucestershire South Feb and Oct 1974. Born Feb 1938; educ. Roan School for Girls Greenwich; East Barnet Grammar School, and King's College, London. Lecturer in philosophy, Bristol University, 1965–76. Member, Commons

Expenditure Committee 1977. PPS to Chief Secretary of the Treasury 1977–79; Member, Select Committee on Employment 1981. Member, industrial policy subcommittee and finance and economic affairs subcommittee of Labour's National Executive Committee. ASTMS.

Miss Julie Tallon, director of her own property refurbishment company; partner in firm of industrial and commercial consultants. Born 1948; educ. Sutton Coldfield High School for Girls; Prince Henry's Grammar School, Evesham. Member, Merton and Wimbledon political committee; past vice-chairman. Member, Foreign Affairs Forum.

Mr Donald Benson, freelance transport lecturer and author. Born Feb 10 1926; educ. Palmers College, Grays. Member, Institute of Transport Administration; was chairman of its national education committee. NATFHE.

Mr Robin Maxwell-Hyslop

TIVERTON Electorate 63 828

*Maxwell-Hyslop, R. (C)	27 101	54.8%
Morrish, D. (L / All)	19 215	38.8%
Gorbutt, D. A. (Lab)	3 154	6.4%
C majority	7 886	15.9%
Total vote 49 470	Turnout 77.5%	

Mr Robin Maxwell-Hyslop was elected in the 1960 by-election; contested Derby North 1959. Former personal assistant to director of sales and service, Rolls-Royce Aero Engine Division, following graduate apprenticeship and two years in Export Sales Department. Born Jun 6 1931; educ. Stowe and Christ Church, Oxford. Joint secretary, Conservative parliamentary aviation committee 1972–79. Member, Select Committee on Procedure for Supply, 1980–81, and of Select Committee on Standing Orders since 1979, and Select Committee on Industry and Trade, since 1979.

Mr David Morrish, lecturer at Exeter University, contested Exeter 1970, Feb and Oct 1974 and Tiverton 1979. Born May 17 1931; educ. Sutton High School, Plymouth, Exeter University and Wisconsin University, USA. Member, Exeter City Council 1961–74; Devon County Council since 1973, leader of Liberal group Member, Devon Sea Fisheries Committee; Governor of Bicton College of Agriculture; former chairman, Devon Liberal Party. AUT.

Mr David Corbutt, lecturer. Born 1941. Vice-chairman, West Devon working party on unemployment. Member, Socialist Educational Assoc; Socialist Environmental and Resources Assoc; Friends of the Earth. NATFHE.

Mr John Stanley

TONBRIDGE AND MALLING Electorate 72 549 same

*Stanley, J. (C)	30 417	56.1%
Freeman, F. (SDP/All)	16 897	31.2%
Bishop, D. J. (Lab)	6 896	12.7%
C majority	13 520	24.9%
Total vote 54 210	Turnout 74.7%	

1979: Total vote 54 149 (79.5%); C 29 534 (54.5%); Lab 13 282 (24.5%); L 10 904 (20.1%); NF 429 (0.8%). C maj 16 252 (30.0%); swing 6.3% to C.

Mr John Stanley was appointed Minister of State for the Armed Forces Jun 1983; Minister for Housing and Construction, with rank of Minister of State at the DoE 1979–83; was PPS to Mrs Thatcher 1976–79. Former consultant to RTZ Industries Ltd. Elected Feb 1974; contested Newton 1970. Born Jan 19 1942; educ. Repton School and Lincoln College, Oxford. Member, Select Committee on Nationalized Industries 1974–76; Secretary, Conservative Industry Committee 1974–75; vice-chairman 1975–76. Former research associate of the International Institute for Strategic Studies.

Mr Roland Freeman contested Nuneaton for the Conservatives Oct 1974. Non-executive director, London Weekend TV and LSE governor. Born May 1927; educ. LSE (President of Union and subsequently NUS). Former GLC finance chairman and GLC member for Finchley until 1981.

Mr David Bishop, technical author specializing in avionics. Born Jan 14 1941; educ. technical college. Member, Rochester City Council. AUEW (TASS).

Mr Thomas Cox

TOOTING Electorate 68 083

*Cox, T. (Lab)	19 640	42.5%
Harris, R. (C)	16 981	37.0%
Neuberger, Mrs J. (SDP / All)	8 317	18.1%
Berbridge, P. (NF)	355	0.8%
Shaw, Ms E. (Eco)	255	0.6%
Lewis, R. E. (Com)	181	0.4%
Patel, H. (Eth Min)	146	0.3%
Redgrave, C. (WRP)	72	0.2%
Lab majority	2 659	5.8%
Total vote 45 947		Turnout 67.5%

Mr Thomas Cox was an assistant Government whip 1974–77; Lord Commissioner of the Treasury (whip) 1977–79. Represented Wandsworth, Tooting Feb 1974–83; Wandsworth Central 1970–74. contested Stroud 1966. Born 1930; educ. state schools and London School of Economics. Electrician. Former alderman, Fulham Borough Council. Sponsored by EETPU.

Mr Robin Harris, consultant director, Conservative Research Department. Born Jun 22 1952; educ. Canford School and Exeter College, Oxford. Member, Oxfordshire County Council 1977–80.

Mrs Julia Neuberger, Rabbi. Born Feb 27 1950; educ. South Hampstead High School, Newnham College, Cambridge, and Leo Baeck College, London.

Sir Frederic Bennett

TORBAY Electorate 67 337

*Bennett, Sir F. (C)	25 721	52.6%
Mitchell, M. (L/All)	19 166	39.2%
Rackley, P. W. (Lab)	3 521	7.2%
Murray, Mrs A. M. L. (Ratepyr)	500	1.0%
C majority	6 555	13.4%
Total vote 48 908		Turnout 72.6%

Sir Frederic Bennett was chosen in Apr 1979 to lead the Conservative delegation to the Council of Europe, having been a United Kingdom delegate to the Council of Europe, and WEU since 1974. Returned in Feb 1974; MP for Torquay 1955–74 and for Reading North 1951–55; contested Birmingham, Ladywood 1950, and Burslem 1945. Barrister. Born Dec 2 1918; educ. Westminster School. Director and consultant to various financial and industrial institutions in United Kingdom and abroad. Member Public Expenditure Committee 1974–79.

Mr Michael Mitchell, teacher. Born Apr 2 1949. Councillor.

Mr Philip Rackley, teacher. Born Apr 28 1949; educ. technical high school, Torquay; Plymouth Polytechnic; Bolton College of Education. NUT.

Mr Leo Abse

TORFAEN Electorate 58 739 1979: 57 187 minor

*Abse, L. (Lab)	20 678	47.3%
Blackburn, G. (L/All)	12 393	28.4%
Martin, P. (C)	9 751	22.3%
Cox, Mrs P. (PlC)	896	2.1%
Lab majority	8 285	19.0%
Total vote 43 718		Turnout 74.4%

1979 (as Pontypool): Total vote 44 811 (78.4%); Lab 27 751 (61.9%); C 10 383 (23.2%); L 5 508 (12.3%); PlC 1 169 (2.6%). Lab maj 17 368 (38.7%); swing 4.0% to C.

Mr Leo Abse, a solicitor, elected in 1983 was MP for Pontypool 1958–83; contested Cardiff North 1955. Born Apr 22 1917; educ. Howard Gardens High School, Cardiff, and London School of Economics. Chairman, Select Committee on Welsh Affairs 1979–81. Chairman, Cardiff Labour Party 1951–53; member, Cardiff City Council 1953–58. Member, Home Office Advisory Council for Penal Reform; Council of Institute for Study and Treament for Delinquency; National Council for the Unmarried Mother and Her Child; departmental committee on adoption; Select Committee on Abortion.

Mr Graham Blackburn, engineer and general manager, BSC Cardiff workshops. Born Mar 25 1939; educ. Newport High School and St Catherine's College, Cambridge. Member, Steel Industry Management Assoc.

Mr Peter Martin, an adviser with the British Institute of Management, has been a member of Richmond Borough Council since 1982. Born 1941; educ. St Anselm's College, Birkenhead, Sheffield University and LSE.

Mrs Phyllis Cox, mature student, is a former book-keeper with the British Steel Corporation.

Mr Norman Atkinson

TOTTENHAM Electorate 67944

*Atkinson, N. (Lab)	22423	52.0%
Murphy, P. (C)	13027	30.2%
L'Estrange, A. (L/All)	6990	16.2%
Hurry, W. G. (Ind C)	652	1.5%
Lab majority	9396	21.8%
Total vote 43092		Turnout 63.4%

Mr Norman Atkinson was treasurer of the Labour Party, with a seat on the national executive 1976–81. Elected in 1964; contested Manchester, Wythenshawe 1955; Altrincham and Sale 1959. Mechanical engineer and chief design engineer. Manchester University 1957–64. Born Mar 25 1923; educ. elementary and technical schools. Member Tribune Group. Former chairman Select Committee on Science and Technology; former member Select Committee on Immigration and Race Relations. Member, Manchester City Council 1945–49. Governor Imperial College of Science and Technology. Sponsored by AUEW.

Mr Peter Murphy, chartered surveyor. Son of Liverpool docker. Educ. St Mary's Roman Catholic School, Crosby. Chairman, Tottenham Conservative Assoc. since 1980.

Mr Alex L'Estrange, clerical officer with London shipbrokers. Born Oct 21 1929; educ. Charterhouse; Collier School, Horsham, Sir John Cass College, London; Kingston Technical College.

Mr David Penhaligon

TRURO Electorate 68514

*Penhaligon, D. (L/All)	31279	57.3%
Buddell, P. (C)	20799	38.1%
Beecroft, Ms J. M. (Lab)	2479	4.5%
L/All majority	10480	19.2%
Total vote 54557		Turnout 79.6%

Mr David Penhaligon, Liberal spokesman on industry since 1981 and energy since 1979; spokesman on employment 1976–81 and on transport 1977–81. Won the seat in Oct 1974; contested it Feb 1974, and Totnes 1970. Chartered mechanical engineer. Born Jun 6 1944; educ. Truro School and Cornwall Technical College. Member, Liberal Party Council, since 1968.

Mr Philip Buddell, chartered surveyor. Born 1943; educ. St Paul's School, Hammersmith and Royal Agricultural College, Cirencester.

Ms Janet Beecroft, youth training officer. Born Dec 12 1947; educ. Irvine Royal Academy, Ayrshire, and Craigie College, Ayr. Member of Socialist Countryside Group. TGWU.

Sir Patrick Mayhew

TUNBRIDGE WELLS Electorate 73 709 1979: 71825 same

*Mayhew, Sir P. (C)	31199	58.3%
Blaine, P. (L/All)	16073	30.0%
Casely, S. J. (Lab)	6042	11.3%
Smith, D. (Oth)	236	0.4%
C majority	15126	28.3%
Total vote 53550		Turnout 72.7%

1979: Total vote 53626 (74.7%); C 31928 (59.5%); Lab 11392 (21.2%); L 9797 (18.3%); NF 509 (0.9%). C maj 20536 (38.3%); swing 6.8% to C.

Sir Patrick Mayhew QC, was appointed Solicitor-General Jun 1983; Minister of State, Home Office 1981–83; Under Secretary of State for Employment 1979–81. Elected in Feb 1974; fought Dulwich, Camberwell in 1970. Born Sep 11 1929; educ. Tonbridge School and Balliol College, Oxford. Member Executive of 1922 Committee, 1976–79, and joint vice-chairman, Conservative home affairs committee 1976–79.

Mr Peter Blaine, engineer, contested Rutland and Stamford 1979. Born Jul 13 1944; educ. Leeds Grammar School, Pembroke College, Oxford, Southampton University and Imperial College, London.

Mr Stephen Casely is a postman. Born 1952.

Mr David Steel

TWEEDDALE, ETTRICK AND LAUDERDALE Electorate 37 075

*Steel, D. L. (L/All)	16 868	58.5%
Ballentine, A. (C)	8 329	28.9%
Saren, M. (Lab)	2 200	7.6%
Macartney, A. (SNP)	1 455	5.0%
L / All majority	8 539	29.6%
Total vote 28 852	Turnout	77.8%

Mr David Steel, was elected Leader of the Liberal Party in Jul 1976, when he also took charge of the party's role on devolution. Former Liberal whip. Member, Select Committee on Privileges since 1979. Won Roxburgh, Selkirk and Peebles from the Conservatives 1965 by-election; contested the seat 1964; won this seat 1983. Sponsored the Abortion Act 1967 and member, Select Committee on Abortion (Amendment) Bill 1975–76. President of the Anti-Apartheid Movement in Great Britain 1966–69. Rector of University of Edinburgh since 1982. Born Mar 31 1938; educ. Prince of Wales School, Nairobi; George Watson's College, Edinburgh and Edinburgh University.

Mr Alastair Ballantine, farmer and director of an agricultural supply company; contested Midlothian Oct 1974. Aged 42; educ. Merchiston Castle, Edinburgh and the East College of Agriculture. Former member, Scottish NFU for 15 years. Former member, Scottish Landowners' Federation National Council; former executive member, Roxborough, Selkirk and Peebles Conservative Assoc.

Dr Michael Saren is a lecturer at Strathclyde University Business School and author. Aged 31; educ. Bath University. Member, Edinburgh District Council since 1980; Co-operative Society; AUT.

Mr Allan Macartney, a staff tutor with the Open University, contested Berwick and East Lothian 1979; Renfrewshire West 1970. Church Elder. Chairman, St Andrew Society. Born Feb 1941; educ. Elgin Academy; Edinburgh and Glasgow universities.

Mr Toby Jessel

TWICKENHAM Electorate 64 116

*Jessel, T. F. H. (C)	25 110	50.4%
Waller, J. (L/All)	20 318	40.8%
Nicholas, Ms P. A. (Lab)	3 732	7.5%
Clarke, J. (Eco)	424	0.9%
Denville-Faulkner, T. (NF)	234	0.5%
Kenyon, R. W. (Ind)	40	0.1%
C majority	4 792	9.6%
Total vote 49 858	Turnout	77.8%

Mr Toby Jessel was elected in 1970; contested Kingston-upon-Hull North at by-election 1966 and at general election two months later; fought Peckham 1964. Born Jul 11 1934; educ. Royal Naval College, Dartmouth, and Balliol College, Oxford. Member GLC for Richmond upon Thames 1967–73, and of Southwark Borough Council 1964–66. Joint vice-chairman, conservative backbench arts and heritage committee, since 1982. Member, Council of Europe and WEU.

Mr John Waller, computer systems engineer and managing director, contested Twickenham 1979. Born Apr 14 1940; educ. Sir Roger Manwood's School, Sandwich, and Caius College, Cambridge. Member, London Borough of Richmond upon Thames Council since 1972.

Mrs Patricia Nicholas, secretary at ACCTT. Born Aug 27 1938; educ. state schools. Member, London Borough of Hounslow Council. APEX.

Mr Harry Cowans

TYNE BRIDGE Electorate 60 808

*Cowans, H. (Lab)	21 127	56.5%
Crawley, R. (C)	9 434	25.2%
Dawson, A. (L/All)	6 852	18.3%
Lab majority	11 693	31.3%
Total vote 37 413	Turnout	61.5%

Mr Harry Cowans, former British Railways technical officer, represented Newcastle upon Tyne Central Nov 1976–83; won this seat in 1983. Member, Select Committee on Transport since 1979. Born Dec 19 1932; educ. Atkinson Road Technical School, Newcastle upon Tyne. Member, Gateshead Borough Council 1970–78; and Tyne and Wear County Council 1972–76. Chairman PLP Northern Group. Opposition whip and secretary for Northern group of Labour MPs since 1982. Sponsored by NUR.

Mr Randall Crawley, owner and director of fine arts business. Born 1950; educ. Harrow and Magdalen College, Oxford. Winner of world doubles rackets championships 1981, and British amateur and open championships 1980, 1981 and 1982. Helped his father, Mr Aidan Crawley, in three campaigns in West Derbyshire.

Mr David Dawson is a builder, landscape gardener, and medical translator. Born 1954. Has acted as election agent.

Mr Neville Trotter

TYNEMOUTH Electorate 74 549

*Trotter, N. (C)	27 029	48.6%
Cosgrove, P. J. (Lab)	17 420	31.3%
Mayhew, D. (L/All)	11 153	20.1%
C majority	9 609	17.3%
Total vote 55 602	Turnout	74.6%

Mr Neville Trotter a practising chartered accountant, has been secretary of the Conservative backbench industry committee since 1979 and also chairman of the shipping and shipbuilding committee; formerly joint secretary of the aviation committee. Parliamentary adviser to British Marine Equipment Council. Elected in Feb 1974; contested Consett 1970. Born Jan 27 1932; educ. Shrewsbury School and King's College, Durham. Member Newcastle City Council, 1966–75; vice chairman, Northumberland Police Authority. Member, Commons Public Expenditure Committee and its trade and industry sub-committee 1974–79; Northern Economic Planning Council 1969–74.

Mr Patrick Cosgrove, barrister and former teacher, contested the seat 1979. Born Apr 1947; educ. St Cuthbert's Grammar School, Newcastle and Leeds University. North Tyneside councillor, since 1970; chairman, Tyne and Wear Socialist Education Assoc. TGWU(ACTS)

Mr David Mayhew, careers officer. Born Jul 31 1951; educ. St Paul's School, London; Christ Church, Oxford; Wycliffe Hall, Oxford, and Newcastle Polytechnic. Church of England lay reader.

The Rev William McRae

ULSTER MID Electorate 63 899

McCrea, Rev R. T. W. (DUP)	16 174	30.0%
Morrison, D. G. (SF)	16 096	29.9%
Haughey, P. D. (SDLP)	12 044	22.4%
Thompson, W. J. (OUP)	7 066	13.1%
Lagan, Dr. J. A. (All)	1 735	3.2%
Owens, T. A. (WP)	766	1.4%
DUP majority	78	0.1%
Total vote 53 881	Turnout	84.3%

The Rev William McRae, minister of Calvary Free Presbyterian Church, Magherafelt, County Londonderry; member, Northern Ireland Assembly since 1982; vice-chairman, education committee, and member, health and social services committee. Member, Northern Health and Social Services Board. Party spokesman on education. Vice-President, Assoc. of Local Authorities. DUP spokesman on education. Member, Magherafelt District Council. Born Aug 6 1948. Elected for this seat, 1983.

Mr Denis Haughey, contested Fermanagh and South Tyrone, Feb 1974. Aged 38; educ. St Patrick's College, Omagh. Queen's University, Belfast. A teacher. Full time agent to John Hume. Executive member, Civil Rights Assoc. 1969–70. Executive member SDLP since its formation in 1970; chairman 1973–78. International Secretary SDLP since 1978. Elected Northern Ireland Assembly 1982.

Sir Nicholas Bonsor

UPMINSTER Electorate 66 445 1979: 65 966 same

*Bonsor, Sir N. (C)	25 153	52.5%
Osman, D. (SDP/All)	12 339	25.8%
Hughes, A. (Lab)	9 829	20.5%
Nobes-Pride, G. (NF)	566	1.2%
C majority	12 814	26.8%
Total vote 47 887	Turnout	72.1%

1979: Total vote 53 036 (80.4%); C 27 960 (52.7%); Lab 18 895 (35.6%); L 5 216 (9.8%); NF 965 (1.8%). C maj 9 065 (17.1%); swing 1.8% to C.

Sir Nicholas Bonsor, barrister, farmer and company director, won the seat 1983; MP for Nantwich 1979–83; contested Newcastle under Lyme Feb and Oct 1974. Born Dec 9 1942; educ. Eton and Keble College, Oxford. Chairman, Wing Branch, Buckingham Conservative Assoc. 1974–76. Fellow, Royal Society of Arts. Member of Lloyd's and NFU. Vice-chairman, Conservative backbench foreign and Commonwealth affairs committee, since 1982 and of tourism sub-committee of Conservative backbench trade and industry committee.

Mr David Osman, economist and director of family publishing company. Born Apr 13 1953; educ. Minchenden Grammar School, London and Nottingham University. Member, Shelter; Amnesty International; West Wales Naturalist Trust.

Mr Alan Hughes, teacher. Born Nov 2 1935; educ. grammar school. Member, Redbridge Borough Council. NUT.

Mr Harold McCusker

UPPER BANN Electorate 60795

*McCusker, H. (OUP)	24888	56.9%
McDonald, J. (SDLP)	7807	17.9%
Wells, J. (DUP)	4547	10.4%
Curran, B. (PSF)	4110	9.4%
French, T. (WP)	2392	5.5%
OUP majority	17081	39.1%
Total vote 43744		Turnout 72.0%

Mr Harold McCusker won the seat 1983; represented Armagh Feb 1974–83. Teacher 1961–68; personnel officer–production manager 1968–72; Born Feb 7 1940; educ. Lurgan College. UUUC chief whip 1975. OUP chief whip 1977–79. Chairman Northern Ireland Gas Employers' Board 1977–81. Elected Northern Ireland Assembly 1982.

Mr Michael Shersby

UXBRIDGE Electorate 61615 1979: 60313 same

*Shersby, J. M. (C)	23 876	53.6%
Russell, P. (SDP/All)	11038	24.8%
Magee, P. J. (Lab)	9611	21.6%
C majority	12 838	28.8%
Total vote 44 525		Turnout 72.3%

1979: Total vote 47565 (78.9%); C 24967 (52.5%); Lab 16972 (35.7%); L 5031 (10.6%); NF 595 (1.3%). C maj 7995 (16.8%); swing 6.0% to C.

Mr Michael Shersby was elected as MP for Hillingdon, Uxbridge 1972 by-election. Has been Director General, British Sugar Bureau since 1977. Born Feb 17 1933; educ. John Lyon School, Harrow-on-the-Hill. Chairman, Conservative trade committee 1974–76; joint secretary, parliamentary scientific committee 1977–80; vice-chairman, Conservative environment committee since 1979; vice-chairman, Conservative smaller businesses committee 1970–80 and 1983; chairman, Conservative food and drink sub-committee since 1979. Vice-chairman Smaller Businesses Committee 1983. Secretary UK Sugar Industry Assoc. since 1978; member, Food and Drink Industries Council; director (unpaid) of World Sugar Research Organization. Member, Paddington Borough Council 1959–64; member, Westminster City Council 1964–71; deputy Lord Mayor 1967–68.

Mr Peter Russell, senior university lecturer. Born April 10 1937; educ. Reading, Brunel and London universities. Former member London Borough of Hillingdon Council and GLC. AUT.

Mr Patrick Magee, a mechanical fitter. Born 1947.

Sir Raymond Gower

VALE OF GLAMORGAN Electorate 62885

*Gower, Sir R. (C)	22421	48.0%
Sharp, M. E. (Lab)	12028	25.8%
Evans, A. (SDP/All)	11154	23.9%
Dixon, J. (PlC)	1068	2.3%
C majority	10393	22.3%
Total vote 46671		Turnout 74.2%

Sir Raymond Gower won the seat 1983; represented Barry 1951–83; contested Ogmore 1950. Solicitor, Vice-president, National Chamber of Trade. Director, Airport Hotels and another company and consultant to British Soil. Born Aug 15 1916; educ. Neath Grammar School; Cardiff High School; University College, Cardiff, and Cardiff School of Law. Vice-chairman Welsh Conservative MPs since 1974. Treasurer, Welsh Parliamentary Party (all-party). Member, Speaker's conference on electoral reform 1967–69 and 1971–74. Member, Select Committee on Welsh Affairs since 1979.

Mr Michael Sharp, probation officer. Born Jun 3 1939; educ. State schools in Derbyshire; Nottingham College of Further Education; Nottingham Technical College; Coleg Harlech Adult College, and Nottingham University. Labour agent for Barry in 1979. Chief whip of Labour group on South Glamorgan County Council. TGWU and National Assoc. of Probation Officers.

Mr Alan Evans, senior educational official, contested Pembroke 1979 for Labour. Born Feb 10 1939; educ. Llanelli Grammar School. Former member, London Borough of Camden and of ILEA. GMBATU.

Mr John Dixon, computer systems analyst, is Plaid Cymru's treasurer. Member, Vale of Glamorgan District Council.

Mr Stuart Holland

VAUXHALL Electorate 64 867

*Holland, S. (Lab)	18 234	46.5%
Manning, K. (C)	10 454	26.7%
Liddle, R. (SDP/All)	9 515	24.3%
Wright, J. (NF)	508	1.3%
Lingard, P. J. (Loony Soc)	266	0.7%
Cook, D. (Com)	199	0.5%
Shorter, G. B. (WP)	38	0.1%
Lab majority	7 780	19.8%
Total vote 39 214	Turnout	60.5%

Mr Stuart Holland, political economist and university lecturer, was chairman of the Public Enterprise Group 1973–75; economist assistant, Cabinet Office 1966–67, and personal assistant to the Prime Minister 1967–68. Elected in 1979. Born Mar 25 1940; educ. Christ's Hospital, University of Missouri, Balliol College, Oxford, and St Antony's College, Oxford. Special adviser, Commons Expenditure Committee 1971–72; consultant, economic and social affairs committee. Council of Europe 1973; Ministry of Overseas Development 1974–75; OECD 1977; UN University 1977–82. ASTMS.

Mr Kingsley Manning, management consultant and company director. Born Feb 11 1952; educ. King Henry VIII School, Coventry; Birmingham University, and London Business School.

Mr Roger Liddle, secretary, Social Sciences Research Trust, member SDP national Committee and policy committee. Born Jun 14 1947; educ. Carlisle Grammar School, Queen's College, Oxford. Member, Oxford City Council 1971–76, deputy leader 1973–76; leader Alliance group, Lambeth Council, since 1982. APEX.

Mr Walter Harrison

WAKEFIELD Electorate 68 416

*Harrison, W. (Lab)	19 166	40.4%
Hazell, N. (C)	18 806	39.7%
Carlton, D. (SDP/All)	9 166	19.3%
Parker, Mrs V. (BNP)	295	0.6%
Lab majority	360	0.8%
Total vote 47 433	Turnout	69.3%

Mr Walter Harrison, Opposition deputy chief whip 1979–83, was Treasurer of the Household and Government Deputy Chief Whip 1974–79. Elected in 1964. Foreman electrician. Born Jan 2 1921; educ. Dewsbury Technical College and School of Art. Opposition deputy Chief Whip 1970–74; a Lord Commissioner of the Treasury (whip) 1968–70 and Assistant Government whip 1966–68. Member, West Riding County Council 1958–64; Castleford Borough Council 1952–66 (alderman 1959–66). Member, Select Committee on House of Commons Services. Sponsored by EEPTU.

Mr Norman Hazell, a design draughtsman. Born Apr 17 1932; educ. Thornes House Grammar School and Wakefield Technical College. Member, Wakefield Metropolitan District Council since 1982. Partner, Titan Flooring Ltd, Wakefield. AUEW (TASS) since 1969.

Dr David Carlton, polytechnic lecturer and SDP founder member. Born Jul 1938; educ. grammar school and LSE. Labour candidate, Tynemouth Feb 1974, and Twickenham 1966.

Mrs Lynda Chalker

WALLASEY Electorate 68 462 1979: 69 211 minor

*Chalker, Mrs L. (C)	22 854	46.0%
Robertson, J. A. (Lab)	16 146	32.5%
Richardson, J. (SDP / All)	10 717	21.6%
C majority	6 708	13.5%
Total vote 49 717	Turnout	72.6%

1979: Total vote 53 475 (77.3%); C 26 548 (49.6%); Lab 21 167 (39.6%); L 5 269 (9.9%). NF 491 (0.9%). C maj 5 381 (10.0%); swing 3.1% to C.

Mrs Lynda Chalker, appointed Minister of State for Transport 1983; Under-Secretary of State for Transport 1982–83; Under-Secretary of State for Health and Social Security 1979–82. An Opposition spokesman on the social services 1976–79. Elected Feb 1974. Born Apr 29 1942; educ. Roedean School, Heidelberg University, Westfield College, London University and Central London Polytechnic. Statistician and former head of international division of Louis Harris International Ltd. Former member, General Advisory Council of BBC. Ex-parliamentary adviser, Market Research Society. Has served on National Union Executive Committee; Conservative Political Centre National Advisory Committee; Select Committee on Immigration and Race Relations.

Mr James Robertson is an economic development officer for Merseyside Council. Born Jul 12 1949; educ. Bristol and Essex universities. Nalgo.

Mr Jon Richardson, head of Cheshire comprehensive school history department. Born 1951; educ. Lancaster and Liverpool universities. Member, European Movement and Wallasey Civic Society.

Mr Edward Garrett

WALLSEND Electorate 76 268

*Garrett, W. E. (Lab)	26 615	49.1%
Leigh, Miss M. (C)	14 101	26.0%
Phylactou, Mrs J. (SDP / All)	13 522	24.9%
Lab majority	12 514	23.1%
Total vote 54 238		Turnout 71.1%

Mr Edward Garrett was elected in 1964. Engineer; secretary, all-party group for chemical industry. Born Mar 21 1920; educ. elementary schools and London School of Economics. Contested Hexham 1955; Doncaster 1959. Parliamentary adviser, Machine Tools Trades Assoc. and International Contact. Chairman, British-Czech parliamentary group. Member, former Select Committee on Expenditure; Northumberland County Council, for 18 years. Sponsored by AUEW engineering section.

Miss Mary Leigh, solicitor. Member, Lambeth Borough Council. Educ. Streatham Hill and Clapham High School.

Ms Joan Phylactou, senior lecturer in indusrial psychology at Newcastle Polytechnic. Born 1947; educ. University College and Birkbeck College, London. Member, North Tyneside MBC, since 1982; area representative, Council for Social Democracy.

Mr David Winnick

WALLSALL NORTH Electorate 68 868

*Winnick, D. (Lab)	20 782	42.5%
Stephens, N. (C)	17 958	36.7%
Bentley, A. (L/All)	10 141	20.8%
Lab majority	2 824	5.8%
Total vote 48 881		Turnout 71.0%

Mr David Winnick, a member, Select Committee on Environment, since 1980, regained seat for Labour in 1979; MP for Croydon South 1966–70; contested Harwich 1964; Croydon Central Oct 1974, and Walsall Nov 1976. Born Jun 26 1933; educ. secondary schools and London School of Economics. Administrative employee. Member, Select Committee on Race Relations and Immigration 1969–70; Willesden Council 1959–64; Brent Council 1964–66. Vice-president, Assoc. of Professional, Executive, Clerical and Computer Staff (APEX).

Mr Nicholas Stephens, chartered accountant and stockbroker. Born May 12 1946; educ. Charterhouse.

Mr Arthur Bentley, retired college lecturer and former local government officer, contested the seat 1979. Born Aug 24 1921; educ. Elmore Green Central School and Open University. Borough Councillor.

Mr Bruce George

WALSALL SOUTH Electorate 67 257

*George, B. (Lab)	21 735	43.5%
Nicholson, D. (C)	21 033	42.1%
Silver, B. (SDP/All)	6 586	13.2%
Parker, J. (BNP)	632	1.3%
Lab majority	702	1.4%
Total vote 49 986		Turnout 74.3%

Mr Bruce George, a member of the Select Committee on Defence since 1979, was elected in Feb 1974; contested Southport 1970. Born Jun 1 1942; educ. Mountain Ash Grammar School, University College, Swansea, and University of Warwick. Senior lecturer in politics, Birmingham polytechnic 1970–74. Member, Select Committee on Violence in the Family; former secretary, all-party parliamentary group on widows and one-parent families. Captain and founder, House of Commons Football Club.

Mr David Nicholson is Home Affairs Director, Assoc. of British Chambers of Commerce; Conservative Research Department 1972–1982. Former Assistant Principal, Department of Employment. Coeditor of *The Diaries of the late L.S. Amery*. Born Aug 17 1944; educ. Queen Elizabeth's Grammar School, Blackburn; Christ Church, Oxford; LSE. Unsuccessfully fought Islington borough elections 1982 and 1978.

Mr Eric Deakins

WALTHAMSTOW Electorate 48324 1979: 49315 minor

*Deakins, E. (Lab)	13241	39.8%
Amos, A. (C)	11936	35.9%
Leighton, P. (SDP/All)	7192	21.6%
Mitchell, P. (NF)	444	1.3%
Lambert, S. (Eco)	424	1.3%
Lab majority	1305	3.9%
Total vote 33237	Turnout	68.8%

1979: Total vote 35135 (71.2%); Lab 17651 (50.2%); C 13248 (37.7%); L 3117 (8.9%); NF 1119 (3.2%). Lab maj 4403 (12.5%); swing 9.1% to C.

Mr Eric Deakins was MP for Waltham Forest, Walthamstow Feb 1974–83. MP for Walthamstow West 1970–74. An Opposition Spokesman on agriculture and food. Member, Select Committee on Foreign Affairs and its overseas development subcommittee 1979–82; was Under Secretary of State, Department of Health and Social Security 1976–79. Under Secretary for Trade 1974–76. Born Oct 7 1932; educ. Tottenham Grammar School and London School of Economics. Contested Finchley 1959; Chigwell 1966 and Walthamstow West 1967. Member, Tottenham Borough Council 1958–61, 1962–63. Author. TGWU.

Mr Alan Amos, teacher. Born Nov 11 1952; educ. St Albans School and St John's College, Oxford. Member, London Borough of Enfield Council since 1978; chairman, education committee.

Mr Peter Leighton, barrister, is a founder member of the SDP. Born Oct 16 1943; educ. local schools and University College, London. Labour councillor, Waltham Forest 1970–78; chairman, education committee, 1972–78. SDP candidate in GLC elections, 1980. Member, governing bodies, North-East London Polytechnic, Waltham Forest College. Secretary, local charity for mentally handicapped children.

Mr John Thompson

WANSBECK Electorate 63398

Thompson, J. (Lab)	21732	47.0%
Thompson, J. A. (L / All)	13901	30.1%
Mitchell, C. (C)	10563	22.9%
Lab majority	7831	17.0%
Total vote 46196	Turnout	72.9%

Mr John Thompson, electrical engineer at Ellington colliery. Born 1928. Labour leader of Northumberland County Council; member, Newbiggin Council.

Mr Alan Thompson, chartered engineer and company director, won the seat 1983; contested East Dunbartonshire 1974, and Morpeth 1979. Born May 8 1936; educ. Dicksons College. District and county councillor; member, Northumbria Police Authority. Former delegate for DATA.

Mr Charles Mitchell, barrister. President, Eye Branch, Suffolk Conservative Constituency Assoc; chairman, municipal district ward of Fulham 1978–80.

Mr Jack Aspinwall

WANSDYKE Electorate 71094

*Aspinwall, J. (C)	28434	50.6%
Denton-White, R. (L / All)	15368	27.4%
Williams, L. (Lab)	12168	21.7%
Stout, A. (W Reg)	213	0.4%
C majority	13066	23.3%
Total vote 56183	Turnout	79.0%

Mr Jack Aspinwall, a director of a family business of retail shops, won this seat 1983; represented Kingswood 1979–83; contested it in Feb and Oct 1974, as a Liberal. Born Feb 1933; educ. Prescott Grammar School, Bootle, and Marconi College, Chelmsford. Member Avon County Council and Kingswood District Council.

Mr Richard Denton-White, teacher. Town councillor. Born Apr 11 1946.

Mr Lynn Williams is an electrician with BP Chemicals, and formerly an NCB colliery apprentice electrician. Born 1949; educ. the Open University. Mayor of Glynneath 1981–82. Member, Neath Borough Council; West Glamorgan Area Health Authority. EETPU.

Mr Patrick Jenkin

WANSTEAD AND WOODFORD

Electorate 57705 1979: 57218 same

*Jenkin, C. P. F. (C)	23765	60.3%
Crawford, K. (L/All)	9411	23.9%
Hilton, Mrs L. S. (Lab)	5334	13.5%
Warth, Mrs C. (Eco)	476	1.2%
Marshall, H. (NF)	456	1.2%
C majority	14354	36.4%
Total vote 39442	Turnout	68.4%

1979: Total vote 42170 (73.7%); C 26214 (62.2%); Lab 8464 (20.1%); L 6535 (15.5%); NF 957 (2.3%). C maj 17750 (42.1%); swing 7.4% to C.

Mr Patrick Jenkin was appointed Secretary of State for the Environment 1983; Secretary of State for Industry in 1981–83; Secretary of State for Social Services 1979–81; chief Opposition spokesman on the social services 1976–79; and on energy 1974–76. Was appointed to the Shadow Cabinet in 1974; Minister of Energy 1974 Chief Secretary, Treasury 1972–74; Financial Secretary to the Treasury 1970–72. Opposition spokesman on finance, economic and trade affairs 1965–70. Elected in 1964. Born Sep 7 1926; educ. Clifton College and Jesus College, Cambridge. Barrister, former industrial adviser and director of companies.

Mr Keith Crawford, a lecturer in politics, contested Enfield North 1979. Born Jun 18 1949; educ. Wolsingham Secondary School, Durham; South Bank Polytechnic, London; LSE. NATFHE.

Mrs Lesley Hilton, housewife. Born Jul 30 1949; educ. Maidstone Grammar School for Girls.

Mr Robert Jackson

WANTAGE

Electorate 63950

Jackson, R. (C)	25992	52.9%
Tumin, Mrs W. (SDP / All)	15867	32.3%
Popper, A. J. D. (Lab)	7115	14.5%
Barrett Mockler, A. P. (W Reg)	183	0.4%
C majority	10125	20.6%
Total vote 49157	Turnout	76.9%

Mr Robert Jackson, political adviser, was elected in 1983; contested Manchester Central Oct 1974. Member, European Parliament for Upper Thames since 1979. Born 1946; educ. Falcon College, near Bulawayo, and St Edmund Hall, Oxford (President of the Union, 1967). Member, Oxford City Council 1969–71.

Mrs Winifred Tumim, freelance writer and lecturer. Born 1936; educ. Oxford and London universities. Has served on council and executive committee, Royal National Institute for the Deaf; and as chairman of the sub-group on confidentiality of the Government inquiry into the education of handicapped children (Warnock Committee). Member, Hammersmith and Fulham District Health Authority and the DHA joint consultative committee and ethical committee. Represents Hammersmith and Fulham on Council for Social Democracy.

Mr Andrew Popper, a solicitor, contested Abingdon 1979. Born Apr 9 1951; educ. St Paul's School and Oriel College, Oxford. Member, Barnet Borough Council 1974–78. APEX.

Mr Andrew Faulds

WARLEY EAST

Electorate 57439

*Faulds, A. (Lab)	18036	45.6%
Whitby, M. (C)	14645	37.0%
Hamer, B. (SDP/All)	6697	16.9%
Randhawa, H. S. (Com)	217	0.6%
Lab majority	3391	8.6%
Total vote 39595	Turnout	68.9%

Mr Andrew Faulds, an actor, was Opposition spokesman on the arts 1970–73, and 1979–82. Elected in Feb 1974; MP for Smethwick 1966–74; contested Stratford upon Avon 1963 and 1964 by-elections. Born Mar 1 1923; educ. George Watsons, Louth Grammar School, Daniel Stewart's Edinburgh, Stirling High School and Glasgow University. Former member, Select Committee on House of Commons (Services). Member, Equity (council member, 1966–69). Joint chairman, all-party heritage group British branch, Parliamentary Assoc. for Euro-Arab Cooperation; Chairman, PLP arts group.

Mr Michael Whitby, a former employee of GKN plc and British Steam Specialists, initiated a group of companies in 1969, including a wholesale business, shops and firm of property developers. Born Feb 1948; educ. James Watt Technical School, College of Michaelshoven, German, and Birmingham University. Steering committee chairman, local branch, National Federation of Self-Employed and Small Businesses. Member, Warley East executive committee; Sandwell Community Council.

Mr Bryn Hamer, owner of sub Post Office and retail business, formerly engaged in banking. Born 1938; educ. Denbigh Grammar School.

Mr Peter Archer

WARLEY WEST Electorate 57 165

*Archer, P. (Lab)	18 272	47.1%
McIntyre, Miss A. (C)	13 004	33.6%
Baines, A. G. (L/All)	7 485	19.3%
Lab majority	5 268	13.6%
Total vote 38 761	Turnout	67.8%

Mr Peter Archer QC, was elected to Shadow Cabinet in 1981, becoming chief Opposition spokesman on legal affairs in 1982 and on trade later that year. Solicitor General 1974–79. Returned Feb 1974; represented Rowley Regis and Tipton 1966–74; contested Brierley Hill 1964 and Hendon South 1959. Born Nov 20 1926; educ. Wednesbury High School, LSE and University College London. Has served on Select Committee on European Legislation. APEX.

Miss Anthea McIntyre, market gardener. Born Jun 29 1954; educ. Queen's College, London. Member, Hereford and Worcester County Council since 1977.

Mr Anthony Baines, information and public relations officer. Born Mar 6 1959; educ. Farnham and Bristol. SCPS.

Mr Douglas Hoyle

WARRINGTON NORTH Electorate 69 850

*Hoyle, D. (Lab)	20 873	41.2%
Sexton, S. (C)	15 596	30.8%
Harrison, D. (SDP/All)	13 951	27.5%
Sloan, I. (BNP)	267	0.5%
Lab majority	5 277	10.4%
Total vote 50 687	Turnout	72.6%

Mr Douglas Hoyle won this seat 1983; retained Warrington for Labour at the 1981 by-election. MP for Nelson and Colne Oct 1974–79; contested it in Feb 1974, and 1970; Clitheroe 1964. member, Labour Party National Executive Committee 1978–82. Born Feb 17 1930; educ. Adlington School, Horwich Technical College and Bolton Technical College. Member, Council of 'Get Britain Out' (of EEC) Campaign. Member, Manchester Regional Hospital Board 1968–74. Member, ASTMS since 1958; member, national executive since 1968, president 1978, and now vice-president. Sponsored by ASTMS.

Mr Stuart Sexton, political adviser to Sir Keith Joseph and Dr Rhodes Boyson. Educ. St Joseph's College, London, and Imperial College of Science. Former member, Croydon Borough Council; past treasurer, vice-chairman and ward chairman, local constituency assoc. Member, National Education Assoc.

Mr David Harrison, head of department, business management and trade union studies at Warrington's North Cheshire College. Chairman, North Cheshire area party. Graduate in economics; fellow of British Institute of Management. Born 1939.

Mr Mark Carlisle

WARRINGTON SOUTH Electorate 72 803

*Carlisle, M. (C)	22 740	41.9%
Colin-Thome, D. (Lab)	16 275	30.0%
Marks, I. (L/All)	14 827	27.3%
Chantrell, N. (Eco)	403	0.7%
C majority	6 465	11.9%
Total vote 54 245	Turnout	74.5%

Mr Mark Carlisle QC, Secretary of State for Education and Science 1979–81; chief Opposition spokesman on education and science 1978–79; Minister of State, Home Office 1972–74, Under-Secretary, Home Office 1970–72. Won this seat 1983; represented Runcorn 1964–83; contested St Helens 1958 by-election and 1959. Born Jul 1929; educ. Radley College and Manchester University. Former chairman Federation of University Conservative and Unionist Assoc; vice-chairman North-West Conservative MPs since 1974. Former member Home Office Advisory Council on the Penal System. Member Executive 1922 Committee until November 1978. Recorder. Bencher, Gray's Inn 1980. Member, General Council BBC 1975–79. Member, National Assoc. for Care and Resettlement of Offenders 1975–79. Member, Franks Committee on Immigration. Treasurer Commonwealth Parliamentary Assoc. since 1982. Vice-chairman CPA UK Branch since 1982. Chairman Conservative Independent Schools Committee since 1982. Vice-chairman NW Group of Conservative MPs since 1982.

Mr David Colin-Thome, general practitoner. Born Oct 5 1943; educ. Hutton Grammar School, Preston, Lancs, and Newcastle University Medical School. Member, Halton Borough Council since 1979; vice-chairman, Halton Health Authority. MPU, ASTMS.

Mr Ian Marks, marketing manager with Fibreglass Ltd, a subsidiary of Piltington Bros plc. Born Apr 12 1948; educ. Bedford School; Churchill College, Cambridge; Liverpool University. Member, Warrington Borough Council.

Sir Dudley Smith

WARWICK AND LEAMINGTON Electorate 70858

*Smith, Sir D. (C)	26512	50.9%
Behrens, R. (SDP/All)	13480	25.9%
Chessum, R. (Lab)	11463	22.0%
Charlton, N. (Eco)	685	1.3%
C majority	13032	25.0%
Total vote 52140		Turnout 73.6%

Sir Dudley Smith, Under Secretary for the Army 1974; Under Secretary for Employment 1970–74. Opposition whip 1964–66. Elected at a by-election 1968. Represented Brentford and Chiswick 1959–66; contested Peckham 1955. Former vice-chairman, Select Committee on Race Relations and Immigration. Born Nov 14 1926; educ. Chichester High School. Management consultant and former journalist. UK delegate to Council of Europe and WEU since 1979; Secretary General of its European Democratic Group since 1983. Member, Middlesex County Council 1958–63. Chairman, Wilderness Foundation (UK) since 1981.

Mr Robert Behrens, senior polytechnic lecturer, is joint secretary, Social Democratic Campaign for Racial Justice. Born 1952; educ. Nottingham and Exeter universities. Senior lecturer in public administration, Lanchester Polytechnic. Member, Council for Social Democracy; SDP representative on Warwick Community Relations Council.

Mr Richard Chessum, unemployed teacher. Aged 40; educ. London University and University of Warwick. Former local government employee.

Mr Francis Maude

WARWICKSHIRE NORTH Electorate 68625

Maude, F. (C)	22452	41.9%
Tomlinson, J. E. (Lab)	19867	37.1%
Kerry, H. (SDP)	11207	20.9%
C majority	2585	4.8%
Total vote 53526		Turnout 78%

Mr Francis Maude, a barrister specializing in criminal law in Sir Michael Havers's chambers, is son of Sir Angus Maude, the former MP for Stratford-on-Avon. Elected in 1983. Born Jul 4 1953; educ. Abingdon School and Corpus Christi College, Cambridge. Member, Westminster City Council since 1978; vice-chairman, housing committee since 1980.

Mr John Tomlinson was Under Secretary, Ministry of Overseas Development 1977–79; Under Secretary, Foreign and Commonwealth Office 1976–79. MP for Meriden Feb 1974–79; contested Walthamstow East 1970, and Bridlington 1966. Born Aug 1 1939; educ. Westminster City School; Cooperative College, Loughborough; Nottingham University. PPS to Prime Minister 1975–76. Senior lecturer in industrial relations and management at Solihull College of Technology since 1979. Political organiser and head of research department, AUEW 1968–70. Former member, Sheffield City Council.

Mr Howard Kerry is a director, UK and USA, freight forwarding and customs agent, and export sales company. Born Feb 17 1943; educ. Yardley Grammar School, Birmingham.

Mr Tristan Garel-Jones

WATFORD Electorate 71992

*Garel-Jones, W. T. (C)	26273	48.0%
Burton, P. (SDP/All)	14267	26.0%
Wilson, I. (Lab)	14247	26.0%
C majority	12006	21.9%
Total vote 54787		Turnout 76.1%

Mr Tristan Garel-Jones, a Government Whip since 1982, was principal of a language school 1966–70; merchant banker 1970–74; and at Conservative Central Office from 1974, being personal assistant to party chairman 1978–79. Gained seat for Conservatives in 1979; contested Caernarvon Feb 1974 and Watford Oct 1974 Former executive member, Hemel Hempstead Conservative Assoc. Born Feb 28 1941; educ. Llangennech Primary School and King's School, Canterbury. Secretary, Conservative backbench constitutional committee until 1982. ASTMS.

Mr Peter Burton, managing director of computer and systems engineering plc, and chairman of Chiltern Radio plc. Born Feb 11 1930; educ. Pinner County School, University College, London and Harvard Business School. Member, St Albans District Council since 1982.

Mr Ian Wilson, teacher, contested Enfield Southgate 1979. Born Mar 2 1951; educ. Colchester Royal Grammar School, Churchill College. London Borough of Islington councillor since 1978. Chairman, National Young Fabian Group 1975. Member, Socialist Educational Assoc. and National Council for Civil Liberties. NUT.

Mr James Prior

WAVENEY Electorate 77 960

*Prior, J. (C)	30 371	51.8%
Lark, J. A. (Lab)	16 073	27.4%
Artis, Ms G. (SDP/All)	12 234	20.9%
C majority	14 298	24.4%
Total vote 58 678		Turnout 75.3%

Mr James Prior became Secretary of State for Northern Ireland in 1981; Secretary of State for Employment 1979–81; chief Opposition spokesman on employment 1974–79, after a short period as spokesman of home affairs. Lord President of the Council and Leader of the House of Commons 1972–74; Minister of Agriculture, Fisheries and Food 1970–72; Deputy chairman, Conservative Party Organization 1972–74. Won this seat in 1983; MP for Lowestoft 1959–83. Vice-chairman, Conservative Party, Apr–Aug 1965, when he resigned to become PPS to Mr Edward Heath until 1970. Farmer and land agent. Born Oct 11 1927; educ. Charterhouse and Pembroke College, Cambridge.

Mr Alan Lark, industrial safety adviser, contested Lowestoft 1979. Born Oct 18 1936; educ. Roman Hill School and Lowestoft College of Further Education. Member, Waveney District and Suffolk County councils.

Ms Gillian Artis, lecturer, is a committee member of Women for Social Democracy and Norfolk SDP county coordinator. Born 1954; educ. Loughborough University of Technology and Wolverhampton Poly.

Sir Geoffrey Johnson Smith

WEALDEN Electorate 69 244

*Johnson Smith, Sir G. (C)	31 296	64.2%
Pace, D. (SDP/All)	14 741	29.6%
Knight, Mrs P. (Lab)	3 060	6.2%
C majority	17 185	34.6%
Total vote 49 727		Turnout 71.8%

Sir Geoffrey Johnson Smith, won this seat 1983; MP for East Grinstead 1965–83; Parliamentary Secretary, Civil Service Department 1972–74; Under Secretary of Defence for the Army 1971–73. Opposition Whip 1965–66. Represented Holborn and St Pancras South 1959–64. Chairman, Conservative backbench Media Committee 1982; vice-chairman, backbench energy committee; Chairman, Select Committee on MPs interests 1979; member, Liaison Committee 1980. Member, Executive 1922 Committee since 1979; North Atlantic Assembly Political and Military Committee since 1980; chairman of subcommittee on conventional weapons. IBA General Advisory Council 1975–80. Governor, British Film Institute from 1980. Former television broadcaster, reporter and interviewer. Born Apr 16 1924; educ. Charterhouse and Lincoln College, Oxford. Member, Still Water Subcommittee, Salmon and Trout Assoc. Chairman, Conservative backbench media Committee, since 1982.

Mr David Pace, lecturer in management. Born Mar 28 1940; educ. Worthing High School, University of East Anglia, and London University.

Mrs Patricia Knight. Born Feb 26 1941; educ. Manchester and Warwick universities. NATFHE.

Mr Peter Fry

WELLINGBOROUGH Electorate 67 598

*Fry, P. (C)	25 715	48.9%
Mann, J. (Lab)	13 659	26.0%
Stringer, L. (L/All)	12 994	24.7%
Garnett, Miss D. M. P. (Oth)	228	0.4%
C majority	12 056	22.9%
Total vote 52 596		Turnout 77.8%

Mr Peter Fry, a former Conservative spokesman on transport, has been a member of the Select Committee on Transport since 1979. Won the seat at 1969 by-election. Company director. Born May 1931; educ. Royal Grammar School, High Wycombe; Worcester College, Oxford. Contested Nottingham North 1964, and Willesden East 1966. Chairman, all-party footwear and leather industries group; joint chairman, all-party roads study group. Chairman, British Bohemian Parliamentary Group; vice-chairman, British Yugoslav Group. Member, Buckinghamshire County Council 1961–67. Partner in Political Research and Communications International, Vice-President, British Yugoslav Society. Director, Peter Fry (Insurance) Ltd.

Mr John Mann is a principal lecturer at Tresham College, Kettering. Born Mar 3 1940; educ. Wellingborough Grammar School and the LSE. Member, Wellingborough Borough Council.

Mr Leslie Stringer, administration manager in industrial relations, contested Wellingborough May 1979. Born Nov 28 1927; educ. Woolwich Polytechnic London. Member, Wellingborough Borough Council.

Mr David Heathcoat-Amory

WELLS Electorate 62159

Heathcoat-Amory, D. (C)	25385	52.7%
Butt-Philip, A. (L/All)	18810	39.0%
Leigh, A. M. (Lab)	3747	7.8%
Livings, G. (Ind)	273	0.6%
C majority	6575	13.6%
Total vote 48215	Turnout	77.6%

Mr David Heathcoat-Amory, chartered accountant and director of agricultural machinery company; elected in 1983; contested Brent South 1979. Born Mar 21 1949; educ. Eton College and Oxford University. Assistant finance director, British Technology. Chairman of housing assoc.

Mr Alan Butt-Philip, university lecturer, contested Wells twice in 1974 and 1979, also contested European election as Liberal for Somerset. Born Aug 15 1945; educ. Eton, St John's College and Nuffield College, Oxford. Author of books, articles and pamphlets. AUT.

Mr Andrew Leigh, local government officer. Born 1947. Former professional rock musician, subsequently trained as teacher and is now with Wiltshire County Council's education department. Elected to Somerset County Council 1981; member, CND, Nalgo.

Mr Christopher Murphy

WELWYN HATFIELD Electorate 72644

*Murphy, C. (C)	27498	47.7%
Granshaw, L. (SDP/All)	15252	26.5%
France, J. (Lab)	14898	25.8%
C majority	12246	21.2%
Total vote 57648	Turnout	79.4%

Mr Christopher Murphy gained seat for the Conservatives in 1979. Member, Select Committee on Statutory Instrument since 1979. Contested Tower Hamlets, Bethnal Green and Bow Feb and Oct 1974. Advertising and marketing consultant. Born Apr 20 1947; educ. Devonport High School and Queen's College, Oxford. Former president, Oxford University Conservative Assoc. Former member, executive committee of the Federation of Conservative Students and of executive committee of the National Assoc. of Conservative Graduates. Vice-chairman, Conservative backbench arts and heritage committee, since 1982, and vice-chairman, Conservative urban and new town affairs committee since 1981.

Dr Lindsay Granshaw, university researcher. Born Aug 21 1954; educ. Brighton and Hove High School; St Anne's College, Oxford; Bryn Mawr College and University of Pennsylvania. AUT.

Mr John France, university lecturer. Born May 22 1941; educ. Ripon Grammar School and Nottingham University. Swansea City councillor, since 1979. AUT (member, national executive).

Mr Peter Hardy

WENTWORTH Electorate 62057

*Hardy, P. (Lab)	25538	59.1%
Norton, R. (C)	9603	22.2%
Tildsley, M. (SDP/All)	8082	18.7%
Lab majority	15935	36.9%
Total vote 43223	Turnout	69.7%

Mr Peter Hardy won the seat in 1983; MP for Rother Valley 1970–83. Born Jul 17 1931; educ. Wath upon Dearne Grammar School; Westminster College, London, Sheffield University. Contested Scarborough and Whitby 1964; Sheffield, Hallam 1966. Chairman, PLP energy group since 1974. Vice-chairman PLP environment group and of all-party nature conservation committee. Sponsored the Badgers Act 1973, the Conservation of Wild Creatures and Wild Plants Act 1975, the Protection of Birds (Amendment) Act 1976 and the Education (Northern Ireland) Act 1978. Sponsored by NACODS. NUPE.

Mr Richard Norton, a merchant banker. Born 1956; educ. Ampleforth College and New College, Oxford.

Mr Max Tildsley, architect. Born 1945; educ. Sheffield University. Chief architect for an Inner London borough. Member, Sheffield Nalgo executive committee. Formed a theatre company in 1982 to take three plays to the Edinburgh Festival Fringe.

Mr Peter Snape

WEST BROMWICH EAST Electorate 59391

*Snape, P. (Lab)	15 892	38.1%
Cole, C. (C)	15596	37.4%
Smith, M. (L/All)	10200	24.5%
Lab majority	296	0.7%
Total vote 41 688	Turnout	70.2%

Mr Peter Snape, an Opposition spokesman on home affairs since 1982 and former spokesman on defence and disarmament. Lord Commissioner of the Treasury (whip) 1977–79; Assistant whip 1975–77. Elected Feb 1974. Clerical officer, British Rail. Born Feb 12 1942; educ. St Joseph's School, Stockport. Member, Bredbury and Romily UDC 1971–74 (chairman, finance committee, leader of Labour group). Member Council of Europe since Jan 1976. Sponsored by NUR. Honorary parliamentary adviser to Musicians' Union.

Mr Charles Cole fought Sheffield Park 1979. Personnel manager, Lucas Electrical Ltd. Born Dec 13 1948; educ. Spalding Grammar School and Bristol University. Member, Holland-with-Boston Conservative Assoc. Member and past treasurer, Sutton Coldfield Conservative Political Centre. Constituency representative on West Midlands Area CPC. Is a Birmingham probation service volunteer; former member, International Voluntary Service.

Mr Martyn Smith, CHC secretary, contested Stoke-on-Trent South Feb 1974; Stoke-on-Trent North Oct 1974, and West Bromwich East 1979. Born Feb 16 1946; educ. Wyggeston Boys' School, Leicester, and Jesus College, Cambridge. Member, Newcastle-under-Lyme Borough Council 1972–74; Sandwell Metropolitan Borough Council since 1980. ASTMS.

Miss Betty Boothroyd

WEST BROMWICH WEST Electorate 58341 1979: 58803 (minor)

*Boothroyd, Miss B. (Lab)	18896	50.7%
Harman, D. (C)	12257	32.9%
Collingbourne, A. (SDP/All)	6094	16.4%
Lab majority	6639	17.8%
Total vote 37247		Turnout 63.8%

1979: Total vote 39465 (67.1%); Lab 23791 (60.3%); C 14323 (36.3%). Lab maj 9468 (24.0%); swing 7.7% to C.

Miss Betty Boothroyd, a member of the Speaker's panel of chairmen, was elected to Labour Party national executive committee 1981. Assistant Government whip 1974–76. Was MP for West Bromwich May 1973–Feb 1974, when she was elected for the new constituency. Member, European Parliament 1975–77. Contested Rossendale 1970; Nelson and Colne by-election Jun 1960; Peterborough 1959; Leicester South-East by-election 1957. Born Oct 8 1929; educ. Dewsbury Technical College. Former member Select Committees on Public Accounts, Abortion (Amendment) Bill, Sound Broadcasting and Select Committee on Foreign Affairs. Sponsored by GMBATU.

Mr David Harman, general sales manager with Domestic Electrical Appliance Co, contested Wednesbury 1964, 1966 and 1970. Born Aug 10 1936; educ. West Bromwich Grammar School and Walsall Technical College. Member, West Bromwich Council 1960–63; Sandwell Council 1975–79.

Mr Anthony Collingbourne, brewer. Born 1947; educ. college. Trained as microbiologist. Contested council elections, Cradley Heath ward, 1982. Former deputy secretary and representative, ACTSS.

Mr Dennis Walters

WESTBURY Electorate 80244

*Walters, D. (C)	31133	51.4%
Hughes, D. (L/All)	22627	37.4%
Thomas, H. W. (Lab)	6058	10.0%
Ekins, P. (Eco)	609	1.0%
Banks, J. C. (W Reg)	131	0.2%
C majority	8506	14.1%
Total vote 60558		Turnout 75.5%

Mr Dennis Walters was elected in 1964; contested Blyth 1959 and 1960 by-election. Born Nov 1928; educ. Downside School and St Catharine's College, Cambridge. Founder member Bow Group; chairman, Federation of University Conservative and Unionist Assoc. 1949–50. Joint secretary, Conservative foreign affairs committee 1965–71 and joint vice-chairman, foreign and Commonwealth affairs committee 1974–79. Chairman, Asthma Research Council since 1969; joint chairman, Council for Advancement of Arab-British Understanding 1970–82. Chairman, Conservative Middle East Council since 1981. Director, Cluff Oil Inc and KCA International Ltd. Trustee, ANAF Foundation, Adviser to Canadian finance company; member, Kuwait Investment Advisory Committee and consultant to Balfour Beatty Construction Ltd.

Mr David Hughes, publishing and marketing consultant and company director. Born Apr 10 1956; educ. St Paul's School, Barnes, Southampton University (former president, student's union). Contested Southampton Test 1979. Former European elections agent.

Mr Haydn Thomas, lecturer. Born Feb 3 1951; educ. Polytechnic of North London and Kings College, London. Member, Westbury Town Council. NATFHE and NUPE; delegate to West Wilts trades union council.

Mr Donald Stewart

WESTERN ISLES

Electorate 22 822 1979: 22 393 same

*Stewart, D. J. (SNP)	8 272	54.5%
Wilson, B. D. H. (Lab)	4 560	30.1%
Morrison, M. (C)	1 460	9.6%
McLeod, N. (L/All)	876	5.8%
SNP majority	3 712	24.5%
Total vote 15 168		Turnout 66.5%

1979: Total vote 15 119 (67.5%); SNP 7941 (52.5%); Lab 4 878 (32.3%); C 1 600 (10.6%); L 700 (4.6%). SNP maj 3 063 (20.2%).

Mr Donald Stewart, leader of the Scottish National Parliamentary Party since 1974, won the seat in 1970. Provost of Stornoway 1958–64 and 1968–70; Hon Sheriff 1960. Member, Council of 'Get Britain Out' (of EEC) Campaign. Born Oct 17 1920; educ. Nicolson Institute, Stornoway.

Mr Brian Wilson, journalist, contested Ross and Cromarty 1974, and Inverness 1979. Born Dec 13 1948; educ. Dunoon School, Dundee University and University College, Cardiff. Director, *West Highland Free Press*.

Mr Murdo Morrison, regional public affairs officer for an oil company, contested the seat 1979. Born 1938; educ. Nicolson Institute, Stornoway. Conservative group leader, Motherwell District.

Mr Neil MacLeod, principal teacher of history, is chairman, Western Isles Liberal Assoc. Born Jun 4 1933; educ. Nicolson Institute and Aberdeen University. Taught in East Africa 1962–68.

Mr John Wheeler

WESTMINSTER NORTH

Electorate 68 988

*Wheeler, J. (C)	19 134	43.2%
Latham, A. (Lab)	17 424	39.4%
Halliwell, G. (SDP/All)	6 956	15.7%
Cooper, T. (Eco)	527	1.2%
Keen, T. L. (TVCabl)	148	0.3%
Fisher, B. (Ind)	73	0.2%
C majority	1 710	3.9%
Total vote 44 262		Turnout 62.2%

Mr John Wheeler, director-general of the British Security Industry Assoc. Ltd, won the seat in 1983; MP for Cities of London and Westminster, City of Westminster, Paddington 1979–83. Assistant governor Wandsworth Prison 1968–72, and Brixton 1972–73. Former research officer at the Home Office. Born May 1 1940; educ. Bury St Edmunds County School and Prison Services Staff College. Director, National Supervisory Council for Intruder Alarms since 1977. Chairman, National Inspectorate of Security Guard Patrol and Transport Services since 1982. Member, Home Office standing committee on crime prevention since 1976; member, Home Affairs Select Committee since 1979; chairman of its subcommittee on race relations and immigration since 1980; vice-chairman, all-party penal affairs group from 1979; vice-chairman, Conservative urban affairs and new towns committee since 1980; joint secretary, Conservative Greater London MPs committee since 1979.

Mr Arthur Latham, was MP for Paddington 1974–79 and Paddington North 1969–74. Born Aug 1930; educ. Romford Royal Liberty School, Garnett College of Education. Lecturer in further education, Southgate Technical College. Chairman, Greater London Labour Party since 1977.

Mr Guy Halliwell, management consultant. Born Feb 2 1929; educ. Charterhouse and Gonville and Caius College, Cambridge. Chairman, Whitehead Consulting Group Ltd; director, Job Creation Ltd.

Mr Michael Jopling

WESTMORLAND AND LONSDALE

Electorate 67 161

*Jopling, M. (C)	29 775	61.3%
Hulls, K. (L/All)	13 188	27.2%
Stott, C. (Lab)	4 798	9.9%
Gibson, R. (Eco)	805	1.7%
C majority	16 587	34.2%
Total vote 48 566		Turnout 72.3%

Mr Michael Jopling was appointed Minister of Agriculture, Fisheries and Food in June 1983. Parliamentary Secretary Treasury and Government Chief Whip 1979–83. An Opposition spokesman on agriculture 1974–79; Government Whip 1971–74. Won the seat in 1983; represented Westmorland 1964–83; contested Wakefield 1959. Farmer and member of Lloyds. Born Dec 10 1930; educ. Cheltenham College and King's College, Durham University. Former member, select committees on science and technology and on agriculture. Member, NFU national council 1962–64; Thirsk RDC 1958–64. Joint secretary, Conservative agriculture committee 1966–70. PPS Minister of Agriculture 1970–71.

Dr Kenneth Hulls, company managing director, contested Westmorland 1979. Born Apr 20 1944; educ. London and Warwick universities.

Mr Christopher Scott is a manager at K Shoemakers Ltd. Aged 49. Member, Kendal Town Council since 1979.

Mr Jerry Wiggin

WESTON-SUPER-MARE Electorate 71 439

*Wiggin, A. W. (C)	27 948	53.6%
Marks, J. (SDP/All)	18 457	35.4%
Berry, R. L. (Lab)	5 781	11.1%
C majority	9 491	18.2%
Total vote 52 186		Turnout 73.1%

Mr Jerry Wiggin, Under Secretary of State for the Armed Forces 1981–83; Parliamentary Secretary, Ministry of Agriculture, Fisheries and Food 1979–81. Returned at a by-election in 1969; contested Montgomeryshire 1964 and 1966. Born Feb 24 1937; educ. Eton and Trinity College, Cambridge. Formerly tenant farmer. PPS to Lord Balniel, Minister of State for Defence 1970–74, and to Sir Ian Gilmour, Minister of State for Defence Procurement 1971–73. Joint Secretary, Conservative defence committee 1974–75; vice-chairman, Conservative agriculture committee 1975–79; chairman, Conservative West Country MPs 1978. General rapporteur, economic committee, North Atlantic Assembly 1976–79. Member of Lloyd's.

Mr Jonathan Marks, barrister, is a member of the steering committee, Social Democratic Campaign for Racial Justice. Born 1952; educ. Harrow and University College, Oxford. Common law practitioner, mostly in contract, personal injuries and industrial relations in London and Exeter.

Mr Roger Barry, economics lecturer at Bristol University. Born Jul 4 1948; educ. Bristol and Sussex universities. Member, Avon County Council since 1981. AUT.

Mr Roger Stott

WIGAN Electorate 72 390

*Stott, R. (Lab)	29 851	54.6%
Piggott, J. (L / All)	12 554	22.9%
Cadman, H. (C)	12 320	22.5%
Lab majority	17 297	31.6%
Total vote 54 725		Turnout 75.6%

Mr Roger Stott, an Opposition spokesman on transport since 1981, won the seat in 1983; MP for Westhoughton 1973–83; contested Cheadle 1970. PPS to Secretary of State for Industry 1975–76; to the Prime Minister, 1976–79; Leader of the Opposition 1979–80. Telephone engineer. Born Aug 7 1943; educ. Rochdale Technical College; Ruskin College. Rochdale Councillor 1970–74 (chairman, housing committee). Sponsored by POEU. Vice-chairman, PLP North-West area group.

Mr John Piggott, production planning manager in the paint industry, contested Westhoughton 1979. Born Feb 21 1947; educ. Hull and Lancaster universities. Member Wigan Metropolitan Borough Council, since 1979 being Liberal Group leader and leader of opposition.

Mr Henry Cadman, a lecturer. Born 1935; educ. Liverpool University and University of Mancheser Institute of Science of Technology.

Mr Richard Needham

WILTSHIRE NORTH Electorate 76 150 1979: 74 519 (minor)

*Needham, R. (C)	30 924	53.1%
Graham, C. S. M. (L/All)	23 692	40.6%
Allsop, S. R. (Lab)	2 888	5.0%
Barham, E. (Eco)	678	1.2%
Baile de La Perrière, H. (JDF)	113	0.2%
C majority	7 232	12.4%
Total vote 58 295		Turnout 76.6%

1979 (as Chippenham): Total vote 59 586 (80.0%); C 29 308 (49.2%); L 24 611 (41.3%); Lab 5 146 (8.6%); Ecol 521 (0.9%). C maj 4 697 (7.9%); swing 7.8% to C.

Mr Richard Needham, represented Chippenham 1979–83; won this seat in 1983; contested Pontefract and Castleford Feb 1974, and Gravesend Oct 1974. Chairman, RGM Print Holdings Ltd; director Radio Somerset Ltd. Personal and political assistant to Mr James Prior 1974–79. Member Public Accounts Committee, since 1982. Joint vice-chairman, Conservative backbench employment committee, since 1982. Chairman all-party productivity committee; joint secretary Anglo-Japanese committee. Member of Lloyd's. Born Jan 29 1942; educ. Eton. Member, Somerset County Council 1967–74.

Mr Christopher Graham, BBC producer of current affairs programmes. Born Sep 21 1950; educ. St Edward's School, Oxford, University of Liverpool. Member, Liberal Party standing committee and coordinator of rural campaign 1982–83. Liverpool City Council 1971–74. ACTT.

Mr Stephen Allsopp, a member of the Society of Civil and Public Servants since 1978. Born Jun 26 1952; educ. Park School, Swindon, Swindon College, and Essex University. Member, Thamesdown Borough Council.

Sir Michael Havers

WIMBLEDON

Electorate 64 132 1979: 65 471 same

*Havers, Sir M. (C)	24 169	52.1%
Twigg, D. (L/All)	12 623	27.2%
Tansey, R. B. (Lab)	8 806	19.0%
Jones, A. (Eco)	717	1.5%
Weakner, E. (PAL)	114	0.3%
C majority	11 546	24.9%
Total vote 46 429	Turnout	72.4%

1979: Total vote 50 035 (76.4%); C 27 567 (55.1%); Lab 14 252 (28.5%); L 7 604 (15.2%); NF 612 (1.2%). C maj 13 315 (26.6%); swing 4.3% to C.

Sir Michael Havers, QC, has been Attorney General since 1979. Opposition spokesman on law, 1974–79. Solicitor-General 1972–74. Former chairman, Conservative Legal Committee. Member, Committee of Privileges, since 1976 and Select Committee on MP's interests 1974–79. Elected in 1970. Born Mar 10 1923; educ. Westminster School and Corpus Christi College, Cambridge. Recorder of Dover 1962–68; Recorder of Norwich 1968.

Mr David Twigg, consulting civil engineer. Born Mar 7 1934; educ. Queen Elizabeth I Grammar School, Alford.

Mr Rock Tansey, barrister, has been a member of Merton Council since 1978. Born Jul 1939. TGWU (ACTS), NCCL, Haldane Society of Socialist Lawyers.

Mr John Browne

WINCHESTER

Electorate 72 792

*Browne, J. (C)	31 908	57.6%
MacDonald, J. (SDP/All)	18 861	34.0%
Allchin, W. H. (Lab)	4 512	8.1%
Winkworth, S. (W Reg)	155	0.3%
C majority	13 047	23.5%
Total vote 55 436	Turnout	76.2%

Mr John Browne was elected in 1979. Member of Westminster City Council 1974–78. Banker and company director. Adviser to Barclays Bank International. Joint secretary, Conservative backbench finance committee since 1981. Born Oct 1938; educ. Malvern College, Royal Military Academy, Sandhurst, Cranfield Institute of Technology, Harvard Business School. Served in Grenadier Guards; retired as captain 1967.

Mr John MacDonald, sixth form teacher at Winchester College. Born Dec 8 1938; educ. Oxford University. Member, Winchester SDP steering group; committee member Mid-Hants area party; Winchester City Council since 1982. Co-founder, Winchester Schools' Archaeological Society and Fellow of the Society of Antiquaries.

Dr William Allchin, a psychotherapist and lecturer, contested Winchester in Feb and Oct 1974 and 1979. Born Mar 1921; educ. Westminster, and Oxford and London universities. Member, Socialist Medical Assoc. and ASTMS.

Dr Alan Glyn

WINDSOR AND MAIDENHEAD

Electorate 78 619

*Glyn, Dr A. (C)	32 191	58.2%
Winner, P. (L/All)	13 988	25.3%
Price, Mrs V. I. (Lab)	6 383	11.6%
Board, W. O. (Ind C)	1 842	3.3%
Gillmore, G. F. C. (NF)	511	0.9%
Illesley, P. B. (Ind)	300	0.5%
Bex, C. R. (W Reg)	68	0.1%
C majority	18 203	32.9%
Total vote 55 283	Turnout	70.3%

Dr Alan Glyn was returned in Feb 1974, having been MP for Windsor 1970–74 and for Clapham 1959–64. Barrister and medical practitioner. Born Sep 29 1918; educ. Westminster School, Caius College, Cambridge, St Bartholomew's Hospital and St George's Hospital. Member, Kensington, Chelsea and Westminster local medical committee; member, board of governors of the heart and chest hospitals special health authority. Former chairman, Conservative foreign affairs sub-committee on Far East; chairman, Danish, Swedish, Mongolian and Indonesian parliamentary groups of the Inter-parliamentary Union.

Mr Paul Winner, managing director of market communication firm, contested Spelthorne 1979, and twice in 1974. Born Jul 1934. educ. St Lawrence College, Ramsgate; Westminster City Schools, Sorbonne; St John's College, Oxford; LSE Department of Business Administration.

Mrs Valerie Price contested the seat in 1979. A purchase administrator. Member, Windsor Borough Council 1971–74; Windsor and Maidenhead District Council 1974–76. Born Jun 7 1940; educ. St Alban's Girls' School. Founder Windsor Peace Group and of Slough Women's Aid for battered women. GMBATU.

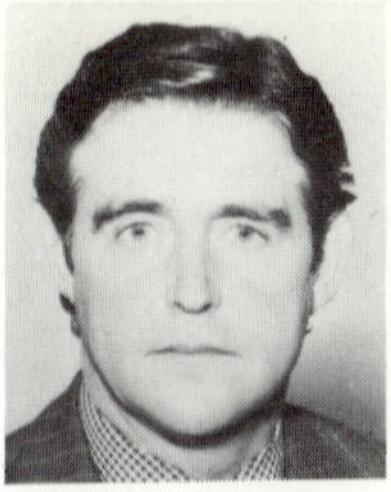

Mr Barry Porter

WIRRAL SOUTH Electorate 60 864

*Porter, B. (C)	24 766	53.7%
Hollingworth, P. (SDP/All)	10 928	23.7%
Rimmer, K. J. S. (Lab)	10 411	22.6%
C majority	13 838	30.0%
Total vote 46 105		Turnout 75.8%

Mr Barry Porter was MP for Bebington and Ellesmere Port 1979–83; won this seat 1983; contested Chorley Oct 1974, and Newton Feb 1974, and Liverpool, Scotland Exchange Apr 1971. Solicitor and company director. Born Jun 11 1939; educ. Birkenhead School and University College, Oxford. Member, Wirral Borough Council 1976–77. Secretary, backbench leisure industries committee and all-party tourism committee; member, Commons transport select committee.

Mr Keith Rimmer is a Post Office engineer. Born 1949. Chairman, Wirral District Labour Party. Former secretary and treasurer, Wirral Constituency Labour Party. POEU.

Mr David Hunt

WIRRALL WEST Electorate 61 646

*Hunt, D. (C)	25 276	55.9%
Mullholland, S. (L/All)	10 125	22.4%
McCabe, J. (Lab)	9 855	21.8%
C majority	15 151	33.5%
Total vote 45 256		Turnout 73.4%

Mr David Hunt, a solicitor, represented Wirral Mar 1976–83; elected for this seat in 1983. Born May 21 1942; educ. Liverpool College, Montpellier University, Bristol University, Guildford College of Law. Solicitor of Supreme Court of Judicature, admitted 1968. Chairman, British Youth Council, 1971–74, National Young Conservatives 1972–73. Vice-chairman, National Union of Conservative and Unionist Assoc. 1974–76. Contested Bristol South 1970, and Kingswood 1974. Vice-chairman, Conservative Group for Europe 1978–81; chairman since 1981; vice-chairman all-party parliamentary youth lobby 1978–79; President, British Youth Council 1978–80; PPS to Secretary of State for Trade 1979–81; PPS to Secretary of State for Defence 1981; assistant Government whip 1981–83; Government whip from Jun 1983.

Mr Stephen Mulholland, senior computer operator. Born Nov 23 1953; educ. Ushaw College, Durham; Kidderminster College of Further Education and Liverpool University. Member, Cheshire County Council since 1981. ASTMS.

Mr John McCabe is a mature student and former bus driver. Born Aug 1947. Member, Merseyside County Council since 1982; member CND, TGWU.

Mr Douglas Hurd

WITNEY Electorate 69 362

*Hurd, D. (C)	28 695	55.4%
Baston, J. (L/All)	15 983	30.8%
Douse, Mrs C. B. (Lab)	7 145	13.8%
C majority	12 712	24.5%
Total vote 51 823		Turnout 74.7%

Mr Douglas Hurd was appointed Minister of State, Home Office in Jun 1983; Minister of State for Foreign and Commonwealth Affairs 1979–83; Opposition spokesman on Europe 1976–79. Head of Mr Heath's political office 1968–74. Won the seat 1983; represented Mid-Oxon Feb 1974–83. Born Mar 8 1930; educ. Eton and Trinity College, Cambridge. Worked in the Foreign Service 1952–66 in China, the United States and Europe, becoming a chief secretary. Conservative Research Department 1966–68. Author of political thrillers. Former member, Advisory panel on Arms Control and Disarmament. Director British section, European League for Economic Co-operation 1977–79.

Mr John Baston, chartered surveyor. Born Feb 27 1928; educ. local schools. Member, Oxfordshire County Council since 1977; leader, Liberal group since 1981. Partner in local firm of surveyors and valuers.

Mrs Carole Douse is an educational adviser for Open University students. Aged 40. Former member, Witney Urban District Council.

Mr Cranley Onslow

WOKING

Electorate 78 327 1979: 76 670 same

*Onslow, C. (C)	32 748	58.3%
Goldenberg, P. (L/All)	16 511	29.4%
Broer, Mrs D. B. (Lab)	6 566	11.7%
Comens, D. (PAL)	368	0.7%
C majority	16 237	28.9%
Total vote 56 193	Turnout	71.7%

1979: Total vote 55 601 (76.5%); C 31 719 (57.0%); Lab 13 327 (24.0%); L 9 991 (18.0%); NF 564 (1.0%). C maj 18 392 (33.0%); swing 5.3% to C.

Mr Cranley Onslow was Minister of State for Foreign and Commonwealth Affairs 1982–83. Chairman, Select Committee on Defence 1981–82; member 1980–82. Member, Public Accounts Committee 1970–72, and 1922 Committee 1968–72; and 1981–82. Chairman Conservative Aviation Committee 1970–72, 1979–82. Under Secretary of State for Trade and Industry (Aerospace) 1972–74. Elected in 1964. Former company director, business consultant and journalist. Born Jun 8 1926; educ. Harrow School, Oriel College, Oxford and Geneva University. Member, UK delegation on Council of Europe 1977–82. Member Dartford RDC, 1960–62; Kent County Council 1961–64. Council member, Anglers' Cooperative Assoc, Salmon and Trout Assoc. and National Rifle Assoc.

Mr Philip Goldenberg, solicitor, contested Eton and Slough Feb and Oct 1974, and 1979. Born Apr 26 1946; educ. St Paul's School, London and Pembroke College, Oxford, Joint vice-chairman, Assoc. of Liberal Lawyers, since 1981; member Liberal Party council since 1975.

Mrs Barbara Broer, aged 40, is employed at the Centre for International Briefing at Farnham Castle. Member, Southern regional executive committee, Labour Party, and the party's political education training team.

Sir William van Straubenzee

WOKINGHAM

Electorate 71 725

*van Straubenzee, Sir W. (C)	32 925	60.4%
Leston, J. (L / All)	17 227	31.6%
Orton, M. (Lab)	4 362	8.0%
C majority	15 698	28.8%
Total vote 54 514	Turnout	76.0%

Sir William van Straubenzee has been second Church Estates Commissioner since 1979; chairman, Conservative backbench education committee since 1979. Chairman, Select Committee on Assistance to Members, 1976–78. Minister of State, Northern Ireland, 1972–74, and Under-Secretary for Education and Science 1970–72. Opposition spokesman on education 1968–70. Elected 1959; contested Wandsworth, Clapham 1955. Solicitor. Born Jan 27 1924; educ. Westminster School. Member, House of Laity of the Church Assembly for the Diocese of Oxford 1965–70 and of the General Synod since 1975. Vice-president National Union of Students.

Mr John Leston, marketing consultant. Berkshire county councillor. Born Nov 26 1953.

Mr Michael Orton is a lecturer. Born 1949.

Mrs Renée Short

WOLVERHAMPTON NORTH EAST

Electorate 63 716

*Short, Mrs R. (Lab)	17 941	40.1%
Burnside, A. (C)	17 727	39.6%
Yarnell, R. (L / All)	8 524	19.0%
Baugh, C. (NF)	585	1.3%
Lab majority	214	0.5%
Total vote 44 777	Turnout	70.3%

Mrs Renée Short has been chairman of Select Committee on Social Services since 1979. Elected in 1964; contested Watford 1959 and St Albans 1955. Born Apr 1919; educ. Notts County Secondary School and Manchester University. Member, Estimates Committee 1964–70; Expenditure Committee 1970–79 (chairman, social services and employment sub-committee). Chairman, British-GDR parliamentary group; secretary, British-Soviet parliamentary group; president, British-Romanian Friendship Assoc. Member, Labour Party NEC 1970–81 and since 1983. Former national president, Nursery Schools Assoc. Chairman, Theatres' Advisory Council 1977–81. Freelance journalist. Sponsored by TGWU, NUJ.

Mr Anthony Burnside, schoolmaster. Born Sep 17 1951; educ. Northumberland Heath Secondary Modern School, Erith; Erith Grammar School, and West Midlands College of Higher Education. Member, Walsall Borough Council 1975–79 and since 1982.

Mr Raymond Yarnell, part-time tutor at the Open University, contested Wrekin 1979. Born Oct 25 1927; educ. at Manchester, the Open and Birmingham universities.

Mr Robert Edwards

WOLVERHAMPTON SOUTH EAST Electorate 56428

*Edwards, R. (Lab)	17440	44.7%
McLoughlin, P. (C)	12428	31.9%
Wernick, J. (L / All)	9112	23.4%
Lab majority	5012	12.9%
Total vote 38980		Turnout 69.1%

Mr Robert Edwards was elected in Feb 1974; represented Bilston 1955–74; contested by-elections Newport 1945 and Stretford 1939, and general election, Chorley 1935. Member European Parliament, 1977–79. Born Jan 6 1906; educ. council schools and technical college. Chairman, Industrial Common Ownership Group. General Secretary, Chemical Workers' Union 1947–71; national officer TGWU 1971–76. Member Liverpool City Council 1929–32. President Britain-Cyprus Committee. Fought in Spain with the Republicans during the Civil War. Sponsored by Co-operative Party.

Mr Patrick McLoughlin, mineworker. Born 1957; educ. Cardinal Griffin Comprehensive School and Staffordshire College of Agriculture. National vice-chairman, Young Conservatives. Member, Staffordshire County Council, Cannock Chase District Council, Society for the Protection of the Unborn Child, Cannock Chase League of Hospital Friends. NUM.

Mr Joseph Wernick, chairman and managing director of Wernick Group, timber framed building manufacturers, contested Wolverhampton South West Feb and Oct 1974 and 1979. Born Aug 28 1920; educ. Wolverhampton Municipal Grammar School.

Mr Nicholas Budgen

WOLVERHAMPTON SOUTH WEST Electorate 68847

*Bugden, N. (C)	25214	50.6%
Jones, R. M. (Lab)	13694	27.5%
Harwood, E. (SDP / All)	10724	21.5%
Deary, J. (ACM)	201	0.4%
C majority	11520	23.1%
Total vote 49833		Turnout 72.4%

Mr Nicholas Budgen, a barrister and farmer, was elected in Feb. 1974, contested Birmingham, Small Heath 1970. Government whip 1981–82. Born Nov 3 1937; educ. St Edward's School, Oxford and Corpus Christi College, Cambridge. Chairman, Birmingham Bow Group 1967–68. Member Public Accounts Committee, 1980–81; secretary, Conservative Finance Committee 1979.

Mr Robert Jones works for the Manpower Services Commission running a local project. Educ. Wolverhampton Municipal Grammar School and Wolverhampton and Trent polytechnics. Member, Wolverhampton Council since 1980.

Mr Edgar Harwood, regional manager for Steel Stockholder. Born 1939; commissioned into Worcestershire Regiment. Spent some years in the Special Air Service Territorial Regiment. Round Table member for 17 years and International Officer for the UK. Chairman of an amateur theatre club in Droitwich and involved with committees of Hospital Friends and Army Cadet Force Welfare.

Mr Paul Dean

WOODSPRING Electorate 71280

*Dean, P. (C)	31932	57.6%
Morgan, R. (L / All)	16800	30.3%
White, D. H. (Lab)	6536	11.8%
Robyns, D. (W Reg)	177	0.3%
C majority	15132	27.3%
Total vote 55445		Turnout 77.8%

Mr Paul Dean was appointed Second Deputy Chairman of Ways and Means and Deputy Speaker in May 1982. Member, Select Committee on Members' Salaries 1981–82; Select Committee on Overseas Development 1978–79, chairman Conservative backbench health and social services committee 1979–82. Member, chairmen's panel 1979–82. Under Secretary, Health and Social security 1970–74. Won seat in 1983; represented Somerset North 1964–83; contested Pontefract by-election, Mar 1962; Born Sep 14 1924; educ. Ellesmere College, Shropshire and Exeter College, Oxford. Former farmer. Resident tutor, Swinton College 1956–57; joined Conservative research department 1958 and assistant director 1962. Chairman, Watchdog group for the self-employed 1975–79. Director, Charterhouse Pensions, Watney Mann and Truman Holdings Ltd. Consultant on pension schemes.

Mr Rowland Morgan, chartered civil engineer and university teacher, contested Bedwellty Feb and Oct 1974, and Weston-super-Mare 1979. Born Dec 2 1934; educ. Tredegar Grammar School and University of Manchester. AUT.

Mr David White is a senior design planner with Rolls-Royce. Born 1934. Member, Avon County Council since 1977. Chairman, Avon Labour Group of Councillors. AUEW.

Mr John Cartwright

WOOLWICH Electorate 56 297 1979: 52 523 minor

*Cartwright, J. (SDP / All)	15 492	40.5%
Wise, Mrs A. (Lab)	12 767	33.4%
Brown, Mrs P. (C)	9 616	25.1%
Fitz-Gerald, T. C. (BNP)	384	1.0%
SDP / All majority	2 725	7.1%
Total vote 38 259	Turnout	68.0%

1979 (as Woolwich East); Total vote 36 822 (70.1%); Lab 21 700 (58.9%); C 11 240 (30.5%); L 2 998 (8.1%); NF 884 (2.4%); Lab maj 10 460 (28.4%); swing 4.7% to C.

Mr John Cartwright, former director, Royal Arsenal Co-operative Society, was elected as Labour MP for Woolwich East in Oct 1974. Resigned party and joined SDP in 1981 becoming spokesman on environment. Contested Bexleyheath Feb 1974 and Bexley 1970. Born Nov 29 1933; educ. Woking County Grammar School. Former chairman Manifesto Group of PLP. Executive civil servant 1952–55; Labour Party organizer 1955–67; political secretary RACS 1967–72. Chairman National Union of Labour Organizers 1969–70. Leader of Greenwich Borough Council 1971–74 and chief whip London Boroughs Assoc. 1971–75. Member Labour Party NEC 1971–75 and 1976–78. Trustee National Maritime Museum. Chairman PLP Defence Group 1979–81. PPS to Secretary of State for Education and Science 1976–77. Vice-president Assoc. of Metropolitan Authorities since 1974.

Mrs Audrey Wise was MP for Coventry South-West 1974–79. Born Jan 1935; educ. Rutherford High School. Former shorthand-typist; borough councillor at 21. Vice-chairman, Institute for Workers' Control. USDAW.

Mrs Philomena Brown, teacher. Born 1935; educ. La Retraite Convent and Philippa Fawcett College of Education. Croydon councillor. Vice-chairman, European Democrat Forum; committee member, Foreign Affairs Forum. Delegate, Nato, SHAPE. Guest and observer, US presidential election, 1980.

Mr Peter Walker

WORCESTER Electorate 66 531

*Walker, P. (C)	24 381	49.5%
Phipps, C. (SDP / All)	13 510	27.4%
Rudd, J. (Lab)	11 208	22.7%
Axon, K. A. (BNP)	208	0.4%
C majority	10 871	22.1%
Total vote 49 307	Turnout	74.1%

Mr Peter Walker became Secretary of State for Energy 1983; Minister of Agriculture, Fisheries and Food 1979–83. Opposition spokesman on defence 1974–75, and on trade and industry 1974. Secretary of State for Trade and Industry 1972–74; Secretary of State for the Environment 1970–72; Minister of Housing and Local Government Jun–Oct 1970. Elected at by-election Mar 1961. Born Mar 25 1932; educ. Latymer Upper School, Hammersmith. Former chairman, Lloyd's insurance brokers and director of other companies.

Mr Colin Phipps, petroleum geologist and oil and gas consultant, was Labour MP for Dudley West from Feb 1974 to 1979. Born Jul 1934; educ. Acton County School, Bishop Gore School, Swansea and London and Birmingham Universities. Petroleum geologist with Shell 1957–65; set up an oil and gas consultancy 1979. Former member, Council of Europe and Western European Union. Chairman, Wyvern area party; member, Council for Social Democracy and of its energy policy group. Contested Walthamstow East 1969 by-election.

Mr John Rudd, is director of a London charitable housing association. Former member, Worcester Council.

Mr Eric Forth

WORCESTERSHIRE MID Electorate 74 254

Forth, E. (C)	28 159	50.9%
Maher, R. E. (Lab)	13 954	25.2%
Fairhead, Mrs M. (SDP / All)	12 866	23.2%
Fletcher, D. W. (NP)	386	0.7%
C majority	14 205	25.7%
Total vote 55 365	Turnout	74.6%

Mr Eric Forth elected in 1983, has been member of the European Parliament for North Birmingham since 1979. Chairman, backbench committee, European Democratic Group. Contested Barking, Feb and Oct 1974. Born Sep 9 1944; educ. Jordanhill College School, Glasgow; Glasgow University, Member, Brentwood UDC 1968–72.

Mr Richard Maher, is a telephone engineer. Born Jan 20 1945; educ. Moseley Grammar School and Ruskin College, Oxford. POEU.

Mrs Margaret Fairhead, retired college lecturer. Aged 59; educ. Nottingham University. Founder member, SDP. Member, Council for Social Democracy.

Mr Michael Spicer

WORCESTERSHIRE SOUTH Electorate 73278

*Spicer, W. H. M. (C)	30095	55.8%
Phillips, D. (L/All)	18706	34.7%
Sandland-Nielsen, P. E. (Lab)	4183	7.8%
Woodford, G. (Eco)	866	1.6%
Pass, G. R. G. (Ind)	113	0.2%
C majority	11389	21.1%
Total vote 53963		Turnout 73.6%

Mr Michael Spicer, an economic consultant was elected in Feb 1974; contested Easington 1966 and 1970; Vice-chairman, Conservative Party since 1981; PPS to Ministers of State for Trade 1979–81. Member, Conservative Research Department 1966–68; director, Conservative Systems Research Centre 1968–70; former deputy chairman, computer subcommittee of Commons Services Committee. Born Jan 22 1943; educ. Wellington College and Emmanuel College, Cambridge. Director, Argus Press Group. Managing director, Economic Models Ltd 1970–80.

Mr David Phillips, company director in electronics industry, contested Worcestershire South 1979. Born Feb 17 1933; educ. Waverley Grammar School, Birmingham. Secretary of Liberal Parliamentary Assoc.; member, Liberal Party Council, and West Midlands Liberal Party Council.

Mr Peter Sandland-Nielsen is a computer project manager. Aged 41; educ. Handsworth Technical School, Birmingham and the School of Peace Studies at the University of Bradford. Member, Hereford and Worcester County Council 1977–82; Worcester County Council. Member, CND; Co-operative Party; European Nuclear Disarmament; Anti-Nuclear Campaign; Third World First; NUS; TGWU.

Mr Dale Campbell-Savours

WORKINGTON Electorate 56119 1979: 55030 same

*Campbell-Savours, D. N. (Lab)	23239	52.0%
Smith, M. (C)	16111	36.1%
Blackshaw. N. (L/All)	5311	11.9%
Lab majority	7128	16.0%
Total vote 44661		Turnout 79.6%

1979: Total vote 46109 (83.8%); Lab 24523 (53.2%); C 18767 (40.7%); L 2819 (6.1%). Lab maj 5756 (12.5%); swing 5.6% to C.

Mr Dale Campbell-Savours regained the seat for Labour in 1979; contested Darwen Feb and Oct 1974. Export and technical agent. Born Aug 1943; educ. Keswick School and Sorbonne. Member Ramsbottom Council 1972–74. TGWU.

Mr Michael Smith, pensions account consultant with Legal and General Assurance Society Ltd. Born Apr 23 1948; educ. Sarah Robinson Secondary School, Crawley, and Leeds University. ASTMS.

Mr Neil Blackshaw, local government town planning officer, contested Workington 1979. Born Jul 17 1948; educ. Hyde Grammar School, University of Manchester and the University of Wales, Institute of Science and Technology. Nalgo branch secretary.

Mr Terence Lewis

WORSLEY Electorate 71987

Lewis, T. (Lab)	21675	40.3%
Windle, S. (C)	17536	32.6%
*Roper, J. F. (SDP/All)	14545	27.1%
Lab majority	4139	7.7%
Total vote 53756		Turnout 74.7%

Mr Terence Lewis elected in 1983 is deputy leader of Bolton Borough Council; education chairman. A personnel officer. District councillor 1971–74. Born Dec 29 1935. ASTMS.

Mr Stanley Windle, electro-plating engineer. Born 1925; educ. St John's School, Heaton Mersey and Engineering Training College, London. Chairman, North West Area Conservative Clubs Advisory Council and Heaton Mersey Ward. Member, executive committee. National Union.

Mr John Roper, chief whip of the SDP since 1981, was elected as Labour MP for Farnworth in 1970; contested High Peak 1964. Resigned party and joined SDP 1981. Labour spokesman on foreign and Commonwealth affairs and the arts. Opposition spokesman on defence. 1979–80. Economist and director of Co-operative Wholesale Society 1969–74. Born Sep 10 1935; educ. William Hulme's Grammar School, Manchester, Reading School, Magdalen College, Oxford and University of Chicago. Member, Select Committee on Procedure (Finance) 1982–83; former member, select committees on European secondary legislation, wealth tax and expenditure. Chairman, Labour Committee for Europe 1976–79; member, Council of Europe, 1973–79, chairman, Committee of Culture and Education. Chairman of the committee on defence questions and armaments, WEU 1976–79. Vice-president, Manchester Statistical Society. Trustee, History of Parliament Trust.

Mr Terence Higgins

WORTHING Electorate 75772 1979: 74961 same

*Higgins, T. (C)	32807	60.9%
Clare, A. (L/All)	17554	32.6%
Minto, A. (Lab)	3158	5.9%
Wingfield, M. (NF)	292	0.5%
Monks, D. (BNP)	103	0.2%
C majority	15253	28.3%
Total vote 53914	Turnout	71.2%

1979: Total vote 54924 (73.3%); C 33624 (61.2%); L 13244 (24.1%); Lab 7163 (13.0%); NF 893 (1.6%). C maj 20380 (37.1%), swing 3.6% to C.

Mr Terence Higgins, an economist has been a member of the Select Committee on Treasury and Civil Service since 1979; chairman Select Committee on Procedure (Finance) since 1980. Opposition spokesman on trade 1974–76, and a spokesman on Treasury and economic affairs during 1974. Financial Secretary to the Treasury 1972–74, and Minister of State, Treasury 1970–72. Elected 1964. Born Jan 18 1928, educ. Alleyn's School, Dulwich, Gonville and Caius College, Cambridge, and Yale. Opposition spokesman on Treasury and economic affairs 1966–70. Director Lex Service Group. Former Olympic and Commonwealth Games athlete. Chairman, Conservative backbench sports and recreation committee 1980–81 and 1982–83; and of backbench transport committee since 1980. Member executive 1922 committee since 1979. Council member Royal Institute of International Affairs since 1978. Council member Institute of Advanced Motorists since 1980. Governor of Dulwich College since 1980.

Mr Arthur Clare, microbiologist employed by Beecham Group plc. Born Feb 13 1941; educ. St John's, Leatherhead and Brunel University. Member, Worthing Borough Council since 1975.

Mr Ashley Minto, social worker. Born Jul 10, 1954; educ. Taunton's School, Southampton; Lanchester Polytechnic, Coventry, and Southampton University. Member, Southampton City Council 1979–82. NUPE (branch secretary).

Mr Warren Hawksley

WREKIN, THE Electorate 77226

*Hawksley, P.W. (C)	22710	39.0%
Grocott, B. (Lab)	21379	36.7%
Biltcliffe, M. (SDP/All)	14208	24.4%
C majority	1331	2.3%
Total vote 58297	Turnout	75.5%

Mr Warren Hawksley, formerly a bank clerk, gained the seat for Conservatives in 1979. Contested Wolverhampton North East in Feb and Oct 1974. Born Mar 10 1943; educ. Mill Mead Shrewsbury, and Denstone College, Uttoxeter. Member, Shropshire County Council 1970–81. Member of West Mercia Police Authority 1977–1981.

Mr Bruce Grocott was MP for Lichfield and Tamworth Oct 1974–79; contested the seat Feb 1974, and South West Hertfordshire 1970. Television journalist and local government officer. Born Nov 1940; educ. Hemel Hempstead Grammar School and Leicester and Manchester universities. Former chairman, Bromsgrove UDC. Former chairman, all-party group on penal reform 1976–79. Member, Select Committee on Overseas Development 1978–79. ASTMS, NUJ.

Mr Mark Biltcliffe, teacher, head of humanities at Springhill Middle School, Chasetown, Staffordshire. Born 1956; educ. Bodafon Primary School, Ysgol John Bright School and West Midlands College of Higher Education, Walsall. Successfully contested for the Alliance in 1981 by-election to Great Worley Parish Council, near Walsall. Former school governor.

Dr John Marek

WREXHAM Electorate 60707

Marek, J. (Lab)	16120	34.3%
Wood, Mrs K. (C)	15696	33.4%
Thomas, M. (L/All)	13974	29.7%
Thomas, J. (Pl C)	1239	2.6%
Lab majority	424	0.9%
Total vote 47029	Turnout	77.5%

Dr John Marek, university lecturer, was elected in 1983; contested Ludlow 1974. Born Dec 24 1940; educ. University of London. Member, Ceredigion District Council. ASTMS.

Mrs Kay Wood, speech therapist, contested Newham North East 1979. Born Mar 21 1943; educ. Queen's School, Chester; Oldrey Fleming College of Speech Therapy; Guys Hospital Medical School, and London University. Honorary treasurer and councillor, College of Speech Therapists 1973–76. ASTMS.

Mr Martin Thomas QC, a barrister and recorder, contested West Flint 1964, 1966 and 1970 and Wrexham Feb and

Oct 1974. Former President of the Welsh Liberal Party; spokesman on Treasury affairs. Born 1937; educ. Grove Park Grammar School, Wrexham and Peterhouse, Cambridge.

Mr John Thomas, deputy headmaster and councillor. Member, Wrexham Maelor District Council, since 1973; mayor of the borough 1981–82.

Mr Raymond Whitney

WYCOMBE Electorate 70065

*Whitney, R. W. (C)	27221	54.2%
Page, A. (SDP/All)	14024	27.9%
Bastin, C. (Lab)	8636	17.2%
Amin, M. (MPP)	327	0.7%
C majority	13197	26.3%
Total vote 50208	Turnout	71.1%

Mr Raymond Whitney was appointed Under Secretary of State for Foreign and Commonwealth Affairs in Jun 1983. Former company chairman and export consultant. Elected at the by-election Apr 1978. Former member diplomatic service. Member Public Accounts Committee since 1979. Joint vice-chairman, Conservative backbench committee on employment since 1980; chairman, Conservative backbench committee on foreign and Commonwealth Affairs since 1981. Born Nov 28 1930; educ. Wellingborough School, Sandhurst, and London University. Head of Chancery, British Embassy, Buenos Aires 1969–72; Assistant Head, East African Department; Foreign and Commonwealth Office 1972–73; Deputy High Commissioner and Economic Counsellor, Dacca 1974–75; head of Information Research Department, Foreign and Commonwealth Office 1973–77 and head of Overseas Information Department 1977–78.

Mr Alan Page, general manager of major motor manufacturer retail franchise. Born Dec 21 1933; educ. local village schools, Tylers Green and Hazlemere C of E. Ran his own company for 20 years.

Mr Colin Bastin, computer consultant. Born 1948.

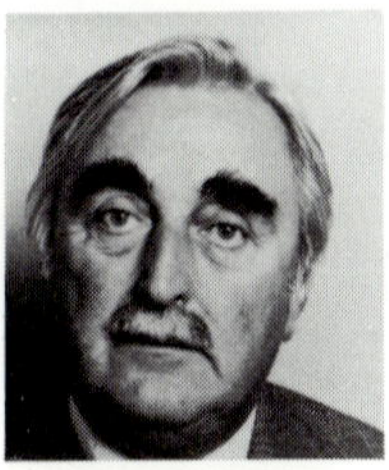

Sir Walter Clegg

WYRE Electorate 65934

*Clegg, Sir W. (C)	26559	56.5%
Murdoch, I. (SDP/All)	11748	25.0%
Goldsmith, W. (Lab)	8743	18.6%
C majority	14811	31.5%
Total vote 47050	Turnout	71.4%

Sir Walter Clegg, Lord Commissioner of the Treasury (whip) 1970–72; Vice-Chamberlain of the Household (whip) 1972–73; Comptroller of the Household (whip) 1973–74. Partner in firm of solicitors. Won the seat in 1983; MP for North Fylde 1966–83; contested Ince 1959. Born Apr 18 1920; educ. Arnold School, Blackpool, Bury Grammar School, and Manchester University. Member, Lancashire County Council 1955–61. Opposition whip Mar to Oct 1974. Member, executive 1922 committee 1975–76, treasurer since 1976. Member, Committee of Selection; chairman all-party solicitors group. On executive IPU and CPA. Chairman, Conservative backbench committee of North-West MPs.

Mr William Goldsmith is a chemical process operator. Leader, Labour group, Wyre District Council. Age 49. GMBATU.

Mr Esmond Bulmer

WYRE FOREST Electorate 68298

*Bulmer, J. E. (C)	24809	48.4%
Batchelor, A. (L/All)	16632	32.4%
Williams, R. B. (Lab)	9850	19.2%
C majority	8177	15.9%
Total vote 51291	Turnout	75.1%

Mr Esmond Bulmer won the seat 1983; MP for Kidderminster Feb 1974–83. Chairman, HP Bulmer Holdings since Apr 1982 and farmer. Member, executive committee, National Trust. Secretary, Conservative employment committee 1975–79. PPS to Minister of State, Home Office, 1979–80. Born May 19 1935; educ. Rugby and King's College, Cambridge. Non-executive director, Wales and West Mid-Regional Board, National Westminster Bank. Member, British Heritage Committee, British Tourist Authority.

Mr Anthony Batchelor a senior lecturer is leader of the Liberal group on Wyre Forest District Council. Born Apr 6 1941; educ. King Charles I School, Kidderminster, University College, London and University of Keele. Contested Worcestershire South 1964; Kidderminster Feb and Oct 1974, and Birmingham South for the European Parliament in 1979. Kidderminster Borough Councillor 1967–74; Wyre Forest District Councillor since 1973. NATFHE.

Mr Roger Williams, lecturer. Born Nov 7 1947; educ. Wolverhampton Polytechnic and Southlands College. Member, Co-operative Party. NATFHE.

Mr Paddy Ashdown

YEOVIL Electorate 66 102

Ashdown, J. J. D. (L/All)	26 608	50.5%
Martin, D. J. P. (C)	23 202	44.0%
Brushett, P. J. (Lab)	2 928	5.6%
L/All majority	3 406	6.5%
Total vote 52 738		Turnout 79.8%

Mr Paddy Ashdown, local government officer with Dorset County Council, won the seat in 1983; contested it 1979. Born Feb 24 1941; educ. Bedford School, Hongkong University. Qualified Chinese interpreter. Joined Foreign Office 1972; First Secretary to the British Mission to the United Nations in Geneva 1974–76. AUEW (TASS).

Mr David Martin, director of family caravan business. Born Feb 5 1945; educ. Norwood School, Exeter, Kelly College, Tavistock, and Fitzwilliam College, Cambridge. Called to the Bar 1969, and practised (Inner Temple) 1969–76. Teignbridge district councillor 1979–83.

Mr Peter Brushett, poultry distributor, contested New Forest Oct 1974 and Bournemouth West 1979. Born Jun 15 1931; educ. Kemp Welch School and Seale Hayne Agricultural College. Member, Dorset County Council and Bournemouth District Council. NUAAW.

Mr Keith Best

YNYS MON Electorate 50 359 1979: 47 726 same

*Best, K. L. (C)	15 017	37.5%
Jones, I. W. (Pl C)	13 333	33.3%
Williams, T. (Lab)	6 791	16.9%
Thomas, D. (SDP/All)	4 947	12.3%
C majority	1 684	4.2%
Total vote 40 088		Turnout 79.6%

1979 (as Anglesey): Total vote 38 746 (81.2%); C 15 100 (39.0%); Lab 12 283 (31.7%); Pl C 7 863 (20.3%); L 3 500 (9.0%). C maj 2 817 (7.3%); swing 12.5% to C. C gain from Lab.

Mr Keith Best, a barrister and lecturer in law, won this seat (then called Anglesey) in May 1979. PPS to Secretary of State for Wales. Member, Welsh Affairs Select Committee; secretary, Welsh Conservative Members' Committee, Conservative Northern Ireland Committee, Conservative Tourism Committee, Parliamentary Scout Assoc. Councillor, Brighton Borough Council (chairman, Lands Committee, Housing Committee) 1976–80. Member, Young Conservatives Advisory Committee 1978. Member of Lloyd's. Born Jun 10 1949; educ. Brighton College, Keble College, Oxford.

Mr Ieuan Wyn Jones, deputy treasurer of Plaid Cymru, is a solicitor in Denbigh. Educ. Ysgol Y Berwyn, Y Bala and Liverpool University. Contested Denbigh 1979, and North Wales for European Parliament 1979. Party spokesman on transport, national chairman 1978–82.

Mr Tudor Williams, solicitor. Born 1939. Member, Fabian Society and Society of Labour Lawyers. TGWU (ACTSS).

Mr David Thomas, barrister. Born Sep 27 1951; educ. Cardigan County Secondary School, Jesus College, Oxford. Gray's Inn.

Mr Conal Gregory

YORK Electorate 78 311 1979: 76 832 same

Gregory, C. (C)	24 309	41.3%
*Lyon, A. W. (Lab)	20 662	35.1%
Cable, V. (SDP/All)	13 523	23.0%
Lister, A. J. (Ind)	204	0.4%
Brattan, T. G. (BNP)	148	0.3%
C majority	3 647	6.2%
Total vote 58 846		Turnout 75.1%

1979: Total vote 59 698 (77.7%); Lab 26 703 (44.7%); C 25 453 (42.6%); L 6 752 (11.3%); Other 569 (1.0%); NF 221 (0.4%). Lab maj 1 250 (2.1%); swing 2.1% to C.

Mr Conal Gregory, international wine consultant, lecturer and wine editor. Won the seat in 1983. Born Mar 11 1947; educ. King's College, Wimbledon, University of Sheffield and Worshipful Company of Vintners (Master of Wine). Member, Norfolk County Council 1977–81; East Anglia Tourist Board.

Mr Alexander Lyon, barrister, was Minister of State, Home Office 1974–76. Member of the Select Committee on Home Affairs, 1979–83. Opposition spokesman on home affairs 1972–74, and Commonwealth Affairs 1970–72. Won this seat in 1966 and contested it in 1964. Born Oct 15 1931; educ. West Leeds High School and University College, London. Chairman, PLP Home Affairs Group 1980–83.

Mr Vincent Cable, an economist and deputy director, Overseas Development Institute. Contested Glasgow, Hillhead 1979, for Labour. Born May 9 1943; educ. Nunthorpe Grammar School, York, and Cambridge and Glasgow universities. Glasgow city councillor 1971–74. ASTMS.

Political party and trade union abbreviations

The following abbreviations for political parties have been used:

C Conservative, Lab Labour, SDP/All Social Democratic Party/Alliance, L/All Liberal/Alliance, SNP Scottish National Party, Pl C Plaid Cymru, OUP Official Unionist Party, Eco Ecology Party, DUP Democratic Unionist Party, SDLP Social Democratic and Labour Party, All Alliance, PSF Provisional Sinn Fein, UPUP Ulster Popular Unionist Party, Ind DUP Independent Democratic Unionist Party, WP Workers Party, Ind Independent, NF National Front, Com Communist, WRP Workers' Revolutionary Party.

The following abbreviations have been used for the smaller parties and individual candidates: AB Assassins Bullet, ACIE Against Cuts in Education, A Corr Anti Corruption, ACM Anti-Common Market, AV Anti-Vivisection, BELLS Ban Every Licensing Law Society, BNP British National Party, Brit Nat British National, CBWU Campaign for Black and White Unity, CD Christian Democrat, CFCP Conservative Favouring Capital Punishment, Comp Dem Computer Democrat, CPPS Committee for Prevention of Police State, CSD Christian Social Democrat, CUI Council for United Ireland, Eth Min Ethnic Minority, FAMP Freddie's Alternative Medicine Party, FD Fancy Dress Party, FTACM Free Trade Anti Common Market, FWD Freedom From World Domination, Ind C Independent Conservative, Ind L Independent Liberal, IFP Islington and Finsbury Party. INP Irish National Party, JAHC Jesus And His Cross JDF Justice for Divorced Fathers, LAO Law and Order, LM Loony Monster, LTU Labour and Trade Union, MDP Modern Democratic Party, MK Meybon Kernow, Mod Lab Moderate Labour, MPP Multiracial Political Party, NA Noise Abatement, Nat Nationalist, Nat Lab National Labour Party, New Brit New Britain, NP Nobody Party, PAL Party of Associates with Licencees, PFA Prosperity For All RAP Radical and Anti-Parliamentarian, Rep Republican, Rev Com Revolutionary Communist, RHCP Reintroduction of Hanging and Corporal Punishment, RCCP Restoration of Capital and Corporal Punishment, SACA Servicemen's And Citizen's Association, SBILP Southport Back In Lancashire Party, SDBP Stop Deportation of Black People, SEE Spare the Earth Ecology, SPGB Socialist Party of Great Britain, Soc Unity Socialist Unity, TEF Traditional English Food, TVCABL Tactically Vote Conservative Annihilate Bennites Livingstonites, UCP United County Party, UP Unemployed Party, VGP Very Good Party, WCPPP Workers Charter Party with Pensioner Power, WFLOE Women for Life on Earth, WP Workers Party, and WPWS Workers Party for a Workers State, W Reg Wessex Regionalist.

Some candidates using unique labels have been described as 'Ind' to avoid further proliferation of one-candidate parties.

The following abbreviations for trade unions and other bodies have been used:

ABTA Association of British Travel Agents, ACTT Association of Cinematograph, Television and Allied Technicians, APEX Asssociation of Professional, Executive, Clerical and Computer Staff, ASTMS Association of Scientific, Technical and Managerial Staff, ASW Amalgamated Society of Woodworkers, AUEW Amalgamated Union of Engineering Workers, AUEW/TASS Amalgamated Union of Engineering Workers/Technical and Supervisory Staff, CBI Confederation of British Industry, CND Campaign for Nuclear Disarmament, CPC Conservative Political Centre, EETPU Electrical, Electronic, Telecommunications and Plumbing Union, FRGS Fellow of Royal Geographical Society, GLC Greater London Council, GMBATU General Municipal Boilermakers Amalgamated Trade Union, ILEA Inner London Education Authority, IOJ Institute of Journalists, LCC London County Council, LSE London School of Economics, MEP Member of European Parliament, MDC Metropolitan District Council, MPU Medical Practitioners' Union, NALGO National Association of Local Government Officers, NAS National Association of Schoolmasters, NATFHE National Association of Teachers in Further and Higher Education, NEC National Executive Committee, NEDC National Economic Development Council, NFU National Farmers' Union, NSPCC National Society for Prevention of Cruelty to Children, NUJ National Union of Journalists, NUM National Union of Mineworkers, NUPE National Union of Public Employees, NUT National Union of Teachers, NUR National Union of Railwaymen, PLP Parliamentary Labour Party, POEU Post Office Engineering Union, PPS Parliamentary Private Secretary, RDC Rural District Council, SLADE Society of Lithographic Artists, Designers, Engravers and Process Workers, TGWU Transport and General Workers Union, TSB Trustee Savings Bank, UDC Urban District Council, USDAW Union of Shop, Distributive and Allied Workers, UCATT Union of Construction, Allied Trades and Technicians, VSO Voluntary Service Overseas, WEA Workers' Educational Association, WEU Western European Union.

Ministers in House of Lords

Lord Bellwin

Lord Gowrie

Lady Young

Lord Cockfield

Lord Hailsham of St Marylebone, the Lord Chancellor since 1979, held the office, 1970–74. Made life peer 1970. As Mr Quintin Hogg, he was chief Opposition spokesman on home affairs, 1966–70. Renounced the Hailsham viscountcy on Nov 20 1963, to return to the Commons and was elected for St Marylebone, 1963. Born October 1907; educ. Eton and Christ Church, Oxford. MP for Oxford City, 1938–50, when he succeeded to the peerage. Under-Secretary for Air, Apr–Jul 1945; First Lord of the Admiralty 1955–56; Minister of Education, 1957; Lord President of the Council, 1957; Lord Privy Seal and Minister for Science 1959; Lord President of the Council and Minister for Science 1960–64; Secretary of State for Education and Science, Apr–Oct 1964. Chairman, Conservative Party Organization, 1957–59.

Viscount Whitelaw, Lord President of the Council and Leader of the House of Lords, from June 1983. Mr William Whitelaw, Home Secretary, 1979–83, was awarded an hereditary peerage in the birthday honours following the general election. He continues as Mrs Thatcher's deputy in the Cabinet. Deputy Leader of the Opposition 1975–79 after unsuccessfully contesting the leadership of the Conservative Party. Chief Opposition spokesman on devolution 1974–76, and on home affairs and broadcasting 1976–79. Chairman of the Conservative Party 1974–75; Opposition spokesman on employment 1974; Secretary of State for Employment 1973–74; Secretary of State for Northern Ireland 1972–73, and Lord President of the Council and Leader of the House of Commons 1970–72. President, National Union of Conservative and Unionists Assoc. 1971. Opposition chief whip 1964–70; Parliamentary Secretary, Ministry of Labour 1962–64. Elected 1955; contested East Dunbartonshire, 1950 and 1951. Born Jun 28 1918; educ. Winchester and Trinity College, Cambridge. Farmer and landowner. Partner, Mount Pleasant Farms, Penrith. Former captain, Royal and Ancient Golf Club..

Lord Cockfield, Chancellor of the Duchy of Lancaster, from June 1983, was Secretary of State for Trade, 1982–83; Minister of State, Treasury, 1979–82. Chairman of the Price Commission 1973–77. Adviser on taxation policy to the Chancellor of the Exchequer, 1970–73. Former Commissioner of Inland Revenue. Born Sep 1916; educ. Dover County; London School of Economics.

Lady Young, Minister of State for Foreign and Commonwealth Affairs from Jun 1983, was Leader of the House of Lords, 1981–83; Lord Privy Seal, 1982–83; Chancellor of the Duchy of Lancaster, 1981–82. Minister of State, Education and Science, 1979–81; Under-Secretary of State for the Environment, 1973–74; Baroness-in-Waiting (Government Whip), 1972–73. Born Oct 1926; educ. Dragon School, Oxford; Headington School, and in the USA. Former Leader, Conservative group, Oxford City Council.

The Earl of Gowrie, Minister of State, Privy Council Office, and Minister for the Arts since Jun 1983; Minister of State, Northern Ireland Office, 1981–83; Minister of State, Employment 1979–81. Lord-in-Waiting (Government Whip), 1972–74. Born Nov 1939; educ. Eton; Balliol College, Oxford. Also has day-to-day responsibilities for Civil Service from Jun 1983.

Lord Cameron of Lochbroom appointed Lord Advocate in May 1984 was President, Pensions Appeal Tribunal for Scotland, 1975–84; chairman, committee of investigations under 1958 Agricultural Marketing Act, 1980–84; Advocate Depute, 1981; Home Advocate Depute, 1982. Born Jun 11 1931; educ. Edinburgh Academy, Oxford and Edinburgh Universities. Admitted to Faculty of Advocates 1958; QC in 1972. Chairman, industrial tribunals in Scotland, 1966–81; member, Legal Aid Central Committee, 1974–81.

Lord Bellwin, Minister for Local Government and Environmental Services since Jan 1983; Under-Secretary of State for the Environment, 1979–82. Vice-chairman Association of Metropolitan Authorities 1978. Elected to Leeds CBC in 1965; alderman 1968; housing committee chairman, 1967–72. Chairman, Leeds City Council policy and finance committee and leader of council, 1975–79. Born Feb 1923; educ. Leeds Grammar School and Leeds University.

Lord Belstead, Minister of State, Agriculture, Fisheries and Food from Jun 1983, was Minister of State, Foreign and Commonwealth Office, 1982–83. Under-Secretary of State, Home Office, 1979–82. Under-Secretary for Education and Science, 1970–73; Under-Secretary, Northern Ireland Office, 1973–74. Born Sep 1932; educ. Eton; Christ Church, Oxford. Deputy Leader of House of Lords from Jun 1983.

The Earl of Mansfield, Minister of State, Northern Ireland Office, from Jun 1983, was

Minister of State, Scottish Office, 1979–83. Member European Parliament, 1973–75. Hon Sheriff of Perth, 1973. Born Jul 1930; educ. Eton; Christ Church, Oxford. Barrister.

Lord Gray of Contin, Minister of State, Scottish Office from June 1983. Mr Hamish Gray was made a life peer in the birthday honours following the general election. His biographical details appear under the Ross, Cromarty and Skye constituency on page 193.

Lord Trefgarne, Under-Secretary of State of Defence for the Armed Forces from June 1983; Under-Secretary of State, Health and Social Security, 1982–83; Under-Secretary of State, Foreign and Commonwealth Affairs, 1981–82. Under-Secretary, Department of Transport, 1981; Lord-in-Waiting (Government Whip), 1979–81; Opposition Whip in Lords, 1977–79. Born Mar 1941; educ. Haileybury and in the USA.

The Earl of Avon, Under-Secretary of State for Energy, since Jan 1983; Government whip and spokesman for the arts, environment and transport, 1980–83; Opposition Whip 1978–79. Born Oct 1930; educ. Eton.

Lord Elton, Under-Secretary of State, Home Office, since 1982; Under-Secretary of State, Department of Health and Social Security, 1981–82; Under-Secretary of State, Northern Ireland Office, 1979–81. Opposition spokesman 1976–79. Born Mar 1930; educ. Eton; New College, Oxford. Publisher.

Lord Glenarthur, Under-Secretary of State for Health and Social Security since June 1983; Lord-in-Waiting (Government Whip), 1982–83. Commissioned 10th Royal Hussars (PWO) 1963, Captain, 1970, Major, 1973, Retired, 1975. Major, the Royal Hussars TAVR, 1976–80. Born Oct 1944; educ. Eton.

Lord Denham, Government Chief Whip and Captain, Gentlemen at Arms, since 1979; Opposition Chief Whip, 1978–79; Opposition Deputy Chief Whip 1974–78; Captain, Yeomen of the Guard, 1971–74. Born Oct 1927; educ. Eton; King's College, Cambridge.

The Earl of Swinton, Captain, Queen's Bodyguard and Yeomen of the Guard. Member North Riding, Yorkshire County Council, 1961–74; member North Yorkshire County Council, 1973–77. Born Mar 1937; educ. Winchester and Royal Agriculture College.

Viscount Long, Lord-in-Waiting (Government whip) since 1979. Opposition whip 1974–79. Born Jan. 1929; educ. Harrow.

Lord Lyell, Lord-in-Waiting (whip) since 1979. Opposition whip, 1975–79. Born Mar 1939; educ. Eton and Christ Church, Oxford. Chartered accountant.

Lord Skelmersdale, Lord-in-Waiting (whip) since 1981. Born Apr 1945; educ. Eton and Lord Wandsworth College. Horticulturist.

Lord Lucas of Chilworth, Lord-in-Waiting (whip). Former member Lords Select Committee, Science and Technology. Born Apr 1926; educ. Peter Symonds School, Winchester and Luton Technical College.

Lady Trumpington, Baroness-in-Waiting (whip), appointed Jun 1983; Cambridge city councillor 1963–73; Mayor of Cambridge 1971–72; Cambridgeshire county councillor, 1973–75. Born Oct 1922; educ. privately in England and France.

How the Nation Voted—June 1983

	C	Lab	All	Scot Nat Pl C	others	Total
England						
Electorate						35 146 369
Votes	11 711 519	6 862 422	6 714 957	–	183 748	25 472 646
% of vote/turnout	46.0	26.9	26.4	–	0.7	72.5
MPs	362	148	13	–	0	523
Candidates	523	523	523	–	431	2 000
						Swing +4.3%
Scotland						
Electorate						3 886 899
Votes	801 354	990 654	692 767	331 975	7 830	2 824 580
% of vote/turnout	28.4	35.1	24.5	11.8	0.3	72.7
MPs	21	41	8	2	0	72
Candidates	72	72	72	72	26	314
						Swing +1.7%
Wales						
Electorate						2 113 854
Votes	499 310	603 858	373 358	125 309	7 151	1 608 986
% of vote/turnout	31.0	37.5	23.2	7.8	0.4	76.1
MPs	14	20	2	2	0	38
Candidates	38	38	38	38	17	169
						Swing +4.2%
N. Ireland						
Electorate						1 050 222
Votes	–	–	–	–	764 925†	764 925
% of vote/turnout	–	–	–	–	100	72.8
MPs	–	–	–	–	17	17
Candidates	–	–	–	–	95	95
United Kingdom						
Electorate						42 197 344
Votes	13 012 183	8 456 934	7 781 082	457 284	963 654	30 671 137
% of vote/turnout	42.4	27.6	25.4	1.5	3.1	72.7
MPs	397	209	23	4	17	650
Candidates	633	633	633	110	569	2 578
						Swing +3.9%

† Separate table on page 285

Swings from Lab to C

How the Nation Voted—May 1979

	C	Lab	L	Scot Nat Pl C	NF	Com	Others	Total
England								
Electorate								34 212 573
Votes	12 255 514	9 526 758	3 876 577	–	189 150	6 622	117 629	25 972 250
MPs	306	203	7	–	–	–	–	516
% of vote/turnout	47.2	36.7	14.9	–	0.7	0.0	0.5	75.9
Candidates	516	516	506	–	297	18	221	2 074
							Swing	+5.8%
Scotland								
Electorate								3 795 865
Votes	916 155	1 211 445	255 095	504 259	104	5 926	23 653	2 916 637
MPs	22	44	3	2	–	–	–	71
% of vote/turnout	31.4	41.5	8.7	17.3	0.0	0.2	0.8	76.8
Candidates	71	71	42	71	1	12	16	284
							Swing	+0.7%
Wales								
Electorate								2 061 109
Votes	526 254	768 458	173 525	132 544	2 465	4 310	29 032	1 636 588
MPs	11	21	1	2	–	–	1*	36
% of vote/turnout	32.2	47.0	10.6	8.1	0.2	0.3	1.8	79.4
Candidates	35	35	28	36	5	8	7	154
							Swing	+5.4%
N. Ireland								
Electorate								1 027 204
Votes	–	–	–	–	–	–	695 887	695 887
MPs	–	–	–	–	–	–	12	12
% of vote/turnout	–	–	–	–	–	–	100	67.7%
Candidates	–	–	–	–	–	–	64	64
United Kingdom								
Electorate								41 096 751
Votes	13 697 923	11 506 661	4 305 197	636 803	191 719	16 858	866 201	31 221 362
MPs	339	268	11	4	–	–	13*	635
% of vote/turnout	43.9	36.9	13.8	2.0	0.6	0.1	2.8	76.0
Candidates	622	622	576	107	303	38	308	2 576
							Swing	+5.2%

*Including the Speaker

Swings from Lab to C

Survey of the voting

Labour and Alliance have mountains to scale

by David Butler, Fellow of Nuffield College, Oxford
and
Robert Waller, Fellow of Magdalan College, Oxford

The re-election of the Conservative Government set new landmarks in history and in psephology. Mrs Thatcher became only the second Conservative Prime Minister ever to be re-elected after a full term (Lord Salisbury in 1900 was the other). Her margin in seats and in votes was the largest won by any party since 1935. Her party's advance from 339 seats in 1979 to 397 seats in 1983 was the largest ever achieved by an incumbent Government (though, when allowance is made for the 21 seats that the Conservatives are estimated to have owed to redistribution, it does not quite match Labour's advance from 1964 to 1966).

The Labour setback was even more striking, statistically, than the Conservative triumph. The party lost over a quarter of its 1979 vote, falling back from 36.9 per cent to 27.6 per cent—the lowest share ever won by the principal opposition party. Never since the Labour Representation Committee was founded in 1900 had the average vote for Labour candidates been so low. The only comparable examples of such slumps in votes are offered by the Conservatives in 1945 and the Liberals in 1924.

But despite the Conservative triumph which offered them utterly secure control of British politics for the next five years, the Government's authority rests on a mere 42.4 per cent of the national vote (or 30.8 per cent of the nominal electorate). The Conservative percentage actually fell 1.5 per cent from the 1979 figure of 43.9 per cent. The only precedents for a government with a House of Commons majority that had so small a measure of popular support are October 1974 (when 39.2 per cent secured a majority of three for Mr Wilson) and November 1922 (when 38.5 per cent secured a majority of 63 for Mr Bonar Law).

The Conservatives could only win this huge victory on so small a vote because the opposition was divided. The new Liberal/SDP Alliance came near to Mr Jenkins's goal of breaking the mould of British politics. It secured 25.4 per cent of the vote compared to Labour's 27.6 per cent. It was in first or second place in 332 seats compared to Labour's 341 but it won only 23 seats compared to Labour's 209.

The anomaly of the Labour party securing nine times as many seats as the Alliance with only 2 per cent more of the vote naturally stirred up discussion of proportional representation. If seats had been allocated exactly in accordance with votes the Conservatives would have won 285 (−111), Labour 180 (−29) and the Alliance 160 (+137). Under any of the electoral systems operating in the other nine EEC countries, Mrs Thatcher would not have had a majority.

The share of the vote won by Conservative and Labour combined was 70.0 per cent far the lowest since 1923. But all the other parties which together received 30.0 per cent of the UK vote, won only 6 per cent of the seats. Northern Ireland, outside the main party stream, distorts these figures. In mainland Britain the other parties with 28.2 per cent of the vote secured only 4 per cent of the seats. In the 523 constituencies in England, the Alliance, with 26.4 per cent of the vote, secured only 2½ per cent of the seats. It is worth setting out some precedents:

	Con		Lab		L(L/SDP)		*other*	*Total*
	votes	*seats*	*votes*	*seats*	*votes*	*seats*	*seats*	*seats*
1983	42.4	397	27.6	209	25.4	23	21	650
1979	43.9	339	36.9	268	13.8	11	17	635
Oct 1974	35.8	277	39.2	319	18.3	13	26	635
1945	39.8	213	47.8	393	9.1	12	22	640
1935	53.7	432	37.9	154	6.4	20	9	615
1923	38.1	258	30.5	191	29.6	159	7	615
1922	38.2	345	29.5	142	29.1	116	12	615

SURVEY OF THE VOTING

Any analysis of the 1983 election results must inevitably be confused by the effects of the statutory redistribution of seats which was completed early in 1983. This produced the most drastic change of parliamentary boundaries in British history. The House of Commons was increased from 635 to 650 seats and only 66 constituencies survived unaltered. Inevitably the changes helped the Conservatives. Over the decade since the previous redistribution, people had moved from the cities to the suburbs and from the North to the South. The areas that lost seats as constituency electorates were equalized were on the whole Labour-inclined and the areas that gained were Conservative.

The GLC area, for example, forfeited eight constituencies and it was reckoned that this cost Labour five seats and the Conservatives two. At the national level, a detailed study conducted by the BBC and ITN suggested that if the 1979 election had been fought on the new boundaries the Conservatives would have won 360 seats (not 339) and Labour would have won 260 (not 268). In other words, the Conservatives went into the election with a gain of 21 seats in the enlarged House. They could have afforded to lose 34 seats and still have kept their majority: Labour needed a 5.5 per cent swing to win an overall majority.

All our calculations are based, necessarily, on the BBC/ITN estimates of what would have happened in 1979 in the new seats which are set out on pages 279 and 280. These estimates, although very carefully calculated, may in a few cases be misleading because of the difficulties of assessing how voters would have divided in subsections of a constituency, particularly when wards have been redrawn, but the general picture can certainly be trusted.

Another problem in analysing the results of the 1983 election comes from the arrival of a genuinely three-party situation. In every election from 1931 to 1979 two parties predominated. The ratio between the two main parties and the Liberals varied from 20:20:1 in 1951 to 2:2:1 in 1974. But always, in at least threequarters of the seats, Conservative and Labour provided the top two at the poll. In 1983 the ratio changed to 1½:1:1 and Conservative and Labour provided the top two in less than half the seats.

With two parties predominant, it has been customary to simplify all movements of votes into one single figure 'swing'. 'Swing', defined as the average of Conservative percentage gain and Labour percentage loss, has become familiar as a simple instrument for assessing electoral tides, as between constituencies or as between regions.

As soon as three parties are seriously in contention, explanation necessarily becomes more complex; the details of three or more sets of percentage change become relevant, and the hypotheses multiply about the components of any movement that is recorded.

The turnout in the election was recorded as 72.7 per cent. The only lower figures have been 71.0 per cent in 1970, 71.1 per cent in 1935, 71.1 per cent in 1923 and 57.2 per cent in 1918. However, the election was in June when, as in 1970, many people were away on early summer holidays. It was also an election in which the polls had made plain that a walkaway victory could be expected. Moreover, as a Census Office report (published in December 1982) had made plain, the quality of the electoral register has become much worse in recent years.

Since 6.5 per cent of the names were wrongly included on the list, even if everybody had voted, the turnout could never have exceeded 93.5 per cent (in 1966 a similar study had shown only 3.5 per cent of 'dead' names). The register was revealed as particularly inefficient in inner city areas; the fact that nine London constituencies were the only ones to have turnouts under 60 per cent may reflect inaccurate registers as much as popular alienation. The highest turnout was, not for the first time, in Fermanagh and South Tyrone (88.6 per cent). In Britain the highest was in Carmarthen (82.1 per cent). The lowest was in City of London and Westminster South (51.8 per cent).

In absolute terms the Conservatives won 13.0m votes (13.7m in 1979) to Labour 8.5m (11.5m in 1979) and the L/SDP Alliance's 7.8m (the Liberals got 4.3m in 1979). Labour got 3m fewer votes than in any post-war election.

The Conservative total of 397 seats represents an increase of 58 over their 1979 figure and an increase of 37 over the 360 seats they would have won on the new boundaries. Four Conservative MPs were defeated: Delwyn Williams in Montgomery, Hamish Gray in the new Ross, Cromarty and Skye, Iain Sproat, who had misguidedly left his Aberdeen seat (which was held comfortably) for the supposedly more promising Roxburgh and Berwickshire, and David Myles who, having had his Banff seat abolished by redistribution, vainly tried to gain Orkney and Shetland. The party also lost Yeovil and Gordon. It is arguable that their failure to win in Crewe and Nantwich, in Birmingham, Erdington, in Glasgow, Cathcart and in Liverpool, Broadgreen should also, in the light of boundary changes, be considered as losses.

Labour's 209 seats represents a fall of 59 from the actual 1979 result or of 51 allowing for the notional effect of the boundary changes. Some 30 sitting Labour MPs were defeated including three who had served in the Cabinet.

The Alliance lost 25 of the seats they held at dissolution but only two of the four MPs who had actually been elected as Liberals or Social Democrats forfeited their seats: the 1981 by-election victories of Shirley Williams at Crosby and of Bill Pitt at Croydon were reversed. But of the 26 SDP MPs who stood again after defecting from the Labour Party (and in one case the Conservatives) only four survived.

Only 314 of the 650 members of the new Parliament were returned on a majority vote. Labour got 50 per cent or more in 68 seats: the Conservatives were similarly dominant in 232 seats and the Alliance in eight seats: only four of the 17 Northern Ireland MPs had a clear majority. It is hard to say how many seats were decided by a split vote: a withdrawal by the candidate who came third would seldom have led to all his votes being transferred to the candidate who came second. Obviously the former Labour MP Ben Ford's 8.6 per cent in Bradford North may have contributed to the Militant Pat Wall's defeat by a margin of 3.4 per cent. James Marshall who lost Leicester South for Labour by seven votes may feel wistful about the 495 which went to an Ecology candidate or even the 161 for a Worker's Party splinter. Arthur Davidson might have similar thoughts about his 21-vote defeat in Hyndburn. William Whitlock lost by 362 in Nottingham North where the Communist polled 1 184. The lowest winning percentage was the Labour's 31.6 per cent in the three-way marginal of Carmarthen.

However the luck of narrow victories and narrow defeat fell fairly equally. Of those who won by under 500 votes six were Conservative, ten were Labour and one was Alliance.

Despite expectations to the contrary, there was a notable degree of uniformity in the results, in all types of constituency and in all regions. It was remarkable that in every region the increase in the Alliance vote lay between 10.6 per cent and 13.2 per cent, except for Scotland where it reached 15.7 per cent. The Conservative vote changed little—it stayed level in the South East and fell by 3.8 per cent in the North West. Labour slumped everywhere; in Scotland the fall was only 6.4 per cent and in the North West only 6.5 per cent but elsewhere it ranged between 8.9 per cent and 12.3 per cent.

Labour's vote actually fell less than the Conservatives in major cities such as Liverpool, Birmingham, Manchester and Glasgow; no Conservative MPs at all were returned by Liverpool or Glasgow. But in Hertfordshire where Labour held four seats in 1974, the party came third in every constituency. The Alliance did very well in the capital cities of London (+12.8 per cent); Cardiff (+14.0 per cent, including notional figures) and, most of all, Edinburgh (+16.3 per cent).

At the constituency level, there were some outstanding performances. The Conservatives gained Basildon, Barrow and Furness and Amber Valley from Labour, all with swings between the two parties of over 9 per cent. They also took the new mining seat of Sherwood and swept the board in nearby Nottingham, winning Nottingham North with a 9.6 per cent swing from Labour.

On the other hand Labour did well in a number of Liverpool seats, including Broadgreen (where they would have won even without the division of the vote between Liberal and SDP candidates). Michael Foot had the compensation of winning 70.1 per cent of the vote and a 23,705 majority in Blaenau Gwent, the highest margins for any MP. (The highest Conservative majority was Peter Hordern's 21 785 at Horsham.)

But the most unexpected results were produced by the Alliance. The Liberals seized Leeds West and Yeovil in each case increasing their vote by nearly 20 per cent. The 24-year-old Charles Kennedy produced the only SDP gain of the election in Ross, Cromarty and Skye, with a remarkable overturn of the Conservative minister, Hamish Gray, who promptly received a life peerage and stayed a minister.

The sitting SDP members performed exceptionally in retaining Plymouth, Devonport, Woolwich, and Caithness and Sutherland (and even the vote for some defeated SDP members merits note—e.g. in Crosby, Islington South and Finsbury, and Erith and Crayford). Finally Enoch Powell did well in his narrowly balanced Down South division, securing five-sixths of the split Protestant vote, to scrape home over the SDLP by 548 votes.

There was once again little consistent evidence for personal votes—either pro- or anti-. But in addition to the achievements of Mr Foot and of the Alliance candidates already mentioned, it is worth noting Ken Weetch's achievement in retaining Ipswich, Labour's last seat in East Anglia, Jeffrey Rooker's swing in Perry Barr against the Conservative tide, and Gerry Fitt's 10,326 votes as an Independent Socialist in Belfast West. Although he lost his seat at Bristol East, Tony Benn did not suffer from a larger swing than the regional average. It might also be noted that in Finchley Mrs Thatcher gained a smaller swing (2.2 per cent) than the norm for London (3.8%) or for England (3.9%).

Rural seats provided the only type of constituency in which the Conservatives actually increased their overall share of the vote and resisted the Alliance tide better than elsewhere; they also did well in seaside resorts. The Government fared disproportionately badly in inner city seats, especially in those with a large non-white population. They also did worse in seats with a high proportion of council housing and in those with a high proportion of unemployed; seats with a concentration of students and academics were good for Labour and for the Alliance.

The Conservatives and the Alliance did very well in New Towns while Labour's vote declined by 12.9 per cent, 3 per cent more than the national average. There is no evidence that in seats with notably left wing Labour candidates the Alliance or the Conservatives benefited. There is some evidence that Labour did particularly badly in Plymouth, Devonport; Portsmouth North; Woolwich and Aldershot. It may be significant that one of the few increases in the Conservative vote was in Newbury, which includes the Greenham Common Air Force base. Newbury also provided one out of the five seats where the Alliance vote actually fell.

The election once again showed that non-white candidates fare worse than their party colleagues. None of the 18 non-white candidates was elected. For the Conservatives Pramila La Hunte suffered a 10.6 per cent drop in the Conservative vote in Birmingham, Ladywood while in supposedly marginal West Hertfordshire, Paul Boateng lost 23.7 per cent of the Labour vote and finished in third place nearly 15,000 votes behind the Conservative victor.

Twenty-three women were elected, compared to 19 in the 1979. Six of them entered parliament for the first time including Ann Winterton of Congleton, whose husband, Nicholas Winterton, was re-elected in next door Macclesfield; Clare Short was elected for Labour at Birmingham, Ladywood while her husband Alex Lyon was defeated at York after 17 years as an MP. Some 498 MPs were re-elected; of the 157 new MPs seven had served in an earlier Parliament.

The oldest member is now the 77 year old Robert Edwards (Lab) of Wolverhampton South East, but nine members over 70 were elected including James Callaghan (71), the new Father of the House, and Ian Mikardo (74) and Michael Foot (69) the only other MPs to have shared in the Labour landslide of 1945. Sir Hugh Fraser (65) is the only Conservative survivor of that election.

For the Scottish and Welsh nationalists there was little change. Each returned their two MPs with increased majorities but neither gained any seats. The Scottish Nationalists stayed within striking distance in three seats in the North East of Scotland but the SNP share of the Scottish vote fell from 17.3 per cent to 11.8 per cent. Plaid Cymru made a strong challenge in Ynys Mon and in Carmarthen but nowhere else; total PLC support in Wales fell from 8.1 per cent to 7.8 per cent.

In Northern Ireland, the Nationalist and Republican parties did not manage to increase their representation despite the award of five extra seats to the province. They won only two of the 17 new seats despite there being a probable Catholic majority in five of the others. The Catholic vote was rather evenly split between SDLP (17.9 per cent) and Sinn Fein (13.4 per cent). This enabled the protestants to win in Fermanagh and South Tyrone, Mid-Ulster, Newry and Armagh and South Down.

The Official Unionists (with 34 per cent of the Northern Ireland vote) won 11 seats while Ian Paisley's Democratic Unionists (with 20.0 per cent) won three and James Kilfedder, as an Independent Unionist, took North Down. The leader of the SDLP, John Hume, won Foyle while Sinn Fein's Gerry Adams took Belfast West from Gerry Fitt.

The 'fringe' parties fared poorly. The National Front polled an average of only 1.0 per cent per candidate (the highest was 3.7 per cent at Newham South); Communists 0.8 per cent (the highest was 2.8 per cent Rhondda) and the Ecologists 1.1 per cent (the highest was 2.9 per cent at Ogmore). None of the three sitting MPs who stood as Independent Labour saved their deposits: Arthur Lewis secured 11.0 per cent in Newham North West; Michael O'Halloran 11.1 per cent in Islington North and Ben Ford 8.6 per cent in Bradford North. Independent Conservatives did well in Bournemouth East (7.7 per cent) and in Spelthorne (where the author Richard Adams won 5.5 per cent on an anti-hunting ticket), and an Independent Labour local councillor achieved 7.5 per cent in Erewash. These were the only six candidates in Britain outside the main parties to get even one twentieth of the vote.

The electors reversed three of the six by-election upsets of 1981–83. Croydon North West and Crosby were recovered by the Conservatives from the Alliance and Northfield from Labour. Ossie O'Brien, whose retention of Darlington for Labour in March 1983 had had such an impact, lost the seat to his Conservative challenger, as did John Spellar (Birmingham, Northfield). Only in Hillhead (SDP), Bermondsey (Liberal), and Mitcham and Morden (Conservative) was a by-election switch confirmed at the general election.

The election gave the Conservatives a very decisive victory. Yet the figures are more startling for the decline of the Labour Party than for any Conservative advance. In only five seats did the Conservative vote rise by over 5 percent (Blyth Valley 10 per cent,

Chertsey and Walton 9 per cent, Brigg and Cleethorpes 8 per cent, Livingstone 7 per cent and Newbury 6 per cent). In threequarters of the seats it fell.

But Labour's record was more spectacular. An average fall of 9.5 per cent concealed nine drops of over 20 per cent and only ten increases. Labour lost 119 deposits (its previous worst was 35 in 1929). The Alliance lost only 11 and the Conservatives only five. Altogether 802 deposits were lost, with the Ecology Party having to pay £150 for each of its 63 candidates.

In the area south of a line from Bristol to Dover the Labour party came third in every seat save Crawley, Brighton Kempton and Southampton Test. Outside the London area Bristol South, Leicester West, Thurrock, and Ipswich provided the only Labour victories south east of a line from Grimsby to the Bristol Channel.

The electoral system worked as had been predicted. On the assumption of uniform swings, Clive Payne had calculated in advance that a division of 43 per cent, Lab 27 per cent, Lib 25 per cent would yield 405 Conservatives, 200 Labour and 18 Alliance. A few spectacular individual performances increased the Alliance total to 23 and Labour held on disproportionately in a few seats in the North West and Scotland. But the logic of uniform swings under first-past-the-post elections held good.

After the election the Conservatives held 77 of its 397 seats by under 10 per cent but were within 10 per cent of victory in 67. Labour held 62 of its 209 seats by under 10 per cent but within 10 per cent of victory in 56. The Alliance held 12 of their 23 seats by under 10 per cent but were within 10 per cent of victory in 26. If the Alliance were to add 10 per cent to its 25.4 per cent, drawn equally from Labour and Conservative, it would gain only 74 more seats.

The Alliance found that it had to contend with the so-called 'plateau effect'—its share increased least in those seats in which it had already obtained a strong second place. This was exemplified in the Liberals' disappointments in Richmond and Barnes, in Chelmsford and in Cornwall North. One explanation is that in the best Liberal hopes, the Labour vote had already been squeezed as much as practicable in previous General Elections. Defections by Labour supporters may well have assisted the Liberals in their strong performances in seats such as Yeovil, Montgomery, Cheltenham, Torbay and Edinburgh West. In Montgomery and Gordon the Conservatives lost their seats despite an increase in their share of the vote; an apparent triumph for 'tactical voting' by squeezed Labour voters.

The performances of the respective partners in the Alliance were worth noting. The Liberals averaged 27.4 per cent and SDP 24.5 per cent but the SDP candidates improved on the 1979 Liberal vote by 12.4 per cent and the Liberal candidates by only 10.5 per cent. This was partly due to the fact that the SDP candidates fought seats where the Liberals had been weaker in 1979. But they did also have the advantage of being able to include the advances (ranging from 9.7 per cent in Liverpool, to 36.5 per cent in Plymouth, Devonport) when sitting SDP MPs were candidates.

It is notable that 273 of the 397 Conservative MPs now have as their principle opponent an Alliance candidate. It will be ironic for those on the Government benches to spend their efforts in fighting a Labour opposition of 209 in the House of Commons when over two-thirds of them have to worry about holding off an Alliance challenge in their constituencies.

If the Labour party is to return to full power it will need to gain 117 seats. It will need a swing of over 10 per cent in votes from Conservative to Labour. This confirms the replacement of the 'cube law' relationship between seats and votes by a 'square law'; whereas once about 18 seats would have changed hands for each swing of 1 per cent between Conservative and Labour now only about 10 would do so. Except in 1945 a 10 per cent swing has never been achieved. It is twice the postwar record swing the Conservatives managed in 1979. Once safe seats such as Mansfield and Dagenham, Thurrock and Burnley, must now be considered as Labour marginals.

Over the years the electoral map of Britain has been redrawn. The Labour Party which once controlled half the seats in East Anglia now has no predominantly rural seats in England and only Carmarthen elsewhere. Its hold on mining and East End seats is much less overwhelming. Contrast these votes with the more or less comparable ones for 1955:

	Lab (percent)	
	1955	1983
Islwyn	82	59
Hemsworth	83	59
Bow and Poplar	81	50
Newham South	81	50
Dagenham	73	39

The Conservatives, governing with 42.4 per cent of support, may hardly seem to be in a strong position. But each of their two major opponents has a mountain to scale if they are to deny the Conservatives another victory.

However, any analysis of this oddly uniform election should contain a warning. The years 1979–83 saw unprecedented volatility in the electorate. The Conservatives had only 27 per cent support in the polls in November 1981. A mere 18 months before the dissolution they had just lost an utterly safe seat like Crosby. Equally, in November 1980, a year earlier, Labour stood at 50 per cent in the opinion polls. At the beginning of the decade, the volatile voters moved first one way and then another. June 1983 was a well-timed election for the Conservatives: as things turned out the electoral system gave them the maximum bonus for their efforts. But that does not, with this fickle electorate, guarantee them power beyond the current Parliament.

Regional, metropolitan, city and county voting patterns

The Times has drawn up the following analyses of voting in the General Election on June 9 1983 in which 650 parliamentary seats were contested in 1983 compared with 635 at the last election in May 1979. The increased number of constituencies flowed from reports, approved by Parliament early this year and last year, by the Boundary Commissions for England, Scotland, Wales and Northern Ireland, although the higher number of seats in the latter was consequent upon an Act of Parliament in 1979.

The number of seats in England increased from 516 to 523, in Scotland from 71 to 72, in Wales from 36 to 38, and in Northern Ireland from 12 to 17.

In England, Scotland and Wales, the commissions set about their task and made their determinations on the basis of not crossing county, London borough, metropolitan county and borough and Scottish region boundaries and of crossing as few local government district boundaries as possible.

This has enabled the following breakdowns of voting to be drawn up to give many perfect and some imperfect voting comparisons between the 1983 and 1979 elections, but if there are no major boundary changes between now and the next election, which seems certain, there is the basis of perfect comparison of voting at that election.

The decade of the seventies saw massive changes in the organization and thus boundaries of local government, and the 1983 election was held with the main parliamentary and local government boundaries truly in line.

The Times was not being published in 1979 but the following voting comparisons build on those set out for the first time in *The Times Guide to the House of Commons, May 1979* published by Times Books Ltd. Swing is between Conservative and Labour.

England

England has been divided into the following 10 regions and when drawn up in 1979 – by the late Mr Frank Roberts, Local Government Correspondent of *The Times* – they were largely based on the Central Office of Information's groupings. For 1979 a few parliamentary seats did cut across county boundaries and these were given to the regions to which they most naturally belonged, a course which has also been adopted for this election in the non-metropolitan counties analysis.

The 10 regions are as follows:

Region	*No. of seats* *1979*	*1983*	*Counties*
London	92	84	Greater London
South Eastern	40	42	Kent, Surrey, East Sussex, West Sussex.
Southern and Wessex	42	47	Berkshire, Buckinghamshire, Dorset, Hampshire, Isle of Wight, Oxfordshire, Wiltshire.
South Western	34	36	Avon, Cornwall, Devon, Gloucestershire, Somerset.
Eastern	45	51	Bedfordshire, Cambridgeshire, Essex, Hertfordshire, Norfolk, Suffolk.
East Midland	40	42	Derbyshire, Leicestershire, Lincolnshire, Northamptonshire, Nottinghamshire.
Midland	56	58	Herefordshire and Worcestershire, Shropshire, Staffordshire, Warwickshire, West Midlands.
North Western	76	73	Cheshire, Greater Manchester, Lancashire, Merseyside.
Yorkshire and Humberside	54	54	Humberside, North Yorkshire, South Yorkshire, West Yorkshire.
Northern	37	36	Cleveland, Cumbria, Durham, Northumberland, Tyne and Wear.
Total	516	523	

REGIONAL ANALYSIS

The constituencies and voting in the 10 regions of England were as follows:

London

1979: 92 seats

	votes	*% votes*	*MPs*	*Candidates*
C	1693844	46.0	50	92
Lab	1458885	39.6	42	92
L/All	438093	11.9	0	92
Others	90136	2.5	0	156
Totals	3680958	100.0	92	432

Electorate: 5147135 Turnout 71.5%

1983: 84 seats

	votes	*% votes*	*MPs*	*Candidates*
C	1 517 105	43.9	56	84
Lab	1 031 539	29.8	26	84
L/All	853 360	24.7	2	84
Others	55 774	1.6	0	151
Totals	3 457 778	100.0	84	403

Electorate 5093471 Turnout 67.9% Swing 3.8% to C

South-Eastern

1979: 40 seats

	votes	*% votes*	*MPs*	*Candidates*
C	1240520	57.2	40	40
Lab	521114	24.0	0	40
L/All	383301	17.7	0	40
Others	23389	1.1	0	42
Totals	2168324	100.0	40	162

Electorate: 2833430 Turnout 76.5%

1983: 42 seats

	votes	*% votes*	*MPs*	*Candidates*
C	1 220 321	57.2	42	42
Lab	301 156	14.1	0	42
L/All	593 547	27.8	0	42
Others	18 964	0.9	0	34
Totals	2 133 988	100.0	42	160

Electorate 2939448 Turnout 72.6% Swing 5.0% to C

Southern and Wessex

1979: 42 seats

	votes	*% votes*	*MPs*	*Candidates*
C	1341703	54.4	38	42
Lab	607586	24.6	3	42
L/All	494435	20.0	1	42
Others	23299	0.9	0	35
Totals	2467023	100.0	42	161

Electorate: 3178340 Turnout 77.6%

1983: 47 seats

	votes	*% votes*	*MPs*	*Candidates*
C	1 359 074	54.5	46	47
Lab	357 291	14.3	0	47
L/All	760 781	30.5	1	47
Others	17 035	0.7	0	44
Totals	2 494 181	100.0	47	185

Electorate 3383089 Turnout 73.7% Swing 5.2% to C

South Western

1979: 34 seats

	votes	*% votes*	*MPs*	*Candidates*
C	962,449	51.0	29	34
Lab	483,075	25.6	4	34
L/All	418,206	22.2	1	34
Others	23653	1.2	0	47
Totals	1887383	100.0	34	149

Electorate 2381148 Turnout 79.3%

1983: 36 seats

	votes	*% votes*	*MPs*	*Candidates*
C	947 409	50.2	32	36
Lab	291 910	15.5	1	36
L/All	634 666	33.7	3	36
Others	12 152	0.6	0	36
Totals	1 886 137	100.0	36	144

Electorate 2475266 Turnout 76.2% Swing 4.7% to C

Eastern

1979: 45 seats

	votes	*% votes*	*MPs*	*Candidates*
C	1395269	51.5	39	45
Lab	864797	31.9	5	45
L/All	428222	15.8	1	45
Others	23,358	0.9	0	43
Totals	2711646	100.0	45	178

Electorate 3446495 Turnout 78.7%

1983: 51 seats

	votes	*% votes*	*MPs*	*Candidates*
C	1 384 958	51.1	48	51
Lab	530 405	19.6	2	51
L/All	782 922	28.9	1	51
Others	10 911	0.4	0	28
Totals	2 709 196	100.0	51	181

Electorate 3621136 Turnout 74.8% Swing 6.0% to C

East Midland

1979: 40 seats

	votes	*% votes*	*MPs*	*Candidates*
C	1034164	46.7	24	40
Lab	845,742	38.2	16	40
L/All	313602	14.2	0	40
Others	20465	0.9	0	35
Totals	2213973	100.0	40	155

Electorate: 2839286 Turnout 78.0%

1983: 42 seats

	votes	*% votes*	*MPs*	*Candidates*
C	1 013 384	47.2	34	42
Lab	600 624	28.0	8	42
L/All	517 098	24.1	0	42
Others	17 266	0.8	0	26
Totals	2 148 372	100.0	42	152

Electorate 2891369 Turnout 74.3% Swing 5.4% to C

Midland

1979: 56 seats

	votes	*% votes*	*MPs*	*Candidates*
C	1334079	47.1	31	56
Lab	1135853	40.1	25	56
L/All	323961	11.5	0	50
Others	36545	1.3	0	56
Totals	2830438	100.0	56	218

Electorate: 3758247 Turnout 75.3%

1983: 58 seats

	votes	*% votes*	*MPs*	*Candidates*
C	1 261 378	45.0	36	58
Lab	874 190	31.2	22	58
L/All	655 982	23.4	0	58
Others	12 464	0.4	0	32
Totals	2 803 994	100.0	58	206

Electorate 3863281 Turnout 72.6% Swing 3.4% to C

North Western

1979: 76 seats

	votes	*% votes*	*MPs*	*Candidates*
C	1577534	43.8	30	76
Lab	1530866	42.5	44	76
L/All	471952	13.1	2	72
Others	23429	0.7	0	53
Totals	3603781	100.0	76	277

Electorate 4743025 Turnout 76.0%

1983: 73 seats

	votes	*% votes*	*MPs*	*Candidates*
C	1 405 451	40.0	36	73
Lab	1 266 103	36.0	35	73
L/All	822 237	23.4	2	73
Others	23 179	0.7	0	44
Totals	3 516 970	100.0	73	263

Electorate 4820148 Turnout 73.0% Swing 1.3% to C

Yorkshire and Humberside 1979: 54 seats

	votes	% votes	MPs	Candidates
C	1 044 165	39.3	19	54
Lab	1 195 808	45.0	34	54
L/All	391 406	14.7	1	54
Others	23 356	0.9	0	53
Totals	2 654 735	100.0	54	215
Electorate	3 564 461		Turnout 74.5%	

1983: 54 seats

	votes	% votes	MPs	Candidates
C	1 013 311	38.7	24	54
Lab	925 084	35.3	28	54
L/All	669 377	25.5	2	54
Others	13 516	0.5	0	30
Totals	2 621 288	100.0	54	192
Electorate	3 690 001	Turnout 71.1%	Swing 4.5% to C	

Northern 1979: 37 seats

	votes	% votes	MPs	Candidates
C	631 787	36.0	6	37
Lab	883 032	50.3	30	37
L/All	213 399	12.2	1	37
Others	25 771	1.5	0	16
Totals	1 753 989	100.0	37	127
Electorate	2 321 006		Turnout: 75.6%	

1983: 36 seats

	votes	% votes	MPs	Candidates
C	589 128	34.6	8	36
Lab	684 120	40.2	26	36
L/All	424 987	25.0	2	36
Others	2 507	0.2	0	7
Totals	1 700 742	100.0	36	115
Electorate	2 369 160	Turnout 71.8%	Swing 4.4% to C	

English Regions: totals 1979

	votes	% votes	MPs	Candidates
C	12 255 514	47.2	306	516
Lab	9 526 758	36.7	203	516
L/All	3 876 577	14.9	7	506
Others	313 401	1.2	0	536
Totals	25 972 250	100.0	516	2074
Electorate:	34 212 573		Turnout: 75.9%	

1983

	votes	% votes	MPs	Candidates
C	11 711 519	46.0	362	523
Lab	6 862 422	26.9	148	523
L/All	6 714 957	26.4	13	523
Others	183 748	0.7	0	432
Totals	25 472 646	100.0	523	2001
Electorate	35 146 369	Turnout 72.5%	Swing 4.3% to C	

Metropolitan analysis

A further basis for comparison between the areas of heaviest population in England has been obtained by using the six Metropolitan counties, plus London which in the boundary commission's report is dealt with separately. Here the Metropolis is divided into two areas – Outer London (57 seats in 1979 and 55 seats in 1983) and Inner London (35 seats in 1979 and 29 seats in 1983).

The six metropolitan counties and 36 metropolitan districts outside London came into existence on local government reorganization in 1974. None of the constituencies fought in 1983 crosses a metropolitan county boundary and only six out of 129 constituencies cross a metropolitan district boundary – four in Greater Manchester, one in Tyne and Wear and one in West Yorkshire.

The number of constituencies making up the metropolitan areas and voting analyses are as follows:

Metropolitan county	*No. of seats* 1979	1983
London	92	84
West Midlands	31	31
Greater Manchester	32	30
Merseyside	16	17
South Yorkshire	13	15
West Yorkshire	23	23
Tyne and Wear	14	13
Totals	221	213

Outer London

1979: 57 seats

Barking Barking, Barking Dagenham, Barnet Chipping Barnet, Barnet Finchley, Barnet Hendon North, Barnet Hendon South, Brent East, Brent North, Brent South, Ealing Acton, Ealing North, Ealing South, Enfield Edmonton, Enfield North, Enfield Southgate, Haringey Hornsey, Haringey Tottenham, Haringey Wood Green, Harrow Central, Harrow East, Harrow West, Havering Hornchurch, Havering Romford, Havering Upminster, Hillington Hayes & Harlington, Hillingdon Ruislip-Northwood, Hillingdon Uxbridge, Hounslow Brentford & Isleworth, Hounslow Feltham & Heston, Newham North East, Newham North West, Newham South, Redbridge Ilford North, Redbridge Ilford South, Redbridge Wanstead & Woodford, Waltham Forest Chingford, Waltham Forest Leyton, Waltham Forest Walthamstow, Bexley Bexleyheath, Bexley Erith & Crayford, Bexley Sidcup, Bromley Beckenham, Bromley Chislehurst, Bromley Orpington, Bromley Ravensbourne, Croydon Central, Croydon North East, Croydon North West, Croydon South, Kingston-upon-Thames Kingston, Kingston-upon-Thames Surbiton, Merton Mitcham & Morden, Merton Wimbledon, Richmond-upon-Thames Richmond, Richmond-upon-Thames Twickenham, Sutton, Sutton & Cheam, Sutton Carshalton.

	votes	*% votes*	*MPs*	*Candidates*
C	1 227 597	48.9	40	57
Lab	906 304	36.1	17	57
L/All	325 393	13.0	0	57
Others	51 687	2.1	0	82
Totals	2 510 981	100.0	57	253
Electorate	3 370 604		Turnout: 74.5%	

1983: 55 seats

Barking, Beckenham, Bexleyheath, Brent East, Brent North, Brent South, Brentford and Isleworth, Carshalton and Wallington, Chingford, Chipping Barnet, Chislehurst, Croydon Central, Croydon North East, Croydon North West, Croydon South, Dagenham, Ealing Acton, Ealing North, Ealing Southall, Edmonton, Enfield North, Enfield Southgate, Erith and Crayford, Feltham and Heston, Flechley, Harrow East, Harrow West, Hayes and Harlington, Hendon North, Hendon South, Hornchurch, Hornsey and Woodgreen, Ilford North, Ilford South, Kingston upon Thames, Leyton, Mitcham and Morden, Newham North East, Newham North West, Newham South, Old Bexley and Sidcup, Orpington, Ravensbourne, Richmond and Barnes, Romford, Ruislip-Northwood, Surbiton, Sutton and Cheam, Tottenham, Twickenham, Upminster, Uxbridge, Walthamstow, Wanstead and Woodford, Wimbledon.

	votes	*% votes*	*MPs*	*Candidates*
C	1 120 328	47.6	44	55
Lab	604 262	25.7	11	55
L/All	601 835	25.6	0	55
Others	25 620	1.1	0	67
Totals	2 352 045	100.0	55	232
Electorate 3 350 019	Turnout 70.2%	Swing 4.6% to C		

Inner London

1979: 35 seats

Camden Hampstead, Camden Holborn & St Pancras South, Camden St Pancras North, Cities of London & Westminster, City of London & Westminster South, City of London & Westminster Paddington, City of London & Westminster St Marylebone, Hackney Central, Hackney North & Stoke Newington, Hackney South & Shoreditch, Hammersmith Fulham, Hammersmith North, Islington Central, Islington North, Islington South & Finsbury, Kensington & Chelsea, Chelsea, Kensington & Chelsea Kensington, Tower Hamlets, Bethnal Green & Bow, Tower Hamlets Stepney & Poplar, Greenwich Greenwich, Greenwich Woolwich East, Greenwich Woolwich West, Lambeth Central, Lambeth Norwood, Lambeth Streatham, Lambeth Vauxhall, Lewisham Deptford, Lewisham East, Lewisham West, Southwark Bermondsey, Southwark Dulwich, Southwark Peckham, Wandsworth Battersea North, Wandsworth Battersea South, Wandsworth Putney, Wandsworth Tooting.

	votes	*% votes*	*MPs*	*Candidates*
C	466 247	39.9	10	35
Lab	552 581	47.2	25	35
L/All	112 700	9.6	0	35
Others	38 449	3.3	0	74
Totals	1 169 977	100.0	35	179
Electorate	1 776 531		Turnout: 65.9%	

1983: 29 seats

Battersea, Bethnal Green and Stepney, Bow and Poplar, Chelsea, City of London and Westminster South, Dulwich, Eltham, Fulham, Greenwich, Hackney North and Stoke Newington, Hackney South and Shoreditch, Hammersmith, Hampstead and Highgate, Holborn and St Pancras, Islington North, Islington South and Finsbury, Kensington, Lewisham Deptford, Lewisham East, Lewisham West, Norwood, Peckham, Putney, Southwark and Bermondsey, Streatham, Tooting, Vauxhall, Westminster North, Woolwich.

	votes	*% votes*	*MPs*	*Candidates*
C	396 777	35.9	12	29
Lab	427 277	38.6	15	29
L/All	251 525	22.8	2	29
Others	30 154	2.7	0	84
Totals	1 105 733	100.0	29	171
Electorate 1 743 452	Turnout 63.4%	Swing 2.3% to C		

West Midlands

1979: 31 seats

Aldridge-Brownhills, Birmingham Edgbaston, Birmingham Erdington, Birmingham Hall Green, Birmingham Handsworth, Birmingham Ladywood, Birmingham Northfield, Birmingham Perry Barr, Birmingham Selly Oak, Birmingham Small Heath, Birmingham Sparkbrook, Birmingham Stechford, Birmingham Yardley, Coventry North-East, Coventry North-West, Coventry South-East, Coventry South-West, Dudley East, Dudley West, Halesowen & Stourbridge, Solihull, Sutton Coldfield, Walsall North, Walsall South, Warley East, Warley West, West Bromwich East, West Bromwich West, Wolverhampton North East, Wolverhampton South East, Wolverhampton South West.

1983: 31 seats

Aldridge-Brownhills, Birmingham Edgbaston, Birmingham Erdington, Birmingham Hall Green, Birmingham Hodge Hill, Birmingham Ladywood, Birmingham Northfield, Birmingham Perry Barr, Birmingham Selly Oak, Birmingham Small Heath, Birmingham Sparkbrook, Birmingham Yardley, Coventry North-East, Coventry North-West, Coventry South East, Coventry South West, Dudley East, Dudley West, Halesowen & Stourbridge, Meriden, Solihull, Sutton Coldfield, Walsall North, Walsall South, Warley East, Warley West, West Bromwich East, West Bromwich West, Wolverhampton North East, Wolverhampton South East, Wolverhampton South West.

	votes	*% votes*	*MPs*	*Candidates*
C	630178	45.4	12	31
Lab	625677	45.1	19	31
L/All	108481	7.8	0	25
Others	23922	1.8	0	39
Totals	1388258	100.0	31	126

Electorate: 1905137 Turnout: 72.9%

	votes	*% votes*	*MPs*	*Candidates*
C	583 767	41.7	13	31
Lab	521 837	37.4	18	31
L/All	285 092	20.4	0	31
Others	6 984	0.5	0	20
Totals	1 396 680	100.0	31	113

Electorate 1984318 Turnout 70.4% Swing 2.0% to C

Greater Manchester

1979: 32 seats

Altrincham & Sale, Ashton-under-Lyne, Bolton East, Bolton West, Bury & Radcliffe, Cheadle, Eccles, Farnworth, Hazel Grove, Heywood & Royton, Ince, Leigh, Manchester Ardwick, Manchester Blackley, Manchester Central, Manchester Gorton, Manchester Moss Side, Manchester Openshaw, Manchester Withington, Manchester Wythenshawe, Middleton & Prestwich, Oldham East, Oldham West, Rochdale, Salford East, Salford West, Stalybridge & Hyde, Stockport North, Stockport South, Stretford, Westhoughton, Wigan.

	votes	*% votes*	*MPs*	*Candidates*
C	580590	40.2	5	32
Lab	671494	46.4	26	32
L/All	184615	12.8	1	29
Others	9155	0.6	–	23
Totals	1445854	100.0	32	116

Electorate: 1899061 Turnout: 76.1%

1983: 30 seats

Altrincham and Sale, Ashton under Lyne, Bolton West, Bolton North East, Bolton South East, Bury North, Bury South, Cheadle, Davyhulme, Denton and Reddish, Eccles, Hazel Grove, Heywood and Middleton, Leigh, Littleborough and Saddleworth, Makerfield, Manchester Blackley, Manchester Central, Manchester Gorton, Manchester Withington, Manchester Wythenshawe, Oldham Central and Royton, Oldham West, Rochdale, Salford East, Stalybridge and Hyde, Stockport, Stretford, Wigan, Worsley.

	votes	*% votes*	*MPs*	*Candidates*
C	508 273	36.2	11	30
Lab	557 563	39.7	18	30
L/All	332 005	23.6	1	30
Others	6 907	0.5	0	21
Totals	1 404 748	100.0	30	111

Electorate 1944856 Turnout 72.2% Swing 1.4% to C

Merseyside

1979: 16 seats

Birkenhead, Bootle, Crosby, Huyton, Liverpool Edge Hill, Liverpool Garston, Liverpool Kirkdale, Liverpool Scotland Exchange, Liverpool Toxteth, Liverpool Walton, Liverpool Wavertree, Liverpool West Derby, St. Helens, Southport, Wallasay, Wirral.

	votes	*% votes*	*MPs*	*Candidates*
C	295586	41.4	6	16
Lab	308419	43.2	9	16
L/All	104572	14.7	1	16
Others	5221	0.7	0	12
Totals	713798	100.0	16	60

Electorate 982 052 Turnout 72.7%

1983: 17 seats

Birkenhead, Bootle, Crosby, Knowsley North, Knowsley South, Liverpool Broadgreen, Liverpool Garston, Liverpool Mossley Hill, Liverpool Riverside, Liverpool Walton, Liverpool West Derby, St Helens North, St Helens South, Southport, Wallasey, Wirral South, Wirral West.

	votes	*% votes*	*MPs*	*Candidates*
C	285452	35.0	5	17
Lab	325170	39.9	11	17
L/All	193137	23.7	1	17
Others	11223	1.4	0	10
Totals	814982	100.0	17	61

Electorate 1140132 Turnout 71.5% Swing 1.5 to Lab

South Yorkshire

1979: 13 seats

Barnsley, Dearne Valley, Doncaster, Don Valley, Penistone, Rotherham, Rother Valley, Sheffield Attercliffe, Sheffield Brightside, Sheffield Hallam, Sheffield Heeley, Sheffield Hillsborough, Sheffield Park.

	votes	*% votes*	*MPs*	*Candidates*
C	205815	31.2	1	13
Lab	374961	56.8	12	13
L/All	74396	11.3	0	13
Others	5297	0.8	0	14
Totals	660469	100.0	13	53

Electorate: 903528 Turnout: 73.1%

1983: 15 seats

Barnsley Central, Barnsley East, Barnsley West and Penistone, Doncaster Central, Doncaster North, Don Valley, Rotherham, Rother Valley, Sheffield Attercliffe, Sheffield Brightside, Sheffield Central, Sheffield Hallam, Sheffield Heeley, Sheffield Hillsborough, Wentworth.

	votes	*% votes*	*MPs*	*Candidates*
C	193 780	28.0	1	15
Lab	337 115	48.8	14	15
L/All	158 924	23.0	0	15
Others	1 464	0.2	0	4
Totals	691 283	100.0	15	49

Electorate 994249 Turnout 69.6% Swing 2.4% to C

West Yorkshire

1979: 24 seats

Batley & Morley, Bradford North, Bradford South, Bradford West, Brighouse & Spenborough, Colne Valley, Dewsbury, Halifax, Hemsworth, Huddersfield East, Huddersfield West, Keighley, Leeds East, Leeds North East, Leeds North West, Leeds South, Leeds South-East, Leeds West, Normanton, Pontefract & Castleford, Pudsey, Shipley, Sowerby, Wakefield.

	votes	*% votes*	*MPs*	*Candidates*
C	409642	37.1	7	24
Lab	521073	47.1	16	24
L/All	165355	15.0	1	24
Others	9590	0.9	0	25
Totals	1105660	100.0	24	97

Electorate 1476293 Turnout: 74.9%

1983: 23 seats

Batley & Spen, Bradford North, Bradford South, Bradford West, Calder Valley, Colne Valley, Dewsbury, Elmet, Halifax, Hemsworth, Huddersfield, Keighley, Leeds Central, Leeds East, Leeds North East, Leeds North West, Leeds South & Morley, Leeds West, Normanton, Pontefract & Castleford, Pudsey, Shipley, Wakefield.

	votes	*% votes*	*MPs*	*Candidates*
C	412 584	37.3	11	23
Lab	394 734	35.7	10	23
L/All	287 454	26.0	2	23
Others	10 196	0.9	0	20
Totals	1 104 968	100.0	23	89

Electorate 1538890 Turnout 71.8% Swing 5.9% to C

Tyne and Wear

1979: 14 seats

Blaydon, Gateshead East, Gateshead West, Houghton-le-Spring, Jarrow, Newcastle-upon-Tyne Central, Newcastle-upon-Tyne East, Newcastle-upon-Tyne North, Newcastle-upon-Tyne West, South Shields, Sunderland North, Sunderland South, Tynemouth, Wallsend.

	votes	*% votes*	*MPs*	*Candidates*
C	210 992	34.0	2	14
Lab	341 605	55.1	12	14
L/All	63 286	10.2	0	14
Others	4 017	0.7	0	6
Totals	619 900	100.0	14	48

Electorate 845 434 Turnout 73.3%

1983: 13 seats

Blaydon, Gateshead East, Houghton and Washington, Jarrow, Newcastle-upon-Tyne Central, Newcastle-upon-Tyne East, Newcastle-upon-Tyne North, South Shields, Sunderland North, Sunderland South, Tyne Bridge, Tynemouth, Wallsend.

	votes	*% votes*	*MPs*	*Candidates*
C	193 966	31.3	2	13
Lab	281 015	45.4	11	13
L/All	144 090	23.3	0	13
Others	478	0.1	0	1
Totals	619 549	100.0	13	40

Electorate 892 200 Turnout 69.4& Swing 3.5% to C

English Metropolitan Counties totals

1979

	votes	*% votes*	*MPs*	*Candidates*
C	4 026 647	41.9	83	222
Lab	4 302 114	44.7	136	222
L/All	1 138 798	11.8	3	213
Others	147 338	1.5	0	275
Totals	9 614 897	100.0	222	932

Electorate 13 158 640 Turnout: 73.1%

1983

	votes	*% votes*	*MPs*	*Candidates*
C	3 693 927	38.9	99	213
Lab	3 448 973	36.3	108	213
L/All	2 254 062	23.8	6	213
Others	93 026	1.0	0	227
Totals	9 489 988	100.0	213	866

Electorate 13 588 116 Turnout 69.9% Swing 2.7% to C

Non-Metropolitan Counties

The 39 non-metropolitan counties were under the boundaries review allocated 310 seats none of which cross county boundaries whereas 31 of the previous constituencies were divided by such boundaries. In view of special geographical circumstances, the commission allocated an additional seat to Cumbria, Lancashire and Northumberland, but kept the Isle of Wight as one seat. Comparison in some counties with voting in the last election is perfect, in others not, but is as near as possible. The analysis is as follows (Isle of Wight is on page 143):

Avon

1979: 10 seats

Bath, Bristol North East, Bristol North West, Bristol South, Bristol South East, Bristol West, Gloucestershire South, Kingswood, Somerset North, Weston-super-Mare. Parts of three in Gloucestershire and Somerset.

	votes	*% Votes*	*MPs*	*Candidates*
C	264 696	47.9	7	10
Lab	191 845	34.7	3	10
L/All	89 434	16.2	0	10
Others	7 230	1.3	0	16
Totals	553 205	100.0	10	46

Electorate 703 253 Turnout: 78.7%

1983: 10 seats

Bath, Bristol East, Bristol North West, Bristol South, Bristol West, Kingswood, Northavon, Wansdyke, Weston-super-Mare, Woodspring.

	votes	*% votes*	*MPs*	*Candidates*
C	251 487	47.3	9	10
Lab	129 026	24.3	1	10
L/All	146 791	27.6	0	10
Others	4 073	0.8	0	13
Totals	531 377	100.0	10	43

Electorate 708 399 Turnout 75.0% Swing 4.9% to C

Bedfordshire

1979: 5 seats

Bedford, Bedfordshire Mid, Bedfordshire South, Luton East, Luton West.

	votes	*% votes*	*MPs*	*Candidates*
C	140 891	51.3	5	5
Lab	90 318	32.9	0	5
L/All	40 516	14.8	0	5
Others	2 814	1.0	0	7
Totals	274 539	100.0	5	22

Electorate 345 739 Turnout 79.4%

1983: 5 seats

Bedfordshire Mid, Bedfordshire North, Bedfordshire South West, Luton North, Luton South.

	votes	*% votes*	*MPs*	*Candidates*
C	141 424	51.0	5	5
Lab	62 686	22.6	0	5
L/All	72 981	26.3	0	5
Others	344	0.1	0	1
Totals	277 435	100.0	5	16

Electorate 364 167 Turnout 76.2% Swing 5.0% to C

Berkshire

1979: 6 seats

Eton and Slough, Newbury, Reading North, Reading South, Windsor and Maidenhead, Wokingham. Also parts of three other constituencies under Oxfordshire and Buckinghamshire.

	votes	*% votes*	*MPs*	*Candidates*
C	182 844	52.4	5	6
Lab	90 239	25.9	1	6
L/All	69 070	19.8	0	6
Others	6 594	1.9	0	8
Totals	348 747	100.0	6	26

Electorate 454 083 Turnout 76.8%

1983: 7 seats

Berkshire East, Newbury, Reading East, Reading West, Slough, Windsor and Maidenhead, Wokingham.

	votes	*% votes*	*MPs*	*Candidates*
C	202 447	54.7	7	7
Lab	59 121	16.0	0	7
L/All	103 957	28.1	0	7
Others	4 514	1.2	0	10
Totals	370 039	100.0	7	31

Electorate 508 697 Turnout 72.7% Swing 6.1% to C

Buckinghamshire

1979: 5 seats

Aylesbury, Beaconsfield, Buckingham, Chesham and Amersham, Wycombe, Part of Beaconsfield in Berkshire.

	votes	*% votes*	*MPs*	*Candidates*
C	178 705	57.4	5	5
Lab	77 921	25.0	0	5
L/All	52 089	16.7	0	5
Others	2 881	0.9	0	4
Totals	311 596	100.0	5	19
Electorate	399 285			Turnout 78.0%

1983: 6 seats

Aylesbury, Beaconsfield, Buckingham, Chesham and Amersham, Milton Keynes, Wycombe.

	votes	*% votes*	*MPs*	*Candidates*
C	176 161	56.8	6	6
Lab	44 564	14.4	0	6
L/All	88 383	28.5	0	6
Others	1 277	0.4	0	4
Totals	310 385	100.0	6	22

Electorate 421 010 Turnout 73.7% Swing 5.0% to C

Cambridgeshire

1979: 5 seats

Cambridge, Cambridgeshire, Huntingdonshire, Isle of Ely, Peterborough.

	votes	*% votes*	*MPs*	*Candidates*
C	157 780	50.1	4	5
Lab	87 030	27.6	0	5
L/All	67 959	21 6	1	5
Others	2 072	0.7	0	4
Totals	314 841	100.0	5	19
Electorate	407 573			Turnout 77.3%

1983: 6 seats

Cambridge, Cambridgeshire North East, Cambridgeshire South East, Cambridgeshire South West, Huntingdon, Peterborough.

	votes	*% votes*	*MPs*	*Candidates*
C	165 272	51.0	5	6
Lab	54 981	17.0	0	6
L/All	102 392	31.6	1	6
Others	1 396	0.4	0	5
Totals	324 041	100.0	6	23

Electorate 435 650 Turnout 74.4% Swing 5.8% to C

Cheshire

1979: 11 seats

Bebington and Ellesmere Port, Chester City of, Crewe, Knutsford, Macclesfield, Nantwich, Newton, Northwich, Runcorn, Warrington, Widnes. It had seven whole constituencies and parts of six others across boundaries with Greater Manchester and Merseyside.

	votes	*% votes*	*MPs*	*Candidates*
C	288 855	46.7	7	11
Lab	246 916	39.9	4	11
L/All	80 215	13.0	0	11
Others	2 641	0.4	0	5
Totals	618 627	100.0	11	38
Electorate	794 641			Turnout 77.9%

1983: 10 seats

City of Chester, Congleton, Crewe and Nantwich, Eddisbury, Ellesmore Port and Neston, Halton, Macclesfield, Tatton, Warrington North, Warrington South.

	votes	*% votes*	*MPs*	*Candidates*
C	237 733	45.6	7	10
Lab	154 931	29.7	3	10
L/All	127 307	24.4	0	10
Others	1 158	0.2	0	3
Totals	521 129	100.0	10	33

Electorate 698 915 Turnout 74.6% Swing 4.6% to C

Cleveland

1979: 6 seats

Cleveland and Whitby, Hartlepool, Teesside Middlesbrough, Teesside Redcar, Teesside Stockton, Teesside Thornaby. Part of one of these in North Yorkshire while it contains small parts of two others under Durham and North Yorkshire.

	votes	*% votes*	*MPs*	*Candidates*
C	123 879	40.0	1	6
Lab	155 713	50.3	5	6
L/All	27 587	8.9	0	6
Others	2 533	0.8	0	7
Totals	309 712	100.0	6	25
Electorate	409 895			Turnout 75.6%

1983: 6 seats

Hartlepool, Langbaurgh, Middlesbrough, Redcar, Stockton North, Stockton South.

	votes	*% votes*	*MPs*	*Candidates*
C	105 910	35.8	1	6
Lab	112 168	37.9	4	6
L/All	77 703	26.2	1	6
Others	412	0.1	0	2
Totals	296 193	100.0	6	20

Electorate 417 197 Turnout 71.0% Swing 4.1% to C

Cornwall

1979: 5 seats

Bodmin, Cornwall North, Falmouth and Camborne, St. Ives, Truro.

	votes	*% votes*	*MPs*	*Candidates*
C	130 149	50.6	4	5
Lab	32 270	12.6	0	5
L/All	87 994	34.2	1	5
Others	6 646	2.6	0	11
Totals	257 059	100.0	5	26
Electorate	316 743			Turnout 81.2%

1983: 5 seats

Cornwall North, Cornwall South East, Falmouth and Camborne, St Ives, Truro.

	votes	*% votes*	*MPs*	*Candidates*
C	126 182	49.3	4	5
Lab	22 838	8.9	0	5
L/All	104 365	40.8	1	5
Others	2 604	1.0	0	7
Totals	255 989	100.0	5	22

Electorate 330 129 Turnout 77.5% Swing 1.1% to C

Cumbria

1979: 6 seats

Barrow-in-Furness, Carlisle, Penrith and the Border, Westmorland, Whitehaven, Workington. Morecambe and Lonsdale under Lancashire.

	votes	*% votes*	*MPs*	*Candidates*
C	119 875	45.5	2	6
Lab	107 520	40.8	4	6
L/All	35 314	13.4	0	6
Others	790	0.3	0	1
Totals	263 499	100.0	6	19
Electorate	333 137			Turnout 79.1%

1983: 6 seats

Barrow and Furness, Carlisle, Copeland, Penrith and the Border, Westmorland and Lonsdale, Workington.

	votes	*% votes*	*MPs*	*Candidates*
C	129 940	46.7	3	6
Lab	86 730	31.2	3	6
L/All	60 654	21.8	0	6
Others	805	0.3	0	1
Totals	278 129	100.0	6	19

Electorate 368 063 Turnout 75.6% Swing 5.4% to C

COUNTY ANALYSIS

Derbyshire

1979: 10 seats

Belper, Bolsover, Chesterfield, Derby North, Derby South, Derbyshire North East, Derbyshire South East, Derbyshire West, High Peak, Ilkeston.

	votes	*% votes*	*MPs*	*Candidates*
C	215 297	40.9	4	10
Lab	240 103	45.6	6	10
L/All	68 219	13.0	0	10
Others	2 521	0.5	0	7
Totals	526 140	100.0	10	37

Electorate 672 387 Turnout 78.3%

1983: 10 seats

Amber Valley, Bolsover, Chesterfield, Derby North, Derby South, Derbyshire North East, Derbyshire South, Derbyshire West, Erewash, High Peak.

	votes	*% votes*	*MPs*	*Candidates*
C	214 730	41.5	6	10
Lab	180 598	34.9	4	10
L/All	117 228	22.6	0	10
Others	5 311	1.0	0	3
Totals	517 867	100.0	10	33

Electorate 691 972 Turnout 74.8% Swing 5.7% to C

Devon

1979: 10 seats

Devon North, Devon West, Exeter, Honiton, Plymouth Devonport, Plymouth Drake, Plymouth Sutton, Tiverton, Torbay, Totnes.

	votes	*% votes*	*MPs*	*Candidates*
C	296 992	53.9	9	10
Lab	121 717	22.1	1	10
L/All	125 880	22.8	0	10
Others	6 659	1.2	0	14
Totals	551 248	100.0	10	44

Electorate 705 031 Turnout 78.2%

1983: 11 seats

Honiton, Devon North, Devon West and Torridge, Exeter, South Hams, Plymouth Devonport, Plymouth Drake, Plymouth Sutton, Teignbridge, Tiverton, Torbay.

	votes	*% votes*	*MPs*	*Candidates*
C	292 254	52.8	10	11
Lab	61 438	11.1	0	11
L/All	196 131	35.4	1	11
Others	3 984	0.7	0	12
Totals	553 807	100.0	11	45

Electorate 727 001 Turnout 76.2% Swing 4.9% to C

Dorset

1979: 6 seats

Bournemouth East, Bournemouth West, Dorset North, Dorset South, Dorset West, Poole. Parts of Christchurch and Lymington and of New Forest, which are under Hampshire.

	votes	*% votes*	*MPs*	*Candidates*
C	189 226	59.2	6	6
Lab	64 766	20.3	0	6
L/All	63 591	19.9	0	6
Others	2 248	0.7	0	5
Totals	319 831	100.1	6	23

Electorate 416 578 Turnout 76.8%

1983: 7 seats

Bournemouth East, Bournemouth West, Christchurch, Dorset North, Dorset South, Dorset West, Poole.

	votes	*% votes*	*MPs*	*Candidates*
C	201 441	58.6	7	7
Lab	35 163	10.2	0	7
L/All	102 097	29.7	0	7
Others	4 944	1.4	0	7
Totals	343 645	100.0	7	28

Electorate 476 807 Turnout 72.1% Swing 4.7% to C

Durham

1979: 7 seats

Bishop Auckland, Chester-le-Street, Consett, Darlington, Durham, Durham North West, Easington. Was five seats and parts of four. Two here; two elsewhere.

	votes	*% votes*	*MPs*	*Candidates*
C	115 518	31.8	0	7
Lab	205 110	56.5	7	7
L/All	41 685	11.5	0	7
Others	444	0.1	0	1
Totals	362 757	99.9	7	22

Electorate 484 968 Turnout 74.8%

1983: 7 seats

Bishop Auckland, Darlington, Durham City of, Durham North, Durham North West, Easington, Sedgefield.

	votes	*% votes*	*MPs*	*Candidates*
C	101 975	30.4	1	7
Lab	152 861	45.5	6	7
L/All	80 275	23.9	0	7
Others	406	0.1	0	2
Totals	335 517	100.0	7	23

Electorate 462 737 Turnout 72.5% Swing 4.8% to C

Essex

1979: 14 seats

Basildon, Braintree, Brentwood and Ongar, Chelmsford, Colchester, Epping Forest, Essex South East, Harlow, Harwich, Maldon, Saffron Walden, Southend East, Southend West, Thurrock.

	votes	*% votes*	*MPs*	*Candidates*
C	435 148	52.5	12	14
Lab	239 393	28.9	2	14
L/All	146 381	17.7	0	14
Others	7 515	0.9	0	11
Totals	828 437	100.0	14	53

Electorate 1 069 077 Turnout 77.5%

1983: 16 seats

Basildon, Billericay, Braintree, Brentwood and Ongar, Castle Point, Colchester North, Colchester South and Maldon, Chelmsford, Epping Forest, Harlow, Harwich, Rochford, Saffron Walden, Southend East, Southend West, Thurrock.

	votes	*% votes*	*MPs*	*Candidates*
C	424 932	51.9	15	16
Lab	145 600	17.8	1	16
L/All	243 679	29.8	0	16
Others	4 937	0.6	0	10
Totals	819 148	100.0	16	58

Electorate 1 122 378 Turnout 73.0% Swing 5.2% to C

Gloucestershire

1979: 5 seats

Cheltenham, Cirencester & Tewkesbury, Gloucester, Gloucestershire West, Stroud. Had small part of Gloucestershire South which is under Avon.

	votes	*% votes*	*MPs*	*Candidates*
C	149 149	51.5	5	5
Lab	80 553	27.8	0	5
L/All	59 034	20.4	0	5
Others	1 139	0.4	0	3
Totals	289 875	100.1	5	18

Electorate 361 369 Turnout 80.2%

1983: 5 seats

Cheltenham, Cirencester and Tewkesbury, Gloucester, Gloucestershire West, Stroud.

	votes	*% votes*	*MPs*	*Candidates*
C	148 692	50.7	5	5
Lab	49 044	16.7	0	5
L/All	94 245	32.1	0	5
Others	1 218	0.4	0	3
Totals	293 199	100.0	5	18

Electorate 382 197 Turnout 76.7% Swing 5.2% to C

Hampshire

1979: 14 seats

Aldershot, Basingstoke, Christchurch and Lymington. Eastleigh, Fareham, 'Gosport, Havant and Waterloo. New Forest, Petersfield, Portsmouth North, Portsmouth South, Southampton Itchen, Southampton Test, Winchester. Parts of Christchurch and Lymington and New Forest in Dorset.

	votes	*% votes*	*MPs*	*Candidates*
C	461 180	55.6	13	14
Lab	222 134	26.8	1	14
L/All	143 633	17.3	0	14
Others	3 176	0.4	0	7
Totals	830 123	100.1	14	49

Electorate 1 072 961 Turnout 77.4%

1983: 15 seats

Aldershot, Basingstoke, Eastleigh, Fareham, Gosport, Hampshire East, Hampshire North West, Havant, New Forest, Portsmouth North, Portsmouth South, Romsey and Waterside, Soutampton Itchen, Southampton Test, Winchester.

	votes	*% votes*	*MPs*	*Candidates*
C	446 697	55.1	15	15
Lab	119 281	14.7	0	15
L/All	242 528	29.9	0	15
Others	1 745	0.2	0	6
Totals	810 251	100.0	15	51

Electorate 1 099 940 Turnout 73.7% Swing 5.8% to C

Hereford and Worcester

1979: 6 seats

Bromsgrove and Redditch, Hereford, Kidderminster, Leominster, Worcester, Worcestershire South.

	votes	*% votes*	*MPs*	*Candidates*
C	187 402	53.2	6	6
Lab	84 667	24.0	0	6
L/All	75 466	21.4	0	6
Others	4 683	1.3	0	5
Totals	352 218	99.9	6	3

Electorate 451 529 Turnout 78.0%

1983: 7 seats

Bromsgrove, Hereford, Leominster, Worcester, Worcestershire Mid, Worcestershire South, Wyre Forest.

	votes	*% votes*	*MPs*	*Candidates*
C	187 965	52.3	7	7
Lab	55 097	15.3	0	7
L/All	112 997	31.4	0	7
Others	3 420	1.0	0	7
Totals	359 479	100.0	7	28

Electorate 478 844 Turnout 75.1% Swing 3.9% to C

Hertfordshire

1979: 9 seats

Hemel Hempstead, Hertford & Stevenage, Hertfordshire East, Hertfordshire South, Hertfordshire South West, Hitchin, St Albans, Watford, Welwyn and Hatfield.

	votes	*% votes*	*MPs*	*Candidates*
C	286 943	51.1	9	9
Lab	193 415	34.4	0	9
L/All	74 164	13.2	0	9
Others	7 132	1.3	0	9
Totals	561 654	100.0	9	36

Electorate 692 103 Turnout 81.2%

1983: 10 seats

Broxbourne, Hertford & Stortford, Hertfordshire North, Hertfordshire South West, Hertfordshire West, Hertsmere, St Albans, Stevenage, Watford, Welwyn, Hatfield.

	votes	*% votes*	*MPs*	*Candidates*
C	279 184	50.3	10	10
Lab	105 213	19.0	0	10
L/All	167 638	30.2	0	10
Others	2 696	0.5	0	6
Totals	554 731	100.0	10	36

Electorate 720 597 Turnout 77.0% Swing 7.4% to C

Humberside

1979: 10 seats

Bridlington, Brigg and Scunthorpe, Goole, Grimsby, Haltemprice, Howden, Kingston upon Hull Central, Kingston upon Hull East, Kingston upon Hull West, Louth. Six whole seats and parts of five which lay across boundaries with Lincolnshire and the three Yorkshire counties.

	votes	*% votes*	*MPs*	*Candidates*
C	224 478	42.4	5	10
Lab	212 674	40.2	5	10
L/All	87 949	16.6	0	10
Others	4 258	0.8	0	9
Totals	529 359	100.0	10	39

Electorate 715 700 Turnout 74.0%

1983: 9 seats

Beverley, Boothferry, Bridlington, Brigg and Cleethorpes, Glanford and Scunthorpe, Great Grimsby, Hull East, Hull North, Hull West.

	votes	*% votes*	*MPs*	*Candidates*
C	200 486	43.9	5	9
Lab	133 356	29.2	4	9
L/All	122 360	26.8	0	9
Others	1 025	0.2	0	2
Totals	457 227	100.0	9	29

Electorate 645 004 Turnout 70.9% Swing 6.2% to C

Kent

1979: 15 seats

Ashford, Canterbury, Dartford, Dover and Deal, Faversham, Folkestone and Hythe, Gillingham, Gravesend, Maidstone, Rochester and Chatham, Royal Tunbridge Wells, Sevenoaks, Thanet East, Thanet West, Tonbridge and Malling.

	votes	*% votes*	*MPs*	*Candidates*
C	443 512	51.6	15	15
Lab	246 675	28.7	0	15
L/All	160 096	18.6	0	15
Others	9 341	1.1	0	18
Totals	859 624	100.0	15	63

Electorate 1 070 032 Turnout 80.3%

1983: 16 seats

Ashford, Canterbury, Dartford, Dover, Faversham, Folkestone and Hythe, Gillingham, Gravesham, Kent Mid, Maidstone, Medway, Sevenoaks, Thanet North, Thanet South, Tonbridge and Malling, Tunbridge Wells.

	votes	*% votes*	*MPs*	*Candidates*
C	437 349	53.9	16	16
Lab	150 703	18.6	0	16
L/All	218 030	26.9	0	16
Others	6 001	0.7	0	15
Totals	812 083	100.0	16	63

Electorate 1 109 631 Turnout 73.2% Swing 6.2% to C

Lancashire

1979: 17 seats

Accrington, Blackburn, Blackpool North, Blackpool South, Burnley, Chorley, Clitheroe, Darwen, Lancaster, Morecambe and Lonsdale, Nelson & Colne, North Fylde, Ormskirk, Preston North, Preston South, Rossendale, South Fylde, Lancashire had 13 whole constituencies and parts of nine others in five neighbouring counties.

	votes	*% votes*	*MPs*	*Candidates*
C	416 297	50.0	12	17
Lab	310 793	37.3	5	17
L/All	99 833	12.0	0	16
Others	6 412	0.8	0	13
Totals	833 335	99.9	17	63
Electorate	1 075 940			Turnout: 77.5%

1983: 16 seats

Blackburn, Blackpool North, Blackpool South, Burnley, Chorley, Fylde, Hyndburn, Lancashire West, Lancaster, Morecambe & Lunesdale, Pendle, Ribble Valley, Preston, South Ribble, Rossendale & Darwen, Wyre.

	votes	*% votes*	*MPs*	*Candidates*
C	373 993	48.2	13	16
Lab	228 439	29.4	3	16
L/All	169 788	21.9	0	16
Others	3 891	0.5	0	10
Totals	776 111	100.0	16	58

Electorate 1 036 245 Turnout 74.9% Swing 3.1% to C

Leicestershire

1979: 8 seats

Blaby, Bosworth, Harborough, Leicester East, Leicester South, Leicester West, Loughborough, Melton.

	votes	*% votes*	*MPs*	*Candidates*
C	234 341	49.7	5	8
Lab	167 421	35.5	3	8
L/All	61 595	13.1	0	8
Others	8 452	1.8	0	8
Totals	471 809	100.0	8	32
Electorate	596 821			Turnout: 79.1%

1983: 9 seats

Blaby, Bosworth, Harborough, Leicester East, Leicester South, Leicester West, Leicester North West, Loughborough, Rutland and Melton.

	votes	*% votes*	*MPs*	*Candidates*
C	244 053	50.6	8	9
Lab	122 069	25.3	1	9
L/All	109 262	22.7	0	9
Others	6 648	1.4	0	14
Totals	482 032	100.0	9	41

Electorate 639 897 Turnout 75.3% Swing 5.6% to C

Lincolnshire

1979: 6 seats

Gainsborough, Grantham, Holland with Boston, Horncastle, Lincoln, Rutland and Stamford. Four whole constituencies and parts of three, two under Humberside and the other under Leicestershire.

	votes	*% votes*	*MPs*	*Candidates*
C	161 514	52.2	6	6
Lab	81 588	26.4	0	6
L/All	63 489	20.5	0	6
Others	2 816	0.9	0	5
Totals	309 407	100.0	6	23
Electorate	401 840			Turnout 77.0%

1983: 6 seats

Gainsborough and Horncastle, Grantham, Holland with Boston, Lincoln, Lindsey East, Stamford and Spalding.

	votes	*% votes*	*MPs*	*Candidates*
C	162 402	53.2	6	6
Lab	46 074	15.1	0	6
L/All	95 802	31.4	0	6
Others	802	0.3	0	2
Totals	305 080	100.0	6	20

Electorate 414 281 Turnout 73.6% Swing 6.2% to C

Norfolk

1979: 7 seats

Norfolk North, Norfolk North West, Norfolk South, Norfolk South West, Norwich North, Norwich South, Yarmouth. (Most of Lowestoft under Suffolk.)

	votes	*% votes*	*MPs*	*Candidates*
C	200 751	50.9	5	7
Lab	140 817	35.7	2	7
L/All	50 567	12.8	0	7
Others	2 234	0.6	0	7
Totals	394 369	100.0	7	28
Electorate	503 895			Turnout: 78.3%

1983: 8 seats

Great Yarmouth, Norfolk Mid, Norfolk North, Norfolk North West, Norfolk South, Norfolk South West, Norwich North, Norwich South.

	votes	*% votes*	*MPs*	*Candidates*
C	200 775	49.8	8	8
Lab	88 871	22.0	0	8
L/All	112 636	27.9	0	8
Others	1 303	0.3	0	5
Totals	403 585	100.0	8	29

Electorate 536 846 Turnout 75.2% Swing 6.3% to C

Northamptonshire

1979: 5 seats

Daventry, Kettering, Northampton North, Northampton South, Wellingborough.

	votes	*% votes*	*MPs*	*Candidates*
C	147 057	50.3	4	5
Lab	106 221	36.3	1	5
L/All	37 353	12.8	0	5
Others	2 040	0.7	0	5
Totals	292 671	100.0	5	20
Electorate	370 200			Turnout: 79.1%

1983: 6 seats

Corby, Daventry, Kettering, Northampton North, Northampton South, Wellingborough.

	votes	*% votes*	*MPs*	*Candidates*
C	146 075	49.0	6	6
Lab	76 079	25.5	0	6
L/All	75 284	25.3	0	6
Others	733	0.3	0	2
Totals	298 171	100.0	6	20

Electorate 395 078 Turnout 75.5% Swing 4.8% to C

Northumberland

1979: 4 seats

Berwick-upon-Tweed, Blyth, Hexham, Morpeth. (Parts of three, including nearly all of Tynemouth, under Tyne and Wear)

	votes	*% votes*	*MPs*	*Candidates*
C	63 253	33.3	1	4
Lab	66 328	35.0	2	4
L/All	42 196	22.2	1	4
Others	17 987	9.5	0	1
Totals	189 764	100.0	4	13
Electorate	238 899			Turnout 79.4%

1983: 4 seats

Berwick-upon-Tweed, Blyth Valley, Hexham, Wansbeck.

	votes	*% votes*	*MPs*	*Candidates*
C	57 337	33.5	1	4
Lab	51 346	30.0	2	4
L/All	62 265	36.3	1	4
Others	406	0.2	0	1
Totals	171 354	100.0	4	13

Electorate 228 963 Turnout 74.8% Swing 2.6% to C

Nottinghamshire

1979: 10 seats

Ashfield, Bassetlaw, Beeston, Carlton, Mansfield, Newark, Nottingham East, Nottingham North, Nottingham West, Rushcliffe. Small part of Bassetlaw in South Yorkshire.

	votes	*% votes*	*MPs*	*Candidates*
C	250 184	45.0	4	10
Lab	238 093	42.8	6	10
L/All	63 875	11.5	0	10
Others	4 375	0.8	0	9
Totals	556 527	100.0	10	39
Electorate	724 774			Turnout: 76.8%

1983: 11 seats

Ashfield, Bassetlaw, Broxtowe, Gedling, Mansfield, Newark, Nottingham East, Nottingham North, Nottingham South, Rushcliffe, Sherwood.

	votes	*% votes*	*MPs*	*Candidates*
C	246 124	45.1	8	11
Lab	175 804	32.2	3	11
L/All	119 522	21.9	0	11
Others	3 772	0.7	0	5
Totals	545 222	100.0	11	38

Electorate 750 141 Turnout 72.7% Swing 5.4% to C

Oxfordshire

1979: 5 seats

Abingdon, Banbury, Henley, Oxford, Oxon Mid. Parts of Abingdon and Henley in Berkshire.

	votes	*% votes*	*MPs*	*Candidates*
C	158 254	53.6	5	5
Lab	83 944	28.4	0	5
L/All	51 116	17.3	0	5
Others	2 018	0.7	0	5
Totals	295 332	100.0	5	20
Electorate	380 011			Turnout: 77.7%

1983: 6 seats

Banbury, Henley, Oxford East, Oxford West and Abingdon, Wantage, Witney.

	votes	*% votes*	*MPs*	*Candidates*
C	150 537	51.5	6	6
Lab	53 866	18.4	0	6
L/All	85 625	29.3	0	6
Others	2 314	0.8	0	9
Totals	292 342	100.0	6	27

Electorate 391 782 Turnout 74.6% Swing 3.9% to C

Shropshire

1979: 4 seats

Ludlow, Oswestry, Shrewsbury, Wrekin The.

	votes	*% votes*	*MPs*	*Candidates*
C	100 677	56.4	4	4
Lab	34 756	19.5	0	4
L/All	42 624	23.9	0	4
Others	460	0.3	0	2
Totals	178 517	100.0	4	14
Electorate	264 575			Turnout: 67.5%

1983: 4 seats

Ludlow, Shrewsbury and Atcham, Shropshire North, Wrekin The.

	votes	*% votes*	*MPs*	*Candidates*
C	101 881	49.0	4	4
Lab	44 268	21.3	0	4
L/All	61 785	29.7	0	4
Others	135	0.1	0	1
Totals	208 069	100.0	4	13

Electorate 280 369 Turnout 74.2% Swing 4.6% to Lab

Somerset

1979: 4 seats

Bridgwater, Taunton, Wells, Yeovil. Nearly all of North Somerset and Weston-super-Mare under Avon.

	votes	*% votes*	*MPs*	*Candidates*
C	121 463	51.5	4	4
Lab	56 690	24.0	0	4
L/All	55 864	23.7	0	4
Others	1 979	0.8	0	3
Totals	235 996	100.0	4	15
Electorate	294 752			Turnout: 80.1%

1983: 5 seats

Bridgwater, Somerton and Frome, Taunton, Wells, Yeovil.

	votes	*% votes*	*MPs*	*Candidates*
C	128 794	51.2	4	5
Lab	29 564	11.7	0	5
L/All	93 134	37.0	1	5
Others	273	0.1	0	1
Totals	251 765	100.0	5	16

Electorate 327 540 Turnout 76.9% Swing 6.0% to C

Staffordshire

1979: 10 seats

Burton, Cannock, Leek, Lichfield and Tamworth, Newcastle-under-Lyme, Stafford and Stone, Staffordshire South West, Stoke-on-Trent Central, Stoke-on-Trent North, Stoke-on-Trent-South.

	votes	*% votes*	*MPs*	*Candidates*
C	266 490	46.0	5	10
Lab	250 561	43.3	5	10
L/All	58 464	10.1	0	10
Others	3 335	0.6	0	5
Totals	578 850	100.0	10	35
Electorate	734 699			Turnout 78.8%

1983: 11 seats

Burton, Cannock and Burntwood, Newcastle-under-Lyme, Stafford, Staffordshire Mid, Staffordshire Moorlands, Staffordshire South, Staffordshire South East, Stoke-on-Trent Central, Stoke-on-Trent North, Stoke-on-Trent South.

	votes	*% votes*	*MPs*	*Candidates*
C	255 472	44.9	7	11
Lab	187 142	32.9	4	11
L/All	125 652	22.1	0	11
Others	716	0.1	0	2
Totals	568 982	100.0	11	35

Electorate 763 045 Turnout 74.6% Swing 4.6% to C

Suffolk

1979: 5 seats

Bury St Edmunds, Eye, Ipswich, Lowestoft, Sudbury and Woodbridge. Part of Lowestoft under Norfolk.

	votes	*% votes*	*MPs*	*Candidates*
C	173 756	51.4	4	5
Lab	113 824	33.7	1	5
L/All	48 635	14.4	0	5
Others	1 591	0.5	0	5
Totals	337 806	100.0	5	20
Electorate	428 108			Turnout: 78.9%

1983: 6 seats

Bury St Edmunds, Ipswich, Suffolk Central, Suffolk Coastal, Suffolk South, Waveney.

	votes	*% votes*	*MPs*	*Candidates*
C	173 371	52.5	5	6
Lab	73 054	22.1	1	6
L/All	83 596	25.3	0	6
Others	235	0.1	0	1
Totals	330 256	100.0	6	19

Electorate 441 498 Turnout 74.8% Swing 6.3% to C

COUNTY ANALYSIS

Surrey

1979: 11 seats

Chertsey and Walton, Dorking, Epsom and Ewell, Esher, Farnham, Guildford, Reigate, Spelthorne, Surrey East, Surrey North West, Woking. Tiny part of Dorking under West Sussex.

	votes	% votes	MPs	Candidates
C	341 052	59.3	11	11
Lab	116 359	20.2	0	11
L/All	114 130	19.8	0	11
Others	3 755	0.7	0	8
Totals	575 332	100.0	11	41
Electorate	745 600			Turnout 77.2%

1983: 11 seats

Chertsey and Walton, Epsom and Ewell, Esher, Guildford, Mole Valley, Reigate, Spelthorne, Surrey East, Surrey North West, Surrey South West, Woking.

	votes	% votes	MPs	Candidates
C	331 879	59.4	11	11
Lab	61 285	11.0	0	11
L/All	159 676	28.6	0	11
Others	5 945	1.1	0	7
Totals	558 785	100.0	11	40

Electorate 770 406 Turnout 72.5% Swing 4.7% to C

Sussex East

1979: 8 seats

Brighton Kemptown, Brighton Pavilion, Easbourne, East Grinstead, Hastings, Hove, Lewes, Rye. Part of East Grinstead under Sussex West.

	votes	% votes	MPs	Candidates
C	234 252	58.6	8	8
Lab	87 168	21.8	0	8
L/All	72 292	18.1	0	8
Others	6 285	1.6	0	10
Totals	399 997	100.1	8	34
Electorate	534 900			Turnout: 74.8%

1983: 8 seats

Bexhill and Battle, Brighton Kemptown, Brighton Pavilion, Eastbourne, Hastings and Rye, Hove, Lewes, Wealden.

	votes	% votes	MPs	Candidates
C	220 859	58.4	8	8
Lab	51 301	13.6	0	8
L/All	103 040	27.2	0	8
Others	3 265	0.9	0	6
Totals	378 465	100.0	8	30

Electorate 533 686 Turnout 70.9% Swing 4.0% to C

Sussex West

1979: 6 seats

Arundel, Chichester, Horsham and Crawley, Shoreham, Sussex Mid, Worthing, East Grinstead under Sussex East.

	votes	% votes	MPs	Candidates
C	221 704	60 0	6	6
Lab	70 876	19.2	0	6
L/All	72 751	19.7	0	6
Others	4 008	1.1	0	6
Totals	369 339	100.0	6	24
Electorate	480 898			Turnout 76.8%

1983: 7 seats

Arundel, Chichester, Crawley, Horsham, Shoreham, Sussex Mid, Worthing.

	votes	% votes	MPs	Candidates
C	230 234	59.9	7	7
Lab	37 867	9.8	0	7
L/All	112 801	29.3	0	7
Others	3 753	1.0	0	6
Totals	384 655	100.0	7	27

Electorate 525 725 Turnout 73.2% Swing 4.6% to C

Warwickshire

1979: 5 seats

Meriden, Nuneaton, Rugby, Stratford-on-Avon, Warwick and Leamington. (Large part of Meriden was in West Midlands.)

	votes	% votes	MPs	Candidates
C	156 678	49.7	4	5
Lab	115 816	36.7	1	5
L/All	38 926	12.3	0	5
Others	4 145	1.3	0	5
Totals	315 565	99.9	5	20
Electorate	402 307			Turnout 78.4%

1983: 5 seats

Nuneaton, Rugby and Kenilworth, Stratford-on-Avon, Warwick and Leamington, Warwickshire North.

	votes	% votes	MPs	Candidates
C	133 293	49.2	5	5
Lab	65 846	24.3	0	5
L/All	70 456	26.0	0	5
Others	1 189	0.4	0	2
Totals	270 784	100.0	5	17

Electorate 356 705 Turnout 75.9% Swing 6.0% to C

Wiltshire

1979: 5 seats

Chippenham, Devizes, Salisbury, Swindon, Wesbury.

	votes	% votes	MPs	Candidates
C	135 957	47.4	4	5
Lab	65 568	22.9	1	5
L/All	79 047	27.6	0	5
Others	6 382	2.2	0	6
Totals	286 954	99.9	5	21
Electorate	364 461			Turnout 78.7%

1983: 5 seats

Devizes, Salisbury, Swindon, Westbury, Wiltshire North.

	votes	% votes	MPs	Candidates
C	146 887	50.3	5	5
Lab	43 468	14.9	0	5
L/All	99 784	34.2	0	5
Others	2 033	0.7	0	7
Totals	292 172	100.0	5	22

Electorate 390 627 Turnout 74.8% Swing 5.4% to C

Yorkshire North

1979: 8 seats

Barkston Ash, Harrogate, Richmond (Yorks), Ripon, Scarborough, Skipton, Thirsk and Malton, York. Four whole constituencies and parts of 10 others which had areas in the adjacent seven counties.

	votes	% votes	MPs	Candidates
C	230 001	55.2	7	8
Lab	99 416	23.9	1	8
L/All	82 777	19.9	0	8
Others	4 472	1.1	0	6
Totals	416 666	100.1	8	30
Electorate	543 085			Turnout 76.7%

1983: 7 seats

Harrogate, Richmond (Yorks), Ryedale, Scarborough, Selby, Skipton and Ripon, York.

	votes	% votes	MPs	Candidates
C	206 461	56.1	7	7
Lab	59 879	16.3	0	7
L/All	100 639	27.4	0	7
Others	831	0.2	0	4
Totals	367 810	100.0	7	25

Electorate 511 858 Turnout 71.9% Swing 4.3% to C

Non-Metropolitan Counties totals (including Isle of Wight)

1979: 294 seats

	votes	% votes	MPs	Candidates
C	8 241 737	50.3	223	294
Lab	5 200 268	31.8	67	294
L/All	2 767 699	16.9	4	293
Others	166 063	1.0	0	261
Totals	16 375 767	100.0	294	1142

Electorate 21 052 810 Turnout 77.8%

1983: 310 seats

	votes	% votes	MPs	Candidates
C	8 017 592	50.2	263	310
Lab	3 413 449	21.4	40	310
L/All	4 460 895	27.9	7	310
Others	90 722	0.6	0	205
Totals	15 982 658	100.0	310	1135

Electorate 21 558 253 Turnout 74.1% Swing 5.1% to C

English Metropolitan Cities and Boroughs

The following statistics for cities and boroughs within the Metropolitan counties are provided for close comparison (London details are in the regional analysis):

Bolton

1979: 2 seats

Bolton: East, West.

	votes	% votes	MPs	Candidates
C	37 325	43.5	0	2
Lab	39 777	46.3	2	2
L/All	7995	9.3	0	2
Others	805	0.9	0	2
Totals	85 902	100.0	2	8

Electorate 108 703 Turnout: 79.0%

1983: 3 seats

Bolton: North East, South East, and West.

	votes	% votes	MPs	Candidates
C	58 594	39.7	2	3
Lab	57 752	39.1	1	3
L/All	30 789	20.8	0	3
Others	586	0.4	0	3
Totals	147 721	100.0	3	12

Electorate 193 799 Turnout 76.2% Swing 1.7% to C

Birmingham

1979: 12 seats

Birmingham: Edgbaston, Erdington, Hallgreen, Handsworth, Ladywood, Northfield, Perry Barr, Selly Oak, Small Heath, Sparkbrook, Stechford, and Yardley.

	votes	% votes	MPs	Candidates
C	214 207	44.7	5	12
Lab	222 487	46.4	7	12
L/All	35 445	7.4	0	10
Others	7624	1.6	0	16
Totals	479 763	100.0	12	50

Electorate 686 175 Turnout 69.9%

1983: 11 seats

Birmingham: Edgbaston, Erdington, Hall Green, Hodge Hill, Ladywood, Northfield, Perry Barr, Selly Oak, Small Heath, Sparkbrook and Yardley.

	votes	% votes	MPs	Candidates
C	179 994	39.0	5	11
Lab	195 597	42.3	6	11
L/All	83 250	18.0	0	11
Others	3 558	0.8	0	11
Totals	462 399	100.0	11	44

Electorate 684 843 Turnout 67.5% Swing 0.8% to Lab

Bradford

1979: 3 seats

Bradford: North, South, West.

	votes	% votes	MPs	Candidates
C	56 107	37.3	0	3
Lab	75 701	50.4	3	3
L/All	16 614	11.1	0	3
Others	1 827	1.2	0	4
Totals	150 249	100.0	3	13

Electorate 210 290 Turnout 71.4%

1983: 3 seats

Bradford: North, South, West.

	votes	% votes	MPs	Candidates
C	50 688	34.8	1	3
Lab	52 533	36.1	2	3
L/All	37 406	25.7	0	3
Others	4 852	3.3	0	5
Totals	145 479	100.0	3	14

Electorate 207 233 Turnout 70.2% Swing 5.9% to C

Coventry

1979: 4 seats

Coventry: North East, North West, South East, South West.

	votes	% votes	MPs	Candidates
C	72 001	40.2	1	4
Lab	88 327	49.4	3	4
L/All	14 609	8.2	0	4
Others	4 052	2.3	0	9
Totals	178 989	100.0	4	21

Electorate 234 327 Turnout: 76.4%

1983: 4 seats

Coventry: North East, North West, South East, South West.

	votes	% votes	MPs	Candidates
C	62 464	36.3	1	4
Lab	70 512	41.0	3	4
L/All	38 227	22.2	0	4
Others	749	0.4	0	3
Totals	171 952	100.0	4	15

Electorate 236 724 Turnout 72.6% Swing 2.2% to C

Dudley

1979: 2 seats

Dudley: East, West.

	votes	% votes	MPs	Candidates
C	44 992	44.5	1	2
Lab	51 540	51.0	1	2
L/All	3639	3.6	0	1
Others	844	0.8	0	1
Totals	101 015	100.0	2	6

Electorate 137 186 Turnout 73.6%

1983: 2 seats

Dudley: East, West.

	votes	% votes	MPs	Candidates
C	45 875	40.8	1	2
Lab	42 968	38.2	1	2
L/All	23 523	20.9	0	2
Others	—	0.0	0	0
Totals	112 366	100.0	2	6

Electorate 152 560 Turnout 73.7% Swing 4.5% to C

Leeds

1979: 6 seats

Leeds: East, North East, North West, South, South East, West.

	votes	*% votes*	*MPs*	*Candidates*
C	86 177	35.2	2	6
Lab	118 481	48.4	4	6
L/All	36 582	14.9	0	6
Others	3 757	1.5	0	10
Totals	244 997	100.0	6	28

Electorate 347 252 Turnout 70.6%

1983: 6 seats

Leeds: Central, East, North East, North West, South and Morley, West.

	votes	*% votes*	*MPs*	*Candidates*
C	91 722	34.8	2	6
Lab	93 719	35.5	3	6
L/All	75 479	28.6	1	6
Others	2 815	1.1	0	8
Totals	263 735	100.0	6	26

Electorate 388 542 Turnout 67.9% Swing 6.2%

Liverpool

1979: 8 seats

Liverpool: Edge Hill, Garston, Kirkdale, Scotland Exchange, Toxteth, Walton, Wavertree, and West Derby.

	votes	*% votes*	*MPs*	*Candidates*
C	100 290	35.9	2	8
Lab	137 202	49.1	5	8
L/All	40 504	14.5	1	8
Others	1 553	0.6	0	7
Totals	279 549	100.0	8	31

Electorate 399 380 Turnout 70.0%

1983: 6 seats

Liverpool: Broadgreen, Garston, Mossley Hill, Riverside, Walton and West Derby.

	votes	*% votes*	*MPs*	*Candidates*
C	79 627	29.3	0	6
Lab	128 467	47.3	5	6
L/All	55 389	20.4	1	6
Others	8 071	3.0	0	5
Totals	271 554	100.0	6	23

Electorate 389 199 Turnout 69.8% Swing 2.4% to Lab

Manchester

1979: 8 seats

Manchester: Ardwick, Blackley, Central, Gorton, Moss Side, Openshaw, Withington, Wythenshawe.

	votes	*% votes*	*MPs*	*Candidates*
C	103 025	36.9	1	8
Lab	151 225	54.1	7	8
L/All	22 942	8.2	0	7
Others	2 299	0.8	0	8
Totals	279 491	100.0	8	31

Electorate 382 267 Turnout 73.1%

1983: 5 seats

Manchester: Blackley, Central, Gorton, Withington and Wythenshawe.

	votes	*% votes*	*MPs*	*Candidates*
C	65 856	30.4	1	5
Lab	109 073	50.3	4	5
L/All	40 382	18.6	0	5
Others	1 477	0.7	0	4
Totals	216 788	100.0	5	19

Electorate 319 540 Turnout 67.8% Swing 1.3% to Lab

Newcastle upon Tyne

1979: 4 seats

Newcastle upon Tyne: Central, East, North, and West.

	votes	*% votes*	*MPs*	*Candidates*
C	49 381	36.4	1	4
Lab	72 489	53.5	3	4
L/All	13 675	10.1	0	4
Totals	135 545	100.0	4	12

Electorate 190 625 Turnout 71.1%

1983: 3 seats

Newcastle upon Tyne: Central, East, and North.

	votes	*% votes*	*MPs*	*Candidates*
C	46 345	33.7	1	3
Lab	54 165	39.4	2	3
L/All	36 352	26.5	0	3
Others	478	0.4	0	1
Totals	137 340	100.0	3	10

Electorate 191 706 Turnout 71.6% Swing 5.7% to C

Sheffield

1979: 6 seats

Sheffield: Attercliffe, Brightside, Hallam, Heeley, Hillsborough, Park

	votes	*% votes*	*MPs*	*Candidates*
C	90 224	33.9	1	6
Lab	144 539	54.3	5	6
L/All	29 014	10.9	0	6
Others	2 403	0.9	–	8
Totals	266 180	100.0	6	26

Electorate 373 602 Turnout 71.3%

1983: 6 seats

Sheffield: Attercliffe, Brightside, Central, Hallam, Heeley, Hillsborough.

	votes	*% votes*	*MPs*	*Candidates*
C	85 726	29.4	1	6
Lab	128 832	44.2	5	6
L/All	75 777	26.0	0	6
Others	1 464	0.5	0	4
Totals	291 799	100.0	6	22

Electorate 420 191 Turnout 69.4% Swing 2.8% to C

Sunderland

1979: 2 seats

Sunderland: North, South.

	votes	*% votes*	*MPs*	*Candidates*
C	37 313	35.2	0	2
Lab	58 616	55.2	2	2
L/All	10 222	9.6	0	2
Totals	106 151	100.0	2	6

Electorate: 152 124 Turnout: 69.8%

1983: 2 seats

Sunderland: North, South.

	votes	*% votes*	*MPs*	*Candidates*
C	34 304	33.5	0	2
Lab	47 048	46.0	2	2
L/All	20 955	20.5	0	2
Totals	102 307	100.0	2	6

Electorate 153 644 Turnout 66.6% Swing 3.8% to C

Walsall

1979: 2 seats

Walsall: North, South.

	votes	*% votes*	*MPs*	*Candidates*
C	41 998	43.2	0	2
Lab	49 452	50.9	2	2
L/All	3 778	3.9	0	1
Others	1 893	1.9	0	2
Totals	97 121	100.0	2	7

Electorate 130 811 Turnout 74.3%

1983: 2 seats

Walsall: North, South.

	votes	*% votes*	*MPs*	*Candidates*
C	38 991	39.4	0	2
Lab	42 517	43.0	2	2
L/All	16 727	16.9	0	2
Others	632	0.6	0	1
Totals	98 867	100.0	2	7

Electorate 136 125 Turnout 72.6% Swing 2.1% to C

Warley 1979: 2 seats

Warley: East, West.

	votes	% votes	MPs	Candidates
C	31 310	38.2	0	2
Lab	46 508	56.8	2	2
L/All	2 864	3.5	0	1
Others	1 204	1.5	0	1
Totals	81 886	100.0	2	6
Electorate	115 961			Turnout 70.6%

1983: 2 seats

Warley: East, West.

	votes	% votes	MPs	Candidates
C	27 649	35.3	0	2
Lab	36 308	46.3	2	2
L/All	14 182	18.1	0	2
Others	217	0.3	0	1
Totals	78 356	100.0	2	7

Electorate 114 604 Turnout 68.4% Swing 3.8% to C

West Bromwich 1979: 2 seats

West Bromwich: East, West.

	votes	% votes	MPs	Candidates
C	31 631	39.3	0	2
Lab	43 070	53.5	2	2
L/All	3 228	4.0	0	1
Others	2 526	3.1	0	2
Totals	80 455	100.0	2	7
Electorate	116 463			Turnout 69.1%

1983: 2 seats

West Bromwich: East, West.

	votes	% votes	MPs	Candidates
C	27 853	35.3	0	2
Lab	34 788	44.1	2	2
L/All	16 294	20.6	0	2
Others	–	0.0	0	0
Totals	78 935	100.0	2	6

Electorate 117 732 Turnout 67.1% Swing 2.7% to C

Wolverhampton 1979: 3 seats

Wolverhampton: North East, South East, South West.

	votes	% votes	MPs	Candidates
C	57 380	42.2	1	3
Lab	60 581	44.6	2	3
L/All	14 198	10.4	0	3
Others	3 735	2.8	0	4
Totals	135 894	100.0	3	13
Electorate	187 938			Turnout 72.3%

1983: 3 seats

Wolverhampton: North East, South East, South West.

	votes	% votes	MPs	Candidates
C	55 369	41.5	1	3
Lab	49 075	36.7	2	3
L/All	28 360	21.2	0	3
Others	786	0.6	0	2
Totals	133 590	100.0	3	11

Electorate 188 991 Turnout 70.7% Swing 3.5% to C

English Metropolitan Cities and Towns totals (including London)

1979: 158 seats

	votes	% votes	MPs	Candidates
C	2 747 205	43.0	65	158
Lab	2 818 880	44.2	92	158
L/All	693 402	10.9	1	151
Others	124 658	2.0	0	232
Totals	6 384 147	100.0	158	699
Electorate	8 920 239			Turnout 71.6%

1983: 145 seats

	votes	% votes	MPs	Candidates
C	2 468 162	40.0	72	144
Lab	2 174 893	35.2	68	144
L/All	1 446 452	23.4	4	144
Others	81 459	1.3	0	199
Totals	6 170 966	100.0	144	631

Electorate 8 988 904 Turnout 68.7% Swing 2.9% to C

Non-Metropolitan Cities and Boroughs

Voting in principal non-metropolitan cities and boroughs of England, Scotland, Wales and Northern Ireland, together with a close comparison with the results in 1979, was as follows:

Aberdeen 1979: 2 seats

Aberdeen: North, South.

	votes	% votes	MPs	Candidates
C	28 477	29.6	1	2
Lab	46 819	48.7	1	2
L/All	10 788	11.2	0	2
Scot Nat	10 157	10.6	0	2
Totals	96 241	100.0	2	8
Electorate	129 837			Turnout: 74.1%

1983: 2 seats

Aberdeen: North, South.

	votes	% votes	MPs	Candidates
C	22 819	28.3	1	2
Lab	31 074	38.6	1	2
L/All	20 490	25.5	0	2
Scot Nat	5 764	7.2	0	2
Others	367	0.5	0	1
Totals	80 514	100.0	2	9

Electorate 120 589 Turnout 66.8% Swing 4.4% to C

Belfast 1979: 4 seats

Belfast: East, North, South, West.

	votes	% votes	MPs	Candidates
OUP	63 745	39.0	1	4
DUP	31 400	19.2	2	3
All (NI)	32 955	20.2	0	4
PSF	—	0.0	0	0
SDLP	27 997	17.1	1	3
Others	7 315	4.5	0	9
Totals	163 412	100.0	4	23
Electorate	268 358			Turnout: 60.9%

1983: 4 seats

Belfast: East, North, South, West.

	votes	% votes	MPs	Candidates
OUP	46 085	28.3	2	4
DUP	32 855	20.2	1	4
All (NI)	22 197	13.6	0	3
PSF	23 619	14.5	1	4
SDLP	20 613	12.6	0	4
Others	17 685	10.9	0	8
Totals	163 054	100.0	4	27
Electorate	230 153			Turnout 70.9%

Blackpool

1979: 2 seats
Blackpool: North, South.

	votes	% votes	MPs	Candidates
C	44 971	52.6	2	2
Lab	25 894	30.3	0	2
L/All	13 184	15.4	0	2
Others	1 467	1.7	0	2
Totals	85 516	100.0	2	8

Electorate 118 172 Turnout 72.4%

1983: 2 seats
Blackpool: North, South.

	votes	% votes	MPs	Candidates
C	40 444	50.9	2	2
Lab	18 444	23.2	0	2
L/All	19 857	25.0	0	2
Others	777	1.0	0	2
Totals	79 522	100.0	2	8

Electorate 113 777 Turnout 69.9% Swing 2.7% to C

Bournemouth

1979: 2 seats
Bournemouth: East, West.

	votes	% votes	MPs	Candidates
C	51 681	61.2	2	2
Lab	16 800	19.9	0	2
L/All	14 415	17.1	0	2
Others	1 542	1.8	0	3
Totals	84 438	100.0	2	9

Electorate 117 741 Turnout: 71.7%

1983: 2 seats
Bournemouth: East, West.

	votes	% votes	MPs	Candidates
C	53 642	55.2	2	2
Lab	10 269	10.6	0	2
L/All	28 895	29.8	0	2
Others	4 322	4.5	0	4
Totals	97 128	100.0	2	10

Electorate 143 068 Turnout 67.9% Swing 1.7% to C

Brighton

1979: 2 seats
Brighton: Kemptown, Pavilion.

	votes	% votes	MPs	Candidates
C	47 730	53.7	2	2
Lab	29 603	33.3	0	2
L/All	10 144	11.4	0	2
Others	1 478	1.7	0	3
Totals	88 955	100.0	2	9

Electorate 121 173 Turnout 73.4%

1983: 2 seats
Brighton: Kemptown, Pavilion.

	votes	% votes	MPs	Candidates
C	43 588	51.3	2	2
Lab	22 766	26.8	0	2
L/All	18 289	21.5	0	2
Others	290	0.3	0	1
Totals	84 933	100.0	2	7

Electorate 120 646 Turnout 70.4% Swing 2.1% to C

Bristol

1979: 5 seats
Bristol: North East, North West, South, South-East, West.

	votes	% votes	MPs	Candidates
C	98 700	42.7	2	5
Lab	100 181	43.3	3	5
L/All	28 616	12.4	0	5
Others	3 735	1.7	0	11
Totals	231 232	100.0	5	26

Electorate 305 880 Turnout 75.6%

1983: 4 seats
Bristol: East, North West, South, West.

	votes	% votes	MPs	Candidates
C	87 266	42.3	3	4
Lab	68 263	33.1	1	4
L/All	48 528	23.5	0	4
Others	2 357	1.1	0	7
Totals	206 414	100.0	4	19

Electorate 284 549 Turnout 72.5% Swing 4.9% to C

Cardiff

1979: 4 seats
Cardiff: North, North-West, South-East, and West.

	votes	% votes	MPs	Candidates
C	50 276	33.7	2	3
Lab	48 667	32.6	1	3
L/All	9 753	6.5	0	2
Pl. Cymru	5 724	3.8	0	4
*Others	28 941	23.3	1	5
Totals	143 361	100.0	4	17

Electorate 198 150 Turnout 72.3%

*Includes Mr Speaker George Thomas who was re-elected in Cardiff West.

1983: 4 seats
Cardiff: Central, North, South and Penarth, and West.

	votes	% votes	MPs	Candidates
C	66 167	40.6	3	4
Lab	48 789	29.9	1	4
L/All	44 427	27.2	0	4
Pl. Cymru	3 199	2.0	0	4
Others	517	0.3	0	2
Totals	163 099	100.0	4	18

Electorate 225 250 Turnout 72.4% Swing 4.8% to C

Derby

1979: 2 seats
Derby: North, South.

	votes	% votes	MPs	Candidates
C	49 436	41.9	0	2
Lab	55 742	47.2	2	2
L/All	11 289	9.6	0	2
Others	1 563	1.3	0	5
Totals	118 030	100.0	2	11

Electorate 159 002 Turnout 74.2%

1983: 2 seats
Derby: North, South.

	votes	% votes	MPs	Candidates
C	40 051	41.2	1	2
Lab	36 966	38.0	1	2
L/All	19900	20.5	0	2
Others	297	0.3	0	1
Totals	97 214	100.0	2	7

Electorate 138 952 Turnout 70.0% Swing 4.3% to C

Dundee

1979: 2 seats
Dundee: East, West.

	votes	% votes	MPs	Candidates
C	21 964	22.0	0	2
Lab	41 632	41.6	1	2
L/All	2 317	2.3	0	1
Scot. Nat.	33 694	33.7	1	2
Others	411	0.4	0	2
Totals	100 018	100.0	2	9

Electorate 128 213 Turnout 78.0%

1983: 2 seats
Dundee: East, West.

	votes	% votes	MPs	Candidates
C	17 310	18.6	0	2
Lab	35 548	38.3	1	2
L/All	11 522	12.4	0	2
Scot. Nat.	28 249	30.4	1	2
Others	302	0.3	0	1
Totals	92 931	100.0	2	9

Electorate 125 455 Turnout 74.1%

Edinburgh

1979: 7 seats

Edinburgh: Central, East, Leith, North, Pentlands, South, West.

	votes	% votes	MPs	Candidates
C	100 334	38.2	4	7
Lab	102 423	39.0	3	7
L/All	32 172	12.3	0	6
Scot Nat	26 647	10.1	0	7
Others	1 025	0.4	0	4
Totals	262 601	100.0	7	31

Electorate 349 655 Turnout 75.1%

1983: 6 seats

Edinburgh: Central, East, Leith, Pentlands, South, West.

	votes	% votes	MPs	Candidates
C	86 286	34.7	4	6
Lab	76 402	30.8	2	6
L/All	70 992	28.6	0	6
Scot Nat	13 456	5.4	0	6
Others	1 256	0.5	0	3
Totals	248 392	100.0	6	27

Electorate 351 644 Turnout 70.6% Swing 2.4% to C

Glasgow

1979: 13 seats

Glasgow: Cathcart, Central, Craigton, Garscadden, Govan, Hillhead, Kelvingrove, Maryhill, Pollok, Provan, Queens Park, Shettleston, Springburn.

	votes	% votes	MPs	Candidates
C	97 499	25.9	1	13
Lab	218 861	58.0	12	13
L/All	15 081	4.0	0	5
Scot. Nat.	43 094	11.4	0	13
Others	2 699	0.7	0	10
Totals	377 234	100.0	13	54

Electorate 533 860 Turnout 70.7

1983: 11 seats

Glasgow: Cathcart, Central, Garscadden, Govan, Hillhead, Maryhill, Pollok, Provan, Rutherglen, Shettlesston, Springburn.

	votes	% votes	MPs	Candidates
C	75 335	18.8	0	11
Lab	207 731	51.9	10	11
Scot. Nat.	30 200	21.2	1	11
L/All	84 724	7.6	0	11
Others	2 011	0.5	0	9
Totals	400 001	100.0	11	53

Electorate 578 938 Turnout 69.1% Swing 0.5% to Lab

Hull

1979: 3 seats

Hull: Central, East, West.

	votes	% votes	MPs	Candidates
C	42 034	29.8	0	3
Lab	81 479	57.7	3	3
L/All	16 268	11.5	0	3
Others	1 481	1.1	0	4
Totals	141 262	100.0	3	13

Electorate 202 313 Turnout 69.8

1983: 3 seats

Hull: East, North, West.

	votes	% votes	MPs	Candidates
C	40 585	30.2	0	3
Lab	60 341	44.9	3	3
L/All	33 128	24.7	0	3
Others	222	0.2	0	1
Totals	134 276	100.0	3	10

Electorate 202 282 Turnout 66.4% Swing 6.6% to C

Leicester

1979: 3 seats

Leicester: East, South, West.

	votes	% votes	MPs	Candidates
C	60 732	39.9	0	3
Lab	74 424	48.9	3	3
L/All	13 511	8.9	0	3
Others	3 633	2.4	0	3
Totals	152 300	100.0	3	12

Electorate 205 192 Turnout 74.2%

1983: 3 seats

Leicester: East, South, West.

	votes	% votes	MPs	Candidates
C	59 666	40.1	2	3
Lab	60 438	40.6	1	3
L/All	25 707	17.3	0	3
Others	3 010	2.0	0	7
Totals	148 821	100.0	3	16

Electorate 208 335 Turnout 71.4% Swing 4.2% to C

Luton

1979: 2 seats

Luton: East, West.

	votes	% votes	MPs	Candidate s
C	39 039	43.9	2	2
Lab	37 946	42.7	0	2
L/All	10 518	11.8	0	2
Others	1 375	1.6	0	5
Totals	88 878	100.0	2	11

Electorate 113 613 Turnout 78.2%

1983: 2 seats

Luton: North, South.

	votes	% votes	MPs	Candidates
C	48 646	45.1	2	2
Lab	32 044	29.7	0	2
L/All	27 164	25.2	0	2
Others	—	0.0	0	0
Totals	107 854	100.0	2	6

Electorate 140 820 Turnout 76.6% Swing 7.1% to C

Nottingham

1979: 3 seats

Nottingham: East, North, West.

	votes	% votes	MPs	Candidates
C	57 956	41.3	0	3
Lab	66 762	47.5	3	3
L/All	12 667	9.0	0	3
Others	3 113	2.2	0	6
Totals	140 498	100.0	3	15

Electorate 203 989 Turnout 68.9%

1983: 3 seats

Nottingham: East, North, South.

	votes	% votes	MPs	Candidates
C	58 609	42.0	3	3
Lab	51 068	36.6	0	3
L/All	27 282	19.6	0	3
Others	2 605	1.9	0	2
Totals	139 564	100.0	3	11

Electorate 209 504 Turnout 66.6% Swing 5.8% to C

Plymouth

1979: 3 seats

Plymouth: Devonport, Drake, Sutton.

	votes	% votes	MPs	Candidates
C	66 195	50.7	2	3
Lab	51 665	39.6	1	3
L/All	12 038	9.2	0	3
Others	725	0.6	0	3
Totals	130 623	100.0	3	12

Electorate 172 463 Turnout 75.7%

1983: 3 seats

Plymouth: Devonport, Drake, Sutton.

	votes	% votes	MPs	Candidates
C	60 828	46.2	2	3
Lab	24 304	18.5	0	3
L/All	45 492	34.6	1	3
Others	1 048	0.8	0	5
Totals	131 672	100.0	3	14

Electorate 174 086 Turnout 75.6% Swing 8.3% to C

Portsmouth

1979: 2 seats

Portsmouth: North, South.

	votes	% votes	MPs	Candidates
C	53 191	51.5	2	2
Lab	39 351	38.1	0	2
L/All	9 841	9.5	0	2
Others	877	0.8	0	3
Totals	103 260	100.0	2	9
Electorate	136 216			Turnout 75.8%

1983: 2 seats

Portsmouth: North, South.

	votes	% votes	MPs	Candidates
C	56 514	52.8	2	2
Lab	23 337	21.8	0	2
L/All	26 180	24.5	0	2
Others	1 005	0.9	0	3
Totals	107 036	100.0	2	9

Electorate 152 460 Turnout 70.2% Swing 8.8% to C

Southampton

1979: 2 seats

Southampton: Itchen, Test.

	votes	% votes	MPs	Candidates
C	53 632	45.0	1	2
Lab	53 111	44.5	1	2
L/All	12 525	10.5	0	2
Totals	119 268	100.0	2	6
Electorate	158 041			Turnout 75.5%

1983: 2 seats

Southampton: Itchen, Test.

	votes	% votes	MPs	Candidates
C	46 594	43.4	2	2
Lab	29 635	27.6	0	2
L/All	31 239	29.1	0	2
Totals	107 468	100.0	2	6

Electorate 146 901 Turnout 73.2% Swing 7.7% to C

Southend

1979: 2 seats

Southend: East, West.

	votes	% votes	MPs	Candidates
C	51 862	57.0	2	2
Lab	19 980	22.0	0	2
L/All	17 829	19.6	0	2
Others	1 356	1.5	0	2
Totals	91 027	100.0	2	8
Electorate	123 995			Turnout 73.4%

1983: 2 seats

Southend: East, West.

	votes	% votes	MPs	Candidates
C	48 103	55.1	2	2
Lab	9 863	11.3	0	2
L/All	29 379	33.6	0	2
Others	—	0.0	0	0
Totals	87 345	100.0	2	6

Electorate 125 176 Turnout 69.8% Swing 4.4% to C

Stoke-on-Trent

1979: 3 seats

Stoke-on-Trent: Central, North, South.

	votes	% votes	MPs	Candidates
C	42 696	30.9	0	3
Lab	81 969	59.4	3	3
L/All	13 083	9.5	0	3
Others	341	0.3	0	1
Totals	138 089	100.0	3	10
Electorate	193 088			Turnout 71.5%

1983: 3 seats

Stoke-on-Trent: Central, North, South.

	votes	% votes	MPs	Candidates
C	45 968	31.3	0	3
Lab	69 526	47.4	3	3
L/All	30 694	20.9	0	3
Others	504	0.3	0	1
Totals	146 692	100.0	3	10

Electorate 212 785 Turnout 68.9% Swing 6.2% to C

Swansea

1979: 2 seats

Swansea: East, West.

	votes	% votes	MPs	Candidates
C	34 463	35.1	0	2
Lab	56 084	57.2	2	2
L/All	3 484	3.6	0	1
Pl Cymru	3 744	3.8	0	2
Others	308	0.3	0	1
Totals	98 083	100.0	2	8
Electorate	126 222			Turnout 77.7%

1983: 2 seats

Swansea, East, West.

	votes	% votes	MPs	Candidates
C	23 772	28.4	0	2
Lab	40 339	48.1	2	2
L/All	16 798	20.1	0	2
PL Cymru	2 326	2.8	0	2
Others	559	0.7	0	2
Totals	83 794	100.0	2	10

Electorate 115 522 Turnout 72.5% Swing 1.1% to C

Teesside

1979: 4 seats

Middlesbrough, Redcar, Stockton, Thornaby.

	votes	% votes	MPs	Candidates
C	72 743	35.9	0	4
Lab	108 856	53.7	4	4
L/All	18 577	9.2	0	4
Others	2 533	1.3	0	7
Totals	202 709	100.0	4	19
Electorate	278 679			Turnout 72.7%

1983: 4 seats

Middlesbrough, Redcar, Stockton North, Stockton South.

	votes	% votes	MPs	Candidates
C	62 712	33.1	0	4
Lab	71 905	37.9	3	4
L/All	54 666	28.8	1	4
Others	412	0.2	0	2
Totals	189 695	100.0	4	14

Electorate 270 464 Turnout 70.1% Swing 6.5% to C

UK Non-Metropolitan Cities and Boroughs totals

	votes	% votes	MPs	Candidates
C	1 165 611	36.9	25	69
Lab	1 358 249	43.0	43	69
L/All	288 100	9.1	0	57
Scot. Nat.	113 592	3.6	1	24
Pl Cymru	9 468	0.3	0	6
Others	227 739	7.2	5	103
Totals	3 162 759	100.0	74	328
Electorate:	4 343 852			Turnout: 72.8%

	votes	% votes	MPs	Candidates
C	1 084 905	35.0	33	66
Lab	1 029 052	33.2	29	66
L/All	715 353	23.1	3	66
Scot. Nat.	77 669	2.5	1	21
Pl Cymru	5 525	0.2	0	6
Others	184 915	6.0	4	81
Totals	3 097 419	100.0	70	306

Electorate 4 391 356 Turnout 70.5% Swing 4.0% to C

Scotland

Arising from the review by its boundary commission, Scotland emerged with 72 constituencies compared with the 71 fought at the last election, a figure which had not changed since the first periodical review in 1954. Provision for 71 seats in Scotland was first made in the Representation of the People Act 1918. The Scottish parliamentary boundary review followed on the Local Government Boundary Commission review of regional electoral arrangements for Scotland's nine regions, three island areas and 53 districts, the structure of local government being radically altered with effect from May 1975.

An analysis of the voting in the nine regions in 1983 is as follows (the voting in the island areas of Orkney and Shetland and Western Isles is in the constituency details elsewhere):

Borders (2 seats): Roxburgh and Berwickshire, Tweeddale Ettrick and Lauderdale.

	votes	*% votes*	*MPs*	*Candidates*
C	20 853	34.5	0	2
Lab	4 526	7.5	0	2
L/All	32 788	54.2	2	2
Scot. Nat.	2 307	3.8	0	2
Others	0			
Totals	60 474	100.0	2	8
Electorate	78 777			Turnout 76.8%

Central (4 seats): Clackmannan, Falkirk East, Falkirk West, Stirling.

	votes	*% votes*	*MPs*	*Candidates*
C	39 114	25.6	1	4
Lab	63 008	41.2	3	4
L/All	30 823	20.2	0	4
Scot. Nat.	19 556	12.8	0	4
Others	334	0.2	0	1
Totals	152 845	100.0	4	17
Electorate	205 391			Turnout 74.4%

Dumfries and Galloway (2 seats): Dumfries, Galloway and Upper Nithsdale.

	votes	*% votes*	*MPs*	*Candidates*
C	36 309	44.6	2	2
Lab	13 228	16.3	0	2
L/All	15 165	18.6	0	2
Scot. Nat.	16 645	20.5	0	2
Totals	81 347	100.0	2	8
Electorate	109 425			Turnout 74.3%

Fife (5 seats): Dunfermline East, Dunfermline West, Fife Central, Fife North East, Kirkcaldy.

	votes	*% votes*	*MPs*	*Candidates*
C	53 329	28.6	1	5
Lab	66 330	35.5	4	5
L/All	50 080	26.8	0	5
Scot. Nat.	15 304	8.2	0	5
Others	1 724	0.9	0	4
Totals	186 767	100.0	5	24
Electorate	256 899			Turnout 72.7%

Grampian (6 seats): Aberdeen North, Aberdeen South, Banff and Buchan, Gordon, Kincardine and Deeside, Moray.

	votes	*% votes*	*MPs*	*Candidates*
C	95 412	37.8	4	6
Lab	47 734	8.9	1	6
L/All	67 106	26.6	1	6
Scot. Nat.	42 063	16.7	0	6
Others	367	0.2	0	1
Totals	252 682	100.0	6	25
Electorate	366 885			Turnout 68.9%

Highland (3 seats): Caithness and Sutherland, Inverness Nairn and Lochaber, Ross Cromarty and Skye.

	votes	*% votes*	*MPs*	*Candidates*
C	30 473	29.5	0	3
Lab	14 674	14.2	0	3
L/All	46 318	44.8	3	3
Scot. Nat.	11 826	11.5	0	3
Totals	103 291	100.0	3	12
Electorate	142 917			Turnout 72.3%

Lothian (10 seats): East Lothian, Edinburgh Central, Edinburgh East, Edinburgh Leith, Edinburgh Pentlands, Edinburgh South, Edinburgh West, Linlithgow, Livingston, Midlothian.

	votes	*% votes*	*MPs*	*Candidates*
C	128 363	30.4	4	10
Lab	150 686	35.6	6	10
L/All	111 323	26.3	0	10
Scot. Nat.	31 481	7.4	0	10
Others	1 455	0.3	0	4
Totals	423 308	100.0	10	44
Electorate	586 116			Turnout 72.2%

Strathclyde (33 seats): Argyll and Bute, Ayr, Carrick Cumnock and Doon Valley, Clydebank and Milngavie, Clydesdale, Cumbernauld and Kilsyth, Cunninghame North, Cunninghame South, Dumbarton, Eastwood, East Kilbride, Glasgow Cathcart, Glasgow Central, Glasgow Garscadden, Glasgow Govan, Glasgow Hillhead, Glasgow Maryhill, Glasgow Pollok, Glasgow Provan, Glasgow Rutherglen, Glasgow Shettleston, Glasgow Springburn, Greenock and Port Glasgow, Hamilton, Kilmarnock and Loudoun, Monklands East, Monklands West, Motherwell North, Motherwell South, Paisley North, Paisley South, Renfrew West and Inverclyde, Strathkelvin and Bearsden.

	votes	*% votes*	*MPs*	*Candidates*
C	317 132	24.2	6	33
Lab	577 727	44.1	26	33
L/All	294 162	22.5	1	33
Scot. Nat.	117 109	8.9	0	33
Others	3 399	0.3	0	14
Totals	1 309 529	100.0	33	146
Electorate	1 789 316			Turnout 73.2%

Tayside (5 seats): Angus East, Dundee East, Dundee West, Perth and Kinross, Tayside North.

	votes	*% votes*	*MPs*	*Candidates*
C	73 685	33.7	3	5
Lab	45 516	20.8	1	5
L/All	34 752	15.9	0	5
Scot. Nat.	64 265	29.4	1	5
Others	541	0.3	0	2
Totals	218 759	100.0	5	22
Electorate	298 264			Turnout 73.3%

Wales

Wales, under the boundary changes, has 38 parliamentary seats in its eight counties compared with the 36 seats fought in 1979 and in every election since 1950. Nine of the previous constituencies crossed the county boundaries established under the reorganization of Welsh local government in 1974. Thirteen constituencies had remained unaltered for over 60 years. Only two Welsh constituencies were left unchanged.

The analysis of voting in the Welsh counties in 1983 is as follows:

Clwyd (5 seats): Alyn and Deeside, Clwyd North West, Clwyd South West, Delyn, Wrexham.

	votes	*% votes*	*MPs*	*Candidates*
C	90 234	39.5	3	5
Lab	67 486	29.5	2	5
L/All	62 372	27.3	0	5
Others	8 563	3.7	0	5
Totals	228 655	100.0	5	20

Electorate 298 103 Turnout 76.7%

Dyfed (4 seats): Carmarthen, Ceredigion and Pembroke North, Llanelli, Pembroke.

	votes	*% votes*	*MPs*	*Candidates*
C	63 804	31.9	1	4
Lab	62 010	31.0	2	4
L/All	45 473	22.7	1	4
Pl Cymru	27 124	13.5	0	4
Others	1 944	1.0	0	6
Totals	200 355	100.0	4	22

Electorate 255 702 Turnout 78.4%

Glamorgan Mid (7 seats): Bridgend, Caerphilly, Cynon Valley, Merthyr Tydfil and Rhymney, Ogmore, Pontypridd, Rhondda.

	votes	*% votes*	*MPs*	*Candidates*
C	55 852	18.6	1	7
Lab	158 940	52.9	6	7
L/All	59 112	19.7	0	7
Pl Cymru	23 239	7.7	0	7
Others	3 216	1.1	0	4
Totals	300 359	100.0	7	32

Electorate 402 015 Turnout 74.7%

Glamorgan South (5 seats): Cardiff Central, Cardiff North, Cardiff South and Penarth, Cardiff West, Vale of Glamorgan.

	votes	*% votes*	*MPs*	*Candidates*
C	88 588	42.2	4	5
Lab	60 817	29.0	1	5
L/All	55 581	26.5	0	5
Pl Cymru	4 267	2.0	0	5
Others	517	0.3	0	2
Totals	209 770	100.0	5	22

Electorate 288 135 Turnout 72.8%

Glamorgan West (5 seats): Aberavon, Gower, Neath, Swansea East, Swansea West.

	votes	*% votes*	*MPs*	*Candidates*
C	53 494	25.3	0	5
Lab	103 726	49.1	5	5
L/All	44 486	21.1	0	5
Pl Cymru	8 675	4.1	0	5
Others	709	0.3	0	3
Totals	211 090	100.0	5	23

Electorate 280 930 Turnout 75.1%

Gwent (6 seats): Blaenau Gwent, Islwyn, Monmouth, Newport East, Newport West, Torfaen.

	votes	*% votes*	*MPs*	*Candidates*
C	71 073	28.2	2	6
Lab	114 865	45.6	4	6
L/All	60 543	24.0	0	6
Pl Cymru	5 761	2.3	0	6
Totals	252 242	100.0	6	24

Electorate 327 686 Turnout 77.0%

Gwynedd (4 seats): Caernarfon, Conwy, Meirionnydd Nant Conwy, Ynys Mon.

	votes	*% votes*	*MPs*	*Candidates*
C	45 815	33.0	2	4
Lab	23 993	17.3	0	4
L/All	23 702	17.1	0	4
Pl Cymru	45 455	32.7	2	4
Totals	138 965	100.0	4	16

Electorate 176 532 Turnout 78.7%

Powys (2 seats): Brecon and Radnor, Montgomery.

	votes	*% votes*	*MPs*	*Candidates*
C	30 450	45.1	1	2
Lab	12 021	17.8	0	2
L/All	22 089	32.7	1	2
Pl Cymru	2 225	3.3	0	2
Others	765	1.1	0	2
Totals	67 550	100.0	2	10

Electorate 84 751 Turnout 79.7%

The statistics in this regional and other analyses were produced by the staff of *The Times* Systems Department led by Mr D. W. Skelsey.

Notional election of 1979

Political commentators, correspondents and the media as a whole made considerable use throughout the election and since of *The BBC/ITN Guide to the New Parliamentary Constituencies* in which members of a joint working party on the new constituency boundaries estimated for each new constituency what the election result might have been in May 1979 had the new boundaries then been in operation. There were 66 constituencies with boundaries unchanged and 43 with only minor change (less than 5 per cent). The following are the BBC/ITN notional majorities in the 541 constituencies in which there were extensive boundary changes:

Aberavon: Lab 17 573. Aberdeen N: Lab 17 516. Aberdeen S: C 541. Aldershot: C 19 395. Aldridge-Brownhills: C 6 992. Altrincham and Sale: C 18 949. Alyn & Deeside: Lab 5 126. Amber Valley: Lab 6 181. Angus E: C 6 161. Antrim E: DUP 5 889. Antrim N: DUP 14 101. Antrim S: UU 18 534. Argyll & Bute: C 4 063. Arundel: C 23 583. Ashfield: Lab 5 832. Aylesbury: C 17 124. Ayr: C 4 284.

Banbury: C 12 979. Banff & Buchan: C 916. Barking: Lab 8 266. Barnsley Cen: Lab 12 172. Barnsley E: Lab 18 592. Barnsley W & Penistone: Lab 14 344. Barrow and Furness: Lab 5 427. Basildon: Lab 8 163. Basingstoke: C 10 438. Bassetlaw: Lab 9 325. Batley & Spen: Lab 1 716. Battersea: Lab 6 963. Beaconsfield: C 20 329. Bedfordshire Mid: C 16 798. Beds N: C 11 415. Beds SW: C 14 077. Belfast E: UU 550. Belfast N: UU 2 525. Belfast S: UU 14 365. Belfast W: SDLP 12 456. Berkshire E: C 15 303. Berwick-upon-Tweed: L 5 265. Bethnal Green & Stepney: Lab 9 460. Beverley: C 17 412. Bexhill & Battle: C 18 393. Bexleyheath: C 10 387. Billericay: C 14 229. Birkenhead: Lab 8 077. Birmingham Edgbaston: C 12 821. B'ham Erdington: C 1 419. B'ham Hall Green: C 8 964. B'ham Hodge Hill: Lab 3 661. B'ham Ladywood: Lab 6 467. B'ham Northfield: C 137. B'ham Perry Barr: Lab 4 497. B'ham Selly Oak: C 6 807. B'ham Small Heath: Lab 16 252. B'ham Sparkbrook: Lab 10 865. B'ham Yardley: C 3 269. B Auckland: Lab 5 321. Blackburn: Lab 2 452. Bl Gwent: Lab 22 847. Blaydon: Lab 11 020. Blyth Valley: Lab 650. Bolsover: Lab 18 522. Bolton NE: C 1 368. Bolton SE: Lab 12 534. Bolton W: C 5 602. Boothferry: C 9 701. Bootle: Lab 15 635. Bosworth: C 14 759. Bournemouth E: C 21 542. Bournemouth W: C 18 915. Bow & Poplar: Lab 12 215. Bradford N: Lab 7 597. Bradford S: Lab 4 962. Bradford W: Lab 7 887. Brecon & Radnor: C 2 446. Brent E: Lab 5 869. Brent N: C 12 001. Brent S: Lab 12 708. Brentwood & Ongar: C 19 267. Bridgend: Lab 4 581. Bridgwater: C 10 948. Bridlington: C 16 945. Brigg and Cleethorpes: C 7 714. Brighton Kemptown: C 7 781. Brighton Pavilion: C 10 346. Bristol E: Lab 4 296. Bristol NW: C 4 021. Bristol S: Lab 10 897. Bristol W: C 12 680. Bromsgrove: C 12 144. Broxbourne: C 15 592. Broxtowe: C 10 859. Buckingham: C 13 634. Burnley: Lab 3 249. Bury N: C 3 017. Bury S: C 414. Bury St Edmunds: C 15 365.

Caerphilly: Lab 19 027. Calder Valley: C 1 317. Cambridge: C 1 695. Cambs NE: L 1 361. Cambs SE: C 15 256. Cambs SW: C 17 399. Cannock & Burntwood: Lab 5 451. Canterbury: C 18 518. Cardiff Cen: C 1 362. Cardiff N: C 7 077. Cardiff S & Penarth: Lab 5 068. Cardiff W: Lab 5 294. Carmarthen: Lab 435. Carrick, Cumnock & Doon Valley: Lab 3 324. Castle Point: C 16 878. Ceredigion & Pembroke N: L 1 025. Cheadle: C 17 071. Chelmsford: C 3 462. Cheltenham: C 12 815. Chesham & Amersham: C 20 562. Chester City of: C 7 723. Chesterfield: Lab 12 009. Chorley: C 5 145. Christchurch: C 19 805. Cirencester & Tewkesbury: C 17 317. City of London & Westminster S: C 15 827. Clackmannan: Lab 3 382. Clwyd NW: C 11 466. Clwyd SW: C 3 006. Clydesdale: Lab 9 677. Colchester N: C 15 279. Colchester S & Maldon: C 13 041. Colne Valley: Lab 2 239. Congleton: C 9 135. Conwy: C 5 606. Corby: Lab 396. Cornwall N: C 5 287. Cornwall SE: C 7 616. Coventry NE: Lab 11 731. Coventry NW: Lab 4 205. Coventry SE: Lab 5 696. Coventry SW: C 5 374. Crawley: C 2 750. Crewe & Nantwich: C 3 634. Crosby: C 19 022. Croydon Cen: C 8 811. Croydon NE: C 7 799. Croydon NW: C 1 409. Cumbernauld & Kilsyth: Lab 7 215. Cunninghame N. Lab 286. Cunninghame S : Lab 9 974. Cynon Valley: Lab 20 918.

Dagenham: Lab 8 849. Dartford: C 4 743. Daventry: C 13 096. Davyhulme: C 10 671. Delyn: C 5 371. Denton & Reddish: Lab 10 178. Derby N: Lab 2 373. Derby S: Lab 3 949. Derbyshire NE: Lab 5 738. Derbyshire S: Lab 862. Derbyshire W: C 15 686. Devon N: C 6 896. Devon W & Torridge: C 15 352. Dewsbury: Lab 5 155. Doncaster Cen: Lab 5 541. Doncaster N: Lab 16 505. Don Valley: Lab 11 553. Dorset N: C 18 745. Dorset S: C 13 587. Dorset W: C 17 245. Dover: C 5 175. Down N: Ind UU 10 469. Down S: UU 566. Dudley E: Lab 9 460. Dudley W: C 2 178. Dulwich: C 450. Dumfries: C 7 730. Dunfermline E: Lab 14 958. Dunfermline W: Lab 6 129. Durham City of: Lab 8 364. Durham N: Lab 23 405. Durham NW: Lab 12 162.

Ealing Acton: C 8 699. Ealing N: Lab 1 421. Easington: Lab 21 536. Eastbourne: C 24 129. E Kilbride: Lab 8 855. Eastleigh: C 12 555. E Lothian: Lab 9 567. Eastwood: C 11 504. Eccles: Lab 9 906. Eddisbury: C 11 596. Edinburgh Cen: C 1 971. Edinburgh E: Lab 6 837. Edinburgh Leith: Lab 8 141. Edinburgh Pentlands: C 6 429. Edinburgh S: C 3 600. Edinburgh W: C 6 382. Edmonton: Lab 863. Ellesmere Port & Neston: Lab 1 770. Elmet: C 3 802. Eltham: C 2 946. Enfield N: C 4 079. Enfield Southgate: C 18 366. Epsom & Ewell: C 23 010. Erewash: C 2 607. Erith & Crayford: Lab 4 521. Esher: C 22 376.

Falkirk E: Lab 11 660. Falkirk W: Lab 8 577. Falmouth & Camborne: C 15 938. Fareham: C 19 932. Faversham: C 10 362. Fermanagh & S. Tyrone: Ind Rep 5 030. Fife Cen: Lab 12 529. Fife NE: C 8 550. Foyle: SDLP 1 995. Fylde: C 22 180.

Gainsborough & Horncastle: C 7 436. Galloway & Upper Nithsdale: C 5 230. Gateshead E: Lab 14 892. Gedling: C 11 835. Glanford & Scunthorpe: C 807. Glasgow Cathcart: C 1 737. Glasgow Cen: Lab 12 911. Glasgow Govan: Lab 13 213. Glasgow Hillhead: Lab 2 020. Glasgow Maryhill: Lab 13 284. Glasgow Pollok: Lab 13 085. Glasgow Rutherglen: Lab 12 686. Glasgow Shettleston: Lab 13 745. Glasgow Springburn: Lab 18 535. Gloucester: C 6 970. Gordon: C 4 731. Gosport: C 17 293. Gower: Lab 6 327. Grantham: C 15 224. Gravesham: C 6 572. Gt Yarmouth: C 3 152. Greenwich: Lab 7 029. Guildford: C 19 430.

Hackney N & Stoke Newington: Lab 9 342. Hackney S & Shoreditch: Lab 11 371. Halesowen & Stourbridge: C 9 793. Halifax: Lab 905. Halton: Lab 5 750. Hamilton: Lab 17 142. Hampshire E: C 19 267. Hampshire NW: C 15 834. Hampstead & Highgate: C 3 845. Harrogate: C 19 787. Harrow E: C 9 121. Harrow W: C 18 473. Harwich: C 15 571. Hastings & Rye: C 12 540. Havant: C 16 092. Hazel Grove: C 11 815. Hemsworth: Lab 20 491. Henley: C 17 928. Hertford & Stortford: C 12 063. Herts N: C 11 591. Herts SW: C 17 525. Herts W: Lab 683. Hertsmere: C 12 613. Hexham: C 7 811. Heywood &

Middleton: Lab 9 143. High Peak: C 6 505. Holborn & St Pancras: Lab 7 933. Holland with Boston: C 10 201. Honiton: C 22 389. Hornsey and Wood Green: C 4 256. Horsham: C 25 155. Houghton & Washington: Lab 20 612. Huddersfield: Lab 4 326. Hull E: Lab 19 268. Hull N: Lab 8 817. Hull W: Lab 11 359. Huntingdon: C 20 046. Hyndburn: Lab 1 991.

Ilford N: C 6 532. Ilford S: C 2 351. Inverness, Nairn and Lochaber: L 1 088. Ipswich: Lab 3 386. Islington N: Lab 6 643. Islington S & Finsbury: Lab 6 296. Islwyn: Lab 21 168: Jarrow: Lab 15 213. Keighley: C 2 357. Kent Mid: C 8 846. Kettering: C 5 731. Kincardine & Deeside: C 9 085. Kingswood: Lab 3 898. Kirkcaldy: Lab 8 667. Knowsley N: Lab 17 205. Knowsley S: Lab 11 033.

Lagan Valley: UU 22 658. Lancs W: C 4 157. Lancaster: C 7 901. Langbaurgh: C 4 613. Leeds Cen: Lab 14 482. Leeds E: Lab 11 807. Leeds NE: C 10 864. Leeds NW: C 11 805. Leeds S & Morley: Lab 11 901. Leeds W: Lab 12 842. Leics. NW: Lab 836. Leigh: Lab 10 852. Leominster: C 9 180. Lewes: C 18 220. Lewisham Deptford: Lab 7 450. Lewisham E: Lab 2 079. Lewisham W: Lab 867. Lincoln: C 3 831. Lindsey E: C 11 407. Linlithgow: Lab 12 092. Littleborough & Saddleworth: C 5 586. Liverpool Broadgreen: C 565. L'pool Garston: Lab 5 229. L'pool Mossley Hill: C 9 086. L'pool Riverside: Lab 19 126. L'pool Walton: Lab 11 074. L'pool W Derby: Lab 11 134. Livingston: Lab 10 283. Llanelli: Lab 20 595. Londonderry E: UU 17 527. Loughborough: C 10 083. Ludlow: C 12 466. Luton N: C 7 397. Luton S: C 885.

Macclesfield: C 20 879. Maidstone: C 14 022. Makerfield: Lab 10 452. Manchester Blackley: Lab 5 785. Man Cen: Lab: 20 478. Man Gorton: Lab 9 872. Man Withington: C 4 734. Mansfield: Lab 8 346. Medway: C 3 689. Meirionnydd Nant Conwy: Pl C 1 789. Meriden: C 10 040. Merthyr Tydfil & Rhymney: Lab 26 060. Middlesbrough: Lab 12 296. Midlothian: Lab 12 544. Milton Keynes: C 6 739. Mole Valley: C 19 585. Monklands E: Lab 12 757. Monklands W: Lab 12 311. Monmouth: C 8 969. Moray: C 267. Morecambe & Lunesdale: C 12 177. Motherwell N: Lab 15 576.

Neath: Lab 16 374. Newark: C 5 092. Newbury: C 8 653. Newcastle-under-Lyme: Lab 5 843. Newcastle-upon-Tyne Cen: C 5 790. Newcastle E: Lab 9 803. Newcastle N: Lab 5 431. New Forest: C 20 877. Newport E: Lab 5 724. Newport W: Lab 3 201. Newry and Armagh: UU 2 338. Norfolk Mid: C 14 658. Norfolk N: C 11 954. Norfolk NW: C 5 894. Norfolk S: C 14 486. Norfolk SW: C 11 041. Normanton: Lab 8 908. Northampton N: C 5 077. Northampton S: C 9 717. Northavon: C 14 181. Norwich N: C 3 371. Norwich S: Lab 2 615. Norwood: Lab 3 330. Nottingham E: Lab 444. Nottingham N: Lab 8 956. Nottingham S: C 594. Nuneaton: Lab 1 396.

Ogmore: Lab 15 026. Oldham Cen & Royton: Lab 6 115. Oldham W: Lab 3 518. Orpington: C 13 043. Oxford E: Lab 235. Oxford W & Abingdon: C 10 508. Paisley N: Lab 10 776. Paisley S: Lab 8 167. Peckham: Lab 10 451. Pembroke: C 6 261. Pendle: C 1 535. Penrith and the Border: C 19 840. Perth & Kinross: C 5 172. Peterborough: C 2 892. Plymouth Devonport: Lab 2 823. Plym Drake: C 6 697. Plym Sutton: C 10 655. Pontefract and Castleford: Lab 17 411. Pontypridd: Lab 11 521. Poole: C 17 979. Portsmouth N: C 6 910. Portsmouth S: C 11 177. Preston: Lab 8 525. Pudsey: C 9 572.

Ravensbourne: C 18 306. Reading E: C 12 777. Reading W: C 8 484. Reigate: C 18 758. Renfrew W & Inverclyde: Lab 1 818. Ribble Valley: C 18 294. Richmond & Barnes: C 2 489. Richmond (Yorks): C 21 190. Rochford: C 20 155. Romsey & Waterside: C 20 831. Ross, Cromarty & Skye: C 5 579. Rossendale & Darwen: C 4 953. Rother Valley: Lab 14 944. Roxburgh & Berwickshire: C 18. Rugby & Kenilworth: C 6 640. Rutland & Melton: C 19 689. Ryedale: C 20 172.

St Albans: C 15 845. St Helens N: Lab 9 122. St Helens S: Lab 11 333. St Ives: C 15 108. Salford E: Lab 11 811. Salisbury: C 7 142. Scarborough: C 12 773. Sedgefield: Lab 13 061. Selby: C 13 846. Sevenoaks: C 18 692. Sheffield Attercliffe: Lab 16 218. Sheff Brightside: Lab 20 557. Sheff Cen: Lab 20 733. Sheff Hallam: C 18 526. Sheff Heeley: Lab 12 673. Sheff Hillsborough: Lab 9 559. Sherwood: Lab 6 252. Shipley: C 11 485. Shoreham: C 21 502. Shropshire N: C 14 023. Skipton & Ripon: C 16 006. Slough: Lab 510. Solihull: C 26 472. Somerton & Frome: C 10 702. Southampton Itchen: Lab 789. Southampton Test: C 2 635. S Hams: C 13 736. S Ribble: C 8 854. S Shields: Lab 9 439. Southwark & Bermondsey: Lab 12 688. Stafford: C 8 415. Staffs Mid: C 7 989. Staffs Moorlands: C 11 738. Staffs SE: C 4 941. Stamford & Spalding: C 16 141. Stevenage: Lab 988. Stirling: C 686. Stockport: C 4 382. Stockton N: Lab 11 923. Stockton S: Lab 940. Stoke-on-Trent Cen: Lab 14 547. Stoke N: Lab 13 403. Stoke S: Lab 12 489. Strangford: Ind UU 7 921. Stratford-upon-Avon: C 21 210. Strathkelvin & Bearsden: C 7 529. Streatham: C 4 833. Stretford: Lab 3 607. Stroud: C 15 522. Suffolk Cen: C 9 870. Suffolk Coastal: C 16 772. Suffolk S: C 13 490. Sunderland N: Lab 12 201. Sunderland S: Lab 9 121. Surrey SW: C 16 961. Sussex Mid: C 22 595. Swansea E: Lab 19 867. Swansea W: Lab 3 371.

Tatton: C 14 663. Tayside N: C 1 951. Teignbridge: C 9 790. Thanet N: C 14 111. Thanet S: C 13 631. Thurrock: Lab 7 305. Tiverton: C 14 399. Tooting: Lab 5 045. Torbay: C 15 974. Tottenham: Lab 9 867. Truro: L 7 548. Tweeddale, Ettrick & Lauderdale: L 4 774. Twickenham: C 12 889. Tyne Bridge: Lab 17 964. Tynemouth: C 7 725. Ulster Mid: UUUP 8 788. Upper Bann: UU 10 487. Vale of Glamorgan: C 2 203. Vauxhall: Lab 8 619.

Wakefield: Lab 5 842. Wallsend: Lab 22 192. Walsall N: Lab 4 193. Walsall S: Lab 4 815. Wansbeck: Lab 10 253. Wansdyke: C 6 391. Wantage: C 13 593. Warley E: Lab 6 312. Warley W: Lab 9 084. Warrington N: Lab 7 189. Warrington S: C 7 235. Warwick & Leamington: C 10 853. Warwickshire N: Lab 3 116. Watford: C 6 759. Waveney: C 5 771. Wealden: C 18 999. Wellingborough: C 7 611. Wells: C 11 935. Welwyn Hatfield: C 2 275. Wentworth: Lab 18 718. West Bromwich E: Lab 2 340. Westbury: C 13 081. Westminster N: C 2 376. Westmorland & Lonsdale: C 14 973. Weston-super-Mare; C 16 903. Wigan: Lab 15 035. Winchester: C 20 156. Windsor & Maidenhead: C 22 759. Wirral S: C 14 223. Wirral W: C 15 220. Witney: C 14 013. Wokingham: C 19 080. Wolverhampton NE: Lab 4 660. Wolve SE: Lab 8 602. Wolve SW: C 10 061. Woodspring: C 20 479. Worcester: C 11 136. Worcs Mid: C 7 047. Worcs S: C 18 270. Worsley: Lab 8 113. Wrekin The: Lab 1 382. Wrexham: Lab 9 617. Wycombe: C 15 742. Wyre: C 15 251. Wyre Forest: C 12 678. Yeovil: C 8 858.

Table of the Polls

Almost every day during the 1983 election campaign, a new poll was published indicating the way a microcosm of the nation, asked in the previous day or two, would have voted. It was clear from the polls throughout the campaign that the Conservatives were well ahead, and although one or two showed the Alliance overtaking Labour in the last days of the campaign, most produced accurate predictions of the result, and Market and Opinion Research International (MORI) in a poll in the London *Evening Standard* on election day gave the result accurately. Polls published during the campaign were:

Data of field work	*Poll (and no. polled)*		**C**	**Lab**	**All**	**other**	**C lead**
May 4–9	**Gallup** (*Daily Telegraph*)	971	49	31.5	17.5	2	17.5
5–6	**Harris** (*The Observer*)	1053	46	38	15	1	8
6	**NOP** (*Mail on Sunday*)	1058	47	34	18	1	13
6	**MORI** (Panorama)	1090	45	34	20	1	11
10	**MORI** (*Daily Star*)	1047	46	31	21	2	15
5–11	**MORI** (*Evening Standard*)	1824	46	32	22	0	14
9–11	**Marplan** (*The Guardian*)	1457	46	34	19	1	12
11	**Harris** (Thames TV)	1048	52	31	17	0	21
12	**MORI** (*Daily Express*)	964	49	34	15	2	15
11–16	**Gallup** (*Daily Telegraph*)	946	46	33	19	2	13
16	**MORI** (*Daily Star*)	1090	44	37	17	2	7
16	**Audience Selection** (TV AM 'phone)	1154	46	31	21	2	15
16–17	**NOP** (*Daily Mail*)	1584	49	31	19	1	18
17	**Audience Sel** (*The Sun*, phone)	507	44	33	21	2	11
18	**Harris** (Thames TV)	1053	45	35	17	3	10
17–18	**MORI** (*Sunday Times*)	960	47	30	21	2	17
19	**MORI** (*Daily Express*)	1100	46	37	16	1	9
19–20	**Harris** (*The Observer*)	1052	45	36	18	1	9
20	**Marplan** (*Sunday Mirror*)	1250	47	34	18	1	13
20–23	**Gallup** (*Daily Telegraph*)	1700	48	33	18	1	15
23	**MORI** (*Daily Star*)	1068	51	33	15	1	18
23	**Audience Sel** (TV AM 'phone)	1071	45	32	20	3	13
23–24	**NOP** (*Daily Mail*)	1104	52	33	14	1	19
24	**Audience Sel** (*The Sun*, phone)	557	45	32	21	2	13
23–25	**MARPLAN** (*The Guardian*)	1422	47.5	32.5	19	1	15
24–25	**Harris** (Thames TV)	1034	48	33	18	1	15
24–25	**MORI** (*Sunday Times*, panel)	1023	46	30	23	1	16
24–26	**Gallup** (*Daily Telegraph*)	2015	49	31.5	18	1.5	17.5
26	**MORI** (*Daily Express*)	1088	51	29	18	2	22
26–27	**Harris** (*The Observer*)	1029	47	30	21	2	17
27	**MARPLAN** (*Sunday Mirror*)	1325	49.5	31	19	.5	18.5
30	**Audience Sel** (TV AM 'phone)	1056	41	30	24	5	11
31	**MORI** (*Daily Star*)	1026	44	32	21	3	12
25–30	**Gallup** (*Daily Telegraph*)	918	47.5	28	23	1.5	19.5
31	**Audience Sel** (*The Sun*)	504	44	29	25	2	15
31–June 1	**Harris** (Thames TV)	1048	46	28	24	2	18
31–1	**MARPLAN** (*The Guardian*)	1276	47	30	22	1	17
31–2	**Gallup** (*Sunday Telegraph*)	1989	45.5	31.5	22	1	14
June 1–3	**MORI** (*Sunday Times*, panel)	942	45	28	25	2	17
2	**MORI** (*Daily Express*)	1067	43	32	23	2	11
2–3	**Harris** (*The Observer*)	1041	47	28	23	2	19
3	**MARPLAN** (*Sunday Mirror*)	1311	44	27	27.5	1.5	17
3	**NOP** (*Mail on Sunday*)	1074	47	29	23	1	18
5	**Audience Sel** (*The Sun*, phone)	1038	45	24	28	3	17
6	**MARPLAN** (*The Guardian*)	1337	47	26	25	2	21
6–7	**NOP** (*Daily Mail*)	1040	46	28	24	2	18
6–7	**MORI** (*Daily Express* and *Daily Star*)	867	47	26	25	2	21
7	**Audience Sel** (*The Sun*, phone)	1100	45	23	29	3	16
7–8	**Harris** (*The Observer*)	567	47	25	26	2	21
7–8	**Gallup** (*Daily Telegraph*)	2003	45.5	26.5	26	2	19
8	**MARPLAN** (*The Guardian*)	1335	46	26	26	2	20
8	**MORI** (*Evening Standard*)	1101	44	28	26	2	16
June 9	**Election result**		**42.4**	**27.6**	**25.4**	**4.6**	**14.8**

Marginal seats

A total of 155 members of the House of Commons represent seats which they won in June 1983 by majorities of less than 10 per cent, comprising 77 Conservative, 62 Labour, 12 Alliance and four in Northern Ireland. The following table shows the percentage majority and voting majority, the third column identifies the party who were runners up, and the final column shows the number of votes cast for the party in third place – Alliance except where indicated.

Conservative marginals

Leicester South	0.0	7	Lab	9 410
Hyndburn	0.0	21	Lab	6 716
Richmond and Barnes	0.2	74	L / All	3 156 Lab
Chelmsford	0.6	378	L / All	3 208 Lab
Nottingham North	0.8	362	Lab	9 200
Edinburgh West	1.1	498	L / All	9 313 Lab
Glanford and Scunthorpe	1.2	637	Lab	12 819
Sherwood	1.3	658	Lab	10 172
Newport West	1.4	581	Lab	10 163
Batley and Spen	1.6	870	Lab	11 678
Leicester East	1.9	933	Lab	10 362
Erith and Crayford	2.2	920	SDP / All	11 260 Lab
Banff and Buchan	2.3	937	SNP	6 084 SDP / All
Wrekin, The	2.3	1 331	Lab	14 208
Swindon	2.5	1 395	Lab	13 743
Edmonton	2.7	1 193	Lab	7 523
Oxford East	2.4	1 267	Lab	10 690
Basildon	3.1	1 379	Lab	11 634
Renfrew W & Inverclyde	3.2	1 322	SDP / All	12 139 Lab
Bridgend	3.2	1 327	Lab	9 630
Kingswood	3.2	1 797	Lab	12 591
Stevenage	3.3	1 755	SDP / All	12 673 Lab
Nottingham East	3.4	1 464	Lab	8 385
Bradford North	3.4	1 602	Lab	10 404
Halifax	3.4	1 869	Lab	11 868
Norwich South	3.5	1 712	Lab	11 968
Clywd South West	3.6	1 551	SDP / All	11 829 Lab
Bristol East	3.7	1 789	Lab	10 404
Westminster North	3.9	1 710	Lab	6 956
Feltham and Heston	3.9	2 148	Lab	8 706
Moray	4.0	1 713	SNP	7 901 L / All
Cannock and Burntwood	4.0	2 045	Lab	11 336
Dewsbury	4.0	2 086	Lab	13 065
Cunninghame North	4.1	1 637	Lab	7 268
Hazel Grove	4.1	2 022	L / All	5 895 Lab
Ynys Mon	4.2	1 684	PlC	6 791 Lab
Cardiff West	4.4	1 774	Lab	10 388
Lewisham East	4.5	1 909	Lab	9 351
Hereford	4.7	2 277	L / All	3 690 Lab
Warwickshire North	4.8	2 585	Lab	11 207
Dulwich	4.9	1 859	Lab	8 376
Newcastle Central	5.0	2 228	Lab	9 923
Manchester, Withington	5.1	2 373	Lab	12 231
Birmingham, Northfield	5.2	2 760	Lab	10 045
Bury North	5.3	2 792	Lab	7 550
Crosby	5.3	3 401	SDP / All	6 611 Lab
Bolton North East	5.4	2 443	Lab	8 311
Keighley	5.5	2 774	Lab	9 951
Lewisham West	5.7	2 507	Lab	7 470
Fife North East	5.9	2 185	L / All	2 442 SNP
Norfolk North West	5.9	3 147	SDP / All	10 139 Lab
Slough	6.0	3 106	Lab	9 519
York	6.2	3 647	Lab	13 523
Amber Valley	6.4	3 318	Lab	10 989
Corby	6.5	3 168	Lab	9 905
Darlington	6.8	3 438	Lab	8 737
Edinburgh Central	6.9	2 566	Lab	9 498
Birmingham, Yardley	6.9	2 865	Lab	8 109
Derby North	6.9	3 506	Lab	9 924
Harlow	6.9	3 674	Lab	12 891
Hornsey and Woodgreen	7.4	3 899	Lab	10 995
Bury South	7.5	3 720	Lab	9 628
Hampstead and Highgate	7.6	3 370	Lab	11 030
Strathkelvin and Bearsden	7.7	3 700	L / All	12 308 Lab
Angus East	8.1	3 527	SNP	4 978 SDP / All
Edinburgh South	8.2	3 655	SDP / All	12 824 Lab
Luton South	8.6	4 621	Lab	13 395
Cardiff Central	8.9	3 452	L / All	9 387 Lab
Barrow and Furness	9.0	4 577	Lab	11 079
Aberdeen South	9.1	3 581	Lab	10 372
Cornwall North	9.4	5 059	L / All	2 096 Lab
Twickenham	9.6	4 792	L / All	3 732
Cheltenham	9.6	5 518	L / All	4 390 Lab
Edinburgh, Pentlands	9.9	4 309	SDP / All	10 390 Lab
Southport	9.9	5 039	L / All	4 233 Lab
Nuneaton	9.9	5 061	Lab	14 264
Pudsey	9.9	5 314	L / All	9 542 Lab

Labour marginals

Carlisle	0.2	71	C	10 471
Bradford South	0.2	110	C	12 143
Wolverhampton NE	0.5	214	C	8 524
Crewe and Nantwich	0.5	290	C	9 820
Birmingham Erdington	0.6	231	C	7 915
West Bromwich East	0.7	298	C	10 200
Wakefield	0.8	360	C	9 166
Derby South	0.9	421	C	9 976
Wrexham	0.9	424	C	13 974
Islington S and Finsbury	1.0	363	SDP / All	9 894 C
Walsall South	1.4	702	C	6 586
Great Grimsby	1.5	731	C	14 552
Burnley	1.5	770	C	11 195
Ipswich	2.1	1 077	C	7 220
Carmarthen	2.2	1 154	C	14 099 PlC
Gower	2.7	1 205	C	10 450
Sheffield, Hillsborough	2.8	1 546	L / All	15 881 C
Alyn and Deeside	3.1	1 368	C	9 535
Greenwich	3.5	1 211	C	8 783
Leicester West	3.7	1 712	C	5 935
Thurrock	3.8	1 722	C	9 761
Stockton North	3.8	1 870	C	14 630
Walthamstow	3.9	1 305	C	7 192
Derbyshire NE	3.9	2 006	C	11 494
Durham City of	4.0	1 973	SDP/All	15 438 C
Copeland	4.3	1 837	C	6 722
Mansfield	4.8	2 216	C	11 036
Dumbarton	4.9	2 115	C	9 813
Doncaster Central	5.0	2 508	C	10 524
Newcastle-upon-Tyne N	5.1	2 556	C	15 136
Cardiff S and Penarth	5.4	2 276	C	8 816
Blackburn	5.4	3 055	C	8 174
Swansea West	5.5	2 350	C	8 036
Newcastle-under-Lyme	5.6	2 804	C	10 916
Tooting	5.8	2 659	C	8 317
Walsall N	5.8	2 824	C	10 141
Hammersmith	6.0	1 954	C	4 925
Hartlepool	6.4	3 090	C	7 428
Newport East	6.5	2 630	C	10 293
Bradford West	6.8	3 337	C	13 301
Dunfermline West	6.9	2 474	C	9 434
Redcar	6.9	3 104	C	11 614
Coventry SE	7.2	2 682	C	9 323
Oldham C and Royton	7.4	3 312	C	11 022
Dagenham	7.5	2 997	C	10 769
Battersea	7.5	3 276	C	7 675
Blyth Valley	7.7	3 243	SDP/All	11 657 C
Worsley	7.7	4 139	C	14 545
Coventry NW	7.8	3 038	C	7 479
Norwood	7.9	2 883	C	6 371
Oldham West	7.9	3 180	C	7 745
Bassetlaw	7.9	3 831	C	8 124
Huddersfield	8.2	3 955	C	12 027
Liverpool, Broadgreen	8.3	3 800	C	7 021 Ind L
Bishop Auckland	8.4	4 306	C	10 070
Warley East	8.6	3 391	C	6 697
Liverpool, Garston	8.7	4 002	C	7 153
Bristol South	8.9	4 419	C	9 674
Stalybridge and Hyde	9.1	4 362	C	8 339
East Kilbride	9.2	4 336	SDP/All	11 483 C
Heywood and Middleton	9.5	3 974	C	9 262
Normanton	9.7	4 183	C	9 741

L/SDP Alliance marginals

Stockton South	0.2	102	C	13 998 Lab
Gordon	1.9	850	C	3 899 Lab
Montgomery	2.3	668	C	2 550 Lab
Glasgow, Hillhead	2.8	1 164	Lab	9 638 C
Leeds West	4.4	2 048	Lab	12 515 C
Isle of Wight	4.7	3 503	C	1 828 Lab
Ross, Cromarty and Skye	4.9	1 704	C	4 901 Lab
Colne Valley	5.9	3 146	C	13 668 Lab
Yeovil	6.5	3 406	C	2 928 Lab
Woolwich	7.1	2 725	Lab	9 616 C
Liverpool, Mossley Hill	9.1	4 195	C	12 352 Lab
Cambridgeshire NE	9.8	5 195	C	4 625 Lab

Official Unionist Party marginals

Antrim East	1.0	367	DUP	7 620 All
Down South	1.1	548	SDLP	4 074 PSF
Newry and Armagh	3.3	1 554	SDLP	9 928 PSF

Democratic Unionist Party marginal

Ulster Mid	0.1	78	SF	12 044 SDLP

Labour's new front bench

Mr Neil Kinnock, who had been chief Opposition spokesman on education since 1979 and a member of the national executive since 1978, was elected Leader of the Labour Party by the party's electoral college at Brighton on October 2, 1983. Mr Roy Hattersley was elected Deputy Leader.

Following the Parliamentary Labour Party elections to the shadow cabinet, Mr Kinnock announced the full Labour Front Bench team as follows (* denotes member of Shadow Cabinet):

Treasury and Economic Affairs	Mr Roy Hattersley* Mr Terry Davis Dr Oonagh McDonald Mr Jeffrey Rooker
Foreign and Commonwealth Affairs	Mr Denis Healey* Mr George Robertson Mr Donald Anderson
Home Affairs	Mr Gerald Kaufman* Mr Denis Howell Mr Alfred Dubs Mr Robert Kilroy-Silk
Trade and Industry	Mr Peter Shore* Mr Bryan Gould Mr Harry Ewing Mr Roger Stott Mr Alan Williams
Employment	Mr John Smith* Mr John Evans Mr Barry Sheerman
Environment	Dr John Cunningham* Dr David Clark Mr Jack Straw
Transport	Mr John Prescott* Mr Peter Snape
Defence and Disarmament	Mr John Silkin* Mr Denzil Davies Mr Kevin McNamara
Northern Ireland	Mr Peter Archer* Mr Clive Soley
Wales	Mr Barry Jones* Mr Roy Hughes
European and Community Affairs	Mr Robin Cook* Mr George Foulkes
Housing and Construction	Mr Eric Heffer* Mr John Fraser
Health and Social Security	Mr Michael Meacher* Mr Frank Dobson Mrs Margaret Beckett Miss Harriet Harman
Education	Mr Giles Radice* Mr Andrew Bennett Mr Barry Sheerman
Energy	Mr Stanley Orme* Mr Edward Rowlands
Agriculture	Mr Robert Hughes Dr Mark Hughes
Arts	Mr Norman Buchan
Disabled	Mr Alfred Morris
Legal Affairs	Mr John Morris
Overseas Development and Cooperation	Mr Stuart Holland
Regional Affairs	Mr John Golding
Science and Technology	Dr Jeremy Bray
Scotland	Mr Donald Dewar Mr Jim Craigen Mr Martin O'Neill
Women's Rights	Miss Jo Richardson

Also members of the Shadow Cabinet are Mrs Gwyneth Dunwoody, with responsibility for coordinating Labour campaigns in Parliament and the country; Mr Michael Cocks, who was re-elected Opposition chief whip, Mr Jack Dormand, who was re-elected chairman of the PLP, Lord Cledwyn of Penrhos, who was re-elected leader of the Opposition peers in the House of Lords, and the Opposition chief whip in the Lords – Lord Ponsonby of Shulbrede.

Mr Peter Shore is also the chief Opposition spokesman on House of Commons affairs. Mr Norman Hogg was elected Opposition deputy chief whip.

How Northern Ireland voted 1979 and 1983

	May 1979				June 1983			
	total votes	% total votes	MPs	candi-dates	total votes	%total votes	MPs	candi-dates
OUP	254 578	36.6	5	11	259 952	34.0	11	16
DUP	70 975	10.2	3	5	152 749	20.0	3	14
All NI	82 892	11.9	0	12	61 275	8.0	0	12
PSF	–	–	–	–	102 701	13.4	1	14
SDLP	137 110	19.7	1	10	137 012	17.9	1	17
Others	150 334	21.6	3	26	51 236	6.7	1	22
Totals	695 889	100	12	64	764 925	100	17	95
Electorate	1 027 204		(turnout 67.8%)		1 050 222		(turnout 72.8%)	

Rise and fall of the parties 1945–83

The following table gives the state of the parties after each election from 1945 to 1983

	1945	1950	1951	1955	1959	1964	1966	1970	Feb 1974	Oct 1974	1979	1983
Conservative	213	298	321	345	365	303	253	330	296	276	339	397
Labour	393	315	295	277	258	317	363	287	301	319	268	209
Liberal/Alliance	12	9	6	6	6	9	12	6	14	13	11	23
Others (*includes the Speaker)	22	3	3	2	–	2*	2*	7*	24*	27*	17*	21
Total	640	625	625	630	630	630	630	630	635	635	635	650

By-Elections

The twenty by-elections since the May 1979 election saw an IRA prisoner elected, the emergence of a new party and a record-breaking 16 candidates standing in one constituency.

In Fermanagh and South Tyrone in Northern Ireland, Mr Robert Sands, serving a 14-year sentence in the Maze Prison for possessing firearms, was six weeks into a hunger strike when he was elected, standing for Anti H-block. He died a month later and the law was changed later that year to preclude prisoners serving sentences of more than a year from standing for election. Four months after Mr Sands was elected, another by-election in the same constituency returned his former election agent, Mr Owen Carron, for the same party. Mr Carron never took his seat.

In Warrington, Mr Roy Jenkins, a founder member of the Social Democratic Party and later its leader, was runner-up. He stood as SDP with Liberal support—the fledgling form of the Alliance which emerged. In Croydon North West three months later, Mr William Pitt, a Liberal, became the first MP standing as a L/SDP candidate to be elected. In Crosby a month after that, Mrs Shirley Williams, another founder member of the SDP and now its President, became the first SDP MP to be elected, although some sitting Labour MPs had already defected to the SDP. Mr Jenkins was returned to Parliament after winning at Glasgow Hillhead four months later.

At Southwark Bermondsey Mr Simon Hughes, for the L/SDP Alliance, beat 15 other candidates. It was the largest number of candidates ever to stand in a single constituency. When the election was announced by-elections were pending in two Welsh seats – Cardiff North West (Conservative) and Rhondda (Labour).

1979

September 27: Manchester Central: R. Litherland (Lab) 7 494 (70.7%); A. Parkinson (L) 1 502 (14.2%); A. Lea (C) 1 275 (12.0%); S. Ala-Ud-Din 187 (1.8%); J. Foster (Eco) 129 (1.2%); W. Boaks (Dem Mon) 12 (0.1%) Lab maj: 5 992 (56.5%). No change.

December 13: Hertfordshire South West: R. Page (C) 17 031 (45.9%); S. Reeves (Lab) 10 259 (27.7%); D. Clouston (L) 8 752 (23.6%); N. Jeskins (Eco) 602 (1.6%); D. Bundy (Anti-EEC) 288 (0.8%); N. Ffooks (Soton rag) 143 (0.4%). C maj: 6 772 (18.2%). No change.

1980

March 13: Southend East: E. Taylor (C) 13 117 (36.8%); C. George (Lab) 12 687 (35.6%); D. Evans (L) 8 939 (25.1%); T. Robertson (New Brit) 532 (1.5%); W. Smedley (Anti-EEC) 207 (0.6%); J. Curry (Ind L) 132 (0.3%); W. Boaks (Public Safety) 23 (0.1%). C maj: 430 (1.2%). No change.

June 26: Glasgow Central: R. McTaggart (Lab) 4 902 (60.8%); G. Paterson (SNP) 2 122 (26.3%) A. McCurley (C) 707 (8.8%); J. MacKenzie (NF) 148 (1.9%); G. Watson (Scot Young L) 134 (1.6%); D. Mellor (Eco) 45 (0.5%); D. Kean (Soc Dem) 10 (0.1%). Lab maj: 2 780 (34.5%). No change.

1981

April 9: Fermanagh and South Tyrone: R. Sands (Anti H-block) 30 492 (51.2%); H. West (Off UU) 29 046 (48.8%). Anti H-block majority: 1 446 (2.4%). Anti H-block gain from Ind.

July 16: Warrington: D. Hoyle (Lab) 14 280 (48.4%); R. Jenkins (SDP with L support) 12 521 (42.3%); S. Sorrell (C) 2 102 (7.1%); N. Chantrell (Eco) 219 (0.7%); D. Hussey (United Democratic Lab) 149 (0.5%); I. Leslie (CB Radio) 111 (0.4%); J. Fleming (Ind Lab) 53 (0.2%); D. Kean (SDP) 38 (0.1%); W. Boaks (Public Safety) 14 (0.0%); H. Wise (English Dem Party) 11 (0.0%); T. Keen (Campaign for Prosperous Britain) 10 (0.0%). Lab maj: 1 759 (6.1%). No change.

August 20: Fermanagh and South Tyrone: O. Carron (Anti H-block) 31 278 (49.1%); K. Maginnis (Off U) 29 048 (45.6%); S. Close (All) 1 930 (3.0%); T. Moore (Workers' Party) 1 132 (1.8%); M. Green (Peace Lover) 249 (0.3%); S. Hall-Raleigh (Amnesty) 90 (0.1%). Anti H-block maj: 2 230. (3.5%). No change.

October 22: Croydon North West: W. Pitt (L/SDP) 13 800 (40%); J. Butterfill (C) 10 546 (30.5%); S. Boden (Lab) 8 967 (26%); N. Griffin (NF) 429 (1.2%); M. Gillies-Carr (Ind Pro-Life) 340 (1%); J. Foster (Eco) 155 (0.4%); S. McKenzie (Const) 111 (0.3%); L. Brooks (War Pensioners) 81 (0.2%); W. Boaks (White Resident) 51 (0.1%); G. Major (Family Law Ref) 31 (0.1%); J. Joseph (Self-Employed) 20 (0.1%); S. Done (Anti-EEC) 11 (0.1%). L/SDP maj: 3 254 (9.5%). L/SDP gain from C.

November 26: Crosby: Mrs S. Williams (L/SDP) 28 118 (49.1%); J. Butcher (C) 22 829 (39.8%); J. Backhouse (Lab) 5 450 (9.5%); R. Small (Eco) 480 (0.8%); T. F'Tang (Cambride Univ Raving Loony Soc) 223 (0.4%); T. Keen (C-L All) 99 (0.2%); W. Boaks (White Resident) 36 (0.1%); J. Kennedy (Middx Poly student) 31 (0.1%); D. Potter (Humanitarian) 31 (0.1%). L/SDP maj: 5 289 (9.3%). L/SDP gain from C.

1982

March 4: Belfast South: Rev M. Smyth (Off U) 17 123 (39.3%); D. Cook (All) 11 726 (26.9%); Rev W McCrea (Dem U) 9 818 (22.6%); A. McDonnell (SDLP) 3 839 (8.8%); J. McMichael (Ul Loy Dem) 576 (1.3%); B. Caul (United Lab) 303 (0.7%); J. Narain (One Hum Fam) 137 (0.3%); S. Hall-Raleigh (Peace State) 12 (0.0%). Off U maj: 5 397 (12.4%). No change.

March 25: Glasgow Hillhead: R. Jenkins (SDP/L All) 10 106 (33.4%); G. Malone (C) 8 068 (26.6%); D. Wiseman (Lab) 7 846 (25.9%); G. Leslie (SNP) 3 416 (11.3%); J. Glass (Protestant against Papal visit) 388 (1.3%); R. Jenkins (Soc Dem) 282 (0.9%); N. Carlow (Eco) 178 (0.6%); W. Boaks (Public Safety) 5 (0.0%). SDP/L All maj: 2 038 (6.8%). SDP/L All gain from C.

May 27: Beaconsfield: T. Smith (C) 23 049 (61.8%); P. Tyler (Alliance) 9 996 (26.8%); A. Blair (Lab) 3 886 (10.4%); M. Byrne (Ind C) 225 (0.6%); W. Boaks (Public Safety) 99 (0.3%); T. Keen (Benn in Ten Unless PR) 51 (0.1%). C maj: 13 053 (35%). No change.

June 3: Merton, Mitcham and Morden: Mrs A. Rumbold (C) 13 306 (43.4%); B. Douglas-Mann (SDP/All) 9 032 (29.4%); D. Nicholas (Lab) 7 475 (24.4%); J. Pearce (NF) 547 (1.8%); E. Larkin (Ind L) 123 (0.4%); R. Sawh (Ethnic Min) 84 (0.3%); W. Boaks (Public Safety) 66 (0.2%); J. Bardwaj (COPS) 22 (0.1%); C. Farnsworth (Computer Dem) 18 (0.1%). C maj: 4 274 (14%). C gain from SDP.

June 24: Coatbridge and Airdrie: T. Clarke (Lab) 19 208 (55.1%); H. deBurgh (C) 9 118 (26.2%); R. Wyllie (Scot Nat) 3 652 (10.5%); A. Henderson (L/All) 2 873 (8.2%). Lab maj: 10 090 (28.9%). No change.

September 16: Gower: G. Wardell (Lab) 17 095 (43.5%); G. Jones (SDP/All) 9 875 (25.1%); T. Llewellyn (C) 8 690 (22.1%); I. Owen (Pl C) 3 431 (8.7%); J. Donovan (Computer Dem) 125 (0.3%); D. Burns (Welsh Poi Prisoner) 103 (0.3%). Lab maj: 7 220 (18.4%). No change.

October 28: Southwark Peckham: Ms H. Harman (Lab) 11 349 (50.3%); D. Taverne (SDP/L All) 7 418 (32.9%); J. Redwood (C) 2 800 (12.4%); M Webster (NF) 874 (3.9%); W. Boaks (Pub Safety) 102 (0.5%). Lab maj: 3 931 (17.4%). No change.

October 28: Birmingham Northfield: J. Spellar (Lab) 15 904 (36.3%); R. Gale (C) 15 615 (35.6%); S. Ridley (L/SDP All) 11 453 (26.1%); I. Anderson (NF) 411 (0.9%); P. Sheppard (Comm) 349 (0.8%); R. Taylor (People's Prog) 63 (0.1%); W. Boaks (Public Safety) 60 (0.1%). Lab maj: 289 (0.7%). Lab gain from C.

December 2: Glasgow Queen's Park: Mrs H. McElhone (Lab) 8 851 (56.0%); P. Mallan (Scot Nat) 3 157 (20.0%); J. Carlaw (C) 1 888 (11.9%); G. Watson (Lib/SDP All) 1 487 (9.4%); J. Kay (Comm) 339 (2.1%); J. Connell (Peace/Socialist) 40 (0.3%); A. Tennent (Scot Repub Socialist) 39 (0.2%). Lab maj: 5 694 (36.0%). No change.

1983

February 24: Southwark Bermondsey: S. Hughes (L/SDP All) 17 017 (57.7%); P. Tatchell (Lab) 7 698 (26.1%); J O'Grady (Real Lab) 2 243 (7.6%); R. Hughes (C) 1 631 (5.5%); J. Sneath (NF) 426 (1.4%); D. Sutch (Loony) 97 (0.3%); J. Birdwood (Ind Pat) 69 (0.2%); M. Keulemans (New Brit) 62 (0.2%); B. Giddings (Ind Lab) 50 (0.2%); R. Gordon (Comm) 50 (0.2%); G. Hannah (Eco) 45 (0.1%); F. Eden (Rev Comm) 38 (0.1%); A. King (Nat Lab) 25 (0.1%); A. Baker (United Dem) 15 (0.1%); D. Wedgwood (Anti-EEC) 15 (0.1%); E. Bevan (Ind) 8 (0.1%). Lib/SDP All maj: 9 319 (31.6%). L/SDP gain from Lab.

March 24: Darlington: O. O'Brien (Lab) 20 544 (39.5%); M. Fallon (C) 18 132 (34.9%); A. Cook (SDP/L All) 12 735 (24.5%); D. Sutch (Loony) 374 (0.7%); A. Clark (Ind) 164 (0.3%); T. Keen (Tactical Voting) 27 (0.1%); J. Bardwaj (Yoga) 15 (0.0%); P. Smith (Repub) 10 (0.0%). Lab maj: 2 412 (4.6%). No change.

Women MPs

A total of 23 women MPs were elected, comprising 10 Labour and 13 Conservative, headed by Mrs Margaret Thatcher, the Prime Minister. Before the dissolution there were also 23 women MPs, comprising 19 elected in May 1979 and a further four who won their seats at by-elections.

Mrs Shirley Williams, a former Labour Secretary of State for Education and Science, having lost her seat at Hertford and Stevenage in May 1979, left the Labour Party and became a founder member and President of the SDP, then won Crosby for the new party at a by-election in November, 1981, but lost it to the Conservatives at this general election.

The other by-election victors were: Ms Harriet Harman, who retained Southwark, Peckham for Labour in October 1982 and held Peckham at the general election; Mrs Angela Rumbold, who won the former Labour seat of Merton, Mitcham and Morden in June 1982 for the Conservatives when the sitting Labour member joined the SDP and caused a by-election, and retained Mitcham and Morden at the general election; and Mrs Helen McElhone, who retained Glasgow, Queen's Park in December 1982 for Labour in a by-election following the death of the sitting member, her husband Frank, but she did not get selected for the general election.

Six women took their seats for the first time and one returned to Parliament after an absence of four years. For the Conservatives: Mrs Ann Winterton won Congleton, joining her MP husband, Nicholas, who retained neighbouring Macclesfield; Mrs Elizabeth Peacock won Batley and Spen; Mrs Marion Roe won Broxbourne; Mrs Edwina Currie won Derbyshire South; and Mrs Anna McCurley won Renfrew West and Inverclyde.

For Labour: Mrs Margaret Beckett, who as Miss Margaret Jackson was MP for Lincoln October 1974–79 and a former Under Secretary for Education and Science, won Derby South; and Ms Clare Short won Birmingham, Ladywood while her husband, Mr Alexander Lyon, Labour MP, was losing York.

The women who had seats in May 1979 and lost them in June 1983 were: Miss Joan Lestor (Eton and Slough, Lab), Opposition spokesman on women's rights and a former Under Secretary for Education and Science, who lost Slough, having held Eton and Slough since 1966; Dr Shirley Summerskill (Halifax, Lab), an Opposition spokesman on home affairs and former Under Secretary, Home Office, who lost the seat she had held since 1964; Mrs Ann Taylor (Bolton West, Lab), an Opposition spokesman on housing and construction and a former assistant Government whip, lost Bolton North East, having held Bolton West since October 1974. Mrs Sheila Faith (Belper, C) and Mrs Sheila Wright (Birmingham, Handsworth, Lab) did not stand.

The women MPs in this Parliament:

Conservative

Mrs Lynda Chalker (*Wallasey*); Mrs Edwina Currie (*Derbyshire South*); Mrs Peggy Fenner (*Medway*); Miss Janet Fookes (*Plymouth, Drake*); Mrs Elaine Kellett-Bowman (*Lancaster*); Mrs Jill Knight (*Birmingham, Edgbaston*); Mrs Anna McCurley (*Renfrew West and Inverclyde*); Mrs Sally Oppenheim (*Gloucester*); Mrs Elizabeth Peacock (*Batley and Spen*); Mrs Marion Roe (*Broxbourne*); Mrs Angela Rumbold (*Mitcham and Morden*); Mrs Margaret Thatcher (*Finchley*); and Mrs Ann Winterton (*Congleton*).

Labour

Mrs Margaret Beckett (*Derby South*); Miss Betty Boothroyd (*West Bromwich West*); Mrs Gwynneth Dunwoody (*Crewe and Nantwich*); Ms Harriet Harman (*Peckham*); Dame Judith Hart (*Clydesdale*); Miss Joan Maynard (*Sheffield, Brightside*); Miss Oonagh McDonald (*Thurrock*); Ms Jo Richardson (*Barking*); Ms Clare Short (*Birmingham, Ladywood*); and Mrs Renée Short (*Wolverhampton North East*).

Defeated Members

In this general election 63 members of the May 1979 to June 1983 Parliament lost their seats. Thirty of them were Labour, four Conservative, 24 members of the SDP/Liberal Alliance, three Labour independents, one independent and one a Provisional Sinn Fein candidate who had never taken his seat.

The defeated Labour MPs included former Cabinet ministers Mr Tony Benn, Mr Albert Booth and Mr David Ennals and former junior ministers Dr Shirley Summerskill, Miss Joan Lestor, Mr Roland Moyle, Mr William Whitlock, Mr Alex Lyon, Mr Neil Carmichael and Mr Robert Cryer, and former Labour Government Whips like Mr Edward Graham, Mrs Ann Taylor and Mr David Stoddart.

The election deprived the Conservatives of Mr Iain Sproat, a junior trade minister in the Government. Another former junior minister, Mr Hamish Gray was luckier. He lost at Ross, Cromarty and Skye, but was made a life peer and transferred from the Department of Energy to the Scottish Office as Minister of State.

The Social Democrat losses included Mrs Shirley Williams (Crosby), Mr William Rodgers (Stockton North) and Dr Dickson Mabon, who failed at Renfrew West and Inverclyde. One of their Liberal allies, Mr William Pitt, was not re-elected at Croydon North West.

Mr Gerard Fitt, standing as an independent at Belfast West, was defeated in a contest won by Mr Gerry Adams, of Provisional Sinn Fein. At Fermanagh and South Tyrone Mr Owen Carron, also of Provisional Sinn Fein, lost the seat he won as Anti H-block candidate in a by-election in 1981.

In some cases, often as a consequence of the boundary changes, MP fought MP. At Glasgow, Hillhead, for example, Mr Roy Jenkins, then Leader of the SDP, beat Mr Carmichael, while at Crosby Mrs Shirley Williams was unseated by Mr Malcolm Thornton, a river Mersey pilot who in the last Parliament represented Liverpool, Garston.

Mr John Tilley, former Labour MP for Lambeth Central was beaten at Southwark and Bermondsey by Mr Simon Hughes, Liberal victor of the Bermondsey by-election earlier this year. Two Labour by-election winners were less fortunate. Mr John Spellar went out at Birmingham, Northfield, the seat he had gained only eight months before, and Mr Oswald O'Brien's triumph at Darlington lasted a mere 11 weeks.

Those not re-elected were:

Labour

Benn, A. W. *Bristol East*
Booth, A. E. *Barrow and Furness*
Carmichael, N. *Glasgow, Hillhead*
Cryer, R. *Keighley*
Davidson, A. *Hyndburn*
Dean, J. *Leeds West*
Ennals, D. *Norwich North*
Garrett, J. *Norwich South*
Graham, T. E. *Edmonton*
Homewood, W. D. *Corby*
Hooley, F. O. *Stratford-on-Avon*
Kerr, R. W. *Feltham and Heston*
Lestor, Miss J. *Slough*
Lyon, A. W. *York*
Marshall, J. *Leicester South*
Moyle, R. *Lewisham East*
Newens, A. S. *Harlow*
O'Brien, O. *Darlington*
Price, C. *Lewisham West*
Roberts, G. E. *Cannock and Burntwood*
Sever, E. J. *Meriden*
Spellar, J. *Birmingham, Northfield*
Stoddart, D. *Swindon*
Summerskill, Dr S. *Halifax*
Taylor, Mrs W. A. *Bolton North East*
Tilley, J. *Southwark and Bermondsey*
White, F. R. *Bury North*
Whitehead, P. *Derby North*
Whitlock, W. *Nottingham North*
Woolmer, K. J. *Batley and Spen*

Conservative

Gray, H. *Ross, Cromarty and Skye*
Myles, D. *Orkney and Shetland*
Sproat, I. *Roxburgh and Berwickshire*
Williams, D. *Montgomery*

Liberal

Pitt, W. H. *Croydon North West*

Social Democrat

Bradley, T. *Leicester East*
Brocklebank-Fowler, C. *Norfolk North West*
Brown, R. W. *Hackney South and Shoreditch*
Crawshaw, R. *Liverpool, Broadgreen*
Cunningham, G. *Islington South and Finsbury*
Davies, E. H. *Basingstoke*
Ellis, R. T. *Clwyd South West*
Ginsburg, D. *Dewsbury*
Grant, J. *Islington North*
Horam, J. *Newcastle upon Tyne Central*
Lyons, E. *Bradford West*
Mabon, Dr J. D. *Renfrew West and Inverclyde*
Magee, B. *Leyton*
McNally, T. *Stockport*
Mitchell, R. *Southampton, Itchen*
Ogden, E. *Liverpool, West Derby*
Rodgers, W. *Stockton North*
Roper, J. F. *Worsley*
Sandelson, N. D. *Hayes and Harlington*
Thomas, J. *Cardiff West*
Thomas, M. *Newcastle upon Tyne East*
Wellbeloved, A. J. *Erith and Crayford*
Williams, Mrs S. V. *Crosby*

Independent Labour

Ford, B. T. *Bradford North*
Lewis, A. *Newham North West*
O'Halloran, M. *Islington North*

Independent

Fitt, G. *Belfast West*

Provisional Sinn Fein

Carron, O. *Fermanagh and South Tyrone*

Retiring Members

Sir Harold Wilson, the former Labour Prime Minister, Mr George Thomas, the Speaker, and Mr Jo Grimond, the former Liberal leader, were among the 77 members of the Commons who did not contest the election. These distinguished parliamentarians headed those who decided to retire from politics but on this occasion they were joined by many others who failed to be selected for seats following upon the huge boundary changes that came into effect. Among those thus affected were Mr Joel Barnett, former Labour Chief Secretary to the Treasury, and Mr Jock Bruce-Gardyne, who was still Economic Secretary. to the Treasury in Mrs Thatcher's Government.

Other former ministers who left the House included Sir John Nott, Secretary of State for Defence at the time of the Falklands crisis, Sir Neil Marten, Minister for Overseas Development, and Mr Frederick Mulley, a former Labour Secretary of State for Defence. Mr John Parker, Father of the House, who first became an MP in 1935, also retired, being succeeded by the former Labour Prime Minister, Mr James Callaghan.

The full list is:

Conservatives

Mr Thomas Benyon (*Abingdon*), Mr Michael Brotherton (*Louth*), Mr Jock Bruce-Gardyne (*Knutsford*), Sir Frederick Burden (*Gillingham*), Sir Albert Costain (*Folkestone and Hythe*), Sir John Eden (*Bournemouth West*), Sir William Elliott (*Newcastle upon Tyne North*), Sir Russell Fairgrieve (*West Aberdeenshire*), Mrs Sheila Faith (*Belper*), Sir Anthony Fell (*Yarmouth*), Sir Nigel Fisher (*Kingston upon Thames, Surbiton*), Sir Charles Fletcher-Cooke (*Darwen*), Sir Victor Goodhew (*St Albans*), Mr Percy Grieve (*Solihull*), Mr Michael Hamilton (*Salisbury*), Sir Stephen Hastings (*Mid Bedfordshire*), Sir Bryant Godman Irvine (*Rye*), Sir Donald Kaberry (*Leeds North West*), Sir Marcus Kimball (*Gainsborough*), Sir Timothy Kitson (*Richmond, Yorks*), Sir John Langford-Holt (*Shrewsbury*), Mr Spencer Le Marchant (*High Peak*), Mr John Loveridge (*Havering, Upminster*), Sir Neil Marten (*Banbury*), Sir Angus Maude (*Stratford-on-Avon*), Mr Ray Mawby (*Totnes*), Mr Geraint Morgan (*Denbigh*), Sir John Nott (*St Ives*), Mr John Peyton (*Yeovil*), Sir Anthony Royle (*Richmond upon Thames, Richmond*), Mr William Rees-Davies (*Thanet West*), Mr Keith Stainton (*Sudbury and Woodbridge*), Sir Derek Walker-Smith (*Hertfordshire East*), Mr Keith Wickenden (*Dorking*).

Labour

Mr Frank Allaun (*Salford East*), Mr Joel Barnett (*Heywood and Royton*), Mr Arthur Bottomley (*Teesside, Middlesbrough*), Mr Robert Cant (*Stoke on Trent, Central*), Mr Stanley Cohen (*Leeds South East*), Mr Clinton Davis (*Hackney Central*), Mr Jack Dunnett (*Nottingham East*), Mr Michael English (*Nottingham West*), Mr Alan Fitch (*Wigan*), Mr Raymond Fletcher (*Ilkeston*), Mr George Grant (*Morpeth*), Mr Leslie Huckfield (*Nuneaton*), Mr Douglas Jay (*Wandsworth, Battersea North*), Mr James Johnson (*Kingston upon Hull West*), Mr Walter Johnson (*Derby South*), Mr Daniel Jones (*Burnley*), Dr Edmund Marshall (*Goole*), Mr Kenneth Marks (*Manchester, Gorton*), Mrs Helen McElhone (*Glasgow, Queen's Park*), Mr Andrew McMahon (*Glasgow, Govan*), Mr Charles Morris (*Manchester, Openshaw*), Mr George Morton (*Manchester, Moss Side*), Mr Frederick Mulley (*Sheffield Park*), Mr Arthur Palmer (*Bristol North East*), Mr John Parker (*Barking, Dagenham*), Mr Reg Race (*Haringey, Wood Green*), Mr Albert Roberts (*Normanton*), Mr Samuel Silkin (*Southwark, Dulwich*), Mr Julius Silverman (*Birmingham, Erdington*), Mr Leslie Spriggs (*St Helens*), Mr Albert Stallard (*Camden, St Pancras North*), Mr Thomas Urwin (*Houghton-le-Spring*), Mr Edwin Wainwright (*Dearne Valley*), Mr David Watkins (*Consett*), Mr Frederick Willey (*Sunderland North*), Sir Harold Wilson (*Huyton*), Mr William Wilson (*Coventry South East*), Mrs Sheila Wright (*Birmingham, Handsworth*).

Liberal

Mr Jo Grimond (*Orkney and Shetland*).

SDP

Mr James Dunn (*Liverpool, Kirkdale*).

Dem U

John McQuade (*Belfast North*).

UUUP

John Dunlop (*Ulster Mid*).

Other

Mr George Thomas (*the Speaker*).

The General Election Manifestos*

The Conservative Party:

'The Challenge of our Times'

Foreword by Margaret Thatcher

In the last four years, Britain has recovered her confidence and self-respect. We have regained the regard and admiration of other nations. We are seen today as a people with integrity, resolve and the will to succeed.

This Manifesto describes the achievements of four years of Conservative government and sets out our plans for our second term.

The choice before the nation is stark: either to continue our present steadfast progress towards recovery, or to follow policies more extreme and more damaging than those ever put forward by any previous Opposition.

We face three challenges: the defence of our country, the employment of our people, and the prosperity of our economy.

How to defend Britain's traditional liberties and distinctive way of life is the most vital decision that faces the people at this election. We have enjoyed peace and security for thirty-eight years – peace with freedom and justice. We dare not put that security at risk. Every thinking man and woman wants to get rid of nuclear weapons. To do that we must negotiate patiently from a position of strength, not abandon ours in advance.

The universal problem of our time, and the most intractable, is unemployment. The answer is not bogus social contracts and government overspending. Both, in the end, destroy jobs. The only way to a lasting reduction in unemployment is to make the right products at the right prices, supported by good services. The Government's role is to keep inflation down and offer real incentives for enterprise. As we win back customers, so we win back jobs.

We have a duty to protect the most vulnerable members of our society, many of whom contributed to the heritage we now enjoy. We are proud of the way we have shielded the pensioner and the National Health Service from the recession. Only if we create wealth can we continue to do justice to the old and the sick and the disabled. It is economic success which will provide the surest guarantee of help for those who need it most.

Our history is the story of a free people – a great chain of people stretching back into the past and forward into the future. All are linked by a common belief in freedom, and in Britain's greatness. All are aware of their own responsibility to contribute to both.

Our past is witness to their enduring courage, honesty and flair, and to their ability to change and create. Our future will be shaped by those same qualities.

The task we face is formidable. Together, we have achieved much over the past four years. I believe it is now right to ask for a new mandate to meet the challenge of our times.

THE ROAD TO RECOVERY

Britain is once more a force to be reckoned with. Formidable difficulties remain to be overcome. But after four years of Conservative government, national recovery has begun.

When we came to office in May 1979, our country was suffering both from an economic crisis and a crisis of morale. British industry was uncompetitive, over-taxed, over-regulated and over-manned. The British economy was plagued by inflation. After only a brief artificial pause, it was back into double figures. This country was drifting further and further behind its neighbours. Defeatism was in the air.

We did not disguise the fact that putting Britain right would be an extremely difficult task. The second sharp oil price increase and the deepest world recession since the 1930s have made those

*The Conservative, Labour and Liberal/SDP Alliance manifestos are published in full with extracts from the manifestos of other parties

difficulties worse. At the same time, the Western world is passing through another transformation – from the age of the smokestack to the era of the microchip. Traditional industries are being transformed by the new technologies. These changes have led to a rapid rise in unemployment in almost every Western country.

Our opponents claim that they could abolish unemployment by printing or borrowing thousands of millions of pounds. This is a cruel deceit. Their plans would immediately unleash a far more savage economic crisis than their last; a crisis which would, very soon, bring more unemployment in its wake.

The truth is that unemployment, in Britain as in other countries, can be checked and then reduced only by steadily and patiently rebuilding the economy so that it produces the goods and services which people want to buy, at prices they can afford.

What we have achieved

This is the task to which we have steadfastly applied ourselves with gradually increasing success. Prices are rising more slowly now than at any time for fifteen years. Britain is now among the low-inflation nations of the Western world. Output is rising.

We are creating the conditions in which trade and industry can prosper. We have swept away controls on wages, prices, dividends, foreign exchange, hire purchase, and office and factory building.

We have returned to free enterprise many state firms, in order to provide better service to the customer and save taxpayers' money.

We have cut income tax rates and raised allowances at all levels.

We have more than protected pensions against rising prices. We have strengthened the National Health Service. We have given council tenants the right to buy their own homes.

We have strengthened the police and the armed forces of the Crown.

We have done all this and more, and still kept our promise to bring public spending under control.

We have paid off nearly half the overseas debts the Labour Party left behind. Once the IMF's biggest borrower, we are now playing a leading part in strengthening international trade and finance – to the benefit of the poorest countries on earth.

And we have acted so that people might live in freedom and justice. The bravery, skill and determination with which Britain's task force recaptured the Falklands reverberated around the world. Many small nations gave thanks for that stand; and our allies in the North Atlantic are heartened by what Britain achieved in the South Atlantic.

Over the past four years, this country has recaptured much of her old pride. We now have five great tasks for the future. They are:

to create an economy which provides stable prices, lasing prosperity and employment for our people;

to build a responsible society which protects the weak but also allows the family and the individual to flourish;

to uphold Parliamentary democracy and strengthen the rule of law;

to improve the quality of life in our cities and countryside;

to defend Britain's freedom, to keep faith with our allies in Europe and in NATO, and to keep the peace with justice.

These tasks will require sustained determination, imagination and effort from Government and people alike.

JOBS, PRICES AND UNIONS

During the years of recession, now coming to an end, even the most successful of our competitors have faced increasingly serious problems and mounting unemployment. Despite all these difficulties, the Conservative Government has been overcoming Britain's fundamental problems: restoring sound money, setting a better balance between trade unions and the rest of society, bringing efficiency to the nationalised industries, and developing effective policies to mitigate the curse of unemployment.

The foundations of recovery have been firmly laid. In the next Parliament, we shall build on this progress.

Success against inflation

Steadier prices and honest money are essential conditions for recovery. Under the last Labour government, prices doubled and inflation soared to an all-time peak – despite the existence of a battery of controls on prices, profits, dividends and pay.

Today, there are no such controls. Yet prices are rising more slowly than at any time since the 1960s. During the last year, inflation has come down faster in Britain than in any other major economy. With lower inflation, businessmen, families, savers and pensioners can now begin at last to plan and budget ahead with confidence.

In the next Parliament, we shall endeavour to bring inflation lower still. Our ultimate goal should be a society with stable prices.

We shall maintain firm control of public spending and borrowing. If Government borrows too much, interest rates rise, and so do mortgage payments. Less spending by Government leaves more room to reduce taxes on families and businesses.

We shall continue to set out a responsible financial strategy which will gradually reduce the growth of money in circulation – and so go on bringing inflation down.

Our opponents are once again proposing the same financial policies that led to such appalling inflation and chaos in the past.

Labour's 'National Economic Assessment' is a stale repeat of the Social Contract which ended so disastrously in the Winter of Discontent. Once again, the Labour Party is committed to carry out trade union leaders' instructions in exchange for mere expressions of goodwill.

Commonsense in pay bargaining

With lower inflation, we have seen a return to commonsense in pay bargaining. Uncertainty and anxiety about rising prices have contributed to the absurdly high pay claims that destroyed so many jobs. As inflation subsides, people in work can see the prospect of real, properly-earned improvements in their living standards – which have gone up by more than 5 per cent on average over the last four years. So long as sensible government policies are matched by sensible attitudes in industry and commerce, these living standards can continue to improve.

The last four years have shown that a bureaucratic machine for controlling wages and prices is quite unnecessary. It simply stores up trouble and breeds inefficiency.

But Government remains inescapably responsible for controlling its own costs. We are committed to fair and reasonable levels of pay for those who work in the public services. We shall therefore continue to seek sensible arrangements for determining pay in the Civil Service and the National Health Service, following the Megaw Report and the resolution of the NHS pay dispute.

It is equally our duty to the nation as a whole to prevent any abuse of monopoly power or exploitation of the sick, the weak and the elderly. So we must continue to resist unreasonable pay claims in the public sector.

Trade union reforms

In the return to more sensible pay bargaining, the trade unions have an important part to play.

They can be powerful instruments for good or harm, to promote progress or hinder change, to create new jobs or to destroy existing ones. All of us have a vital interest in ensuring that this power is used democratically and responsibly.

Both trade union members and the general public have welcomed the 1980 and 1982 Employment Acts, which restrain secondary picketing, encourage secret ballots, curtail abuse of the closed shop, and restore rights of redress against trade unions responsible for committing unlawful acts.

But some trade union leaders still abuse their power against the wishes of their members and the interests of society. Our 1982 Green Paper, *Democracy in Trade Unions*, points the way to give union members control over their own unions. We shall give union members the right to:

- hold ballots for the election of governing bodies of trade unions;
- decide periodically whether their unions should have party political funds.

We shall also curb the legal immunity of unions to call strikes without the prior approval of those concerned through a fair and secret ballot.

Political levy

Consultations on the Green Paper have confirmed that there is widespread disquiet about how the right of individual trade union members not to pay the political levy operates in practice, through the system of contracting-out. We intend to invite the TUC to discuss the steps which the trade unions themselves can take to ensure that individual members are freely and effectively able to decide for themselves whether or not to pay the political levy. In the event that the trade unions are not willing to take such steps, the Government will be prepared to introduce measures to guarantee the free and effective right of choice.

Essential services

The proposal to curb immunity in the absence of pre-strike ballots will reduce the risk of strikes in essential services. In addition, we shall consult further about the need for industrial relations in specified essential services to be governed by adequate procedure agreements, breach of which would deprive industrial action of immunity. The nation is entitled to expect that the operation of essential services should not be disrupted.

Involving employees

Good employers involve their employees by consulting them and keeping them fully informed. This is vital for efficiency as well as harmony in industry. We shall continue to encourage it. Many employers have already done much in recent years to establish a long-needed sense of common purpose with their workforces. We shall resist current attempts to impose rigid systems of employer/employee relations in Britain. We will continue to encourage workers to identify with the success of the firm for which they work, by the promotion of share-ownership and profit-sharing.

In each of the last two years, largely as a result of tax changes we have introduced, about a quarter of a million employees have acquired shares in the companies that employ them.

When state industries are offered to the private sector, we have given their employees the chance to buy shares in them, and many have exercised this right.

Unemployment: coping with change

During the last four years, unemployment in the industrialised countries has risen more sharply than at any time since the 1930s. Britain has been no exception. We have long been one of the least efficient and most over-manned of industrialised nations. We raised our own pay far more, and our output far less, than most of our competitors. Inevitably, this pushed prices up and drove countless customers to buy from other countries, forcing thousands of employers out of business and hundreds of thousands of workers out of jobs.

At the same time, there has been a rapid shift of jobs from the old industries to the new, concentrated on services and the new technologies. Tragically, trade unions have often obstructed these changes. All too often this has delayed and reduced the new and better-paid jobs which could replace those that have been lost.

This Government has an impressive record in helping the unemployed who, usually through no fault of their own, are paying the price of these past errors.

We have committed over £2,000m. this year to training and special measures for the unemployed. This is supported by substantial help from the European Community's Social Fund, amounting to over £250m. in 1982. As long as unemployment remains high, we shall maintain special measures of this kind, which bring effective help to many of those who have no job.

This year, some 1,100,000 people are being trained or helped by the most comprehensive programme of its kind in Europe.

For the first time, the new Enterprise Allowance Scheme offers many thousands of unemployed people the support they need, but previously could not get, while they start their own businesses. We will maintain special help for the long-term unemployed through the Community Programme, and for the older unemployed through early retirement schemes.

Removing the barriers to jobs

We shall go on reducing the barriers which discourage employers from recruiting more staff, even when they want to. And we shall help to make the job market more flexible and efficient so that more people can work part-time if they wish, and find work more easily.

That is why we have amended the Employment Protection Act and why we shall continue to:

minimise the legal restrictions which discourage the creation of new jobs;

encourage moves towards greater flexibility in working practices, such as Part-Time Job Release, which makes it financially possible for people nearing retirement age to go part-time; and the Job-Splitting Scheme which helps employers to split a whole-time job into two part-time jobs;

improve the efficiency of the employment services in identifying and filling job vacancies;

ensure that Wages Councils do not reduce job opportunities by forcing workers to charge unrealistic pay rates, or employers to offer them.

Training

If we are to make the most of the employment opportunities that present themselves in an age of rapid change and more varied patterns of work and occupation, up-to-date training is essential.

Training for work must start with better, more relevant education at school. For school-leavers, we have provided the most imaginative and far-reaching scheme in our history. The Youth Training Scheme offers every 16-year old a year of serious training for work. It should help 350,000 youngsters by the autumn of this year. From now on, no one leaving school at 16 need be unemployed in his first year out of school.

This is only a part of our wider strategy to ensure effective training for the skills and jobs of tomorrow – on a scale and of a quality to match the world's best. At its heart is our reform of industrial training and the apprenticeship system.

We are improving the scope and quality of our training for the employed and unemployed alike; tackling problems which the Labour Party has never had the courage to face.

We shall continue to provide for, and improve, the special employment and training needs of the disabled, and to reform our training agencies to meet more effectively the needs of industry and workers alike.

The nationalised industries

Reform of the nationalised industries is central to economic recovery. Most people who work in these industries work hard and have a sense of public service. Since 1979, we have gone to great lengths to improve the performance of the state sector, to appoint top-class managers and work closely with them to tackle each industry's problems.

But for all this, few people can now believe that state ownership means better service to the customer. The old illusions have melted away. Nationalisation does not improve job satisfaction, job security or labour relations – almost all the serious strikes in recent years have been in state industries and services. We have also seen how the burden of financing the state industries has kept taxes and government borrowing higher than they need have been.

A company which has to satisfy its customers and compete to survive is more likely to be efficient, alert to innovation, and genuinely accountable to the public. That is why we have transferred to private ownership, in whole or in part, Cable and Wireless, Associated British Ports, British Aerospace, Britoil, British Rail Hotels; Amersham International, and the National Freight Corporation. Many of their shares have been bought by their own employees and managers, which is the truest public ownership of all.

We shall continue our programme to expose state-owned firms to real competition. In telecommunications, we have licensed a new independent network, Mercury, and have decided to license two mobile telephone networks. We have allowed competition in commercial postal services. Already, standards of service are beginning to improve. Investment is rising. And better job opportunities are being opened up.

We shall transfer more state-owned businesses to independent ownership. Our aim is that British Telecom – where we will sell 51 per cent of the shares to the private sector – Rolls-Royce, British Airways and substantial parts of British Steel, of British Shipbuilders and of British Leyland, and as many as possible of Britain's airports shall become private sector companies. We also aim to introduce substantial private capital into the National Bus Company. As before, we will offer shares to all those who work in them.

We shall also transfer to the private sector the remaining state-owned oil business – the British Gas Corporation's offshore oil interests.

We have abolished the Gas Corporation's statutory monopoly of the supply of North Sea gas to industry. Already there has been a vigorous new lease of life for gas exploration and development in the North Sea, which had ground to a complete halt under Labour. In the last Parliament, we passed a law to encourage the private generation of electricity. In the next Parliament, we shall seek other means of increasing competition in, and attracting private capital into, the gas and electricity industries.

Merely to replace state monopolies by private ones would be to waste an historic opportunity. So we will take steps to ensure that these new firms do not exploit their powerful positions to the detriment of consumers or their competitors. Those nationalised industries which cannot be privatised or organised as smaller and more efficient units will be given top-quality management and required to work to clear guidelines.

ENCOURAGING FREE ENTERPRISE

We want to see an economy in which firms, large and small, have every incentive to expand by winning extra business and creating more jobs. This Conservative Government has been both giving these incentives and clearing away the obstacles to expansion: the high rates of tax on individuals and businesses; the difficulties facing the small firm trying to grow, and the self-employed man trying to set up on his own; the blockages in the planning system; the bottlenecks on our roads; the restrictions on our farmers and fishermen; and the resistance to new ideas and technologies.

In the last four years, many British firms have made splendid progress in improving their competitiveness and profitability. But there is some way to go yet before this country has regained that self-renewing capacity for growth which once made her a great economic power, and will make her great again.

Only a government which really works to promote free enterprise can provide the right conditions for that dream to come true.

Lower and simpler taxes

In the last four years, we have made great strides in reducing and simplifying taxes. We have:

cut the basic rate of income tax; raised tax allowances above the level we inherited *after* allowing for price rises; brought the higher rates of income tax down to European levels; and made big reductions in the investment income surcharge, which have particularly helped the old;

removed many of the worst features of Capital Transfer Tax, Capital Gains Tax and Development Land Tax;

cut business taxes, in particular the National Insurance Surcharge, Labour's tax on jobs, from 3½ per cent to 1 per cent; and improved stock relief for businesses;

much reduced the taxes on, and increased the incentives for, gifts to charities;

greatly reduced tax bureaucracy. Manpower in the Inland Revenue and Customs & Excise has fallen from 113,400 in April 1979 to 98,500 in April 1983, and is set to fall further.

This dramatic progress is all the more striking when compared with the vast increases in taxation which our opponents' policies would inevitably bring.

The changes to this year's Finance Act on which Labour have insisted show that they intend just this. We shall reverse those changes at the earliest opportunity.

Further improvements in allowances and lower rates of income tax remain a high priority, together with measures to reduce the poverty and unemployment traps.

We want to encourage wider ownership. This means lowering taxes on capital and savings; encouraging individuals to invest directly in company shares; and encouraging the creation of more employee share schemes.

More small firms

We have reduced the burdens on small firms, especially in employment legislation and planning, and cut many of the taxes they pay, particularly Corporation Tax. Our Loan Guarantee Scheme has already backed extra lending of over £300m. to about 10,000 small firms. The new Business Expansion Scheme, a major extension of the Business Start-up Scheme, will encourage outside investment in small companies by special tax reliefs. The construction of new premises for small businesses has more than doubled.

To help the engineering industry and the areas most dependent on it, we have introduced and now extended a very successful scheme of grants (SEFIS) to smaller firms, which help them to buy new machinery.

Thanks to these policies and over one hundred other important measures, the climate for new and smaller businesses in the UK has been transformed and is now as favourable as anywhere in the world.

Help for the new technologies

Even during the recession, our new industries and technologies made remarkable progress. Britain has more micro-computers in relation to its population than any other country. We have speeded this progress by supporting research and spreading knowledge of the technologies of tomorrow; and by increasing government support for the new technologies from £100m. in 1978–9 to over £350m. in 1983–4. But that is only the beginning. We will now:

promote in partnership with industry, the Alvey programme for research into advanced information technology;

accelerate the transfer of technology from the university laboratory to the market place, especially by the encouragement of science parks;

help firms to launch new products through pilot schemes and public purchasing;

build on the successes of our 'Micros-in-Schools' scheme and our network of Information Technology Centres for the young unemployed so that they are equipped with tomorrow's skills;

sanction the launch of new cable networks to bring wider choice to consumers, not just for entertainment, but for the whole new world of tele-shopping and tele-banking.

Regions, enterprise zones and freeports

We shall continue to maintain an effective regional policy which is essential to ease the process of change and encourage new businesses in areas which have been dependent on declining industries. We do not propose sudden changes in regional policy. But we will:

make sure that these policies are economical and effective in creating genuine jobs;

secure more effective co-ordination between central and local government and the European Community's Regional Development Fund to ensure that their actions offer the greatest help to communities in need;

further develop local self-help initiatives, the 24 Enterprise Zones and, our latest innovation, duty free trading zones, which will be established in certain experimental 'Freeports';

diversify regional economies by encouraging the fullest use of our schemes for innovation.

Planning

In our crowded country the planning system has to strike a delicate balance. It must provide for the homes and workplaces we need. It must protect the environment in which we live.

One particular way to achieve this is by bringing back into use the thousands of acres lying derelict and unused, so much of which is in the ownership of local authorities or other public bodies. We have set up Land Registers to identify this land, and we shall now use our powers to bring it into use. The more this land can be used, the less the need to build on Green Belts and the countryside.

We will also bring open-cast coalmining within normal proper planning control, and we shall establish more control over intensive livestock units near residential areas.

Energy

Britain has come from nowhere to be the world's fifth largest oil producer. The North Sea success story has been a triumph of private enterprise for the nation's benefit. We shall continue to ensure that our taxation and licensing policies encourage development in the North Sea.

In the next Parliament, the interests of the whole country require Britain's massive coal industry, on which we depend for the overwhelming bulk of our electricity generation, to return to economic viability.

We shall press ahead with the development of safe nuclear power. It is an important way of securing lower-cost electricity for the future. We shall set up an Energy Efficiency Office to co-ordinate the Government's conservation effort, so as to ensure that the taxpayer gets the best value for money.

We recognise that some energy users have special needs. This is why we have:

ensured that standing charges no longer dominate the bills of small gas and electricity consumers;

increased help for the needy with their fuel bills, leading to many fewer disconnections; and introduced more favourable terms for the energy-intensive industries.

Better transport for industry

The national motorway and trunk road network will continue to be developed and improved to high-quality standards. This will not only make driving much safer for all, but also speed and cheapen the transport of goods. We will also seek to make rail freight more competitive.

Many of our ports have now been returned from state control to independent ownership. We intend that they should provide profitable and efficient services without the taxpayers' support.

Tourism

Our hotels, resorts and tourist attractions are important because they provide hundreds of thousands of jobs, earn valuable foreign exchange, and provide holidays for millions of our own people. We shall continue to support the Tourist Boards and tourism projects throughout the country.

Farming and fishing

British farming and horticulture have improved dramatically since 1979. Exports have leapt to £2,500m. a year. Since 1978, our self-sufficiency in food has risen by more than a sixth, from 53 per cent to 62 per cent.

In Europe, our tough negotiating stance has doubled our farmers' share of the help available under the Common Agricultural Policy. The cost of the CAP to British taxpayers doubled under Labour. Under us, it has been falling in real terms. We have reversed the Labour Government's disastrous policy for the Green Pound which harmed British farmers. At the same time, we have not neglected the consumers' interest. Food prices more than doubled under Labour and rose faster than other prices. Under the Conservatives, they have risen less than other prices. Last year they grew by less than one per cent, the smallest rise for nearly twenty years.

We have given special help to Britain's hill farmers, and agreed very worthwhile Community schemes for beef and sheepmeat. These have all brought great benefits to Wales, Scotland, Northern Ireland and the uplands of England. We have launched successfully the 'Food from Britain' campaign, which should help us sell far more of our products both at home and in the rest of the Community.

We shall help the glasshouse industry to sell more fruit and vegetables, and to make use of the best possible arrangements for heating and insulation.

We welcome the fact that, after long negotiations, the National Farmers' Union and the Country Landowners' Association have agreed on the best way to make more farm tenancies available for young people. We shall legislate on these lines at an early opportunity. We intend to make sure that British agriculture and horticulture continue to make the greatest possible contribution to our economic success.

We have successfully negotiated a Common Fishing Agreement that provides British fishermen with the greatest advantages in our waters in the industry's history. For the first time since we joined the Community, we now have effective conservation measures, and can look forward to expanding, rather than declining, stocks of fish. During the next Parliament, we shall introduce measures to restructure the fishing industry and to encourage investment and better marketing.

RESPONSIBILITY AND THE FAMILY

Freedom and responsibility go together. The Conservative Party believes in encouraging people to take responsibility for their own decisions. We shall continue to return more choice to individuals and their families. That is the way to increase personal freedom. It is also the way to improve standards in the state services.

Conservatives believe equally strongly in the duty of Government to help those who are least able to help themselves. We have more than carried out our pledges to protect pensioners against price rises and to maintain standards in the National Health Service. This rebuts the totally unfounded charge that we want to 'dismantle the Welfare State'. We are determined that our public services should provide the best possible value both for people they seek to help and for the taxpayer who pays the bill.

A free and independent society is one in which the ownership of property is spread as widely as possible. A business which is partly or wholly owned by its workers will have more pride in performance. Already firms like the National Freight Company, where managers and workers joined together to take over the business, are thriving.

Under this Government, the property-owning democracy is growing fast. And the basic foundation of it is the family home.

Housing: towards a home-owning democracy

We have given every council and New Town tenant the legal right to buy his or her own home. Many Housing Association tenants have been granted the same right, too. This is the biggest single step towards a home-owning democracy ever taken. It is also the largest transfer of property from the State to the individual. No less than half a million council houses and flats were sold in the last Parliament to the people who live in them. By our encouragement of private housebuilding and our new range of schemes to help first-time buyers, there are a million more owner-occupiers today than four years ago.

The Labour Party has met these proposals with vicious and prolonged resistance and is still fighting a rearguard action against wider home ownership. A Labour government would take away the tenant's right to buy his council house, would prevent councils selling even voluntarily at a discount, and would force any former tenant who wanted to sell his house to sell it back to the council.

In the next Parliament, we will give many thousand more families the chance to buy their homes. For public sector tenants, the present 'Right to Buy' scheme will be improved and extended to include the right to buy houses on leasehold land and the right to buy on a shared ownership basis. The maximum discount will be increased by one per cent a year for those who have been tenants for between twenty and thirty years, taking the maximum discount to 60 per cent. We shall also help first-time buyers who are not council tenants through our various low-cost home-ownership schemes: 'home-steading', building for sale, improvement for sale, and shared ownership.

Britain needs more homes to rent, too, in the private sector as well as the public sector. For years, the blind prejudice of the Labour Party has cast a political blight on privately rented housing. But our assured tenancy scheme has encouraged builders to start building new homes to rent again, and our shorthold scheme is helping the private sector to meet the needs of those who want short-term rented accommodation.

We shall extend our Tenants' Charter to enable council tenants to get necessary repairs done themselves and be reimbursed by their councils. Housing Improvement grants have been increased substantially in the last two years and will continue to play an important role.

We shall conduct early public consultation on proposals which would enable the builing societies to play a fuller part in supporting the provision of new housing and would bring upto date the laws which govern them.

Our goal is to make Britain the best housed nation in Europe.

Protecting the pensioner

Over the last four years, the retirement pension has risen from £19.50 to £32.85 a week for a single person and from £31.20 to £52.55 for a married couple. Even after allowing for price rises, pensioners can buy more with their pension today than they could under the last Labour government. We have ended Labour's unreliable system of relying on forecasts of price rises to decide by how much to increase the pension. In five of the last seven years, those forecasts turned out to be wrong. In future, pensions will be related to actual and not estimated price increases.

In the next Parliament, we shall continue to protect retirement pensions and other linked long-term benefits against rising prices. Public sector pensioners will also continue to be protected on the basis of realistic pension contributions. In this Parliament, we raised to £57 a week the amount pensioners may earn without losing any of their pension. It remains our intention to continue raising the limit and to abolish this earnings rule as soon as we can. The Christmas Bonus, which Labour failed to pay in 1975 and 1976, will continue to be paid every year in accordance with the law we passed in 1979.

Over 11.5m people – half the working population – are now covered by occupational pension schemes. We will consider how the pension rights of 'early leavers', people who change jobs, can be better protected and how their members may be given fuller information about their pension schemes.

Social security

Supplementary benefits, too, have been raised ahead of prices. To encourage thrift, instead of penalising it, the Government has also raised the amount of savings people can keep without losing any supplementary benefit. At the same time, we have clamped down firmly on fraud and abuse of social security.

Expenditure on cash benefits to the disabled is 21 per cent higher than under Labour, even after allowing for rising prices. There has been extra help, too, for those who are least able to afford their fuel bills.

We have introduced — and extended — a widows' bereavement allowance. We have kept the war widows' pension ahead of prices and removed it from tax altogether.

Child benefit and one-parent benefit are to be raised in November to their highest-ever level in real terms. We have also improved the family income supplement scheme to help low-paid working families.

Our record shows the strength of our commitment. But our ability to help depends on the wealth which the country produces. In Britain today, over 40p in every pound of public spending is already devoted to health and social security. It is hypocritical for the Labour Party to pretend that they could raise public spending on benefits by thousands of millions of pounds without admitting the vast increases in taxation and national insurance contributions that would be needed, or the increased inflation that would result.

The National Health Service

We have more than matched our pledge to maintain spending on the National Health Service and secure proper value for money. Even after allowing for price rises, the nation is spending substantially more on health, and getting better health care.

By last year, there were 45,000 more nurses and midwives, and over 6,500 more doctors and dentists, working for the NHS than in 1978. This has helped to make it possible to treat over two million more patients a year in our hospitals. Until last year's futile strike, waiting lists for treatment fell sharply.

We intend to continue to make sure that all patients receive the best possible value for the money that is spent on the Health Service. The treatment of the elderly, the mentally handicapped and the mentally ill will continue to command our particular attention. We shall continue to make extra provision for those parts of the country in the North and the Midlands which have always been comparatively short of resources.

Unlike the last Labour government which actually cut the hospital building programme by one-third, we have committed £1,100m. to our large-scale programme for building new hospitals. There are now 140 new hospitals in that programme being designed or built. We shall continue to upgrade existing hospitals and brighten up shabby wards.

To release more money for looking after patients, we will reduce the costs of administering the Health Service. We are asking health authorities to make the maximum possible savings by putting services like laundry, catering and hospital cleaning out to competitive tender. We are tightening up, too, on management costs, and getting much firmer control of staff numbers.

Most people who are ill or frail would prefer to stay in or near their own homes, rather than live in a hospital or institution. Helping people to stay in familiar surroundings is the aim of our policy 'Care in the Community'. The Government has given extra powers and extra cash to health authorities to enable them to finance such community care for individual patients on a long-term basis.

Partnership in care

Conservatives reject Labour's contention that the State can and should do everything.

We welcome the growth in private health insurance in recent years. This has both made more health care available, and lightened the load on the NHS, particularly for non-urgent operations. We shall continue to encourage this valuable supplement to state care. We shall promote closer partnership between the State and the private sectors in the exchange of facilities and of ideas in the interests of all patients.

We also welcome the vital contribution made by voluntary organisations in the social services. We shall continue to give them strong support. The Conservative Government has already made many radical changes in law and taxation which have greatly improved the way charities and voluntary bodies are financed. The terms governing gifts under covenants have been much improved, and the liability to capital taxation has been lightened or swept away.

We shall continue to support our highly successful 'Opportunities for Volunteering' scheme. In the next Parliament, we shall develop other new ways to encourage more private giving.

Schools: the pursuit of excellence

For a long time now, parents have been worried about standards and discipline in many of our schools. This Conservative Government has responded to that worry with the Parents' Charter and the 1980 Education Act. For the first time:

local authorities were obliged to take account of parents' choice of school for their children;

schools were obliged to publish prospectuses, giving details of their examination results;

parents were given the right to be represented on school governing bodies;

the Government offered Assisted Places to enable less-well-off parents to send bright children to some of the best independent schools.

Giving parents more power is one of the most effective ways of raising educational standards. We shall continue to seek ways of widening parental choice and influence over their children's schooling.

We shall defend Church schools and independent schools alike against our opponents' attacks. And we shall defend the right of parents to spend their own money on educating their children.

This country is now spending more per child in school than ever before, even after allowing for price rises. As a result, the average number of children per teacher is the lowest ever. Exactly how the money is spent, and how schools are run, is up to local education authorities.

But the Government can help improve standards and make sure that children are taught and trained for the world they will grow up into.

Until now, HM Inspectors' reports have remained secret. Now we are publishing them and making sure they are followed up, too.

We are not satisfied with the selection or the training of our teachers. Our White Paper sets out an important programme for improving teacher training colleges.

We shall switch the emphasis in the Education Welfare Service back to school attendance, so as to reduce truancy.

We have given special help for refresher courses for teachers, research into special schools, and play groups and nursery schools where they are most needed.

We shall also encourage schools to keep proper records of their pupils' achievements, buy more computers, and carry out external graded tests. The public examination system will be improved, and O-level standards will be maintained.

We are setting up fourteen pilot projects to bring better technical education to teenagers. The success of these will play a vital part in raising technical training in Britain to the level of our best overseas competitors.

Higher education

Our universities and polytechnics, too, must generate new ideas and train the skilled workforce of the next generation. We have unrivalled institutions and unrivalled inventive genius — as the number of British Nobel prize-winners shows. What matters is to bring the two close together and make the best practical use of both.

Britain has more students in professional training than Japan, and a greater proportion of young people in higher education than France or West Germany. More of our young people are now entering full-time degree courses than under the last Labour government. And a larger proportion of them complete their courses than in most other countries.

The very large sums of public money now going to higher education must be spent in the most effective way. Within that budget, we want to see a shift towards technological, scientific and engineering courses.

We have set aside money for 700 new posts for young lecturers over three years to bring new blood into research.

Over the next three years, we will provide for more teaching and research on information technology, with new posts for lecturers, and 2,200 new places for students.

Sport and recreation

The Government has increased the real level of funding for the Sports Council. The Urban Aid and Derelict Land Programmes have also contributed to new sporting projects. By these means, and by offering one pound of government money for every one pound raised locally, we have begun to transform sports facilities in the inner cities.

But there are still plenty of sports facilities which could be opened up to the general public. In particular, to reinforce our initiatives for better use of schools and playing fields, we shall urge every local education authority to make school and college premises available for use outside school hours and in the holidays. In all these initiatives, voluntary bodies will be enabled to play a bigger part.

We have kept up the pressure for public access to parks and reservoirs for anglers and all those who enjoy and respect the countryside.

Safety, quality and value for money

The best way to protect the consumer is to bring price rises down and keep them down, and to increase competition. We have achieved both, and so helped the housewife far more than any bureaucratic system of controls. We have also brought the state industries under the scrutiny of the Monopolies and Mergers Commission, and exposed many of them to competition to prevent them from exploiting their customers.

We shall remain vigilant in defence of the quality and safety of the products people buy. But we shall also reduce government intervention wherever it is unnecessary or harmful to the interests of the customer.

The provisions of our Data Protection Bill will meet public concern that computers pose a particular threat to privacy, and will enable us to ratify the European Convention on Data Protection.

Supporting family life

It is not for the Government to try to dictate how men and women should organise their lives. Our approach is to help people and their families fulfil their own aspirations in a rapidly changing world. As an employer, this Government is fulfilling its commitment to equal opportunities for men and women who work in the public services. We have brought forward for public discussion proposals for improving the tax treatment of married women, whether or not they go out to work.

We are reviewing the family jurisdiction of the courts, including their conciliation role, with a view to improving the administration of family law. We shall also reform the divorce laws to offer further protection to children, and to secure fairer financial arrangements when a marriage ends.

LAW, DEMOCRACY AND THE CITIZEN

The rule of law matters deeply to every one of us. Any concession to the thief, the thug or the terrorist undermines that principle which is the foundation of all our liberties. That is why we have remained firm in the face of the threats of hijackers and hunger strikers alike. The defeat of the occupation of the Iranian Embassy is only one example of our determination to be patient but still unyielding.

Backing the crime-fighters

We recognised from the start the immense and continuing public concern about lawlessness, particularly in some of our larger cities. We acted immediately to fulfil our pledges to give the hard-pressed police every possible backing.

The strength of the police force now stands at record levels: 9,000 extra policemen have been recruited in England and Wales alone since 1979. They are much better paid and equipped than ever before. We shall be ready to increase police establishments where necessary in the war against crime.

Thousands more policemen are back on the beat, where the public wishes to see them, instead of being isolated in panda cars. It takes time for any reform in police training and methods to achieve its full effect, but already street crime is being reduced and public confidence improved in some of the worst inner-city areas.

The proposals embodied in our Police and Criminal Evidence Bill will help the police to bring criminals to justice. At the same time, they will reinforce public support for the police by laying down clear rules for the proper treatment of suspects. We shall also build more courtrooms to reduce delays in trying criminal cases.

Last year's Criminal Justice Act has given the courts tougher and more flexible sentencing powers. This Act makes parents more responsible for crimes committed by their children, and improves compensation for the victims of crime.

Courts will also continue to impose Community Service Orders which compel offenders to make amends by doing useful work for the local community. We shall set up more compulsory attendance centres to which the courts can send young hooligans. The invaluable work of the Probation Service will continue to be supported.

There must be enough prison places to cope with sentences imposed by the courts. We shall complete our major programme of building which will provide another 4,800 places in ten new prisons. And we are recruiting more prison officers to staff them.

We will also respond to the increasing public concern over obscenity and offences against public decency, which often have links with serious crime. We propose to introduce specific legislation to deal with the most serious of these problems, such as the dangerous spread of violent and obscene video cassettes.

We accept the case for an independent prosecution service, and will consider how it might best be set up.

We intend to extend substantially the grounds that disqualify those with criminal records from serving on juries.

Dealing with crimes, civil disobedience, violent demonstrations and pornography are not matters for the police alone. It is teachers and parents — and television producers, too — who influence the moral standards of the next generation. There must be close co-operation and understanding between the police and the community they serve.

Immigration: firm and fair

We are utterly opposed to racial discrimination wherever it occurs, and we are determined to see that there is real equality of opportunity. The Conservative Party is, and always has been, strongly opposed to unfairness, harassment and persecution, whether it be inspired by racial, religious or ideological motives.

To have good community relations, we have to maintain effective immigration control. Since 1979, immigration for settlement has dropped sharply to the lowest level since control of immigration from the Commonwealth began more than twenty years ago. By passing the British Nationality Act, we have created a secure system of rights and a sound basis for control in the future; and we will continue to pursue policies which are strict but fair.

The supremacy of Parliament

Th British Constitution has outlasted most of the alternatives which have been offered as replacements. It is because we stand firm for the supremacy of Parliament that we are determined to keep its rules and procedures in good repair.

We have modernised the Select Committees to improve Parliament's ability to keep a check on the actions of the Executive. We shall continue to pursue sensible, carefully considered reforms where they are of practical value.

Labour want to abolish the House of Lords. We will ensure that it has a secure and effective future. A strong Second Chamber is a vital safeguard for democracy and contributes to good government.

Northern Ireland

In Northern Ireland, building upon the courage, commitment and increasing success of our security forces, we will give the highest priority to upholding law and order. We will continue to give the support essential for the Province to overcome its economic difficulties.

The people of Northern Ireland will continue to be offered a framework for participation in local democracy and political progress through the Assembly. There will be no change in Northern Ireland's constitutional position in the United Kingdom without the consent of the majority of people there, and no devolution of powers without widespread support throughout the community. We believe that a close practical working relationship between the United Kingdom and the Government of the Republic can contribute to peace and stability in Northern Ireland without threatening in any way the position of the majority community in the Province.

The quality of government

This country is fortunate to have a Civil Service with high standards of administration and integrity. The Civil Service has loyally and effectively helped to carry through the far-reaching changes we have made to secure greater economy, efficiency and better management in Government itself. It is a tribute to this spirit of co-operation that the number of civil servants has been reduced from 732,000 to 649,000 with the minimum of redundancies and with higher standards of service to the citizen. This has saved the taxpayer about £500m. a year, and is helping us to improve civil service working conditions.

The efficiency 'scrutinies' launched by Lord Rayner and other money-saving techniques have now identified savings worth £400m. a year to the taxpayer. We have abolished 500 Quangos and done away with no less than 3,600 different types of government forms.

We are successfully putting out to tender more services needed by central government. We shall press on with this wherever public money can be saved and standards of service maintained or improved.

Public spending is now planned in terms of hard cash instead of so-called constant prices, and the discipline of cash limits on spending has been extended. As a result, public spending is firmly under control.

Local government: saving ratepayers' money

We have checked the relentless growth of local government spending, and manpower is now back down to the level of 1974. The achievement of many Conservative authorities in savings ratepayers' money by putting services like refuse collection out to tender has played a major part in getting better value for money and significantly reducing the level of rate increases. We shall encourage every possible saving by this policy.

There are, however, a number of grossly extravagant Labour authorities whose exorbitant rate demands have caused great distress both to businesses and domestic ratepayers. We shall legislate to curb excessive and irresponsible rate increases by high-spending councils, and to provide a general scheme for limitation of rate increases for all local authorities to be used if necessary.

In addition, for industry we will require local authorities to consult local representatives of industry and commerce before setting their rates. We shall give more businesses the right to pay by instalments. And we shall stop the rating of empty industrial property.

The Metropolitan Councils and the Greater London Council have been shown to be a wasteful and unnecessary tier of government. We shall abolish them and return most of their functions to the boroughs and districts. Services which need to be administered over a wider area — such as police and fire, and education in inner London — will be run by joint boards of borough or district representatives.

IMPROVING OUR ENVIRONMENT

The Conservative Party has a long record of practical and effective action to improve the quality of life in our cities and countryside and to preserve our heritage. Since 1979, no government in Western Europe has done more for the environment — a clumsy word for many of the things that make life worth living.

Reviving Britain's cities

We have to cure the disastrous mistakes of decades of town-hall Socialism by striking a better balance between public and private effort. Our approach to reviving the rundown areas of our great cities is to use limited public money to stimulate much larger investment by private enterprise. The £60m. we have earmarked for the Urban Development Grant this year will be matched by up to four times that sum from private firms investing in new developments. On Merseyside, Operation Groundwork has brought together landowners, local industry and local authorities to tackle the squalor and dereliction on the edge of towns. The lessons of this and many other Merseyside initiatives will now be applied in other urban areas.

We have encouraged people to move back into the inner cities. Builders are not being helped to build homes of the type that young couples in particular can afford. We shall promote the revival of our inner cities, both by new building, and by sales by local councils of some of their rundown property to homesteaders who will restore the homes themselves.

We shall encourage greater opportunity for all those who live in our inner cities, including our ethnic minorities.

Our small business schemes are helping to bring firms back into the city centres, and the Enterprise Zones we have set up are already bringing new life to some of the hardest-hit places in industrial Britain.

We shall continue to give priority to the areas most in need. Our programme for the reclamation of derelict land will continue. We shall increase our efforts to secure the disposal of under-used public sector land, using the powers available to us in order to require sites to be sold for homes and jobs.

Public transport

We have already taken important steps to improve the standards of public transport. We have lifted restrictions on long-distance coach services. As a result, about one hundred new express coach services have been started, fares have been substantially reduced and comfort improved. We shall further relax bus licensing to permit a wider variety of services. We shall encourage the creation of smaller units in place of the monolithic public transport organisations which we have inherited from the Socialist past, and encourage more flexible forms of public transport. City buses and underground railways will still need reasonable levels of subsidy. But greater efficiency and more private enterprise will help keep costs down.

The GLC has grossly mismanaged London Transport. We shall set up a new London Regional Transport Authority for the underground, buses and commuter trains in the London area. This will provide the opportunity to split the different types of transport into separate operating bodies, put more services out to private tender and offer the passenger better performance.

In the country, we shall ensure better use of school and special buses for local communities. Restrictions on minibuses will be cut. So will the red tape which makes it so difficult for small firms and voluntary bodies to provide better ways to get around for those without cars, particularly the very old and the disabled.

We want to see a high-quality, efficient railway service. That does not mean simply providing ever-larger subsidies from the taxpayer. Nor, on the other hand, does it mean embarking upon a programme of major route closures. There is, however, scope for substantial cost reductions in British Rail which are needed to justify investment in a modern and efficient railway.

Fewer restrictive practices and much more attention to the customer are also essential. Rail services are now facing vigorous competition from coaches and cars, and they need to respond with more innovative and more modern work methods. We shall examine ways of decentralising BR and bringing in private enterprise to serve railway customers.

To make life more agreeable in our towns and villages, we will push ahead our bypass programme, which will help to take more lorries away from them.

Rural policy and animal welfare

Conservatives understand the need for a proper balance between the strengthening of the rural economy and the preservation of the beauty and habitat of our countryside. Economic development will be encouraged in areas where this balance can be best maintained. At the same time, we have introduced the Wildlife and Countryside Act — the most important piece of legislation yet affecting the countryside — to safeguard areas of natural beauty and sites of scientific interest.

We have taken the lead in the much acclaimed measures to save the whale from extinction and to protect seals, and we shall co-operate fully in the important international work to protect all endangered species.

Since 1979, we have been working to achieve full European agreement on the treatment of animals. We have introduced measures to improve the conditions of farm animals being transported or exported. There is nòw a European Convention on the Protection of Animals. We welcomed this agreement, and immediately introduced a White Paper on Animal Welfare to foreshadow changes in the law. We now propose to introduce legislation to update the Cruelty to Animals Act 1876 which will ensure more humane treatment of laboratory animals in scientific and industrial research. The sale of pet animals in street markets has been banned.

Controlling pollution

We intend to remove lead from petrol, and are taking the initiative with our European partners to achieve this at the earliest possible date. We will press ahead with our plans to reduce lead in paints, food and drinking water.

We will continue our policy to reduce river pollution — the length of polluted rivers has been halved in the last ten years, and this work will continue. We shall tighten up the controls on the disposal of hazardous waste and continue to support the movement for recycling and reclamation.

The worst problems of air pollution have been resolved. But in some areas the levels of smoke and sulphur dioxide need to be further reduced.

The peaceful application of nuclear energy, if properly controlled (as it always has been in this country), will be beneficial to the environment as well as to the economy. We intend to make sure that the safety record of the British nuclear industry continues to be second to none. The Sizewell Inquiry into Britain's first Pressurised Water Reactor is well under way. The project will go ahead only if both the independent inspector and the Government are satisfied it is safe.

Arts and the heritage

Despite the recession, this Government has strengthened its support for the best of our heritage and for the performing arts. We have created the National Heritage Memorial Fund, which fulfils the long-delayed wish to commemorate the dead of two world wars in a permanent and tangible way. We are building a new British Library. The new Commission for Ancient Monuments and Historic Buildings will both safeguard our heritage and give more people a chance to enjoy it. Under the Conservatives, Britain's opera, theatre and ballet continue to win world-wide renown. And our tax changes have helped to revive the British film industry. We shall keep up the level of government support, including a fair share for the regions. We shall also examine ways of using the tax system to encourage further growth in private support for the arts and the heritage.

BRITAIN IN THE WORLD

For nearly four decades, Europe has been at peace. The strength of the Western Alliance has kept our own freedom secure. The possession of nuclear weapons by both sides has been an effective deterrent to another war in Europe.

The policies which our Labour opponents now propose would put at risk all this hard-won security.

The protection of peace

The invasion of Afghanistan and the suppression of dissent in Poland remind us of the true nature of the Sovet Union. It remains a threat to the liberty and security of the West. The Soviet Union maintains massive armed forces in Europe, and is extending its naval power throughout the world. Soviet nuclear strength continues to grow, despite the false assurances of their propaganda machine.

Labour's support for gestures of one-sided disarmament is reckless and naive. There is no shred of evidence to suggest that the Soviet bloc would follow such an example.

Labour would give up Britain's nuclear deterrent and prevent the United States from using its bases in Britain which are part of its nuclear shield over Europe. That would shatter the NATO Alliance, and put our safety in the greatest jeopardy.

We will fully support the negotiations to reduce the deployment of nuclear weapons. But we will not gamble with our defence.

The Soviet Union now has over one thousand SS20 warheads, two-thirds of which are targeted on Europe. If the Soviet Union does not recognise over the coming months the legitimate anxieties of the West by agreeing to our proposals to eliminate this class of weapons, we will start deploying cruise missiles by the end of this year. Even after this, the West will remain entirely ready to negotiate for the removal of some or all of the missiles which we deploy, on the basis of a balanced and fair agreement with the Soviet Union.

The Western Alliance can keep the peace only if we can convince any potential aggressor that he would have to pay an unacceptable price. To do so, NATO must have strong conventional forces backed by a nuclear deterrent. And we in Britain must maintain our own independent nuclear contribution to British and European defence. At the same time, we shall continue to support all realistic efforts to reach balanced and verifiable agreements with the Soviet Union on arms control and disarmament.

We have substantially increased our defence expenditure in real terms. We have honoured our promise to give our regular and reserve forces proper pay and conditions and the equipment they need to do the job.

There could be no greater testimony to the professional dedication and the quality of equipment of the British Armed Services than the brilliant recapture of the Falkland Islands in just 74 days. We take pride in their achievement.

Civil defence

Our overriding desire and policy is to go on preserving peace.

However, no responsible government can simply assume that we shall never be attacked. To plan for civil defence is a humanitarian duty — not only against the possibility of nuclear, but also of conventional attack.

That is why we must take steps to provide the help that could be vital for millions. To proclaim a nuclear-free zone, as some Labour councils have, is a delusion.

The Conservative Government has accordingly carried out a thorough review of civil defence, brought forward new regulations to require local authorities to provide improved protection, strengthened the UK Warning and Monitoring Organisations, and nearly doubled spending on civil defence.

We propose to amend the Civil Defence Act 1948 to enable civil defence funds to be used in safeguarding against peacetime emergencies as well as against hostile attacks.

Britain in Europe

The creation of the European Community has been vital in cementing lasting peace in Europe and ending centuries of hostility. We came to office determined to make a success of British membership of the Community. This we have done.

Our first priority in 1979 was to cut our financial contribution to the Community Budget to a fairer level. Labour made a song and dance about renegotiating the terms, but had achieved nothing. The bill to British taxpayers soared.

We have stood up for Britain's interests, and substantially reduced our net contribution to the Community Budget. We have tenaciously sought a permanent alternative to the annual wrangles about refunds. Until we secure a lasting solution, we shall make sure of proper interim safeguards for this country. Meanwhile, with the help of Conservatives in the European Parliament, we shall continue to try to shift the Community's spending priorities away from agriculture and towards industrial, regional and other policies which help Britain more.

We shall continue both to oppose petty acts of Brussels bureaucracy and to seek the removal of unnecessary restrictions on the free movement of goods and services between member states, with proper safeguards to guarantee fair competition.

The Labour Party wants Britain to withdraw from the Community, because it fears that Britain cannot compete inside and that it would be easier to build a Socialist siege economy if we withdrew. The Liberals and the SDP appear to want Britain to stay in but never to upset our partners by speaking up forcefully. The Conservatives reject both extreme views.

The European Community is the world's largest trading group. It is by far our most important export market. Withdrawal would be a catastrophe for this country. As many as two million jobs would be at risk. We would lose the great export advantages and the attraction to overseas investors which membership now gives us. It would be a fateful step towards isolation, at which only the Soviet Union and her allies would rejoice.

A trading nation

Our most important contribution to a healthy world economy is to manage our own affairs successfully. We shall also build on our important role in promoting international action to encourage recovery through the IMF and other international organisations. With the other leading industrial nations, we shall continue with our realistic initiatives to improve currency stability in the Western world, and assist nations with excessive debts to regain stability. Together with the

Community, we are also playing a leading part in preserving an open world trading system, while safeguarding our most vulnerable industries.

While world trade declined last year, our exports and share of world trade increased, and we enjoyed a healthy balance of payments surplus, despite the pessimists who said the pound was uncompetitive. We believe in reinforcing success. This Government has given wholehearted support to British companies tendering for major overseas projects, and helped them secure many important contracts in the face of the toughest competition.

We will build on these initiatives to help our exporters, and vigorously promote the interests of British trade and industry in international negotiations — where we have already made our presence very effectively felt. We have no intention of becoming a dumping ground for the goods of other nations. We shall continue to challenge other nations' unfair barriers, whether in the shape of tariffs or trading practices.

Our wider role

In a troubled world, Britain is increasingly respected because we stand up for our own interests. But we are also respected because we stand up for the cause of freedom and the spread of prosperity throughout the world.

We resisted unprovoked aggression in the Falkland Islands, when the loyal support of our friends throughout the world reminded us of our common heritage of freedom. We will continue to uphold the principles for which we fought.

We shall continue to give our full support to the Commonwealth and to play an active and constructive part at the United Nations.

Our generous but carefully controlled aid programme is both an investment in the freedom and prosperity of the poorer countries and in a stable and expanding world economy. That programme helps us as well as those who receive it, since most of it is spent on British goods and services. More than many other nations, we direct our aid to the poorest countries, particularly in the Commonwealth.

But government aid is only a part of the total help we give the developing world. Unlike the Labour Party, we believe in permitting a free and profitable outflow of British investment. That flow to poorer countries has now grown far larger than British Government aid, bringing with it an invaluable transfer of skills and technology.

THE RESOLUTE APPROACH

This Government's approach is straightforward and resolute. We mean what we say. We face the truth, even when it is painful. And we stick to our purpose.

Most decisions worth taking are difficult. Cutting a clear path through the jungle of a modern bureaucracy is hard going. The world recession of the past four years, and the high level of unemployment throughout the industrial world, have made the going harder.

During these difficult years, we have protected the sick and the elderly. We have maintained Britain's defences and her contribution to the Western Alliance. And at the same time, we have laid the foundations for a dynamic and prosperous future.

The rewards are beginning to appear. If we continue on our present course with courage and commonsense, those rewards should multiply in the next five years.

We shall never lose sight of the British traditions of fairness and tolerance. We are also determined to revive those other British qualities — a genius for invention and a spirit of enterprise.

Under Conservative government, confidence is brushing aside pessimism at home. Abroad, Britain is regarded for the first time in years as a country with a great future as well as a great past.

We mean to make that future a reality.

The Labour Party:

'The New Hope for Britain'

Foreword by Michael Foot

Here you can read Labour's plan to do the things crying out to be done in our country today.

To get Britain back to work. To rebuild our shattered industries. To get rid of the ever-growing dole queues. To protect and enlarge our National Health Service and our other great social services. To help stop the nuclear arms race. Here you can see what Labour is determined to do, and how we shall set about it.

But at once the objection is raised: Can we afford it? Where will the money come from? Are we not just making promises which cannot be fulfilled?

You will find the detailed answers here. But let us emphasise a few of them at once.

The first short, sharp answer is that what Britain cannot afford is the present policy of accepting mass unemployment. Mass unemployment on the scale Mrs Thatcher and her government have been prepared to tolerate — worse than we have ever known before and worse than any other industrial country has experienced — imposes a crushing burden on the whole community.

Of course it hits hardest the young denied work altogether, and their mothers and fathers thrown out of their jobs with little chance of getting another. But it also hits the whole country.

Mass unemployment costs the country £15 billion, £16 billion, £17 billion a year, astronomic figures never conceived possible before, and they move higher still every month. Mass unemployment is the main reason why most families in Britain, all but the very rich, are paying more in taxes today than they did four years ago when the Conservatives promised to cut them for everybody. Mass unemployment is the main reason why we are wasting our precious North Sea oil riches. Since 1979 Mrs Thatcher's government has had the benefit of £20 billion in tax revenues from the North Sea. It has all been swallowed by the huge, mounting cost of mass unemployment. And the oil won't last for ever, although, according to Mrs Thatcher's economics, the unemployment will.

Our country, no civilised country, can afford the human waste, the industrial and economic waste, involved in these policies. We in the Labour Party reject them absolutely, and we describe in this Manifesto the real constructive alternative, *and how we shall pay for it.*

See, first, our Emergency Programme of Action to be started immediately we are given the power. Most of these measures are designed to start the drive for expansion, and the cost of them has been added up. How fast can the country escape for the present stagnant rut? That is the *real* question.

Just a week before Sir Geoffrey Howe, the Tory Chancellor, produced his last Budget to keep us in the rut, Peter Shore, Labour's Shadow Chancellor, produced his budget for expansion. The costs he set out — an £11 billion expansion — would cover, as they were designed to cover, the items we have listed in the Emergency Programme, the promises we have tabulated. So little is it true that Labour has not counted the cost. No party in opposition has ever stated its intentions so clearly and comprehensively.

Then what happens? What happens after the first expansion is launched? Here in these pages we describe the conditions for success, the pace we can move forward, how that will depend on the response we can secure from all sections of the community, on the partnership we have established with the trade unions. Without that continuing partnership to rebuild our country, all else will fail. True enough; but Labour is the only party which has worked for this partnership and pledges it for the future.

And where will the money come from? Some of it will come from those oil revenues now pouring down the drain. Some of it will come from the billions we waste on the dole queues. Some of it will come from the billions now being allowed to be exported in investment abroad. Yes, and some of it will be *borrowed*, Mrs Thatcher's dirty word.

But borrowing in that sense is what every intelligent government since the war in Britain has done — including even Conservative governments. Borrowing in that sense is what has been done by other governments in this world slump who have kept their unemployment much lower than ours — and their inflation rates low too.

Of course the slump can be beaten, if we have the will and the right policies. The European governments which have survived it best have been mostly socialist governments rejecting Thatcherite nostrums. And the whole wider experience of the Western world since 1945 *proves* what can be done when governments set before them full employment as a target. Is it truly realistic and practical to cast all that knowledge aside? It is just not true that mass unemployment must be accepted.

Rather, if nothing can be done about unemployment, nothing truly enduring can be done about anything else. Allow it to persist and it will corrode the rest of our society. It will make more deeply endemic than ever the injustices, the bitter hardships, which afflict so many of our people. So let's put a stop to defeatism, and put a stop too to all those sermons about Victorian values. The Labour movement — the Labour Party and the trade unions acting together — came into being, as one of our poets, Idris Davies, said, to end "the long Victorian night". It was a fight to introduce civilised standards into the world of ruthless, devil-take-the-hindmost individualism.

Particularly after our 1945 victory, when Labour had a majority, we set to work creating a real community in which the strong would come to the aid of the weak, in which the profit test would have to make way for the human test. It was the Labour Party which created — to take just one example — the National Health Service, in the teeth of bitter Tory opposition. Labour will come to the rescue of that service and make it worthy of those who founded it, those who serve it, and the patients who need it most of all. It is a commonsense example of democratic socialism in action.

Of course, we know that the full work of rebuilding will not be easy. Of course we know that, thanks to world conditions and the Conservative years of destruction and decay, our task is made much harder.

But the programme of socialist reconstruction outlined in these pages, can be carried through if a Labour government commands the support of the other great democratic institutions in the land — in particular the local authorities and the trade unions. Labour is the only party which desires and can secure the working partnership between the government and the trade unions essential to national recovery.

Above all, the new Labour government will play a much more ambitious part in helping to guide the nation towards peace, and, as an essential part of the process, in establishing a sensible defence policy for our country. One bunch of smears and scares with which Tory propagandists have already disfigured this election campaign suggests that the Labour Party proposes to throw away our defences, to abandon our alliances. It is just not true. And it should not be forgotten that one of the last acts of Mrs Thatcher's government was to stop the debate in the House of Commons when these slanders could have been nailed.

What we do propose to do is to get rid of the nuclear boomerangs which offer no genuine protection to our people but, first and foremost, to help stop the nuclear arms race which is the most dangerous threat to us all.

One of the most wretched features of the present government's record has been the low interest they have devoted to the work of securing international disarmament. No British initiative of any significance in this field has been taken. Instead, the programme for establishing American-controlled Cruise missiles on our soil has been accepted without question, and the Trident programme for the expansion of the British-controlled nuclear force has been accepted without reference to the possibilities of disarmament. Indeed, the logic of the case of the nuclear deterrent, presented by British Conservative Ministers, is that all peace-loving countries should equip themselves with the same protection. It is a logic which would intensify the race and destroy the universe.

The first task of a new Labour government will be to restore a sense of sanity in dealing with these supreme questions. We offer a combined programme of action by this country and of action in association with other countries. We are the only party that offers such a programme to meet the scale of the challenge. We are the only party that offers a non-nuclear defence policy. But we are not alone in our plans and our aspirations. Multitudes of people in many other lands, on both sides of the Atlantic, in Asia and Africa and Europe too, are ready to join us in the campaign for a nuclear freeze, for fresh exertions to stop the proliferation of these weapons, to stop the whole monstrous nuclear race to destruction.

In this campaign document we set out Labour's alternative to mass unemployment. We explain how a Labour government will help to stop the nuclear arms race. We provide a radical programme of action, for a full, five-year parliament, to save British industry and rebuild the welfare state.

The years of Tory failure

When the Tories took office in May 1979, unemployment was falling and the economy growing. Living standards had gone up by a sixth in two years, and North Sea oil held out the prospect of economic growth, high levels of employment and better social services. All this was thrown away by the Tories. Nearly three and a quarter million men and women are now out of work, even on the official count. Plant after plant forced to close. Manufacturing production down by a fifth.

Investment cut by a third. Our domestic markets captured by imports of manufactured goods.

After four years of Mrs Thatcher, Britain is a poorer country. We have fared far worse than any other major industrial country. The unprecedented advantage of North Sea oil and gas — worth, in tax revenues alone, 8p in the pound on income tax — has been squandered, with nothing whatsoever to show for it.

What have all these sacrifices achieved? Our economy today is weaker, not stronger, than in 1979. There is no prospect of real economic growth. Indeed, the Tories no longer dare to predict when unemployment will begin to fall. True enough, inflation, after being forced to record levels by the Tories, has been brought down. But look at the cost in jobs, in poorer housing, in living standards, and in lost opportunities for our youth. And now inflation is set to increase again, with interest rates and mortgate rates likely to rise too.

The legacy of four Tory years goes beyond unemployment and industrial decline; beyond the damage done to our social services; beyond even the dangerous commitment to new nuclear weapons. It is expressed in the deep sense of bitterness, distrust and despair now felt among so many sections of the community. Our task will be to heal these wounds and rekindle among the British people a new sense of unity and common purpose.

EMERGENCY PROGRAMME OF ACTION

Within days of taking office, Labour will begin to implement an emergency programme of action, to bring about a complete change of direction for Britain. Our priority will be to create jobs and give a new urgency to the struggle for peace. In many cases we will be able to act immediately. In others, which involve legislation, they will take longer to bring into effect. But in all cases we shall act swiftly and with determination. This is what we plan to do. We will:

Launch a massive programme for expansion. We will:

Provide a major increase in public investment, including transport, housing and energy conservation.

Begin a huge programme of construction, so that we can start to build our way out of the slump.

Halt the destruction of our social services and begin to rebuild them, by providing a substantial increase in resources.

Increase investment in industry, especially in new technology — with public enterprise taking the lead. And we will steer new industry and jobs to the regions and the inner cities.

Ensure that the pound is competitive; and hold back prices through action on VAT, rents, rates and fares.

Introduce a cash programme of employment and training, with new job subsidies and allowances.

Begin to rebuild British industry, working within a new framework for planning and industrial democracy. We will:

Agree a new national economic assessment, setting out the prospects for growth in the economy.

Prepare a five-year national plan, in consultation with unions and employers.

Back up these steps with a new National Investment Bank, new industrial powers, and a new Department for Economic and Industrial Planning.

Repeal Tory legislation on industrial relations and make provision for introducing industrial democracy.

Begin the return to public ownership of those public industries sold off by the Tories.

Start to create a fairer Britain, with decent social services for all. We will:

Raise child benefits by £2 a week, and give special help to one-parent families and families with disabled dependants.

Uprate the pension in November 1983 by the full amount needed to protect against inflation; and increase pensions by £1.45 a week for a single person and £2.25 for a married couple.

Provide more resources for the health service with an increase of at least 3 per cent a year in real terms.

Improve the personal social services, such as meals on wheels and home helps, with an increase of at least 4 per cent a year in real terms.

Spend more on education, including on essential books and equipment; and the assisted place scheme; and stop selection in secondary schools.

Begin to develop comprehensive care for the under-fives.

Begin to develop a strategy to eliminate low pay.

Introduce positive action programmes to promote women's rights and opportunities, and appoint a cabinet minister to promote equality between the sexes. We will:

Strengthen the Equal Pay Act and the Sex Discrimination Act.

Improve child care and other social services.
Take steps to end discrimination in education and training.
Reverse Tory cuts in maternity rights.
Increase the maternity grant.

Encourage and assist local authorities to begin a massive programme of *house-building and improvement*, through an immediate 50 per cent increase in their housing investment programmes. Priority will go to the urgent repair and replacement of run-down estates. We will freeze all rents for the first full year.

Begin a major programme to stop the waste of *energy*. We will stop Sizewell and abandon the Tory PWR programme; and open urgent discussions, with the unions and management in the coal industry, on a new Plan for Coal.

Give more help to public transport, with funds to increase investment — especially in rail electrification and better freight facilities. Councils will be given new powers to support local services.

Act to *improve the environment and deal with pollution* — including a ban on lead in petrol. An urgent start will be made on improving our inner cities, including action on derelict land and buildings.

Introduce a positive action programme for the *ethnic minorities*. We will also introduce citizenship and immigration laws which do not discriminate against either women or black and Asian Britons.

Give a new priority to *open government* at local and national levels, and give local communities greater freedom to manage their own affairs. We will also introduce an early Bill to abolish the legislative powers of the House of Lords.

In *international policy*, we shall take new initiatives to promote peace and development. We will:

Cancel the Trident programme, refuse to deploy Cruise missiles and begin discussions for the removal of nuclear bases from Britain, which is to be completed within the lifetime of the Labour government.
Ban arms sales to repressive regimes.
Increase aid to developing countries towards the UN target of 0.7 per cent.
Re-establish a separate Ministry of Overseas Development.
Take action to protect the status of refugees in Britain.

We will also open immediate negotiations with our EEC partners, and introduce the necessary legislation, to prepare for *Britain's withdrawal from the EEC*, to be completed well within the lifetime of the Labour government.

A five-year programme

Labour's emergency programme of action will get Britain on the road to recovery. But on its own it will not be enough to establish a fairer, more prosperous, more caring Britain.

The programme we set out in the pages which follow is, therefore, for a full, five-year term of office. Clearly, we cannot do everything at once. The economy has been dangerously weakened by the Tories, and Britain is considerably poorer than when we were last in government. The world recession could hamper our plans for economic revival.

Moreover, our proposals add up to a considerable increase in public spending. Our programme is thus heavily dependent upon the achievement of our basic objectives: namely, a large and sustained increase in the nation's output and income on a matching decline in the numbers out of work. It is this that will make the resources available for higher public spending programmes and cut the enormous cost of unemployment. Even so, some of our commitments will be phased in over a number of years. At each stage, clearly, we shall have to choose carefully our priorities.

Ending mass unemployment

The present hideous level of unemployment is not an accident. It is the direct result of the policies of this government. The Tories have cut public investment and services, and increased taxes, taking spending power out of the economy and destroying jobs in both public and private sectors alike. They have forced up interest rates and kept the pound too high — a combination that has crippled British industry, and helped lose us markets at home and abroad.

Our approach is different. We will expand the economy by providing a strong and measured increase in spending. Spending money creates jobs. Money spent on railway electrification means jobs, not only in construction, but also in the industries that supply the equipment — as well as faster and better trains. If we increase pensions and child benefits, it means more spending power for the elederly and for parents, more bought in shops, more orders for goods, and more jobs in the factories. More spending means that the economy will begin to expand: and growth will provide the new wealth for higher wages and better living standards, the right climate for industry to invest, and more resources for the public services.

Our central aim will be to reduce unemployment to below a million within five years of taking office. We recognise the enormous scale of this task. When we set this as our target, unemployment was 2.8 million, according to the official figures. On this basis, it is now at least 3.2 million. Our target will thus be all the more difficult to achieve. It remains, however, the central objective of our economic policy.

To achieve it we will need five years of economic growth, with a Labour government carrying through all of the industrial, financial and economic policies outlined here. But we will also work with other governments — especially socialist governments — to bring about a co-ordinated expansion of our economies.

Economic expansion will make it possible to end the waste of mass unemployment. But it will also reduce the human costs of unemployment — the poverty, the broken homes, the increase in illness and suicides. And it will provide the resources we need to increase social spending, as we must, at least in line with the growth of the economy.

How will we pay for it?

Given our commitment to increase public spending, it is right that people should ask: how will we pay for it?

It would be wrong to finance the initial boost to spending by increasing taxation. Only if ours was a fully employed economy would this be the right way of doing it. But our economy today is chronically under-employed. We have people out of work, idle plant, and unused savings. To finance expansion by increasing taxation in these circumstances would be wrong. For the increased spending in one part of the economy would be cancelled out by decreased expenditure elsewhere. Of course, once the economy gets much nearer to full employment, some taxes will have to be increased, both to shift the tax balance towards those who can best afford to pay, and to help finance our social programme.

Like any other expanding industrial enterprise, we shall borrow to finance our programme of investment. This is better than borrowing, as the Tories are doing, in order to pay for the dole queue or to provide finance for the Argentine government to buy arms.

There is no shortage of savings in the country available for borrowing today. Indeed, vast amounts of British money — more than the government's total borrowing requirement last year — are flowing into overseas investment. For with our present slump, there is not the demand for investment here.

But the scale of borrowing will not be nearly as great as the increase in spending. Spending generates new income and new savings. As the economy recovers we shall be able to spend less on keeping people unemployed. And when people get jobs they will also pay income tax and spend more on goods which are taxed. Last year benefit payments, and tax revenues foregone — because of unemployment — cost the nation some £17,000 million. There are also important savings to be made by cancelling the present government's massive expenditure programmes on Trident and on PWR nuclear reactors.

WORKING TOGETHER

At the heart of our programme is Labour's new partnership with the trade unions. Our policies have been worked out with them. The Tories take pride in rejecting any chance of constructive co-operation with the trade unions. But it is the nation that has paid the price — the economy in ruins, and industrial relations a battlefield. We believe that there is a better way: to harness the goodwill and co-operation of working people and to work together to create a better life for all.

Our starting point in government will be to discuss and agree with the trade unions a national economic assessment, as described in our joint statement with the TUC, *Partners in Rebuilding Britain*. This will set out the likely growth in the national output and how it could be shared. It will cover the allocation of resources, and the distribution of income between profits, earnings from employment, rents, social benefits and other incomes. It will also take into account our policies on the redistribution of income and wealth, not least through the reform of taxation. It will take a view on what changes in costs and prices would be compatible with our economic and social objectives, and help to ensure that our plan for expansion is not undermined by inflation. We will not, however, return to the old policies of government-imposed wage restraint. The assessment will thus play a crucial part in our national plan.

The assessment will also play an important role in Labour's plans for the redistribution of wealth and power in our society. For, as we emphasise in *Labour's Programme*, our aim is nothing less than to bring about 'a fundamental and irreversible shift in the balance of power and wealth in favour of working people and their families'.

An offensive against low pay

The next Labour government will launch an offensive against low pay as part of our strategy for equality. The problem of low pay remains acute both in relative and absolute terms. If low pay at present is defined as less than two-thirds of average male manual earnings, there were 3 million full-time low-paid workers in 1982, of whom over 2 million were women workers. Adding to these figures young workers, part-time workers and homeworkers produces a total in the region of almost 6 million — a great majority of whom are women.

We will work together with the unions to tackle low pay and extend the concept of fair wages and arbitration. We will strengthen the Equal Pay Act. We strongly emphasise the principles of fairness and proper comparability, and will ensure machinery is available for the trade unions to establish these principles. We will also discuss with the TUC the possibility of introducing a statutory minimum wage.

Industrial democracy

Industrial democracy is vital to the success of the national plan. We believe that working people must have clear and definite rights to a say in running their firms — and to an influence in economic planning. We will give new statutory rights to workers — through their trade unions — on information, consultation and representation within their companies. These are described in our joint statement with the TUC, *Economic Planning and Industrial Democracy*. But we will work out with the unions concerned what this means for the individual industries and firms.

We will repeal the divisive Tory 'employment' laws and provide new statutory support for collective bargaining. We will also give proper employment protection to women and to home-workers, part-time workers and temporary workers.

The Tories' cut-backs in the work of the Health and Safety Commission will be reversed. Labour will actively support the commission and the role of joint safety committees in the work place.

SAFEGUARDS FOR EXPANSION

Increased spending will not be enough to ensure sustained economic growth. Spending will not create jobs if it is soaked up by imports. We must not allow firms to use a return to growth as an excuse to put up prices. It will, in addition, be essential to co-ordinate expansion so proper investment is made for the future.

First, we will see that our financial and monetary policies support expansion. We will make sure that public borrowing is financed, through the financial institutions and national savings, without disruptive or damaging changes in interest rates.

Second, exchange controls — maintained by successive British governments since 1939; and so foolishly scrapped by the Tories in 1979 — will be re-introduced. This will help to counter currency speculation and to make available — to industry and government in Britain — the large capital resources that are now flowing overseas.

Third, we must ensure that our trade and balance of payments contribute to our expansion. This means maintaining the pound at a realistic and competitive rate. Tory monetary policies have kept interest rates far too high, pushing the pound beyond its competitive value. An overpriced pound taxes exports and subsidises imports. Our balance of trade, other than North Sea oil, has been seriously damaged as a result. A competitive exchange rate will assist British exports abroad and make British goods more competitive at home.

A policy for imports

But we must also plan ahead so that, as the economy expands, we keep our exports and imports in balance. We must therefore be ready to act on imports directly: first, in order to safeguard key industries that have been seriously put at risk by Tory policy; and second, so as to check the growth of imports should they threaten to outstrip our exports and thus our plan for expansion. We will:

Use agreed development plans, which we shall negotiate with the large companies that dominate our economy, so as to influence their purchasing and development policies. Our aim will be to prevent excessive import penetration and promote our own exports.

Use public purchasing policy to help support our strategy.

Introduce back-up import controls, using tariffs and quotas, if these prove necessary, to achieve our objective of trade balance — upon which sustained expansion depends.

Our purpose in trade policy is not to reduce trade but to make possible an orderly expansion of imports, paid for by our growing export trade. We will thus be able to replace the present policies of deflation, which restrict world trade, by policies of expansion, which increase world trade. We will also encourage international action for expansion and increased world trade.

Within the framework of an orderly expansion of trade, we will also seek to give real preferences to imports from developing countries, particularly from the poorest countries, except where this will create acute problems for particular industries in this country.

Prices — controlling inflation

The Tories have used mass unemployment to control inflation. We completely reject this approach. We believe it is madness to keep people out of work deliberately. Our priority will be to expand the economy and create jobs. But we are also determined to prevent soaring prices. Expansion will in itself help cut the costs of production and therefore hold back prices. But we will use other measures to help restrain inflation. We will:

Use direct measures of price restraint, such as cutting VAT, and subsidies on basic products, to cut into inflation as and when necessary.

Stop using public sector charges, such as gas prices — up by 116 per cent since 1979 — as a back-door way of raising taxes, as the Tories have done.

Buy our food where it is cheaper, on world markets, following Britain's withdrawal from the EEC.

Give powers to a new Price Commission to investigate companies, monitor price increases and order price freezes and reductions. These controls will be closely linked to our industrial planning, through agreed development plans with the leading, price-setting firms.

Take full account of these measures in the *national economic assessment*, to be agreed each year with the trade unions. The assessment will also take account of the impact of cost increases on the future rate of inflation.

Value for money

The Tories say that 'competition' ensures that shoppers get a fair deal. The customers know better. Stronger legal safeguards are essential to protect customers — not least from shoddy goods. And shoppers must know their rights and be able to enforce them. We will undertake an urgent and comprehensive review of consumer law and reform it. We will also bring in new safeguards on advertising. We will:

Establish a major public service facility — a Product Research Unit — to test products and manufacturers' claims about them, and to publicise the results widely.

Set up consumer advice centres in all main shopping centres, with mobile units for rural areas.

Provide simple court procedures for small claims, stronger trade codes of practice placed on to a statutory basis, and adequate penalties for trading offences.

See that all public enterprises give a high priority to dealing with consumer complaints and needs — and back them with stronger consumer councils.

Introduce a code of advertising practice, on a statutory basis, to be administered by the office of Fair Trading; and provide powers to order advertisements to be substantiated, withdrawn or corrected with equal prominence.

REBUILDING OUR INDUSTRY

The Tories have been a disaster for British industry. Plants and companies have closed, skilled workers have been laid off, markets at home and abroad have been lost to our competitors. Industry has not invested enough, and it has failed to develop and exploit the new technologies as successfully as other industrial countries.

We must rebuild our industrial strength — and we can do so under a Labour Government working together with unions and managers, to plan Britain's industrial development. Our aim is not just to save companies and factories from closing down. We intend to create new companies and new science-based industries — using new public enterprise to lead the way, and supported by the development of industrial democracy.

In our joint statement with the TUC, *Economic Planning and Industrial Democracy*, and in *Labour's Programme 1982*, we show how it can be done. We will:

Develop a new five-year national plan to coordinate expansion and public spending with plans for individual industries and regions. We will create a powerful new Department of Economic and Industrial Planning.

Involve the trade unions and management in planning at every level with a new, tripartite National Planning Council.

Link planning at all levels firmly to a radical extension of industrial democracy. New statutory rights will enable workers to draw up plans for their own enterprise and sectors of industry, which we will seek to incorporate into our strategy.

Make our planning flexible, so that it is able to respond quickly to changing circumstances and take full account of changing needs and preferences. We are opposed to any kind of rigid planning from the centre. But we will seek to develop a firm sense of strategic direction.

Negotiate agreed development plans with all leading companies — national and multinational, public and private — so that such companies play a constructive role in supporting the national plan and our plans for individual regions and sectors.

Support these agreed development plans with new industrial powers, including discretionary price controls, financial support and access to credit; and take powers to invest in individual companies, to purchase them outright or to assume temporary control.

Monitor closely the activities of multinational companies, through a Foreign Investment Unit. All UK-based multinationals will have to operate within clearly laid-down guidelines.

Develop regional development plans, with plans also being drawn up at local level by local authorities. Regional development agencies will be established, extending our present commitment to a Northern Development Agency to other English regions in need of them. These agencies will have similar powers and resources to those in Scotland and Wales. We will also consider using new regional job subsidies.

Strengthen the NEB, the Scottish and Welsh Development Agencies, and the Industrial Development Board in Northern Ireland. We will give them, and the new development agencies, adequate resources for investment and acquisition.

Public and co-operative enterprise

We will use public and co-operative enterprise to support our planning and as a major source of technical innovation. We will:

Encourage and help existing public enterprises to expand and diversify. They will be given far more freedom to raise funds on capital markets.

Return to public ownership the public assets and rights hived off by the Tories, with compensation of no more than that received when the assets were denationalised. We will establish a significant public stake in electronics, pharmaceuticals, health equipment and building materials, and also in other important sectors, as required in the national interest.

Give generous encouragement and help to worker co-operatives and local enterprise boards. We will establish a Co-operative Investment Bank. The development agencies and local authorities will be empowered to support and to help establish co-operatives and local enterprise boards. We will give new rights to workers to convert their firms into co-operatives.

Labour will also support key industries in the public sector. We will:

Prevent the further decline of both public and private sectors of the *steel industry* so that the industry can, through planned investment, meet the rising demand from economic expansion. We will retain the five major BSC plants and see that a larger share of the home market is met from UK production. A major public presence will also be established in the steel stock-holding industry.

Develop our *aerospace industries*. We will ensure that proper levels of research, development and investment take place, and that the industries have the capacity and skills needed to compete as equals in the world market. The British Aerospace Corporation will be re-established as a major public enterprise.

Support the *shipbuilding industry*, which is vital for a maritime nation such as Britain, with interests in merchant shipping, the Navy, offshore oil and gas resources and fishing. Labour will establish a maritime strategy embracing both shipbuilding and shipping interests. We will re-establish the British Shipbuilding Corporation as a public sector company with a new financial basis and adequate resources for investment.

Telecommunications

A national cable system will make possible a wide range of new telecommunications services, greater variety in the provision of televison, and a major stimulus to British technology and industry. But it must be under firm public control. A publicly-owned British Telecommunications will thus be given the sole responsibility to create a national, broadband network (including Mercury, the new privately-owned telecommunications system for business), which integrates telecommunications and broadcasting.

Science and technology

Science and technology are essential to Britain's economic and social regeneration. The Tories have undermined research and development in the science-based research industries of the future. Cuts in higher education threaten our fundamental research. Industry devotes less to research and development than any other of our major industrial competitors. Defence accounts for over 80 per cent of government research funds in industry.

The fall in output, together with the lack of planning and retraining, has meant that new technology has brought major job losses in some sectors. Only Labour can plan new technology to meet our commitment to full employment. We will:

Guarantee adequate funding for higher education, the research councils and government research establishments.

Use the National Investment Bank to channel funds from the financial institutions into long-term investment in new technology.

Work together with trade unions to plan an expansion of new technology, in particular using it to aid a product-based recovery of the economy. New technology agreements, for proper safeguards and retraining for the work-force, will be extended.

Strengthen the links between research by higher education and industry to help greater industrial innovation.

Increase technological literacy in schools and give boys and girls equal opportunities to study science and technology.

Promote the supply of engineers and technicians, including women, to meet the needs of industry and the community.

Ensure that research and development are directed towards society's needs, with a reduction in the present high proportion of defence research.

Promote the development and use of new information and communication services to support a wider democracy.

Finance for industry

It is essential that industry has the finance it needs to support our plans for increased investment. Our proposals are set out in full in our Conference statement, *The Financial Institutions*. We will:

Establish a National Investment Bank to put new resources from private institutions and from the government — including North Sea oil revenues — on a large scale into our industrial priorities. The bank will attract and channel savings, by agreement, in a way that guarantees these savings and improves the quality of investment in the UK.

Exercise, through the Bank of England, much closer direct control over bank lending. Agreed development plans will be concluded with the banks and other financial institutions.

Create a public bank operating through post offices, by merging the National Girobank, National Savings Bank and the Paymaster General's Office.

Set up a Securities Commission to regulate the institutions and markets of the City, including Lloyds, within a clear statutory framework.

Introduce a new Pension Schemes Act to strengthen members' rights in occupational pension schemes, clarify the role of trustees, and give members a right to equal representation, through their trade unions, on controlling bodies of the schemes.

Set up a tripartite investment monitoring agency to advise trustees and encourage improvements in investment practices and strategies.

We expect the major clearing banks to co-operate with us fully on these reforms, in the national interest. However, should they fail to do so, we shall stand ready to take one or more of them into public ownership. This will not in any way affect the integrity of customers' deposits.

EMPLOYMENT AND TRAINING

The long-term unemployed — the men and women who have suffered most from the Tory onslaught — will benefit directly from economic expansion and our policies on regional development. But special measures are also needed. By the end of our first five years, our aim is that no-one will be out of work for more than a year without receiving an offer of a job or training place.

We will act quickly to save jobs and stop the further destruction of industry. We will expand the schemes for compensating firms that avoid redundancy and provide temporary jobs for the long-term unemployed. We will widen the Job Release Scheme and offer employment subsidies to firms, linked to agreements with them to preserve and create jobs. We will also provide major increases in youth and adult training, with special provision for women, ethnic minorities and the disabled; and integrate a reformed Youth Training Scheme into our scheme for a two-year student-traineeship.

Industry has been badly hit by the collapse of training under the Tories. Expansion must not be held back by shortages of skilled labour; and people without work must have the skills needed to take up the available jobs. We will:

Introduce a new statutory framework, linking adult training with initial training. This will also place a statutory duty on employers to carry out training and establish joint workplace training committees. Adequate funds will be provided jointly by industry and government.

Give the Manpower Services Commission the authority and resources it needs to do the job. The commission will develop its regional and local structures, advise companies on their plans for manpower, and get advance notice of redundancies.

Ensure that the MSC develops a national job centre network and reverses the cutbacks in occupational guidance and help for disadvantaged job seekers. We will take urgent steps to abolish private employment agencies.

Working time in Britain, over the life-time of individual workers, is among the highest in industrial countries. We will work through collective bargaining to reduce working time; and this will include more flexible working arrangements, more time off for study, longer holidays, earlier voluntary retirement with adequate pensions — with progress towards our aim of a common pension age of 60 — and a 35 hour week.

Equal rights at work

Labour's aim is to create equal rights at work for women and to overcome the effects of past discrimination. We will:

Expand *Positive Action Programmes* to eliminate discrimination, change employment practices and introduce special training schemes to equip women to enter non-traditional areas of work.

Carry out these programmes throughout the public sector, ensure that public-sector contracts include a commitment to positive action, and press employers and unions to negotiate these programmes through joint equal opportunities committees at the workplace. These proposals will be backed, if necessary, by a statutory duty on employers.

Strengthen the Sex Discrimination and Equal Pay Acts to make them more effective. We will shift the burden of proof from the complainant to the alleged discriminator, incorporate the concept of indirect discrimination and introduce the principle of equal pay for work of equal value.

End the distinction between part-time and full-time workers in terms of rights, hourly pay-rates and conditions, and extend greater employment protection to homeworkers and women on maternity leave.

We also aim to create equality of opportunity and treatment for black workers, and similar positive action programmes will be carried through on their behalf.

ENERGY

Energy is vital to our future as an industrial nation. We will plan its supply and demand more carefully and save more of the energy we use. As outlined in *Labour's Programme 1982*, we will:

Ensure that everyone can afford adequate heat and light at home.

Give priority to the coal industry and the use of coal as a fuel. We will seek to re-establish the tripartite machinery set up under Labour and prepare a new Plan for Coal. We will also replace old plant with coal-fired stations.

Assist major towns and cities to set up combined heat and power schemes.

Begin a massive conservation programme, led by insulation for council housing, and giving incentives to industry on agreed plans to save energy. The programme will be managed by a new Energy Conservation Agency.

Greatly increase spending on the development of renewable sources.

Stop Sizewell and scrap the Tory PWR programme. The need for a continuing nuclear programme based on the British AGR will be reassessed when we come to office.

Re-establish the Energy Commission to advise on the preparation and annual review of a comprehensive energy plan.

Transfer the whole of the National Nuclear Corporation to the public sector.

Energy costs now represent a major part of family budgets. We will aim to reduce these costs, both by conservation and by introducing new fuel allowances.

We will bring Britoil back into public ownership and combine it with BNOC to create a powerful national oil corporation with full powers to engage in all aspects of oil-related activities. We will restore to the new corporation a minimum 50 per cent stake in all fields discovered since 1975; and, in line with our objective to bring North Sea oil into public ownership and control, the public sector will have the dominant role in all future oil and gas exploration and development in the North Sea. We reaffirm our commitment to achieving full public control and ownership of British Petroleum, in order to make it an effective agent of a nationally directed oil policy.

FOOD, FISHING AND AGRICULTURE

Britain needs a food and agriculture policy much more in line with our needs — and this is one of the prime reasons for leaving the EEC. Instead of the inflated prices of the EEC's Common Agricultural Policy, we will support our agriculture through deficiency payments — coupled, where necessary, with limited intervention buying and direct income support.

As we describe in *Labour's Programme 1982*, we will conduct an 'annual assessment' of the industry, after consultation with all those concerned. This will set the level of support given to the industry. Labour will also negotiate long-term supply agreements with agricultural producing nations; establish commodity agencies and support marketing co-operatives; and, where helpful, extend marketing boards to other sectors.

Together with the trade unions we will work to close the gap between agricultural and industrial earnings, and replace the Agricultural Wages Board with a statutory joint industrial council. We will also act to improve farm safety, provide statutory support for workers' safety representatives, and end pay discrimination against women workers.

We will give a new deal to the fishing industry. We will draw up a National Fisheries Plan so as to take full advantage of our withdrawal from the EEC. We will also provide public investment for the industry and improved conditions of employment — including safety conditions — and introduce a licensing system for registered fishing vessels and fishermen.

We will end the de-rating of agricultural land. We will also defend the agricultural environment by giving a new priority to the effect on the environment of our agricultural policies. We will make all agricultural aid subject to environmental criteria and extend development controls to agriculture.

We shall take tougher measures to control the use of pesticides and herbicides. We shall establish a body with statutory powers to supervise their use, and in particular we shall ban the use of 245-T. We shall strengthen controls on the use of additives in feedstuffs, and in food, and ensure better labelling.

Our aim is to make it easier for new entrants, such as young farmers, to come into the industry and obtain a tenancy. We will do this with the help of a new Rural Land Authority, which will administer rural land already publicly-owned and begin to extend public ownership to tenanted land.

For the forestry industry, we intend to reconstitute the Forestry Commission, as described in *Labour's Porgramme 1982*, so that it operates as an expanding public enterprise. The commission would cease to act as a spokesman for the private sector; and it will be expected to extend its activities to include the processing side of the industry. We will also seek to increase tree plantings.

A BETTER DEAL FOR WOMEN

Labour's objective is to achieve equality between women and men. Over half the population are women; yet in our society, paid employment is seen as important while domestic skills — involving caring for children — do not enjoy their proper status. Women should have a genuine choice between staying at home to look after the family or going to work. Men and women should be able to share the rights and responsibilities of paid employment and domestic activities, so that job segregation within and outside the home is broken down.

Tory attacks on women's rights and opportunities have more than doubled the numbers of unemployed women and destroyed services which women in particular depend upon. Labour will do more than reverse these policies. We will:

Expand current positive action programmes as well as introduce wide-ranging new schemes in order to encourage women to train and apply for new job opportunities, particularly in the area of new technology.

Provide equal pay for work of equal value by amending the Equal Pay Act; and take action, together with the trade unions, against low pay.

Strengthen the Sex Discrimination Act to include direct and indirect discrimination on the grounds of family status, and shift the burden of proof from the complainant to the alleged discriminator.

Strengthen and expand the role of the Equal Opportunities Commission.

Restore and extend women's employment rights to include part-time and home-workers.

Reverse the Tory attack on employment, social services and maternity rights.

Improve the level of financial support to families with children and disabled dependants. The household duties test will be abolished. Extra help will be given to one-parent families.

Establish an integrated system of child care with priority for children in the most deprived areas. Our aim will be to introduce, as soon as possible, a statutory duty on local authorities to provide nursery education for all pre-school children whose parents wish it.

Take steps to end discrimination in education and training, as set out in *Labour's Programme 1982*.

Provide the resources to make a major improvement in the personal social services for the care of elderly, sick and disabled people.

Within the NHS, improve community services, extend preventive measures including screening, and develop child health services.

Increase the maternity grant to at least £100.

Provide fair treatment for widows.

Increase the death grant to at least £200.

Work to establish equal treatment in tax and social security.

End VAT on sanitary protection.

Appoint a cabinet minister to promote equality between the sexes.

Review the whole question of divorce and maintenance.

Establish a fairer system of family law, and introduce Family Courts.

Give more support for victims of rape; and provide an urgent review of police and court procedures in cases of rape and violence against women.

Improve ante-natal and maternity services, and respect the wishes of women in childbirth.

Support the provision of family crisis centres and more refuges for battered women.

While continuing to defend and respect the absolute right of individual conscience, we will improve NHS facilities for family planning and abortion, including counselling and day-care; and we will remove barriers to the implementation of the existing right of choice for women in the termination of a pregnancy.

FAIR SHARES

Our plan for expansion must be supported by measures to create a fairer Britain. We shall reform taxation so that the rich pay their full share and the tax burden on the lower paid is reduced. By progressively increasing the real value of the personal allowance, we will help the lower paid and those on average earnings. We intend also to bring down the starting point of the highest rates of tax, and to remove the present ceiling on earnings-related National Insurance contributions.

In *Labour's Programme 1982*, we explain how we will reduce tax avoidance. This will include action on family trusts and children's investment income. We also intend to limit the open-ended availability to higher-rate tax payers of various tax reliefs. A determined attack will be mounted on illegal tax evasion.

We shall also reform indirect taxation. We will extend zero-rating under VAT, with different rates for essentials and non-essentials.

Capital taxes will be used to reduce the huge inequalities in inherited wealth. We shall reverse most of the Tories' concessions on capital transfer tax and introduce a new annual tax on net personal wealth, along the lines set out in *Labour's Programme 1982*. This will ensure that the richest 100,000 of the population make a fair and proper contribution to tax revenue.

HELPING FAMILIES

Labour will give families a better deal. Our first priority will be to help families with children in order to support them in the task of parenthood. The Tories refuse to accept the wide variety in the type and size of families. Their policies restrict choice for members of families — in particular they reduce the freedom of men and women to choose whether to work or to stay at home and look after their families. At the same time, Tory policy has trapped more and more families in poverty through a combination of means-tested benefits and tax system which bites hardest on the lowest paid.

We aim to recast the tax and benefit system, so as to redistribute resources to families with children. Our priority is child benefit. We will increase it by £2.00 a week, make it index-linked, and subsequently improve it in real terms, as resources allow. In the longer term, we shall aim to raise child benefit to the level of child support given to those on long-term benefits. We shall also restore the rights to weekly payment of child benefit; increase the maternity grant to £100; and give extra help to one-parent families.

We shall continue to help family budgets throughout the parliament:

By increasing personal tax allowances — thus taking the poorest families out of the tax net;

By making further increased in child benefit;

By extending and improving the Invalid Care Allowance for those who care for disabled people.

To help pay for these improvements we shall, over the lifetime of the parliament, phase out the married man's additional tax allowance for those under the age of retirement. Married couples with dependants will clearly benefit considerably from these changes — whilst the overall change for those without dependants, given the increases in personal allowance, will be small in any one year. However, we recognise that the loss of the allowance could cause financial difficulty for those couples where one of the spouses is not in work. We shall therefore consider how best to give support to these married couples where there are no dependants. Our aim is to end sex discrimination in taxation. We favour the principle of separate taxation and are examining how best to implement this.

A new deal for pensioners

We believe that elderly people, both today's pensioners as well as those who will benefit in future from labour's pension scheme, should share as of right in our future prosperity. We shall:

Uprate the pension in November 1983 by the full amount necessary to protect its real value against the rise in inflation to that date.

Increase pensions, as soon as practicable, by £1.45 for a single person and £2.25 for a married couple. This is the amount pensioners have lost through the Tories breaking the link between pensions and earnings.

Link pensions and average earnings, when these are rising faster than prices, and extend this to all benefits.

Make progress towards our aim of a common pension age of 60.

Double the Christmas bonus to £20.

Phase out the TV licence for pensioners, during the lifetime of the Labour government.

Give women the additional tax allowance for the elderly — the age allowance — at 60 instead of 65.

Increase the Death Grant to £200 and extend it to cover all deaths.

Introduce a Pension Schemes Act that will more adequately protect occupational pensions from the effects of inflation than they are at present; protect the position of early leavers; and extend to members of schemes, rights to participation and to greater information.

Introduce, in areas where more favourable concessionary travel on local transport does not exist, a nationwide, off-peak, half-fares scheme for pensioners.

Reform the harsh supplementary benefit rules introduced by the Tories.

Reduce energy costs, for pensioners, both through support for conservation and by introducing new fuel allowances.

Help for the unemployed

Working people are entitled to a decent income when they lose their job through circumstances beyond their control. An improved earnings-related supplement will once again be paid during the first months of unemployment. We shall end the discrimination whereby the unemployed are not entitled to the long-term rate of supplementary benefit after a year. We shall also consider how best to improve unemployment benefit for the longer-term unemployed so that large-scale supplementation is not required.

Help for people with disabilities

The last Labour government established, for the first time, the basis for eliminating poverty among disabled people. We intend to build on this. We will:

Introduce a £10 a week blindness allowance, as a first step towards the introduction of a new cash benefit for disabled people, which will vary according to the degree of disability.

Bring up the non-contributory invalidity pension to the level of the flat-rate contributory invalidity benefit, and restore the 5 per cent cut in invalidity benefit.

Help the many disabled people who are capable of working part-time or for limited periods, but discouraged by present benefit regulations. We shall amend these to take account of their needs.

Abolish the household duties test for housewives' non-contributory invalidity pension and extend invalid care allowance to all those women presently excluded.

Continue to pay mobility allowance to existing recipients as they reach the age of 75.

Ensure the full implementation of the Chronically Sick and Disabled Persons Act.

For those who require long-term care — elderly, mentally handicapped, mentally ill and disabled people — develop services within both the health service and the local authority services, based on support for them and their families within the community.

Make proper provision for the 20 per cent of children requiring various forms of special education. We will promote and provide the resources for the integration within mainstream schooling of those children whose needs are best met by ordinary schools.

Labour will also aim to overcome discrimination against the disabled at work. We will reverse the Tory cuts, which have caused unnecessary suffering for people with disabilities. We shall increase the number of disablement resettlement officers; extend capital grants to adapt employer's premises; strengthen existing schemes — especially rehabilitation — to help disabled people back to work; and introduce new legislation, including quotas, to secure employment opportunities and job protection for disabled people.

A fairer benefit system

The new supplementary benefit scheme introduced by the Tories is harsh and unfair. We shall reform it. The families of those involved in industrial disputes will be entitled to full benefits — less any strike pay actually paid. We shall return to a sliding scale for assessing capital and the surrender value of insurance policies will be excluded. The anomaly which prevents some widows from claiming long-term supplementary benefit will be removed. We shall give extra help to families with children.

We shall improve staffing levels and physical conditions in social security offices so as to provide a more humane and responsive service for claimants. Many people fail to claim benefit to which they are entitled. We shall aim to increase take-up by improvements in publicity and the provision of advice.

All the social security changes made by the Tories, including the new sick pay and housing benefit schemes, will be reviewed. If they do not treat working people and their families fairly, we will replace them.

Forty years have elapsed since the Beveridge Report which led to the setting up of the National Insurance scheme by the post-war Labour government. We shall conduct a thorough review of the scheme in the light of today's circumstances.

THE RIGHT TO HEALTH CARE

The creation of the National Health Service is one of the greatest achievements of the Labour Party. It now faces a double threat from the Tories: a lack of resources for decent health care; and the active encouragement of private practice. Labour will act to defend the basic principles of the service. We will ensure that it is free at the point of use and funded out of taxation, and that priority depends on medical need not ability to pay.

To meet rising costs due to improved medical technology and the age composition of the population, and to allow for a general expansion of our under-funded health services, we shall increase health service expenditure by 3 per cent per annum in real terms. We will also seek a fairer distribution of these resources at both regional and district level. Since the election, prescription charges have increased from 20p to £1.40 per item. Labour will phase out health charges. We shall also ensure that NHS staff receive a fair reward for their work and dedication; and we will discuss with the TUC new arrangements for pay determination and the resolution of disputes.

Our overriding aim will be to reduce inequalities in standards of health care for all who need it. We will:

Give greater emphasis to prevention, both within the health and personal social services. We will come forward with proposals to help prevent accidents and disease, including action on advertising.

Give priority to improving our primary health care services, especially in the inner cities.

Continue to improve the ante-natal and maternity services and develop our child health services; and we will respect the wishes of women in child birth.

Introduce an independent complaints system in both hospital and family practitioner services.

Recognise the importance of community health councils and ensure that they have the power and facilities to represent fully the consumer point of view.

Abolish the special charges for overseas visitors, and end passport checks.

Take a major public stake in the pharmaceutical industry — and ensure that the drugs available are safe, effective and economic.

The present expansion in private medicine is a serious threat to our priorities in health care. We will not allow the development of a two-tier health service, where the rich can jump the queue. We shall remove private practice from the NHS and take into the NHS those parts of the profit-making private sector and prevent it expanding further. We will give proper recognition to those consultants who make a full-time commitment to the NHS; and we will provide incentives to those choosing to work in under-doctored areas and specialities.

While continuing to defend and respect the absolute right of individual conscience, we will improve NHS facilities for family planning and abortion, including counselling and day-care; and we will remove barriers to the implementation of the existing right of choice for women in the termination of a pregnancy.

Personal social services

Personal social services — such as childcare, home helps, meals on wheels and residential and day care for the elderly and handicapped, are a vital part of our welfare state. And it is those who are most vulnerable in our society who depend most upon them.

The Tory cuts in the social services have hit women hardest. They have meant lost jobs for many women and a loss of support for the elderly and disabled, thus forcing women to stay at home as unpaid carers. A major improvement in personal social services will be necessary, not only to raise the standard of living of those who depend upon them, but also to give women an equal right to work. Labour will reverse the Tory cuts, improve and expand services so that they can complement the much better community health services we shall provide. This will involve increasing spending by at least 4 per cent a year in real terms. We will:

Increase joint finance and extend it to cover other agencies.

Require social services departments to plan and develop services for children jointly with education and health authorities.

Strengthen the Chronically Sick and Disabled Persons Act so that it provides a Charter of Rights for disabled people everywhere.

Require local authorities to develop preventive services for children at risk.

Give greater attention to the needs of ethnic minorities.

Encourage the growth of local, independent advice and advocacy services.

EDUCATION FOR THE FUTURE

If individuals are to achieve their full creative potential, and our society is to advance, we must substantially improve educational provision and opportunity. The Tories' cuts have shown that they have no commitment to a free and fair education system. The fact is, however, that economic and social progress will depend on our success in making use of the abilities of the whole of our population.

For the under-fives, our goal is to achieve comprehensive provision, with priorities for children in the most deprived areas. We will unify education and care services for the under-fives, both nationally and locally. Our aim will be to introduce a statutory duty on local authorities to provide nursery education, as soon as possible, for all pre-school children whose parents wish it.

Schools in the community

Primary education is fundamental to all educational and social development, as any parent knows. We will restore funds to local education authorities to reduce class sizes; and improve learning materials and facilities in primary schools so that our children receive the best possible start in their schooling.

Secondary education is a period during which all young people must prepare themselves as the workers and citizens of the future. We shall encourage a higher standard of achievement among all pupils in the variety of academic and other activities which are essential parts of fully comprehensive education. We will:

Repeal the Education Act 1979 and prohibit all forms of academic selection, such as the eleven plus, as a condition of admission to secondary schools.

Require local education authorities to maintain a broad, balanced and comprehensive curriculum, providing genuinely equal opportunities for boys and girls, and for the ethnic minorities to meet the needs of our multi-cultural society.

Establish a common system of assessment for all 16 year olds which will encourage effort and accurately record achievement at school.

Throughout the *whole of schooling*, we will:

Determine a supply of appropriately qualified teachers to reduce class sizes. No class size should be over 30. The quality and frequency of teacher in-service training must be improved so that teachers receive no less than one school term of training in every five years of service.

Discuss with the local authorities ways of developing a reformed system for funding education. Whilst safeguarding local democracy in education, this must secure and maintain improved national standards of provision in essential areas.

Abolish corporal punishment; and help local authorities and schools to develop other methods, already successfully practised in many schools, for dealing with bad behaviour.

Positively encourage parental understanding and participation in the education of their children by increasing parental representation on school governing bodies and increasing the links between home and school.

Re-establish the school meals and milk services, cut back by the Tories. This will help to offset the inequalities, for ecample in nutrition, highlighted by the Black Report.

Private schools are a major obstacle to a free and fair education system, able to serve the needs of the whole community. We will abolish the Assisted Places Scheme and local authority place buying; and we will phase out, as quickly as possible, boarding allowances paid to government personnel for their children to attend private schools, whilst ensuring secure accommodation for children needing residential education.

We shall also withdraw charitable status from private schools and all their other public subsidies and tax privileges. We will also charge VAT on the fees paid to such schools; phase out fee changing; and integrate private schools within the local authority sector where necessary. Special schools for handicapped pupils will retain all current support and tax advantages.

Post 16 education

For 16 and 17 year olds, we will introduce a two years' student-traineeship within a third or 'tertiary', stage of education, as described in the section on young people. A 'tertiary awards council' will be established to develop and validate a proper system of educational assessment for the whole of the age group. Our aim is to replace the rigid 'A' level system with a broader programme of study within the student-traineeship, thus preventing over-specialisation and promoting flexibility and breadth in learning.

Our policy for *education after eighteen* is expansion with change. We will reverse the Tory cuts and restore the right for all qualified young people seeking higher education to secure places. We will also substantially expand opportunities for adults in both further and higher education.

We reject the Tory proposals for student loans; and we will ensure students are given adequate financial support. We will also provide proper financial support for those on non-advanced, part-time advanced, and Open University courses.

Adult education

We are determined to give priority to adults who have been denied educational opportunity on leaving school. We will:

Give statutory backing to paid educational leave for workers.

Phase in a new, adult educational entitlement that will provide one year of education, backed by financial support for adults who have never received education after eighteen.

Require educational institutions to be more flexible in their admissions procedures and methods of study.

Establish a proper legal basis for adult education; and create a development council to promote adult and continuing education.

Establish machinery to plan and co-ordinate all post 18-education together and ensure that the bodies funding universities, and planning local authority further, higher and continuing education, are more accountable and representative.

A NEW DEAL FOR YOUNG PEOPLE

Labour will end the scourge of youth unemployment and prepare young people to take up the jobs that we will create. We will also encourage all young people in employment to join a trade union. Our radical new scheme for young people will establish a new, two year student-traineeship for all 16 and 17 year olds. It will bring together, for the first time, the first years of apprenticeships, other training schemes for young workers and the young unemployed and courses in full-time education in schools and colleges. We will:

Give to young people who are at work the right to be released to college or school, on full pay. Employers will be given a statutory duty to provide opportunities for their young employees to receive systematic education and training and to release student-trainees at their request. Premiums will be paid to them to recruit young people and provide them with such opportunities.

Abolish the so-called Young Workers' Scheme, set up by the Tories to reduce youth wages. Labour rejects completely the Tory argument that young people have priced themselves out of jobs.

Offer all young people without work a place on new youth training schemes, with proper education and training opportunities — which can best be guaranteed by active monitoring by the trade unions; and give them an allowance of at least £30 per week — the level of which will be agreed annually with the TUC — with trade unions being free to negotiate better terms.

Provide student-trainees, in full-time education, with an educational maintenance allowance of £25 a week, at 1983 prices, covering 52 weeks in a year.

Labour will establish new rights and provide more resources for youth. We will:

Expand and improve the youth service so that it meets the social, cultural and recreational needs of young people — especially the unemployed, young women, the ethnic minorities and the young disabled.

Establish a 'youth initiatives fund' to give greater recognition and support to organisations which represent young people's interest.

Encourage local authorities to support representative local youth councils as one of the means of enabling young people to influence public affairs as young adults.

Expand funding and staffing for the provision of social studies and education for citizenship in youth clubs and schools with the aim of informing young people of their civil, political and trade union rights and responsibilities as citizens. Accredited trade union representatives should be involved with secondary school students in the context of such education, with full facilities for such representatives at all career days.

HOMES FOR EVERYONE

Britain faces a major housing crisis. The Tories have slashed public spending on housing by half and house building is at its lowest since the 1920s. Houses are falling into disrepair faster than they can be repaired, while homelessness and waiting lists continue to grow. Labour will reverse this decline. Our aim is a decent home for all with real freedom of choice between renting and owning, on terms people can afford.

Labour governments have done more than any others to assist owner occupiers; and we will extend this by giving special assistance to first-time buyers and council tenants.

Labour will immediately increase by half the total housing investment programmes for local authorities. This will be a first step in increasing resources for council housing repairs and improvements and for new public sector house building. We will also give a new priority to getting empty council owned housing back into use. We will overhaul and extend the renovation grant and area improvement programme to tackle properly the decay of our older houses. New and better housing and environmental standards will be developed and greater provision will be made for hitherto neglected groups, such as single people.

Council housing

The Tories have forced council rents to more than double. The number of council homes for rent is falling because of the rundown of new building and enforced sales. Thousands have to cope with leaking roofs and damp, inadequate heating, broken down lifts, noise, lack of security, increasing disrepair and neglect.

Labour will give council tenants a new deal. In addition to a freeze on rents for a full year, and the restoration of subsidies, Labour will:

fund a national action programme to repair and improve or replace run-down estates, especially the system-built developments in which so many defects have been revealed.

Strengthen tenants' rights on security, repairs and improvements, access to files, exchanges, transfers, moves between local authority areas, and rehousing rights on breakdown of relationship;

Encourage more responsive and decentralised housing management and maintenance, and promote tenant participation and democracy, including housing co-operatives;

End all residential and other qualifications, which unfairly exclude people from council housing in the area where they live, extend the 'priority' groups under the Housing (Homeless Persons) Act and strengthen the rights of homeless people;

End enforced council house sales, empower public landlords to repurchase homes sold under the Tories on first resale and provide that future voluntary agreed sales will be at market value.

Home ownership

Labour believes in real home ownership at prices people can afford. Under the Tories the mortgate rate reached its highest ever level at 15 per cent and is still at 10 per cent. They have done little to help low income groups become owners.

We support financial assistance for owner-occupation and will maintain mortgage tax relief for existing house purchasers at the current rate. The unfairness of mortgage tax relief above the basic rate, which gives most benefit to the highest incomes, will be phased out. We will also examine the possibility of a new and substantial form of financial help for first time buyers, with special consideration for council and new town tenants, aimed at easing the heavy initial burdens of house purchase.

Labour will act to help home-owners. We will:

Simplify and reduce the cost of house purchase, ending the solicitors' conveyancing monopoly, and require full disclosure of mortgage lending terms and practices;

Make it easier for lower income groups to borrow funds on secure terms by greatly expanding council mortgage lending and providing the funds needed. This will be financed primarily by onlending from the building societies, at least 10 per cent of whose funds should be made available in this way;

Allow and encourage councils to provide a unified house-purchase service, including estate agency, surveying, conveyancing and mortgage lending;

End the leasehold system for houses, strengthen the rights of leaseholders of flats and increase protection to mobile home residents.

Privately rented housing

The worst housing conditions are in privately rented housing. The Tories have loosened the controls on rents and security of tenure and pushed up rents. If they get the chance, they would abolish all controls.

Labour will ensure that tenants are fully protected. We will:

Actively encourage the transfer of all property owned by absentee private landlords to the public or owner-occupied sectors, with local authorities setting the pace. This will not apply to owner-occupiers letting all or part of their home.

Repeal the Tories' shorthold scheme and close other loopholes in security of tenure; and strengthen tenants' rights on deposits and harassment.

Strengthen councils' powers to enforce repairs and improvements and the standards of management, particularly in multi-occupied properties; and launch a programme of action against property held empty without justification.

Bring forward measures to strengthen tied tenants' rights and improve their access to secure housing when they leave their job.

Bring service charges for private tenants and leaseholders within the fair rents scheme.

Help for all tenants

Tenants in both the public and private sectors are plagued with difficulties caused by all-too frequent failure of landlords to carry out repairs satisfactorily and speedily. Tenants recognise that major structural repairs, for example to blocks of flats or maisonettes, can only be dealt with by large-scale improvement projects. But they rightly see no reason why routine repairs should be neglected. Labour will launch a new initiative aimed at tackling this troublesome problem.

We will introduce a right to repair for all tenants — council, new town, housing associations and private landlord. This will give tenants the right to force landlords, including councils, to get routine repairs done, with landlords footing the cost. Where there are council direct labour organisations, these will be responsible for doing this work. Major structural work will not be included, but the Labour government will assist councils to carry out such work through much larger capital investment allocations and reinstatement of an adequate housing subsidy system.

We also intend to reform the system of housing benefits for low income groups. A new Housing Tribunal will be established to replace the present confusing jumble of courts, tribunals and committees, as an accessible means of resolving landlord-tenant disputes.

CONSTRUCTION

The Tory recession has seriously damaged the construction industry. Company after company has gone bankrupt. Nearly 400,000 construction workers are on the dole. Labour's plan for expansion will help the industry back to its feet. But we will also introduce changes to the industry, as described in *Labour's Programme, 1982* — not least to help stabilise the industry's workload. We will also provide greater job security for employees; and we will work out, with the agreement of the trade unions, a system of decasualisation.

We also believe that a major new role should be played in the industry by public and co-operative enterprise — to provide a new source of enterprise, initiative and innovation. We will establish a new, publicly-owned company, as a major pace-making public enterprise, for large and medium-sized construction projects. In additon, to help protect the public ownership into the building materials industry, in which a small number of large companies now enjoy near monopoly conditions.

We will also give generous and active support to the development of workers' co-operatives, especially at the 'jobbing' end of the industry. We will reverse Tory policies towards local authority direct labour organisations. We will give them more scope by allowing them to compete for other work in their locality, while ensuring that they are efficiently run as municipal enterprises. We will oppose the contracting out of government services to privately-owned companies.

PLANNING FOR PEOPLE

The way we plan for the use of our land affects every one of us. It determines where we build our housing, the kind of shopping centres which are available, and where new jobs and factories are sited. We are determined to strengthen local planning and ensure greater participation by ordinary people over the decisions which affect their lives.

The Tories have always put the interests of property developers before the needs of local people. Labour will change this. We will ensure that local authorities are able to decide on the positive use of land in their areas instead of having to respond to the initiatives of developers. And we shall take explicit powers to link land-use planning firmly with the economic and social planning of local authorities.

A key issue in planning at local level is the ownership and use of land. We are determined to stop land speculation and make sensible and comprehensive planning possible. We will establish new land authorities, similar to the successful Land Authority of Wales, with the powers and funds needed to acquire development land — at its current use value — so that local plans can be fulfilled. Our proposals do not apply to owner-occupiers, whose homes and gardens will be safeguarded.

We intend also to widen democratic participation in the planning system by:

Codifying and extending public rights of consultation, and of appeal against planning decisions;

Improving access to public planning inquiries and broadening their terms of reference;

Ensuring that, before the inquiry stage of certain major development proposals, the environmental effects are subject to detailed analysis and the report is published;

Creating a new fund to help objectors at major public inquiries, with an independent board to decide who should be helped and by how much.

The inner cities

The decay, squalor and level of unemployment in our inner cities are a national disgrace. Labour is determined to reverse their decline. We will provide more resources, more investment and more jobs. We will act to ensure, through the policies set out in this campaign document, that people living in the inner cities have access to decent homes, health and education — and that there is proper accountability for the police.

In addition to providing a major increase of funds for the Urban Programme, we will:

Use agreed development plans, negotiated at national level with major firms — public and private — to locate investment and jobs in the inner cities.

Use regional development agencies to prepare sites, encourage municipal and co-operative enterprise, and help improve transport and other facilities.

Get local authorities to prepare local economic and social plans. We will also support the development of well-financed local enterprise boards in areas which need them — and enable local authorities to conclude agreed development plans with small and medium-sized local firms.

THE ENVIRONMENT

Labour believes that the countryside should be preserved and enhanced as a source of recreation for town and country dwellers alike and as a habitat for wild creatures and plants. Everyone has a right to a decent living and working environment.

We intend to monitor closely — and publicly — the nation's progress in improving the environment. We shall therefore present to parliament each year a major report on the 'State of the Environment'. We will also safeguard our heritage by:

Supporting rights of access to common land. We will stop landed interests from preventing access for anglers;

Strengthening the planning laws to ensure that the countryside is protected from damaging development;

Strengthening the legislation which protects endangered species;

Providing increased resources so that the Nature Conservancy Council and Countryside Commission can function effectively;

Enacting a new Wildlife and Countryside Act and providing proper protection for sites of special scientific interests.

We will also act to curb pollution. We will:

Proceed with the implementation of the 1974 Control of Pollution Act.

Undertake a comprehensive review of the effectiveness of the present machinery and powers on pollution control.

Eliminate lead in petrol by setting a date after which all new cars will be required to use only lead-free petrol. The interests of motorists will be safeguarded.

Restore those environmental agencies abolished by the Tories with a responsibility for monitoring air and noise pollution.

Develop a programme for eliminating toxic substances from our living and working environments.

We will reform the water industry by repealing the Tories' Water Act and restoring democratic accountability in the industry. We will re-establish a national authority charged with responsibility for the strategic planning and use of all water resources. The canal system will be brought under a new national authority, so that it can be developed and maintained as an essential water resource. We will also consider how best to provide help, for those on low incomes, with paying their water rates.

RURAL AREAS

Tory policies have seriously harmed the rural areas. Bus services have disappeared. Rail links are under threat. Jobs have been axed. Houses are not being built. Village halls and sub-post offices have been closed. Labour will act to improve the quality of life in the rural areas; and we have outlined our plans in *Labour's Programme 1982* and in our statement *Out of Town, Out of Mind*. We will give greater priority to rural problems. And ministers will be expected to bring about greater co-ordination in promoting our policies. We will:

Ensure that the Development Commission, and its counterparts in Scotland and Wales, become actively involved in implementing our policies for rural regeneration.

Take measures to increase employment by encouraging the expansion of light industry and tourism in the rural areas, while safeguarding the rural nature of the countryside.

Improve the rural public transport network by a major injection of public funds and a better use of existing resources.

Wherever possible retain village schools and generally improve educational provision for all age groups; and mobile 'all purpose' community services offices.

Take extensive measures to expand the provision of all types of housing in the rural areas, which will also help to deal with the 'Second Home' problem.

TRANSPORT

Four years of Tory government has meant serious damage to Britain's transport system. Profitable elements have been sold off. Important but unprofitable sections left in public hands are being starved of investment. The quality of public transport service has fallen disastrously.

Another Tory government would mean even poorer services, higher fares and lower safety standards. Labour repudiates this whole approach. We believe that the improvement of public transport must be a major social priority, which can only be achieved by a sensibly integrated transport system. We describe our proposals in *Labour's Programme 1982*.

We will maintain and improve the rail network, invest in the electrification of the main lines and replace worn-out railway stock. We will encourage the use of the railways for freight traffic by extending grants for rail freight facilities and encouraging the development of trans-shipment depots.

Heavy lorries will be made to bear their full share of road costs, including environment costs. We will cut to a minimum noise and pollution from goods vehicles and introduce national routeings and restrictions to take lorries away from people. Vehicle Excise Duty for private cars will be abolished and the revenue secured by a higher tax on petrol.

Labour believes that, together with a properly enforced licensing system, a publicly-owned share of the road haulage industry is essential. It would clearly be sensible for the National Freight Company to form part of this sector; and we are examining how best to bring this about.

We will ensure that local authorities are able to give proper support to public transport. In areas where more favourable concessionary travel on local transport does not exist, we shall bring in a nationwide, off-peak half-fares scheme for pensioners. A proper licensing system, to safeguard the network of bus services, will be reintroduced. We shall also ensure that a basic minimum level of service is provided throughout the country. In addition, we will:

Encourage the development of effective traffic management schemes to alleviate the problems of traffic congestion.

Improve facilities and safety standards for cyclists and increase financial incentives to local authorities to assist these improvements.

Give a high priority to building by-passes.

Establish a national shipping organisation able to acquire and operate shipping services; and protect our shipping and jobs from unfair foreign competition.

Invest in inland waterways, and encourage the greater use of them — and of coastal shipping — in the interests of taking freight off our roads.

Establish a new National Ports Authority to take ports into public ownership and to develop a new overall strategy for these.

Create a National Transport Authority to develop transport policy and good practice, secure integration and facilitate comprehensive planning.

LAW, ORDER AND JUSTICE

Labour's aim is to ensure that all sections of the community are safe on the street and at home, free from the fear that crime generates. We believe that the police should have the support of the community, have their rights safeguarded, and be fairly paid. But we also believe that it is as much in the interests of the police, as of their local communities, that they are properly accountable and fully subject to the law. We will ensure that, throughout the country, the police are encouraged to return to the beat and therefore closer to the communities they serve. That is the best way of preventing and detecting crime.

We intend to protect the rights of individual suspects, while providing the police with sufficient powers to do their job effectively whilst not infringing the civil rights of individual suspects. We aim to create elected police authorities in all parts of the country, including London, with statutory responsibility for the determination of police policy within their areas. We will also:

Launch a major initiative to help victims, including extending and simplifying the present Criminal Injuries Compensation Scheme.

Give priority to crime prevention as part of our action programme for rundown estates.

Bring about better co-ordination in the technical, support and information services of the police.

Replace the present police complaints procedure with an independent system accountable to local communities, with minority police representation.

Create community police councils to provide an opportunity for open discussion between police and the community as to the quality and manner of police provision.

Introduce strict limits on searches of people in the street, searches of premises, the use of the power of arrest, and on the time a prisoner can be held in custody before being charged.

Protect the rights of those in police custody, by giving revised Judges Rules, which safeguard those under arrest or interrogation, the force of law and, in England and Wales, take the role of prosecutor away from the police by implementing a public prosecutor system, on the Procurator Fiscal model.

Repeal the Police and Criminal Evidence Bill, because it infringed the rights and freedoms of individuals.

Disband the London Special Patrol Groups and local SPGs, which have increasingly been deployed in aggressive public order roles.

Access to legal services

We will not allow people's legal rights to go by default. Accessible legal services are essential to protect human rights. As described in *Labour's Programme 1982*, we will increase central government spending to set up new law centres and help existing ones, and to improve the legal aid scheme by widening its provisions. We will also introduce a system of appeals against the refusal of legal aid in criminal cases.

We will speed the extension of duty solicitor schemes to all magistrate courts and police stations in England and Wales. We will also introduce measures to help citizens to secure their legal rights in the areas of tribunal and welfare rights law.

We will co-ordinate the responsibility for advice and legal services so that ministerial responsibility is clearer and more direct. We will also establish a new Legal Services Commission to be responsible for the provision and financing of public legal services. Our aim is to ensure that the expertise and training of the legal profession should be geared far more than at present to those legal problems affecting ordinary people.

The penal system

No one concerned for human dignity and civil rights can find our prison system acceptable. We are determined to improve conditions. We do not accept that wives and children should be punished together with the prisoners. We will:

Reduce the prison population by cutting many maximum sentence lengths for non-violent offenders. We will stop putting petty offenders into prison. We will expand non-custodial alternatives, and examine new penalties involving reparation and restitution to the victim. We will also introduce a maximum period of custody for those on remand, along the lines of the provisions in Scotland.

Treat prisoners as human beings by providing reasonable conditions in our prisons. We will incorporate, in new, legally enforceable prison rules, minimum standards on such matters as cell space. And we will reduce unnecessary restrictions — for example on prisoners' correspondence.

Refurbish urban prisons.

Hand over all specialist services in prisons, such as medical care, to the normal community agencies.

Establish a genuinely independent complaints and disciplinary procedure to replace the current board of visitors system; and provide better aftercare for those leaving prison, to help them resettle in the community.

Improve the training, working conditions and job opportunities of prison officers.

Examine the additional problems faced by women prisoners, especially those with young children.

EQUAL RIGHTS

The next Labour government will lead a political offensive against racial disadvantage, discrimination and harassment; and we have set out our proposals in *Labour's Programme 1982*. To encourage equality and reduce discrimination, we will greatly expand funding to ethnic minority projects. We will also encourage local authorities, in selecting projects under the Urban Programme, to provide for greater ethnic minority participation. We will also:

Stimulate a wide range of positive action programmes to ensure that ethnic minorities receive a fair deal — in employment, education, housing and social services: and encourage the keeping of ethnic records, in order to assess the needs of ethnic minorities and take steps to meet them.

Launch a major public education initiative aimed at eliminating prejudice.

Strengthen the existing Race Relations Act — in particular, to enable us to deal more effectively with racialist literature, speeches and marches; and to remove the exception for seamen recruited abroad.

Appoint a senior minister to lead the offensive against racial inequality.

We are concerned that homosexuals are unfairly treated. We will take steps to ensure that they are not unfairly discriminated against — especially in employment and in the definition of privacy contained in the 1967 Act — along the lines set out in *Labour's Programme, 1982*.

Nationality and immigration

Through their immigration and nationality laws, the Tories have divided families and caused immense suffering in the immigrant communities. We accept the need for immigration controls. But we will repeal the 1971 Immigration Act and the 1981 British Nationality Act and replace them with a citizenship law that does not discriminate against either women or black and Asian Britons.

Under our Nationality Act, we will restore rights removed by the Tories, such as the right to automatic citizenship if born in Britain. The Act will enable other Commonwealth and foreign nationals to acquire citizenship if they qualify by objective tests, and provide a right of appeal against the refusal of an application for citizenship. We will also ensure that the cost of acquiring citizenship will no longer be an obstacle to those who wish to apply.

Under our new Immigration Act we will liberalise the age limit criteria for children and the criteria for elderly parents and other relatives. We will simplify the procedures and commit the resources necessary for all applications to be processed promptly; and allow medical examinations, including x-rays, only for medical, not administrative purposes. The race and sex discrimination in the husbands and fiances' rules will be ended: we will restore the entitlement to admission to join a woman settled here irrespective of her citizenship, birthplace or ancestry. We will also ensure that immigration officials fully respect the human rights of those seeking entry. We will also:

Consult Commonwealth governments so as to resolve the question of the other British nationals from independent countries who possess no other citizenship.

Provide a right of appeal for those who the Home Secretary proposes to deport or exclude on security grounds.

Establish a more independent and balanced panel of adjudicators for immigration appeals.

A WIDER DEMOCRACY

Labour will take action to enhance democratic rights and ensure greater openness and accountability in the institutions of government. We have set out our policies in *Labour's Programme, 1982*. We shall:

Introduce a Freedom of Information Bill, providing for a genuine system of open government and placing the onus on the authorities to justify withholding information.

Bring in data protection legislation to prevent the abuse of confidential information held on personal files; and, subject to certain exceptions, allow individuals access to their personal records.

Reform the administration of government and the civil service machine so that it meets modern needs and is properly accountable to elected representatives. We recognise the damage done to the morale and efficiency of the civil service by this government. We will work to repair this damage, together with the unions, and to give proper recognition to the importance of the work of the service.

Take action to abolish the undemocratic House of Lords as quickly as possible and, as an interim measure, introduce a Bill in the first session of parliament to remove its legislative powers — with the exception of those which relate to the life of a parliament.

Make improvements in the legislative process and procedures in the House of Commons.

Reform the procedures for appointments to public bodies to ensure they are more open and genuinely representative of the community.

Overhaul the outdated honours system.

Give a new priority to making our public services more responsive to the needs and wishes of those who use them. Wherever possible we will decentralise services to make them as close as possible to those who use them. We will also provide more effective procedures for complaints — with clear rights for users — and ensure better training and status for those in contact with the public.

Labour believes that state aid for political parties is now essential for the working of our parliamentary democracy. We will introduce such aid, along the lines set out in the Houghton Report, with the funds available adjusted to today's prices and index linked.

The security services

There is now widespread concern about our security services. We intend that they should become properly accountable institutions — and that the civil rights of individuals are fully protected. We outline in *Labour's Programme, 1982* our proposals for a new Security Act, to define the powers and responsibilities of the services, including those concerned with the interception of communications. We will also extend parliamentary accountability — including over the accounts of the services — which will be assisted by a new select committee; prohibit, under the Security Act, unauthorised surveillance; and abolish 'D' notices.

LOCAL DEMOCRACY

Labour is determined to strengthen local democracy. We will shift radically the balance between central and local government and give local communities much more say about how their services are run.

First, we will give local authorities freedom to implement comprehensive local plans, covering economic, social and environmental policies. We explain elsewhere in this document, and more fully in *Labour's Programme, 1982*, our proposals to assist local authorities to create jobs, to establish local enterprise boards and engage in local economic planning. We will reverse Tory policies on the privatisation of local authority services.

Second, we will expand the scope for local democracy. Instead of local councillors never being completely sure what is permitted and what is *ultra vires*, we shall give a power of general competence to all local authorities to carry out whatever activities are not expressly forbidden by statute. We shall also seek to define the relationship between central and local government — as part of our consideration of the universal application of realistic minimum standards — so that basic provision of key services is available in all parts of the country. We will also:

Take action to encourage councils to make their services more responsive to the needs and wishes of their clients and of the local community.

Extend workers' rights and industrial democracy in local government, by enabling non-voting employee representatives to be co-opted on to committees, and encouraging the introduction of formal procedures for participation in decisions on the implementation of policy. We will also allow all but the most senior officers the right to become elected or co-opted members of the authority which employs them.

Pay proper allowances and provide adequate administrative support, to local councillors.

We are examining how best to reform local government. We believe that services such as health, water and sewerage should become answerable to a much greater extent to elected members; and we aim to end, if we can, the present confusing division of services between two tiers of authority. Unitary district authorities, in England and Wales, could be responsible for all of the functions in this area that they could sensibly undertake. We will also ensure that the City of London is absorbed into a reformed democratic system of local government. For Scotland, any reform of local government will be a matter for our proposed Scottish Assembly.

Local government finance

Labour will reverse the Tory government's attacks on local authority services. We shall provide finance, through the rate support grant, to allow local authority expenditure to grow in line with our plans for economic expansion; and the hard-pressed urban areas will benefit especially from an increased share of the resources available.

Labour believes in active local democracy. We will therefore repeal the Tory legislation which allows the government to impose ceilings on local authority spending, and to impose penalties on local authorities whose spending exceeds those ceilings. We shall repeal the ban on supplementary rates. We will restore the right of local authorities to spend additional amounts from revenue on capital expenditure in excess of loan sanction limits. The rate support grant system will be recast to give fairer treatment to areas in greatest need and the maximum freedom of action for local authorities to control their own budgets.

Labour will also enact legislation to abolish the penalty of personal surcharge on individual councillors. Instead councillors, like others in the community, will be liable at law for any unlawful or illegal acts. Public audit will be confined to that purpose and auditors will not be permitted to involve themselves in judgements on politics or policies.

DEVOLUTION TO SCOTLAND

Labour is determined to decentralise power in decision-making. In Scotland, the people have shown their support for devolution in a referendum and at successive general elections; and we have set out our proposals for devolution in a major statement, *Scotland and Devolution*. Labour will:

Establish a directly elected Scottish Assembly, with an executive drawn from members of the assembly.

Provide the Assembly with legislative and executive powers over a wide range of domestic policy, including matters such as health, education and social welfare.

Ensure a major role for the Assembly in assisting in the regeneration of Scottish industry — including the preparation and implementation of a Plan for Scotland — within the context of our overall national plan.

As well as receiving grants from central government, the Scottish Assembly will have tax-raising powers, thus ensuring that the level of services provided can be determined in Scotland.

NORTHERN IRELAND

Labour believes that Ireland should, by peaceful means and on the basis of consent, be united, and recognises that this will be achieved with the introduction of socialist policies. We respect and support, however, the right of the Northern Ireland people to remain within the UK, although this does not mean that Unionist leaders can have a veto on political development; and we accept that, to achieve agreement and consent between the two parts of Ireland, we must create greater unity within the Northern Ireland community.

In our 1981 conference statement and in *Labour's Programme 1982*, we set out in full Labour's policy on Northern Ireland. We will aim to establish an agreed, devolved administration. In the meantime, we will continue with direct rule. We will also initiate early discussions between the British government, the Irish government, the Irish Labour Party, and the trade unions on both sides of the border, and political representatives of the people of Northern Ireland, on how best to proceed with our policy of unification by consent.

Tory policies have been a disaster for the Northern Ireland economy. Unemployment has soared. The economy is in ruins. Housing and the social services are in desperate straits. Labour will give new hope to Northern Ireland. We will create jobs and provide investment. We will use all of the economic planning powers and institutions set out in this document — together with a massive injection of public resources — to rebuild the economy.

We will also act on security and civil rights, along the lines set out in our 1981 statement. We will repeal the Prevention of Terrorism Act and the Payment of Debt Act and reform the system of Diplock courts. We will provide equal rights for women, including rights to abortion, and make progress towards an integrated comprehensive system of education.

LEISURE FOR LIVING

Labour believes that a comprehensive approach is needed, at national and local levels, to provide services and facilities for leisure.

The arts

A crucial part will be played in this by the arts. Labour's aim is to make the arts, in their broadest sense, an accepted part of everyday life for the whole population. We will place special emphasis on their availability to the young, the handicapped and the retired. Substantial extra funds will be provided, with priority being given to the regions and to access for those on low incomes. Local authorities will have a statutory duty to provide adequate arts and entertainments facilities; and the arts will be zero-rated in respect of VAT.

We will retain a Minister of the Arts, whose first task will be to undertake a major survey on the disparities in provision between regions and to produce proposals for action. The public bodies which support the arts will also be made more open and accountable, and include more representation from workers in the arts, local authorities and consumers. The Craft Council will be strengthened, and regional museums and galleries supported through a Museums and Galleries Council.

For the film industry, we will establish a British Film Authority, responsible for the National Film Finance Corporation. This will ensure that revenue from a levy on ticket sales goes to British film-makers who produce British films. We will also ensure that the profits from British film-making and distribution are channelled back into British films — and that the present two-company monopoly of film distribution in Britain is ended. The new British Film Authority will be responsible for extending public ownership into film distribution.

Sport and recreation

Labour will accept responsibility for the provision of a broadly-based leisure service. We will:

Encourage greater participation in sport and recreation.

Give incentives to voluntary bodies to involve themselves more widely in the provision of sporting and community facilities.

Encourage local authorities and other owners of facilities to make them much more available to public use.

Set up an immediate enquiry into the financial basis of sport and recreation.

Review the provision of national sporting facilities, so as to secure a fairer geographical distribution.

Ensure that the sporting talent of the nation receives sufficient support to enable them to bring sporting success to Britain.

We will also provide for the wider use of the countryside for recreational purposes, such as angling and other water-based sports. Angling will be given additional support, by ensuring wider access to rivers and lakes, financial assistance to provide a wider ownership of fishing waters, improvements in respect of conservation, and action to prevent pollution.

The media

Our aims in the media are to safeguard freedom of expression, encourage diversity and establish greater accountability. For all the media, we will introduce a statutory right of reply to ensure that individuals can set the record straight. We will introduce stronger measures to prevent any further concentration in the media.

For the press, we will encourage diversity by:

Setting up a launch fund to assist new publications.

Ensuring that all major wholesalers accept any lawful publication, and arrange for its proper supply and display, subject to a handling charge.

Preventing acquisition of further newspapers by large press chains.

Protecting freedom of expression by prohibiting joint control of the press, commercial radio and television.

Breaking up major concentrations of press ownership, by setting an upper limit for the number of major publications in the hands of a single proprietor or press group.

Replacing the Press Council with a stronger, more representative body.

In broadcasting, we will aim to make both broadcasting itself, and the organisations responsible, more accountable and representative — and to provide greater public access. Our aim is to promote a more wide-ranging and genuine pluralism in the media, and we set out our proposals in *Labour's Programme 1982*. We will also seek to introduce a genuinely independent adjudication of grievances and complaints. The licence fee will be phased out for pensioners, during the lifetime of the Labour government.

The high standards of British public service broadcasting are threatened by Tory plans to introduce cable TV on free-market principles. We will regulate satellite and cable provision and foster the same principles of diversity and pluralism as conventional broadcasting authorities. To avoid wasteful duplication, we will entrust the provision of the national cable system to British Telecom.

Animal protection

The Labour Party was the first major political party to publish a policy statement, in 1978, on animal protection — *Living Without Cruelty*; and these policies are reaffirmed in *Labour's Programme 1982*. We believe that all animals — whether in the wild, domesticated or farmed — should be properly treated.

To achieve our aims we will transform the Farm Animal Welfare Council into a Standing Royal Commission on Animal Protection. We will also urgently review the 1876 Cruelty to Animals Act. A high priority will be given to research into alternatives to using live animals in experiments, and to restrictions on the use of live animals in experiments — with proper control and supervision in order to avoid pain.

Hare coursing, fox hunting and all forms of hunting with dogs will be made illegal. This will not, however, affect shooting and fishing. The use of snares will also be made illegal.

We will lay down clear conditions on freedom of movement for livestock; and we will ensure that our legislation meets, at least, the requirements of the European Convention for the Protection of Animals kept for Farming Purposes. We will also ban, over a phased period, all extreme livestock systems and introduce legislation to ensure that animals are slaughtered as near as possible to the point of production. We will ban the export of live food animals.

Animals kept in zoos, circuses and safari parks will be included in our animals protection legislation. Health and safety at work legislation will be reviewed in order to better protect people employed on such premises.

BRITAIN AND THE COMMON MARKET

Geography and history determine that Britain is part of Europe, and Labour wants to see Europe safe and prosperous. But the European Economic Community, which does not even include the whole of Western Europe, was never devised to suit us, and our experience as a member of it has made it more difficult for us to deal with our economic and industrial problems. It has sometimes weakened our ability to achieve the objectives of Labour's international policy.

The next Labour government, committed to radical, socialist policies for reviving the British economy, is bound to find continued membership a most serious obstacle to the fulfilment of those policies. In particular the rules of the Treaty of Rome are bound to conflict with our strategy for economic growth and full employment, our proposals on industrial policy and for increasing trade, and our need to restore exchange controls and to regulare direct overseas investment. Moreover, by preventing us from buying food from the best sources of world supply, they would run counter to our plans to control prices and inflation.

For all these reasons, British withdrawal from the Community is the right policy for Britain — to be completed well within the lifetime of the parliament. That is our commitment. But we are also committed to bring about withdrawal in an amicable and orderly way, so that we do not prejudice employment or the prospect of increased political and economic co-operation with the whole of Europe.

We emphasise that our decision to bring about withdrawal in no sense represents any weakening of our commitment to internationalism and international co-operation. We are not 'withdrawing from Europe'. We are seeking to extricate ourselves from the Treaty of Rome and other Community treaties which place political burdens on Britain. Indeed, we believe our withdrawal will allow us to pursue a more dynamic and positive international policy — one which recognises the true political and geographical spread of international problems and interests. We will also seek agreement with other European governments — both in the EEC and outside — on a common strategy for economic expansion.

The process of withdrawal

On taking office we will open preliminary negotiations with the other EEC member states to establish a timetable for withdrawal; and we will publish the results of these negotiations in a White Paper. In addition, as soon as possible after the House assembles, we will introduce a Repeal Bill: first, in order to amend the 1972 European Communities Act, ending the powers of the Community in the UK; and second, to provide the necessary powers to repeal the 1972 Act, when the negotiations on withdrawal are completed.

Following the publication of the White Paper, we will begin the main negotiations on withdrawal. Later, when appropriate and in the same parliament, we will use our powers to repeal the 1972 Act and abrogate the Treaty of Accession — thus breaking all of our formal links with the Community. Britain will at this point withdraw from the Council of Ministers and from the European Parliament.

There will need to be a period of transition, to ensure a minimum of disruption — and to phase in any new agreements we might make with the Community. This will enable us to make all the necessary changes in our domestic legislation. Until these changes in UK law have taken place, the *status quo* as regards particular items of EEC legislation will remain. And this period will, of course, extend beyond the date when we cease, formally, to be members.

THE INTERNATIONAL DIMENSION

The Labour Party is working to create a democratic socialist society in Britain, but we realise to achieve this we must enjoy the fullest international co-operation. There is a real interdependence between nations, and, if Britain under Labour is not to stand on the sidelines, we must co-operate to survive. Our foreign policy is a logical extension of our work at home.

A deep crisis now afflicts the world economy. In the developed world, recession has meant lengthening dole queues and a falling standard of life; for the peoples of the Third World, recession has added to an already intolerable burden of poverty. Unlike the Tories, Labour believes that there is a way out of the crisis, and that we need not accept an international status quo so manifestly riddled with injustice, inefficiency and waste. Labour will pursue and win international support for policies designed to stimulate trade, investment, and growth; and we shall work inside the appropriate institutions to end the financial chaos which now threatens the stability of so many countries. There can be no sure prospect of peace in a world wracked by an enduring economic crisis. Labour's policies will help bring that crisis to an end.

Labour recognises the urgent need to restore detente and dialogue between the states and the peoples of the world. We will actively pursue dialogue with the Soviet Union and China, and will urge the American government to do so. We will work consistently for peace and disarmament, and devote all our efforts to pulling the world back from the nuclear abyss. Labour will dedicate some of the resources currently wasted on armaments to projects designed to promote both security and human development.

An essential difference between the Labour and the Tory approach is that we have a foreign policy that will help liberate the peoples of the world from oppression, want and fear. We seek to find ways in which social and political progress can be achieved and to identify the role that Britain can play in this process.

Our objectives cannot be pursued in isolation; we will work with the international agencies, friendly governments, and with socialist parties and genuine liberation movements in order to convert these objectives into concrete achievements.

DISARMAMENT — THE INTERNATIONAL CONTEXT

The pursuit of peace, development and disarmament is central to our policy. We wish to strengthen the process of detente, which means the easing of political as well as military tension between East and West. A third world war would destroy civilisation, yet the danger of a nuclear holocaust grows alarmingly.

Labour is determined that Britain should play its full part in the struggle for peace. Now in 1983, in what is a critical year for peace, we can begin to influence events by the way we present the imperative case for disarmament. In government we can carry that influence much further, by example and by common action with others. We must use unilateral steps taken by Britain to secure multilateral solutions on the international level. Unilateralism and multilateralism must go hand in hand if either is to suceed. It is for this reason that we are against moves that would disrupt our existing alliances, but are resolved on measures to enable Britain to pursue a non-nuclear defence policy.

To achieve our paramount aim — stopping the nuclear arms race itself, and the other arms races pursued beneath its shadow — we need stronger international institutions. First and foremost is a United Nations organisation with real and growing authority. Labour is determined to sustain and fortify the United Nations. All our recent experience re-emphasises how necessary it is to have an international Charter against aggression. It is a tragedy that the 1982 UN Special Session on Disarmament was allowed to disband in failure and disappointment. We shall work to recall a new session on a more ambitious and hopeful basis. We will support the commitments of the UN Special Sessions on Disarmament and the UN Committee on Disarmament.

We shall seek to restore the Final Document on Disarmament, approved by the 1978 United Nations Special Session, as the long-term objective. But, of course, as the international tension sharpens, we must pursue other more immediate aims. Labour has always opposed Soviet deployment of SS20s. We want to see the Geneva talks on intermediate weapons succeed. Labour was arguing that they should begin long before President Reagan and Mrs. Thatcher came round to the idea. It is imperative that the SALT II agreement is ratified. We shall work for this. We strongly support the reduction of strategic weapons in the START talks. We will propose urgent action to make the Non-Proliferation Treaty effective and to keep it effective. The uncontrolled proliferation of nuclear weapons would enormously increase the danger to us all.

Following the steps taken by the last Labour government in such fields as non-proliferation and the Mutual and Balanced Force Reduction talks, Britain must again take a lead in disarmament negotiations.

DEFENCE POLICY

The overriding task for Britain, as for the rest of the world, is to draw back from the nuclear abyss. Britain must act on her own account as well as seeking agreement with other countries on nuclear disarmament.

One immediate step our government must take is to insist on implementing the recent United Nations call for a freeze on the production, deployment and testing of nuclear weapons, and for a comprehensive test ban. That the Tory government should have voted against these propositions in the United Nations is deplorable, and betrays our country's capacity to play a leading role as an advocate of world disarmament. Labour's proposals will help to restore that opportunity.

Labour believes in effective defence through collective security but rejects the present emphasis on nuclear weapons. Britain and her allies should have sufficient military strength to discourage external aggression and to defend themselves should they be attacked. Labour's commitment is to establish a non-nuclear defence policy for this country. This means the rejection of any fresh nuclear bases or weapons on British soil or in British waters, and the removal of all existing nuclear bases and weapons, thus enabling us to make a direct contribution to an eventually much wider nuclear-free zone in Europe. However, all this cannot be done at once, and the way we do it must be designed to assist in the task to which we are also committed — securing nuclear disarmament agreements with other countries and maintaining co-operation with our allies.

The most pressing objective must be to prevent the deployment here or elsewhere in Western Europe of Cruise or Pershing missiles. This deployment would mark a new and dangerous escalation in the nuclear arms race. It would make the achievement of effective disarmament agreements covering these and other weapons much more difficult in the future. We will therefore not permit the siting of Cruise missiles in this country and will remove any that are already in place.

The next Labour government will cancel the Trident programme. Apart from the huge, persisting and distorting burden it would impose on our defence budget and our economy as a whole, it would not offer security but would rather help to intensify the arms race. We will propose that Britain's Polaris force be included in the nuclear disarmament negotiations in which Britain must take part. We will, after consultation, carry through in the lifetime of the next parliament our non-nuclear defence policy.

Labour believes in collective security. The next Labour government will maintain its support for NATO, as an instrument of detente no less than of defence. We wish to see NATO itself develop a non-nuclear strategy. We will work towards the establishment of a new security system in Europe based on mutual trust and confidence, and knowledge of the objectives and capabilities of all sides. The ultimate objective of a satisfactory relationship in Europe is the mutual and concurrent phasing out of both NATO and the Warsaw Pact.

We oppose any attempt to expand the role of the alliance into other continents. We condemn the doctrine that nuclear war can be limited, and the notion that somehow the West must catch up with a supposed nuclear superiority in the East. We are opposed to the introduction into Europe of any new nuclear systems such as the neutron bomb. We oppose, too, the storage, research and production of chemical and biological weapons, and call for the withdrawal of all forward stocks of chemical weapons.

Labour will reduce the proportion of the nation's resources devoted to defence so that the burden we bear will be brought into line with that of the other major European NATO countries, without increasing the reliance on nuclear weapons. A Labour government will plan to ensure that savings in military expenditure do not lead to unemployment for those working in defence industries. We shall give material support and encouragement to plans for industrial conversion so that the valuable resources of the defence industries can be used for the production of useful goods.

The emphasis of our defence priorities in the 1980s and 1990s must be to create military forces that are clearly equipped and deployed for defensive purposes, and tailored more to Britain's geography and economic resources. This will mean maintaining adequate conventional forces, at present threatened by the extravagant expenditure on Trident.

We are alarmed by the growth of the arms trade. Labour will limit Britain's arms sales abroad and ban the supply of arms to repressive regimes such as South Africa, El Salvador, Chile, Argentina and Turkey. We will not supply arms to countries where the chances of international aggression or internal repression would be increased. Labour will ensure that all arms sales are under strict ministerial control, subject to parliamentary accountability.

THE COMMONWEALTH AND THE DEVELOPING WORLD

We shall continue to work for the peaceful and just settlement of disputes and the strengthening of international organisations, particularly the Commonwealth, as well as the United Nations. Labour has always attached a special significance to the Commonwealth — a unique form of nations, cutting across ethnic, cultural and ideological barriers. We will strengthen Britain's political and material commitment to the Commonwealth.

The future prosperity of Britain, as well as that of other industrialised countries, is inextricably linked to the future of the developing world. At the moment some 30 per cent of Britain's manufacturing exports are destined for Third World countries with which we enjoy a very healthy balance of trade. If their economies could be stimulated, the gain would be ours as well as theirs. Countless British jobs have already come about as a consequence of our trading relationship with the poorer countries. That relationship must be strengthened and expanded in the interests of working people both in Britain and overseas.

The war that Labour will wage on poverty in Britain will be extended to the developing world. A primary objective of the next Labour government's foreign policy will be to help revive the North-South dialogue. That some 800,000,000 people should be condemned to a life of absolute poverty in the Third World is an affront to any version of civilised values, as well as a constant threat to international peace and stability.

Labour sets a high priority on attacking the causes of mass poverty. A Labour government will reach the UN sponsored aid target of 0.7 per cent of Gross National Product and work towards a further target of 1.0 per cent. We will also re-establish the principle that aid must be used in the interests of the poorest people in the poorest countries and, in our efforts to bring this about, we will fund as appropriate, both governments and independent organisations. Labour will set up once again a separate Ministry of Overseas Development with a cabinet minister.

Labour will plan an expansion of trade with the developing world and will work to bring about changes in the international trading system that will be of benefit to poor countries, allowing them to receive stable prices for their commodity exports and to diversify their production. In trade agreements, Labour will insist upon workers' rights and will bring in legislation to control the activities of British-based multinational companies operating overseas.

Labour believes that, in order to enhance the prospects of the Third World economies, it will be vital to ensure that organisations such as the World Bank and the International Monetary Fund receive adequate funding from the world community, and provide loans in a way that, taking into account the economic difficulties faced by each developing country, will improve the condition of their peoples.

There is much Britain can do to lift people out of absolute poverty, and a Labour Britain will once again speak out in solidarity with the poor and the oppressed everywhere.

We will ensure that provision for overseas students is based on a major expansion of the ODA programme for student sponsorship giving preference to entrants on grounds of origin, income level and availability of courses in Britain and elsewhere.

THE LAW OF THE SEA

Labour welcomes the recently concluded United Nations Conference on the Law of the Sea and fully supports the UNCLOS proposal for a new international regime covering every aspect of ocean use. Unlike either the Tory government or the Reagan administration, Labour will endorse the Law of the Sea, which will see as a crucial element in the North-South dialogue, and will ensure that Britain participates actively in the future progress of UNCLOS.

NEAR AND MIDDLE EAST

The Labour Party is committed to the promotion of peace, democracy and socialism in the Middle

East, and to the principle of national self-determination. The Arab-Israeli conflict remains a major element in the continuing conflict and tension in the region, though not the only one. The core of the conflict is the struggle between the Israeli and Palestinian peoples for the realisation of national self-determination. We shall therefore:

Support the right of all Israelis to live in peace and security in the state of Israel, within secure internationally recognised borders.

Support the right of Palestinians to self determination, including the establishment of a Palestinian state.

The suffering of the Lebanese people and their continued occupation by foreign forces demands our attention, and we shall work for the restoration of the independence, sovereignty and territorial integrity of the Lebanon, and play a full part in its reconstruction.

The Turkish dictatorship is of special concern to Britain, given Turkish membership of NATO and its status in Europe. We deplore the constitution imposed upon the Turkish people and will work for the restoration of freedom and democracy. Until this is achieved we shall oppose assistance to the Turkish junta.

Labour is deeply concerned by the continuing violation of human rights throughout the Middle East. Labour will do what it can to help those struggling for freedom, democracy, civil and trade union rights.

We support genuine guarantees for the independence, sovereignty and territorial integrity of Cyprus, and the pursuit of intercommunal discussions sponsored by the UN for as long as both communities are committed to those talks.

AFRICA

We are totally opposed to apartheid and will unequivocally support its opponents, giving financial and material assistance to the liberation movement in South Africa and SWAPO of Namibia. Labour will also work with our trade union colleagues to assist the non-racial trade unions in South Africa.

We will carry through a systematic programme of economic disengagement from South Africa by supporting comprehensive mandatory sanctions at the UN and curtailing our economic relations with the regime. The details of our policy towards Southern Africa are set out in *Labour's Programme 1982.*

LATIN AMERICA

Latin America is a continent in crisis. The world recession and severe financial difficulties have added to the burden of already frail economies. Democracy is established in very few countries; torture and death are instruments of control in many areas.

Central America is of particular concern. Treated for decades by the United States as its backyard, the countries of this region have almost without exception failed to establish a tradition of representative democracy. Millions of people have endured a lifetime of oppression and deprivation. In recent years, the pressure for social change to respond to basic needs has grown intense, but has met with the firm resistance of the wealthy and the powerful, invariably backed by Washington. This is true of El Salvador, Nicaragua and Guatemala. Labour rejects US policy in Central America. Regrettably, the Tory government has connected Britain with that policy by its slavish support for everything the Reagan administration says and does. This applies even in the case of Guatemala, which the US is re-arming, when it lays claim to Belize, to whose defence we are committed.

Labour will do everything in its power to weaken Latin America's repressive governments by, for example, withdrawing diplomatic representation, opposing multilateral loans, banning arms sales and drawing international attention to human rights violations. Our detailed policy is set out in *Labour's Programme 1982.*

FALKLAND ISLANDS

Mrs Thatcher's policy of *Fortress Falklands* is imposing an intolerable burden both on the British people and on the inhabitants of the Falklands themselves. The war, which wiser policies could have avoided, have already cost us £1,000 million. On top of that the Conservative government plans to spend £600 million a year for the indefinite future on garrisoning the islands — £1½ million per year for every Falklands family.

With four British servicemen on the islands to every adult male Falklander, the traditional way of life of this rural community is being destroyed. Yet at the same time Mrs Thatcher is allowing British firms to equip warships for the Argentine dictatorship and is lending money to General Bignone to spend on arms. A Labour government would not sell arms to any Argentine government which was hostile to Britain or denied civil rights and democratic freedoms to its own people. Labour believes that Britain must restore normal links between the Falklands and the Latin American mainland, and that the United Nations must be involved in finding a permanent settlement of the problem.

ASIA

Emotional as well as political ties exist between Britain and many of the countries of Asia. It was the 1945 Labour government which gave independence to India and Pakistan.

Labour is concerned about the suppression of human and civil rights in many of the countries of Asia, and we will support every extension of democracy in the region. A Labour government will end military involvement with those countries that have repressive regimes.

The Labour Party is concerned that the Tory policy on overseas students' fees has already affected the ability of students from Asia, as well as elsewhere, to undertake courses in Britain. Steps will be taken to improve the position, as laid out in a previous section.

Labour believes in a closer understanding with China, and hopes that China can become more directly involved in international discussions on peace, disarmament and the world economy. We will hold talks with China with the aim of securing a peaceful and prosperous future for the people of Hong Kong.

Japan is a major power in the world economy. We hope to persuade Japan to play a more active part in a concerted expansion of the economies of the industrial nations, and to remove the obstacles that her trade policies now create. We also hope that Japan will help to bridge the division between North and South by increasing her aid to the Third World.

HUMAN RIGHTS

Labour gives the highest priority to the protection of human dignity, civil rights, democracy and freedom, which will be reflected in all that a Labour government does.

We uphold the rights of all nations to self-determination. Accordingly, we condemn the Soviet invasion of Afghanistan and US support for repressive regimes in Central America. We warn against all military interventions contrary to the UN Charter. We condemn violations of human rights wherever they occur, whether in Poland, Turkey or Nigeria, and whatever the complexion of the government concerned. Labour will further the cause of human rights in all international organisations. We will press for suspension from NATO of any dictatorship.

We will protect the opponents of regimes from harassment by their government's representatives in Britain. Our policy on refugees will be more compassionate than that of the Tory government. We will not deport individuals who would face arrest or death in their own countries.

We will also take into account human rights considerations when giving aid. Official aid will not be given to governments that persistently violate civil and trade union rights. Help will instead be given to the victims of repression.

The Liberal/SDP Alliance:

'Working together for Britain'

PROGRAMME FOR GOVERNMENT

An introduction by Roy Jenkins and David Steel

The General Election on June 9th 1983 will be seen as a watershed in British politics. It may be recalled as the fateful day when depression became hopelessness and the slide of the post-war years accelerated into the depths of decline. Alternatively it may be remembered as the turning point when the people of this country, at the eleventh hour, decided to turn their backs on dogma and bitterness and chose a new road of partnership and progress.

It is to offer real hope of a fresh start for Britain that the Alliance between our two parties has been created. What we have done is unique in the history of British parliamentary democracy. Two parties, one with a proud history, and one born only two years ago out of a frustration with the old systems of politics, have come together to offer an alternative government pledged to bring the country together again.

The Conservative and Labour parties between them have made an industrial wasteland out of a country which was once the workshop of the world. Manufacturing output from Britain is back to the level of nearly 20 years ago. Unemployment is still rising and there are now generations of school-leavers who no longer even hope for work. Mrs Thatcher's government stands idly by, hoping that the blind forces of the marketplace will restore the jobs and factories that its indifference has destroyed. The Labour Party's response is massive further nationalisation, a centralised state socialist economy and rigid controls over enterprise. The choice which Tories and Socialists offer at this election is one between neglect and interference. Neither of them understands that it is only by working together in the companies and communities of Britain that we can overcome the economic problems which beset us.

Meanwhile the very fabric of our common life together deteriorates. The record wave of violence and crime and increased personal stress are all signs of a society at war with itself. Rundown cities and declining rural services alike tell a story of a warped sense of priorities by successive governments. Our social services have become bureaucratic and remote from the people they are supposed to serve. Mrs Thatcher promised 'to bring harmony where there is discord'. Instead her own example of confrontation has inflamed the bitterness so many people feel at what has happened to their own lives and local communities.

Our Alliance wants to call a halt to confrontation politics. We believe we have set an example by working together as two separate parties within an alliance of principle. Our whole approach is based on co-operation: not just between our parties but between management and workers, between people of different races and above all between government and people. Because we are not the prisoners of ideology we shall listen to the people we represent and ensure that the good sense of the voters is allowed to illuminate the corridors of Westminster and Whitehall. The TUC and CBI, each paying the bills for the party it supports, have been too much listened to and ordinary people have been heard too little.

We do not believe that all wisdom resides in one party, or even in the two parties of the Alliance. There are men and women of sense and goodwill in both the other parties. But they opted out and allowed the demands of the old party politics to make the House of Commons the most noisily partisan assembly in the Western World.

Our concern is for the long-term, not just for tomorrow. We do not want to solve our immediate problems by piling up new crises for future generations. So when we plan for industrial recovery, we are not simply seeking growth for growth's sake. We want an increase in the sort of economic activity which will provide real jobs, which will rebuild our decaying infrastructure, which will conserve energy, and which will re-use and recycle materials rather than wasting them. We want to invest in education and housing since our long-term future depends upon the skill and maturity of the next generation. The lavish promises and the class-war rhetoric of the Conservative and Labour manifestos have no place in our Programme for Government. We offer instead a sober assessment of the first steps back to economic health and social well-being. But the vision which unites us is of a nation of free people working together in harmony, respecting each other's rights and freedom and sharing in each other's success. To achieve these hopes, we must not only change failed policies. We must reform the institutions which produced them.

When we advocate a fairer voting system we are therefore talking neither about a constitutional abstraction nor the self-interest of a new political force. Of course we want fairness for ourselves, but even more do we demand a change in the interests of the majority, whose wishes are increasingly distorted by the pull of the extremes. This is in the interests of the cohesion of the country, for it is wrong and dangerous that one big party should be a stranger to the areas of prosperity and the other an incomprehending alien in the areas of deprivation. It is also in the interests of a more stable political and economic direction, without which those who work in industry, public or private, or in the community services, will not have the framework within which to plan for the future.

We believe that Britain needs the fresh start of the Alliance even more in 1983 than it did in the heady days of our birth in 1981. The Labour Party has not become more moderate. The extremists have been taken out of the shop window; they have not been removed from the shop. The policies of nationalisation, attacks on private enterprise, withdrawal from Europe, with its devastating effect upon our exports and investment prospects, and alienation of our international friends and allies, are all enthroned and inviolate. Jobs and national safety would be at risk.

Mrs Thatcher offers no alternative of hope or of long-term stability. Some of her objectives were good. Britain needed a shake-up: lower inflation, more competitive industry and a prospect of industrial growth to catch back the ground we had lost over the years. But the Government has not succeeded. After a bad start it has got lower inflation, but the prospects even of this year are not good. And the price paid has been appalling. British industry has seen record bankruptcies and liquidations. Unemployment has increased on twice the scale of the world recession.

Prospects for the future are more important than arguing about the failures of the past. The last four years could be forgiven if we now had a springboard for the future. We do not. At best we have a prospect of bumping along the bottom. On present policies the 80's will be a worse decade for unemployment than the 30's. Nearly a half of those without a job in 1933 got one by 1937. By 1987, if we continue as we are, unemployment will be at least as bad as in 1983. As a reaction, if the old two-party system is allowed to continue, we shall then lurch into the most extreme left-wing Government we have ever known.

The Alliance can rescue us from this. There is no need for hopelessness. By giving a moderate and well-directed stimulus to the economy, accompanied by a firm and fair incomes policy, we can change the trend and begin to get people back to work. Unlike the Labour Party, we would do it in a way which encouraged private business. We believe in enterprise and profit, and in sharing the fruits of these.

Beyond that, further success will depend upon the international climate. That is not wholly ours to command. But it does not intimidate us. The world is looking for a lead. Concerted expansion, greater currency stability, a recognition of interdependence between poorer and richer countries are all possible and necessary. We need the vision and sense of enlightened self-interest which produced the Marshall Plan and pulled post-war Europe together.

It is an opportunity for Britain. We yearn for a world role and are qualified by our history and experience to perform one.

The Alliance is unashamedly internationalist. We cannot live in a bunker. We are for a British lead in Europe, for multilateral disarmament and for a new drive to increase our own prosperity by co-operating with others to reduce poverty and squalor throughout the world. We offer reconciliation at home and constructive leadership abroad. We are not ashamed to set our sights high.

THE IMMEDIATE CRISIS: JOBS AND PRICES

Our economic crisis demands tough immediate action. It also requires a Government with the courage to implement those strategic and structural reforms which alone can end the civil war between the two sides of industry.

The immediate priority is to reduce unemployment. Why?

To the Alliance unemployment is a scandal; robbing men and women of their careers, blighting the prospects for a quarter of all our young people, wasting our national resources, aborting our chances of industrial recovery, dividing our nation and fuelling hopelessness and crime.

Much of the present unemployment is a direct result of the civil war in British industry, of restrictive practices and low investment. But in addition Conservative Government policies have caused unemployment to rise. An Alliance Government would cause unemployment to fall. How? Can it be done without releasing a fresh wave of inflation?

We believe it can. We propose a carefully devised and costed jobs programme *aimed at reducing unemployment by 1 million over two years*. This programme will be supported by immediate measures to help those hardest hit by the slump – the disadvantaged, the pensioners, the poor.

Ours is a programme of mind, heart and will. It is a programme that will work! The Programme has three points: Fiscal and Financial Policies for Growth; Direct Action to provide jobs; An Incomes Strategy that will stick.

Sustained policies for growth

These will be based on carefully selected increases in public spending and reductions in taxation. Despite the impression Mrs Thatcher gives, the Conservative Government is borrowing £8 billion a year. It is costing us £17 billion to keep over 3 million people on the dole. In view of the depth of the slump, we think it right to increase public borrowing to around £11 billion and to use this money in two basic ways:

to reverse the reduction in public investment which over the last decade has been little short of catastrophic, through a selective programme of capital investment in the water and sewerage systems, electrification of railways, building and repairing roads, rebuilding and refurbishing hospitals, investing in housing, improving transport services and developing energy conservation schemes.

To concentrate the funds available for *tax reductions* in areas where tax cuts have a direct impact on prices such as the abolition of the National Insurance Surcharge (the 'tax on jobs') and in this way keep prices down as growth is stepped up. We will stop the nationalised industries being forced to raise prices for gas and electricity merely to increase Government revenue.

Such action to rekindle growth without inflation, buttressed by a less restrictive monetary policy and management of the exchange rate to keep our exports competitive, will be pursued so as to reduce unemployment by 400,000 over our first two years.

Direct action to provide jobs

The immediate action we propose is targeted on those among the unemployed in greatest need, the long-term unemployed and the young. It does not throw money wildly about, but has been carefully drawn up to achieve the biggest early fall in unemployment we can manage at the lowest practicable cost. Our main proposals are:

to provide jobs for the long-term unemployed in a programme of housing and environmental improvement – house renovation and insulation, land improvements; these jobs are real jobs crying out to be done. There will also be a major expansion of the Community Programme. We will back programmes of this kind with great determination to ensure that they generate at least 250,000 jobs over two years;

to extend the Youth Training Scheme so that it is available to all 16 and 17 year olds and give real help to those who want to stay on at school after 16 or go to college or take a training course. Our long term aim is to see all 16–19 year olds either as students with access to work experience, or as employed people with access to education and training. But the extension of training proposed here would alone reduce youth unemployment by 100,000;

to create more jobs in labour-intensive social services. There is a great need for extra support staff in the NHS and the personal social services. These services are highly labour-intensive and their greatest need for extra people is in regions of high unemployment. We propose the establishment of a special £500 million Fund for the health and social services in order to create an additional 100,000 jobs of this kind over two years;

to give a financial incentive to private firms to take on those longest out of work – To boost jobs in the private sector, we propose to pay a grant to companies for every *extra* job they provide and fill with someone unemployed for over six months. The scheme will be for employment pay, not unemployment pay. The Government loses about £100 per week (in unemployment benefit and lost tax revenues) for every person unemployed, so it is not extravagant to pay £80 a week for each additional job. According to the best estimates this incentive could increase employment by around 175,000 jobs within two years of its introduction.

In sum, our immediate programme of direct action would reduce unemployment by well over 600,000 in two years. What is more, it will do so in a highly cost-effective way by switching the money which is now paid to people to do nothing, into payment for useful jobs instead, and it therefore will not involve irresponsible increases in public spending or borrowing.

Taken together these proposals should reduce unemployment by 1 million by the end of our second year in government.

An incomes strategy that will stick

We do not pretend that a lasting return to high levels of employment can be achieved painlessly, or without a re-emergence of the inflationary pressures which record unemployment has temporarily damped down. We are convinced there is no hope of a lasting return to full employment unless we can develop ways of keeping prices down which do not involve keeping unemployment up. And unlike either of the two old parties, we are prepared to face up to this by pursuing a fair and effective pay and prices policy that will stick. It is Labour's refusal to face up to the need to restrain incomes, at the dictates of its union paymasters, which above all makes Labour's claim to have a solution to unemployment so utterly bogus, and it is Mrs Thatcher's refusal to contemplate anything other than unemployment as an incomes policy which condemns the country to permanently high unemployment if she wins another term.

In drawing up its counter-inflation programme, the Alliance has faced the question of pay and prices policy head on. Unlike other parties, the Alliance will seek a specific mandate from the electorate in support of an incomes policy. We shall campaign for a series of arrangements to keep price rises in check whilst unemployment comes down. Specifically we propose:

to establish a range for pay settlements. The Government will discuss with representatives of commerce and industry, trade unions and consumers, the prospects for the economy as a whole, and will establish the desirable range within which pay settlements should be negotiated given the outlook for unemployment. The Government will provide forecasts of the implications for unemployment, inflation and growth, of pay settlements at different levels, and the objective will be to arrive each year at an agreed norm or range for pay settlements. In the absence of agreement the government will announce its own view and tailor its policies accordingly, but every effort will be made to minimise disagreement and establish a common view.

a fair deal for pay in the public services. The agreed norm or range will provide the background to a fair and systematic approach to pay in the public services. A single, independent Assessment Board for public service pay will be set up to provide fair comparisons. Agreed arrangements for arbitration will be needed. As a result, public service sector pay will grow at broadly similar rates to that of comparable groups in the private sector.

new arrangements to discourage excessive pay settlements in the private sector – Pay settlements in the private sector will be negotiated with no direct interference in settlements made by small and medium sized businesses. We intend to set up a Pay and Prices Commission to monitor pay settlements in large companies, with powers to restrict price increases caused by wage settlements which exceed the agreed range. At the same time, we shall legislate to introduce a Counter Inflation Tax, giving the Government the power to impose the tax if it becomes necessary. The tax will be levied by the Inland Revenue on companies paying above the pay range. It will be open to successful companies where productivity increases have been high to pay above the agreed range if they do so through the distribution of shares which are not immediately marketable.

the nationalised industries will be subject to similar restraints, on excessive wage settlements; and will not be permitted to evade the consequences of excessive wage settlements and counter-inflation tax payments simply by raising prices.

We would, if we were convinced it was necessary in the prevailing circumstance, be prepared to introduce a fully statutory incomes policy to cover the interim period whilst these new arrangements are being introduced.

Previous incomes policies have been short term reactions to crisis. They have been reversals of earlier policies. They have had no mandate from the electorate. The Alliance presents its policy now because that is both honest and necessary. To work, a pay and prices framework must be understood and supported. The framework we propose can last. It is flexible. It will encourage growth and reward productivity and initiative. *It offers the only way of regaining growth without refuelling inflation*.

STRATEGY FOR INDUSTRIAL SUCCESS

The Alliance is alone in recognising that Britain's industrial crisis cannot be solved by short term measures such as import controls or money supply targets. Our crisis goes deep. Its roots lie in the class divisions of our society, in the vested interests of the Tory and Labour parties, in the refusal of management and unions to widen democracy in industry, in the way profits and risks are shared.

The policies offered by the two class-based parties will further divide the nation North v South, Management v Labour. Our greatest need is to build a sense of belonging to one community. We are all in it together. It is impossible for one side or the other in Britain to 'win'. Conflict in industrial relations means that we all lose.

But how do we reduce conflict? How do we end class war in industry? Not by intimidating the unions through unemployment. Not by nationalising, denationalising, re-nationalising. Not by pretending the problem doesn't exist.

The Alliance is committed to policies which will invest resources in the high-technology industries of the future. We are committed to a major new effort in education and training. We are pledged to trade union reform, to tough anti-monopoly measures. Above all we will act to share profits and responsibility in industry far wider than ever before.

We need to do these things to ensure Britain's economic success in a brutally competitive world. But the aim is not merely economic growth for its own sake. To live fulfilled and meaningful lives we each need challenge, reward and responsibility. In British industry far too many feel they have no stake in success, no role to play, nothing to contribute. It is that feeling which leads to bitterness, and conflict. The time has come to change these things – now, before it is too late.

Partnership in industry

Britain has made little progress towards industrial democracy, yet several of our European partners have long traditions of participation and co-operation backed by legislation. They do not face the obstacles to progress with which our divisive industrial relations present us. To be fully effective, proposals for participation in industry need to be buttressed by action on two fronts: a major extension of profit sharing and worker share-ownership to give people a real stake where they work as well as the ability to participate in decision-taking, and reform of the trades unions to make them genuinely representative institutions.

Participation at Work

We propose enabling legislation that will offer a flexible and sensible approach:

an Industrial Democracy Act to provide for the introduction of employee participation at all levels, incentives for employee share-ownership, employee rights to information, and *an Industrial Democracy Agency* (IDA) to advise on and monitor the introduction of these measures;

Employee Councils covering each place of work (subject to exemption for small units) for all companies employing over 1,000 people. Smaller companies would also be encouraged to introduce Employee Councils;

Top level representation will, for example, be through directors elected jointly by employees and shareholders, or a Representative Council with rights to co-determination on a range of issues;

No 'single channel' appointments by trade unions: every employee must have a vote and be able to exercise it secretly.

Profit-sharing and Employee Share-Ownership

We propose:

through the Industrial Democracy Act to encourage companies to develop collective share ownership schemes based on profit sharing as an essential component of industrial democracy. We will also increase the exemption limit for Corporation Tax relief on Inland Revenue approved profit-sharing and share-ownership schemes to £3,000 per employee;

to give specific encouragement to co-operatives through increased funding for the Co-operative Development Agency – to provide advice and financial support for those setting up co-operatives.

Giving the Unions back to their Members

Employee democracy in industry can only be extended if trade unions are made genuinely representative of their members since they are bound to have an important role in participation. It is for that reason, and not in any spirit of 'union bashing' that we propose further democratization of the unions themselves. We want to see effective, representative and responsible trade unions playing their full part in industry, and in this we stand apart from the Conservative Party, which has no interest in participation, and which wants to reform the unions only in order to weaken them.

We will legislate to provide for:

compulsory secret individual ballots, normally on a postal basis, for the election of the national executives of unions and, where appropriate, union general secretaries;

the right for a certain proportion – 10 per cent – of the relevant bargaining unit to require a ballot before an official strike can be called;

maximum encouragement of arbitration, as a fair and constructive means of settling disputes, including a legal requirement in essential public services that any dispute be taken to impartial arbitration operating on common principles for all public service groups, before industrial action shall commence;

measures to provide for a more efficient and more effective trade union movement: tax exemption for union contributions to encourage a better level of funding, a Trade Union Development Fund to assist union mergers and rationalisation, statutory rights to recognition for unions that have won majority support from the relevant workforce; adequate facilities at the workplace and reasonable time off for union representatives to perform their duties; and increased support for education and training for shop stewards and representatives. We propose an Employees' Charter clearly safeguarding trade union and workers' rights.

We favour a careful balance of collective and individual rights on existing closed shops, with action against the pre-entry closed shop matched by retention of legal provision from union membership agreements on condition the latter rests on substantial workforce support and that exemption from union membership is available on grounds on conscience.

Government and industry

Priority for Industry

We cannot restore employment or achieve the standards we want in our social services unless we first reverse our industrial decline. So the rebuilding of our industry and commerce must be given priority in the formulation of government policies.

Government and Private Industry
The role of an Alliance government in relation to private industry will be to provide selective assistance taking a number of forms:

an industrial credit scheme, to provide low-interest, long-term finance for projects directed at modernising industry;

a national innovation policy, to provide selective assistance for high-risk projects, particularly involving the development of new technologies and for research and development in potential growth industries (with a corresponding reduction in R and D spending on defence);

public purchasing policies to stimulate innovation, encourage the introduction of crucial technologies and aid small businesses;

Government assistance in export promotion, with increased efforts to reduce non-tariff barriers to trade;

we will establish a Cabinet Committee chaired by the Prime Minister at the centre of decision-taking on *all* policies with a bearing on the performance of industry.

The Alliance will strengthen the Monopolies and Mergers Commission to ensure its ability to prevent monopoly and unhealthy concentrations of industrial and commercial power. The aim is to guarantee fair competition and to protect the interests of employers, consumers and shareholders.

Government and Public Industry
We must get away from the incessant and damaging warfare over the *ownership* of industry and switch the emphasis to how well it performs. Thus we will retain the present position of British Aerospace but will not privatise British Telecom's main network nor sell off British Airways. But we will make the nationalised industries successful and efficient as well as properly responsible to their consumers. Specifically, we propose that:

where nationalised industries are operating viably in competitive conditions, Government regulation and control should largely be removed. Their borrowing on the market should not be subject to external financing limits (EFLs), and they should effectively be run as independent enterprises;

where public industries are not subject to market forces – eg the public utilities – or where they are dependent on public finance – eg the railways – alternative means of exerting pressure to ensure operational efficiency are required, and we will set up an Efficiency Audit Commission to report regularly and publicly to a Select Committee of Parliament on the overall management and discharge of their responsibilities by the industries concerned;

we will seek to distance the Government from direct involvement in nationalised industries. They must be free to run their industries according to the criteria laid down for them, without political interference.

New and Small Businesses
To encourage the growth of new and small businesses, we will attack red tape and provide further financial and management assistance by:

extending the Loan Guarantee Scheme, in the first instance raising the maximum permitted loan to £150,000; and the Business Start-Up Scheme, raising the upper limit for investment to £75,000; and introducing Small Firm Investment Companies to provide financial and management help;

zero-rating building repairs and maintenance for VAT purposes and reducing commercial rates by 10 percent;

making sure the Department of Industry co-ordinates and publicises schemes for small businesses and that government aid ceases to discriminate against small businesses;

tailoring national legislation such as the Health and Safety Regulations to the needs of small businesses and amending the statutory sick pay scheme to exclude small businesses.

Agriculture and Fisheries
Agriculture is an important industry and employer. To encourage its further development we will:

increase Government support for effective agricultural marketing at home and abroad and continue support for 'Food from Britain';

ensure that agriculture has access like other industries to the industrial credit scheme we propose;

encourage greater access to farming, especially by young entrants.

We believe that the provision of alternative sources of employment is the key to many other problems of the rural areas. To this end, we will promote moves at local level to establish rural development agencies.

The Alliance is determined to safeguard the future of our fishing industry which needs help to re-build after years of uncertainty and the drastic consequences for the deep-sea fleet of 200-mile limits in the waters they used to fish. We believe:

that in order to conserve stocks for the future, EEC inspection must be strengthened to ensure that conservation measures are fairly enforced on the fleets of all member states;

that better marketing and promotion, better vocational training, and reasonable credit terms would all help the future of the industry;

that government measures must take account of the special importance of our inshore industry to rural communities.

Energy

The first priority of the Alliance energy policy is the conservation and efficient use of energy. A programme of house insulation is part of our jobs plan and a programme to encourage increased energy efficiency in industry will lead to a substanial increase in employment and savings to the economy.

For the foreseeable future, coal will continue to supply a large part of our major energy needs. To ensure the continued prosperity of the coal industry we will make substantial investments in the modernisation of techniques and capacity. This does not mean a dramatic schedule of pit closures. There will be some employment problems – where the oldest deep pits are coming to the end of their economic life. The Alliance plans for jobs and industry are designed to give particular help to areas like these where new employment is needed.

The North Sea currently produces the oil and gas we need. But we want to make sure that there are enough reserves to keep up British oil and gas production. So we will encourage the exploration for and development of new reserves. We want to link Britain up by pipeline with the rest of the North Sea gas-fields so that, together with our European partners, we can make the best use of the gas that is there.

We will invest as a matter of urgent priority in different types of energy and new technologies, especially the use of sources of energy like the sun, wind, waves and the heat below the earth's surface and the development of combined heat and power systems. We are determined to maintain a British power plant industry.

The power stations we have and are currently building will be enough for our needs for some considerable time to come. We see no evidence including anything yet submitted to the Enquiry to justify the building of Sizewell or other PWR generating stations. However research into nuclear waste disposal must be continued in order to cater for existing needs and we would develop Britain's research programme and expertise in the field of nuclear power and the possibilities presented by fast-breeder technology and fusion.

Education and training

The third basic condition for industrial success is a people with the skills and self-confidence that will be needed for the challenges of new technology. The education and training systems are not providing enough people with the skills necessary to make them employable and the country successful in competition with its rivals. We are falling further behind. Japan on present plans will be educating all its young people to the age of 18 by 1990. More than 90 per cent of the 16–19 age group in Germany gain recognised technical qualifications. And it is not just a matter of school-leavers. Our managers are less professionally qualified than our main competitors'. From the bottom to top we are underskilled, and this has to be put right if we are to prosper in future. To do this, to raise standards in education and training and to improve their effectiveness, is the object of proposals set out in the next Section.

CREATING ONE COMMUNITY

A fundamental purpose of the Alliance is to reduce the divisions which over the last two decades have been fragmenting our society, and restore our sense of being one community.

The gap between rich and poor is as wide today, as it was forty years ago when the Beveridge Report was written. There has been a big increase in poverty and urban squalor as a result of the present slump. The pressures of the recession have placed an increasing burden on women in particular. The trend towards two nations in health, education and the social services is accelerating as those who can pay increasingly opt for private provision. To combat these trends will require determined action across a wide front:

immediate help for those bearing the burden of unemployment;

a determined attack on poverty, aimed at releasing those locked in the poverty trap, by raising the living standards of the hardest-pressed families;

action to raise standards in education and the quality of health care provided by the NHS and remove the inadequacies in the state services which lie behind the trend to private provision;

increased investment in housing, drawing on wider sources of finance to build new communities of mixed ownership, together with urgent attention to the rehabilitation of existing council estates, the decentralisation of housing management and tenants' rights;

giving serious priority to the environmental aspects of actions and policy changes at the earliest possible stage;

creating one nation will also require positive action to tilt the balance more in favour of disadvantaged and depressed minority groups and to focus assistance on inner city areas.

This must be backed by firm action to strengthen the rule of law, with support for an effective police force commanding the confidence of the community in the fight against vandalism and crime.

Immediate help for those in need

The burden of the slump is being borne quite disproportionately by those now in long-term unemployment and by the poor, especially poor families with children. We propose to take the following measures straight away:

help for families with children by increasing Child Benefit by £1.50 per week; increasing the Child Allowance in Supplementary Benefit by £1.50 per week; increasing the extra child allowance of one-parent families;

help for pensioners. We will up-rate the pension twice a year because the present system gives rise to serious injustices. We will make sure pensioners can earn money without losing pension; we will increase the death grant to £250 for those of lesser means; standing charges for gas, electricity and basic telephone services will be abolished;

help for the unemployed and sick by increasing Unemployment Benefit, Sickness Benefit and sick pay by 5 percent; giving long-term Supplementary Benefit to the long-term unemployed; changing the rules so people are not forced to spend their redundancy money before they can get Supplementary Benefit;

help for the disabled by spending an extra £200 million a year to make a start on many reforms which will help disabled people. These will include the extension of the invalid care allowance and full rights under the non-contributory invalidity pension to married women and the abolition of the age limit on the mobility allowance;

finance. The total cost of these proposals is approximately £1,750m. This will be financed by: raising the upper limit at which National Insurance contributions are paid to £315 per week; reversing the recent increases in the high rate tax bands; and by the first stage of phasing out the married man's tax allowance. Therefore this programme does not require an increase in public borrowing.

Attacking poverty

The Alliance proposes to carry through a major overhaul of the welfare system. The original grand design of the Liberal reformer, William Beveridge, has been mutilated over the years. Instead of a basic benefit which was to secure for the old, the sick and the unemployed, a tolerable minimum standard of living as of right, we have a complex network of benefits dependent on 44 different means tests. Many people are dependent on benefits which are woefully inadequate. Millions are in poverty because they fail to apply for benefits to which they are entitled. Others find that they are worse off if they earn more.

Mass unemployment has made the scale of our problems greater than at any time since the war. We believe that we can offer a better, simpler structure of social security which would be the most important reform since Beveridge. In the long term, we plan a complete integration of the tax and benefit systems. We aim in the next Parliament to bring together all the major benefits – Family Income Supplement, housing benefits, free school meals, Supplementary Benefits, and to replace with a simpler, single benefit, the size of which for each family will depend basically on the number of children, and their housing costs.

The levels of benefit we propose mean that:

a working family with two children, currently earning £100 per week, will be around £24 per week better off;

single parents with two children, currently helped by Supplementary Benefit, will be around £10 per week better off;

single pensioners only getting the state pension will be £5.50 per week better off, and pensioner couples in the same position £10 per week better off;

help will especially be concentrated on poor families with children since these are the real centres of hardship.

The benefit will be used to supplement people's income – whether from a job, unemployment or sickness benefit or a pension – and the amount people actually get will depend on their income. The benefit will be gradually withdrawn as incomes rise – but in a steady way so that as people earn more they do end up better off despite the reduction of benefit – and the overall effect will be a substantial boost to the incomes of those suffering most hardship.

The additional spending which the new welfare system will involve will be paid for from three sources. First, by the continued phasing out of the married man's extra tax allowance (over at least three years). This is part of the removal of sex discrimination in taxation and will allow us to introduce the principal of separate taxation of earned income for all men and women. Second, by not fully indexing personal tax allowances, and third, by a relatively small increase in public borrowing – around £600–£700 million over the final programme.

This attack on poverty is basic to the Alliance strategy for creating in Britain a more united and caring community. The Conservatives speak only of an efficient and competitive society. We seek a civilized community using the resources provided by a revived economy to guarantee to all the security and self-respect that are every citizen's right.

Education, Health and Housing

Building a united, civilized community requires decent standards in education, health and housing for everyone. The Tories have imposed savage cuts in the social services and an Alliance Government would increase spending to restore and improve standards.

But it will not be enough just to spend money. The social services are too centralised, too bureaucratic. They are often insensitive and unaccountable. We will aim to make the social services more democratic, attuned to the needs of the individual. In this way, also they will become more efficient.

Education and Training

The principal need in education and training is to release the full potential of the individual. It is on the skills and energies of our people that our survival depends. An increasingly complex and technical society places great demands on the educational system and as falling school numbers continue to release resources these must not be withdrawn but invested to create better education opportunities. The needs of the *under-fives* have to be met by both education and the social services. We will ensure that at least one year of pre-school educational experience is available for all children under five; we will *act to raise standards* in the primary and secondary schools in three ways:

by involving parents, teachers and local people more in the running of schools – these are the people who really care about standards;

by ensuring that children study a broader range of subjects than they do now right through to eighteen, putting more stress on maths, science and technical subjects as well as practical skills to make them better equipped for life in today's world. It is especially important to ensure that these opportunities are equally available to girls as well as boys;

by improving the in-service training of primary teachers and of others with specialist skills eg in maths.

We will develop *a broader bridge between school and work*, including more part-time schooling, and more work experience and better technical education for all pupils; we will undertake *a major re-organization of education and training for the 16–19s*, so that school leavers are not faced with the dole but can opt for either education and training or employment or a combination of the two. Present arrangements are disjointed. Britain is well behind its competitors, resources have been devoted to ad hoc schemes not necessarily leading to employment, and many young people are unable to acquire skills and qualifications. So we propose:

a single Ministry of Education and Training combining the youth training functions of the MSC and the responsibilities of the Education Departments;

full-time vocational courses offering sustained and properly planned periods of work experience, and the replacement of the time-served apprenticeship with training to set national standards;

greater access to work experience for all 16–19 year old students and a right to further education and training for those of this age-group in work;

expansion of the YTS to enable all 17 year olds not covered by the above to participate in a Government training scheme;

a new system of educational maintenance allowances to ensure that help is available to those who stay on at school, those who opt for further education and those who opt for further training.

We will *increase access to Higher and Further Education*. We shall also review the structure of higher education to see that people who are keen to work in industry are provided with the right range of skills at this level. This may mean for example students typically taking a wider range of courses before moving on to a job or more specialist education; we will actively support *Adult and Continuing Education*. Initial education alone cannot prepare people adequately for life. It must be made easier for them as part of their normal development to acquire new skills and to re-train as technology advances. We will ensure further public support for the voluntary and statutory sectors of the youth service. Improvement in training facilities provided by the State will be accompanied by fiscal and other incentives to companies to increase their training efforts.

Health and Social Services

The Alliance is wholly committed to sustaining and strengthening the NHS. The Health Service must be funded to ensure that extra help goes to those most in need and that sufficient resources are available to meet the needs of our ageing population. The Alliance is commited to the steady increase in the real level of funding for the health and personal social services required to *maintain standards* in the face of demographic changes such as the increasing numbers of old people.

In addition, the Alliance will set up a *special Fund with £500 million each year* to pay for new schemes and ideas submitted by area health authorities, local authorities and other voluntary organisations to help the poorest areas and the neediest people. The funding of this scheme will count as part of the Alliance's immediate employment programme, and employment as well as other criteria will govern the choice of projects by the fund. The areas of greatest need in the health and social services are also high unemployment areas, so that such a special fund is an ideal use of available money.

Within the health programme, action will be taken to make better use of the health budget by:

increased emphasis on primary care, health education and preventive medicine;

emphasising community care, not as a cheap option but because of the improved quality of care this brings;

re-allocating funds between areas and between users to increase equality of access to services for people in need whatever their means or wherever they happen to live. Particular attention will be given to the traditionally under-funded services such as those for the elderly, the chronically disabed and the mentally handicapped;

encouraging local experiments and plans to improve services;

reducing the drugs bill by extending the practice of generic prescribing, saving over one hundred million pounds.

The quality of care will also be improved by our policies in three related areas. First, the continuing commitment of all NHS staff is vital if the health service is to deliver the best care it can. This means NHS staff must be propery and fairly treated. We gave our commitment in the second section to determine pay in the public services by a new system based on *fair comparison* with other groups and a fair arbitration procedure which will also apply to NHS staff. Second, we will pay far more attention to *prevention* of accidents, illness and stress, making sure that health and safety legislation is properly applied and reducing environmental risks, for example by removing lead in petrol. Third, we will work for much closer co-operation between public and private services, to maximise the amount and coverage of health care available to the community as a whole. As with private schools, we have no wish to ban private health services, but nor will we subsidise them.

In the *personal social services*, the Alliance is determined to make the welfare state less bureaucratic and more responsive to people's needs, charting a more imaginative way forward by creating community-orientated services, incorporating a much greater degree of voluntary effort, and making much better use of the dedication and enthusiasm of professional staff, working with and through voluntary groups. We favour caring for people in the community – for example, helping the elderly to live among family friends and neighbours. We will support and sustain the family in particular by helping those, especially women, who carry the burden of this care. We will encourage the development of supportive care in the community for children through a wide range of facilities including pre-school play schemes and nursery centres, and will support training for child-minders. Imaginative grants can produce value for money and high community involvement.

Housing

Housing standards have fallen under the Tory Government, and fewer houses have been built. Council tenants have been able to buy their own houses but face almost impossible financial difficulties if trying to move out of council estates into private housing.

Alliance housing policy has three basic aims: to restore the housing stock where this is needed, to provide wider genuine choice for consumers and to allocate available funds with greater fairness.

This will mean increased investment. Britain's building industry has been one of the worst hit by the recession. 1 in 8 of the unemployed are in construction. Higher investment here will not only help the tenant, the home buyer and the home-owner: it will help the whole country by creating jobs and boosting the economy.

Investment. There is an urgent need for increased investment in housing. The Housing Programme has suffered more than any other under this government, falling in cash terms from £4,514m in 1979/80 to £2,792m now which represents a fall of almost two-thirds in real terms. The all-party Environment Select Committee predicts a shortage of nearly half a million houses by 1985. And not enough is being spent even to maintain the standard of existing houses. More than 2 million houses are now 'unfit for habitation' or 'in serious disrepair', and the figure is rising. We propose:

a steady expansion of local Council and housing association building programmes, particularly for the single and the elderly, local council programmes to be in low density, human scale developments;

vigorous programmes of repair, improvement and rehabilitation of existing Council estates;

scrapping VAT on repairs;

maximum use of improvement grants to the private sector with particular help for elderly owner-occupiers who face difficulties in maintaining their houses;

attracting institutional investment in a new type of non-profit making rented housing to be managed by housing associations;

encouraging partnership schemes between local councils and private builders to provide houses to rent; and low cost house ownership opportunities on the same estates.

The last two proposals will involve new non-public money in housing, and cut down the public expenditure costs of increasing housing investment.

Widening Choice in Housing. We propose:

changing council allocation and transfer procedures to give tenants far more choice about where they live;

encouraging shared purchase and other schemes which bring owner occupation within the reach of lower income families;

providing new sources of rented housing to compete with local councils;

breaking up the large monolithic council housing departments into Neighbourhood Housing Trusts run jointly by tenants and Council representatives;

decentralising the management of the remaining Council housing to local offices responsible to local boards composed of Councillors and tenants;

introducing a new Tenants Charter to define standards of repairs, maintenance and amenities to which tenants are entitled;

giving tenants the right to call in an outside contractor from an approved list when they are dissatisfied with the Council's performance on repairs and sending the bill to the Council;

establishing a single national scheme to help tenants wanting to move from one area to another.

The Right to Buy should be retained. After the introduction of proportional representation and hence greater accountability, Councils could be given more discretion to decide their housing policy. However, there should be a right of appeal in which Councils would justify to the local Government Ombudsman any proposed restriction on the individual's right to buy such as in areas of housing need or in certain rural areas where cheap rented housing is necessary to keep an adequate proportion of young people in the community.

Major Extension of the Capital Home Loan Scheme

At present this scheme to help first time buyers is a paltry thing adding at most £110 capital for £1,000 saved by the buyer. The Alliance wants to give far more substantial aid to those determined to buy their own homes but without the means to do so under present arrangements.

We will extend the scheme so that anyone saving £1,000 over 2 years will receive an extra £1,000 at the end of that period. Rents paid over more than five years by Council tenants will count as equivalent to £1,000 saving and will also qualify for the additional £1,000. 10 years rent will entitle the tenant to £1,500 and 15 years to £2,000. We will seek to devise similar arrangements for private tenants.

Of course the present limits on the maximum value of properties which can qualify for such assistance will be maintained. The scheme is to help those who cannot otherwise become home-owners, not to benefit those with adequate resources. This will be strictly enforced.

This measure is imaginative and bold. It opens up new prospects and hope for many who are determined to save and work for a better way of life.

Greater Fairness

Housing subsidies must be distributed more according to need. Council tenants have been particularly hard hit by the government's policy of deliberately forcing up rents far faster than the rate of inflation. Central government subsidies to local authority housing fell from £1,274m in 1980/81 to £370m in 1983/84 with the result that in most parts of the country, housing accounts are now moving into surplus. The Alliance says this process must stop. Council rents should be fixed so that housing accounts balance. Any surplus should be reinvested in improved management and maintenance, and not used to subsidise the general rates.

For owner-occupiers, the Alliance's long-term policy is to reform mortgage tax relief so that it relates to individual income rather than the size of the loan. In the meantime, tax relief will be limited to the standard rate of income tax. The Alliance also intends to encourage 'low start' mortgages and other schemes to bring home-ownership within the reach of more people.

The Environment

There can be no healthy economy without a healthy environment. For far too long we have been wasting irreplaceable resources and amenities, both natural and manmade on which our community's prosperity and well-being depend. In all public decision-making the environmental aspects of changes should be assessed and taken into account from the beginning.

Pollution

We endorse the 'Polluter Pays' principle – that those responsible for pollution should pay for the resultant environmental damage. Existing pollution control legislation must be enforced and extended as recommended by the Royal Commission on Environmental Pollution.

Limiting Waste

We will encourage the manufacture of products to last longer than at present and the manufacture of those goods which cannot be re-used from materials which can be re-cycled. We will provide financial incentives for authorities with responsibility for waste disposal to construct new plants to re-cycle waste material.

Transport

Without an effective public transport system the environment will suffer serious damage and energy resources will be wasted. We believe that new investment should be linked with modernised operating practices to ensure a future for our railways, and we therefore reject the negative philosophy of the Serpell Report. Careful planning and co-ordination is required to meet the different public transport needs of both the cities and the countryside.

Land use

We need a fundamental change in the way in which we plan our cities, towns and villages to develop greater participation by those directly affected, to protect, create and develop living communities.

Farming and Conservation

We will give increased responsibility to local bodies representative of farming and environmental interests which would be based on the present Farming and Wildlife Advisory Groups, in the award of agricultural grants and subsidies, and which would seek to reconcile different interests in the use of land.

Animal welfare

Cruelty to animals and unnecessary suffering by animals demean our society and the Alliance would, as a matter of priority, establish an advisory Standing Commission on Animal Welfare. This would keep under constant and rigorous examination all issues of animal welfare including experimentation on live animals, the treatment of farm animals, the transportation of animals and the regulations covering the use of animals for entertainment. A caring community must care for animals as well as for human beings.

TRANSFORMING THE POLITICAL SYSTEM

Electoral reform

The introduction of Proportional Representation is the linchpin of our entire programme of radical reform. Alone of the political parties the Liberal Party and the SDP recognise that our economic crisis is rooted in our political system. As class based parties, Labour and Conservative represent and intensify our divisions. The 'first-past-the-post' voting system ensures that under-representation of all those who reject class as the basis of politics. Electoral reform is thus a pre-condition of healing Britain's divisions and creating a sense of community. It is also a change we must make if we are, in the full sense of the word, to be a democracy.

The national interest demands electoral reform. The Alliance will not hesitate to use its strength in the next Parliament to ensure the introduction of a system which will strengthen the power of the voters.

A system based on proportional representation will provide a stable political framework in two ways. First, in order to form a government, political parties combining together will need to command the support of about half the voters. The policies such a government will pursue can only be less dogmatic and extreme than those likely to be followed under our present system where governments can be elected with the support of no more than one quarter of the electorate. Secondly, the political parties will have to aim much more for the centre ground and will be much more reluctant to adopt the divisive policies we see at present.

Specifically we propose to *replace the existing electoral system with a system of Community Proportional Representation*. It will be based on multi-member constituencies which correspond to natural communities. It will use a system of preferential voting under which people list candidates in the order of their choice. The outcome will be that the share of seats gained by the parties in Parliament will reflect their support among the voters.

Thus natural communities like cities (eg Hull, Plymouth, Leeds, Edinburgh), and counties (eg Somerset, Northumberland) will be single multi-member constituencies of different size, represented by different numbers of MPs. Preferential voting by single transferable vote (STV) will enable the voter to distinguish between candidates of a particular party and thus to affect the character of that Party in Parliament. A single Party will not be able to gain a parliamentary majority unless it secures nearly 50 percent of the votes. There will be a spread of representation in every part of the country and will see the end of the increasing political polarisation between North and South.

Electoral reform is no academic matter. While this is our preferred system it is not the only acceptable system of fairer voting. It is necessary to strengthen and restore faith in our democratic process, under which the relationship between seats and votes is becoming entirely arbitrary. A switch to proportional representation will transform the character of our politics, producing a more constructive political dialogue, and it will change the nature of the policies pursued by successive governments. As the fundamental reform required for continuity of policy – crucial if we are gradually and steadily to overcome our basic economic problems – it is no less than the precondition for economic recovery and future prosperity.

Decentralising Government

In addition to electoral reform, the Alliance is committed to two further constitutional reforms: decentralisation to make government more accountable to the electorate, and basic legislation to protect fundamental human rights and freedoms.

Our system of government is inefficient because it is over-centralised. Departments, Ministers and Parliament are hopelessly overloaded and Parliament cannot adequately control the executive; there is great reliance on non-elected quangos, particularly at regional level – such as Regional Health Authorities, and Regional Water Authorities which together with the regional 'outposts' of central government departments now constitute an undemocratic regional tier of government; local government is too dependent on and dominated by central government – which has eroded not only its independence but also its sense of responsibility – and the Tories have made the spending of individual local authorities subject to central control. The overall result is lack of efficiency and lack of accountability, and the concentration of political power in London leads to a concentration of economic power there too, accentuating the trend to two nations – a relatively prosperous South, and a relatively deprived North. We need to disperse power in order to help spread prosperity.

In the light of these deficiencies in the structure of government, we propose:

to transfer substantial powers and responsibilities, currently exercised by the centre, to the nations and regions of Britain. The demand for devolution is clearly stronger in Scotland than in Wales or in some of the English regions, and we do not believe that devolution should be imposed on nations or regions which do not wish it. But there is a strong practical case, especially in terms of regional development, for relevant public expenditure to be allocated between and within regions in line with regional needs. We therefore propose:

immediate action to set up a Scottish Parliament with a full range of devolved powers, including powers to assist economic development and powers to tax, but not to run a Budget deficit;

to enact Scottish devolution in an Act which would also provide the *framework for decentralisation to assemblies in Wales and the English regions as demand develops*;

in the English regions to set up *economic development agencies with substantial powers*. To make these development agencies, and other nominated regional authorities which already exist, accountable in the first instance to *regional committees of a reformed Second Chamber*.

in Northern Ireland to encourage a non-sectarian approach to the problems of the province. We support the present Northern Ireland Assembly and will work towards a return to devolved power in place of direct rule from Westminster. We favour the early establishment of an Anglo-Irish consultative body at parliamentary level representing all parties at Westminster, Belfast and Dublin.

to revitalise local government, restoring its independence and its accountability to the local electorate by:

introducing proportional representation at local level to make local government representative of its electorate and responsive to currents of opinion in that electorate;

simplifying the structure of local government to make it more effective by abolishing one of the existing tiers of local government. This will be done by stages against the background of our proposals for the development of regional government. It would inevitably involve the eventual abolition of the Metropolitan Counties, and the GLC (but not ILEA) and would also allow for the restoration of powers to some of the former County boroughs;

paving the way to the abolition of domestic rates and reducing local government's dependence on central grant, by introducing a local income tax. This change in the structure of local government finance will increase the independence of local government;

extending the right of local communities to have statutory Parish or Neighbourhood Councils.

to increase the accountability of Government to Parliament by reforming the operation and procedures of the House of Commons, to make its control of the executive more effective and to reform the powers and composition of the House of Lords, which must include a significant elected element representative of the nations and regions of Britain.

This set of proposals amounts to an extensive decentralisation of power from the centre, both to the nations and regions and to local government, and to a considerable strengthening of democratic accountability at all levels of government.

Promoting individual rights

Resting on our laurels as the oldest modern democracy, we have become smug and complacent with the result that the rights we have taken for granted are being increasingly threatened. The third major area of constitutional reform therefore includes a series of measures to buttress our now shaky structure of liberties and rights and guarantee them by law. Changes in the power of the State, the media and in technology require specific protection of rights by statute. Such action will be coupled with determined action to strengthen the rule of law, giving full backing to the police subject to a proper system of accountability.

Individual rights

The following are our proposals:

a new Bill of Rights. It is shaming that our citizens have so frequently had to go to the European Court to have basic rights enforced. We shall incorporate the rights and freedoms of the European Convention of Human Rights into English, Scottish and Northern Ireland law by means of a new Bill of Rights Act which will be paramount over all inconsistent statutes and common law;

we shall create a *UK Commission of Human Rights* to help people bring proceedings under the Bill of Rights to secure compliance with its provisions. This will incorporate the existing Equal Opportunities Commission and Commisson for Racial Equality and will deal with discrimination on grounds of sex or race;

The Alliance believes that *sex and race equality* are fundamental to our society. They will be promoted by positive action in relation eg to public employment policies which will be monitored in central and local government. Anti-discrimination legislation will be actively enforced;

nationality and immigration: we believe the British Nationality Act 1981 to be offensive and discriminatory. We will revert to the simple concept that all those born in Britain are entitled to British Citizenship. There should be objective tests for citizenship and a right of appeal against refusal. Immigration control will be applied without discrimination on grounds of sex, race or colour, and rules on dependents will be revised to promote family unity;

we shall legislate for public *access to official information*, including the right of individuals to have access to information on themselves, subject to a Code of Practice defining exceptions and limitations;

we support state financing of political parties. Trade Union members must have the right to 'contract-in' on the political levy and to determine their union's party political affiliation by secret postal ballot. There should be equivalent action to regulate company donations to political parties.

The rule of law

We are dedicated to extending individual rights but rights also carry responsibilities. We need to restore our traditions of responsible citizenship. There is great concern about rising crime. The number of serious cases has this year risen above 3 million for the first time in our history. The rise in the crime rate has accompanied the rise in unemployment. As the Conservative Government has put more and more men and women out of work, the family has been undermined, whole communities have lost their self-respect and good and neighbourly values have been forgotten. Many citizens now live in terror of the vandal, the mugger and the thief. Old people particularly are cruelly exposed to violence and abuse. The causes of crime are complex but we all have an obligation to resist the dangerous slide to lawlessness that has brought fear to our streets. The Alliance believes that it is vital to support and reinforce the police in their efforts to prevent and detect crime.

But policing can only be effective if it is responsive to and carries the support and confidence of local communities. We therefore propose:

to support *community policing* with local policemen on the beat and living locally, small local police stations and reforms to police recruitment and training policy;

support for local liaison committees which will involve local people in helping the police to do their job;

to enhance confidence in the police by introducing a *conciliation service* and *an independent system for the investigation of serious complaints.* We will establish a new police disciplinary offence of racially prejudiced behaviour and introduce lay visitors into police stations;

to improve police accountability outside London by strengthening the community element on Police Authorities and encouraging community representation at the level of police divisions for the Metropolitan Police, we shall as an iterim measure establish a Select Committee drawn from London MPs.

Action to protect and promote individual and minority rights is an essential part of the Alliance's determination to heal division and enhance Britain's awareness of being one, inter-dependent Community. Prejudice against racial and other minorities, discrimination against them and against women in job opportunities and in pay, all threaten the creation of this community. The Alliance is born of Liberal and Social Democratic values. In government it would be true to those values.

The Alliance recognises that the expansion of television technology through cable, video cassettes and satellite offers great opportunities in the creation of a better informed society and provides new opportunities for the Arts.

However these technologies also carry dangers to our society if they become vehicles for pornography and violence. This must not be allowed to happen, and the State must have particular regard to its responsibilities for the young.

PEACE AND SECURITY

Alliance policies in the field of foreign policy and defence are uncompromisingly internationalist. They are based on the view that Britain must play a full and leading role in the community of nations.

The Alliance holds that Britain's security as a country depends on the cohesion and effectiveness of the NATO alliance; that our political and economic interests require us to play our full part in the European Community, and that the poorest countries of the world can best be helped if the industrial nations pursue more expansionary economic policies in concert.

The Alliance's commitment to internationalism and its recognition of the interdependence of nations clearly differentiates its approach from that of both the Labour and Tory parties. In a dangerous and complex world there is a temptation to withdraw into narrow and nationalistic attitudes. This is what both the class-based parties have done.

Labour is now pledged to policies which would isolate and weaken Britain – import controls, unilateral withdrawal from the EEC, one-sided disarmament. If these policies were enacted our Allies would lose all confidence in us, the Western Alliance would be badly undermined and as an economically debilitated and less influential country we would be quite unable to launch the international initiatives now desperately needed to help the poor of the world through concerted economic expansion and aid.

The Conservative Party specifically refuses to recognise the true inter-dependence of nations in its approach to both development and peace. It has failed utterly to respond to the challenge of the Brandt Report. Their refusal to countenance the inclusion of Britain's nuclear systems in any disarmament negotiations displays their lack of real commitment to multilateral disarmament; their determination to spend vast sums on Trident betrays their lack of confidence in any commitment to our alliance with the United States.

The Alliance sees little prospect for progress towards a more peaceful, prosperous and just world unless inter-dependence is accepted as the basis of international relations. This leads us to radically different policies from those advocated by the class based parties in three key areas:

Defence and Disarmament

The Alliance believes Britain must be properly defended and our forces equipped for that task. We pay tribute to the courage and determination of our armed forces in the Falklands and in Northern Ireland. Our defence policies reject both Labour's one-sided disarmament and the Conservatives' escalation of the nuclear arms race. The main points of our policies for defence are:

to adhere firmly to the principles of collective security. Britain cannot defend herself alone, and the NATO Alliance has made a decisive contribution to the maintenance of peace in Europe. *Participation in NATO* must be the cornerstone of the country's defence policy, and in order to consolidate the NATO Alliance we reaffirm our commitment to the NATO target for strengthening conventional forces in Europe;

we accept the need for a nuclear component in the NATO deterrent whilst the USSR has nuclear weapons. NATO should however move away from its present excessive dependence on the early use of nuclear weapons. We therefore support raising the nuclear threshold in Europe and moving towards a *'no first use' policy* by strengthening NATO's conventional forces and establishing a 150km Battlefield Nuclear Weapon-Free Zone at the central front. An Alliance Government would regard such a zone as the basis for negotiations with the Russians on a wider verifiable nuclear weapon-free zone;

we strongly back *multilateral disarmament* and arms control efforts, in particular the Geneva negotiations for reduction in both sides strategic (START) and intermediate range (INF) nuclear weapons. More specifically, the START and INF talks should be merged or at least closely linked so that trade-offs can be made across weapons systems: *Trident* should be cancelled to avoid a new and provocative contribution to the nuclear arms race and demonstrate our commitment to arms control; *Polaris* should be included in the merged START and INF talks as a further contribution to the prospects of multilateral disarmament.

The Geneva negotiations should be pursued to a successful conclusion. Before deciding whether or not to oppose the deployment of Cruise missiles in Britain, an Alliance Government will take account in particular of the negotiating position of the Soviet Union and the United States; the attitude of our NATO partners in Europe and whether arrangements for a double safety-catch system have been agreed;

if successful progress in nuclear weapons reductions has not been achieved in the negotiations at Geneva, an Alliance Government *will explore the opportunities for a verifiable, mutual freeze on the production and deployment of all nuclear weapons*;

we strongly support an agreement between East and West to *ban* the production and possession of *chemical weapons* and we would work for mutual and balanced force reductions in Europe and a comprehensive test ban to strengthen the Non-Proliferation Treaty;

on *international security*, we support the recommendations in the Palme Report, and wish to see the UN's peace-keeping role strengthened, and increased powers given to the UN Secretary-General. An Alliance Government will press for a European initiative to register the sale of arms to third world countries, and will act to end sales of British arms to regimes which persistently and brutally violate human rights.

This set of policies – stressing disarmament on both sides, a nuclear weapon-free zone in Europe, strengthened conventional forces for NATO and reduced NATO reliance on nuclear weapons, the cancellation of Trident and the inclusion of Polaris in disarmament negotiations – *will reduce the danger of nuclear conflict* and increase Britain's security.

Membership of the European Community

The Alliance is wholly committed to continuing UK membership of the European Community. Membership has increased our political influence with our European neighbours and in the world beyond. Continued membership is so unequivocally to our economic advantage. The community is by far Britain's largest trading partner, with over half of our exports going to community countries or countries with whom they have Free Trade Agreements. It also provides an influential framework for the discussion of the Irish problem between two member states, ourselves and the Irish Republic. Withdrawal, to which Labour is committed, would have a highly destructive effect on exports and hence on jobs. We would also use a great deal of foreign, particularly US investment which has come here because we are in the Community. The Alliance advocates further development of the Community and new common policies. At the same time however, there is a great deal wrong with the structure of existing policies, and we will take the lead in putting things right.

First, we support political development of the Community through adoption of the common electoral system for the 1984 direct elections to the European Parliament; more majority voting in the Council of Ministers; and greater involvement of the European Parliament in the appointment of the Commission.

Second, to correct the imbalance in existing activities, an Alliance Government will press for expansion of Community activity on regional and social policies, industrial innovation, energy conservation and the development of renewable sources of energy. To develop new policies we accept the need for an increase in community revenues on a more diversified and fairer basis. We will work for some reduction in the agriculture budget first by holding back intervention prices for agricultural products in surplus and if need be by setting a limit on the quantities of production eligible for intervention support.

These are important policies which will help to solve the British budget problem, help solve some of Europe's most chronic difficulties such as the imbalance of wealth and development between regions, and switch the balance of Community activities more directly in line with Britain's needs.

Third, we will take the lead in advocating the development of new policies where Europe has everything to gain from standing together. We must increasingly stand together in trade talks, following the pattern of the recent Multi-Fibre Arrangement talks and GATT talks in which the Commission spoke for the Community. We must increase political co-operation to reach consensus on foreign policy questions and be prepared to move into new areas such as a common procurement policy for defence. We need to develop a Community industrial policy to spend money on easing the pain for areas dependent on declining industries and also in encouraging new, high technology investment. And we need to develop and back initiatives at European level through the Social Fund aimed at reducing youth unemployment from 25 per cent to the level of general unemployment. There is great scope fo launching joint economic policies and an Alliance government will take the lead in advocating them. Fourth, an Alliance government will make Britain a full member of the European Monetary System in order to iron out the wild fluctuations in the exchange rate which have done such damage to exports and jobs over the last few years.

Helping the world's poor

Conservative policy towards the poor countries of the world has been mean and short-sighted, reducing the level of British aid and effectively excluding Third World students from our higher education system. The widespread pursuit of restrictive policies has plunged the world into the worst slump for 50 years, and the poor countries have suffered most. On the other hand, Labour's restrictive trade policies would be extremely damaging to the developing world. There is no hope for them or the rest of the world if protection leads on to waves of retaliation and countries destroy each others' markets, sending the whole economy spiralling further downwards.

We want to do two things. First, to advocate joint policies, to be developed and implemented by the major industrial countries, to take the world out of slump. We advocate co-ordinated action:

joint expansionary measures following the example of the 1978 Bonn Economic Summit, so that the main countries expand together, so managing to avoid balance of payments difficulties and the inflationary consequences of collapsing currencies;

monetary stability. Co-operation between the three main currency blocs – the US, Japan and the EMS (including Britain) – to keep their currencies stable;

additional finance for the developing world so that general expansion is not frustrated by credit constraints – increased resources for the IMF and World Bank, and fresh issues of international money (Special Drawing Rights).

International policies of this kind could chart the way out of recession. In so doing, they would help developing countries – and, indeed, the developed countries, alike – more than any foreseeable increases in levels of aid. However, Britain has a significant individual contribution to make to Third World development through its own aid programme. An Alliance government would:

increase the proportion of GNP spent on aid over 5 years to 0.7 percent;

concentrate aid on the poorest countries and on the poorest people in those countries;

increase financial support for the work of voluntary agencies, stressing urgent projects;

promote more generous funding for overseas students, especially those from the poorest countries and the poorest students from other countries;

support the principles of the Brandt Report, and in particular the proposals for increased credit through the international institutions.

Plaid Cymru

In its manifesto *The Only Alternative*, Plaid Cymru said:

The people of Wales face a straight choice—between the dead-end policies of the London-based parties, and the new hope and challenge presented by Plaid Cymru. Plaid Cymru believes that the people of Wales should accept the responsibility of self-government. We believe that Wales should be free to join the world as a nation in our own right.

Thatcher insists that "there is no alternative", but in reality unemployment has not hit everyone as it has hit Wales. Small, self-governing countries like Norway, Sweden and Austria have contained the depression and maintained full employment.

Mass unemployment is nothing new for Wales. Overdependence on a few major industries, a dangerous reliance on branch factories controlled from outside Wales, poor roads and rail links have all damaged our country's economic life. Plaid Cymru believes that the people of Wales should take control of our own economic life.

With the true level of unemployment in Wales now in the region of a quarter of a million people, Plaid Cymru calls for an investment programme by the next government of £2,000m, only twice the level of Wales' contribution every year to British defence policy and arms spending.

London's obsession with nuclear weapons makes Wales a certain target for Soviet nuclear weapons. While no country could isolate itself from nuclear conflict, a self-governing Wales would be a safer country as well as a voice for peace in the world.

Plaid Cymru rejects the idea that our economic life should be owned and controlled by absentee shareholders or by state bureaucrats. Our economic difficulties and industrial relations problems indicate that there should be a far-reaching shift towards decentralisation of economic activity and towards industrial democracy.

Plaid Cymru aims at greater European unity – but not by the methods employed by the EEC. Plaid Cymru believes in a Europe of the Peoples which accords a role to all the nations rather than being based on narrow commercial interests. We believe in a decentralised and nuclear-free Europe which is not part of any military power-bloc.

Wales remains one of Europe's most energy-rich countries. Yet, despite these resources, Wales remains one of the most deprived areas of the British State, because we have no government of our own. Plaid Cymru has developed a comprehensive energy policy and demands the establishment of an Energy Authority for Wales to govern the supply and use of energy in Wales.

The spread of second homes has added to the cost of housing, especially in rural areas of Gwynedd and Dyfed. The present Tory government has wilfully intensified the colonisation of Wales by refusing to check the spread of second home ownership. The provision of first homes must have priority over second homes in the use of the community's housing stock.

The Scottish National Party

The Scottish National Party manifesto *Choose Scotland—the Challenge of Independence* said:

The British political system offers Scotland no hope of improvement. A further term of Thatcherism will devastate the Scottish economy, concentrating more wealth and power in the South-East of England. The weak and divided Labour Party is powerless to protect Scotland, and has failed us too often in the past to be trusted.

But there is an alternative—to choose Scotland. Never has the need for an independent Scottish Parliament and a Scottish Government been greater.

Only with our own Government will Scotland have the will and the resources to reverse our economic decline and end mass unemployment. Only a Scottish Government will remove all nuclear weapons from our soil. Only a Scottish Government will be able to tackle the appalling social conditions in which many of our people have to live.

The Scottish people have the right to self-determination – only by exercising that right will we have control over our country's destiny.

When the SNP wins a majority of the Scottish seats in the UK Parliament, we will invite the other Scottish MPs to co-operate in negotiating the orderly transfer of power from Westminster to Scotland and the preparation of a Constitution.

The SNP rejects the belief that mass unemployment is inevitable, and has produced a detailed, fully-costed plan to reduce unemployment to the low levels found in other small European countries.

The SNP Jobs Plan, with a net cost of less than one-tenth of revenues from Scottish oil, would aim to create 220,000 new jobs within three years, reducing Scottish unemployment to about 5 per cent.

Scotland has seen little benefit from the oil bonanza. An SNP Government will set up an Oil Development Fund to invest oil revenues in job creation and industrial regeneration and establish a Scottish National Oil Company to ensure direct benefit to the Scottish public from oil development.

The SNP will build no more nuclear power stations, but retain existing stations and prevent the dumping of any foreign nuclear waste in Scotland.

We propose to introduce a statutory minimum wage to protect low earners and introduce a programme of industrial democracy, including worker-participation and profit-sharing in private and nationalised industries.

A Scottish Government will cancel the Trident nuclear programme, which will only fuel the arms race and increase our danger, and remove all nuclear weapons and foreign military establishments from Scottish soil and territorial waters.

The Ecology Party

The Ecology Party manifesto *Politics For Life* said:

In a nutshell, this is what we mean by Green Politics:

PEACE—through unilateral nuclear disarmament, complete withdrawal from the arms trade, a reduction in international tension through resource conservation, and a secure and credible alternative defence strategy.

WORK—guaranteeing basic material security and good work for all, based on renewable resources, human-scale technology, and the sustainable economics of self-reliance, recycling, rehabilitation and repair.
LAND—with a deep reverence for the Earth, and for all its creatures, leading to radical land reform, changes in farming practice, and comprehensive measures to control all forms of pollution.
PEOPLE AND SOCIETY—living in decentralized communities, with a proper balance between feminine and masculine values, protected by a Bill of Rights, working near home, leading healthier lives and ensuring that our children get a creative, constructive education.
THE WORLD—working for One World by helping the Third World, stabilising world population through genuine redistribution of wealth, eliminating our wasteful resource and energy depletion, and protecting the global environment.
THE SPIRIT—responding to people's hunger for meaning, placing less emphasis on material values, and more on personal growth and spiritual development – the life and the soul of Green Politics.

We believe that a programme like this is both radical and realistic.

This is not Utopian dreaming, it is already happening in Germany, Belgium, Italy and other countries. Green Politics is the single most significant international movement since the birth of Socialism at the end of the 19th century.

No Cruise, No Trident. No Polaris. No nuclear weapons of any description. No chemical or biological weapons. No American bases. No involvement in Nato. This makes the Ecology Party the only uncompromisingly unilateralist party in this election.

Phase in a National Income Scheme to remove the poverty trap.

Animal Rights Charter: introduce mandatory protection for endangered species and ban the importation of whale products and seal skins. Take immediate action against battery farming, and move as rapidly as possible to abolish vivisection. Ban all hunting and coursing with hounds.

We should withdraw from the EEC. We would seek instead to establish a European Federation, non-aligned in defence matters, opposed to reliance on economic growth, with its emphasis on the regions of Europe, and not its nation states, and committed to sustainability and justice, both in Europe and the Third World. The repsonsible adult use of cannabis should be legalized.

The National Front

The National Front manifesto entitled *Let Britain Live* states: We will put an end to a multi-racial society in Britain and make it a land fit for our children to grow up in.

The streets of our larger towns and cities—once safe for all, the old, the weak, and the infirm—have become jungles plagued by gangs of vicious—predominantly though not exclusively Black—muggers who hunt down our old folk for pitiful sums of money.

Clearly the greatest single contribution which a National Front Government will make to law and order will be the repatriation of coloured immigrants and their descendants and dependants. In the case of Black criminals, they will not join the financially assisted queue; they will be deported immediately upon conviction. Pending repatriation, there will be no 'kid gloves' treatment for rioters. They will be hammered from the streets most vigorously by a police force equipped with water cannon and such other non-lethal equipment as is deemed necessary.

In order to guarantee Britain's sovereignty—in other words, our control over our own affairs and destiny—we propose to withdraw from all internationalist bodies, including the United Nations, the Common Market, Nato, the International Monetary Fund and other international financial bodies.

A National Front Government would remove all foreign military bases from British soil . . . and would see to it that Britain is self-sufficient for all the strategic and tactical nuclear and conventional weaponry that the British forces required. A National Front Government therefore would not purchase or provide facilities for American Cruise or Trident missiles.

A National Front Government would recognize the Palestine Liberation Organization as the only authentic representative of the Palestinian people. We do not subscribe to the view that the Jews have any ancestral right to occupy Palestine.

We shall ensure that the Falklands remain British for all time and are adequately protected so as to prevent another invasion by Argentina or any other country.

We do not believe there is any real advantage in keeping Hongkong British. As far as we are concerned, China is welcome to it.

A National Front Government would maintain a foreign aid programme but for a period of a decade or more this would be deployed solely as an integral part of our programme to repatriate to their lands of ethnic origin the coloured immigrants and their offspring presently residing in our country.

Index to Candidates

Those elected are named in bold type.

A

B

C

D

E

F

G

H

I

J

M

N

O

P

Q

R

S

Y

Z

By-election statistics taken from *The Times*

Mr David Maclean

PENRITH AND THE BORDER July 28 1983

Polling on July 28 1983 in this by-election caused by the elevation to the House of Lords of Mr William Whitelaw resulted in the election of **Mr David Maclean** as the new Conservative MP for the seat. He was a candidate in the June 1983 election at Inverness, Nairn and Lochaber. (*See page 142*)

Maclean, D. (C)	17 530
Young, M. (L/All)	16 978
Williams, L. (Lab)	2 834
Others	738
C majority	552

	July 1983 %	General Election %	Change %
C	46.0	58.8	−12.8
L/All	44.6	27.9	+16.7
Lab	7.4	13.3	−5.9
Others	2.0	–	–
Poll	55.9	73.1	
Electorate	68 122	68 164	
Total votes	38 080	49 799	

Mr Tony Benn

CHESTERFIELD March 1 1984

Benn, A. N. W. (Lab)	24 633
Payne, M. (L/All)	18 369
Bourne, N. (C)	8 028
Anscomb, Miss H. (Death off Roads)	34
Bardwaj, J. (Yoga)	33
Bentley, D. (Four Wheel Drive)	116
Butler, D. (Chesterfields in Theme)	24
Cahill, D. (Reclassify Sun Newspaper)	12
Connell, J. (Peace)	7
Davey, J. (No dental increases)	83
Hill, C. (Prisoner: I am not a number)	17
Layton, T. A. (Spare the Earth)	46
Maynard, B. (Ind.)	1 355
Nicholls-Jones, P. (Ind, the Welshman)	22
Piccaro, G. R. (Official Acne)	15
Shaw, S. (Elvis Presley)	20
Sutch, D. (Monster Raving Loony)	178
Lab majority	6 264

	March 1984 %	General Election %	Change %
Lab	46.5	48.1	−1.6
L/All	34.7	19.5	+15.2
C	15.1	32.4	−17.3
Poll	75.8	72.6	
Electorate	69 822	68 486	
Total votes	52 992	49 704	

Mrs Ann Clwyd

CYNON VALLEY May 3 1984

Clwyd, Mrs A. (Lab)	19 389
Aubel, F. (SDP/All)	6 554
Jones, C. (PLC)	3 619
Arbuthnot, J. (C)	2 441
Nicholls-Jones, P. (Ind)	122
Recontre, N. (Ind Womble)	215
Winter, Mrs M. (Com)	642
Lab majority	12 835

	May 1984 %	General Election %	Change %
Lab	58.8	56.0	+2.8
SDP/All	19.9	20.6	−0.7
PLC	10.9	9.3	+1.6
C	7.4	14.2	−6.8
Others	1.0	–	–
Poll	65.6	73.4	
Electorate	50 267	50 284	
Total votes	32 982	36 923	

Mrs Ann Clwyd, broadcaster and journalist, was member of the European Parliament for Mid and West Wales, 1979–84. Elected to Labour Party National Executive Committee 1983. Vice-chairman Arts Council of Wales 1975–79 and of the Arts Council of Great Britain 1975–80. Born Mar 21 1937; educ. Holywell Grammar School, Queen's School Chester, and University College, Bangor. Unsuccessfully contested Denbigh 1970, and Gloucester Oct 1974. Member, Royal Commission on the National Health Service, which reported in 1979. NUJ, TGWU.

Mr William Cash

STAFFORD May 3 1984

Cash, W. (C)	18 713
Dunn, D. (SDP/All)	14 733
Poulter, M. (Lab)	12 677
Teasdale, C. (Soon to be unemployed)	210
C majority	3980

	May 1984 %	General Election %	Change %
C	40.4	51.2	−10.8
SDP/All	31.8	24.7	+7.1
Lab	27.4	23.7	+3.7
Soon to be unemployed	0.4	–	–

Poll	65.5	76.5	–
Electorate	70 688	70 570	–
Total votes	46 333	54 002	–

Mr William Cash, a solicitor, was elected at the by-election in 1984. Born May 10, 1940; educ. Stonyhurst College and Lincoln College Oxford. A director of Community Task Force and of Ironbridge Gorge Museum Trust.

Mrs Virginia Bottomley

SURREY SOUTH WEST May 3 1984

Bottomley, Mrs V. (C)	21 545
Scott, G. (L/All)	18 946
Roche, Mrs B. (Lab)	2 949
Anscomb, Miss H. (Freight off roads)	82
Litvin, V. (Pro Nuclear Holocaust)	117
Smith, P. (Votes for full hearing)	29
C majority	2 599

	May 1984 %	General Election %	Change %
C	49.3	59.7	−10.4
L/All	43.4	32.1	+11.3
Lab	6.7	8.2	−1.5
Others	0.2	–	–
Poll	61.7	74.5	
Electorate	70 832	69 875	
Total votes	43 668	52 022	

Mr Michael Hancock

PORTSMOUTH SOUTH June 14 1984

Hancock, M. T. (SDP/All)	15 358
Rock, P. R. J. (C)	14 017
Thomas, Mrs S. T. (Lab)	10 846
Andrews, A. N. (Vote Educ)	42
Evens, A. J. (Ind Lib)	113
Knight, G. A. (NF)	226
Layton, T. A. (Spare Earth)	50
Mitchell, T. A. F. (Ecology)	190
Smith, P. R. (New Nat)	41
SDP/All majority	1341

	June 1984 %	General Election %	Change %
SDP/All	37.6	25.4	+12.2
C	34.3	50.0	−15.7
Lab	26.5	22.6	+3.9
Others	1.6	–	–
Poll	54.5	67.3	
Electorate	74 977	74 537	
Total votes	40 883	50 196	
